Praise for 'The Complete Walt Disn

"Seriously thorough." —*Family Circle*

"Highly recommended." —*New York Dail*

"Should leave fans of Mickey smiling from ear to ear." —*Chicago Tribune*

"A thorough overview, with inside tips. With more than 500 color photos, it also makes a nice souvenir." —*Boston Globe*

"A fantastic planning tool... A guidebook series marked by stunning photography and depth of information... Unusual details that matter to families... So beautifully illustrated, vacationers will want to save it as a keepsake." —*Orlando Sentinel*

"In-depth insider knowledge... The magic of Disney radiates from the pages... All the information needed to ensure your vacation is the experience of a lifetime... Definitely the book to purchase to help plan out your trip." —*Midwest Book Review*

"Our favorite Disney guidebook."—*Ft. Worth Star Telegram*

"Endless tips and trivia."—*Knoxville News-Sentinel*

"Very detailed descriptions of each ride, show and attraction. Among the gems are fun facts, suggested itineraries and little things to look for."—*Florida Times Union*

"The ultimate Walt Disney World guidebook... Everything you could possibly need to know to plan and pull off the best Disney trip ever... Colorful, easy-to-navigate... Leaves no stone unturned." —*Writer's Digest*

"Visually engaging... What sets apart the Neals' book are the 550 color photographs of rides, rooms and characters" —*Library Journal*

"In this case, 'complete' is not hyperbole, it is a fact. *The Complete Walt Disney World* makes a trip to Disney seem more like an adventure full of surprises, instead of a whine-filled money drain." —*MomMostTraveled.com*

"The best reference available for planning a Disney vacation." —*Orlando Vacation Rentals*

"Well-written and illustrated, with sumptuous colour photographs." —*Florida Review and Travel Guide, United Kingdom*

"Truly comprehensive. As much a small-format coffee-table book as it is tour guide... Stuffed to the gills with startling photography." —*Kevin Yee, Disney author and columnist*

"A guidebook to end all guidebooks... An absolute joy to have with us... A 'dive right in' kind of book... If you're looking for a Disney guidebook, this is the one to get." —*Claudine Wolk, author of "It Gets Easier... And Other Lies We Tell New Mothers"*

Awards and honors

Outstanding Family Product. Disney's iParenting Media Awards

Travel/Family Activity Book of the Year. 2010 Living Now Book Awards

Travel Guide of the Year. 2010 International Book Awards

Travel Guide of the Year. 2010, 2009, 2008 National Independent Excellence Book Awards

Travel Guide of the Year, Silver Medalist. 2010 Benjamin Franklin Awards

Best Interior Design, Finalist. 2010 International Book Awards

Nonfiction Book of the Year. 2009 National Independent Excellence Book Awards

Nonfiction Book of the Year. 2008 Writer's Digest International Book Awards

Travel Guide of the Year, Silver Medalist. 2009 ForeWord Reviews Awards

Travel/Family Activity Book of Year, Silver Medalist. 2009 Living Now Book Awards

Reference Book of the Year, Silver Medalist. 2009 Writer's Digest International Book Awards

Travel Guide of the Year, Finalist. 2008 National Best Book Awards

Best Southeast Nonfiction, Silver Medalist. 2008 Independent Publisher Book Awards

The Complete Walt Disney World 2011

ISBN 978-0-9709-5962-1
ISSN 1547-8491
Library of Congress Control No. 2010914555

Writing and research: Julie Neal
Photography: Mike Neal
Additional photography and research: Micaela Neal
Illustrations: Vince Burkhead

Acknowledgments
Our thanks to Dave Herbst, Jason Lasecki, Jonathan Frontado, Juliana Cadiz, Bebee Frost, Darrell Fry, Matt Gottfried, David Hillstrom, Laura Spencer, Charles Stovall and Benjamin Thompson for a variety of assistance, as well as: Craig Albert, Ngǫnba Anadou, Mandee Andrichyn, Odalys Aponte, Karen Aulino, Kevin Baker, Michelle Baumann, Liz Benz, David Brady, Mike and Carolyn Burkhead (and El too!), Jodi Chase, John Chenciner, Lee Cockerell, Mike Colangelo, Michael Colavolpe, John Corbett, Brian Cotten, Amy and Mitch Crews, Alan Cumming, the Dix family, Jason Dobbins, Todd Ferrante, Andrea Finger, Jay Garcia, Kayce Giglio, Phran Gauci, Lorraine Gorham, Matt Hathaway, Holland Hayes, Kisha Howard, Mary Hutchison, Walter Iooss, Rob Iske, Eric Jacobson, Kristie A. Jones, Kristine Jones, Kathy Mangum, Roberto Martinez, Bob Miller, Tony Morreale, Doobie and Rebekah Moseley, Nenette Mputu, Laura Murphy, Thabo Pheto, Charles Ridgway, Wally Robinson, Kathy Rogers, Joe Rohde, Debbie Sacleux, Hanns-Claudius and Monika Scharff, Steve Schussler, Ryan Seacrest, Theron Skees, Brian Spitler, Jason Surrell, Rheo Tan, Paul Tomayko, Kendra Trahan, the Turners (Jeff, Anna, Laura, Michael, Andrew), Alicia Vaughn, Jenn Wakelin, Terry Ward, Chris Weaver, John Wetzel, Consuelo Wint, Herb and Debbie Wright, Kevin Yee and all the Disney resort managers and park duty managers.

To Mike Burkhead, for going above and beyond.

The Complete Walt Disney World® 2011

Julie and Mike Neal

coconut
press™

COCONUT PRESS
Sanibel Florida

Contents

Mickey Mouse and Donald Duck star in Mickey's PhilharMagic at Magic Kingdom

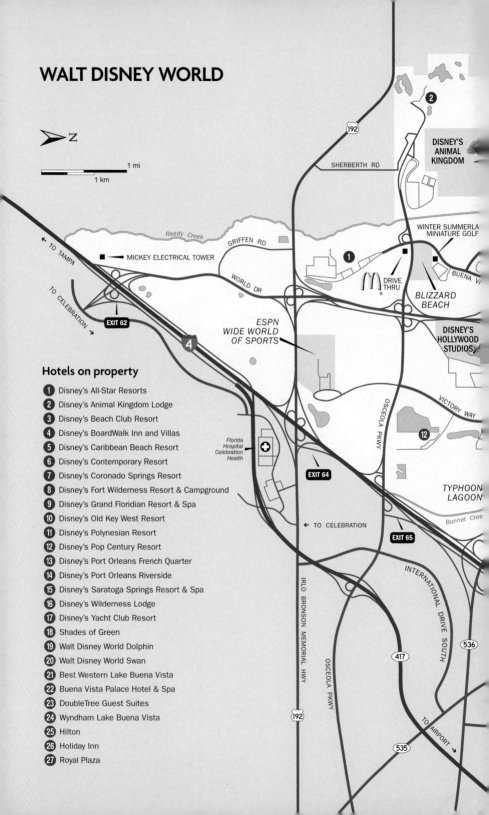

WALT DISNEY WORLD

N

1 mi
1 km

MICKEY ELECTRICAL TOWER

Reedy Creek

GRIFFEN RD

WORLD DR

TO TAMPA

TO CELEBRATION

EXIT 62

4

ESPN
WIDE WORLD
OF SPORTS

Florida
Hospital
Celebration
Health

EXIT 64

← TO CELEBRATION

192

SHERBERTH RD

WINTER SUMMERLA
MINIATURE GOLF

DRIVE
THRU

BLIZZARD
BEACH

BUENA VI

DISNEY'S
ANIMAL
KINGDOM

DISNEY'S
HOLLYWOOD
STUDIOS

OSCEOLA PKWY

VICTORY WAY

12

TYPHOON
LAGOON

Bonnet Cree

EXIT 65

INTERNATIONAL DRIVE SOUTH

536

417

OSCEOLA PKWY

IRLO BRONSON MEMORIAL HWY

192

TO AIRPORT

535

Hotels on property

1 Disney's All-Star Resorts
2 Disney's Animal Kingdom Lodge
3 Disney's Beach Club Resort
4 Disney's BoardWalk Inn and Villas
5 Disney's Caribbean Beach Resort
6 Disney's Contemporary Resort
7 Disney's Coronado Springs Resort
8 Disney's Fort Wilderness Resort & Campground
9 Disney's Grand Floridian Resort & Spa
10 Disney's Old Key West Resort
11 Disney's Polynesian Resort
12 Disney's Pop Century Resort
13 Disney's Port Orleans French Quarter
14 Disney's Port Orleans Riverside
15 Disney's Saratoga Springs Resort & Spa
16 Disney's Wilderness Lodge
17 Disney's Yacht Club Resort
18 Shades of Green
19 Walt Disney World Dolphin
20 Walt Disney World Swan
21 Best Western Lake Buena Vista
22 Buena Vista Palace Hotel & Spa
23 DoubleTree Guest Suites
24 Wyndham Lake Buena Vista
25 Hilton
26 Holiday Inn
27 Royal Plaza

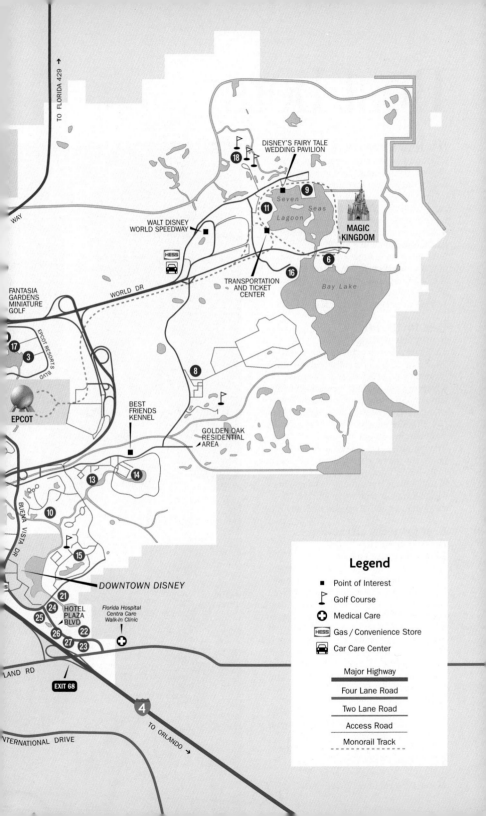

Best bets

It's like Christmas. You plan and save and anticipate for weeks and months. You yearn for a magical time with your family, full of memories and unforgettable moments. It certainly runs up the balance on your credit cards, but when it's over you're most likely glad you did it. Yes, a vacation to Walt Disney World has a lot in common with Christmas, at least the secular American version. But how do you decorate your particular tree? Which presents do you choose? Following are the author's Best Bets; 24 of Disney World's most seminal experiences:

Best thrill ride:
Space Mountain (p72)

This wild ride seems to fill everyone with joy. Zoom through the dark with reckless abandon on this indoor roller coaster, which zips you through space as twinkling stars and shooting comets race by. New sound effects make the experience seem faster than ever, with whooshing noises as you turn corners and plunge down drops. The low-sided, one-person-wide rocket is one of the narrowest coaster vehicles ever built, barely interfering with your feeling of a solo flight through the cosmos. This Magic Kingdom institution still has the magic it had when it opened back in 1975.

Best princess attraction:
Beauty and the Beast—
Live on Stage (p150)

This dazzling musical stage show (shown at right) is both touching and laugh-out-loud funny. While romantics swoon over the love story between Belle and her Beast, everyone will love the cartoonish slapstick humor; children will giggle at the silly enchanted characters. The music? Some of Disney's best songs, the Howard Ashman classics "Belle," "Gaston," "Be Our Guest," "Something There," "The Mob Song" and "Beauty and the Beast." Villain Gaston is a hoot, funnier and less threatening than in the movie. When bookworm Belle and her Beast embrace at the conclusion, the happy ending makes some onlookers cry. The show plays throughout the day at Disney's Hollywood Studios.

Best overall attraction: Soarin' (p98)

The sense of soaring is well realized at this indoor Epcot attraction (above). Buckled in to what resembles a hang glider, you lift in the air in front of a concave projection screen; a 5-minute video takes you over California. Swaying and dipping in the breeze, breathing in scents of pines and orange groves, your senses are fully immersed. With no narration or plot, Soarin's only accompaniment is its beautiful, uplifting music. It's a rush.

Best theatrical show: Festival of the Lion King (p176)

Energetic performers bring to life the best songs from Disney's 1994 movie "The Lion King" at this in-the-round musical spectacle at Disney's Animal Kingdom. Creative costumes turn dancers into antelopes, warthogs, zebras and other beasts. Similar to a great circus, there is almost too much to look at; during the joyful "Circle of Life" finale singers belt out their numbers center stage while a human bird soars overhead, wisecracking host Timon mimes his reactions, animal dancers and stilt-walkers circle the action and four huge puppets react in each corner of the theater.

Best vintage ride: Peter Pan's Flight (p58)

You fly over London and head off to Never Land in this classic dark ride at Magic Kingdom. Dusted with pixie dust and led by Tinker Bell, guests board pirate ships, lift off from Wendy Darling's home as they cruise over—and through—a variety of scenes from Disney's 1953 animated film, "Peter Pan." Designed more than 50 years ago, the ride's imaginative engineering and overdose of black lights conjure an experience that still charms all ages.

Best toddler attraction: it's a small world (p56)

This classic Magic Kingdom boat ride (shown at right) creates a child's view of the world, one of a million colors, patterns, shapes, sparkles, textures and twinkly lights. Nearly 300 smiling dolls sing and play musical instruments, while whimsical animals have flower-shaped spots, jeweled eyes and twirling heads. Butterflies, clowns, jugglers and magic carpets float overhead like giant crib mobiles. The gentle attraction holds nothing threatening, and its reassuring message of unity and friendship resonates with guests of all ages.

Best animal attraction: Kilimanjaro Safaris (p178)

Nirvana for animal lovers, this bouncy, open-air safari ride offers unpredictable beastly encounters as it roams through wide-open grasslands and forests. A giraffe may peek in your truck. Lions may roar. Giant armored rhinos may calmly—or not so calmly—block the road in front of you. Each "two-week" tour is different, as the scores of spectacular animals are always busy living their own lives—feeding, fighting, nursing, running, even raising babies. It's best to ride during a rain shower, when the elephants like to play in their watering holes and all the animals are typically most lively. Covering 110 acres, the ride is the largest Disney attraction in the world, and the signature experience at Disney's Animal Kingdom.

Best educational attraction: The Hall of Presidents (p40)

President Barack Obama speaks, as do George Washington and Abraham Lincoln at this venerable Magic Kingdom attraction that was completely redone in 2009.

Created as lifelike Audio-Animatronics figures, all 43 American leaders are represented as breathing, fidgeting, murmuring individuals... a mirror of our unsettled selves, the American people. Before the curtain raises on the presidents, a high-definition, ultra-widescreen film tells the illuminating tale of our country's origins, complete with interesting portraits of Andrew Jackson and Teddy Roosevelt. Morgan Freeman narrates. Note: the presentation doesn't take a political stand; hardcore haters of either Democrats or Republicans may want to skip it.

Best fireworks: Wishes (p78)

You're likely to tear up. Not the typical reaction to a fireworks show, perhaps, but this Magic Kingdom evening extravaganza is anything but typical. Though often subtle and understated, its synchronized starbursts, music and dialogue pack an emotional punch, bringing back childhood dreams and memories. The show begins quietly—a lone shooting star arches over Cinderella Castle—and slowly builds to a spectacular finish.

Best 3-D movie:
Mickey's PhilharMagic (p54)

Donald Duck finds himself in the dining hall from "Beauty and the Beast," the undersea grotto of "The Little Mermaid" and other classic Disney settings in this dazzling Magic Kingdom experience (above) that all ages will love. When the duck steals the sorcerer's hat Mickey Mouse needs to conduct his musician-free orchestra, the foul-minded fowl gets swept up into a long, strange trip. Combining high-tech animation with great music, innovative effects and punchy comedy, the movie grows wider as it progresses and eventually fills your entire field of vision. In-theater wind, water and aromatic effects add to the fun. Don't miss Donald's attempt to kiss Ariel—it's electrifying.

Best scary attraction:
The Twilight Zone Tower of Terror (p154)

"The next time you check into a deserted hotel on the dark side of Hollywood, make sure you know just what kind of vacancy you're filling." That's the lesson host Rod Serling teaches you at this remarkable ride at Disney's Hollywood Studios. From its abandoned, weed-filled grounds to its eerie music to its cobweb-covered lobby to its unwelcoming boiler room, the Tower of Terror is designed expressly to freak you out. And all that is *before* you board the creaky freight elevator for a randomly-selected series of violent plunges and sudden ascents. Waiting in the dark silence for the first sudden drop—or lift—is especially tense.

Best ride at night:
Big Thunder Mountain Railroad (p50)

Magic Kingdom's "wildest ride in the wilderness" is even wilder at night, as the scenery is lit but the track is so pitch black that each curve and dip comes as a surprise. Crystals glow in the bat cave, and sulphur pools swirl in vivid colors you can't see during the day. At the mining town of Tumbleweed, sharp-eyed riders will spot drunks and dance-hall dames partying behind the lit windows at the Gold Dust Saloon.

Best character meal: Cinderella's Happily Ever After Dinner (p253)

It says a lot that Cinderella is *not* the most entertaining character at this Grand Floridian Resort experience. Little girls love her, of course, but for adults the real treats are in the supporting cast: regal Prince Charming proposes to moms; squabbling stepsisters Anastasia and Drizella flirt with little boys; haughty Lady Tremaine disapproves of everything. The buffet is delicious, especially the roasted prime rib and chilled strawberry soup.

Best bar: Raglan Road (p257)

Hidden in a corner of Pleasure Island at Downtown Disney, this spirited Emerald Isle pub features step-dancers, a live band and a stock of Irish beers and whiskeys. Four grand bars, each more than 130 years old and imported from Ireland, feature marble adornments, leaded glass and ornate detailing. All ages are welcome, and the modern-Irish fare—the huge place is also a restaurant—offers something for every taste.

Best live band: Mariachi Cobre (p117)

This quality Mariachi band formed in Tucson, Ariz., way back in 1971 and played with Linda Ronstadt on her Spanish-language albums. Led by trumpets, violins and exuberant vocals backed by harmonizing guitars, the band expresses the romantic soul of Mexico in a way even the most whitebread *gringo* can appreciate. The group plays at Epcot's Mexico pavilion.

Best improv troupe: Citizens of Hollywood (p158)

This motley crew of street performers channels the mythical residents of a 1940s Tinseltown at Disney's Hollywood Studios. Performing impromptu skits on Hollywood and Sunset Boulevards, they incorporate willing park guests in makeshift dating games, celebrity spelling bees and other silly setups. Characters include director Alberto Dante ("often imitated, never nominated"), script girl Paige Turner ("I'm not a wannbe, I'm a gonna be!"), card shark Jack Diamond and dumb-blond starlet Evie Starlight.

Best Pixar attraction: Finding Nemo—The Musical (p202)

You don't have to be a child to love this musical version of Pixar's "Finding Nemo" (shown at left). Playing at Disney's Animal Kingdom, the stage show taps into the underlying bonds between fathers and sons and is a visual delight. Costumed live singers act out their roles as they operate large puppets, some the size of cars. Toothy shark Bruce shimmies across the stage, his actor-operator covered with seaweed.

Best water-park ride: Crush 'n' Gusher (p216)

There's nothing quite like this Typhoon Lagoon water coaster (below), which powers its riders up lifts and down dips, tunnels and many tight turns. You literally feel the thrust of the water jets, since there is nothing between you and the power source but your plastic blow-up tube. Tubes seat two, or even three, people apiece, which makes the ride great for families. The waiting line is out of the sun, unusual for a water park attraction.

Best playground: The Boneyard (p198)

Children can excavate dinosaur bones at Disney World's biggest playground. Kids can pick from lots to do at this calm spot at Disney's Animal Kingdom, including playing archeologist in no-stick sand, exploring a multi-level maze, climbing on a real Jeep and scrambling through tunnels. Tucked into the sides are hidden interactive surprises like musical "xylobones" and dinosaur footprints that trigger dino roars. Parents appreciate the shady seating area.

Best place to meet 'locals': Main Street U.S.A. (p79)

Get fashion advice from stylish Miss Inga DaPointe. Have the mayor sing Happy Birthday to you. Trade Disney pins with Main Street Gazette Reporter Scoop Sanderson. Learn to sing from ebullient voice teacher Victoria Trumpetto. These are just a few of the Citizens of Main Street, the living, breathing embodiment of the town, who dance, joke, sing, pose for photos and sign autographs for Magic Kingdom guests.

© Disney

Best parade:
Mickey's Jammin' Jungle Parade (p204)

A giant chameleon may try to nab a fly off your head in this wildly creative procession at Disney's Animal Kingdom (shown at right). Accompanied by colorful stilt-walkers, dancers, drummers and a catchy world-music soundtrack ("Iko Iko," "Mas Que Nada"), huge mechanical animals are joined by Disney characters in whimsical SUVs. The park's narrow walkways bring you amazingly close to the action.

Best splurge:
Pirates League (p312)

Although at Magic Kingdom you can't "drink up me 'earties" with anything stronger than Diet Coke, you can certainly have a swashbuckling time, thanks to this pirate-makeover salon (below), which adjoins the Pirates of the Caribbean attraction. For about $30 adults and children alike can select either a pirate style—complete with beard, scars, earrings, eye patches—or go the skeleton route. Yo ho, yo ho, a pirate's life for… you!

Best place to stay:
Disney's Yacht Club Resort (p286)

With comfortable rooms, good food at all price levels, its own miniature water park and a location that's just a short boat ride to both Epcot and Disney's Hollywood Studios, this beautiful lakeside resort is tough to beat. The adjacent Beach Club offers much the same experience, with less restaurants, a less formal atmosphere and more sandy shore.

Best restaurant: Boma (p250)

No, it doesn't serve roast zebra. Ignore the misconceptions about the food at this beautiful buffet restaurant at Animal Kingdom Lodge; the fare is a mix of non-exotic African dishes with traditional American comfort food. You'll have a wide variety of foods to pick from both at breakfast and dinner. Outstanding choices include the creamy pap for breakfast, homemade soups for dinner, and the carving stations at both meals. The artistic decor features hand-cut tin, hand-blown glass and thatched roofs. Servers are outstanding.

© Disney

What's new

Magic Kingdom

A new nightly projection show filled with special effects, **"The Magic, The Memories, and You!"** transforms Cinderella Castle into a canvas for playful animated sequences as well as images of park guests taken in the park that day. The show is part of a new Walt Disney World marketing campaign, "Let the Memories Begin."

Other Magic Kingdom changes: New characters to meet include **Rapunzel and Flynn Rider** from the 2010 movie "Tangled"... The vintage **Main Street Electrical Parade** evening procession returns after a 9-year hiatus. It takes the place of its original replacement, SpectroMagic... Nearly all **architectural facades** on Main Street U.S.A. have been refurbished with more elaborate detailing... A new interactive queue at **The Many Adventures of Winnie the Pooh** features hands-on activities for children... At **Space Mountain**, new sound effects simulate the whoosh of passing asteroids. New techno music thumps and throbs... The vintage Tomorrowland Transit Authority ride has been renamed the **PeopleMover**. It debuted as the WEDway PeopleMover in 1975.

Now underway, the largest expansion in Magic Kingdom history will nearly double the size of **Fantasyland**. Included will be the indoor ride Under the Sea—Journey of the Little Mermaid (guests travel with Ariel and her friends through adventures above and below the waves), Enchanted Tales with Belle (guests meet Belle and Lumiere and share in an interactive re-telling of the "tale as old as time"), a Be Our Guest restaurant, a Seven Dwarfs Mine Train roller coaster (a musical ride with vehicles that swing back and forth), two circling carousels of Dumbo the Flying Elephant and a re-imagined version of the Barnstormer kiddie coaster featuring Goofy as The Great Goofini. The new area is scheduled to open in phases beginning in late 2012.

Epcot

At the Canada pavilion, **Le Cellier** is now a Disney Signature Restaurant; in Italy new pizzeria **Via Napoli** offers traditional Neapolitan pies; in Germany new candy store **Karamelle-Küche** has replaced Glas und Porzellan. At the Mexico pavilion, a new **La Hacienda de San Angel** waterfront café has a new outdoor La Cantina fast-food spot... The France pavilion has a new fragrance boutique, **Parfums Givenchy**... A new exhibit at the Japan pavilion, **"Spirited Beasts: From Ancient Stories to Anime Stars,"** shows the connection between Japanese myths and modern entertainment... In Future World, most attractions are now open until 9 p.m. One has changed: The 3-D film Honey, I Shrunk the Audience has been replaced with **Captain EO**, a moldy Michael Jackson space fantasy that originally ran in the theater from 1986 to 1994.

Disney's Hollywood Studios

Opening in May, 2011, the park's Star Tours motion simulator has been redone as the

The Magic, The Memories, and You!

Star Tours: The Adventures Continue

3-D **Star Tours: The Adventures Continue.** It features new video and multiple destinations... A budget version of the park's former Block Party Bash street party, the brief **Pixar Pals: Countdown to Fun** parade includes Remy and Emile from "Ratatouille" and Carl, Dug and Russell from "Up" but no guest interaction... A live street concert with a supporting dance troupe, **Disney Channel Rocks** features songs from the television movies "Camp Rock," "High School Musical" and "StarStruck." It replaces the similar High School Musical 3: Right Here! Right Now!... Virtual video arcade **Toy Story Mania!** now includes characters from "Toy Story 3." New game Rex and Trixie's Dino Darts has replaced Bo Peep's Baaa-loon Pop.

Disney's Animal Kingdom
Baby animals born at the park in 2010 include a female Western lowland gorilla, a female African elephant, the park's 28th gerenuk calf, two male scimitar-horned oryx calves (one delivered by Caesarean section in view of guests at Conservation Station), three male warthogs, a female white rhino and a male white-cheeked gibbon.

Downtown Disney
New quick-service restaurant **Pollo Campero** features citrus-flavored Latin chicken and organic offerings... The **AMC 24 theater** now offers the first Enhanced Theater Experience (ETX) in the U.S.... **La Nouba** acts now include a speedy juggler and a playful jumprope segment... the new shop **D Street** features Vinylmation collectibles and stylish apparel.

Activities
A new extra-cost adventure within the Kilimanjaro Safaris landscape, **Wild Africa Trek** takes small groups on personalized guided tours through a remote forest and off the beaten path in the savanna... A new tour, **Through Walt's Eyes,** explores how Walt Disney achieved his dreams... Disney's series of endurance races has been rebranded **runDisney.** Trainer Jeff Galloway is now the official consultant.

Accommodations
Some villas at Disney's **Old Key West Resort** now have sleeper chairs, granite countertops and flat-panel televisions... Disney guests can now get **wake-up calls** in French, German, Japanese, Portuguese and Spanish... The Regal Sun resort is now the **Wyndham Lake Buena Vista**... Set to open in 2012, the **Art of Animation** Value Resort will have many family suites.

Pets, payments and palaces
A **Best Friends Pet Care Resort** kennel has opened near the Port Orleans resorts; all other Disney kennels have closed... A one-day "base" **theme-park ticket** now costs $82 for adults, up from $79 in 2010... Florida residents can now pay for their **annual passes** monthly... **Golden Oak,** a residential subdivision on Disney property, offers single-family homes for $1.5–$8 million.

Opening of the Best Friends Pet Care Resort

Disney Channel Rocks!

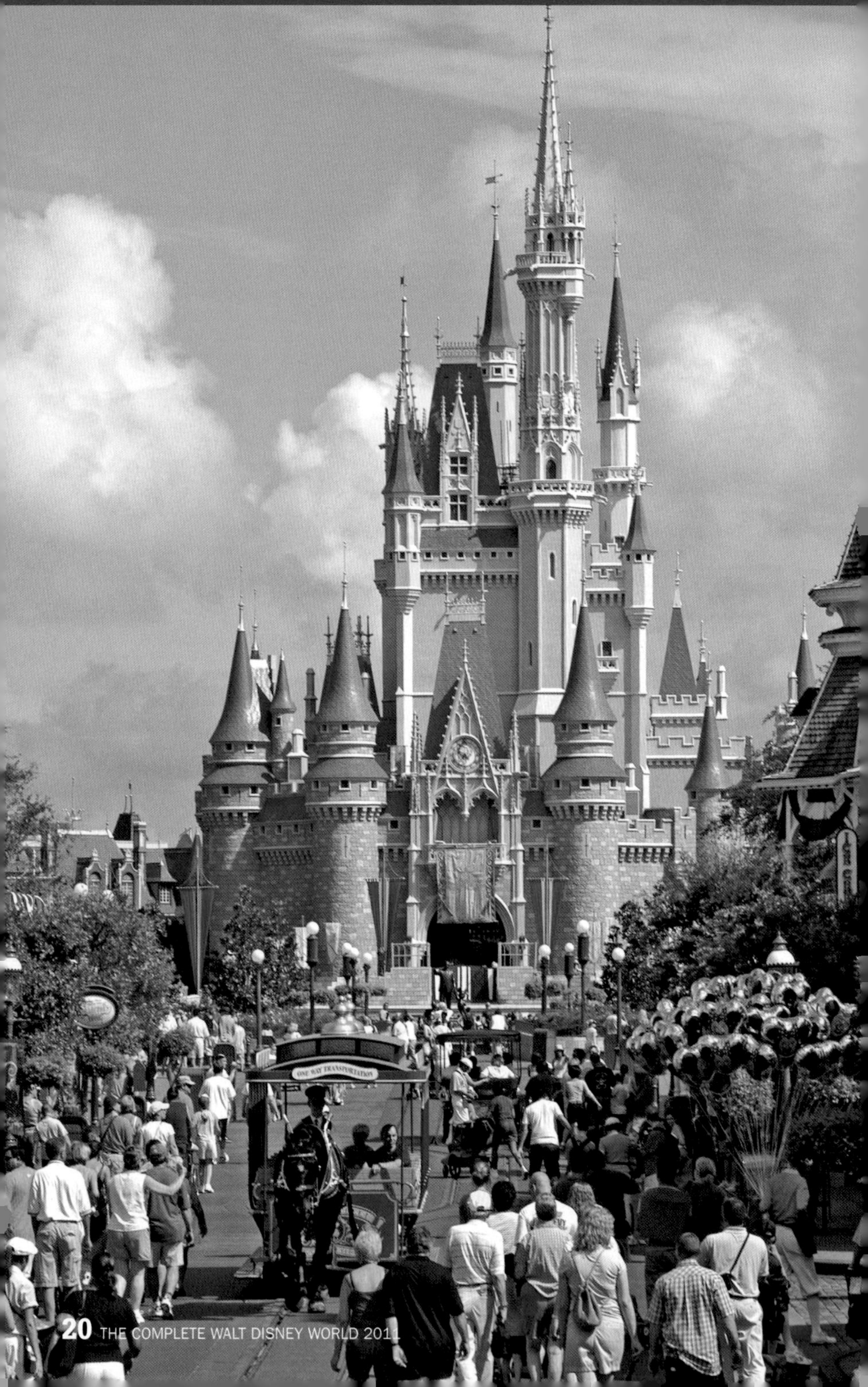
ONE WAY TRANSPORTATION

Magic Kingdom

The world's most popular theme park, Magic Kingdom is a place for adventure, fantasy and nostalgia. Celebrating "Once upon a time…" and "…happily ever after," its appeal lies in memories and imagination, in childhood dreams, of being the prettiest girl at the ball. The rose-colored world includes the friendliest small town ever, an achingly beautiful castle, flying elephants and pirate ships, and an open-cockpit ride through space.

The first theme park opened at Walt Disney World, Magic Kingdom resembles California's Disneyland. During planning, Walt Disney used many of the ideas from his Anaheim park, but on a grand scale. Though Disney unexpectedly died before construction began, his brother Roy ensured that Walt's Magic Kingdom was completed. It opened October 1, 1971.

The most child-focused Disney World park, Magic Kingdom is relatively condensed and easy to navigate. For the most part, its attractions are placed closely together.

Best reasons to go
Main Street U.S.A.: This slice of Americana re-creates a small town boulevard from a century ago. Elaborately detailed from its architecture and music to the costumes of its engaging "citizens," the dreamlike lane triggers nostalgia. In the mornings vintage vehicles shuttle guests back and forth.
Lots of rides: Magic Kingdom has about twice the attractions of any other Disney World park. The range includes everything from a classic merry-go-round to household-name headliners such as Space Mountain.
Iconic fireworks: An unrivalled fireworks display, Wishes bursts above Cinderella Castle in perfect time to a soundtrack of Disney tunes and character voices.
Classic Disney movies: From Dumbo the Flying Elephant to Mickey's PhilharMagic to Peter Pan's Flight, Magic Kingdom is filled with attractions inspired by Disney's legendary animated films.
The monorail: This complimentary "highway in the sky" makes it easy for guests to visit

Facing page: A world-famous landmark, Cinderella Castle faces Main Street U.S.A.

a nearby Disney resort for a meal or other activity, and whoosh back.
The character cup runneth over: More Disney characters appear in Magic Kingdom than any other park, by far. These bonafide celebrities greet guests at many designated outdoor spots, during a street party and in two character meals. They also star in various parades, shows and attractions.
The master's touch: Although he didn't live to see Walt Disney World completed, Walt Disney was heavily involved with its overall planning as well as several of its attractions. Those include Carousel of Progress, The Haunted Mansion, It's a Small World, Jungle Cruise, PeopleMover, Peter Pan's Flight, Pirates of the Caribbean, the Prince Charming Regal Carrousel and the Walt Disney World Railroad.

Worst aspects of the park
The crowds: Attraction capacity: 9,500. Park capacity: 60,000. You do the math. Afternoons are worst; holidays can be jam-packed.
The inconvenience: Getting to the Magic Kingdom can be an adventure in itself, as its parking lot does not adjoin the park. Visitors coming from non-Disney hotels have to first drive or ride a bus, then board a monorail or ferry boat to get to the park entrance.
Afternoons in Tomorrowland: Apparently the future holds little shade and a huge expanse of asphalt. Not good on a warm day.
Tom Sawyer Island: A good idea never fully realized, this small wooded island offers little fun for most young'uns, an exhausting trip to nowhere for their parents.

Getting oriented
Magic Kingdom is divided into six distinctly themed areas:
  Main Street U.S.A.: After entering the park under a train station, guests find themselves in the bustling Town Square of a turn-of-the-century American town. A boulevard leads to Cinderella Castle. From there walkways spoke out to five attraction-packed lands.
  Adventureland: An eclectic mix of African jungles, Arabian nights, Caribbean architecture and South Seas landscaping, this

Many of the 51 building facades of Main Street U.S.A. use Cape Cod clapboarding and gingerbread trim. Each has its own elaborate window framing, frieze work and cornice.

land is home to two boat rides—one indoor, one out—and several smaller adventures.

Liberty Square: Honoring our Colonial heritage, this land's Federal and Georgian architecture brings back the time of the Revolutionary War. The best attractions here: a special-effects laden haunted house and a robotic stage show starring all of America's presidents.

Frontierland: The Old West, the old Midwest, the Old South. Twangin' banjo and fiddle music welcome you to this fun look at 19th-century rural America. It's home to two big thrill rides.

Fantasyland: Set within the stone walls of Cinderella's castle estate, Fantasyland resembles a royal courtyard during a Renaissance fair. Ideal for preschoolers, it holds eight attractions, most of which are based on fairy tales or classic Disney movies. Guests can dine inside Cinderella Castle. Currently the land is in the middle of the biggest expansion in Magic Kingdom history. When the project is finished, the park will have a new "Little Mermaid" ride, a "Beauty and the Beast," restaurant and character experience, a rollicking Seven Dwarfs Mine Train roller coaster and a re-imagined version of the Barnstormer coaster and a double dose of Dumbo the Flying Elephant.

Tomorrowland: Themed to be an intergalactic spaceport, today's version of tomorrow is a trip back to the future of the 1930s. Except for some of it, which is the 1990s as seen from the 1970s. Confused? You betcha. At least it looks cool, especially at night. Attractions include Space Mountain.

What if it rains?

Ducking out of the rain is pretty easy at Magic Kingdom, as stores and counter-service restaurants line most walkways. Big Thunder Mountain Railroad closes when it rains, and parades, street parties, outdoor shows and fireworks can be cancelled. Eleven attractions close when lightning is in the area—Astro Orbiter, Dumbo the Flying Elephant, Jungle Cruise, Liberty Square Riverboat, Magic Carpets of Aladdin, Main Street Vehicles, Splash Mountain, Swiss Family Treehouse, Tomorrowland Speedway, Tom Sawyer Island and the Walt Disney World Railroad.

Family matters

All three thrill rides have height minimums—40 inches for Big Thunder Mountain Railroad and Splash Mountain; 44 inches for Space Mountain. Stitch's Great Escape has a height minimum of 40 inches. Children need to be 54 inches to drive alone on Tomorrowland Speedway; 32 inches to ride as a passenger.

Resembling a royal courtyard during a Renaissance Fair, Fantasyland is home to eight toddler-friendly attractions, and will soon add two more. On most days, the area gets mobbed by crowds after about 11 a.m.

Except for the Speedway, all rides with height minimums have scary elements. Others include Astro Orbiter (fast, high, tilted flight); The Haunted Mansion (dark, with an ominous atmosphere, some screams, pop-up heads); Pirates of the Caribbean (dark, short drop, realistic cannon battle, simulated fire); and Snow White's Scary Adventures (dark, threatening scenes).

Located next to the Crystal Palace restaurant, the park's Baby Care Center provides complimentary changing rooms and nursing areas as well as use of a microwave and playroom. The center sells diapers, formula, pacifiers and over-the-counter medications.

Restaurants and food

Magic Kingdom has a variety of places to eat, with four table-service restaurants, a character-meal buffet and seven indoor fast-food spots. The most memorable eatery—and the toughest reservation to nab in all of Walt Disney World—is Cinderella's Royal Table. Every restaurant has a children's menu. Make reservations at 407-939-3463 or online at disneyworld.com/dining. No alcohol is served in the park.

See the chapter **Restaurants and Food.**

A closer look

Filmmakers by day, the designers of Magic Kingdom expressly created the experience of entering the park so that it mirrors going to the movies. At the turnstiles a train station blocks the view of what's to come, much like a huge curtain used to hide a theater's movie screen from its audience. As guests walk under the station, they pass posters of the park's rides and shows—in other words, its coming attractions. A popcorn stand sits on

A Magical Day

8:30a: Arrive at the entrance turnstiles. As you wait for the gates to open (typically 8:55 a.m.), pick up a Times Guide from Guest Relations at your right.

8:55a: Rush to Fantasyland. See, in this order: Dumbo the Flying Elephant, Peter Pan's Flight, It's a Small World, Mickey's PhilharMagic. (The key to making this work? Getting on one of the first two Dumbo flights of the day.)

9:55a: Get Fastpasses for The Many Adventures of Winnie the Pooh.

10:00a: Ride The Haunted Mansion.

11:15a: Use your Fastpasses to ride The Many Adventures of Winnie the Pooh.

11:45a: Get Space Mountain Fastpasses.

Noon: Lunch at Liberty Tree Tavern.

1:00p: Get Fastpasses for Buzz Lightyear's Space Ranger Spin.

1:10p: Ride Pirates of the Caribbean.

1:45p: Get Splash Mountain Fastpasses.

2:05p: Use your Fastpasses to ride Buzz Lightyear's Space Ranger Spin.

2:45p: Use your Fastpasses to ride Space Mountain.

3:45p: Get Fastpasses for Big Thunder Mountain Railroad.

4:45p: Use Fastpasses at Splash Mountain.

5:30p: See the Move It! Shake It! Celebrate It! street party.

6:10p: Take the monorail to the Grand Floridian Resort to have dinner with Cinderella at 1900 Park Fare.

8:45p: Return to Magic Kingdom to watch the Wishes fireworks show.

9:30p: Use your Fastpasses to ride Big Thunder Mountain Railroad.

Wacky Tomorrowland is best appreciated at night, when the brushed-metal curves of its building trim are lit by rotating beacons, flashing lights and colorful neon

the corner, with its evocative buttery smell. Rounding a small corner, the view opens and the park's feature attraction is revealed—a majestic storybook castle.

Cinderella Castle. Combining the looks of a medieval fortress and Renaissance castle, this concrete-and-fiberglass hexagon magically serves as a perfect icon of the park. Ostensibly the home of the little cinder girl whose rags-to-riches tale made her a princess, in reality the interior holds a restaurant, gift shop and luxurious apartment occasionally offered to chosen guests.

Though the castle appears to be a 300-foot-tall stone fortress, it is actually a 189-foot-tall steel frame covered in a fiberglass shell. The structure was designed to be seen from up close as well as a mile away, so guests arriving on ferries and monorails can spot it early.

A beautiful mosaic decorates the walls of the breezeway. Created out of 500,000 bits of glass in 500 colors, the five-panel artwork tells the Cinderella story. A third of the pieces are fused with silver or gold. The 15- by 10-foot sections were crafted by a team led by acclaimed artist Hanns-Joachim Scharff, based on a design by Disney's Dorothea Redmond. The mosaic took two years to complete.

The castle serves as the backdrop for stage shows, the centerpiece of a fireworks spectacular and the canvas of a new-for-2011

light show that projects photographs of guests onto its walls along with startling animated effects.

The Underworld. Underneath Magic Kingdom is a hidden world; nine acres of warehouse-sized rooms, hallways and work space. The park's nerve center, the "utilidor" is a network of interconnected service areas, including one-and-a-half miles of color-coded tunnels that allow cast members to travel out of view of guests.

Rooms off to the sides include an employee lounge (with lockers, ping-pong tables and video games), a barber shop, a cafeteria, paycheck and wardrobe centers, merchandise storage areas and utility hubs. A huge computer center controls virtually everything in the park, from attraction audio files and projection systems, to the water pressure needed to push boats through It's a Small World and Pirates of the Caribbean, to all parade operations.

Mounted on the ceiling is a fancy trash system—Magic Kingdom's Automated Vacuum Assisted Collection tubes. Every 15 minutes, after above-ground maintenance workers empty the park's trash cans into several backstage collection sites, the garbage is drawn through the tubes at speeds up to 60 miles per hour, on its way to a giant central trash terminal behind Splash Mountain.

Capt. Jack Sparrow trains crew members at his Pirate Tutorial, a street show in front of the Pirates of the Caribbean ride. Children can also participate in the park's Frontierland Hoedown square dance and Move It! Shake It! Celebrate It! street party.

Fun finds. Main Street U.S.A.: ❶ "Well, howdy!" a statue of Goofy says every 30 seconds. It sits on a bench in front of Tony's Town Square Restaurant. ❷ The stars of 1955's "Lady and the Tramp" have put their paw prints in the sidewalk in front of the restaurant patio. ❸ A window at the Emporium identifies its proprietor as Osh Popham, the general-store owner (Burl Ives) in the 1963 movie "Summer Magic." ❹ A singer and dancer can be heard from two Center Street windows marked "Voice and Singing Private Lessons" and "Music and Dance Lessons, Ballet, Tap & Waltz." ❺ Swan topiaries still mark the entrance to the Plaza Swan Boats, a ride that closed in 1983. **Adventureland:** ❻ In front of the Jungle Cruise, six Tikis sync squirts to rhythms. **Liberty Square:** ❼ Streams of brown pavement symbolize sewage that often flowed down 18th-century streets. ❽ Stocks for adults and kids stand in front of the boat dock. ❾ A 1987 cast of the Liberty Bell sits across from the Hall of Presidents. ❿ Adjacent is the Liberty Tree, a 160-year-old live oak that recalls a historic Boston elm. ⓫ Two lanterns in a Hall of Presidents window facing The Haunted Mansion recall the 1860 Longfellow poem "Paul Revere's Ride." ⓬ A rifle sits in a nearby window, a message that the owner is home and ready to fight. ⓭ A marble step beneath a door (No. 26) symbolizes Thomas Jefferson entering the hall to write the Constitution. ⓮ Showing four interlocking hands, a fireman's fund plaque is mounted on a set of green stable doors to the Hall's left. ⓯ The hanging sign outside the Columbia Harbour House includes a U.S. shield with its eagle crying and holding arrows in its right claw, signs the country is at war on

Notable Shops

The Art of Disney: Lithographs, oils, porcelain. Books. Main Street U.S.A.

Bibbidi Bobbidi Boutique: Children's hair, makeover salon. Reservations req. 407-939-7895. Fantasyland.

The Chapeau: Caps. Custom Mickey ears. Main Street U.S.A.

Crystal Arts: Glass. Artisans work in view of guests. Main Street U.S.A.

Disney Clothiers: Fashion apparel. Main Street U.S.A.

The Emporium: Main souvenir store. Main Street U.S.A.

Firehouse Gift Station: Firefighter, police-themed items, pet products. Main Street U.S.A.

Frontier Trading Post / Prairie Outpost & Supply: Pin central, candy, coffee. Frontierland.

Harmony Barber Shop: 9a–4:30p. Res: 407-939-3463. Main Street U.S.A.

Island Supply: Fashion apparel, jewelry. Adventureland.

La Princesa de Cristal: Crystal, glass. Adventureland.

Main Street Confectionery: Candy. Main Street U.S.A.

Sir Mickey's: Disney sundries. Custom Mickey ears. Fantasyland.

Tinker Bell's Treasures: Character costumes. Fantasyland.

Town Square Exposition Hall: Photo, PhotoPass shop. Main Street U.S.A.

Uptown Jewelers: Fine jewelry, watches. Main Street U.S.A.

Ye Olde Christmas Shoppe: Christmas items. Liberty Square.

Stately City Hall holds the park's Guest Relations office. Visitors can ask questions, make dining reservations, exchange currency and pick up maps, Times Guides and disability pamphlets. The office also stores lost items found in the park that day.

Park Resources

ATMs: By the lockers (park entrance), at City Hall, in the Adventureland–Frontierland breezeway, near the Pinocchio Village Haus restrooms, at the Tomorrowland arcade.

First Aid: For minor emergencies. Registered nurses. Next to the Crystal Palace, Main Street U.S.A.

Guest Relations: Walk-up window outside turnstiles, office at City Hall inside. General questions, dining reservations, currency exchange. Maps, Times Guides for all WDW parks. Stores items found in park that day. Multilingual.

Locker rentals: Just inside the park entrance on the right ($7/day plus $5 deposit). Lockers are adjacent.

Package pickup: The building left of City Hall. No charge; allow 3 hours.

Parking: $14/day per car. Free for Disney hotel guests.

Stroller rentals: At Stroller Shop inside park entrance (Singles $15/day, $13/day length of stay. Doubles $31, $27).

Tip Board: Shows attraction wait times. Main Street U.S.A.

Transportation: Monorails to Epcot; Contemporary, Grand Fla., Polynesian resorts. Boats to Ft. Wilderness, Grand Fla., Polynesian, Wilderness Lodge. Buses to Animal Kingdom, Blizzard Beach, Hollywood Studios, all other Disney hotels; no direct service to Downtown Disney, Typhoon Lagoon, ESPN Wide World of Sports.

Wheelchair, scooter rentals: At Stroller Shop inside park entrance. Wheelchairs $12/day, $10/day length of stay. 4-wheel electric scooters $50/day, $20 deposit.

its soil. **Fantasyland:** ⓰ In the mosaic in the castle breezeway, stepsister Drizella's face is green with envy, stepsister Anastasia's is red with anger. ⓱ Columns alongside the mosaic are topped with Cinderella's animal friends. ⓲ Cinderella's wishing well is to the right of the castle, on a walkway that leads to Tomorrowland. ⓳ Cinderella's fountain is behind the castle to the left. Thanks to a wall sketch behind it, youngsters who stand in front of the fountain see the princess wearing her crown. **Tomorrowland:** ⓴ A topiary of Elliot, the star of 1977's "Pete's Dragon," swims through the grass of the entrance plaza. ㉑ Standing between the entrances of the Tomorrowland Transit Authority PeopleMover and Astro Orbiter, a Galaxy Gazette hawker talks ("Extra Extra! Read all about it! Ringleader caught on Saturn!") when a guest stands directly in front of him.

Hidden Mickeys. Entrance area: ❶ Inside Tony's Town Square, as bread loaves in a basket on a server. **Adventureland:** ❷ On the entrance bridge, as white flowers on the first shield on both sides of the walkway. **Liberty Square:** ❸ In the Columbia Harbour House restaurant, as circular wall maps in the room across from the order counter. ❹ In Liberty Tree Tavern, as painted grapes at the top of a spice rack in the lobby, to the right of the fireplace. **Tomorrowland:** ❺ As a softball-sized impression in the concrete between the entrances of the Tomorrowland Transit Authority PeopleMover and Astro Orbiter. In a Mickey's Star Traders mural as ❻ loops of a highway, ❼ train headlights, ❽ glass domes of the building, ❾ satellite dishes, ❿ clear domes covering a city and ⓫ Mickey ears on top of two windows.

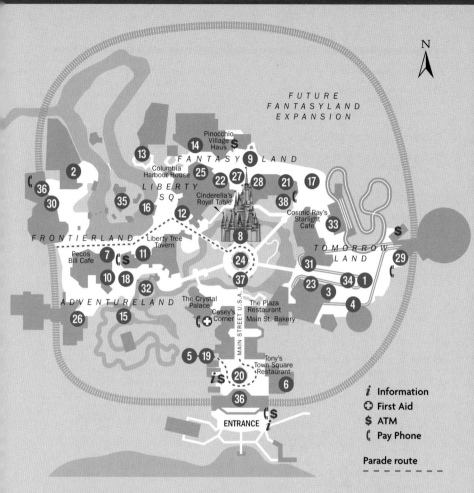

N

FUTURE
FANTASYLAND
EXPANSION

FANTASYLAND
LIBERTY SQ.
FRONTIERLAND
ADVENTURELAND
TOMORROWLAND
MAIN STREET U.S.A.

Pinocchio Village Haus
Columbia Harbour House
Cinderella's Royal Table
Cosmic Ray's Starlight Cafe
Liberty Tree Tavern
Pecos Bill Cafe
The Crystal Palace
Casey's Corner
The Plaza Restaurant
Main St. Bakery
Tony's Town Square Restaurant
ENTRANCE

i Information
✛ First Aid
$ ATM
(Pay Phone

----- Parade route

① Astro Orbiter
② Big Thunder Mountain Railroad
③ Buzz Lightyear's Space Ranger Spin
④ Carousel of Progress
⑤ Celebrate a Dream Come True Parade (start)
⑥ Character Greetings
⑦ Country Bear Jamboree
⑧ Dream Along with Mickey
⑨ Dumbo the Flying Elephant
⑩ The Enchanted Tiki Room— Under New Management
⑪ Frontierland Shootin' Arcade
⑫ The Hall of Presidents
⑬ The Haunted Mansion
⑭ it's a small world
⑮ Jungle Cruise
⑯ Liberty Square Riverboat
⑰ Mad Tea Party
⑱ Magic Carpets of Aladdin
⑲ Main Street Electrical Parade (start)
⑳ Main Street Vehicles
㉑ The Many Adventures of Winnie the Pooh
㉒ Mickey's PhilharMagic
㉓ Monster's, Inc. Laugh Floor
㉔ Move It! Shake It! Celebrate It! Street Party
㉕ Peter Pan's Flight
㉖ Pirates of the Caribbean
㉗ Prince Charming Regal Carrousel
㉘ Snow White's Scary Adventures
㉙ Space Mountain
㉚ Splash Mountain
㉛ Stitch's Great Escape!
㉜ Swiss Family Treehouse
㉝ Tomorrowland Speedway
㉞ Tomorrowland Transit Authority PeopleMover
㉟ Tom Sawyer Island
㊱ Walt Disney World Railroad
㊲ Wishes (best viewing spot)

Attractions at a Glance

Carnival game

🕤 **Frontierland Shootin' Arcade:** ★★★
Shooting gallery Midway game has infrared rifles.
Extra charge. Allow 5 min. No wait. Frontierland.

Character-greeting attractions

6 **Character greetings:** ★★★ **Indoor meet-
and-greet areas** Stars include Mickey Mouse,
Minnie Mouse, princesses. Allow 30 min. Town
Square Exposition Hall, Main Street U.S.A.

Exhibits

32 **Swiss Family Treehouse:** ★★★ **Improvised
home, shipwreck artifacts** Climb-through "Swiss
Family Robinson" home. Allow 20 min. No wait.
Adventureland.

35 **Tom Sawyer Island:** ★ **Two wooded islands**
Connected by bridge, have walk-through cave,
mine, calvary fort. Rafts carry guests across water.
Allow 1 hr. Avg wait 15 min. Frontierland.

Fireworks

37 **Wishes:** ★★★★★ ✔ **Fireworks** Creative pyro
syncs with dialogue, music; life lesson. 12 min.
Loud. Best view is in front of Cinderella Castle.

Parades

5 **Celebrate a Dream Come True Parade:**
★★ **Character procession** Half-hearted floats,
music; many Disney characters. 30 min. 3p. Travels
Main Street U.S.A., Liberty Sq, Adventureland.

19 **Main Street Electrical Parade:** ★★
Evening light procession Retro floats, characters
covered in bulbs. 25 min. Travels Main Street
U.S.A., then Liberty Square, Adventureland.

Rides

1 **Astro Orbiter:** ★★★ ✔ **Elevated hub-and-
spoke rockets** Vehicles circle at 45-degree angle.
2 min. Avg wait 25 min. Steep tilt. Tomorrowland.

2 **Big Thunder Mountain Railroad:**
★★★★★ ✔ **FASTPASS Outdoor roller coaster**
Runaway train twists, turns through mountain
landscapes, mining town. 4 min. Avg wait 35 min.
Height min 40 in. No steep drops. Frontierland.

3 **Buzz Lightyear's Space Ranger Spin:**
★★★ **FASTPASS Ride-through shooting gallery**
Vehicles rotate, guns use laser beams. 5 min. Avg
wait 30 min. Tomorrowland.

9 **Dumbo the Flying Elephant:** ★★★ ✔
Hub-and-spoke ride Two-seat baby-elephant
vehicles. 2 min. Avg wait 30 min. Fantasyland.

13 **The Haunted Mansion:** ★★★★★ ✔
Indoor dark ride "Doom buggies" tour ghostly
retirement home. 11 min. Avg wait 20 min. Dark,
ominous; some screams, pop-up heads. Liberty Sq.

14 **it's a small world:** ★★★★★ ✔ **Indoor boat
ride** Dark gentle ride tours world cultures. Snging
dolls, whimsical animals front colorful abstract
settings. 11 min. Avg wait 15 min. Fantasyland.

15 **Jungle Cruise:** ★★★ **FASTPASS Outdoor
boat ride** Shady journey past dated props, settings; played for laughs. 10 min. Avg wait 30 min.
Adventureland.

16 **Liberty Square Riverboat:** ★★ **Outdoor
boat ride** Paddlewheeler circles Tom Sawyer
Island. 13 min. Avg wait 20 min. Liberty Square.

17 **Mad Tea Party:** ★★★ ✔ **Outdoor spinning
teacups** Canopy-covered; riders control spinning. 2
min. Avg wait 15 min. You'll get dizzy. Fantasyland.

18 **Magic Carpets of Aladdin:** ★★★ **Hub-
and-spoke ride** Four-seat vehicles. 90 sec. Avg
wait 10 min. Adventureland.

20 **Main Street Vehicles:** ★★★★ ✔ **Antique-
style vehicle** Horse trolleys, motorized vehicles
shuttle between Town Square, Cinderella Castle. 3
min. No wait. Mornings only. Main Street U.S.A.

21 **The Many Adventures of Winnie the
Pooh:** ★★★★ ✔ **FASTPASS Indoor dark ride**
Storybook ride recalls Blustery Day. Modern ef-
fects. 3 min 30 sec. Avg wait 30 min. Fantasyland.

25 **Peter Pan's Flight:** ★★★ ✔ **FASTPASS
Indoor dark flight** Vintage ride offers aerial views
of London, Never Land; based on 1953's "Peter
Pan." 3 min. Avg wait 45 min. Fantasyland.

26 **Pirates of the Caribbean:** ★★★★ ✔
Indoor boat ride Dark elaborate settings with
robotic pirates. 9 min. Avg wait 10 min. Short dark
drop, realistic cannon fire. Adventureland.

27 **Prince Charming Regal Carrousel:** ★★★
Merry-go-round Canopy-covered antique carousel. 90 sec. Avg wait 8 min. Fantasyland.

28 **Snow White's Scary Adventures:** ★★★
Indoor dark ride Reenacts scary moments of
1937's "Snow White and the Seven Dwarfs." 2 min
30 sec. Avg wait 20 min. Threatening. Fantasyland.

29 **Space Mountain:** ★★★★★ ✔ **FASTPASS
Indoor roller coaster** Dark, simulates space trip.
2 min 30 sec. Avg wait 45 min. Height min 44 in.
Doesn't go upside down. Tomorrowland.

30 **Splash Mountain:** ★★★ **FASTPASS Indoor/
outdoor boat ride, steep splashdown** Soggy
flume ride travels through robotic indoor scenes,
falls 52 feet. Tells tale of Brer Rabbit (from 1946
film "Song of the South"). 12 min. Avg wait 50
min. Height min 40 in. Most riders get wet, some
soaked. Frontierland.

Goofy dances with guests during the Move It! Shake It! Celebrate It! street party. Held in front of Cinderella Castle throughout the day, it's an easy way to interact with Disney characters.

㉝ Tomorrowland Speedway: ★★ **Kiddie cars** Old-fashioned race cars on a rail top out at 7 mph. 5 min. Avg wait 30 min. Height min 32 in. to ride; 54 in. to take car out alone. Tomorrowland.

㉞ Tomorrowland Transit Authority PeopleMover: ★★★★ ✔ **Elevated indoor, outdoor ride** Open-air tour, goes through four buildings. 10 min. No wait. Tomorrowland.

㊱ Walt Disney World Railroad: ★★★ **Train ride** Steam locomotive circles park. Wooded route. 20 min (round trip). Avg wait 5 min. Main Street U.S.A., Frontierland.

Street party

㉔ Move It! Shake It! Celebrate It!: ★★★★ ✔ **Dance party with characters** Interactive show stars Disney and Pixar characters, dancers, stilt-walkers; guests boogie with performers. 12 min. Cinderella Castle hub.

Theatrical shows

❹ Carousel of Progress: ★★★ ✔ **Audio-Animatronics stage show** Robotic family shows how electricity has improved life. Rotating theater. 21 min. Avg wait 13 min. Tomorrowland.

❼ Country Bear Jamboree: ★★ **Audio-Animatronics stage show** Lowbrow musical revue. 16 min. Avg wait 10 min. Frontierland.

❽ Dream Along with Mickey: ★★★ **Stage show** With Mickey, Minnie Mouse; Donald Duck; Goofy; princesses; "Peter Pan" stars. 20 min. No seats, no shade. Fireworks burst. Cinderella Castle forecourt. Fantasyland.

❿ The Enchanted Tiki Room—Under New Management: ★★ **Audio-Animatronics musical revue** Iago ("Aladdin"), Zazu ("The Lion King") take over, mock, Disney's vintage robotic bird show. 9 min. Avg wait 5 min. Scary Tiki goddess, realistic thunderstorm. Adventureland.

⑫ The Hall of Presidents: ★★★★★ ✔ **Audio-Animatronics stage show** Widescreen film followed by robotic presentation of every U.S. president, including speaking Washington, Obama. 20 min. Avg wait 12 min. Liberty Square.

㉓ Monsters, Inc. Laugh Floor: ★★★ **Improvisational video show** Animated characters interact with audience in live comedy club. 15–20 min. Avg wait 15 min. Tomorrowland.

㉛ Stitch's Great Escape!: ★ *FASTPASS* **Dark stage show** In-the-round show creates the illusion of Experiment 626 skittering around you. 18 min. Avg wait 15 min. Height min 40 in. Restrictive harness, dark periods. Tomorrowland.

3-D movie

㉒ Mickey's PhilharMagic: ★★★★★ ✔ *FASTPASS* **3-D film tours Disney musicals** Donald Duck travels through Disney's best animated films. Delightful. 12 min. Avg wait 15 min. Some sudden images. Briefly totally dark. Fantasyland.

The Walter E. Disney steam engine pulls an open-air passenger train around Magic Kingdom. The vintage locomotive is one of four at the theme park. All were built between 1916 and 1928.

Walt Disney World Railroad

★★★ **Stations at Main Street U.S.A., Frontierland, Fantasyland** 20 min round trip (1.5 mi). Capacity: 360. Outdoor covered queue. Fear factor: None. No eating, drinking, smoking. Idle during parades, fireworks, thunderstorms. Folding strollers OK, no Disney rental strollers. Access: Must be ambulatory; handheld captioning. Debuted: 1971.

Chugging around Magic Kingdom, these full-size trains stop to pick up passengers at Main Street U.S.A., Frontierland and, once it's completed, the park's new Fantasyland area. As most of the journey is heavily wooded, riders get few views of the park. There are glimpses of the indoor riverboat scene of Splash Mountain, the Big Thunder Mountain Railroad and the Tomorrowland Speedway. Guests also pass two small Indian camps and some faux wildlife.

Though a folksy pre-recorded narrator warns "Be on the lookout!" the trip offers no surprises. In general the best views are on the right, though live alligators sometimes swim in a canal on the left, behind Fantasyland. Trains pull in to each station once every 7 to 10 minutes.

Pulled by authentic steam locomotives, the open passenger cars look like Industrial Age street trolleys. The Main Street station replicates a small-town depot from the turn of the 20th century. Its waiting room has working mutoscopes and other antique amusements (bring pennies to play). The station's lower level has vintage railway maps and placards that detail the histories of the engines.

A closer look. Built by Philadelphia's Baldwin Locomotive Works between 1916 and 1928, the four steam engines hauled passengers, jute, sisal and sugar cane for the United Railway of the Yucatan for decades. Acquired by Disney in 1970, they were restored at the Tampa Shipbuilding and Dry Dock Co. in 1971.

Fun facts. ❶ The trains reach a top speed of between 10 and 12 mph. ❷ One of the track's bridges—the steel one just past Frontierland—is half of a two-track bridge from the old Florida Flagler route. ❸ The trains have four sets of passenger cars, each set a different color. The green cars appear only during the park's opening ceremony in front of the Main Street U.S.A. station. In order for performers to exit that train's left side, its cars are missing their left safety rails.

Queasy the Clydesdale waits for guests to board his Main Street horse trolley, shown here decorated for Halloween. Other Main Street Vehicles include a double-decker bus and a fire truck.

Main Street Vehicles

★★★★ ✓ **Main Street U.S.A.** Apx 3 min. Typically mornings only. No horse petting. Fear factor: None. Access: Must be ambulatory. Debuted: 1971.

These old-fashioned vehicles shuttle passengers between Town Square and Cinderella Castle. The rides are free, and there's never a wait. The vehicles are only out in the mornings. The fleet consists of:

Horse trolley. This 22-seat streetcar runs on a track embedded in the street, operated by a driver who has a set of reins, a brake pedal and a foot bell. Morning passengers are often joined by the Dapper Dans barbershop quartet. The horses consist of a Percheron (Charlie), a Belgian (Fritz) and a Clydesdale (Qes, nicknamed, for phonetic reasons only, "Queasy"). Formerly a lawnmower horse in Amish country, laid-back Fritz has been pulling the trolley for 12 years. All geldings, the horses are stabled at Fort Wilderness. A Clydesdale colt, Jacob, is being groomed to join the group. Disney has four trolleys, but uses only one at a time.

Motorized vehicles. A replica of vehicles used in New York City in the 1920s, a 40-seat double-decker bus has a loud horn to keep pedestrians out of its way. Bright red, an 8-seat miniature fire truck carries a giant spotlight as well as a ladder and fire hose. Three horseless carriages are based on luxury Franklin automobiles built between 1903 and 1907; each has two benches and seats six. Topless paddy wagons, two 8-seat jitneys resemble small buses that once shuttled tourists along the boardwalk of Atlantic City, N.J.

Built specifically for the Disney company, the vehicles are the same ones that debuted at Magic Kingdom when it opened in 1971. They run on natural gas. The vehicles' license plates are dated "1915," a reference to the first year the state of Florida issued automobile license plates.

A closer look. America's first horse trolley started service in 1832 and ran along Bowery Street in New York City. The vehicles started to lose popularity three decades later, after a horse lost its footing on a slippery road in San Francisco in 1869, causing a deadly accident. The invention of the cable car (San Francisco, 1873) and the electric streetcar (Richmond, 1888) sealed the horse trolley's fate.

Family matters. Children enjoy sitting up front by the trolley driver; sometimes they can ring the bell.

A winding staircase leads guests through the Swiss Family Treehouse, the makeshift home of a shipwrecked family. The six-story structure includes a living room, two bedrooms and a kitchen.

Swiss Family Treehouse

★★★ **Adventureland** Allow 20 min. Capacity: 300. Shaded queue. Fear factor: None. Access: Must be ambulatory. Debuted: 1971 (Disneyland 1962).

You climb six stories at this walk-through treehouse, which takes guests through the improvised home of the shipwrecked family from the 1960 movie "Swiss Family Robinson."

Remnants of the ship are everywhere—a lantern, log book, ornate railings, benches of various designs and, standing prominently in the living room, the ship's wheel. Ropes from the ship appear to hold the home together. Rooms adapt found objects into everyday effects; giant clamshells form sink basins.

Though ingenious contraptions are found throughout the home—a water-wheel system lifts water up to the tree in bamboo buckets, a barrel in the kitchen cools a refrigerator—the treehouse shows its age. It has no interactive elements, and its 62 steps can exhaust guests who aren't fit.

A closer look. Based on a banyan tree—a tropical fig that grows aerial prop roots to support its outlying branches—the 200-ton, 60-foot-tall, 90-foot-wide *Disneyodendron eximus* ("out-of-the-ordinary Disney tree") is made of concrete, stucco and steel. Its 330,000

leaves are polyethylene, but its Spanish moss is real, as are its lush surroundings. (The first banyan in the U.S. was planted by inventor Thomas Edison in 1925 at his winter home in Fort Myers, Fla. Today it is 400 feet wide.)

In the movie "Swiss Family Robinson," a father, mother and three sons are the sole survivors of a shipwreck on an uncharted tropical island. They use salvage from the ship to build an imaginative home in a huge banyan tree. The story is based on morality tales Swiss pastor Johann Wyss wrote for his sons in 1812. The boys were fans of Daniel Defoe's 1719 novel "Robinson Crusoe."

Family matters. Children will like spotting the wild giant bullfrogs that live in the water under the suspension bridge.

Fun finds. ❶ A living-room Bible is one of two "good books" displayed at Disney World attractions (the other: the Gutenberg Bible at Spaceship Earth). ❷ Rafters above it hold a cask of brandy. Other park displays of alcohol include Pirates of the Caribbean rum, toasting Haunted Mansion ghosts, a Country Bear Jamboree wine glass, Splash Mountain "Muskrat Moonshine" and crates of whiskey at Big Thunder Mountain Railroad.

Micaela Neal

A carnival-style hub-and-spoke ride similar to Dumbo the Flying Elephant, Magic Carpets of Aladdin puts riders in four-seat flying carpets that circle within a palm-lined plaza

Magic Carpets of Aladdin

★★★ **Adventureland** 90 sec. Capacity: 64. Shaded queue. Fear factor: None. Closed during thunderstorms. Access: ECV users must transfer to a wheelchair. Debuted: 2001.

Camels "spit" on riders of this carnival-style hub-and-spoke ride. Inspired by Disney's 1992 animated feature "Aladdin," it's a fun diversion for all ages. Circling around a giant genie bottle, guests fly magic carpets which climb, dip and dive at their command. It's a nice use of 90 seconds, especially when there's little or no wait.

Just another Dumbo the Flying Elephant? Not really. Each carpet seats four, not two, which means the waiting line moves twice as fast and small families can ride together. As guests fly, they control their carpet's pitch as well as its height, thanks to a "magic scarab" controller. The carpets ride rougher than Dumbo, too; they sort of bounce.

A closer look. For a basic carnival ride the attraction offers a lot of detail. The carpets travel over a pool of water—camel heads drool water into it—so as you fly you can look down at your reflection just as Aladdin and Jasmine do in the film. On the bottle, cartwheeling images of Abu the monkey recall early zoetrope animation. Tall palms and ambient "Aladdin" music lend a tropical air.

Princess and pauper. In the film "Aladdin," a beetle-shaped amulet leads its holder to the Cave of Wonders, where a street orphan finds a magic carpet. It later takes Aladdin and princess Jasmine on a romantic flight.

Family matters. Children love to be "spit on" by a camel statue that stands behind the ride's sign. On the ride, fly about halfway high to be hit by a second spitter.

Average wait times

Time	Standby line	Fastpass time
9:00a	0 min	(n/a)
10:00a	5 min	(n/a)
11:00a	5 min	(n/a)
Noon	15 min	(n/a)
1:00p	15 min	(n/a)
2:00p	10 min	(n/a)
3:00p	5 min	(n/a)
4:00p	10 min	(n/a)
5:00p	10 min	(n/a)
6:00p	10 min	(n/a)
7:00p	15 min	(n/a)
8:00p	10 min	(n/a)
9:00p	10 min	(n/a)

A vintage robotic flower-and-bird revue, the Enchanted Tiki Room is 'Under New Management' with owners Iago and Zazu. Facing page: Nearby statues spray guests with water.

The Enchanted Tiki Room

★★ **Adventureland** 9 min. Capacity: 250. Opens 10a. Covered outdoor queue. Fear factor: A threatening goddess, thunderstorm effects. Access: Guests may remain in wheelchairs, ECVs; assistive listening; handheld captioning, Audio Description. Debuted: 1998 (current 'Under New Management' version); original version 1971 (Disneyland 1963).

When parrot Iago (the sarcastic sidekick of Jafar in 1992's "Aladdin") and hornbill Zazu (Mufasa's fastidious majordomo in 1994's "The Lion King") take over this robotic flower-and-bird revue, Iago wants to toss it for something more current. But when he insults the Tiki gods, the parrot learns that "you cannot toy with the Enchanted Tiki Room." Songs include "Hot Hot Hot," "Conga," and, from the mouths of Tiki poles, "In the Still of the Night." If you can, sit on the left side of the theater. You'll face a Tiki goddess.

Parrot Pierre is voiced by the late Jerry Orbach, Det. Lenny Briscoe on TV's "Law & Order." He used the same accent to voice Lumiere in the 1991 movie "Beauty and the Beast." The preshow birds are voiced by Don Rickles and the late Phil Hartman.

A closer look. Conceived as a restaurant, the first Tiki Room debuted at California's Disneyland in 1963 as Disney's first Audio-Animatronics attraction. Guests sang along to 18 minutes of old-time tunes as moving-mouth Tiki poles added grunts and shouts. A duplicate version opened at Walt Disney World in 1971. Disney redid the show in 1998, creating today's shorter, sarcastic storyline with more familiar songs and characters.

Unchanged over the years, the show's bird calls were all voiced by one man. A. Purvis Pullen was also the voice of Cheetah in the 1930s Johnny Weissmuller Tarzan films, the birds in Disney's 1937 "Snow White and the Seven Dwarfs" and 1959's "Sleeping Beauty" and a member of the novelty band Spike Jones and His City Slickers. "It's my favorite accomplishment," Pullen said of his Tiki Room work, "the one that's gonna last."

Fun find. "Boy, I'm tired," Iago says just before the exit doors close. "I think I'll head over to the Hall of Presidents and take a nap."

Hidden Mickeys. ❶ On the entrance doors, as 2-inch berries on a stem underneath a bird's tail, 4 feet off the ground. ❷ On the bottom of Iago's perch, where a small carved face is wearing Mickey ears.

© Disney

An elephant bathing pool is filled with playful pachyderms on the Jungle Cruise. Wise-cracking guides tell guests "If you want to take pictures go ahead—all the elephants have their trunks on."

Jungle Cruise

★★★ **FASTPASS** **Adventureland** 10 min. Capacity: 310. Covered outdoor queue. Fear factor: A trip through a dark temple gets close to some unrealistic snakes. Closed during thunderstorms. Access: Guests may remain in wheelchairs, ECVs; assistive listening, handheld captioning. Debuted: 1971 (Disneyland 1955).

Elephants squirt water from their trunks, headhunters shake their spears, hungry hippos threaten to attack… and they're all fodder for jokes on this outdoor boat ride. Your skipper, a crazed stand-up comic, rattles off corny puns and one-liners at every turn. Other sights include plastic butterflies the size of chickens, gorillas sacking a camp, a treed safari party and a flooded temple with a monkey shrine guarded by pythons. Canopied crafts take guests on a tropical tour down four mighty—and mighty narrow—rivers: the Amazon, Congo, Nile and Mekong.

A closer look. Designed more than a half-century ago, the ride isn't exactly modern. Many of its animals don't move; the ones that do never change expression. Premiering at California's Disneyland in 1955, the ride was originally a serious educational tour of regions most Americans had never seen, even in pictures. The jokes began with the addition of the elephant pool (1962). By the time the Florida version opened (1971) the entire thing was being played for laughs.

Worth your time? It depends on the skipper. Some are terrific—Steve Martin and Robin Williams started with this gig—but others are apathetic or just plain lame. Go twice and you'll probably have two completely different experiences.

Family matters. Ask nicely and your child may be able to "steer" the boat.

Average wait times

Time	Standby line	Fastpass time
9:00a	5 min	9:10a
10:00a	10 min	10:10a
11:00a	20 min	11:30a
Noon	35 min	12:35p
1:00p	35 min	1:40p
2:00p	40 min	2:55p
3:00p	40 min	3:35p
4:00p	30 min	4:40p
5:00p	30 min	5:30p
6:00p	30 min	6:45p
7:00p	25 min	7:35p
8:00p	20 min	8:45p
9:00p	20 min	9:20p

Wild-eyed skippers pilot their vessels past signs of headhunters and other dangers on the Jungle Cruise. Boat names include Volta Val, Zambezi Zelda and Wamba Wanda.

Fun finds. ❶ A sign along the queue honors the cruise company's latest Employee of the Month: E.L. O'Fevre. ❷ Near the dock, a cage holds a giant (faux) tarantula. It jerks and rears up. ❸ A chalkboard on the dock lists the crew's weekly lunch menu: fricassee of giant stag beetle, BBQ'd 3-toed skink, consomme of river basin slug and fillet of rock python. All are reported to taste like chicken. ❹ On the ride, the dancing headhunters shout "I love disco!" though it's tough to hear.

❺ Next to the exit, a list of missing persons include "Ilene Dover" and "Ann Fellen."

Hidden Mickeys. ❶ The queue-area radio plays Cole Porter's 1935 hit "You're the Top," including the lyrics "you're a Bendel bonnet, a Shakespeare sonnet, you're Mickey Mouse!" ❷ On the side of the crashed plane, between and below the windows. ❸ As yellow spots on the back of a giant spider in the temple, on the right just past the snakes.

"The crocodile on the right is Ginger. Watch out... Ginger snaps!" Perhaps realistic in 1971, faux animals along the riverbanks of the Jungle Cruise also include giant butterflies, spiders, tigers and a pride of lions snacking on a hapless zebra.

A dark boat ride through scenes of pirates sacking a village, the Pirates of the Caribbean attraction has inspired a series of feature films. Robotic figures include Capt. Jack Sparrow.

Pirates of the Caribbean

★★★★ ✔ **Adventureland** 9 min. Capacity: 330 (15 per boat). Indoor, air-conditioned queue. Fear factor: Darkness, cannon fire may scare toddlers. Access: ECV and wheelchair users must transfer; handheld captioning, Audio Description. Debuted: 1973, revised 2006 (Disneyland 1967).

Drunk pirates "pillage and plunder... rifle and loot... kidnap and ravage and don't give a hoot" in this rowdy, rum-soaked attraction, a dark, indoor ride in which guests take open-air boats through scenes of robotic pirates ransacking a Caribbean port. There's plenty to look at, as riders pass dozens of vignettes and sight gags. Special effects simulate fire, lightning, wind, splashing cannon balls and a ghostly appearance by Davy Jones (the evil spirit of the deep, not the Monkee).

The inspiration for the "Pirates of the Caribbean" movies, the ride keeps a light-weight tone; the pirates have such caricatured features they seem straight from a cartoon. Updated in 2006, the ride now features Capt. Jack Sparrow and other movie characters. Its cool, dim queue winds through a stone fort.

Aye, a tale there be! The attraction's storyline is a morality tale, told in flashback form. It begins in the present, as guests pass through a watery grotto lined with pirate skeletons, then goes back in time to show what led the pirates to their doom. Scenes include Capt. Barbossa attacking a Caribbean port as he and his men search for Capt. Jack and Jack outsmarting them all as he claims the town's treasure.

Historic it be. The last ride Walt Disney helped design, the attraction combines a farm boy's view of high-seas adventure with a Hollywood showman's use of theatrics.

Average wait times

Time	Standby line	Fastpass time
9:00a	0 min	(n/a)
10:00a	5 min	(n/a)
11:00a	15 min	(n/a)
Noon	15 min	(n/a)
1:00p	20 min	(n/a)
2:00p	15 min	(n/a)
3:00p	20 min	(n/a)
4:00p	15 min	(n/a)
5:00p	5 min	(n/a)
6:00p	10 min	(n/a)
7:00p	10 min	(n/a)
8:00p	15 min	(n/a)
9:00p	10 min	(n/a)

Micaela Neal

Clockwise from top left: The ride's infamous redhead is, in reality, just a pole from the waist down. Capt. Jack learns the location of the town's treasure... and later lolls among the booty.

Conceived as a wax museum, the attraction became an Audio-Animatronics boat ride after the success of two Disney-designed efforts at the 1964 New York World's Fair. It drew from Carousel of Progress, with its then-revolutionary robotic characters, and It's a Small World, which debuted a water-jet system that propelled boats through scenes.

PC it be not. The ride's story is all in good fun, but even the most carefree parent may wonder if scenes showing torture, heavy drinking and the selling of women send the best messages to a wide-eyed child. "There is nothing politically correct about Pirates of the Caribbean," admits Imagineer Eric Jacobson. "In fact, much of it is patently offensive."

In fairness, the ride does imply the consequences of such behavior. As the first scene illustrates, the pirates end up murdered, their bodies left behind to rot. And it is more sensitive than it used to be. A barrel that today hides Capt. Jack once contained a nearly naked young woman. As the pirate in front of her held her slip in his hand, he spoke of his wish to "hoist me colors on the likes of that shy little wench. I be willin' to share, I be!"

Fun facts. The Davy Jones fog screen is made of microscopic water droplets held in place by columns of air. The voices of Davy Jones, Capt. Barbossa and Capt. Sparrow are those of actors Bill Nighy, Geoffrey Rush and Johnny Depp. The auctioneer is voiced by Paul Frees, the Haunted Mansion's "ghost host." The exterior facade is based on the 16th-century El Morro fortress in San Juan, P.R.

Fun finds. ❶ Along the right entrance queue, two chess-playing skeleton pirates stare at the board. ❷ In the harbor, a sign on the ship's stern reveals its name: the Wicked Wench. ❸ At the bridal auction, the first woman in line is beaming, happy to be sold. The auctioneer refers to her portly body as "stout-hearted and cornfed" and asks her to "shift yer cargo, dearie. Show 'em yer larboard side." ❹ Impatient to be next, a buxom redhead pulls up her skirt. The auctioneer responds "Strike yer colors you brazen wench! No need to expose yer superstructure!" ❺ In the next room, a drunken pirate invites two cats to join him in "a little ol' tot of rum." ❻ As you leave the burning town, the hairy leg of a pirate above dangles toward you; a parrot with him squawks "A parrot's life for me!" ❼ Frustrated that the dog in front of the jail won't respond, one prisoner tells another "Hit him with the soup bone!" As the dog looks at you, another captive says "Rover, it's us what needs yer ruddy help, not them blasted lubbers." ❽ Painted on the exit ramp, "shoe prints" that indicate where to step consist of a normal right shoe and peg-leg left mark.

© Disney

A unique theatrical attraction, The Hall of Presidents includes Audio-Animatronics versions of every American commander-in-chief. Above, President Obama recites the oath of office.

The Hall of Presidents

★★★★★ ✔ **Liberty Square** 20 min. Capacity: 740. Open 10a–park close. Every 30 min. on hr, half hr. Indoor, air-conditioned queue. Fear factor: None. Access: Guests may stay in wheelchairs, ECVs. Assistive listening, reflective captioning. Debuted: 1971, revised 2009.

A robotic version of President Barack Obama speaks in this uplifting theatrical show, which also features Abraham Lincoln standing up to recite the Gettysburg Address and a short speech by an Audio-Animatronics version of George Washington. Every president of the United States makes a memorable, robotic appearance. Fans of American history, parents wanting to inspire their children or perhaps just anyone longing for a return to civility in American politics should love every minute.

The presentation begins with a large-format film. Starting with George Washington's struggle to build a new nation, the movie scans U.S. history through the start of the 21st century, highlighting presidents who have reached out to the American people during times of strife. Those featured include Franklin Roosevelt during the Great Depression, Lyndon Johnson after the assassination of John F. Kennedy, Bill Clinton in the aftermath of the Oklahoma City bombing and George W. Bush encouraging citizens at Ground Zero after 9-11.

Midway through the film, a screen rises to reveal Abraham Lincoln sitting alone on the stage. He stands, then delivers his full (ten-sentence) Gettysburg Address. When the film ends, a curtain rises to show every president on stage simultaneously—43 life-sized animated figures, stretching out three-deep across the 100-foot-wide podium. They are introduced one by one.

Each president nods at the audience as he is introduced, and fidgets, shifts his weight, looks around or even whispers to his colleagues as the roll call continues. Warren G. Harding nervously bounces his foot.

Soon, George Washington stands. Using portions of his second inaugural address, he explains the importance of the presidential oath of office. Washington is voiced by actor David Morse, who played our first president in the award-winning 2008 HBO miniseries "John Adams." Standing nearby, Obama recites that oath and then offers his thoughts about the American dream.

Disney says its Obama robot is the most dynamic Audio-Animatronics figure the

Clockwise from top left: The Hall of Presidents lobby features a stately rotunda; a robotic George Washington is voiced by actor David Morse; lobby displays include a vintage teddy bear.

company has ever created. It has an array of subtle movements and facial expressions. After reciting the oath, it checks its notes before continuing.

Disney officials traveled to the White House to record Obama (in the Map Room) and film him for reference. They worked with White House staff to create the clothing and accessories worn by the Obama figure, including an appropriate lapel pin, watch and braided wedding band.

The refurnished lobby has many new artifacts. Display cases exhibit personal presidential belongings such as George Washington's tea caddy and George W. Bush's inaugural cowboy boots. Other cases hold dresses and objects worn by several first ladies, including Edith Roosevelt (Teddy's wife), Elizabeth Monroe and Nancy Reagan, as well as painted Easter eggs from a White House egg hunt.

A closer look. The brainchild of Walt Disney himself, the Hall of Presidents exists only at Walt Disney World. Its widescreen projection system was initially invented by Ub Iwerks, the original animator of Mickey Mouse. His three side-by-side screens are each 18 feet tall and 30 feet wide.

The Lincoln figure is a simplified remake of Disney's original problematic Honest Abe that debuted at the State of Illinois exhibit at the 1964 New York World's Fair, "Great Moments with Mr. Lincoln." With any spike in current, Disney's first Lincoln would flail its arms, hit itself repeatedly in the head and then slam itself back down in its chair.

The malfunction inspired a scene in a 1993 episode of "The Simpsons." In "Selma's Choice," Aunt Selma takes Bart and Lisa to the Walt Disney World-like Duff Gardens, where every attraction is themed to Duff Beer. At the Duff Hall of Presidents, Lincoln holds up a Duff can and takes a swig, then mindlessly smashes it onto his head.

Today's Lincoln recites the Gettysburg address using the original recording, which was voiced in 1963 by character actor Royal Dano. Walt Disney directed the taping.

A Walt Disney World publicist used to tell visiting reporters that some of the presidents were real people—that since there were always a few robots out for repairs, each show had at least one human stand-in. When he once asked the late Walter Cronkite to spot the live actor, the veteran newsman just laughed. A minute later he turned back and said, "Jefferson?"

Family matters. The show is a great opportunity for parents to talk with their children about the American concept that anyone can grow up to be president. Is it true? Would they want to be one?

Especially spooky at night, The Haunted Mansion grounds include a ghostly hearse with an invisible horse, the sounds of a howling wolf, a graveyard, a mausoleum and a pet cemetery

The Haunted Mansion

★★★★★ ✔ **Liberty Square** 11 min. Capacity: 320. Covered queue. Fear factor: Dark, some screams. A few ghosts and some scenes are scary. Access: Must be ambulatory. Handheld captioning, Audio Description. Debuted: 1971, revised 2007.

Ghosts duel, fly, guzzle booze, play an organ, sing, sip tea, waltz, even hitchhike in this dark indoor ride. Touring a ghostly retirement home, guests slowly travel room by room past many inhabitants, who are brought to life by age-old visual tricks, Disney's Audio-Animatronics robot technology and some cool high-tech effects. Although some of the imagery may be too intense for preschoolers, the ride is never truly scary. Anyone who enjoys the ghosts in the Harry Potter movies—think of Nearly Headless Nick, not the dementors—will be tickled by the experience.

According to the attraction's "ghost host" narrator, the mansion's residents are trying to recruit a new member. "We have 999 happy haunts here," he intones, "but there's room for a thousand. Any volunteers?"

Bubble-shaped "doom buggy" vehicles take visitors through a library and conservatory, then to a parlor where a spiritualist conducts a seance—she appears only as a head in a floating crystal ball. The haunts materialize in the dining hall. Twirling spirits dance; boozing spooks swing from chandeliers. The attic holds a ghostly bride who has killed off many husbands, then it's out to a graveyard for a rollicking wake. After a few ghosts appear to hop in your buggy with you, a tiny female spirit urges you to come back again someday. "Hurry back... hurry back..." she coos, dead bouquet in her arms, her veil and flowing robe blowing in the breeze.

Average wait times

Time	Standby line	Fastpass time
9:00a	0 min	(n/a)
10:00a	10 min	(n/a)
11:00a	10 min	(n/a)
Noon	20 min	(n/a)
1:00p	20 min	(n/a)
2:00p	25 min	(n/a)
3:00p	25 min	(n/a)
4:00p	25 min	(n/a)
5:00p	25 min	(n/a)
6:00p	20 min	(n/a)
7:00p	20 min	(n/a)
8:00p	15 min	(n/a)
9:00p	15 min	(n/a)

Transforming before your eyes, a portrait in the foyer depicts a young man aging into a corpse. It's inspired by Oscar Wilde's 1890 novel "The Picture of Dorian Gray."

Family matters. Some images could disturb young children. They include a hanging body, portraits with eyes that track guests as they pass, a person trapped in a coffin, someone burying himself alive and many discomfiting visions of the devil.

A closer look. Many Mansion moments are inspired by movies and literature. Motion picture influences include the 1946 French version of "Beauty and the Beast" ("La Belle et la Bete"), in which human statues follow guests with their gazes and wall sconces are held by human arms, and 1963's "The Haunting," which includes a tapping, thumping corridor of doors. Literary inspirations include Oscar Wilde's 1890 novel "The Picture of Dorian Gray," which features a transforming portrait in which a young man becomes old and skeletal. Edgar Allen Poe fans will find allusions to his 1845 poem "The Raven" and 1846 novel "The Cask of Amontillado," in which a live man is trapped in a brick tomb.

Haunted Mansion voice talents include:

Paul Frees: The voice of the "ghost host" played Boris Badenov in the 1959–1964 TV series "The Adventures of Rocky and Bullwinkle." At the Pirates of the Caribbean Frees voices the auctioneer, Carlos, the concertina player and the nearby dog, and the bridge parrot.

Eleanor Audley: The voice of the spiritualist was the voice of Lady Tremaine in 1950's "Cinderella" and Maleficent in 1959's "Sleeping Beauty." She played the mother of Oliver Douglas in the 1960s television series "Green Acres."

The Mellomen: The quartet that sings "Grim Grinning Ghosts" sang backup on Rosemary Clooney's 1954 hit "Mambo Italiano" and was Elvis Presley's supporting group in "It Happened at the World's Fair" (1963), "Roustabout" (1964) and "Paradise Hawaiian Style" (1966).

Thurl Ravenscroft: The second singing bust from the left in the graveyard, Ravenscroft sang "You're A Mean One, Mr. Grinch" in the 1966 TV special "How the Grinch Stole Christmas!" and was the voice of Tony the Tiger for Kellogg's Frosted Flakes.

Candy Candido: The graveyard executioner was the apple tree in 1939's "The Wizard of Oz" ("Are you hinting my apples aren't what they ought to be?") and the Indian chief in Disney's 1953 movie "Peter Pan."

Fun facts. ❶ A real Civil War antique, the hearse appeared in the 1965 John Wayne film "The Sons of Katie Elder." **❷** The ride's theme song, "Grim Grinning Ghosts" is performed in eight styles, including a dirge that plays as you enter. **❸** The mansion's "dust" is made from fuller's earth, an ingredient in kitty litter. **❹** Except for a few books, the library bookcase is simply a flat painted backdrop. **❺** So is the back wall of the dining hall. **❻** Inspired by a white Styrofoam wig holder, Disney's Ub Iwerks (the original animator for Mickey Mouse) devised the floating head of the spiritualist and the graveyard's singing busts. **❼** You never go in the home. The entire ride takes place in a building behind it.

Fun finds. ❶ Outside the ride, horseshoe and wheel tracks lead from a barn to the hearse; dead roses lie inside it. **❷** Madame Leota's eyes open on her tombstone face, which tilts. **❸** In the queue room, the fireplace grate forms a cross-eyed, arrow-tongued face; grates on the floor form monstrous faces. **❹** Chain stanchions in the loading area are toothy brass bats. **❺** On the ride, a woman in a painting transforms into Medusa. **❻** The paneling in the library between the busts has carved bat faces. **❼** The window frame in the music room has coffin trim. **❽** In the endless hallway, fang-baring serpents extend from

Outside the Haunted Mansion exit, each of 20 occupants of a mausoleum has a pun for a name. The grave of the pirate Bluebeard, and all but one of his "loving" wives, stands around the corner.

the frame molding. **9** Conservatory coffin handles are bats. **10** In the corridor of doors, the grandfather clock is a demon. The casing forms hair and eyes; the clock-face a mouth; the pendulum a tail. **11** On the mantle in the dining hall, a ghost in a top hat has his arm around a bust. **12** The fireplace grate includes two black-cat silhouettes. **13** In front of the fireplace, an old woman knits in a rocking chair. **14** Five ghosts float out of a coffin which has fallen out of a hearse. **15** Mr. Pickwick (from the 1836 Charles Dickens novel "The Pickwick Papers") swings from the chandelier; legendary lovers Marc Antony and Cleopatra sit next to him. **16** Julius Caesar sits at the left end of the table. **17** The sheet-music stand is a leering bat. **18** In the graveyard, a medieval minstrel band includes a flutist emerging from his tomb, a drummer playing bones, a kilt-wearing bagpiper, a soldier playing a small harp and a pajama-clad trumpeter. **19** When the trumpeter rears, so do two owls above him. **20** Five tomb-sitting cats yowl and hiss to the beat. **21** A skeletal dog howls on a hill. **22** A king and queen ride a makeshift seesaw. **23** Swinging from a tree branch, a princess sips tea. **24** A duke and duchess toast at a candlelit table. **25** Four ghosts circle on bicycles behind them. **26** Behind a grave, an earringed pirate raises his teacup, and sometimes his head. **27** A floating teapot pours

tea into a cup. **28** A hearse driver chats with a duchess, who sits atop the vehicle sipping tea. **29** A ghost sits up from the fallen hearse coffin to chat with a sea captain. **30** A dog sniffs an Egyptian sarcophagus; its mummy is sitting up, stirring his tea and mumbling. **31** "What's that? Louder! I can't hear you! Eh?" says an old bearded man to the mummy, holding a horn to his ear. **32** The Grim Reaper floats inside a tomb on the extreme far right. **33** Dressed in Viking gear, male and female opera singers belt out solos. **34** Holding his severed head, a knight cheerfully sings a duet with his executioner. **35** A pint-sized shackled prisoner harmonizes with them. **36** Sensing the party's over, an arm of a ghost trowels itself back into a tomb. **37** Human arms hold up wall sconces in the tomb and in the unload area. **38** Outside the exit, each mausoleum occupant has a pun for a name. **39** Dogs and snakes appear in the frames of benches in front of a hillside pet cemetery. **40** Mr. Toad (of the late Mr. Toad's Wild Ride) is buried there.

Hidden Mickeys. 1 The foyer and stretching rooms form the shape. **2** As the left-most place setting on the near side of the dining table. **3** As a silhouette at the end of the arm of the Grim Reaper. **4** On the right side of the souvenir cart, on the index finger of a painted hand beneath the word "Parlour."

A real paddlewheeler, the Liberty Square Riverboat takes guests on a tour of Magic Kingdom's "Rivers of America," a wide waterway that circles Tom Sawyer Island

Liberty Square Riverboat

★★ **Liberty Square** 13 min. Capacity: 400. Typically operates 10a–dusk, with rides every half hour on the half hour. Outdoor covered queue. Fear factor: None. Access: Guests may remain in wheelchairs, ECVs. Debuted: 1971, updated 2007.

"Steady as she goes!" With recorded narration by an actor playing the role of author Mark Twain, this three-story steamwheeler offers a taste of life on the Mississippi. Circling Tom Sawyer Island, the peaceful half-mile journey passes scenes and props that depict rural American life in the 1800s.

Unfortunately, the sights are nothing special. They include a wilderness cabin, a barely robotic Native American camp and a few remarkably stoic woodland creatures. Better are views of Frontierland and Liberty Square; passengers come close to the track of the Big Thunder Mountain Railroad and get a great glimpse of The Haunted Mansion.

Another downer: the boat has few seats, especially shaded ones. Morning voyages offer a nice diversion from thrill rides, but afternoon trips are often hot and crowded. On sunny days the best places to stand are on the shady second-floor bow. The best views, of course, are from the top deck.

A closer look. Despite its flaws as a ride, the boat offers a decent look at a forgotten way of American life. Though guided by an underwater rail, Disney's Liberty Belle is a true steamwheeler. Pumped full before each trip, its diesel boiler turns river water into steam, then pipes it to an engine which drives a large paddlewheel (as well as the boat's electrical system). A steam whistle and smokestack tops the ship.

Much like railroads, paddle steamers were a major means of transporting goods and passengers in the 1800s. Vulnerable to fire, many of the wooden vessels were destroyed by boiler explosions, events which led to the concept's demise. Invented by the Romans, the paddlewheel was the first practical form of mechanical boat propulsion.

Family matters. Show your children the steam engine. It's located on the lower deck, just in front of the paddlewheel. Where else will they see one?

Fun facts. ❶ The boiler is kept at 700 degrees. **❷** The leadsman is exaggerating when he calls out "Mark Twain!" indicating the water is two fathoms (12 feet) deep. These "Rivers of America" are only 9 feet deep.

'Jamboree' house band The Five Bear Rugs consists of (clockwise from left) homemade-"Thing" player Tennessee, mouth-harpist Big Fred, jug-blower Ted, fiddler Zeb and banjo-strumming Zeke

Country Bear Jamboree

★★ **Frontierland** 16 min. Capacity: 380. Opens 10a. Indoor, air-conditioned queue. Fear factor: None. Access: Guests may remain in wheelchairs, ECVs. Assistive listening, reflective captioning. Debuted: 1971.

Goofy mechanical bears perform in this cornpone musical revue. Set in the union hall of an 1880s lumber camp, it features 18 life-sized performers singing snippets of 14 country and cowboy songs. The bears' exaggerated faces are funny, as are a couple of the songs—Tex Ritter's 1950 "My Woman Ain't Pretty (But She Don't Swear None)" and Homer & Jethro's 1964 "Mama Don't Whip Little Buford (I Think You Should Shoot Him Instead)." Unfortunately, however, the show has lousy pacing and lame jokes.

The best bear is sad-eyed Big Al, who warbles the 1960 tongue-in-cheek Tex Ritter dirge "Blood on the Saddle" (Ritter himself provided the voice). Others include tutu-clad Trixie singing the 1966 Wanda Jackson hit "Tears Will Be the Chaser for my Wine" and Mae West clone Teddi Barra cooing Jean Shepard's 1967 tune "Heart, We Did All That We Could." Mounted on a side wall, talking trophy heads Buff (a buffalo), Max (a deer) and Melvin (a moose) bicker and banter.

A closer look. Designed in the 1960s, the Jamboree was intended for a proposed Disney resort in California's Sequoia National Forest. Sung here by the all-male Five Bear Rugs, "Devilish Mary" was, in real life, the first country song recorded by a female; 14-year-old Roba Stanley sang it in 1924.

Family matters. For parents with older kids the show provides a good springboard for a conversation about how society treats women. While the host often praises the other males for their musical skills, the female bears are described only as either fat or sexy, and portrayed only as flirtatious, emotional or, in one case, drunk. Is that right?

Frontierland Shootin' Arcade. ★★★ Allow 5 min. Capacity: 16. Fear factor: None. Access: Guests may remain in wheelchairs, ECVs. Debuted: 1971. $1 for 25 shots. Just down the walkway from the Bears, this old-fashioned arcade is filled with more than 50 silly targets. Direct hits trigger sight and sound gags—a prisoner escapes from a jail, a grave-digging skeleton pops out of a hole. Ideal for children, the infrared rifles are easy to hold and the targets easy to hit. Guns mounted in the center of the arcade have the best view of the most targets.

No spell check, no problem: Tom Sawyer himself appears to have written signs that direct guests around Tom Sawyer Island. The area features a series of small walk-through adventures.

Tom Sawyer Island

★ **Frontierland** Allow 1 hr. Capacity: 400. Closes at dusk. Outdoor covered queue. Fear factor: The cave has side niches where young children can get temporarily lost. No rafts during thunderstorms. Access: Must be ambulatory. Debuted: 1973.

Tom Sawyer would be bored to death on this small wooded island, which is meant to recall the classic 1876 novel by Mark Twain, "The Adventures of Tom Sawyer." Though children have plenty of things to walk through—a small cave, a mine, a windmill and a watermill—there's little chance for free-spirited adventure. Across a footbridge, a second island features a frontier fort with lookout towers outfitted with toy rifles. The only way to reach the islands is aboard a powered raft.

A closer look. The island has some interesting details. Games of checkers are often set up on tables at the raft landings and the fort. Water appears to run uphill in the mine. The women's restroom at Fort Langhorne is cleverly labeled "Powder Room." Noises inside the watermill create a creaky, squeaky version of "Down By The Old Mill Stream"; the bird trapped in the mill's cogs re-creates a scene from the 1937 cartoon "The Old Mill."

In the novel, Tom Sawyer is a carefree 12-year-old who lives with his Aunt Polly in a small town on the Mississippi (in essence, Hannibal, Mo.). The boy's friends include Huckleberry Finn and Joe Harper. Tom's adventurous life includes cleverly persuading other children to whitewash a fence for him, getting lost in a cave with girlfriend Becky Thatcher, finding gold in the cave left behind by the evil Injun Joe, and running away from home to live on a river island.

Average wait times

Time	Standby line	Fastpass time
9:00a	0 min	(n/a)
10:00a	5 min	(n/a)
11:00a	5 min	(n/a)
Noon	15 min	(n/a)
1:00p	20 min	(n/a)
2:00p	20 min	(n/a)
3:00p	20 min	(n/a)
4:00p	15 min	(n/a)
5:00p	5 min	(n/a)
6:00p	5 min	(n/a)
7:00p	5 min	(n/a)
8:00p	(closed)	(n/a)
9:00p	(closed)	(n/a)

Everyone's got a laughing place: After Brer Fox captures Brer Rabbit by slamming a beehive over his head (below), the helpless bunny cons his enemy into flinging him back into his briar patch. Experiencing the toss firsthand, riders plunge 52 feet to a watery splashdown.

Splash Mountain

★★★ *FASTPASS* **Frontierland** 12 min. Capacity: 440. Covered queue. Fear factor: One small drop is completely dark. The big drop can scare adults. Guests should be free from motion sickness; pregnancy; high blood pressure; heart, back or neck problems. Closed during thunderstorms. Access: Must be ambulatory. Height min: 40 in. Debuted: 1992 (Disneyland 1989).

You plunge 52 feet into a soaking splashdown during this half-mile flume ride, which recalls the animated story told in Disney's 1946 film "Song of the South." A hollowed-out log takes you through bayous, swamps, a cave and a flooded mine as you witness a fox and bear's attempts to snare a wily rabbit. The bright colors, many Audio-Animatronics characters and peppy music will appeal to young children; the big fall to thrill-seekers.

The logs reach 40 mph on the fall, making it the fastest Magic Kingdom moment. For the driest drop choose the back seat and sit on the left; duck down on the drop and stay down until after the slosh. New for 2011, lap bars keep riders safe.

Story. The ride's storyline demonstrates how the weak can outwit the strong. Based on folk tales popular with slaves in the antebellum South, tiny Brer ("brother") Rabbit gets in trouble with the bigger Brer Fox and Brer Bear, but outsmarts them at the end.

It starts with the rabbit packing to leave his home. "I've had enough of this old briar patch," he sings. "I'm lookin' for a little more adventure." Overhearing, Brer Fox and Brer Bear scheme to catch him, but fail time and time again. In his final escape, the hare tricks

After the plunge, Splash Mountain riders circle back into the mountain as Brer Rabbit returns to his home. Many of his friends gather on a showboat to sing "Zip-a-Dee-Doo-Dah." A Hidden Mickey appears in the clouds behind the boat.

his enemies into tossing him safely back to his briar patch. The ride heads back into the mountain after the fall, as a showboat of friends welcomes the bunny back home.

A closer look. The attraction depicts three Brer Rabbit folk tales, all of which show how reverse psychology can be used to help the weak battle the strong.

In "Mr. Rabbit and Mr. Bear," the hare gets caught in a rope trap. Saying he's earning a dollar a minute as a scarecrow, the rabbit convinces the bear to switch places. "Ya know, you'd make a mighty fine scarecrow, Brer Bear. How'd ya like to have this job?"

In "Brother Rabbit's Laughing Place," the rabbit leads his enemies to what he describes as an ideal spot—his "laughing place." When it turns out to be a hollow tree full of stinging bees (through which the rabbit escapes) he explains to the others that it is *his* laughing place, not theirs. In "How Mr. Rabbit Was Too Sharp for Mr. Fox," the fox captures the rabbit by slamming a beehive over his head. As the fox prepares to kill him, the rabbit says to go ahead and cook him, hang him, roast him or skin him, just don't throw him in the briar patch. To be mean, Brer Fox does just that, and the rabbit escapes for good.

Oddly, only one of the three tales ("Mr. Rabbit and Mr. Bear") appears in the movie.

Controversy. Based on African folk tales, the stories were published in "The Complete Tales of Uncle Remus," an 1895 compilation of slave stories by Joel Chandler Harris, a white Atlanta newspaper columnist who became a polarizing figure. In the introduction to his book, the white Harris described his narrator, a freed slave he named Uncle Remus, as having "nothing but pleasant memories of the discipline of slavery." At the time, some Americans used the word "uncle" as a patronizing term to refer to elderly black men. Walt Disney never publicly commented on Harris, but loved the original tales. "These stories have been my special favorites," he said in 1946.

Because of its racial overtones, Disney does not sell "Song of the South" on DVD or show it in theaters or on television. A 1987 compilation "The Tales of Uncle Remus" by Julius Lester offers most of the tales in a more unadulterated state.

Family matters. The Laughin' Place, a very basic playhouse for children ages 2–5, sits behind the ride's Fastpass machines.

Hidden Mickeys. ❶ As stacked barrels along the right side of the second lift hill. **❷** As a hanging rope in the flooded cavern, just past a turtle. **❸** As a full figure reclining in the sky to the right of the riverboat, the upper outline of a cloud. Mickey's head is to the right.

Average wait times

Time	Standby line	Fastpass time
9:00a	0 min	10:05a
10:00a	20 min	10:30a
11:00a	20 min	11:35a
Noon	50 min	12:55p
1:00p	60 min	2:35p
2:00p	80 min	4:30p
3:00p	60 min	5:35p
4:00p	60 min	6:55p
5:00p	70 min	7:50p
6:00p	50 min	8:55p
7:00p	60 min	9:15p
8:00p	45 min	(out)
9:00p	30 min	(out)

All curves all the time, Big Thunder Mountain Railroad scoots riders into each other. The ride's trains are named U.B. Bold, U.R. Daring, U.R. Courageous, I.M. Brave, I.B. Hearty and I.M. Fearless.

Big Thunder Mountain Railroad

★★★★★ ✔ *FASTPASS* Frontierland 4 min. Capacity: 150. Outdoor covered queue. Fear factor: Jerky, violent turns toss riders around in their seats. Many sharp hills and sudden dips. Closed during thunderstorms. Access: Must be ambulatory. Height minimum: 40 in. Debuted: 1980 (Disneyland 1979).

It's all curves all the time on this rollicking roller coaster. Full of humor and not threatening in any way, this "wildest ride in the wilderness" is ideal for those who like fast turns but don't enjoy big drops or going upside down. Top speed is 36 mph. For the wildest ride ask for the back seat.

A crisscrossing trip through a Utah desert, the ride travels around, and through, a mountain that's filled with detail. Two baby opossum twirl overhead as the coaster enters the flooded town of Tumbleweed. A mine shaft is ready to collapse, with shaking rocks and timbers. Other sights include live cactus, bubbling hot springs and swarming bats. At the end, the coaster travels underneath a dinosaur skeleton before passing steaming hot springs and spurting geysers.

Nearly 20 fairly realistic animals dot the landscape, including big-horned sheep, bobcats and javelinas. Authentic mining gear—including buckets, cogwheels and ore carts—lies scattered around the grounds.

Night time is the right time to ride. The scenery is lit but the track is pitch black, which makes every swerve and plunge a surprise. Like many other coaster vehicles, the trains run faster late in the day, after their track grease fully melts. Tumbleweed comes alive after the sun sets, when silhouettes of boozing miners and dance-hall dames party upstairs at the Gold Dust Saloon.

Average wait times

Time	Standby line	Fastpass time
9:00a	0 min	10:05a
10:00a	20 min	10:30a
11:00a	30 min	11:35a
Noon	35 min	12:35p
1:00p	45 min	1:40p
2:00p	60 min	2:45p
3:00p	50 min	3:50p
4:00p	40 min	5:00p
5:00p	35 min	5:45p
6:00p	45 min	6:45p
7:00p	45 min	7:40p
8:00p	55 min	8:55p
9:00p	40 min	(out)

The railroad winds through a rocky desert mountainscape meant to recall Utah's Monument Valley. Above left, a box along the entrance walkway reads "Lytum & Hyde Blasting Caps."

A closer look. Big Thunder Mountain Railroad is the rare roller coaster that tells a story, a tale of a frontier mining town whose citizens' relentless pursuit of riches upset the spirits of nature. During the Gold Rush, according to Disney lore, men in the desert town of Tumbleweed were prospecting on a nearby mountain, which was a Native American burial ground. Though the ridge rumbled whenever any mining took place—Native Americans called the peak Big Thunder Mountain—the gold diggers were persistent. Adding insult to injury, the miners partied hard at night, drinking, playing poker and dancing with parlor girls.

Eventually the spirits had enough. One day a mining train spun out of control, flying around the mountain like a bat out of hell. Moments later a flash flood hit the town, then an earthquake. Some miners were too drunk to notice. After the tragedies, Tumbleweed lost its mining chops. No gold was ever found.

In reality, Big Thunder Mountain is a painted cement and wire-mesh skin over a concrete-and-steel frame. Inside are the ride's computers, electronics and water pumps. The coaster's support structure is hidden under the landscape.

The "Howdy partners!" announcer is Dallas McKennon, the voice of Ben Franklin at Epcot's American Adventure. A longtime Hollywood voice talent, he also voiced the 1960s television versions of Gumby and Archie Andrews, and the Rice Krispies characters Snap, Crackle and Pop.

Fun finds. ❶ Queue lights continuously flicker and dim. ❷ Some entranceway crates are from the "Lytum & Hyde" explosives company. ❸ A crate above the boarding area ramp holds whiskey. ❹ In Tumbleweed, a prospector on the right side of the track has washed into town in his bathtub, while on the left ❺ rainmaker Professor Cumulus Isobar bails himself out. ❻ The proprietors of the dry goods store are D. Hydrate and U. Wither. ❼ Inside the Gold Dust Saloon, an alcohol-fueled game of poker has been flooded out. ❽ Around a bend on the left, a "Flood-ometer" reads "Flooded Out." ❾ If guests exit the ride from the left track, they walk alongside the office of the railroad's telegraph manager, Morris Code. ❿ The right exitway has a canary in a cage (he's not moving) and, above a "Blasting in Progress" sign, a plunger. It's pushed in.

Hidden Mickey. The three-circle shape appears toward the end of the ride as three rusty gears laying on the ground on the right side of the coaster track, not long after the train travels under a dinosaur rib cage.

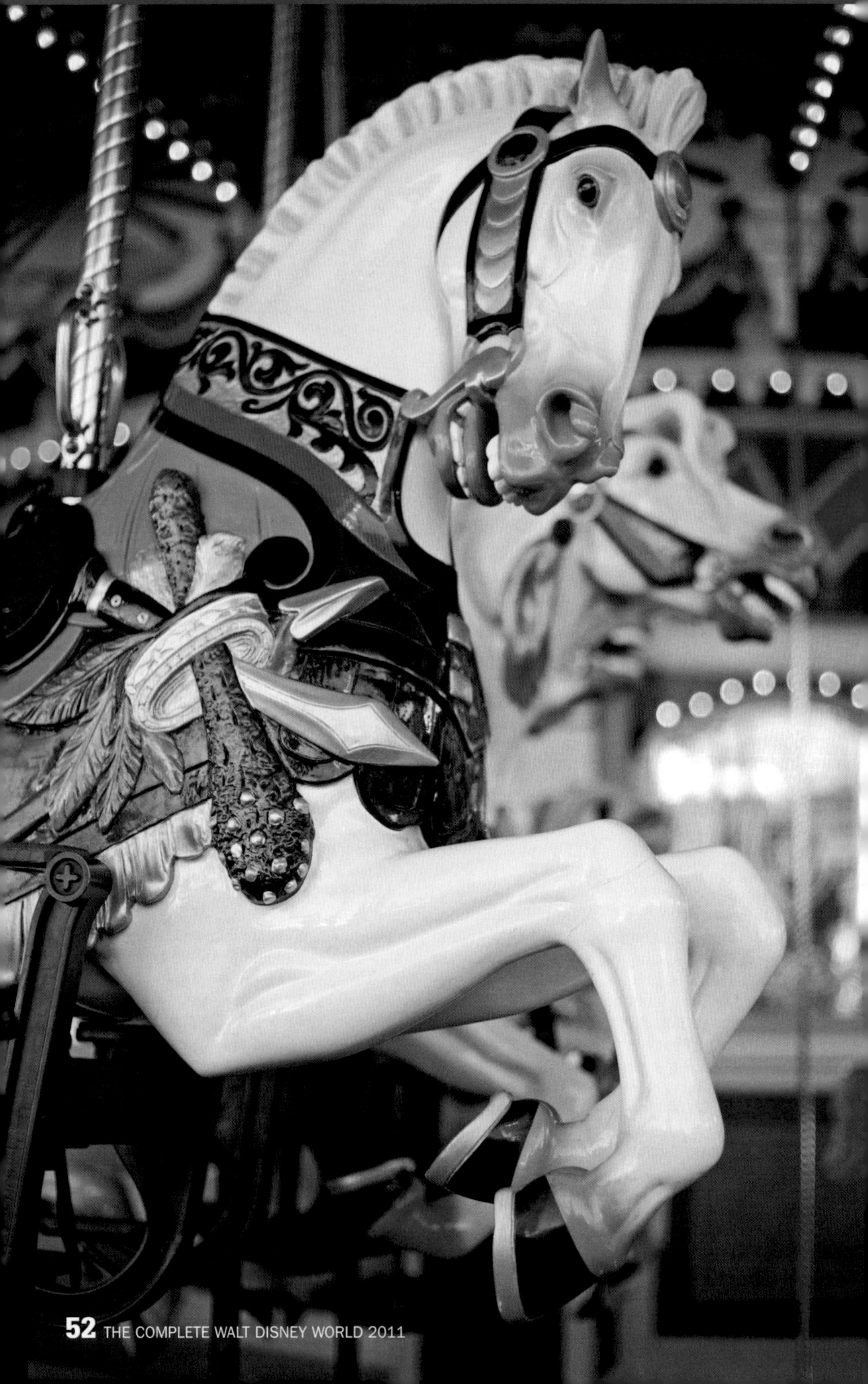

One of the largest vintage merry-go-rounds still operating today, the Prince Charming Regal Carrousel features five rows of horses in five sizes. The largest steeds circle the outside rim.

Prince Charming Regal Carrousel

★★★ **Fantasyland** 90 sec (4 revolutions). Capacity: 91 (87 horses, four-seat chariot), apx 1000 riders per hour. Shaded queue. Fear factor: None. All horses have safety belts. Access: Must be ambulatory. Debuted: 1971.

Designed to fit every member of the family, this large outdoor merry-go-round has five sizes of horses, each one unique. A calliope-like medley of Disney tunes adds ambience. At night the attraction is outlined by hundreds of tiny white lights.

A closer look. The ride was built in 1917 by the Philadelphia Toboggan (i.e. roller coaster) Co., a shop that also sold hand-carved merry-go-rounds. One of only four five-row units the company ever built, this patriotic Liberty model featured images of Miss Liberty, a regal blonde clad in a robe and sandals.

Created for Michigan's Detroit Palace Garden Park, the ride later moved to Olympic Park in Maplewood, N.J. In 1967 the Disney company bought it for Walt Disney World, which had just broken ground. To honor Walt Disney's belief that every carousel rider should feel like a hero, workers repainted the horses white, repositioned their legs to canter instead of prance and removed the chariots to add more horses. To give the ride a girly

appeal, the company painted its trim pieces—even Miss Liberty's patriotic duds—blue, gold, pink and purple. Disney gave the ride a manly name in 2010. Today's horses are fiberglass replicas, but one original wooden chariot has returned. The ride uses the French spelling of the word "carousel."

Family matters. Nervous toddlers should choose an inside horse. Because of the ride's wide diameter, outside horses move twice as fast (7 mph) as those on its inner rim.

Average wait times

Time	Standby line	Fastpass time
9:00a	0 min	(n/a)
10:00a	0 min	(n/a)
11:00a	0 min	(n/a)
Noon	5 min	(n/a)
1:00p	10 min	(n/a)
2:00p	10 min	(n/a)
3:00p	10 min	(n/a)
4:00p	5 min	(n/a)
5:00p	10 min	(n/a)
6:00p	5 min	(n/a)
7:00p	5 min	(n/a)
8:00p	0 min	(n/a)
9:00p	5 min	(n/a)

Donald Duck gets trapped in musical moments from six feature films in the 3-D movie Mickey's PhilharMagic. Above, the duck appears in the "Be Our Guest" scene from "Beauty and the Beast."

Mickey's PhilharMagic

★★★★★ ✔ **Fantasyland** 12 min. Capacity: 450. Indoor, air-conditioned queue. Fear factor: Sudden images, briefly totally dark. Access: Viewers may stay in wheelchairs, ECVs. Assistive listening, reflective captioning. Debuted: 2003.

Donald Duck steals a smooch from the Little Mermaid (or at least tries to), battles the brooms from "Fantasia" and causes chaos in the dining room from "Beauty and the Beast" in this delightful 3-D movie. Action-packed yet never scary, funny but also touching, it's a treat for any age. The plot? When maestro Mickey Mouse runs late for a concert with a musician-free orchestra, Donald attempts to replace him. But when the duck loses the secret to controlling the ensemble—Mickey's Sorcerer's Hat—the result is a madcap adventure as Donald gets swept into signature scenes from classic Disney musicals.

The show plays on the world's widest 3-D screen. Some objects appear to leave the screen and hang directly in front of the audience. Hidden odorizers, air guns and water misters help immerse guests in the action, while a wrap-around sound system and innovative lighting effects complement startling imagery.

Scene transitions are terrific. The "Beauty and the Beast" feast falls into the Sorcerer's Apprentice workshop from "Fantasia"; that room's water washes into Ariel's grotto; sunlight above the mermaid turns into the African sun of "The Lion King."

A closer look. The movie references six Disney movies and one television show:

    "Beauty and the Beast": The enchanted staff of a castle puts on a floor show as they prepare dinner for Belle (1991).

Average wait times

Time	Standby line	Fastpass time
9:00a	0 min	(n/a)
10:00a	10 min	(n/a)
11:00a	5 min	(n/a)
Noon	5 min	(n/a)
1:00p	10 min	(n/a)
2:00p	10 min	(n/a)
3:00p	15 min	(n/a)
4:00p	20 min	(n/a)
5:00p	20 min	(n/a)
6:00p	15 min	(n/a)
7:00p	15 min	(n/a)
8:00p	15 min	(n/a)
9:00p	10 min	(n/a)

Illustration © Disney

in the 1944 cartoon "Commando Duck" when Donald, while learning to parachute, masters bending his knees when he lands. One line of the duck's dialogue isn't really Donald at all. In the movie, when he orders his magic carpet to fly "Faster! Faster!" the voice is actually that of *Donna* Duck, an early version of Daisy. In 1937's "Don Donald" she says it to Donald while riding in his car.

Fun finds. ❶ There's always a murmur in the theater before the show begins, as faint audience noise plays from hidden speakers. **❷** As stage manager Goofy walks behind the curtain, he hums the "Mickey Mouse March" and steps on a cat ("Sorry little feller!"). **❸** In the movie, when Lumiere rolls out toward the audience he's on a tomato that wasn't there a moment earlier. It arrived when Donald briefly blocked the view to ask, "Where's my hat?" **❹** Ariel giggles as she swims onscreen. **❺** Strobes in the ceiling flash when Donald kisses the electric eel. **❻** When a crocodile sends Donald flying during "I Just Can't Wait to be King," guests hear the duck circle behind them. **❼** When Simba sings that he's "in the spotlight," so are some members of the audience. **❽** When a pull chain falls into view, Zazu pulls it to turn Simba's light off and respond, "Not yet!" **❾** Jasmine waves to an audience guest as she starts to sing "A Whole New World." **❿** When she and Aladdin wave goodbye to Donald, so does their carpet. **⓫** Once Mickey regains control of his orchestra, the flute wakes up the tuba and then trips Donald into it. **⓬** As guests exit past the gift shop, Goofy says goodbye in five languages ("Sigh-a-NAIR-ee!").

Hidden Mickeys. ❶ In the lobby mural, as seven 1-inch-wide white paint splotches. From the right, they appear between the third and fourth bass violin, between the second and third clarinet, above the second trumpet, below the second trumpet, to the left of the fourth trumpet, and twice to the left of the sixth clarinet. **❷** On the theater's right stage column, in the French horn tubing. **❸** In the film's "Be Our Guest" scene, as brief shadows on the dining table, visible as Lumiere sings the word "it's" in "Try the gray stuff, it's delicious!" Lumiere's hands cast Mickey's ears; his base Mickey's face. **❹** As a hole made in a cloud as Aladdin's carpet flies through it. **❺** When the carpets dive toward Agrabah, as three domes atop a tower on the left. **❻** In the gift shop, as music stands along the top of the walls.

"Fantasia": Sorcerer's apprentice Mickey avoids washing a floor by wearing his mentor's hat and enchanting a broom (1940).
"The Little Mermaid": Teenage mermaid Ariel collects human objects; fish friend Flounder keeps her company (1989).
"The Lion King": A lion cub just can't wait to be king of beasts, though his father's hornbill advisor remains skeptical (1994).
"Peter Pan": A boy can fly, and his friends can too after they get a sprinkling of dust from pixie Tinker Bell; in London they pause on the minute hand of Big Ben (1953).
"Aladdin": An Iraqi "street rat" wins the heart of Princess Jasmine on a magic-carpet ride despite the efforts of Iago, a cranky pet parrot of her dad's evil advisor (1992).
"The Mickey Mouse Club": In the 1950s every child knew the last line of the theme song of a weekday TV show: "M-I-C... See ya real soon! K-E-Y... Why? Because we like you! M-O-U-S-E."
Déjà Donald. For the most part, the words spoken by Donald Duck are not new recordings. Instead, they come from vintage Disney cartoons, and are voiced by the classic voice of Donald, the late Clarence "Ducky" Nash.

The duck's line "I'll show you who's boss!," shouted at an unruly flute he tosses into the audience, comes from the 1941 cartoon "Early to Bed," when Donald yells at a noisy alarm clock he tosses across his bedroom. When the duck proclaims "Nothin' to it!" after pixie dust gives him the ability to fly, it's from a scene

© Disney

Disney's It's a Small World attraction takes guests on a cultural tour of the globe. Colorful landscapes include overhead flowers that symbolize clouds.

it's a small world

★★★★★ ✓ **Fantasyland** 11 min. Capacity: 600. Indoor queue. Fear factor: None. Access: ECV users must transfer to a wheelchair; handheld captioning, Audio Description. Debuted: 1971, renovated 2010 (New York World's Fair 1964, Disneyland 1966).

Promoting world harmony with dolls that sing in unison, this indoor boat ride takes you on a colorful, cultural trip around the globe. Abstract sets, whimsical animals and hundreds of singing dolls fill your field of vision in six huge dioramas, each of which represents a region of the world.

"The happiest cruise that ever sailed" starts off in Europe, then crosses Asia, Africa, Latin America and Polynesia. The finale heads back to Europe to Copenhagen's Tivoli Gardens—Walt Disney's inspiration for the look of California's Disneyland and, hence, the Magic Kingdom—where all the planet's children come together to celebrate the "world that we share" by dressing in white and singing in unison.

There's a lot to like. To infants the ride is a wide-eyed journey filled with happy faces, funny animals, gentle music and the largest crib mobiles they've ever seen. To preschoolers it's a place to bond with their parents, as there's no narration and lots of time to chat. ("Where are we now, mom?" "Hawaii!").

As a political statement, It's a Small World argues that you can honor diversity while still celebrating the commonality of mankind. Though the dolls speak different languages they all sing the same song, and though they wear different costumes their faces are nearly identical.

As designed by illustrator Mary Blair—she did the backgrounds of the Disney

Average wait times

Time	Standby line	Fastpass time
9:00a	0 min	(n/a)
10:00a	5 min	(n/a)
11:00a	10 min	(n/a)
Noon	15 min	(n/a)
1:00p	20 min	(n/a)
2:00p	20 min	(n/a)
3:00p	30 min	(n/a)
4:00p	25 min	(n/a)
5:00p	20 min	(n/a)
6:00p	15 min	(n/a)
7:00p	15 min	(n/a)
8:00p	5 min	(n/a)
9:00p	5 min	(n/a)

Clockwise from top left: A queue-line clock tower comes to life every 15 minutes. Jousting lances form canopy supports. The ride has 289 singing dolls and dozens of whimsical animals.

movies "Cinderella" (1950) and "Alice in Wonderland" (1951)—the modernist sets have a sophisticated sensibility, forming a playful pop-art collage that combines both organic and geometric shapes as well as cultural motifs. For ideas, Blair tried out combinations of wallpaper cuttings, cellophane and acrylic paint.

As for flaws...the dolls' lips barely move, the short song repeats ad nauseum, the Latin American and South Pacific sets are skimpy and the ride concludes with glitter-board good-byes that must have cost all of $1.98.

A closer look. The ride was initially created for the UNICEF pavilion at the 1964 New York World's Fair. One of 50 attractions that charged a fee, It's a Small World accounted for 20 percent of paid admissions, more than any other attraction. It also inspired some political merchandise, as The Women's International League for Peace and Freedom sold It's a Small World-style dolls to help fund protests against the Vietnam War.

'Anything But That!' In "Selma's Choice," a 1993 episode of "The Simpsons," Aunt Selma takes Bart and Lisa to Duff Gardens, a theme park where every attraction is themed to Duff Beer. On the boat ride Little Land of Duff, they find hundreds of dolls singing a one-verse song ("Duff Beer for me, Duff Beer for you, I'll have a Duff, You have one, too!"). "I want to get

off!" Bart yells. "You can't," says Selma. "We have five more continents to visit!" After Lisa takes a drink of the water, she hallucinates that the dolls are coming after her.

Even Disney cracks jokes. Some Jungle Cruise skippers tell guests that any children left on board will be taken to It's a Small World, have their feet glued to the floor and be forced to sing the theme song "over and over for the rest of their lives." At Disney's Hollywood Studios, Small World dolls help destroy the theater in the finale of Jim Henson's MuppetVision 3-D.

The song is also dissed in the 1994 film "The Lion King." When hornbill Zazu begins to sing "Nobody Knows the Trouble I've Seen," Scar demands something more upbeat, the bird chirps "It's a small world after all; It's a small world after all..." "No, no, no!" cries Scar. "Anything but that!"

Fun finds. ❶ A bespectacled Mary Blair doll is under the Eiffel Tower. **❷** Crazy-eyed Don Quixote tilts at a windmill while Sancho Panza looks on in alarm. **❸** Singers include an ax-wielding yodeler in Europe. **❹** Cleopatra winks at you from an African barge.

Hidden Mickey. The three circles appear as 6-inch purple flower petals in Africa, on a vine between the giraffes on your left.

Flying over a moonlit London, Peter Pan's Flight guests travel in miniature pirate galleons as they head off to Never Land. The vintage indoor dark ride hasn't changed since debuting in 1971.

Peter Pan's Flight

★★★ ✔ *FASTPASS* Fantasyland 3 min. Capacity: 60. Covered outdoor queue. Fear factor: None. Access: Must be ambulatory; handheld captioning, Audio Description. Debuted: 1971 (Disneyland 1955).

You'll fly over London and swoop through Never Land on this indoor dark ride, which uses an overhead track to suspend two-seat pirate ships. Designed in 1954 for California's Disneyland and essentially unchanged since, the ride has a throwback charm that gets sweeter with age. To avoid a long wait, go on it first thing in the morning or use a Fastpass.

The ride depicts key moments of Disney's 1953 movie "Peter Pan." You start off in the Darling nursery, then get a bird's-eye view of nighttime London, its roads filled with moving vehicles. Never Land includes a trio of mermaids (one a dead ringer for Ariel, star of 1989's "The Little Mermaid"). Sailing through Capt. Hook's ship, you witness the pirate's battles with Peter and a ticking crocodile.

The ride's dated technology is easy to spot; the glow from a volcano comes from clearly visible sheets of aluminum foil.

Flights, fights and tights. Based on a 1904 play by James Matthew Barrie, Disney's movie is the story of a boy who refuses to grow up. One night he arrives at the London home of the Darling family and convinces daughter Wendy and her two brothers to fly off with him to Never Land, a remote island. Sprinkled with magic dust from moody pixie Tinker Bell, the kids join Peter's gang of Lost Boys for a series of adventures.

Hidden Mickey. As scars on the fourth painted tree trunk on your left as you face the turnstile, 4 feet off the ground.

Average wait times

Time	Standby line	Fastpass time
9:00a	0 min	10:10a
10:00a	15 min	10:30a
11:00a	35 min	11:40a
Noon	40 min	1:15p
1:00p	55 min	3:10p
2:00p	60 min	4:35p
3:00p	55 min	6:20p
4:00p	55 min	8:00p
5:00p	55 min	9:05p
6:00p	45 min	9:40p
7:00p	45 min	10:40p
8:00p	55 min	11:25p
9:00p	45 min	(out)

Appealing to children of all ages, Dumbo the Flying Elephant puts its guests in single-bench baby pachyderms that circle slowly and level. The ride recalls the finale of the classic 1941 film.

Dumbo the Flying Elephant

★ ★ ★ ✔ **Fantasyland** 2 min. Capacity: 32. Small shaded queue. Fear factor: None. Closed during thunderstorms. Access: Must be ambulatory. Debuted: 1971, revised 1993 (Disneyland 1955).

Flying baby elephants become cozy ride vehicles on this classic hub-and-spoke attraction, which spins like a top as its arms move up and down. A perfect ride for toddlers, it offers a gentle sensation of flight—the Dumbos stay level as they climb and circle, move just fast enough to provide a small thrill and are controlled, to some extent, by an easy-to-use lever. For older guests the ride is certainly iconic, but doesn't justify a long wait.

Topped with a spinning key, the attraction looks like an elaborate antique windup toy, its hub decorated in gilt and pinwheels. Built in 1993, the Jules Verne-style contraption was at first intended for Disneyland Paris.

This version of the attraction will soon close. Now under construction, an expanded Fantasyland will feature two new Dumbo rides set in circus grounds.

Jumbo Jr. When a stork delivers a baby to circus elephant Mrs. Jumbo (in, appropriately, central Florida) in 1941's "Dumbo," she names him Jumbo Jr., though his huge ears soon earn him the nickname Dumbo. At first he's an outcast, but when a mouse convinces the elephant that holding a magic feather will allow him to fly, Dumbo becomes a star. Later he learns he can fly whenever he wants, feather or not.

Family matters. Children love spotting the flying storks (in picture frames hanging off the hub), cartwheeling gophers (on the ride's arms) and Timothy Mouse (on top of the hub, holding Dumbo's feather).

Average wait times

Time	Standby line	Fastpass time
9:00a	0 min	(n/a)
10:00a	20 min	(n/a)
11:00a	25 min	(n/a)
Noon	25 min	(n/a)
1:00p	25 min	(n/a)
2:00p	30 min	(n/a)
3:00p	35 min	(n/a)
4:00p	35 min	(n/a)
5:00p	35 min	(n/a)
6:00p	30 min	(n/a)
7:00p	30 min	(n/a)
8:00p	30 min	(n/a)
9:00p	20 min	(n/a)

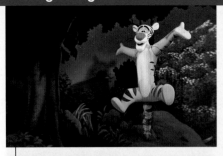

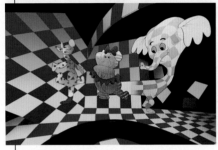

Clockwise from top left: Tigger nearly bounces "clear out of the ride"; a gust of wind blows Rabbit into a wheelbarrow; heffalumps and woozles star in Pooh's surreal nightmare

The Many Adventures of Winnie the Pooh

★★★★ ✓ **FASTPASS** Fantasyland 3 min, 30 sec. Capacity: 48. Shaded queue. Fear factor: Some sudden, mild, effects. The nightmare scene can be disorienting for toddlers. Access: ECV users must transfer to a wheelchair; Audio Description. Debuted: 1999.

You'll bounce with Tigger, float in a flood and see Pooh drift off to dreamland on this dark indoor ride, which uses imaginative special effects to create a memorable experience. Traveling past the animated pages of a storybook in a four-person "Hunny Pot," you witness the weather woes and surreal hefflalump-and-woozle nightmare told in the 1968 featurette "Winnie the Pooh and the Blustery Day." Hidden behind swinging doors, each scene comes as a surprise.

A new standby queue has an interactive playground. Highlights include hands-on activities in Rabbit's garden and "honey-dripping" walls that reveal hidden scenes when guests swipe them with their fingers.

Winnie, windy and wet. Based on a story by A.A. Milne about his son's stuffed animals, "Winnie the Pooh and the Blustery Day" tells of the toys' adventures in a windstorm, thunderstorm and flood. Leader Pooh is a cheerful bear who loves honey. His pals include excavation expert Gopher (a Disney creation), timid Piglet, fastidious gardener Rabbit, motherly Kanga and her adventurous son Roo, gloomy donkey Eeyore, self-important Owl and the ebullient Tigger, who loves to bounce. Pooh's enemies, he believes, are heffalumps and woozles, the elephants and weasles Tigger says steal honey. The film became part of the 1977 full-length movie, "The Many Adventures of Winnie the Pooh."

A closer look. You get drunk, steal a car, mouth off to a cop, then go to hell. Believe it or not, that was the story told by this building's former attraction, Mr. Toad's Wild Ride, a ride based on Disney's 1949 movie "The Adventures of Ichabod and Mr. Toad." The action-packed roadtrip had ardent fans; when Disney announced plans to convert it into a Winnie the Pooh ride in 1997, Toad lovers picketed its entrance. On Mr. Toad's last day, one fan held a sign that read "Here lies dear old J.T. Toad, he hit some Pooh upon the road." Today Mr. Toad rests in peace in the pet cemetery outside the Haunted Mansion.

The silly old bear gets happily stuck in a "hunny" tree during the storybook ride The Many Adventures of Winnie the Pooh. The attraction's new stand-by entrance (below) features interactive fun and games, including a "honey wall" where children can write their names.

Family matters. The attraction offers a nice opportunity for parents to talk to their children about fear. Scenes depict the Pooh characters being afraid of two things they should be (a windstorm and a flood) and one thing they shouldn't (a nightmare based on rumors).

Fun finds. ❶ A boarding-area mirror makes the Hunny Pots disappear into the storybook. ❷ The words blow off the ride's first page. ❸ Along the side of the first diorama, Pooh grips a balloon string to float up to a beehive, a scene from the 1966 featurette "Winnie the Pooh and the Honey Tree." ❹ A framed photo of Mr. Toad handing Owl the deed to the space hangs on the left wall of Owl's house. ❺ A picture of Toad's friend Mole bowing to Pooh lays on the right floor. ❻ The air chills at the Floody Place. ❼ Words wash off the Floody Place storybook.

Hidden Mickeys. ❶ At the attraction's entrance, on the transom of the front door of the Mr. Sanders treehouse. ❷ On the ride, on the radish marker in Rabbit's garden.

Average wait times

Time	Standby line	Fastpass time
9:00a	0 min	10:10a
10:00a	10 min	10:30a
11:00a	25 min	11:30a
Noon	35 min	12:35p
1:00p	30 min	1:40p
2:00p	35 min	2:50p
3:00p	35 min	4:00p
4:00p	30 min	4:50p
5:00p	30 min	6:00p
6:00p	45 min	7:10p
7:00p	35 min	8:05p
8:00p	35 min	9:10p
9:00p	30 min	9:40p

Love's first kiss: Prince Charming awakens Snow White in the final scene of Snow White's Scary Adventures. The rest of the ride depicts the most frightening moments from the 1937 movie.

Snow White's Scary Adventures

★★★ **Fantasyland** 2 min, 30 sec. Capacity: 66. Shaded queue. Fear factor: Scares many young children. Access: Must be ambulatory. Handheld captioning, Audio Description. Debuted: 1971, revised 1994 (Disneyland 1955).

A young girl is chased through the woods and poisoned by her stepmom in this vintage spookhouse-style dark ride, which re-creates the nightmarish moments of the 1937 movie "Snow White and the Seven Dwarfs." The creepy, Shakespearean vibe scares many children, but older riders can find much to enjoy in the attraction's creative depth. In its forest scene Snow White's emotions are brought to life from her point of view: her terror at being left alone turns trees into predators, logs into alligators and every glint of moonlight into a glaring eye. As she calms down the forest gets friendly, the eyes becoming those of little animals.

Though the ride's tech is badly dated, its transformation of the queen into the witch still seems magical.

Note: This ride will permanently close soon, as part of the Fantasyland makeover.

A closer look. At first the ride was a point-of-view experience, designed to have guests live Snow White's adventures for themselves.

The princess didn't appear until the end, lying on her bier. Children who didn't know the story thought Snow White had died.

Hidden Mickeys ❶ In a loading-area mural, as hearts on a pair of boxer shorts and ❷ on the cottage chimney under two flowers. ❸ In the ride, on top of the magic mirror. ❹ On the lower right of the entrance to the dwarfs' mine, a full-figure dwarf-nosed Mickey wears dwarf clothes and holds a shovel.

Average wait times

Time	Standby line	Fastpass time
9:00a	0 min	(n/a)
10:00a	15 min	(n/a)
11:00a	15 min	(n/a)
Noon	15 min	(n/a)
1:00p	20 min	(n/a)
2:00p	25 min	(n/a)
3:00p	30 min	(n/a)
4:00p	25 min	(n/a)
5:00p	35 min	(n/a)
6:00p	25 min	(n/a)
7:00p	30 min	(n/a)
8:00p	25 min	(n/a)
9:00p	20 min	(n/a)

Micaela Neal

Taking a spin: Orlando's Kisha Howard and Jay Garcia spin their teacup on the Mad Tea Party. The ride is one of the few Disney World attractions in which guests control their experience.

Mad Tea Party

★★★ ✔ **Fantasyland** 2 min. Capacity: 72 (18 4-person teacups). Shaded queue. Fear factor: None. Access: Must be ambulatory. Debuted: 1971 (Disneyland 1955).

"If I had a world of my own, everything would be nonsense," says Alice, a well-mannered schoolgirl, in Disney's 1951 movie "Alice in Wonderland." "Nothing would be what it is because everything would be what it isn't. And contrary-wise; what it is it wouldn't be, and what it wouldn't be, it would. You see?"

You'll be as confused as Alice as you get off this classic carnival ride, which puts you in an oversized teacup that spins as it circles within a circling floor. Most guests get dizzy, and most love it. Covered by a huge canopy, the Mad Tea Party operates in any weather.

A wheel in the center of each teacup allows riders to control how fast it spins. To avoid getting dizzy, stare at the wheel.

"My favorite Disney World ride has always been the teacups," NASCAR driver Kyle Petty tells us. "From the time I was little I've loved to jump in and make people sick."

A closer look. In the film, young Alice grows bored listening to her older sister read aloud from an oh-so-sensible history book, and dreams of a world where nothing makes

sense. After falling through a rabbit hole and eating a magic mushroom, she attends an Unbirthday Party, a nonsensical tea time that leaves her dazed and confused.

The movie's soused mouse pops out of the attraction's central teapot; its Japanese tea lanterns hang overhead.

Family matters. The cups give parents an excuse to get silly with their children. Most kids love it when mom or dad scoots into them or playfully spins the wheel.

Average wait times

Time	Standby line	Fastpass time
9:00a	0 min	(n/a)
10:00a	5 min	(n/a)
11:00a	5 min	(n/a)
Noon	10 min	(n/a)
1:00p	10 min	(n/a)
2:00p	15 min	(n/a)
3:00p	15 min	(n/a)
4:00p	15 min	(n/a)
5:00p	15 min	(n/a)
6:00p	20 min	(n/a)
7:00p	10 min	(n/a)
8:00p	10 min	(n/a)
9:00p	10 min	(n/a)

© Disney

Experiment 626 is one steamed Stitch, unhappy with his detainment at Planet Turo's Prisoner Teleport Center. When the lights go out, the mischievous alien appears to roam the room.

Stitch's Great Escape!

★ *FASTPASS* Tomorrowland 18 min. Capacity: 240 (2 120-seat theaters). Indoor, air-conditioned queue. Fear factor: Restrictive harnesses, dark periods scare some children. Access: ECV users must transfer. Handheld captioning, assistive listening. Height min: 40 in. Debuted: 2004.

Stitch burps in your face in this in-the-round theatrical show, geared to those familiar with the early moments of the 2002 movie "Lilo & Stitch." A low-budget makeover of the attraction that preceded it (The ExtraTERRORestrial Alien Encounter), the show includes a cool Stitch robot, but spends most of its time showing uninspired videos.

Mostly told on video screens, the story is set before Stitch arrives on Earth, when he was known as "Experiment 626." Just like in the movie, Stitch escapes a prison by tricking DNA-tracking cannons into blasting his spit, which causes the power to short out. This plunges the prison—the theater—into darkness. Thanks to some special effects, the little monster seems to skitter about the dark room, lingering, and belching, near each guest.

The show's robotic technology is impressive. The best part is a pre-show sergeant, a transparent robocop who shifts his weight and counts on his fingers.

Creature feature. In the movie, a mad scientist uses the genes of ferocious beasts to create a tiny six-limbed creature who can think faster than a supercomputer and see in the dark. Guarded by robotic cannons that track genetic signatures, it ingeniously coughs on the floor, which confuses the guns and knocks out the jail's power grid.

Family matters. Children should sit in the back of the theater. The 39-inch character sits high off the floor, above the front rows.

Average wait times

Time	Standby line	Fastpass time
9:00a	0 min	10:10a
10:00a	5 min	10:40a
11:00a	10 min	11:45a
Noon	25 min	12:40p
1:00p	20 min	1:40p
2:00p	15 min	2:50p
3:00p	15 min	3:45p
4:00p	10 min	4:40p
5:00p	15 min	6:00p
6:00p	10 min	6:50p
7:00p	15 min	7:50p
8:00p	10 min	8:40p
9:00p	10 min	(out)

Monsters, Inc. Laugh Floor sits within a whimsical Buck Rogers-style Tomorrowland (right). Alongside a queue room, a faux vending machine (below) offers such treats as Sugar, Salt & Fat, Same Old Raccoon Bar and a Polyvinyl Chloride candy bar, which the small print on its wrapper notes is artificially flavored.

Monsters, Inc. Laugh Floor

★ ★ ★ **Tomorrowland** 15–20 min. Capacity: 400. Indoor, air-conditioned queue. Fear factor: None. Access: Guests may stay in wheelchairs, ECVs. Reflective captioning, assistive listening. Debuted: 2007.

An animated monster may tell your joke during this high-tech improvisational show. Three large video screens front a comedy-club-style theater, where characters from the world of the 2001 film "Monsters, Inc." chat with, tease and joke with the audience just like real people. The host is Mike Wazowski, who wants to generate electricity for his utility company by gathering laughter in bulk.

Every performance is different, as the characters base some of their routines on guests in the audience. The best shows are those with a full house, which are typically those in the middle of the day. Early morning shows can be stale, as jokes often fall flat in a near-empty theater.

Guests can text jokes to the show to be used onstage, using a password shown in the waiting area.

The show pulls off its magic thanks to hidden cameras, real-time animation technology and backstage actors. To increase the odds of having a character speak to you, wear a colorful shirt or a big hat.

In the movie, the Monsters, Inc. utility company generates energy from the screams of human children. Key characters include eyeball-on-legs Mike Wazowski, a "scare floor" worker; and Roz, a surly secretary. As the film ends, the company learns that laughter is ten times more powerful than fear.

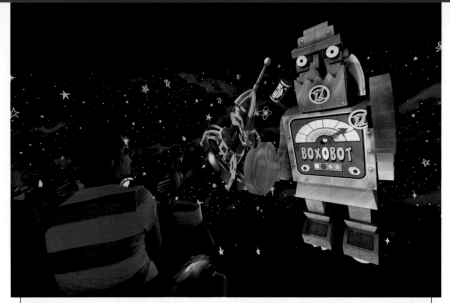

Zurg's lead henchman channels a Rock 'Em Sock 'Em Robot in Buzz Lightyear's Space Ranger Spin. Guests—er, "new recruits in the Galactic Alliance"—rack up points by shooting at the "Z" targets.

Buzz Lightyear's Space Ranger Spin

★ ★ ★ **FASTPASS** Tomorrowland 5 min. Capacity: 201. Indoor, air-conditioned queue. Fear factor: None. Access: ECV users must transfer to a wheelchair. Handheld captioning, Audio Description. Debuted: 1998.

Guests use laser guns to shoot at over a hundred cartoon targets at this ride-through video arcade. It turns the idea of a shooting gallery inside out: here the targets stay in one place while shooters move on a track, riding in two-seat "space cruiser" vehicles equipped with laser guns. Mostly made up of silly cartoon aliens, the black-lit targets often move, make noise or light up as guests hit them. A dashboard display tracks each shooter's score. Though the ride is a little low-tech by today's standards, children and video-game junkies should still enjoy it.

Note that, despite the attraction's name, the vehicles do not spin. They swivel.

The plot—yes, there is one, even in a shooting arcade—involves an epic battle between Buzz Lightyear and the Evil Emperor Zurg. The queue area is Star Command Headquarters, where Buzz mistakes guests for new recruits in his Galactic Alliance.

And there is a crisis: In order to power his new space scooter, Zurg's robotic henchmen

are stealing all "crystallic fusion power cells" (batteries, in Buzz-speak) from the world's toys. To fight back, Buzz orders the Little Green Men to recapture the batteries, and his new recruits —that's you—to destroy the robots.

Although it is fun, the experience does have drawbacks. Every rider's laser light is the same color (red), which makes it tough to get feedback on your aim. Targets are not labeled with point values, so serious gamers

Average wait times

Time	Standby line	Fastpass time
9:00a	0 min	10:20a
10:00a	10 min	10:35a
11:00a	20 min	11:40a
Noon	35 min	12:35p
1:00p	45 min	2:15p
2:00p	35 min	3:10p
3:00p	30 min	4:10p
4:00p	40 min	5:00p
5:00p	35 min	5:45p
6:00p	35 min	6:50p
7:00p	40 min	7:55p
8:00p	40 min	8:50p
9:00p	30 min	9:55p

Zurg powers his secret weapon space scooter with stolen batteries from other toys. Though it is not publicized, riders earn 100,000 points a pop by hitting the lone "Z" target at the bottom of the scooter. Other targets in the scene are worth far less.

waste a lot of shots. And instead of being rewarded by working together (like in the more modern Toy Story Mania at Disney's Hollywood Studios), here players compete against each other. Whoever controls the vehicle's joystick gets a huge advantage.

How to get a high score. The maximum point total possible on the ride is 999,999. Here's how your score can get close to that:

Call dibs on the joystick, so you can keep your vehicle facing the right targets.

Sit on the right side of your vehicle. That side has two-thirds of the targets.

Once your gun is activated, pull the trigger and hold it in for the entire ride. The flashing laser beam will help you track your aim. It will fire about once a second.

Aim only at targets with big payoffs: As you enter Room 1, aim for the left arm of the left robot (each hit is 100,000 points).

As you pass that robot, turn your vehicle to the left and hit the other side of that same arm (25,000 points).

As you leave the first room, turn backwards and aim at the overhead claw of the other robot (100,000 points).

As you enter the second room, aim at the top and bottom targets of the large volcano (25,000 points).

As soon as you see Zurg, hit the bottom target of his space scooter (100,000 points) by firing early and late; you can't aim low enough to hit it straight on.

As you go into the third room, aim about six feet to either side of the top of the exit to hit an unmarked target in the middle of a rectangular plate (25,000 points).

If the ride stops, keep your blaster fixed on a high-value target and keep firing. You'll rack up points.

A closer look. The entire ride takes place in a world of toys. Buzz gets his information from a Viewmaster; Zurg's lead henchman looks like a classic Rock 'Em Sock 'Em Robot. The space cruiser gets its power from a backpack of batteries; its remote control sits on the right as riders cruise in to the exit area.

The track layout is unchanged from its days as "If You Had Wings." Sponsored by Eastern Airlines, the 1970s attraction took passengers through a series of sets that portrayed Caribbean or Latin American destinations. One area created the sensation of speed by combining a slight breeze with wraparound point-of-view video clips of high-speed sports. The ride was a guest favorite, in part because it rarely had a long line and didn't require the use of a ticket. At the time, Disney charged only a token fee to enter Magic Kingdom but required the purchase of a ticket book to ride most attractions.

Hidden Mickeys. ❶ In the queue, a Mickey profile appears on a poster as a green land mass on the planet Pollost Prime. The planet and its mass also appear three more times—to the left of the Viewmaster in the queue, on the ride as guests fight the video Zurg and in the final battle on the left. ❷ Another profile appears on the left as guests enter Zurg's spaceship, behind the battery-delivering robot and under the words "Initiate Battery Unload." ❸ The three-circle shape appears across from the souvenir-photo monitors as an image on a painted monitor on a mural. ❹ Also in that room, on a painted window to the left of the full-size pink character Booster, as a cluster of three stars at the top center of a star field. ❺ As a second star cluster at the bottom right of that field.

Retro rockets: Astro Orbiter's machine-age spacecraft circle high above Tomorrowland. At night, the two-seat rockets glow green from their nose cones and red from their "exhaust fire."

Astro Orbiter

★★★ ✔ **Tomorrowland** 2 min. Capacity: 32. Runs during light rains; grounded by downpours, lightning. Partially shaded queue. Fear factor: Height, steep angle bother even some adults. Access: Must be ambulatory. Debuted: 1971, updated 1994 (Disneyland 1955).

Fast, high and a little scary, open-air rockets twirl five stories above Tomorrowland on this hub-and-spoke ride. Perched atop the boarding station of the elevated PeopleMover ride, Astro Orbiter lifts its riders 55 feet off the ground. Guests take an elevator to reach it.

But there's more to this ride than just height. Top speed is 20 mph—plenty zippy when you're in a tight circle—and your rocket tilts at 45 degrees. At night the rockets' nose cones glow green, their exhaust fires red. Flying within a huge kinetic model of rings, planets and moons, riders make about 20 revolutions around a towering retro antenna.

Unfortunately, the waiting line is usually awful. Astro Orbiter loads very slowly, and guests wait on hot asphalt with absolutely nothing to do. Those who arrive first thing in the morning, however, often get right on and can ride two, sometimes even three times in a row. At night, guests who time it right get a unique view of the Wishes fireworks display.

A closer look. Unchanged from the ride's original incarnation as space-age Star Jets, the ride's green, steel-mesh elevator looks just like the rocket gantries that were used in early manned launches at nearby Cape Canaveral, Fla.

Family matters. Astro Orbiter is Walt Disney World's most exhilarating ride that doesn't have a height minimum. Young thrill-seekers who are too short for the roller coasters will love it.

Average wait times

Time	Standby line	Fastpass time
9:00a	5 min	(n/a)
10:00a	10 min	(n/a)
11:00a	25 min	(n/a)
Noon	40 min	(n/a)
1:00p	25 min	(n/a)
2:00p	25 min	(n/a)
3:00p	25 min	(n/a)
4:00p	40 min	(n/a)
5:00p	35 min	(n/a)
6:00p	45 min	(n/a)
7:00p	30 min	(n/a)
8:00p	35 min	(n/a)
9:00p	20 min	(n/a)

Offering a breezy, elevated tour of Tomorrowland, the PeopleMover travels into Space Mountain and the building holding Buzz Lightyear's Space Ranger Spin. It moves through linear induction.

PeopleMover

★★★★ ✓ **Tomorrowland** 10 min. Capacity: 900 (4 per car). Covered outdoor queue. Fear factor: None. Access: Must be ambulatory. Handheld captioning, Audio Description. Debuted: 1975, revised 1996, 2009.

Zip around above Tomorrowland on this breezy tour, Disney World's most underrated attraction. The elevated track snakes alongside and through four buildings, including Space Mountain, and passes a real piece of Disney future past: the centerpiece of Walt Disney's model of his proposed Experimental Prototype City of Tomorrow.

It's a great escape from a rain; since the entire track is covered, riders only get damp if the wind is blowing the rain sideways. When Space Mountain is closed, they get a peek at that dark ride with its work lights on.

A closer look. While planning his dream EPCOT city, Walt Disney thought a system of small electric trains would give its residents an efficient way to run errands or get to work. It would wind alongside, and sometimes circle over, convenience stores, offices and mass-transit stations without creating pollution or traffic problems.

Driven by Walt, the Disney company formed a separate division—Community Transportation Services (CTS)—to sell PeopleMovers to cities. This ride was the demonstrator. But without Walt's vision (he died during development) the idea went nowhere. EPCOT the city was shelved, and CTS sold only one train—in 1981, to what is today the George Bush Intercontinental Airport in Houston. That train is still running, shuttling travelers under the airport's main terminal.

Efficient and easy to maintain, the train's power system has no moving parts except its wheels. Every six feet or so a magnetic coil embedded in the track pulses with electricity in a carefully timed rhythm, turning on to pull a car to it, then off to let the car roll over it, creating a near-silent glide of linear induction. Loading is fast, as each train slows but never stops. The idea won a design achievement award from the National Endowment for the Arts and the U.S. Dept. of Transportation.

Family matters. PeopleMover is one of the few Disney rides where travelers sit across from one another, making for good photo—and conversation—opportunities.

Hidden Mickey. On a belt buckle in a beauty salon in the Buzz Lightyear's Space Ranger Spin building.

Micaela Neal

"We've now got gas lamps, telephone and the latest design in cast-iron stoves." A turn-of-the-20th-century father raves about "new" technology in Walt Disney's Carousel of Progress.

Walt Disney's Carousel of Progress

★★★ ✓ **Tomorrowland** 21 min. Capacity: 1,440. Outdoor queue. Fear factor: None. Access: Guests may remain in wheelchairs, ECVs; assistive listening; handheld and activated video captioning. Debuted at NY World's Fair 1964, Walt Disney World 1975; revised 1994.

Robotic families welcome you into their homes of yesterday and today in this vintage theatrical show, which demonstrates how electricity has improved family life. Four scenes depict the 1900s, 1920s, 1940s and 1990s. First presented at the 1964 New York World's Fair, the attraction uses a unique circular theater in which the seating area rotates from scene to scene. Last updated in 1994, the show is woefully out-of-date but still offers a wide-eyed charm.

'Don't bark at him, Rover.' The attraction has a fascinating pedigree. Disney created the first Carousel of Progress for the fair's General Electric pavilion, which in keeping with GE's slogan at the time—"Progress Is Our Most Important Product"—was called Progressland. Starring Disney's first Audio-Animatronics people, the show promoted GE appliances as having a history of helping families and, in a Christmastime finale, pitched a modern "GE push-button kitchen

that all but runs itself." The sponsor's name was woven through the script. "Don't bark at him, Rover," the dad told the dog when it barked at a stranger. "He might be a good customer of General Electric."

Walt Disney wrote much of the dialogue himself, and insisted its robots perform not only basic movements but also "business," small supplemental actions that would make them more real. Thanks to Walt, when 1920s house guest Cousin Orville relaxes in a bathtub, he also wiggles his toes.

To bridge the scenes, Disney songwriters Robert and Richard Sherman ("It's a Small World") wrote "There's a Great Big Beautiful Tomorrow." Its lyrics captured a blind optimism that was promoted throughout the fair: "There's a great big beautiful tomorrow, shining at the end of every day. There's a great big beautiful tomorrow, just a dream away!"

After the fair closed Disney moved the attraction to California's Disneyland. A revamped finale featured a home video-cassette recorder, a product that wouldn't appear in stores for more than a decade.

That '70s show. A third Carousel script tied the show into the women's movement when the show moved again in 1975, this

Daughter Patty gets ski boots for Christmas in the Carousel of Progress finale. The Audio-Animatronics character is voiced by Debi Derryberry, the voice of Nickelodeon's Jimmy Neutron.

Micaela Neal

time to Walt Disney World. In a new 1920s scene, the daughter searched Help Wanted ads though her father warned "It's a man's world out there." The 1940s wife demanded equal pay for wallpapering the rumpus room, asking her husband "If you hired a man to do this, wouldn't you pay him?" A new finale showed dad as the family cook.

To meet GE's demand that the Florida show focus on the present, the Shermans wrote a new theme, "Now is the Time." Dissing the future as "still but a dream," it proclaimed "Now is the time! Now is the best time! Now is the best time of your life!"

Though the show had rotated clockwise in its earlier incarnations, it switched directions for the Florida setup. It also returned to using wigs made from human hair. Nylon versions had been used at Disneyland, but over time klieg lights above the father had melted his hair into what one Disney Imagineer described as "a sticky pile of goo."

Lumbago and laser discs. Losing GE as a sponsor, in 1994 Disney created a fourth version of the show, which plays today. Though it keeps much of its 1970s banter, its script is also peppered with old-fashioned sayings— the wife "gets to the core of the apple;" the husband knows it won't rain because "my lumbago isn't acting up." Peering into his dad's stereoscope, the son exclaims "Ooh la la! So that's Little Egypt doing the hoochie-koochie!" a reference to an exotic dancer at the 1893 Chicago World's Fair. Today's finale takes place in the great big beautiful tomorrow of, well, 1994. While mom stays busy with a laptop computer, Grandpa longs for the days before "car phones" and laser discs.

Cousin Bugs. Mel Blanc, the voice of Bugs Bunny and other Warner Bros. cartoon characters, provides the voice of Cousin Orville. Other voice talents include Jean Shepherd (narrator of 1983's "A Christmas Story") as the dad, Debi Derryberry (voice of Nickelodeon's Jimmy Neutron) as the daughter, Janet Waldo (daughter Judy in the 1960s cartoon series "The Jetsons" and Josie in the 1970s "Josie and the Pussycats") as the Christmas grandma and 1950s singing cowboy (and voice of the original Carousel of Progress dad) Rex Allen as the Christmas Grandpa.

'Bigger than Toad!' In the fall of 2001, less than a month after Disney World started a 15-month celebration of Walt Disney's 100th birthday, it closed his beloved Carousel of Progress. The reason: dwindling attendance. Within days, fans organized a protest. "Let's make this bigger than Toad!" wrote one blogger, referring to an earlier failed attempt to save the attraction Mr. Toad's Wild Ride. This time, however, the protest worked. Disney reopened the Carousel a few months later.

Fun facts. The six auditoriums rotate at 2 feet per second on large steel wheels and tracks, just like a train car on a railroad. The show's first grandma also rocks in front of the fireplace in the Haunted Mansion ballroom.

Family matters. Children love watching the dogs. One appears in each scene, listening and reacting to the action.

Hidden Mickeys. ❶ In the 1940s scene, the sorcerer's hat from 1940's "Fantasia" sits on a stool near the exercise machine. Mickey items in the finale include: ❷ a nutcracker on the mantel, ❸ a plushie under the Christmas tree, ❹ a salt shaker on the bar and ❺ an abstract painting of the Sorcerer's Apprentice. ❻ At the start of the video game, the three circles appear as engines of a spaceship.

Riders travel down a flashing-blue "energizing portal" before launching into a starry night on Space Mountain, a dark indoor roller coaster. Its open-air rockets are just one-person wide.

Space Mountain

★★★★★ ✔ *FASTPASS* **Tomorrowland** 2 min, 30 sec. Capacity: 180. Indoor, air-conditioned queue. Fear factor: Dark drops and turns, but you don't go upside down. Guests should be free from motion sickness; pregnancy; high blood pressure; heart, back or neck problems. Access: Must be ambulatory. Height min: 44 in. Debuted: 1975, revised 2009.

"Daddy, did you hear me scream?!" beamed the 6-year-old girl, hopping out of her rocket. "That! Was! Cool!" said her 10-year-old brother. The parents shared a look. "Let's ride again!" exclaimed the wife.

Open-air rockets zoom through a dark universe inside this circular building, which holds the world's oldest, and arguably still best, roller coaster in the dark. Sitting in low-slung ride vehicles that are just a single seat wide, guests hurtle through an inky abyss filled with shooting stars. Every dip, drop and turn comes as a surprise. Top speed is 28 miles per hour, plenty fast in the dark.

The best seat is the front one, which is labeled Row 1 on the boarding platform. It's worth asking for. Those with long legs will prefer seats that line up with either Row 1 or 4.

The ride's story begins as guests walk into the building, a futuristic spaceport and repair center that's orbiting above the earth. Passing the departure board, a long, dark queue tunnel leads to a launch platform. After you climb into your rocket, a sign flashes "Have a Nice Flight" and off you go down into the "energizing portal," a flashing blue tunnel that supposedly powers your machine and ignites its engine. Climbing the launch tower (the chain lift), you pass under a large ship that has come in for service; as mechanics work on its engines, control-room

Average wait times

Time	Standby line	Fastpass time
9:00a	0 min	10:10a
10:00a	25 min	11:15a
11:00a	35 min	12:35p
Noon	50 min	3:00p
1:00p	60 min	5:05p
2:00p	65 min	5:55p
3:00p	55 min	7:20p
4:00p	60 min	8:50p
5:00p	65 min	(out)
6:00p	75 min	(out)
7:00p	65 min	(out)
8:00p	65 min	(out)
9:00p	50 min	(out)

Space Mountain gets its sweeping-pillar look from Israel's Kennedy Memorial. Its shape comes from Japan's Mt. Fuji.

operators monitor their progress. Then you blast off, on a journey through what an early Disney press release called "the void of the universe." When landing your ride triggers a sonic boom in a red de-energizing tunnel.

A major 2009 update made the ride darker and smoother and added video games to the standby queue. Disney added ambient techno music and sound effects in 2010.

A closer look. As it has always been, much of Space Mountain is a subtle tribute to the 1968 film, "2001: A Space Odyssey." The queue's eerie music recalls the movie's early scenes of a moon transport shuttle. The hall's angled plastic clapboard walls duplicate those of the film's transport interior.

The movie's Discovery One spacecraft shows up three times. In the ride's boarding area, the spool-like corners the rockets pass by look just like the axle of Discovery One's rotating living quarters. The blue strobe tunnel recalls its hexagonal corridor that leads to its EVA pods. On the lift hill, the docked ship has the craft's unique head-spine-and-hip shape. The docked ship also appears in an entranceway window.

'Where's Mr. Smee?' With its first passengers astronauts Scott Carpenter, Gordon Cooper and Jim Irwin, the coaster debuted on Jan. 15, 1975. Though Disney declared it "the nation's most breathtaking thrill ride," not every guest got the message. As they climbed in their rockets, many expected something along the lines of Peter Pan's Flight, since at the time Disney didn't do roller coasters. Moments later, up came their lunches and out flew their hats, purses, eyeglasses and, on more than one occasion, false teeth. Disney's response included discreetly ironing out some of the most violent jerks and jolts.

Though it opened during a recession, Space Mountain was an instant smash. When summer came, families with teens, many of whom would have not considered a Disney vacation before, began crowding Magic Kingdom turnstiles early each morning.

Fun facts. The blue energizing portal has a practical function: its strobes shrink your pupils, so your space flight seems darker than it really is. Why do the docked ship's engine nozzles look like plastic caps of spray-paint cans? Because they are. Used by an artist on a pre-production model, real spray-paint caps were accidentally reproduced perfectly on the full-scale prop. The sonic boom heard in the red re-entry tunnel is actually the reversed sound of a jet engine starting up. The building gets its sweeping-pillar look from Israel's Kennedy Memorial; its shape comes from Japan's Mt. Fuji. Space Mountain is the oldest roller coaster in Florida.

Family matters. If your child is nervous about riding but still wants to go, sit behind him. You'll be able to hold his hand, or offer a comforting shoulder hug, throughout the trip.

Fun finds. ❶ Panels inside the mountain refer to it as "Star Port Seven-Five," a nod to the attraction's opening year. ❷ Intergalactic route maps along the queue contain references to the Little Mermaid, Mickey's pet dog and the 1937 movie "Snow White and the Seven Dwarfs." ❸ The chain-lift spaceship is named MK-1, a reference to the fact that this Magic Kingdom version of Space Mountain is the original ride. Similar versions have been built in California, China, France and Japan. The spaceship is marked "H-NCH 1975," a reference to the ride's designer, John Hench, as well as the year the ride opened.

Children drive "race" cars at the Tomorrowland Speedway. Above, Andrew Turner, age 6, of Ft. Myers, Fla., is cheered on by his dad, Jeff, as they head for the finish line.

Tomorrowland Speedway

★★ **Tomorrowland** 5 min. Capacity: 292 (146 2-seat vehicles). Outdoor partially covered queue. Fear factor: None. Closed during thunderstorms. Access: Must be ambulatory. Height min: 54 inches to take a car out alone; 32 inches to ride. Debuted: 1971 (Disneyland 1967). Revised 1996.

Race cars rumble and bump around corners, little boys and girls at the wheel in these small-scale open vehicles, which have a top speed of only 7.5 mph. The winding track has four lanes; its half-mile course takes drivers around five turns, down one short straightaway and under and over a bridge. The track meanders past beautiful live oak and magnolia trees on a green park-like lawn. Children under age 8 will like it best.

The waiting line is one of the worst in the park. Umbrellas provide some shade, but on peak days wait times can exceed an hour. There's no wait first thing in the morning, or sometimes late at night. A small covered grandstand offers those not riding a place to wait that overlooks the boarding area.

A closer look. Why is this old-time attraction in Tomorrowland? For a reason that could only make sense to Disney: When it opened in 1971, the track was a version of the Disneyland attraction Autopia, which, when that California ride premiered in 1955, was a simulation of the limited-access highways destined for that era's future. A 1994 redo as an alien race confused the theme further. Today the attraction has little theme at all.

Family matters. Let your child drive if he can reach the pedals. There's no danger; each car is guided by a rail and slows quickly as soon as its driver takes his foot off the gas pedal.

Average wait times

Time	Standby line	Fastpass time
9:00a	0 min	(n/a)
10:00a	20 min	(n/a)
11:00a	25 min	(n/a)
Noon	30 min	(n/a)
1:00p	30 min	(n/a)
2:00p	35 min	(n/a)
3:00p	30 min	(n/a)
4:00p	35 min	(n/a)
5:00p	35 min	(n/a)
6:00p	35 min	(n/a)
7:00p	30 min	(n/a)
8:00p	40 min	(n/a)
9:00p	25 min	(n/a)

The ebullient Genie from the 1992 Disney movie "Aladdin" greets onlookers of the Celebrate a Dream Come True Parade. The procession features dozens of Disney characters.

Celebrate a Dream Come True Parade

★★ **Travels Main Street U.S.A., then Liberty Square, Frontierland** 30 min. 3p daily. Arrive 20 min early for good spot. Cancelled during rain. Fear factor: None. Access: Special viewing areas for those in wheelchairs, ECVs. Debuted: 2009.

Want to slap hands—er, paws—with Pluto? Want to high-five Sheriff Woody? Don't care that much about floats? Look no further than this afternoon procession. Though its floats are, by Disney standards, unimaginative and often downright cheap, many characters dance down the street and they pause often to greet guests who line the route. Among those who come up to the crowd: Chip 'n Dale, Donald Duck, Goofy, Lady Tremaine and her daughters Anastasia and Drizella ("Cinderella," 1950), Genie and Abu ("Aladdin," 1992), Pluto, Stitch and Woody (from the "Toy Story" series).

Riding the floats are Mickey and Minnie Mouse, nearly every Disney princess and the stars of "Alice in Wonderland" (1951), "Mary Poppins" (1964), "Peter Pan" (1953), "Pinocchio" (1940), and "Snow White and the Seven Dwarfs" (1937). Cinderella rides on a vivid blue float festooned with orange pumpkins; another float has Ariel and Eric ("The Little Mermaid, 1989), Belle and the Beast ("Beauty and the Beast," 1991) and Tiana and Naveen ("The "Princess and the Frog," 2009). As each float passes by, spectators hear songs that match its characters. Snow White arrives to "Whistle While You Work," Mary Poppins gets "Supercalifragilisticexpialidocious."

A closer look. "Created" in 2009, the procession is a halfhearted update of the Disney Dreams Come True Parade (2006–2008), itself a budget makeover of the Share a Dream Come True Parade (2001–2006). Floats, which once were topped with giant snowglobes, now have party-favor confetti and balloon decorations, a holdover look from Disney's 2010 celebration-themed marketing campaign.

Best viewing spots. The parade's best viewing spot is along the shady western side of Main Street U.S.A. Curb seats get taken about 2:30 p.m, earlier during peak periods.

Family matters. As guests wait for the procession, cast members keep children entertained with hula hoops, jump ropes and street games such as Red Light Green Light.

Hidden Mickey. On the Snow White float as a dark mark on the organ, above the middle keys.

Inspired by the Pleasure Island sequence in Disney's 1940 movie "Pinocchio," a giant smiling float lights up like a Christmas tree in the Main Street Electrical Parade

Main Street Electrical Parade

★★ **Travels Main Street U.S.A., then Liberty Square, Frontierland** 25 min. Arrive 30 early for a good seat, an hour early for the best spots. Fear factor: None. Cancelled during rain. Access: Special viewing areas for guests in wheelchairs and ECVs. Debuted: 1977, revised 1999, 2010 (Disneyland 1972).

A giant hookah-smoking caterpillar creeps down the street, followed by a pink-winged dragon and an elephant-sized smiling head. All are floats in this vintage procession, joining twirling snails, Cinderella's coach and dozens of Disney characters. Shimmering with light, the floats and costumes are covered with tiny colored bulbs, much like those on a Christmas tree.

Though the nighttime parade will seem cheesy to many guests—its repetitive Moog music can fry your brain—it will appeal to nostalgic adults and young children, especially those familiar with the movies it depicts: 1951's "Alice in Wonderland," 1950's "Cinderella," 1953's "Peter Pan," 1940's "Pinocchio," 1937's "Snow White and the Seven Dwarfs" and the obscure 1977 Disney film "Pete's Dragon."

Tinker Bell kicks things off, sprinkling pixie dust that leaves a golden swirl on all the floats that follow. Goofy drives a train holding Mickey and Minnie Mouse. Snails, turtles and lightning bugs twirl by to introduce the Alice in Wonderland segment, with Alice perched atop a giant mushroom. Cinderella glides by in her pumpkin carriage.

Peter Pan and Captain Hook duel on a pirate ship, followed by Mr. Smee in a rowboat. Dopey drives a gem-filled mine train to lead in Snow White and the rest of the dwarfs. Next comes a huge smoke-snorting Elliott from "Pete's Dragon," ridden by Pete himself.

Donkey-eared boys dance in front of the Pinocchio float, a decadent Pleasure Island carnival setting. Bringing up the rear is a long patriotic float supported by high-stepping chorus girls.

Returning to Magic Kingdom after a hiatus of over a decade, the parade replaces the similar SpectroMagic.

Where to watch it. A good spot is in front of Tony's Town Square Restaurant along Main Street U.S.A. It offers a good view of the front and side of every float, and is right next to the park exit.

Family matters. Children can play before the parade starts. Cast members provide hula hoops, jump ropes and hopscotch games.

Goofy shakes his tail feather during the "Move It! Shake It! Celebrate It!" street party. The dippy dog-man is one of eight Disney characters who get down and boogie with park guests.

Move It! Shake It! Celebrate It!

★★★★ ✓ **Cinderella Castle hub** 12 min. Floats travel Main Street U.S.A., stop at Cinderella Castle hub for show, then return. Cancelled during rain. Fear factor: None. Access: Special viewing areas for those in wheelchairs, ECVs. Debuted: 2009.

You can dance with a Disney character in this colorful street party, which takes place a few times a day in front of Cinderella Castle. If you're not shy about dancing in public, it's an easy way to have a fun character experience.

After an energetic emcee leads the crowd in a roll-call of celebrations ("If you're having a birthday… raise your hands!"), giant gift boxes open to reveal Sebastian the crab (from 1989's "The Little Mermaid"), Lumiere (1991's "Beauty and the Beast"), the Mad Hatter (1951's "Alice in Wonderland") and Genie (1992's "Aladdin"). Then everyone is invited into the street to "move it like this and shake it like that." Dance leaders make it easy for even the most novice booty shaker to join in.

Characters dancing with guests include cartoon chipmunks Chip 'n Dale directly in front of the castle, Mr. Incredible and Frozone (2004's "The Incredibles") near the entrance to Tomorrowland, Goofy and Donald Duck at the lower right side of the hub, King Louie and Baloo (from 1967's "The Jungle Book") near the Adventureland entrance and "Toy Story" stars Woody and Jessie near the walkway to Liberty Square.

Songs include the Baha Men's "Move It Like This (Shake It Like That)," Peaches & Herb's disco ditty "Shake Your Groove Thing" and the Ray Charles classic "Twist It (Shake Your Tail Feather)." A conga line forms to Buster Poindexter's "Hot, Hot, Hot."

The procession rolls out down Main Street U.S.A. to a reworked version of the Hannah Montana tune "Pumpin' Up the Party." The floats head back to "High School Musical" star Corbin Bleu's "Celebrate You." The show's theme comes from Disney's 2010 celebration-focused marketing campaign.

"Shake It Bake It." On most days, this is one party that's truly hot, as the party takes place in direct sunlight on asphalt pavement. Street temperatures routinely top 105 degrees for shows performed between May and August; when they do Disney usually cuts the conga line out of concern for the performers. Privately, some dancers refer to the show as "Shake It Bake It."

Characters in this show don't formally pose for pictures or sign autographs.

Dozens of rockets and nearly 700 explosions light up the sky behind Cinderella Castle during Wishes, Walt Disney World's signature fireworks show. Visuals synchronize to a symphonic score.

Wishes

★ ★ ★ ★ ★ ✓ **Behind Cinderella Castle** 12 min. Fear factor: Loud explosions. Cancelled during thunderstorms. Access: Special viewing areas for wheelchair and ECV users. Debuted: 2003.

Tinker Bell flies from Cinderella Castle in Disney's signature fireworks show. The beginning may be the ultimate Disney moment: a lone glowing star arching over Cinderella Castle. After narrator Jiminy Cricket (from 1940's "Pinocchio") talks about wishing upon a star, starbursts coordinate precisely with Disney music and the voices of beloved Disney stars.

Though it launches $200,000 worth of pyro each night—683 pieces from 11 locations—Wishes paints delicate strokes as well as bold. Sometimes the sky sparkles, sometimes it flashes. Explosions form starbursts, of course, but also stars, hearts, even a face. Comets shoot off individually and by the dozen.

Synchronizing its visuals to a symphonic score, Wishes packs an emotional punch too, as it teaches a heart-tugging lesson about believing in yourself. The finale, with children singing about their wishes coming true, often makes parents tear up. It's a perfect way to end a Magic Kingdom day.

Where to watch it. Though the fireworks are visible throughout the park, the symmetrical nature of the show means Wishes is best seen from in front of the castle. The perfect spot is on the crest of the Main Street bridge, between the Tip Board and the castle hub. Stay away from Town Square (the lights stay on) and the Main Street U.S.A. train station balcony (there's no audio). The closest dark spot to the exit is in front of the Emporium. Disney offers a Wishes "dessert party" ($26 adults, $14 children 3–9) on the patio of the Tomorrowland Noodle Station, which is off to the side.

A closer look. In 1940's "Pinocchio," the Blue Fairy, symbolizing patient wisdom, appoints Jiminy Cricket to serve as the boy's conscience. "Starlight, Star Bright" is a 19th-century American nursery rhyme. It's based on the notion that if you see the first star of the night sky before any others have appeared, any wish you make will come true.

Family matters. Instead of fighting the huge crowd that leaves the park immediately after the show, embrace the magical mood, get some ice cream and relax. Your children will be happy; why not talk with them? Ask about their dreams and wishes. Tell them yours.

Main Street Thespian Society chairman Beatrice Starr (left), suffragette Hildegard Olivia Harding (center) and choir director Victoria Trumpetto (right) are among the Citizens of Main Street

Street performers and castle shows

Captain Jack Sparrow's Pirate Tutorial
★★★★★ ✔ **Adventureland** 20-minute shows. Across from Pirates of the Caribbean. Comical Capt. Jack Sparrow and first mate Mack recruit aspiring pirates among youngsters in the crowd. After administering the Pirate Oath, they teach the kids how to be rescued from a desert island, use a swordplay trick to flee an enemy, and sing the Disney tune "Yo Ho (A Pirate's Life for Me)."

Casey's Corner Pianist ★★★★ ✔ **Main Street U.S.A.** 20-minute shows, Casey's Corner patio. A skilled entertainer bangs out honky tonk, ragtime, Disney tunes and, yes, requests on a white upright piano.

Citizens of Main Street ★★★★★ ✔ **Main Street U.S.A.** 20-minute shows. A troupe of improvisational actors, the Citizens of Main Street portray the boulevard's townsfolk, strolling the street to chat, dance, joke, sing and pose for pictures with guests. Characters include the mayor, fire chief and a councilman as well as socialites and suffragettes Hildegard Olivia Harding and Beatrice Starr. Guests get fashion advice from style maven Miss Inga DaPointe and voice lessons from choir director Victoria Trumpetto. Disney pin traders exchange wares with Main Street Gazette reporter Scoop Sanderson.

Dapper Dans ★★★★★ ✔ **Main Street U.S.A.** 20-minute shows. Barbershop quartet mixes harmonically perfect repertoire with chimes, tap dancing and corny humor. The group will sing "Happy Birthday" on request. Sometimes they'll serenade guests getting their hair cut at the Harmony Barber Shop, or hop on the horse trolley to harmonize while traveling down Main Street U.S.A. The group participates in the Flag Retreat ceremony every day at 5 p.m.

Dream Along with Mickey ★★★ **Cinderella Castle forecourt** 20-minute shows. No seats, no shade. Mickey Mouse throws a party to celebrate the power of dreams in this elaborate song-and-dance show, which includes Donald Duck, Goofy and Minnie Mouse; princesses Cinderella, Snow White and Aurora (Sleeping Beauty); and nearly the entire cast of 1953's "Peter Pan." Evil fairy Maleficent crashes the party, but to no avail. "Take the dream with you wherever you may go," says Mickey at the finale, as fireworks burst overhead.

Micaela Neal

The men of Main Street U.S.A. include, from left, the Casey's Corner pianist, Main Street Gazette Reporter (and Disney pin enthusiast) Scoop Sanderson and Mayor Christopher George Weaver

Songs include "A Dream is a Wish Your Heart Makes," "So This is Love," "Some Day My Prince Will Come" and "A Pirate's Life." Unlike in most shows, the eyelids of these "fur" characters open and close (Donald's expressions are hilarious; Goofy's half-lidded look suits him to a T). The mouths move, too.

Main Street fashion maven Miss Inga DaPointe

Fantasyland Woodwind Society ★★★★ ✓
Fantasyland 20-minute shows. Sax quartet plays whimsical Disney tunes. Quartet of saxophonists appears in the morning as the Main Street Saxophone Four on Main Street U.S.A.

Flag Retreat ★★ Main Street U.S.A. 20-minute ceremony, 5p daily. Town Square. Patriotic ceremony performed daily by the Park Security Color Guard as it lowers the U.S. flag, often with a guest military veteran. Ceremony includes the Main Street Philharmonic and the Dapper Dans. Guests interested in being the Veteran of the Day should check in with Guest Relations first thing in the morning.

Frontierland Hoedown ★★★ Adventureland 20-minute show at 4:45p; some days have add'l later shows. In front of Prairie Outpost and Supply Shop. Guests square dance and do the hokey pokey from friendly country-western couples. Country Bears characters play washboard and spoons. Brer Rabbit greets guests.

Magic Kingdom Welcome Show ★★★★ ✓
Park entrance 8-minute show. Stage is the train station. A Citizen of Main Street (see previous page) welcomes Mickey Mouse, other characters and a randomly selected guest family who arrive on the Walt Disney World show train to open the park. From the Main Street U.S.A. railroad station, Mickey and friends welcome guests amid a spray of confetti and pixie dust. Main Street Trolley Parade couples (see below) lip-sync a medley of "Good Morning" (from 1952's "Singin' in the Rain"), "Casey Junior" (from 1941's "Dumbo")

Clockwise from top left: The Main Street Philharmonic marching band, the Dapper Dans barbershop quartet, the Main Street Trolley Parade, the Dream Along with Mickey castle show

and "Zip-A-Dee-Doo-Dah" (from 1946's "Song of the South"). It's a nice start to the day.

Main Street Philharmonic ★★★★ ✔ Main Street U.S.A. 20-minute shows. Americana revue with 12-piece comedic brass and percussion ensemble. Tunes include turn-of-the-century favorites such as "Alexander's Rag Time Band." Finale "volunteers" a guest to honk a horn as the band plays "Hold That Tiger."

Main Street Saxophone Four ★★★★ ✔ Main Street U.S.A. 20-minute shows. Sax quartet harmonizes deftly on ragtime, jazz and Disney tunes. The same group appears in the afternoon as the Fantasyland Woodwind Society.

Main Street Trolley Parade ★★★★ ✔ Main Street U.S.A. Three 5-minute shows per parade. Mornings. Gay '90s couples hop off the horse trolley to perform a soft-shoe pantomime; it's more of a song-and-dance street show than a parade. While dancing they lip-sync "The Trolley Song" (from 1944's "Meet Me in St. Louis") and a service number that exalts Magic Kingdom ("The place was made with a magical plan! And just around the corner is a Fantasyland!"). So strange, yet oh so Disney.

The Notorious Banjo Brothers and Bob ★★★★ ✔ Frontierland 20-minute shows. Two banjo pickers and a tuba player perform Disney tunes, bluegrass and cowboy melodies such as "Back in the Saddle Again."

PUSH, The Talking Trashcan ★★★★ ✔ Tomorrowland 20-minute shows. On walkway between Indy Speedway and Auntie Gravity's Galactic Goodies. Roving trash can chats and jokes with guests.

The Magic, The Memories and You! ★★★★ ✔ Cinderella Castle 10-minute shows, once or twice nightly. No seats. Smile, you're on… Cinderella Castle! A giant version of your face may end up on the walls of the famous icon in this special-effects spectacle, a new-for-2011 light show that projects images of theme-park guests onto Cinderella Castle. Up to 500 same-day guest photos are used in each show, most for only a few seconds. Beyond all those, however, the show includes some stunning animated effects that will delight every child-at-heart. Vines grow up the walls of the castle, doves fly out of its breezeway, the largest turret turns into a rocket that blasts off, the castle even catches fire. The finale morphs the building into a video of Walt Disney.

A closer look: The show uses 16 high-powered projectors. Images come from those taken by Disney Photopass photographers earlier each day. Unusual, unposed photos are more likely to make the cut.

Epcot

Human achievement rules at this inspiring theme park, which celebrates science, technology and cultural diversity. Much like a world's fair, Epcot's rides and shows are grouped into pavilions and focus on subjects such as communication, energy, farming, transportation and world cultures. Appealing most to the curious and educated, the park tends to be more interesting than out-and-out fun.

Divided into two distinct sections—Future World and World Showcase—Epcot has a split personality. With its abundance of concrete buildings and scientific themes, Future World is a logical thinker, the nerdy corporate guy with a pocket protector. World Showcase, on the other hand, is a people person, a music-loving shopaholic with a $12 margarita in her hand. She also sleeps late.

Best reasons to go

Soarin': You fly over California in this breathtaking ride, perhaps the best attraction in all of Walt Disney World.

The dolphins: A trio of the mesmerizing mammals live at The Seas with Nemo & Friends pavilion. Training sessions spotlight their remarkable intelligence.

An international cast: Each World Showcase pavilion is staffed by natives of its country. Hand-picked by Disney and flown to the United States especially to work here, these young friendly people love talking with guests about their homelands.

Eating and drinking around the World: Good food and drink—and lots of variety—distinguish this park. No other spot in Disney World has so many eateries.

Unusual shopping: Stores brim with wares in most World Showcase pavilions, offering goods as varied as Japanese bonsai trees to bottles of Mexican tequila. Complimentary delivery to your (Disney-only) resort makes shopping convenient.

Worst aspects of the park

An impersonal Future: Curiously devoid of Disney cast members, the wide walkways

The symbol of Epcot, Spaceship Earth is a 180-foot-tall geodesic sphere

and public spaces in Future World are relatively free of Disney smiles.

No parade: The last one, Tapestry of Dreams, shut down way back in 2003.

What's the matter with kids?: With its emphasis on science, technology and international culture, Epcot has relatively few child-focused experiences.

Limited breakfast choices: The only breakfast restaurant is a princess character meal; the only sit-down fast-food spot is inside The Land pavilion.

Corporate Sponsorland: Many of Epcot's attractions are sponsored by corporations. Spaceship Earth has the name of its sponsor, Siemens, projected onto it as guests leave the park after the nightly fireworks display. If Magic Kingdom had this mindset, Wishes would conclude with Cinderella Castle plastered with the logo of… Barbie?

The walking: This is a big park. Hike out to World Showcase and you've still got 1.3 miles to go to get around it.

Getting oriented

Epcot is the combination of two distinct areas. The front of the park is Future World, with six pavilions circling a central plaza. In back is World Showcase, with 11 pavilions circling a lake.

What if it rains?

Epcot is a mixed blessing on rainy days. Though the park is comprised of indoor pavilions with multiple activities, the pavilions are spread out. Test Track closes when lightning is nearby. IllumiNations can get cancelled due to rain.

Family matters

Four rides have height minimums—44 inches for Mission Space, 40 inches for Soarin' as well as Test Track, 48 inches for The Sum of All Thrills at Innoventions. Other attractions that might scare children include Ellen's Energy Adventure (loud noises, bright flashes, darkened dinosaur habitat); IllumiNations (loud explosions, fire); Journey Into Imagination… with Figment (loud noises, a sudden flash) and Maelstrom (dark, with scary faces).

When break time comes, a trio of Future World janitors transforms into the Jammitors, a witty percussion group. World Showcase musicians include Canada's kilt-wearing Off Kilter, Mexico's Mariachi Cobre and Morocco's Mo'Rockin.

A Magical Day (Future World)

8:00a: Arrive at the parking lot, then be first in line at the entrance turnstiles (and later, the rope line at Innoventions Plaza). As you wait for the turnstiles to open (typically at 8:50 a.m.), pick up a Times Guide from Guest Relations at your far right.

9:00a: Ride Test Track.

9:45a: Get Fastpasses for Soarin'.

10:00a: Have pastries and coffee at Sunshine Seasons food court.

10:25a: Ride Living with the Land.

10:55a: Head to Innoventions West to play Liberty Mutual's Where's the Fire? and IBM's Runtime.

11:45a: Lunch at Coral Reef; ask for a table by the aquarium. As you wait, have one member of your party get a second set of Soarin' Fastpasses.

1:00p: See the dolphins, manatees and other underwater creatures at The Seas with Nemo & Friends pavilion.

2:15p: Use the first set of your Soarin' Fastpasses to ride that attraction.

3:00p: Ride Mission Space and play the post-show games.

4:00p: Treat yourself to handmade ice cream sandwiches or waffle cones at the Fountain View ice-cream shop.

4:30p: Browse at MouseGear (Innoventions Plaza) or The Art of Disney shop (left of Spaceship Earth as you face the exit).

5:00p: Ride Spaceship Earth. Stop at the Project Tomorrow postshow to email your "future" to yourself.

5:50p: Use your remaining Fastpasses to ride Soarin' a second time.

Every Epcot restaurant offers a children's menu except Bistro de Paris in the France pavilion. Epcot has two character meals: Akershus Royal Banquet Hall in Norway (princesses) and Garden Grill in The Land pavilion (Mickey Mouse and pals).

A Baby Care Center inside Future World's Odyssey Center provides changing rooms, nursing areas, a microwave and a playroom. Diapers, formula, pacifiers and over-the-counter medications are available for purchase.

Restaurants and food

Epcot has the most restaurants of any Disney World theme park, with 11 table-service restaurants, one buffet, two character meals and seven indoor fast-food spots. Le Cellier is the park's lone Disney Signature restaurant. Make reservations at 407-939-3463 or online at disneyworld.com/dining.

See the chapter **Restaurants and Food.**

Kim Possible World Showcase Adventure

Ever have the urge to turn tiny townsfolk into red-eyed zombies? This secret-agent scavenger hunt can make it happen. A cell-phone-like "Kimmunicator" allows players to trigger hidden effects at seven World Showcase pavilions. The mission: Save the world, by helping Disney Channel's teenage crime fighter and her friends vanquish a silly villain. Guests make a reservation to play. The adventure is included in Epcot's park admission price.

To get started, players stop by one of three Recruitment Stations (9a–7p, located in both Innoventions buildings as well as on the bridge between Future World and World Showcase) to pick up a Mission Pass,

A Moroccan cashier plays a darbouka drum while waiting out a thunderstorm. Natives of the countries they represent, World Showcase sales clerks, servers and attraction hosts are chosen for their friendly personalities.

a Fastpass-style reservation ticket for use later in the day. One pass is good for up to three handsets. At the assigned time, players report to a Field Station (11a–9p, at the International Gateway, Italy and Norway) to pick up their handsets and get their mission.

To carry out their assignments guests follow instructions on the device. Focused on a particular pavilion (China, France, Germany, Japan, Mexico, Norway or the U.K.), "secret agents" search for clues and eventually capture a cartoon bad guy. Each pavilion has a different mission, with different clues and effects. Among other things, players can make a jade monkey appear in China, a chimney smoke in Norway, a waterfall emerge in Japan, a volcano erupt in Mexico, a beer stein yodel in Germany and the eyes of the tiny residents of that pavilion's miniature train glow.

Each mission takes about an hour, and can be paused (and backed up) at any time.

A closer look

In 1965, flush with success after decades in the entertainment industry, 63-year-old Walt Disney still had one dream left to explore: to find a fix for America's urban areas.

His idea: Combine corporate sponsorships with the money he had just made from the 1964 movie "Mary Poppins" and then—using all 43 square miles of land he had secretly just purchased in Florida—build an experimental city. Filled with technological advancements, it would demonstrate how communities could solve their housing, pollution and transportation problems. Disney called the project the Experimental Prototype Community of Tomorrow. "EPCOT" for short.

The design called for a 50-acre town center enclosed in a dome, an internationally

A Magical Day (World Showcase)

Prior to 10:30a: Take advantage of the late start by sleeping in, having a leisurely breakfast or perhaps an early-morning dip in your hotel pool.

10:30a: Arrive at the park. Pick up a Times Guide as you enter.

10:45a: Stop at Innoventions to sign up for the Kim Possible World Showcase Adventure. Reserve a time for later in the day, then alter the following plan to accommodate it (allow 1 hour).

11:00a: U.K. pavilion. Shop for tea. See the World Showcase Players.

Noon: France pavilion. Shop for perfume. Have a pastry. Watch the movie Impressions de France.

12:40p: Morocco pavilion. Shop for a lamp. See the exhibit at the Gallery of Arts and History, "Moroccan Style: The Art of Personal Adornment."

1:15p: Lunch at the Japan pavilion's Tokyo Dining restaurant. Shop for candy. Before or after lunch, watch Miyuki create her candy-art animals.

3:00p: See the American Adventure Audio-Animatronics show.

3:45p: Germany pavilion. Shop for cuckoo clocks and beer steins. See the miniature train village.

4:30p: China pavilion. Shop for puppets. See the "Tomb Warriors" exhibit. For a treat, try the ice cream.

5:30p: Norway pavilion. Ride Maelstrom. Shop for trolls.

6:30p: Dinner at Mexico's La Hacienda de San Angel. Have a margarita. Or two.

8:30p: See IllumiNations. The best viewing spot is the World Showcase Plaza.

Cell-phone-like "Kimmunicators" trigger hidden effects during the Kim Possible World Showcase Adventure, a high-tech scavenger hunt geared to children. Players help Disney Channel's teenage crime fighter vanquish villains and save the world.

Park Resources

ATMs: Park entrance on far left; on World Showcase-Future World bridge; near American Adventure restrooms.

First Aid: For minor emergencies. Registered nurses. Odyssey Center.

Guest Relations: Walk-up window outside the turnstiles on the far right, office inside left of Spaceship Earth. General questions, dining reservations, currency exchange. Maps, Times Guides for all WDW parks. Stores items found in park that day. Multilingual.

Locker rentals: At the Camera Center, Future World ($7/day plus $5 deposit).

Package pickup: Merchandise bought in the park can be sent to an entrance to pick up later. No charge; allow 3 hours. Packages can be delivered the next day to Disney hotels or shipped nationally.

Parking: $14/day per car. Free for Disney hotel guests.

Stroller rentals: At each entrance (Singles $15/day, $13/day length of stay. Doubles $31, $27). Replacements at the Germany pavilion.

Tip Board: Shows attraction wait times. Innoventions Plaza.

Transportation: Boats serve Hollywood Studios; Epcot-area resorts. Monorail to TTC, connects to Contemporary, Grand Fla., Polynesian resorts; Magic Kingdom. Buses serve all other Disney resorts, theme parks. No direct service to Downtown Disney, Typhoon Lagoon, ESPN Wide World of Sports.

Wheelchair, scooter rentals: At each entrance. Wheelchairs $12/day, $10/day length of stay. 4-wheel scooters $50/day, $20 deposit.

themed shopping area, a 30-story hotel and convention complex, office space, apartments, single-family homes, monorail and PeopleMover systems, an airport, underground roads for cars and trucks, even a nuclear power plant.

There would be a theme park, too, a larger version of Disneyland.

On Nov. 15, 1965, Walt and his brother, Roy, held a press conference in Orlando to announce the project. "I'm very excited about it," he said, "because I've been storing these things up over the years. I like to create new things."

"We think the need is for starting from scratch on virgin land, building a community that will become a prototype for the future," Disney said in a videotaped sales pitch to potential corporate sponsors. "EPCOT will be a community of tomorrow that will never be completed, but will always be introducing and testing and demonstrating new materials and new systems."

Monsanto was interested.

General Electric, too.

But little more than a year later, Walt Disney died unexpectedly. Smoking had caught up with him.

After his death, the Disney company took two of Walt's EPCOT ideas—a corporate-sponsored science center and an international exposition that would showcase other cultures—and reworked them into a theme park.

Epcot opened on October 1, 1982.

Fun finds. ❶ The layout of Future World mimics the left-right division of the human brain. As you enter the park, pavilions on the left are themed to analytical, linear or

Walt Disney World's largest theme-park gift shop, MouseGear stocks a plethora of Disney, Disney World and Epcot merchandise. Located in the center of Future World, the store sits in front of the large fountain at Innoventions Plaza.

engineering issues and sit within a landscape of straight-lined walkways. Those on the right cover more natural topics in a hilly, meandering, watery landscape. ❷ Voices inside a trash can talk to you inside the Electric Umbrella restaurant. Swing open the lid of the only receptacle marked "Waste Please" (it's usually sitting next to a topping bar to the left of the order counter) and you may hear a surfer dude complain "Like, your trash just knocked off my shades!" or a Frenchman exclaim "Zis ees my lucky day! French fries!" ❸ Every 30 minutes the Innoventions fountain offers a five-minute show choreographed to music. ❹ Three Future World drinking fountains imitate submarine sounds, sing opera and offer wisecracks such as "Hey, save some for the fish!" when water hits their drains. One sits in front of MouseGear along the east side of the Innoventions fountain. A second is near the play fountain between Future World and the World Showcase. A third drinking fountain sits close to the restrooms behind Innoventions West. ❺ Always on, fiber-optic lights are embedded in the sidewalks in front of the Innoventions buildings. Pinpoints of shimmering, flickering stars hide in dozens of small squares. ❻ Larger, colorful changing patterns appear in three 6-foot squares in front of Innoventions West. ❼ Thirty-eight discoveries and inventions are honored in the rarely noticed Epcot Inventor's Circle, five concentric rings embedded into the walkway that leads from Innoventions Plaza to The Land pavilion. Inner-ring discoveries lead to outer-ring ones. For example, the inner Alphabet leads to the outer World Wide Web.

Hidden Mickey. As wall gauges behind the main cash registers in MouseGear.

Notable Shops

The Art of Disney: Lithographs, oils, porcelain, 2-ft. character figurines. Innoventions Plaza.

Casablanca Carpets: Furnishings. Traditional carpets, henna-dyed lamb skin lamps. Morocco pavilion.

Club Cool: Coca-Cola items. Free samples of foreign soft drinks. Innoventions Plaza.

Guerlain Paris: Perfume, makeup. Some fragrances in bee bottles. Cosmetics applied on the spot. France pavilion.

Inside Track: Automobile merchandise. Test Track souvenirs. Test Track.

La Bottega: Wine, housewares. Artisan creates stunning papier-mâché, fabric Carnivale masks. Italy pavilion.

Mitsukoshi: Japanese department store. Japan pavilion.

MouseGear: Main Epcot souvenir store. Innoventions Plaza.

Plaza de los Amigos: Mexican market with many items. Mexico pavilion.

The Puffin's Roost: Apparel, perfume, troll toys. Norway pavilion.

The Toy Soldier: Toys. Alice in Wonderland, Peter Pan, Thomas the Tank Engine and Winnie the Pooh items. United Kingdom pavilion.

Village Traders: Souvenirs. Carved art from wood and soapstone sculptor Andrew Mutiso. The Outpost, between the Germany and China pavilions.

Volkskunst: Housewares, watches. Beer steins, cuckoo clocks. Germany pavilion.

Yong Feng Shangdian: Chinese department store. China pavilion.

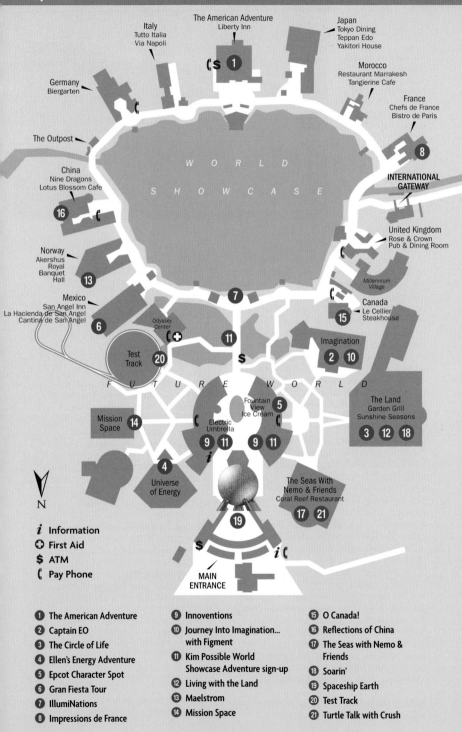

Italy
Tutto Italia
Via Napoli

The American Adventure
Liberty Inn

Japan
Tokyo Dining
Teppan Edo
Yakitori House

Germany
Biergarten

Morocco
Restaurant Marrakesh
Tangierine Cafe

France
Chefs de France
Bistro de Paris

The Outpost

WORLD SHOWCASE

INTERNATIONAL GATEWAY

China
Nine Dragons
Lotus Blossom Cafe

United Kingdom
Rose & Crown
Pub & Dining Room

Millennium Village

Norway
Akershus
Royal
Banquet
Hall

Canada
Le Cellier
Steakhouse

Mexico
San Angel Inn
La Hacienda de San Angel
Cantina de San Angel

Odyssey
Center

Imagination

Test
Track

FUTURE WORLD

The Land
Garden Grill
Sunshine Seasons

Mission
Space

Fountain
View
Ice Cream

Electric
Umbrella

The Seas With
Nemo & Friends
Coral Reef Restaurant

Universe
of Energy

N

MAIN
ENTRANCE

i Information
✪ First Aid
$ ATM
(Pay Phone

1. The American Adventure
2. Captain EO
3. The Circle of Life
4. Ellen's Energy Adventure
5. Epcot Character Spot
6. Gran Fiesta Tour
7. IllumiNations
8. Impressions de France

9. Innoventions
10. Journey Into Imagination... with Figment
11. Kim Possible World Showcase Adventure sign-up
12. Living with the Land
13. Maelstrom
14. Mission Space

15. O Canada!
16. Reflections of China
17. The Seas with Nemo & Friends
18. Soarin'
19. Spaceship Earth
20. Test Track
21. Turtle Talk with Crush

Attractions at a Glance

Character-greeting attraction

5 **Epcot Character Spot:** ★★★ Indoor meet-and-greet areas Characters can include Goofy, Mickey and Minnie Mouse, Pluto. Avg wait 15 min. Innoventions Plaza, Future World.

Exhibits

9 **Innoventions:** ★★★★ ✓ Exhibits, activities Interactive corporate displays. Unlimited. Wait times vary. Height min for Sum of All Thrills ride: 48 in. Innoventions Plaza, Future World.

Fireworks

7 **IllumiNations: Reflections of Earth:** ★★★★ ✓ Outdoor spectacle Fireworks, laser, music show is abstract world-history lesson. 15 min. 9p. Explosions, fire. World Showcase lagoon.

Movies

3 **The Circle of Life:** ★★★ Ecology lesson Stars characters of 1994 film "The Lion King." 13 min. Avg wait 7 min. The Land, Future World.

8 **Impressions de France:** ★★★★ ✓ Travelogue Honors French art, landscape, music. 18 min. Avg wait 10 min. France, World Showcase.

15 **O Canada!:** ★★★ CircleVision 360 travelogue Comedian Martin Short hosts comedic tour. 14 min. Avg wait 10 min. Canada, World Showcase.

16 **Reflections of China:** ★★★★ CircleVision 360 travelogue Celebrates Chinese culture, geography, history. 15 min. Avg wait 10 min. China, World Showcase.

Rides

4 **Ellen's Energy Adventure:** ★★ Indoor dark ride, film Dated oil-company view of energy exploration stars Ellen DeGeneres; includes widescreen films, slow-moving ride past dinosaurs. 45 min. Avg wait 10 min. Loud Big Bang. Universe of Energy, Future World.

6 **Gran Fiesta Tour:** ★★★ Dark indoor boat ride Videos of Donald Duck and friends from 1944's "The Three Caballeros" cheapen a tour of Mexican cultural history. 8 min. No wait. Mexico, World Showcase.

10 **Journey Into Imagination... with Figment:** ★★ Indoor dark ride Mischievous dragon wrecks Eric Idle's tour of Imagination Institute. 6 min. No wait. Loud noises, skunk smell, sudden flash. Imagination pavilion, Future World.

12 **Living with the Land:** ★★★★ FASTPASS Indoor boat ride Greenhouse tour of unusual plants, farming techniques. 14 min. Avg wait 40 min. The Land, Future World.

13 **Maelstrom:** ★★★ FASTPASS Indoor boat ride, film Ride past trolls, goes backwards. Optional 5-min. Norwegian travelogue. 15 min. Avg wait 25 min. Scary faces. Short steep drop. Norway, World Showcase.

14 **Mission Space:** ★★★★ ✓ FASTPASS Motion simulator Centrifuge simulates trip to Mars; 6 min. Avg wait 30 min. Height min 44 in. Original (Orange Team) version is seriously intense; alternate (Green Team) version tame. Future World.

17 **The Seas with Nemo & Friends:** ★★★★ ✓ Indoor dark ride Calm, retells 2003's "Finding Nemo"; vehicle leads to aquariums, exhibits, Turtle Talk with Crush. 5 min. Avg wait 5 min. The Seas with Nemo & Friends pavilion, Future World.

18 **Soarin':** ★★★★★ ✓ FASTPASS Hang-gliding simulator Delightful simulated hang-glider tour of California. 5 min. Avg wait 65 min. Height min 40 in. Virtual and actual heights can disturb some. The Land, Future World.

19 **Spaceship Earth:** ★★★★ ✓ Indoor dark ride Slow-moving dark ride teaches communications history via Audio-Animatronics scenes. 14 min. Avg wait 20 min. Future World.

20 **Test Track:** ★★★★★ ✓ FASTPASS Indoor-outdoor vehicle ride Simulated automotive proving ground. 5 min. Avg wait 70 min. Height min 40 in. High speeds, sharp turns. Future World.

Scavenger hunt

11 **Kim Possible World Showcase Adventure:** ★★★★ ✓ Interactive scavenger hunt Cell-phone-like device causes actions. Allow 45–60 min. World Showcase.

Theatrical shows

1 **The American Adventure:** ★★★★★ ✓ Audio-Animatronics stage show Film, robotic cast tell U.S. story. 30 min. Avg wait 20 min. American Adventure pavilion, World Showcase.

21 **Turtle Talk with Crush:** ★★★★★ ✓ Improvisational animated video Real-time conversations with animated sea turtle from 2003's "Finding Nemo." 12 min. Avg wait 15 min. The Seas with Nemo & Friends pavilion, Future World.

3-D movie

2 **Captain EO:** ★ Musical Creaky space adventure stars Michael Jackson; originally ran 1986–1994. 17 min. Avg wait 17 min. Imagination pavilion, Future World.

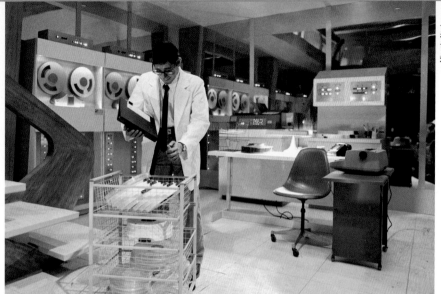

Micaela Neal

A Spaceship Earth scene imagines a 1960s computer room complete with its programmers. The slow-moving dark ride passes 22 dioramas on its trip through the history of communications.

Spaceship Earth

★★★★ ✔ 14 min. Allow up to 45 min for postshow activities. Capacity: 308. Partially covered outdoor queue. Fear factor: None. Access: Must be ambulatory. Stops intermittently to load mobility-impaired guests. Vehicles offer a choice of narration languages: English, French, German, Japanese, Portuguese and Spanish. Audio Description. Debuted: 1982; revised 1994, 2008.

That huge silver sphere is more than the park icon. It's also a ride—a time trip through the history of communications. A four-seat vehicle spirals guests slowly past detailed Audio-Animatronics dioramas populated with 56 realistic robots.

Twenty-two dioramas depict communication advances through human history. At one point, visitors travel through a 1960s IBM computer room where two programmers tend to a gigantic reel-to-reel mainframe; the young woman sports a miniskirt and giant Afro. Another scene shows a 1976 Silicon Valley garage where a young man creates the first PC. Narrator Dame Judi Dench emphasizes the roots of technology, while an ambient score features a 62-piece orchestra and 24-voice choir.

Guests shape their own future as the ride nears its finish. Using a touch-screen inside their ride vehicle, riders decide how they would like to live or work in the years ahead. A few seconds later, guests see their future portrayed on the screen, with their faces superimposed on cartoon bodies. Children in particular love this moment.

A post-show area, "Project Tomorrow" features interactive exhibits which showcase Siemens, the attraction's sponsor. A giant globe pinpoints the hometowns of that day's Spaceship Earth passengers, while video

Average wait times

Time	Standby line	Fastpass time
9:00a	5 min	(n/a)
10:00a	10 min	(n/a)
11:00a	15 min	(n/a)
Noon	15 min	(n/a)
1:00p	25 min	(n/a)
2:00p	20 min	(n/a)
3:00p	25 min	(n/a)
4:00p	15 min	(n/a)
5:00p	10 min	(n/a)
6:00p	10 min	(n/a)
7:00p	5 min	(n/a)
8:00p	5 min	(n/a)
9:00p	(closed)	(n/a)

screens show their future selves. Guests can e-mail the images free of charge.

A closer look. Disney got the idea for the structure from the Perisphere, the icon of the New York World's Fair of 1939. Very much like Spaceship Earth, the 180-foot-tall globe held a slow-moving, educational, futuristic ride. It portrayed Democracity, a "perfectly integrated garden city" from the year 2068.

Spaceship Earth can also trace its parentage to the 1940s geodesic domes designed by engineer R. Buckminster Fuller. Billed as homes of tomorrow, his space-age half-circles were composed of self-bracing triangles. The "Bucky balls" caught on as weather stations and airport radar shelters, but never got beyond a cult following as private homes. One reason: they leaked water.

Fuller also coined the phrase "Spaceship Earth." His 1963 treatise, "An Operating Manual for Spaceship Earth," argued that all the world's peoples must work together as a crew to guide our planet's future.

Fun facts. ❶ Science-fiction author Ray Bradbury ("Fahrenheit 451") helped design the attraction. ❷ Guest "work" futures predict "a great big beautiful tomorrow," the theme song to Magic Kingdom's Carousel of Progress. ❸ A 180-foot-high geodesic sphere, Spaceship Earth does not drip water: a 1-inch gap between each panel flows rainwater into two interior gutters. ❹ The building weighs 16 million pounds. That's 158 million golf balls.

Fun finds. ❶ A placard on the right of the computer room reads "Think," the slogan of IBM founder Thomas J. Watson. It inspired the

The Spaceship Earth attraction winds through the inside of Epcot's iconic "golf ball"

Apple slogan, "Think Different." ❷ Nearby: a 1960s Selectric typewriter and a manual for IBM's System 360 Job Control Language used on 1964 mainframes. ❸ A garage snapshot resembles a classic Microsoft photo.

Hidden Mickeys. ❶ As parchment blots made by a sleeping monk. ❷ As bottle rings on the table of the first Renaissance painter.

In its most famous scene, Spaceship Earth depicts Michelangelo flat on his back, painting the Sistine Chapel. Other scenes include cavemen painting on walls, Egyptians pounding papyrus and a modern young man inventing the first PC.

Innoventions features interactive corporate exhibits. Guests search for household hazards at Liberty Mutual's Where's the Fire? game and assess product durability at UL's Test the Limits Lab.

Innoventions

★★★★ ✔ Presentations avg 20 min. Allow 2–3 hrs for all exhibits. Wait times vary by exhibit. Height min for Sum of All Thrills: 48 in. Indoor, air-conditioned queues. Fear factor: None. Access: Varies by exhibit. Audio Description. Debuted: 1994, revised 2009.

Guests play games inside these two buildings, which house interactive corporate exhibits. Lines are often short, though the buildings get crowded during bad weather. New exhibits debut regularly. Each building also has a Kim Possible World Showcase Adventure Recruitment Center (see Overview).

Sum of All Thrills: Raytheon's math-based exhibit is the first-ever Innoventions ride. After designing their very own virtual roller coaster, jet plane or bobsled experience, guests ride it atop a slow-moving robotic arm (Innoventions East).

Don't Waste It: Guests push garbage-truck-like carts filled with virtual trash to a sorting station, incinerator and landfill at this Waste Management game. Children love to push the carts, which beep when they back up (Innoventions East).

StormStruck: A Federal Alliance for Safe Homes exhibit combines a theatrical show with a display that compares how two Florida homes fared during 2004's Hurricane Charley (Innoventions East).

Test the Limits Lab: Guests swing a hammer at a TV, smash a 55-gallon drum onto a helmet and cause other havoc at this Underwriters Laboratories area (Innoventions East).

Environmentality Corner: Guests make primitive paper (Innoventions East).

Runtime: Guests walk, jump and dance while being recorded at this IBM exhibit. The video clips are combined into a game guests can e-mail to themselves (Innoventions West).

The Great Piggy Bank Adventure: A T. Rowe Price lesson helps guests set financial goals (Innoventions West).

Where's the Fire?: Guests use flashlight-like devices to uncover home fire hazards at this Liberty Mutual game. A companion tour teaches fire safety to children (Innoventions West).

Segway Central: Free Segway test drives (1–7p, riders must be at least 16 years old. Those under 18 require legal consent. Innoventions West).

PlayStation arcade: No-charge Disney games (Innoventions West).

Disney's Universe of Energy pavilion holds Ellen's Energy Adventure. The elaborate oil-company presentation stars robotic dinosaurs and comedian Ellen DeGeneres.

Ellen's Energy Adventure

★★ 45 min (new shows begin every 17 min). Capacity: 582. Outdoor, unshaded queue. Fear factor: The Big Bang portrayal is loud. Access: ECV users must transfer. Assistive listening, handheld captioning, Audio Description. Debuted: 1996.

An outdated attraction that features robotic dinosaurs, a funny comedian and a skewed corporate picture of the 'Universe of Energy." What is... Ellen's Energy Adventure! Based on the game show "Jeopardy," this 45-minute presentation about the history and future of energy combines three theatrical films with a tram ride past Audio-Animatronics dinos.

The story begins on a series of video screens, with Ellen DeGeneres displaying the same loopy wit she used as Dory in 2003's "Finding Nemo." She is in her apartment when friend and neighbor Bill Nye stops by to ask for some aluminum foil, a clothes pin and a candle (she replies "Another hot date, huh?"). Later, while watching her snooty old college roommate and rival (Jamie Lee Curtis) compete on "Jeopardy!" Ellen falls asleep.

Dreaming she's a contestant on the show, Ellen learns that all of her categories deal with one thing she knows nothing about: energy. Frustrated, Ellen decides to "freeze"

her dream and ask Nye for help. He takes her back in time for a crash course in Energy 101.

Moving into a large theater, guests watch as three huge screens dramatically display the Big Bang and the creation of the Earth: billions of years compressed into one stunning minute. As the seating area divides itself into ride vehicles, guests travel into the Mesozoic Era to witness the beginning of fossil fuels. Eventually guests return to the theater to see Ellen become a "Jeopardy" champion.

Produced when the average price of a gallon of gasoline was $1.30, the show ignores the problems of fossil fuels. There's no mention of the Middle East, no talk of global warming, oil spills or fuel efficiency. The show was created in conjunction with Exxon-Mobil, its sponsor until 2004.

A former engineer, Nye hosted "Bill Nye the Science Guy," a 1992-1998 PBS preteen program which Disney sold as a video series.

Fun finds. ❶ After Trebek says to Ellen, "Your first correct response!" her lips don't move when she yells "Freeze!" **❷** Nye's lips stay shut when, in front of a solar mirror, he says "all right." **❸** Michael Richards, who played Kramer in "Seinfeld," portrays a caveman.

Guests choose from two versions of Disney's space-flight simulator Mission Space—the original intense adventure or a mild alternative. Crowds are often light after lunch and after dark.

Mission Space

★★★★ ✔ *FASTPASS* 6 min. Capacity: 160. Indoor, air-conditioned queue. Fear factor: Orange "spinning" version—Intense, can cause disorientation, headaches, nausea. Take warnings seriously; do not ride if you have serious health issues or head cold. Access: ECV, wheelchair users must transfer. Activated video captioning. Height min: 44 in. Debuted: 2003.

So intense it includes motion-sickness bags, this flight simulator offers realistic sensations of space travel. Developed with NASA and the Jet Propulsion Laboratory, it's set in the year 2036 at the International Space Training Center, where "future astronauts" train for a mission to Mars. After liftoff, some unexpected troubles complicate things. The ride comes in two versions.

Orange version. The original ride is a rapidly rotating centrifuge with capsules on its spokes. G-forces mimic those of a rocket launch and the feeling of weightlessness. It's the same way NASA trained astronauts for decades. The ride can make guests sick: common complaints are dizziness and a lingering headache. For the best experience stare at your monitor; keep your eyes open.

Green version. This version doesn't spin. It has no side effects, and is safe for anyone.

The first queue room holds a 35-foot Gravity Wheel, a slowly rotating prop from the year-2000 film "Mission to Mars." Nearby is a Lunar Roving Vehicle display unit on loan from the National Air and Space Museum.

Hidden Mickeys. ❶ As craters on the courtyard moon, near the Luna 8 site. **❷** As tiny tiles in the patio, 40 feet from the Fastpass entrance. **❸** In the queue, as Mars craters on the left and right monitors above the desks.

Average wait times

Time	Standby line	Fastpass time
9:00a	0 min	9:50a
10:00a	20 min	10:50a
11:00a	30 min	11:30a
Noon	40 min	12:50p
1:00p	45 min	2:35p
2:00p	45 min	3:50p
3:00p	15 min	5:15p
4:00p	20 min	6:15p
5:00p	35 min	7:10p
6:00p	30 min	8:00p
7:00p	20 min	8:30p
8:00p	10 min	(out)
9:00p	(closed)	(closed)

© Disney

The fastest ride at Walt Disney World, Test Track reaches speeds up to 65 mph. Guests play the roles of crash dummies as they speed over hills, around corners and through barriers.

Test Track

★★★★★ ✔ *FASTPASS* 5 min. Capacity: 192. Indoor, air-conditioned queue. Fear factor: Intense for those scared by speed. Closed during thunderstorms. Access: Must be ambulatory. Assistive listening; activated captioning. Height min: 40 in. Debuted: 1999.

Guests serve as crash-test dummies at this fun thrill ride. Open-topped cars reach 65 mph as they travel through an automobile proving ground. With 34 turns but no falls or loops, the mile-long course is perfect for those who like speed but hate roller coasters.

The queue area is filled with testing exhibits. Lines lead to a Briefing Room, where engineers Bill and Sherry greet arrivals on a video link. As Bill plans your test schedule, Sherry programs it into a computer. "And depending on how you and your vehicle hold up," Bill adds, "we'll even throw a few surprise tests in there."

"Surprise tests?" Sherry asks.

"Yeah. Pick one." With a mischievous grin, Sherry chooses... a barrier test. (Oh no!)

The first few tests run smoothly, but soon things start to go wrong. Did Sherry forget to turn off those robots? Did you miss that "Turn On Headlights" sign? And remember that surprise test?

Fun Finds. ❶ In the anticorrosion room, the left robot is labeled "CRUS-T." ❷ The right one is "RUS-T." ❸ In the post show, a house of mirrors re-creates a GM truck plant.

Hidden Mickeys. ❶ As washers on the side of a desk near queue area 7b. ❷ In the Corrision Chamber, as fender and door stains. ❸ As stickers on an open gas-tank filler door on a car to your left in the Barrier Test area. ❹ As a coil of hoses on that floor, just before the wall.

Average wait times

Time	Standby line	Fastpass time
9:00a	0 min	10:00a
10:00a	25 min	11:45a
11:00a	45 min	1:40p
Noon	55 min	4:15p
1:00p	100 min	6:40p
2:00p	85 min	8:20p
3:00p	90 min	(out)
4:00p	105 min	(out)
5:00p	90 min	(out)
6:00p	65 min	(out)
7:00p	60 min	(out)
8:00p	55 min	(out)
9:00p	(closed)	(closed)

The Imagination pavilion contains a toddler-friendly ride (Journey Into Imagination... with Figment) and a 3-D movie starring the late Michael Jackson as a dramatic dancing spaceman

Imagination pavilion

Fountain waters play leapfrog, waterfalls splash uphill, rooms turn upside down and Michael Jackson vanquishes the forces of evil with a space monkey named Fuzzball.

Sounds promising, but this "Imagination" pavilion is the least creative in the park. Home to an uninspired ride only preschoolers will love and a recycled 3-D movie, it's a pavilion withering on the vine. The fountains out front are this pavilion's best bet. The Leapfrog Fountain has water that "jumps" from one circular base to another, occasionally over the heads of guests. An adjacent waterfall flows up. In August 2010 Kodak ended its sponsorship of the pavilion after 28 years.

Journey into Imagination... with Figment
★★ 6 min. Capacity: 224. Indoor, air-conditioned queue. Fear factor: A dark room has the loud clamor of an oncoming train; a blast of air projects the odor of a skunk; the last room has a sudden flash. Access: Guests may remain in wheelchairs, ECVs. Handheld captioning, Audio Description. Debuted: 1983, revised 1998, 2001. Mischievous dragon Figment keeps interrupting this slow-moving dark tour of the stuffy Imagination Institute. The ride stops at various labs, where Institute director Dr. Nigel Channing (Monty Python's Eric Idle) attempts to demonstrate how his outfit is

attempting to "capture and control" imagination. Freethinking Figment, however, believes imagination works best when it's set free. Though the ride is one of the few at Epcot for young children, it's—ironically— one of Disney's least imaginative attractions. There is, however, one great effect: in a cage past the Sight Lab, a huge butterfly appears to disappear as you go by.

A closer look. And just who, you may ask, is Figment? In Disney's original Journey Into Imagination ride (1983–1999), he was the creation of Dreamfinder, a jolly wizard-like scientist, composed of elements Dreamfinder found in his travels, including the horns of a steer, the snout of a crocodile and the delight at a child's birthday party.

Figment was originally voiced by legendary character actor Billy Barty. Busby Berkeley movie buffs will remember Barty as a 9-year-old who played a baby Peeping Tom in "The Gold Diggers of 1933" and a lecherous baby who tries to ruin a wedding night in "Footlight Parade." Figment's voice since 2001 has been that of another legend, Dave Goelz, the long-time voice and puppeteer of Muppets Gonzo, Dr. Bunsen Honeydew, Waldorf and Zoot. He also built the first Animal.

Two parents and a small child can sit side-by-side in the ride vehicles for Journey into Imagination... with Figment. Other family choices at Epcot include Turtle Talk with Crush, Gran Fiesta Tour and the Kim Possible World Showcase Adventure.

Family matters: Children will get a kick out of trying to read the color chart hanging on a wall just past the Sight Lab; it's nearly impossible.

Captain EO ★ 17 min, 3 shows an hour; 10 min wait before 6-min pre-show. Capacity: 570. Indoor, air-conditioned queue. Fear factor: None. Access: Guests may stay in wheelchairs, ECVs. Handheld, reflective captioning; assistive listening. Debuted: 1986, reintroduced 2010. And you thought Jar Jar was bad. Developed by "Star Wars" creator George Lucas and directed by Francis Ford Coppola, this 1986 3-D musical film stars singer Michael Jackson at his most Wacko. Though it may be diverting for those wearing very rosy nostalgic glasses, for a typical audience the show wallows in numbing '80s excess.

The story is set in space. Jackson, aka Captain EO, and an oddball puppet crew discover a colorless planet ruled by an evil sorceress (Oscar-winner Anjelica Huston) and her forces of darkness. Using the power of music, dance and light, Captain EO transforms his crew into musicians and musical instruments, and turns the black-and-white land into a world of color (matching Jacko's rainbow T-shirt). Huston's minions defect to Jackson's side, and everyone grooves in a boogie wonderland.

Even before you see Captain EO, you've seen it all before—the same "Thriller"-style dance moves and overdone military fashion from Jackson, the same robots and Death Star trench George Lucas used in "Star Wars." Sadly, the music is forgettable, too.

It's hard to believe the combined talents of Coppola, Jackson and Lucas came up with such self-indulgent drivel. Perhaps all three were at a point in their careers when no one told them "No."

Fun finds. ❶ In the ride queue a page for Merlin Jones seeks the chimp teacher in 1965's "The Monkey's Uncle." ❷ Tennis shoes sit outside the ride's computer room, a reference to 1969's "The Computer Wore Tennis Shoes."

Hidden Mickeys. ❶ In the ride, a Mickey Mouse-eared headphone sits in the Sight Lab, on top of the left wheeled table. ❷ As two small circular carpets and a flowered toilet seat in Figment's bathroom.

The original poster for Captain EO announces "We are here to change the world"

Soarin' flies guests high both literally and virtually. Rising 40 feet in front of a concave screen, riders appear to glide 800 feet above the sights of California, including the Golden Gate Bridge.

The Land pavilion

Epcot's most fully realized pavilion contains two good attractions—including one of the most popular in all of Walt Disney World—and a movie, a dinner restaurant with characters and an outstanding food court. Guests walk in the building between two entry mosaics, each 134 feet long with 150,000 individual pieces of glass, gold, granite, marble and slate to represent the layers of the Earth.

Soarin' ★★★★★ ✓ *FASTPASS* 5 min. Capacity: 174. Indoor, air-conditioned queue. Fear factor: Gentle, but troubling for some who fear heights. Access: ECV and wheelchair users must transfer. Handheld captioning. Height min: 40 in. Debuted: 2005 (Disneyland 2001). Soarin' may take you by surprise. More than just a 5-minute film, it uses an innovative theater to immerse guests in its experience. Exhilarating but not scary, it's a smooth, fun fantasy everyone will love.

After boarding a multi-seat "hang glider," you lift up to 40 feet into an 80-foot IMAX projection dome. Your field of vision filled with the beauty of California, you get the impractical delight of swooping over the Golden Gate Bridge, El Capitan, an aircraft carrier and the evening traffic of Los Angeles. The glider tilts as you travel; your legs dangle underneath.

Special effects provide gentle breezes and fragrances.

The best Soarin' seats are top-row center. Ask the gate attendant for Row 1, Gate B.

Along the standby queue, video screens and hidden motion detectors encourage guests to fly a bird through a river canyon and launch paint balls at a digital canvas.

A closer look: The Soarin' entranceway, waiting area and theater resemble an airport. The theater has runway lights.

Average wait times (Soarin')

Time	Standby line	Fastpass time
9:00a	0 min	11:05a
10:00a	25 min	12:40p
11:00a	55 min	3:30p
Noon	60 min	5:25p
1:00p	65 min	7:00p
2:00p	75 min	(out)
3:00p	70 min	(out)
4:00p	75 min	(out)
5:00p	85 min	(out)
6:00p	80 min	(out)
7:00p	70 min	(out)
8:00p	55 min	(out)
9:00p	(closed)	(closed)

The Living with the Land boat ride travels through fragrant greenhouses filled with exotic plants. Boats also pass through an aquaculture hut where catfish, eels, shrimp, sturgeon and young alligators swim in elevated glass tanks.

Living with the Land ★★★★ *FASTPASS* 14 min. Capacity: 20 per boat. Indoor, air-conditioned queue. Fear factor: None. Access: ECV users must transfer. Handheld captioning, Audio Description. Debuted: 1982 (as Listen to the Land); revised 1993, 2009. This ride takes a subject usually thought of as dull as dirt—agricultural science—and presents it in an entertaining way. A trip through four working greenhouses, the tour is filled with weird plants and odd growing techniques. Crops include coconuts, 2-foot jackfruit, 3-foot winter melons and 500-pound Atlantic giant pumpkins. Many plants hang from strings or trellises, roots in the air. Others grow on overhead conveyor belts, touring their greenhouses like suits in a dry cleaner.

An aquaculture hut has eye-level catfish, eels, shrimp, sturgeon, even young alligators.

The boat first meanders past dioramas of a rainforest, African desert and American farm; some have realistic robotic animals.

The greenhouses grow much of the produce used in Epcot restaurants.

Average wait times (Living with the Land)

Time	Standby line	Fastpass time
9:00a	0 min	9:45a
10:00a	5 min	10:30a
11:00a	15 min	11:35a
Noon	25 min	12:30p
1:00p	45 min	1:30p
2:00p	50 min	2:40p
3:00p	45 min	3:30p
4:00p	50 min	4:30p
5:00p	55 min	5:40p
6:00p	55 min	6:40p
7:00p	45 min	(closed)
8:00p	25 min	(closed)
9:00p	(closed)	(closed)

The Circle of Life: An Environmental Fable ★★★ 13 min. Capacity: 482. Indoor, air-conditioned queue. Fear factor: None. Access: Guests may stay in wheelchairs, ECVs. Handheld, reflective captioning; assistive listening. Debuted: 1995. "Dam!" exclaims the warthog. "Pumbaa, watch your language," says meerkat Timon. This movie uses humor and the stars of 1994's "The Lion King" to teach environmental protection. When Timon and Pumbaa start to clear the savanna to build the "Hakuna Matata Lakeside Village," Simba tells them about a creature—man—who first lived in harmony with nature, but now often forgets that everything is part of the circle of life. Live-action scenes show smokestacks, clogged highways and an oil-soaked bird, but also wind turbines, electric cars and recycling.

Fun facts. ❶ In Soarin' cast members may name your flight "No. 5-5-0-5," a reference to the ride's opening date of May 5, 2005. ❷ A hang glider over Yosemite is computer generated. ❸ So is an errant golf ball.

Hidden Mickeys. In Soarin', ❶ as a blue balloon in the Palm Springs scene, held by a man behind a golf cart at the far lower left; ❷ as a small Mickey silhouette on that errant golf ball. Flinch and you'll miss it; and ❸ in the second burst of Disneyland fireworks, in the center of the screen. In Living with the Land, ❹ in the queue area mural (as bubbles under the word "nature," a Mickey profile); ❺ in the mural behind the loading area, an angled Mickey formed by green and blue circles (near the right wall, near the floor); ❻ in the quonset hut as algae behind the sturgeon; and ❼ in the last greenhouse, as green test-tube caps behind lab windows.

Audio-Animatronics gulls outside the Seas pavilion squawk "Mine! Mine! Mine!" just as they do in "Finding Nemo." The voice is that of "Finding Nemo" director Andrew Stanton.

The Seas with Nemo & Friends

★★★★ ✔ Allow 60 min. Indoor, air-conditioned queue. Fear factor: None. Access: Guests may remain in wheelchairs, ECVs. Reflective captioning, assistive listening, Audio Description. Debuted: 1982, revised 2007.

Dolphins smile, sharks lurk, manatees float, a sea turtle talks! Themed to the 2003 Disney/Pixar film "Finding Nemo," this two-story pavilion surrounds guests with marine life real and animated. The building includes a large tropical aquarium, various exhibits and a fascinating live show.

Visitors enter the pavilion on "clam-mobiles"—three-seat ride vehicles which pass animated dioramas and synchronized videos of Nemo and his pals, who magically appear to swim in the aquarium itself. Experiences inside the building include:

Turtle Talk with Crush ★★★★★ ✔ 12 min; shows every 20 min. Capacity: 210. Indoor, air-conditioned queue. Fear factor: None. Access: Guests may remain in wheelchairs, ECVs. Reflective captioning, assistive listening, Audio Description. Debuted: 2004. Children have real-time conversations with the animated sea turtle at this theatrical show, as a huge video screen resembles a viewing window into an ocean. Crush addresses kids by name ("Elizabeth, your polka-dot shell

is totally cool!"), asks specific questions ("Austin, is that your female parental unit in the fourth row?") and reacts to responses. He also welcomes Dory the blue tang, who speaks whale perhaps a little too well. Hidden cameras, real-time animation and a back-stage impersonator make the show possible. A queue area holds jellyfish, stingrays and fish from the Great Barrier Reef.

Family matters: Crush mostly talks to children near the screen, but sometimes

Average wait times

Time	Standby line	Fastpass time
9:00a	0 min	(n/a)
10:00a	15 min	(n/a)
11:00a	10 min	(n/a)
Noon	15 min	(n/a)
1:00p	15 min	(n/a)
2:00p	20 min	(n/a)
3:00p	10 min	(n/a)
4:00p	5 min	(n/a)
5:00p	5 min	(n/a)
6:00p	5 min	(n/a)
7:00p	0 min	(n/a)
8:00p	0 min	(n/a)
9:00p	(closed)	(n/a)

© Disney

seeks out guests along the theater's center aisle. To maximize the odds that he speaks to your child, have her sit on the floor in front of the theater and wear a funny hat.

Nemo & Friends. This first-floor room displays live versions of many "Finding Nemo" stars, including clownfish (Nemo), regal blue tangs (Dory) and Moorish idols (Gill).

Bruce's Shark World. Geared to children, this re-creation of the film's sunken submarine has child-friendly interactive displays and photo props.

Caribbean aquarium. On the second floor, a huge saltwater aquarium simulates a coral reef. It's filled with blacknose, brown and sand tiger sharks; some angelfish, cobia, snapper and tarpon; schools of lookdown; a Goliath grouper; sea turtles; and a few rays. Lined with floor-to-ceiling windows, an observation tunnel extends into the tank.

Dolphins: A side area holds a bachelor herd of dolphins—Rainer (born in 1986), Calvin and Kyber (1997) and Malabar (2001). Huge bars keep the mammals in their area; otherwise they hassle the fish.

Dolphin training sessions: Stop by at 10:45 a.m., 2:15 p.m. or 4:15 p.m. as trainers conduct identity-matching, rhythm-identification or echolocation lessons.

Fish feedings: A diver unloads his food pouch in front of guests while a narrator adds educational trivia. Feedings occur at 10 a.m., 1 p.m. and 3:30 p.m.

Manatee aquarium. Guests watch Florida sea cows munch lettuce heads from above the surface on the second floor or through a first-floor underwater window. Docents give talks at 15 and 45 minutes after each hour.

The sea-turtle star of "Finding Nemo" chats with children at Turtle Talk with Crush

Fun finds. ❶ As clam-mobile guests pass her by, "Finding Nemo" sea star Peach clings to the aquarium glass as the fish around her continue to sing the theme song "Big Blue World." "Hey wait! Take me with you!" she begs. "It's a nice song but they just never stop! Never, never, ever, ever, ever!" ❷ Rub Bruce's sandpapery skin in Bruce's Shark World and he'll say "Oooooooo! That's good!"

A bottlenose dolphin interacts with the author's daughter at the Caribbean aquarium inside The Seas with Nemo & Friends. The amazing mammals often notice guests watching them and swim over to get closer looks.

Bracketed by totems, the entrance to the Canada pavilion has two interconnected gift shops on the left. In back, Disney's Hotel du Canada facade recalls Ottawa's Chateau Laurier.

World Showcase

Canada

Rockers wear kilts at this pavilion, a woodsy 3-acre salute to our northern neighbor. It holds a movie theater, two shops, a restaurant and a stage for the band Off Kilter. A pretty flower garden and rolling landscape add to its appeal. Fans of Martin Short will enjoy the film "O Canada!" a travelogue which stars the comedian.

Entertainment. Besides the movie, the pavilion also features a live band.

O Canada!: ★★★ 14 min. Capacity: 600. No seats. Covered outdoor queue. Fear factor: None. Access: Guests may stay in wheelchairs, ECVs. Reflective captioning, assistive listening, Audio Description. Debuted: 1982, revised 2007. In this CircleVision 360 film, host Martin Short corrects the misconception that Canada is simply a Great White North. The movie mixes scenes of mountains and redwoods with stops in the country's urban centers. Short is a bumbling participant in dogsledding and toboggan racing. Unfortunately, the scenes don't wrap around you, the signature feature of Disney's CircleVision 360 concept. Instead, multiple versions of the same image repeat around the theater.

Off Kilter: ★★★ ✓ 20-min shows, promenade stage. This kilt-wearing Celtic rock band combines guitars, a bagpipe and quirky humor ("Sweet Home Alabama"). Some guests twirl with Deadhead joy.

Restaurants. Steakhouse Le Cellier is Epcot's only Disney Signature eatery. See chapter **Restaurants and Food.**

Shopping. Two interconnected gift shops offer some authentic Canadian merchandise:

Northwest Mercantile/Trading Post: NHL jerseys, maple treats, dreamcatchers, Canadian-animal plushies. Amusing Hatley aprons, shirts, sleepwear.

Wood cart: Personalized leather, Goofy lumberjack beanbag. Promenade.

Architecture. The grounds are dominated by a three-dimensional French Gothic facade of the "Hotel du Canada." Based on Ottawa's Chateau Laurier, it sits behind a flower garden inspired by Victoria's Butchart Gardens. A native village is represented by a log cabin and a trading post. Carved by a Tsimshian Indian in 1998, the totem on the far left of the area shows the Raven folkbird releasing the sun, moon and stars from a carved cedar chest. Up the steps, a stone building reflects British styles of the Canadian East Coast.

The back of the pavilion recalls the Canadian Rockies; a 30-foot waterfall flows into a stream. The opening to a mine shaft (the entrance to the theater) is trimmed with shoring and Klondike equipment.

Family matters. All ages will find the movie funny. A Kidcot table sits next to Le Cellier's front door.

Hidden Mickeys. ❶ On both sides of the left totem underneath the top set of hands. ❷ As wine-rack bottles behind Le Cellier's check-in counter.

United Kingdom

Friendly Brits serve authentic brews and sing Beatles tunes in this mythical village. Two streets are lined with shops, restaurants and gardens. Stores stock everything from pub coasters and rugby balls to fine bone china and tartan sweaters. Those who enjoy Disney's British films such as 1951's "Alice in Wonderland" and 1964's "Mary Poppins" will find their favorite characters on hand.

Entertainment. An array of live talent performs throughout the grounds:

World Showcase Players: ★★★ ✓ 20-min shows, promenade, Tudor Street. Also Italy pavilion central plaza. Street skits star audience volunteers as this hilarious improvisational troupe butchers classic literature; "Romeo and Juliet" becomes "Romeo and Edna."

The British Invasion: ★★★ ✓ 20-min shows, back green. Tribute band does spot-on Beatles hits. Each set of the day features a different Beatles era.

'Hat Lady' Carol Stein: ★★★ ✓ 20-min shows, Rose & Crown Pub. 12 seats have direct view.

United Kingdom cast members chalk out a "Bounce with Tigger" hopscotch course

Piano entertainer sings Irish anthems and Cockney show tunes.

Restaurants. The Rose & Crown Dining Room has an adjacent pub and outdoor lakeside tables. A fast-food window, the Yorkshire County Fish Shop, sells fish and chips.

See chapter **Restaurants and Food.**

Shopping. Half a dozen pretty little stores offer a variety of merchandise:

The United Kingdom pavilion re-creates many facades of Olde England. One street has a half-timbered 15th-century Tudor leaning with age on its left, the Abbotsford estate of Sir Walter Scott and Henry VIII's red-brick Hampton Court on its right.

VINS FINS

LES VINS DE FRANCE

VINS FINS

LES VINS DE FRANCE

The Crown & Crest: Family name, coat of arms. Beatles and Rolling Stones items.
The Magic of Wales: Tartan apparel. Fine silver.
The Queen's Table: Perfume. Lotions, toiletries. Brands such as Bronnley, Burberry, Miller Harris, Taylor of London. Heavenly aroma.
Sportsman's Shoppe: Sports apparel; tennis shoes; rugby and soccer shoes, balls, books. Pub coasters. Treats include Cadbury dairy milk caramel candy bars.
Tea Caddy: Fine bone china by Dunoon, Royal Albert. Nice teapots; many varieties of Twinings tea, loose and in bags. Biscuits, candy.
The Toy Soldier: Alice in Wonderland, Peter Pan, Thomas the Tank Engine and Winnie the Pooh toys. Children's books. Alice costumes.
Wood cart: T-shirts, U.K. souvenirs. Outdoor stand, promenade.
Architecture. Each building represents a different period in U.K. history. The brick turrets and medieval crenulation of the Sportsman's Shoppe mimic Henry VIII's 16th-century Hampton Court. Its white-stone side is Abbotsford, the 19th-century Scottish estate where Sir Walter Scott wrote novels. Across a street is the 16th-century thatched-roofed cottage of Anne Hathaway, the wife of William Shakespeare. Further down the street sits a half-timbered 15th-century Tudor leaning with age, a plaster 17th-century pre-Georgian, a stone 18th-century Palladian and a home built of angled bricks. Bordering the World Showcase lagoon, the Rose & Crown Pub is divided vertically into three styles—a medieval rural cottage, a 15th-century Tudor tavern and an 1890s Victorian bar.
Family matters. Children will enjoy the street performers, browsing the toy shop and stopping at its Kidcot table, and meeting characters Winnie the Pooh, Tigger, Mary Poppins and Alice (from "Alice in Wonderland"). Cast members often chalk out a promenade hopscotch game about 11 a.m.

France

A good spot to get off your feet, this pavilion offers a nice film in a cozy theater, a sidewalk cafe and some good restaurants. Fine perfume and wine highlight the shopping; the fragrance shops have heavenly aromas.

Facing page: Epcot's France pavilion recalls "the beautiful time" from 1870 to 1910

Entertainment. A lovely travelogue and a comedic acrobatic routine entertain visitors.
Impressions de France: ★★★★ ✔ 18 min. Capacity: 325. Indoor, air-conditioned queue. Fear factor: None. Access: Guests may stay in wheelchairs, ECVs. Reflective captioning, assistive listening, Audio Description. Debuted: 1982. "My Frahnce awakens with the early dawn." Well, duh! A narrator's stuffy intonation is the only sour note in this lovely film. Set to an ethereal score, it uses a 200-degree screen to fill your field of vision with a fairy-tale landscape. Starting off over Normandy, your trip stops at four chateaus, a church, market, vineyard, the gardens of Versailles, a rural bicycle tour and an antique Bugatti race through Cannes... and that's just the first five minutes. Still to come are hot-air balloons, fishing boats, a train, Notre Dame and the Alps. Based on Napoleon III's royal theater in Fontainebleau, the intimate auditorium has padded, if petite, seats.
Serveur Amusant: ★★★ ✔ 20-min shows, in front of Chefs de France. An "amusing server" and chef mime a balancing act with a table, five chairs and five bottles of champagne.
Restaurants. France has both casual (Chefs de France) and formal (Bistro de Paris) table-service restaurants. Boulangerie Patisserie offers a tempting array of pastries. See chapter **Restaurants and Food.**
Shopping. Shops specialize in perfume, cosmetics, food and wine:
Guerlain Paris: Limited-edition and exclusive fragrances, some in signature bee bottles. Cosmetics applied on the spot.
L' Esprit de la Provence: Cookware, cookbooks, kitchen items. Cozy store channels a homey village kitchen.
Les Vins de France: Wine by bottle, glass.
Plume et Palette: Perfume brands include Annick Goutal, Chanel, Dior, Givenchy.
Parfums Givenchy: This tiny boutique is the only store in the U.S. with the full line of Givenchy fragrances, skincare and make-up. Each year it has a U.S. exclusive on one perfume. For 2011 it's eaudemoiselle, a floral fragrance with Asian notes.
Souvenirs de France: General French souvenirs. Berets have "Made in China" tags.
Promenade stands: Parasols, portraits.
Architecture. Visitors approach the Paris of La Belle Époque ("the beautiful time" from 1870 to 1910) on a replica of the Pont des Arts footbridge. Three-story facades have copper and slate mansard roofs, many with chimney pots. A rear shop is based on the Les Halles fruit and vegetable market, an 1850

Tucked into the rear of the Morocco pavilion, Restaurant Marrakesh serves traditional cuisine such as lamb shank with couscous. A belly dancer entertains diners, inviting children to join her.

iron-and-glass-ceilinged Parisian structure. Towering behind it all is a replica of the Eiffel Tower with a period-correct tawny finish.

Family matters. For children, Belle and the Beast, Princess Aurora and sometimes Marie (from 1970's "The AristoCats") pose for pictures and sign autographs. A Kidcot table sits in the Souvenirs de France gift shop.

Morocco

This exotic pavilion features food, merchandise and music that is little-known in the West. Alongside the promenade is a cafe with a tiny sweet shop and an exhibit room; behind them are some small stores and a restaurant. Created by the Kingdom of Morocco, the pavilion is managed independently of Disney. Wafting incense will remind some baby boomers of a head shop.

Entertainment. A robed belly dancer fronts the hypnotic band **Mo'Rockin** (★★★ ✔ 20-min shows, promenade bandstand), which uses a violin, Zendrum and passionate vocals to blend North African rhythms and melodies. Songs include Sting's 1999 hit "Desert Rose."

Exhibit. "Moroccan Style: The Art of Personal Adornment" displays ornate costumes, elaborate jewelry and everyday clothing. Heavily tiled and molded, the Gallery of Arts and History has an intricate

raised ceiling. Easy to overlook, it sits to the left of the front courtyard.

Restaurants. A belly dancer entertains at Restaurant Marrakesh. A fast-food spot, Tangierine Café, has a pastry counter that serves teas and coffees.

See chapter **Restaurants and Food.**

Shopping. Morocco's five shops offer items rarely seen in the United States:

The Brass Bazaar: Handmade brass plates, platters; packaged couscous, spices; ceramic, wooden cookware; rosewater bottles. Aromatic bowls, boxes of thuya, a burled-root wood grown only in Morocco.

Casablanca Carpets: Moroccan carpets, rugs. Lamps that filter light through henna-dyed lamb skin, incense holders, leather chairs, colorful sequined pillows.

Marketplace in the Medina: Open-air alley with belly-dancer kits, seagrass baskets, ceramic-topped furniture, scarves. Two strange drums: ceramic tam-tams covered in camel skin; open-top darboukas with flounder-skin bottoms.

Souk-Al-Magreb: This promenade stand has a mix of merchandise from the other shops. The name means "The Flea Market of Northern Africa."

Tangier Traders: Traditional caftans, gandouras and other robes and wraps, handmade leather slippers.

Architecture. Meant to evoke a desert city, buildings are made of brick, tan plaster and reddish sandstone. Like traditional Moroccan cities, the pavilion is divided into two sections, the Ville Nouvelle (new city) and the medina (old town).

In front, the pavilion's new city recalls Casablanca and Marrakesh. It's anchored by the Koutoubia Minaret prayer tower.

The medina of Fez lies in back, behind the 8th-century Bab Boujouloud Gate. On the left is the central courtyard of a traditional Moroccan home, complete with the sounds of the family. On the right is an open-air market, its bamboo roof lashed to thick beams.

Restaurant Marrakesh is a Southern Moroccan fortress. Nearby is the Nejjarine Fountain. Rising above the old city is the Chellah Minaret, a 14th-century necropolis found in Morocco's capital city of Rabat.

Landscaping represents Morocco's agriculture—date, olive and sour orange trees; mint and ornamental cabbage plants. Along the World Showcase lagoon is a working replica of an ancient waterwheel, an ingenious contraption that shuttles water from the lake to a grid of nearby gardens.

Moroccan artists created the pavilion's detailed tiles from nine tons of ceramic pieces. Deliberate flaws reflect the Muslim belief that only Allah creates perfection.

Seen from across the lagoon—specifically, from the promenade area to the right of the Mexico pavilion—the pavilion appears to include a large, tall building in the distance behind it. Actually that's The Twilight Zone Tower of Terror at Disney's Hollywood Studios, which shares a Spanish influence.

A Moroccan mannequin sports the traditional beaded headdress used in belly dancing

Family matters. Kids can meet Aladdin, Princess Jasmine and Genie in a room behind the shops. A Kidcot table sits in the market.

Hidden Mickeys. ❶ As brass plates on a green door of the Souk-Al-Magreb promenade shop. ❷ As a dome window in a minaret on the photo backdrop in Aladdin's meeting area. Mickey's in the upper right-hand segment, next to a small ladder.

The Gallery of Arts and History holds "Moroccan Style: The Art of Personal Adornment." The exhibit includes costumes, everyday clothing and jewelry. The room itself is a piece of art, heavily tiled and molded with an intricate raised ceiling.

A torii gate in front of the Japan pavilion is a picture-perfect replica of the famed "floating" torii just off the shore of the island of Itsukushima. A torii marks the entrance to a sacred space.

Japan

An authentic Japanese department store highlights Epcot's friendliest exotic pavilion, which also includes three good restaurants and an exhibit gallery. Anime, Hello Kitty and Pokémon aficionados will especially enjoy the shop. The pavilion is run by the Mitsukoshi company, Japan's oldest retail business.

Entertainment. Three unique street performers appear throughout the day.

Honobono Minwa: ★★★ 20-min shows, courtyard. Geared to children, enthusiastic storyteller tells Japanese folk tales and teaches a few words of basic Japanese.

Matsuriza Taiko Drummers: ★★★★ ✓ 20-min shows, pagoda. Intense trio creates propulsive beats on hand-made instruments.

Miyuki: ★★★★★ ✓ 20-min shows, at store entrance. Tokyo native demonstrates remarkable skill at snipping animal-shaped lollipops out of taffy-like rice dough.

Exhibit. "Spirited Beasts: From Ancient Stories to Anime Stars" shows the connection between Japanese myths and modern anime. Filled with more than 100 objects, displays showcase nine creatures from Japanese folklore that have inspired characters in popular video games and television shows. Kappa the water sprite, an inspiration for the Pokémon character Golduck, appears

several times. The exhibit is located at the left rear of the pavilion, in the Bijutsu-kan Gallery.

Restaurants. The pavilion has two table-service restaurants, Teppan Edo and Tokyo Dining. The fast-food option is Yakitori House. See chapter **Restaurants and Food.**

Shopping. A 10,000-square-foot Mitsukoshi department store has four sections. The largest area, Interest, has a Pick-A-Pearl bar, Lucky Cats, transforming Rhythm and Seiko clocks, Hello Kitty items and quirky toys. A Harmony zone bridges Japanese and Western cultures with glass-bead jewelry, sandals and Mikimoto pearl jewelry. The store's Silence area has household items: bonsai trees, lanterns, rice paper and tatami mats. Apparel includes tenugui head coverings and silk kimonos. In back, a Festivity zone stocks chopsticks, porcelain dishes, teas and sweets. A sake-tasting bar offers five microbrews.

Out front, a Mitsukoshi kiosk sells candy, snacks and inexpensive souvenirs.

Architecture. An 83-foot pagoda recalls the 8th-century Horyuji Temple in Nara. Its five stories represent the five elements of creation—earth, water, fire, wind and sky. A hill garden's evergreens symbolize eternal life, its rocks the long life of the earth and its koi-filled water the brief life of animals and man. In the garden, the rustic Yakitori House is modeled on Kyoto's 16th-century

Katsura Imperial Villa. Housing the store and restaurants, the structure on the right recalls the ceremonial Shishinden Hall of the 8th-century Gosho Imperial Palace at Kyoto.

In back, a (very thin) 17th-century wood and stone Nijo castle includes sculptures of mounted samurai warriors. A moat fronts the Shirasagijo (White Heron) castle, a 14th-century feudal fortress.

Family matters. Children will enjoy candy artist Miyuki and listening to the storyteller. A Kidcot table is located in the exhibit room.

Hidden Mickeys. ❶ In the metal tree grates in the courtyard. ❷ As the center of a koi-pond drain cover, near a bamboo fence.

American Adventure

Historic Americans come to life at this pavilion's attraction, which uses Audio-Animatronics figures to tell our nation's story. Fans of Ken Burns documentaries will especially enjoy the show, which uses a similar storytelling technique. The area also has some nice live entertainment and an interesting small exhibit.

Entertainment. The United States pavilion has many good entertainment choices. Its attraction justly gets most of the attention, but the live performers are also worthwhile:

The American Adventure: ★★★★★ ✓ 30 min. Capacity: 1,024. Indoor, air-conditioned queue. Fear factor: None. Access: Guests may remain in wheelchairs, ECVs. Assistive listening, reflective captioning, Audio Description. Debuted: 1982, revised 1993, 2007. Boldly honest for a theme-park attraction, this theatrical presentation does America proud. It combines film footage

The rear of the Japan pavilion resembles the country's historic Nijo and Shirasagijo castles

with robotic historic figures. Ben Franklin and Mark Twain narrate, leading guests from the time of the Pilgrims through World War II, with help from icons like George Washington, Thomas Jefferson, Will Rogers and Rosie the Riveter. The only World Showcase attraction that is critical of its country, the show embraces the triumphs of America and the optimism

Japanese potato sticks and gummy candy hangs in the Mitsukoshi department store. Other merchandise includes bonsai trees, chopsticks, Mikimoto pearl jewelry, silk kimonos, tatami mats and quirky knickknacks.

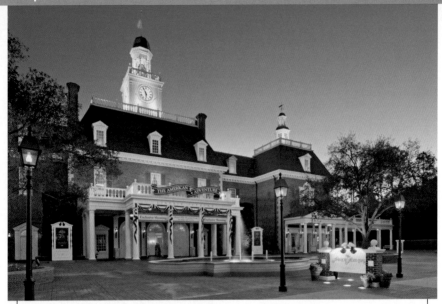

Disney's English-Georgian American Adventure structure was built with 110,000 hand-formed bricks. It holds a huge theater, exhibit gallery, fast-food spot and gift shop.

of its people, but doesn't shy away from our country's flaws and challenges. Chatting with Franklin after the Revolutionary War, Twain says "You Founding Fathers gave us a pretty good start... [but then] a whole bunch of folks found out that 'We the People' didn't yet mean all the people." Subsequent scenes cover slavery and the persecution of Native Americans. The film, a combination of real and re-created images, pans across paintings and photographs. The robots move convincingly. For a moment Franklin appears to walk.

America Gardens concerts: ★★★ 20-min shows. The open-air America Gardens amphitheater holds complimentary concerts sporadically throughout the year.

Spirit of America Fife & Drum Corps: ★★★ ✓ 10-min shows, promenade. Led by a town crier, this dramatic group performs "The Battle Hymn of the Republic," "God Bless America" and similar tunes. Children join to recite Pledge of Allegiance.

The Voices of Liberty: ★★★★ ✓ 20-min shows, pavilion rotunda. Spirited a cappella group harmonizes on Americana tunes such as "Amazing Grace," "Ol' Man River" and "This Land Is Your Land."

Exhibit. A "National Treasures" exhibit displays artifacts from famous Americans. It includes a stovepipe hat worn by Abraham Lincoln; a kinetoscope, kinetophone and tinfoil phonograph made by Thomas Edison; chairs from the homes of Benjamin Franklin and George Washington; and a pool cue from Samuel Clemens' den.

Restaurant. The pavilion has one uninspired fast-food spot, Liberty Inn. Snack kiosks sell turkey legs and funnel cakes. See chapter **Restaurants and Food**.

Shopping. Small Heritage Manor Gifts stocks patriotic apparel, books and various Americana, much of which comes from China. A wood cart out front sells T-shirts.

Architecture. The English-Georgian building uses 110,000 hand-formed bricks, laid with an old-fashioned one-then-a-half technique. In a departure from typical Disney design, the giant structure uses *reversed* forced perspective to appear just three stories tall.

A closer look. The attraction's staging system is a mechanical marvel. Just beneath the sight line of the audience, a 175-ton scene changer (a steel frame 65 feet long, 35 feet wide and 14 feet high) wheels in 13 sets horizontally, raising them into view on telescoping hydraulic supports. Other devices bring in side elements. The show uses 35 Audio-Animatronics characters, including three Ben Franklins and three Mark Twains.

Family matters. A Kidcot table is outside, by the gift shop.

Robotic versions of Benjamin Franklin and Mark Twain host the American Adventure attraction. They lead guests from the time of the Pilgrims through World War II. Other icons include Thomas Jefferson, Will Rogers and Rosie the Riveter.

Italy

Created on site, handmade Carnivale masks sparkle in a corner of a cozy shop at this lovely little pavilion. One of the most attractive World Showcase facades, a Venetian entrance area disguises the fact that this version of *Lo Stivale* ("the boot") is really nothing more than two shops and two restaurants. Well-heeled fans of authentic pasta and pizza will enjoy the food.

Entertainment. Humorous mime **Sergio** (★★★ 20-min shows, promenade) puts child volunteers into his juggling act.

Restaurants. Tutto Italia is a pricey but delicious eatery. New Via Napoli is a classy Neopolitan pizza spot.

See chapter **Restaurants and Food.**

Shopping. The two shops specialize in wine, perfume and decorative items:

Il Bel Cristallo: Fontanini creches, Murano glass, jewelry, Christmas ornaments, Bulgari and Ferragamo perfumes, Puma sportswear, soccer books.

La Bottega: Wine by bottle, glass; Perugina candy; books. Artisan creates papier-mâché, fabric Carnivale masks.

Architecture. A town square resembles the Piazza San Marco. Two freestanding columns recall 12th-century monuments, one topped by the city's guardian, the winged lion of St. Mark the Evangelist, the other crowned by St. Theodore, the city's former patron saint. He's shown killing a dragon, an act that gave him the courage to declare himself a Christian. The 10th-century Campanile (bell tower) dominates the skyline, though this version is just 100 feet tall, less than a third the height of the original. Gold-leafed ringlets decorate an angel on top.

With the 10th-century Campanile dominating its skyline, the front of Epcot's Italy pavilion recalls the cityscape of Venice. Two freestanding columns mimic 12th-century monuments. In reality the buildings have only one story.

The Germany pavilion's quaint cobblestone plaza recalls a 16th-century village. In the center is a fountain topped with a statue of dragon-slaying St. George. A variety of shops line the courtyard.

On the left of the square is a replica of the 14th-century Doge's (leader's) Palace. Its facade replicates many details of the original. The first two stories rest on realistic marble columns that front leaded-glass windows. The third floor is tiled and topped by marble sculptures, statues, reliefs and filigree. Adjoining the palace, a stairway and portico reflect Verona. The La Bottega shop is a Tuscany homestead. A sculpture behind it recalls Bernini's 1642 fountain in Florence.

With the World Showcase lagoon doubling as the Adriatic Sea, a waterfront area includes replicas of Venice bridges, gondolas and striped pilings.

Family matters. A Kidcot table is located behind the La Bottega gift shop.

Germany

Guests indulge at this jolly pavilion, where beer flows and a new caramel shop has lines winding out the door. No fewer than nine stores offer everything from pickle ornaments to teddy bears. The restaurant, though pricey for a buffet, is lots of fun.

Restaurant. An oompah band entertains at the Biergarten, a German buffet. Outside, a popular Sommerfest counter offers good bratwurst and German beer.

See chapter **Restaurants and Food.**

Shopping. Eight stores line a central courtyard; there's one promenade stand:

Das Kaufhaus: Apparel, backpacks, balls, sandals and sporting goods.

Der Teddybar: Children's items, including Steiff bears, Schleich toys, Playmobil sets, plushies, Snow White costumes, customized Engle-Puppen dolls.

Die Weihnachts Ecke: Christmas shop sells classic pickle ornaments, handmade Steinbach nutcrackers.

Glaskunst: Personalized figures, frames, glassware, steins. Promenade stand.

Karamelle-Küche: Old World German caramel shop. Werther's Original candy.

Kunstarbeit in Kristall: Jewelry, personalized glassware, Swarovski crystal pins. Arribas Brothers collectibles.

Sussigkeiten: Candy; cookbooks; cookies; fresh baked pastries, fudge. Imported packaged candy includes Haribo gummies.

Volkskunst: Beer steins, Schneider cuckoo clocks, glassware, pewter, Troika watches. Egg artist Jutta Levasseur often works in the corner; a $1200 ostrich egg is on display.

Weinkeller: Wines and schnapps offered by the bottle or glass.

Architecture. The centerpiece of the plaza depicts St. George slaying a dragon in the Middle East. A clock comes to life hourly with a 3-minute animated display. The Das

At the China pavilion, a miniature Hall of Prayer for Good Harvests recalls the circular main building of Beijing's Temple of Heaven, a 15th-century summer retreat for emperors

Kaufhaus shop was inspired by the Kaufhaus, a 16th-century merchants' hall in the Black Forest town of Freiburg. Three statues on its second story recall Hapsburg emperors. The rear facade combines two 12th-century castles, the Eltz and the Stahleck.

Family matters. Children will enjoy the miniature outdoor train village, located to the right of the pavilion. A walkway leads over track tunnels and alongside a town, which has its own wee little live landscape. Four trains roam over the rivers and through the woods, each on its own track. Snow White and Dopey appear to the left of the pavilion. Germany's Kidcot table sits inside Der Teddybar.

Hidden Mickeys. ❶ In the center of the crown of the left-most Hapsburg emperor statue on the second story of Das Kaufhaus. ❷ A three-dimensional Mickey Mouse often hides in the train village. Usually he stands in a window of a hilltop castle.

China

Global superpower? Communist state? There's no hint of *that* China in this peaceful, pretty pavilion. The attraction—Disney's last true CircleVision 360 movie—is a fascinating travelogue. An exhibit showcases the country's ancient history. The pavilion also has a department store and a good restaurant.

Entertainment. Options include a movie and a unique musician.

Reflections of China: ★★★★ 20 min. Capacity: 200. No seats. Indoor, air-conditioned queue. Fear factor: None. Access: Guests may stay in wheelchairs, ECVs. Reflective captioning, assistive listening, Audio Description. Debuted: 1982, revised 2003. You stand up to watch this poetic travelogue. It includes 30 wrap-around vistas, all crisp and clear. Sights include everything from the Great Wall and the Forbidden City to the cityscapes of Hong Kong and Shanghai to rural Tibet and Inner Mongolia. One scene was filmed by a camera hanging from a banking helicopter. The host portrays 8th-century Chinese poet Li Bai. Developed in the 1950s by video engineer (and original Mickey Mouse animator) Ub Iwerks, CircleVision 360 theaters use nine projectors to display video from a nine-lens camera onto nine screens. (Why nine? Because the concept only works with an odd number—each projector sits in a gap between two screens, and lines up with one screen across from it.)

Si Xian: ★★★ 20-min shows, inside hall. A qin zitherist (instrument is a sound box with curved surface, tight strings) plays ethereal silk-music folk tunes.

Exhibit. "Tomb Warriors—Guardian Spirits of Ancient China" re-creates the

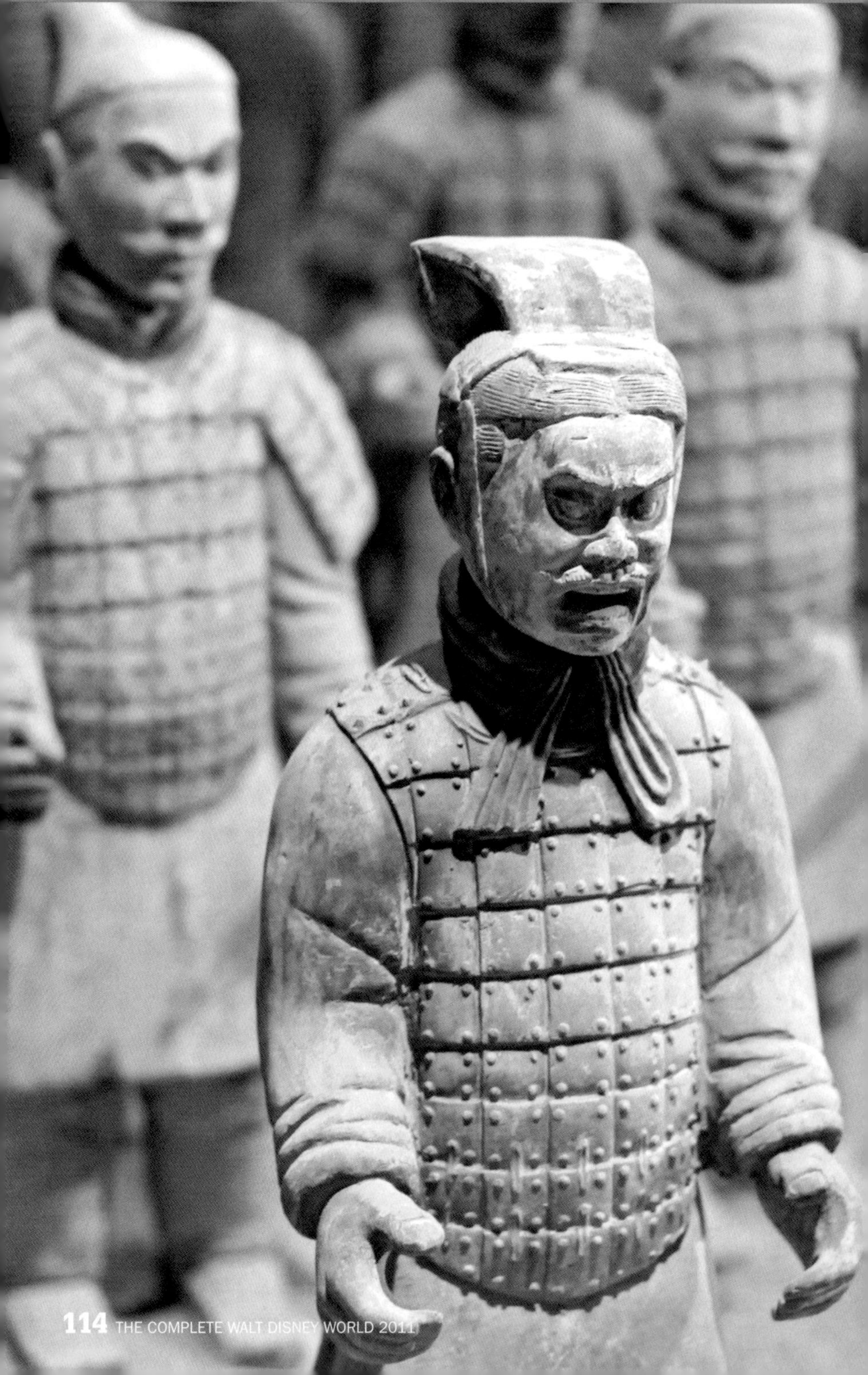

terra cotta "spirit army" found in the tomb of China's first emperor Qin Shi Huang (259–210 B.C.). The largest archeological find in the world, the 22-square-mile site contains 8,000 full-size statues arranged in military formations. An army of 200 half-size reproductions offers a sense of the real thing. The exhibit also includes two dozen small tomb artifacts from the Han, Six, Sui and Tang Dynasties (through 906 A.D.). The exhibit is in the Gallery of the Whispering Willow, in the rear center of the pavilion.

Restaurants. Choose from the table-service Nine Dragons Restaurant or the counter-service Lotus Blossom Cafe.

See chapter **Restaurants and Food.**

Shopping. The sprawling Yong Feng Shangdian department store is packed with imported goods. Prices range from a dollar or so for trinkets to thousands of dollars for intricately carved furniture and jade antiques. Other items include a range of apparel, silk fans, snack food, fountains, housewares, jewelry, prints, silk rugs and tea sets. The store also has a small souvenir stand and a promenade wood cart selling marionettes and personalized parasols.

Architecture. The pavilion is anchored by a triple-arched gate. Behind it sits the Hall of Prayer for Good Harvests, the circular main building of Beijing's 1420 Temple of Heaven, a summer retreat for emperors. Its rotunda columns and beams allude to the cycles of nature. A floor stone is cut into nine pieces, as, in China, nine is a lucky number.

The main walkway also includes facades of an elegant home, a school house and shop fronts reflecting European influences. The gallery has a formal saddle-ridge roof line.

A Suzhou-style pond garden symbolizes nature's order and discipline. Keeping with Chinese custom, it appears old and unkempt. Alongside the lagoon, pockmarked boulders demonstrate a tradition of designing surprising views in landscapes by creating holes in waterside rock formations.

Family matters. Mulan and Mushu from Disney's 1998 film "Mulan" appear. A Kidcot table sits at the back of the store.

Norway

Beauties and beasts dominate this pavilion—pretty princesses at a Disney character meal, three-headed trolls inside a dark boat ride.

Facing page: An army of ancient "tomb warriors" is replicated in the China pavilion

Chiseled Nordic cast members greet guests at the store, restaurant and fast-food spot. A bizarro attraction includes polar bears, trolls and a very bright-eyed god.

Entertainment. Themed to Norway's rich seafaring heritage, **Maelstrom** (★★★ *FASTPASS* 5 min ride, 5 min wait, 5 min film. Capacity: 192. Indoor, air-conditioned queue. Fear factor: Often dark, with a few scary faces. In the film, two loud flashes will jolt those of any age. Access: ECV and wheelchair users must transfer. Assistive listening; handheld and reflective captioning. Debuted: 1988) is an indoor boat ride and movie with a quirky appeal. Sailing in a dragon-headed longboat, guests head up a chainlift as ancient Norse god Odin urges them to "seek the spirit of Norway." The hunt starts off peacefully as the boat passes a 10th-century fishing village. It becomes a confused chaos (a "maelstrom") after trolls commandeer the ship. The boat makes landfall at a modern fishing village.

The second half of Maelstrom is optional. A short film, "The Spirit of Norway" portrays the daydreams of a young boy. As he examines an old Viking ship, the boy imagines many successful Norwegians—businessmen, oil riggers, scientists, seafarers, ski jumpers and ordinary citizens at a Constitution Day parade. The point? "The spirit of Norway... is in its people!" (Cynics will note that, based on the gender of the actors, the spirit of Norway is mostly in its males.)

Exhibit. Axe in hand, a lifesize Rögnvald the Raider stares you down in "Vikings: Conquerors of the Seas," a five-case exhibit inside a model Stave Church. The displays also include figures of Erik the Red and King Olaf, a detailed scale model of the 9th century Viking ship and authentic swords, arrows and axe blades, some of which date back more than 1,000 years.

Average wait times (Maelstrom)

Time	Standby line	Fastpass time
9:00a	(closed)	(closed)
10:00a	(closed)	(closed)
11:00a	5 min	11:45a
Noon	5 min	1:00p
1:00p	10 min	1:45p
2:00p	15 min	2:45p
3:00p	20 min	3:55p
4:00p	25 min	5:10p
5:00p	35 min	5:55p
6:00p	25 min	6:50p
7:00p	30 min	7:40p
8:00p	20 min	8:50p
9:00p	(closed)	(closed)

Opposite page photo: Micaela Neal

Gift shop facades at Epcot's Norway pavilion recall coastal cottages in a village square. A Stave church replicates the 13th-century Gol Church of Hallingdal. The pavilion also includes Maelstrom, an indoor boat ride populated with trolls.

Restaurants. Character meals at the Akershus Royal Banquet Hall feature Disney princesses. The Kringla Bakeri Og Kafe fast-food eatery offers sandwiches and pastries. See chapter **Restaurants and Food**.

Shopping. Norway has just one gift shop, but it has a variety of items:

The Puffin's Roost: Stylish, if pricey Helly Hansen, Dale of Norway apparel. Christmas ornaments, Geir Ness perfume, puffin plushies, toys, plastic trolls. Viking Donald Duck plushie. Silly plastic Viking helmets, all with horns, some with braids.

Architecture. The grounds combine many architectural styles. Standing at the entrance is a replica of the 13th-century Gol Church of Hallingdal, one of Norway's Stave churches that played a key role in the country's movement to Christianity. Next door, a small bakery has a sod roof, a traditional way to insulate homes in Norwegian mountains. Gift shop facades recall coastal cottages. The restaurant and rear facade of the pavilion re-create Akershus, a 14th-century Oslo castle and fortress.

Family matters. Children will enjoy the Kidcot table, which sits inside The Puffin's Roost. Many girls will love the restaurant's princess character meals.

Hidden Mickeys. ❶ Images of Mickey Mouse appear three times in the mural behind the Maelstrom loading area: As Mickey ears on a Viking in the middle of a ship toward the left, as shadows on a cruise-line worker's blouse (her right pocket is Mickey's head, her clipboard ring is his nose) and at the far right on the watch of a bearded construction worker wearing a hardhat. ❷ As black circles on King Olaf II's tunic embroidery in the Stave Church.

© Disney

Princess Aurora ("Sleeping Beauty") and Snow White meet young fans at Norway's Akershus Royal Banquet Hall. Other characters can include Ariel ("The Little Mermaid"), Belle ("Beauty and the Beast"), Cinderella, Jasmine, Mary Poppins and Mulan.

The front of the Mexico pavilion resembles the temple of the Aztec serpent god Quetzalcoatl, part of the ancient city of Teotihuacan. Inside the building is a restaurant, ride and tequila bar.

Mexico

Margaritaville! Young adults in particular enjoy the party hearty atmosphere at this pavilion. Everyone will like the mariachi music, fun shopping and nice (if pricey) dining experiences. Those of Hispanic descent will either appreciate, or be offended by, the pavilion's mutant freak of an attraction.

Entertainment. Mexico's entertainment choices are its aftermentioned boat ride and, much better, live band.

Gran Fiesta Tour: ★★★ 8 min. Capacity: 250. Indoor, air-conditioned queue. Fear factor: None. Access: ECV users must transfer. Handheld captioning, Audio Description. Debuted: 1982, revised 2007. Donald Duck is a wolf in this dark boat ride. An update of the old El Rio Del Tiempo ride, it is still a tour through the cultural history of Mexico, but now its video screens tell a story based on Disney's 1944 movie "The Three Caballeros." When three "happy chappies with snappy serapes"—red-blooded Donald, suave Brazilian parrot José Carioca and hyper Mexican cowboy rooster Panchito—plan to reunite for a concert in Mexico City, Donald disappears to take in the sights and flirt with the females as his friends try to find him. Like the film, the ride is a strange trip. In Acapulco, Donald's bathing suit falls off. At night, he heads to a bar to smooch live-action human señoritas. It's all in good fun, of course, but some guests are not amused. "If the Gran Fiesta Tour is supposed to be a showcase of Mexico, it is a disrespectful one," a Latin American friend tells the authors. "It seems to me just like a big party, with birds running around looking for a duck." As for reliving the cultural history of Mexico, guests who can look past the insistent videos will note they start off in the country's 1st century A.D., sailing through a rainforest before passing a Mayan pyramid and drifting into a temple. A Small World-style celebration includes the Day of the Dead, Mexico's annual fall festival when late ancestors traditionally come back to visit. In modern Mexico guests pass Acapulco's cliffs and grottos, then travel to Mexico City's Reforma Boulevard, where the Three Caballeros' concert takes place. To get the most legroom in the boat, ask for the first row.

Mariachi Cobre: ★★★★ ✔ 20-min shows, inside pyramid. Led by trumpets, violins and confident vocals, backed by harmonizing guitars, this outstanding 11-piece group is Epcot's best live band. The performers have played with, and recorded with, singer Linda Ronstadt.

Animation art © The Walt Disney Co.

Red-feathered rooster Panchito and green parrot José Carioca catch up to Donald Duck in the finale of the Gran Fiesta Tour (left). The stars of Disney's "The Three Caballeros" appear on video screens throughout the boat ride.

Restaurants. With two table-service restaurants (waterside La Hacienda de San Angel and the San Angel Inn), an outdoor fast-food spot (waterside La Cantina de San Angel) and separate tequila bar, Mexico has some of the most popular dining in Epcot.

See chapter **Restaurants and Food.**

Shopping. The pavilion offers a huge variety of Mexican merchandise:

La Princesa Cristal: Crystal, figurines, jewelry. Off Plaza de los Amigos.

La Tienda Encantada: Accessories, fashion apparel, fine jewelry, leather, fleece ponchos, throws. Off Plaza de los Amigos.

Plaza de los Amigos: Blankets, books, candy, glassware, musical instruments, paper flowers, creative handmade ceramic piggy banks, piñatas, ponchos, salsa, sombreros, tequila, toys. Day of the Dead items. Many inexpensive choices.

Animalés Fantasticos Spirits in Wood: Working in the pavilion lobby just inside the pyramid, artisans use machetes and pocketknives to carve animals, humans and mythical creatures from copal wood, then paint them in vivid colors with brushes, cactus spines and syringes.

El Ranchito del Norte: Outdoor stand has a sampling of merchandise from other pavilion shops. Along promenade.

Architecture. The pyramid facade is modeled on the Aztec temple of serpent god Quetzalcoatl in the ancient city of Teotihuacan. Traditionally the god of the morning and evening star, Quetzalcoatl later became known as the patron of priests. Quetzalcoatl himself is depicted by heads along the priests' steps of Disney's pyramid.

Inside the building, the portico to the "outdoor" market resembles a Mexican mayor's mansion. Surrounding facades represent the 16th-century silver mining town of Taxco.

A closer look. The most bizarre movie in the Disney canon, "The Three Caballeros" combines live video, psychedelic animation and a storyline that makes Donald Duck a ladies man. Its point? The charms of Latin America. Here's the plot: When Donald has a birthday, his presents are pop-up books that include a Brazilian playboy parrot named José Carioca and a six-gun-shooting Mexican cowboy rooster named Panchito. As Panchito tosses sombreros to his new friends, he proclaims the trio "three gay caballeros" and takes it on a flying-serape tour of his country. When the group reaches Acapulco, Donald keeps losing his swimsuit but nonetheless goes ga-ga for various live-action bathing beauties ("Come to Papa!" he says to one woman. "Come here, my little enchilada!"). At night the duck can't stay away from the clubs, where he dances with more real-life señoritas.

Surreal animation includes illogical color changes and an overdose of morphing gags, though some scenes are beautiful Mary Blair gems that would later inspire the films "Cinderella" and "Alice in Wonderland" as well as the classic Disney attraction It's a Small World. The movie was produced as part of the U.S. government's Good Neighbor Policy, an effort to promote pro-American feelings in Latin America during the 1930s and 1940s. It increased the region's support for the United States during World War II.

Family matters. A Kidcot table sits just inside the entrance. Donald Duck signs autographs and poses for pictures in his "Three Caballeros" garb. Though the boat ride makes little sense, it's fine for even the youngest child—there's nothing scary.

A fiery ballet of chaos highlights the IllumiNations laser and fireworks spectacle. Directed to Spaceship Earth; the symmetrical show is best viewed from World Showcase Plaza.

IllumiNations: Reflections of Earth

★★★★ ✓ **World Showcase Lagoon** 14 min. Preshow: 30 min of instrumental world music from Japan, South America, Scandinavia and Spain. Fear factor: Loud, bright explosions and fire can be intense for toddlers, some preschoolers. Cancelled during thunderstorms. Access: Guests may remain in wheelchairs, ECVs. Debuted: 1988; revised 1997, 1999.

IllumiNations sets its sights high: to tell the story of planet Earth. Synchronized to a symphonic world-music score, this nightly fireworks and special-effects extravaganza uses the entire World Showcase as its stage. Strobe lights flash, laser beams fly and fireworks burst in a choreographed spectacle. A rotating Earth moves across the lagoon and shows moving images on its continents.

Though there's no narration, the show tells the history of the world in three acts.

"Chaos": The dawn of time begins the Big Bang and the creation of Earth. A lone shooting star explodes into a fiery "ballet of chaos."

"Order": Earth comes under control as scenes on the globe depict primal seas and forests, the development of cultural landmarks such as the Sphinx and historical figures such as the Dalai Lama, Mother Teresa and (of course) Walt Disney. The coolest image: a video of a running horse that transforms into a cave painting.

"Celebration": The globe unfurls and a 40-foot torch emerges. A fireworks finale heralds a new age of man—the 21st century.

Where to watch it. The symmetrical show is directed toward Spaceship Earth. The best viewing spot is World Showcase Plaza, where guests see everything as the designers intended it. An added plus: the plaza is the closest viewing spot to Epcot's front exit, so guests there will be ahead of the masses when the show ends.

Fun facts. ❶ Two-thousand eight-hundred fireworks launch from 750 mortar tubes in 34 locations. **❷** Wrapped in more than 180,000 LEDs, the 28-foot steel globe was the world's first spherical video display. **❸** The pavilions are outlined in 26,000 feet of lights. **❹** The Morocco pavilion does not participate in the show. **❺** The show's music supervisor was Hans Zimmer, the composer for the 1994 Disney movie "The Lion King." **❻** Nineteen torches around the lagoon symbolize the first 19 centuries of modern history. The 20th torch, in the globe, represents the Millennium.

Disney's Hollywood Studios

Love movies and television? If so, you'll enjoy this theme park, Disney's valentine to show business. Chock full of attractions based on movies and television shows, it also offers many inside glimpses on how the magic is made. Fans of old-style glamour can encounter Humphrey Bogart and James Cagney. Animation buffs get the Muppets and

"Toy Story." Guests enter the world of television with attractions based on "American Idol" and "The Twilight Zone." A revamped Star Tours ride will delight fans of the Force.

Visitors also get to *do* things at this theme park, which offers many interactive experiences. At the most popular ride in all of Disney World—Toy Story Mania—guests

Ready for its closeup, Sunset Boulevard glows with neon marquees. Palm trees line the street, which leads to the park's thrill rides.

Best reasons to go

Great thrill rides: Fully realized and truly memorable, Rock 'n' Roller Coaster Starring Aerosmith and the Twilight Zone Tower of Terror hurl guests in the dark.

Disney's best attraction for preschoolers: A lively gem of a puppet show, Disney Junior—Live on Stage speaks directly to young children without being condescending.

Outstanding live shows: Beauty and the Beast—Live on Stage is a touching spectacle. In Voyage of the Little Mermaid, the live Ariel belts out her song with flair. The American Idol Experience is always fun.

Toy Story Mania: This high-tech video arcade is especially rewarding if you try it more than once. By working together, partners open hidden levels of game play.

You'll laugh: No Disney park has a bigger sense of humor. In fact, many Studios experiences are almost guaranteed to put a smile on your face. Examples include watching the preening Gaston of Beauty and the Beast—Live on Stage, witnessing the antics of Dr. Bunsen Honeydew and Beaker at Jim Henson's MuppetVision 3-D, or being a target of a sadistic server at the 50's Prime Time Café.

It won't wear you out: Unlike other theme parks, the Studios doesn't make you spend all day on your feet. The smallest Disney theme park, it has the most sit-down shows as well as some time-consuming rides.

Good choices for lunch and dinner: Aside from Epcot's World Showcase foodfest, the Studios has Disney's best park eateries.

The Citizens of Hollywood: Impersonating Hollywood stereotypes with unfettered glee, this improv troupe spreads silliness up and down Hollywood and Sunset Boulevards.

Worst aspects of the park

Studio Backlot Tour: This sorry vestige of the great earlier Studio Tour still pretends there is a working backlot at the park. Guests get an eyeload of sad, rusting movie props.

Lights, Motors, Action: Distinctly un-Disney gunplay and a lack of humor mar this headachy presentation of automotive stunts.

Journey Into Narnia: A total waste of time, this small room shows the trailer to 2008's "The Chronicles of Narnia: Prince Caspian."

Limited breakfast choices: The only indoor breakfast choice is a Disney Junior character meal at Hollywood & Vine. The only outdoor breakfast spot with hot food is the uninspired Sunset Ranch Market. The best breakfast food is at Starring Rolls, a takeout bakery.

shoot targets in a virtual 3-D video arcade. Audience votes determine the winner of "American Idol" contests. Parkgoers sketch a Disney character at The Magic of Disney Animation and keep the result. Many stage and street shows offer visitors a chance to indulge their celebrity fantasies by volunteering to join the performers.

The park icon is a giant version of the hat worn by Mickey Mouse in the "Sorcerer's Apprentice" segment of the 1940 movie "Fantasia." The headpiece is flanked by a pair of stylized Mickey ears and a gloved Mickey hand that tips it to one side.

A Magical Day

8:00a: Arrive at the parking lot, then be first in line at the turnstiles (and later, the rope line). As you wait for the gates to open (typically at 8:50 a.m.), pick up a Times Guide and Citizens of Hollywood schedule from Guest Relations at your left.

9:00a: As one member of your party gets Fastpasses for Toy Story Mania, the rest gets rolls and coffee at the Starring Rolls Café.

9:10a: Ride Rock 'n' Roller Coaster.

9:25a: Ride Tower of Terror.

9:45a: Use your Fastpasses to ride Toy Story Mania. Get Fastpasses for a second ride later in the day.

10:10a: Arrive for the 10:30 a.m. show of Beauty and the Beast—Live on Stage.

11:00a: See the Citizens of Hollywood.

11:45a: Shop in the stores along Hollywood or Sunset Boulevard.

12:30p: Hamburgers and milkshakes at the Sci-Fi Dine-In, or Cobb salad and cake at the Hollywood Brown Derby.

1:40p: Arrive for the 2 p.m. show of The American Idol Experience.

2:45p: Draw a Disney character at The Magic of Disney Animation.

3:45p: See Mulch, Sweat & Shears perform on New York Street.

4:15p: See MuppetVision 3-D.

4:35p: Get a snack at the Writer's Stop.

5:00p: Ride The Great Movie Ride.

6:00p: Use your Fastpasses to ride Toy Story Mania a second time.

6:45p: Dinner at the 50's Prime Time Café. Ask for a server with "lots of theming."

Getting oriented

Disney's Hollywood Studios has two distinct areas. The front is Old Hollywood; its architecture and street entertainment embody Los Angeles during the glory days of Tinseltown—the 1920s through 1940s. Core attractions sit on a mythical Sunset Boulevard. The rear of the park captures backstage Hollywood, with faux soundstages and backlots that hold more rides and shows.

What if it rains?

With its relatively small size and plethora of indoor attractions, the park is relatively easy to enjoy during a shower. Only the Indiana Jones and Lights Motors Action stunt shows, the Studio Backlot Tour and the playground close due to rain. Fantasmic is cancelled when lightning is in the area.

Family matters

All of the park's thrill rides have height minimums—48 inches for Rock 'n' Roller Coaster Starring Aerosmith, 40 inches for Twilight Zone Tower of Terror as well as the Star Tours motion simulator. Other attractions that may be too intense for youngsters include the Fantasmic evening spectacle (loud noises, bright flashes, fire, villains), The Great Movie Ride (the "Alien" creature moves toward you), Journey Into Narnia: Prince Caspian (violent movie clips), Voyage of the Little Mermaid (giant villain Ursula threatens), and the Studio Backlot Tour (a canyon scene simulates fire and flood disasters).

Every park restaurant offers a children's menu. Disney Junior characters appear at Hollywood & Vine for breakfast and lunch.

A Baby Care Center (located next to Guest Relations) provides changing rooms, nursing

Constantly updated, the Studios Tip Board lists each attraction's wait time, hours of operation and other relevant information. It stands at the intersection of Hollywood and Sunset Boulevards. All Walt Disney World parks have tip boards.

areas, a microwave and a playroom. Diapers, formula, pacifiers and over-the-counter medications are available for purchase.

Restaurants and food

The park has a nice variety of places to eat, with four table-service restaurants, a buffet and three indoor fast-food spots. The most memorable eateries are the Sci-Fi Dine-In Theater and, especially, the '50s Prime Time Café. Make reservations at 407-939-3463 or online at disneyworld.com/dining.

See the chapter **Restaurants and Food.**

A closer look

Real movies and television shows were once produced at the park, as at first the Disney company planned to operate it as an actual television and motion picture production center as well as a tourist attraction.

In 1988, a year before the park opened to the public, the movies "Ernest Saves Christmas" and "Newsies" were filmed on the backlot. Soon, three soundstages hosted shows such as the Disney Channel's "New Mickey Mouse Club." Produced inside the building that today holds the Toy Story Mania ride, the 1989–1994 show starred youngsters Christina Aguilera, Ryan Gosling, Britney Spears and Justin Timberlake. Today's Streets of America area was used for Touchstone's 1990 Warren Beatty/Madonna vehicle "Dick Tracy."

Third-party productions included Ed McMahon's "Star Search"—a talent show in which 11-year-old Timberlake and 10-year-old Spears both appeared (neither won).

Meanwhile, a separate animation studio (Walt Disney Feature Animation Florida) produced sequences for such classics as 1991's "Beauty and the Beast" and later

Park Resources

ATMs: Outside the entrance turnstiles; also in Toy Story Pizza Planet Arcade.

First Aid: For minor emergencies. Registered nurses. Park entrance.

Guest Relations: Walk-up window outside the turnstiles, office inside. General questions, dining reservations, currency exchange. Maps, Times Guides for all WDW parks. Stores items found in the park that day. Multilingual.

Locker rentals: At the Crossroads of the World kiosk inside the park entrance ($7/day plus $5 deposit). Lockers are nearby at Oscar's Super Service.

Package pickup: Merchandise bought in the park can be sent to the entrance to pick up later. No charge; allow 3 hours. Packages can be delivered the next day to Disney hotels or shipped nationally.

Parking: $14/day per car. Free for Disney hotel guests.

Stroller rentals: At Oscar's Super Service inside the park entrance (Singles $15/day, $13/day length of stay. Doubles $31, $27). Replacements at Tatooine Traders.

Tip Board: Shows attraction wait times. Hollywood Blvd. at Sunset Blvd.

Transportation: Boats, walkways lead to Epcot and the BoardWalk, Yacht and Beach Club, Swan and Dolphin resorts. Buses serve all other Disney resorts, Magic Kingdom (via TTC), Epcot, Animal Kingdom, Blizzard Beach and ESPN Wide World of Sports; no direct service to Downtown Disney, Typhoon Lagoon.

Wheelchair, scooter rentals: At Oscar's Super Service. Wheelchairs $12/day, $10/day length of stay. 4-wheel scooters $50/day, $20 deposit.

Re-creating the look of Hollywood in its heyday, the park features replicas of Los Angeles buildings of the era. Many display a 1930 Streamline Moderne style that emphasized curving forms and horizontal lines. Disney's Legends of Hollywood shop (above) recalls the 1939 Academy Theater. At the far left is the original building; at left is how it has appeared since the 1960s, after much of its facade was removed.

complete films such as 1998's "Mulan" and 2002's "Lilo & Stitch." A radio studio was the home of the first children's radio network (Radio Aahs) and later Radio Disney.

Over time, Disney management decided to downsize and eventually close all aspects of its Florida production center. Today, no television or motion-picture work is done at the park except special broadcasts during events such as the annual ESPN—The Weekend. Radio Disney is now based in Burbank, Calif.

An old-fashioned Hollywood gala, the 1989 Grand Opening for what was then called the "Disney-MGM Studios" theme park featured appearances by many Tinseltown legends, including Lauren Bacall, George Burns, Audrey Hepburn and Bob Hope. The event was aired as a two-hour special on NBC-TV.

Fun finds. Hollywood Blvd: ❶ Second-story offices above the second entrance to Keystone Clothiers include those of tailor Justin Stitches. **Echo Lake:** Offices behind that building include ❷ the acting-and-voice studio Sights and Sounds (motto: "We've Finished Some of Hollywood's Finest"), run by master thespian Ewell M. Pressum, voice coach Singer B. Flatt and account executive Bill Moore and ❸ those of dentists C. Howie Pullum, Ruth Canal and Les Payne. ❹ Crates left of Min & Bill's snack stand refer to films "Casablanca," "Citizen Kane," "Gone With the Wind," "It's a Wonderful Life" and "The Producers." **Streets of America:** ❺ A back corner of the Stage 1 Company Store includes the Muppet lockers and Happiness Hotel front desk from 1981's "The Great Muppet Caper." ❻ Nearly

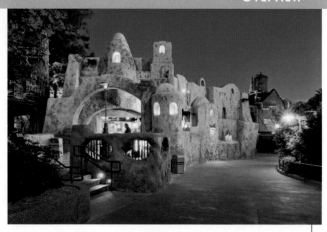

The exit to the Star Tours attraction, the Tatooine Traders gift shop holds a plethora of "Star Wars" merchandise as well as souvenirs of the ride. The desert-planet home of Anakin and Luke Skywalker, Tatooine appears in nearly every "Star Wars" movie.

two dozen silly signs in that shop include one over a doorway that reads "Absolutely no point beyond this point." **Sunset Blvd:** ❼ An office above Villains in Vogue is home to the International Brotherhood of Second Assistant Directors (say it slowly: IBSAD), a union with the motto "We're standing behind you." During the Great Depression "Second Assistant Director" was a mercy title given to go-fers, who were often told to "Get coffee and stand behind me."

Hidden Mickeys. Hollywood Blvd: ❶ In the black decorative molding below the second-floor windows of Cover Story. **Echo Lake:** ❷ As washers used to secure tops of coffee tables in the Tune-In Lounge. **Streets of America:** Outside the Stage 1 Company Store ❸ as purple paint drips on a recessed light under a bronze lion head. Inside the store, ❹ as green drips on a wood bureau shelf. ❺ Mickey's red shorts hang above the hotel desk. Inside Mama Melrose's Ristorante Italiano, ❻ as a spot on the right shoulder of a dalmatian in a lobby statue, and ❼ as a leaf on a vine to the right of the check-in podium, at the bottom right of a lattice fence. Inside Toy Story Pizza Planet, ❽ as star clusters in a mural above the cash registers, near the pizza-slice constellation, left of the spaceship; ❾ a three-quarter profile appears as moon craters in a mural above the arcade. ❿ In the Writer's Stop as yellow stickers on ceiling stage lights. **Sunset Blvd:** ⓫ Behind the Rosie's All-American Cafe counter as three gauges on a welding torch. ⓬ Along the walkways, impressions along the curbs read "Mortimer & Co. Contractors 1928," a reference to Walt Disney's original name for the mouse that became Mickey, which Disney created in 1928.

Notable Shops

Adrian & Edith's Head to Toe: Embroidered, monogrammed items. Custom Mickey ears. Hollywood Blvd.

AFI Showcase Shop: Show-biz items. At the exit to the Studio Backlot Tour. Streets of America.

Animation Gallery: Lithographs, oils, porcelain, 2-ft. character figurines, Disney books. Animation Courtyard.

It's a Wonderful Shop: Christmas items. Streets of America.

Keystone Clothiers: Fashion apparel, jewelry. Hollywood Blvd.

L.A. Cinema Storage: Children's wear, toys. Hollywood Blvd.

Legends of Hollywood: Boys toys. Sunset Blvd.

Mickey's of Hollywood: Main souvenir store. Hollywood Blvd.

Once Upon a Time / Mouse About Town / Sunset Club Couture: Fashion apparel, fine jewelry, watches. Sunset Blvd.

Rock Around the Shop: Rock 'n' Roller Coaster apparel, toys. Sunset Blvd.

Sid Cahuenga's One-Of-A-Kind: Show-biz memorabilia, autographs. Hollywood Blvd.

Stage 1 Co. Store: Children's, Muppets items. Housewares. Streets of America.

Sweet Spells / Villains in Vogue: Candy, Disney Villain items. Sunset Blvd.

Tatooine Traders: "Star Wars" items. Star Tours souvenirs. Streets of America.

Tower Gifts: Tower of Terror, "Twilight Zone" items. Sunset Blvd.

The Writer's Stop: Coffee shop, books, housewares. Streets of America.

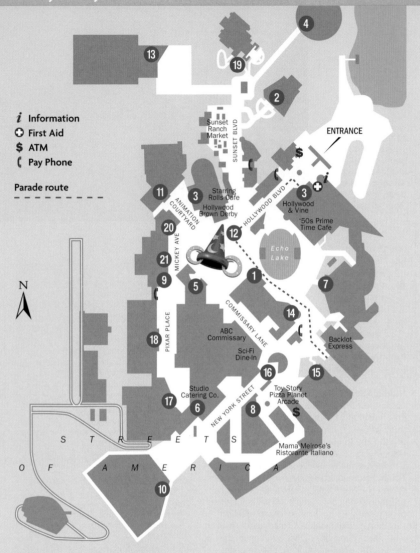

Information

i Information
O First Aid
$ ATM
(Pay Phone

Parade route

ENTRANCE

Sunset Ranch Market
SUNSET BLVD
Starring Rolls Cafe
Hollywood Brown Derby
HOLLYWOOD BLVD
Hollywood & Vine
'50s Prime Time Cafe
ANIMATION COURTYARD
MICKEY AVE
Echo Lake
PIXAR PLACE
ABC Commissary
COMMISSARY LANE
Sci-Fi Dine-In
Backlot Express
Studio Catering Co.
NEW YORK STREET
Toy Story Pizza Planet Arcade
Mama Melrose's Ristorante Italiano

N

S T R E E T S
O F   A M E R I C A

1. The American Idol Experience
2. Beauty and the Beast—Live on Stage
3. Disney Junior—Live on Stage!
4. Fantasmic!
5. The Great Movie Ride
6. "Honey, I Shrunk the Kids" Playground
7. Indiana Jones Epic Stunt Spectacular!
8. Jim Henson's MuppetVision 3-D
9. Journey Into Narnia Prince Caspian
10. Lights! Motors! Action!
11. The Magic of Disney Animation

12. Pixar Pals Countdown to Fun Parade
13. Rock 'n' Roller Coaster Starring Aerosmith
14. Sounds Dangerous
15. Star Tours: The Adventures Continue
16. Streets of America cityscapes
17. Studio Backlot Tour
18. Toy Story Mania!
19. The Twilight Zone Tower of Terror
20. Voyage of the Little Mermaid
21. Walt Disney: One Man's Dream

Attractions at a Glance

Exhibits

9 Journey Into Narnia Prince Caspian: ★ **Movie promo** Glorified trailer. Some props. Allow 15 min. Avg wait 15 min. Violent video. Mickey Ave. next to Pixar Place.

11 The Magic of Disney Animation: ★★★★ ✔ **Animation exhibits, activities** Short film, computer games, character meet-and-greet, exhibits, drawing lesson. Allow 45 min. Avg wait 15 min. Animation Courtyard.

16 Streets of America cityscapes: ★★★ **Simulated backlot** Movie-set-style facades replicate New York City, San Francisco. Unlimited; allow 15 min. No wait. Streets of America.

21 Walt Disney: One Man's Dream: ★★★★ ✔ **Personal, park artifacts; movie** Walt Disney, Disney Co. memorabilia; short biographical film. Allow 35 min. No wait. Mickey Ave.

Parade

12 Pixar Pals Countdown to Fun Parade: ★ **Character procession** Gutted former Block Party Bash. 6 min. Hollywood Blvd, Echo Lake.

Playground

6 'Honey, I Shrunk the Kids' Playground: ★★★ **Themed play area** Soft-floored outdoor spot has tunnels, oversized props themed to movie. Unlimited; allow 15–30 min. No wait. Streets of America.

Rides

5 The Great Movie Ride: ★★★★ ✔ **Indoor tram ride** Tours classic film scenes that feature robotic characters. 22 min. Avg wait 30 min. "Alien" creature moves toward you. Gunshots, fire. Hollywood Blvd.

13 Rock 'n' Roller Coaster Starring Aerosmith: ★★★★★ ✔ FASTPASS **Powered indoor roller coaster** Dark, corkscrews, goes upside down, blares rock music. Very fast start. 1 min 22 sec. Avg wait 70 min. Height min 48 in. Sunset Blvd.

15 Star Tours: The Adventures Continue: ★★★★ ✔ FASTPASS **3-D motion simulator** Wacky adventure aboard "Star Wars" spaceship. Redone for 2011. 7 min. Avg wait 25 min. Height min 40 in. Can cause motion sickness. Echo Lake.

18 Toy Story Mania!: ★★★★★ ✔ FASTPASS **Shooting gallery** Ride-through series of 3-D video games. 7 min. Avg wait 90 min. Pixar Place.

19 The Twilight Zone Tower of Terror: ★★★★★ ✔ FASTPASS **Indoor drop tower** Sudden, swift drops, dark lift; creepy atmosphere. Out-of-control elevator falls 13 stories. 4 min. Avg wait 55 min. Height min 40 in. Sunset Blvd.

Sound-effects show

14 Sounds Dangerous: ★ **Dark 'movie'** Sound-effects headphone show. Stars Drew Carey. 12 min. Avg wait 7 min. Scary sounds. Seasonal. Echo Lake.

Special-effects tour

17 Studio Backlot Tour: ★ **Tram tour** Backlot-themed walking/tram tour includes a stop in effects-filled Catastrophe Canyon. 30–40 min. Avg wait 20 min. Water demo uses fire; canyon has disasters. Streets of America.

Theatrical shows

1 The American Idol Experience: ★★★★ ✔ **Talent show** Singing contest stars park guests; audience members pick winner. Realistic "Idol" atmosphere. 20–25 min. Finale 45 min. Echo Lake.

2 Beauty and the Beast—Live on Stage: ★★★★★ ✔ **Stage musical** Musical tale old as time. 25 min. Gaston stabs the Beast. Sunset Blvd.

3 Disney Junior—Live on Stage!: ★★★★★ **Puppet show** Preschooler show stars Disney Junior TV characters. 22 min. Avg wait 20 min. Animation Courtyard.

4 Fantasmic!: ★★★★ **Outdoor spectacle** Evening extravaganza has dozens of Disney characters, lasers, dancing fountains, water screens, fireworks. 25 min. Arrive 90 min early. Loud noises, bright flashes, fire, villains. Sunset Blvd.

7 Indiana Jones Epic Stunt Spectacular!: ★★★★ NEXT-SHOW FASTPASS **Physical stunts** Performers re-enact scenes from 1981's "Raiders of the Lost Ark." 30 min. Avg wait 10 min. Echo Lake.

10 Lights, Motors, Action! Extreme Stunt Show: ★★ **Automotive stunts** Outdoor show features action-movie chase scenes with jumping cars, motorcycles. 33 min. Avg wait 20 min. Streets of America.

20 Voyage of The Little Mermaid: ★★★★ ✔ FASTPASS **Puppet and stage show** Musical stage show tells Ariel's story with puppets, live singer, effects. 17 min. Avg wait 20 min. Giant puppet Ursula threatens. Animation Courtyard.

3-D movie

8 Jim Henson's MuppetVision 3-D: ★★★★ ✔ **Comedic tour of 3-D lab** Muppet cast, many in-theater effects. Fun, detailed queue. 25 min. Avg wait 15 min. Streets of America.

Off to see the Wizard, Dorothy and her "Wizard of Oz" cohorts approach the Emerald City in a scene at The Great Movie Ride. Dog Toto stands near the bottom right corner.

The Great Movie Ride

★★★★ ✔ **Hollywood Boulevard** 22 min. Capacity: 560. Indoor, air-conditioned queue. Fear factor: Contains gunshots, sometimes fire; the "Alien" creature appears suddenly; the Wicked Witch looks real. Access: ECV users must transfer; assistive listening, handheld captioning. Debuted: 1989.

The stars of classic films sing, swing, fly, cower, sneer and threaten in this indoor tram tour. A robotic tribute to Tinseltown, it travels through soundstage sets that depict nine major films. Unfortunately, its scenes only include movies made before 1989, and its video clips are distinctly low-res.

Guests pass Gene Kelly "Singin' in the Rain" (1952) and "Public Enemy" James Cagney (1931), encounter a stalking "Alien" (1979) with Sigourney Weaver and confront the Wicked Witch from "The Wizard of Oz" (1939), a figure that flexes its backbone, swivels its hips and points its finger.

Additional sets portray the Fountain of Beauty from "Footlight Parade" (1933), the jungle of "Tarzan and His Mate" (1934), the airport finale of "Casablanca" (1942), the rooftops of "Mary Poppins" (1964) and the Well of Souls from "Raiders of the Lost Ark" (1981). Comedy comes from the tram

operator, a self-absorbed movie buff; a second live performer hijacks your vehicle. The ride concludes with a montage of film clips.

An opulent queue includes a carousel horse used in "Mary Poppins." A second room shows clips from vintage movie trailers that serve as the ride's coming attractions.

The entrance facade is a full-scale reproduction of the landmark Grauman's Chinese Theatre. Celebrity handprints (all real except those of Judy Garland) fill the entrance plaza.

Average wait times

Time	Standby line	Fastpass time
9:00a	0 min	(n/a)
10:00a	20 min	(n/a)
11:00a	30 min	(n/a)
Noon	40 min	(n/a)
1:00p	35 min	(n/a)
2:00p	35 min	(n/a)
3:00p	30 min	(n/a)
4:00p	35 min	(n/a)
5:00p	30 min	(n/a)
6:00p	35 min	(n/a)
7:00p	35 min	(n/a)
8:00p	25 min	(n/a)
9:00p	25 min	(n/a)

"Well, that's a mighty tough territory you're headin' into, pilgrim," a robotic John Wayne warns passersby in The Great Movie Ride. Quoting Wayne's mantra from 1954's "Hondo," he adds "A long time ago, I made me a rule: let people do what they want."

Where's the wizard? Though the ride has only one scene from "The Wizard of Oz," Disney built it to have three. A clip from the 1940 Disney movie "Fantasia" plays in what was meant to be Dorothy's tornado; riders can still spot its sepia-toned funnel. After guests leave Munchkinland, they were to go off to see the wizard in the Emerald City, where they would be told to "pay no attention to that man behind the curtain." Last-minute copyright snags forced the cutbacks.

Where to sit. The first few seats in either the first or second row of the tram will put you next to the hijacker, who may direct a few unscripted lines your way ("Hiya doll!"). Request these seats at the boarding area.

Fun finds. ❶ During a 1995 handprint ceremony for Charlton Heston, a photographer yelled "Charlton!" just as the then-72-year-old star was drawing the "R" in his first name, causing him to look up. When Heston got back to work, he accidentally skipped the "L" in his name, creating a signature that reads "Charton" Heston. ❷ Along the left floor of the Nostromo spaceship, inside jokes on the first video monitor include the ride's "estimated time till next special effects failure." ❸ The third Nostromo monitor lists an astronaut as "still programming the witch."

Hidden Mickeys. ❶ As a silhouetted profile in the second-story windows on your left as your tram enters Gangster Alley. ❷ On a partially covered poster on the alley's left wall. ❸ As a profile on a broken gray stone below the Ark in the Well of Souls. ❹ A Mickey pharaoh appears on the Well's left wall, just past the second statue of Anubis. An Egyptian Donald Duck is serving him cheese. ❺ Other hidden characters: Minnie Mouse hides in the boarding-area mural, above and to the right of a central tile roof, tucked under palm fronds. On the left wall of the Well of Souls, a central carving shows a pharaoh holding R2-D2 while C-3PO repairs his friend with a screwdriver. As many "Raiders" fans know, the carving appears on the same wall in the movie.

An Old West bank catches fire in a scene from The Great Movie Ride (above left). An inside joke in the ride's "Alien" scene, a video screen (right) lists an astronaut as "still programming the witch."

Clockwise from top left: Contestants await their fate, judges react to a singer, Callie Craig rushes out of the audition center after winning a spot in the show, armrest keypads tally audience votes.

The American Idol Experience

★★★★ ✓ **Echo Lake** 20–25 min, finale 45 min. Show times at 11a, noon, 1p, 2p, 4p, 5p, 6p. Finale 7p (times may vary during peak and slow periods). Capacity: 1040. Covered outdoor queue. Fear factor: None. Access: Guests may remain in wheelchairs, ECVs; assistive listening. Debuted: 2009.

The audience selects the winners of this unique live talent show, where amateur singers compete for a chance to be first in line at a real "American Idol" audition. Just like on television, an entertaining emcee hosts with the help of a panel of judges, and singers compete on a flashy stage in front of roving camera operators. In this case, though, the winners are determined by guests in the theater. Audience members vote using electronic keypads that are on the armrests of their seats. The indoor auditorium is comfortable and air-conditioned.

Each day a series of qualifying contests leads to a championship finale, which is almost always the best show. Longer than the preliminary rounds, it pits the earlier winners against each other. They compete for a pass that puts them first in line at an audition for the television program. Those who have made it onto the TV show include Aaron Kelly, who finished fifth in Season 9 (2010) and Victoria Huggins, who made it to Hollywood Week in Season 10 (2011).

Though the judges are occasionally too cruel or suggestive given the age of the contestants (many of which are young teens), the show is fun to watch. Singers may flub lyrics, sing off key or awkwardly try to dance; every now and then someone belts out a performance that earns a standing ovation.

The stage looks just like the one on TV, with spiral-staircase catwalks and an overdose of video monitors. Dramatic lighting includes color-shifting LED strips that look like neon tubes. Thanks to small transmitters performers wear, spotlights automatically track them as they move about the stage.

Aspiring contestants audition backstage early each day (minimum age 14; tryouts 9 a.m.–2 p.m.). The process begins with an a capella song performed in a small room in front of a Disney screener. Those making the cut sing to a backing track, using their choice of tunes from a list of about 100. Those passing that test meet with a voice coach and hair and make-up artists before heading onstage.

Crowds. For the first show of the day guests can usually show up at the last minute and

Teenager Victoria Huggins (right) performs at the American Idol Experience. She later appeared on the 2011 season of the "American Idol" television show, where judge Randy Jackson remarked "You have the most personality on 'American Idol' — ever!" Below, Meta Summer wins a "Golden Ticket."

still get a good seat. For other performances arrive about 20 minutes early.

Family matters. The show gives children a rare sense of empowerment. Since every seat has a voting keypad, their votes count just as much as those from adults.

Hidden Mickeys. As dark splotches on both the left and right side of the onstage arch (hidden among other splotches).

ATAS Hall of Fame Showcase. Located in front of the theater, this small plaza has 15 bronze busts of television stars, all members of the Academy of Television Arts and Sciences Hall of Fame. Included are Lucille Ball, Andy Griffith and Mary Tyler Moore. Plaques on a back wall list all the inductees for each year. The plaza draws little attention, even from Disney. The company stopped adding busts and plaques in 1996.

Sounds Dangerous. ★ 12 min. Capacity: 240. No wait. Outdoor covered queue. Fear factor: Some scary sounds. Access: Guests may stay in wheelchairs, ECVs. Assistive listening. Debuted: 1999. Open only during peak periods. Love Drew Carey? Then you might like this sound-effects show, located next to The American Idol Experience. Seated in a dark theater, you're part of a test audience for a television pilot that stars Carey as a klutzy TV investigator. When he shorts out his spy cam, the theater goes dark and you're at the mercy of your imagination as Carey opens a jar of bees, gets a shave and bumps an elephant. With few visuals, the show's slapstick comedy often falls flat. Better is the postshow, SoundWorks, which lets you dub your voice to cartoon and movie stars and create old-fashioned sound effects with help from late Disney legend Jimmy MacDonald. Walls display the actual gadgets he used for 20 classic Disney films.

Fistfights and fireballs spice up the Indiana Jones stunt show. Out front, gift stands display wares on trucks from the movie, while an underground archeologist hopes passersby don't pull his rope.

Indiana Jones Epic Stunt Spectacular

★★★★ *NEXT-SHOW FASTPASS* Echo Lake 30 min. Capacity: 2,000. Covered outdoor theater. Show times vary. Fear factor: Billowing fire. Closed during rain. Access: Guests may remain in wheelchairs, ECVs. Assistive listening; handheld captioning; Audio Description. Debuted: 1989, revised 2000.

Fireballs, gunshots, spears, swords, a great big boulder and a muscle-bound Nazi threaten Indiana Jones and his girlfriend Marion in this outdoor scheduled stage show, which re-creates physical stunts from the 1981 movie "Raiders of the Lost Ark." Between scenes guests witness how backdrops can be quickly set up and dismantled, how heavy-looking props can be feather-light and how stunt actors fake a punch.

Basically unchanged since its debut in 1989, the show is still entertaining and often funny, especially if you've never seen it before.

Just like the movie, the show opens as an Indy stunt double explores a Mayan temple to pursue a golden idol only to be chased by a 12-foot rolling boulder. Next, Indy fights off Cairo villains while Marion makes a death-defying escape out of a flipping, flaming truck. The finale takes place on a North African Nazi airfield. When a Flying Wing rolls in for fuel, Indy and Marion fight Nazis in, on and around the plane, fleeing to safety just as leaking fuel sparks a fiery explosion.

For flavor, Disney pretends the show is a real film shoot. Mock cameramen peer through mock cameras; a fake director barks out fake directions. When the "Assistant Director of the Second Unit" decides "We're going to shoot 36 instead of 24 frames per second," his boss declares "I like it!"

The show also uses a handful of adult audience volunteers, who don costumes to portray Cairo villagers. To be picked, arrive at least 15 minutes early, then jump up, wave and scream with wild abandon when the "casting director" asks for volunteers.

Film producer George Lucas oversaw the show's creation; "Raiders" stunt coordinator Glenn Randall designed the stunts. The performance uses 17 live actors.

Crowds. The first performance of the day usually has the smallest crowd; midday shows can fill to capacity 20 minutes before show times. The last show is often the best looking, as the darker sky makes the explosions more dramatic. Arrive early to sit in the first few rows; you'll get a closer view and feel heat from the fires.

Indiana Jones and girlfriend Marion Ravenwood flee to safety just before a fiery explosion in the finale of the Indiana Jones Epic Stunt Spectacular (right), which re-creates scenes from the 1981 movie "Raiders of the Lost Ark." Below, selected audience volunteers portray Cairo villagers.

A closer look. "Raiders of the Lost Ark" starts its story in 1936. Archaeology professor Dr. Henry "Indiana" Jones Jr. has just returned from Peru, where he has failed to recover a golden idol. But when the Army learns that Nazi Germany wants to find the Ark of the Covenant (a casket used by ancient Hebrews to hold the original Ten Commandments) it sends Indy to find it first.

Reuniting with gutsy former girlfriend Marion Ravenwood, Jones soon arrives in Cairo, where Nazi henchmen kidnap Marion and steal her medallion, which can reveal the Ark's location. As Indy fights off a gang of assassins, Marion knocks one out with a handy frying pan, but soon is taken away in a truck, which explodes.

Indy later finds Marion being held captive at an excavation camp where Nazis are about to fly the Ark to Germany on a Flying Wing. While the plane is fueling, the couple takes it over. Marion shoots Nazis from the cockpit while Indy's fight with a mechanic ends with the bad guy shredded by a propeller. When leaking fuel catches fire, Indy and Marion run to safety just before everything blows up.

Family matters. Consider seeing the movie first to make sure your children are familiar with the 30-year-old story.

Fun finds. ❶ Out front, just to the left of the Fastpass machines, a British archeologist has dug a hole and lowered himself down to the bottom of it. Pull on his rope (it's next to a sign that reads "Warning! Do Not Pull Rope") to hear him get irritated ("I say! Stop mucking about up there!"). ❷ On the exitway behind the Outpost gift shop sits a Nazi staff car and truck, as well as the "Steel Beast" tank (its side gun barrel still exploded from being stuffed with a rock) used in the filming of 1989's "Indiana Jones and the Last Crusade."

A podrace through the desert canyons of Tatooine highlights Star Tours: The Adventures Continue. At several points during the journey the audience can change where the story is going.

Star Tours: The Adventures Continue

★★★★ ✓ **FASTPASS Echo Lake** 7 min. Capacity: 240. Indoor, air-conditioned queue. Fear factor: The vehicle's unpredictable dives and sways can cause nausea in guests of any age. Guests should be free from motion sickness; pregnancy; high blood pressure; heart, back or neck problems. Access: ECV guests must transfer to wheelchairs; guest activated captioning available. Height min: 40 in. Debuted: 1989 (Disneyland 1987), updated 2011.

Riders travel to multiple destinations in this high-definition 3-D motion simulator, which will debut in the summer of 2011. A rollicking ride through the universe of the "Star Wars" motion pictures, it updates an attraction which has been a park staple since 1989. Now incorporating characters and scenes from the three "Star Wars" prequel films released between 1999 and 2005, the ride has a new plot and new 3-D video. Its story takes place between 2005's "Episode 3: Revenge of the Sith" and the original 1977 film now known as "Episode 4: A New Hope."

The most unique aspect of the new ride is its variable flight route. At several points during the journey the audience can change where the story is going. "There are an incredible number of different variations," explains Al Weiss, president of Walt Disney Parks and Resorts. Adds Imagineer Tony Baxter, "You'll be able to go on it a million times without seeing all the stuff we've put in there." (The actual number of different experiences: 54.)

Highlights include a podrace on the desert planet of Tatooine (the home of Anakin and Luke Skywalker) and a trip through a cityscape on the planet of Coruscant (the capital of both the old and new "Star Wars" republics). At one point, the StarSpeeder shuttle vehicle—now a StarSpeeder 1000, a

Average wait times

Time	Standby line	Fastpass time
9:00a	0 min	10:00a
10:00a	15 min	11:00a
11:00a	30 min	12:00p
Noon	40 min	1:00p
1:00p	35 min	2:00p
2:00p	40 min	2:50p
3:00p	45 min	4:00p
4:00p	40 min	5:00p
5:00p	25 min	5:50p
6:00p	20 min	6:30p
7:00p	15 min	7:25p
8:00p	20 min	(out)
9:00p	20 min	(out)

A lifesize vehicle maintenance bay sits alongside the Star Tours queue. Attended by Audio-Animatronics versions of "Star Wars" droids C-3PO and R2-D2, a StarSpeeder shuttle vehicle undergoes tests.

precursor to the 3000 of the original ride—is chased by rogue bounty hunter Boba Fett.

Rebel Alliance Supreme Commander Admiral Ackbar communicates with the vehicle holographically. Scenes include prequel characters such as citizens of Naboo (home planet of Queen Amidala and Jar Jar Binks) and insectoid Geonosians from 2002's "Episode 2: Attack of the Clones." A few aliens from the original trilogy also pop up, including tusked Aqualish and big-brained Bith, the latter best known as cantina musicians in "A New Hope."

Characters created specifically for the attraction include Aly San San, a spokesdroid modeled after the WA-7 "Waitress Droid" from "Attack of the Clones" voiced by Allison Janney (best known for her role as C. J. Cregg on the television series "The West Wing") and new StarSpeeder pilot Ace, a new AC-38 droid who gets replaced by C-3PO. Former Star Tours pilot Rex makes a cameo appearance.

Serving as the attraction's executive producer, "Star Wars" creator George Lucas worked on the update for more than three years. "Star Wars" actors who participated include Anthony Daniels, who recorded new dialogue for C-3PO, James Earl Jones (Darth Vader) and Peter Mayhew (Chewbacca).

As before, an indoor queue weaves through a StarSpeeder maintenance bay where C-3PO and R2-D2 repair a StarSpeeder, then winds through a Droidnostics Center as a robotic mechanic assembles pilots and navigators. Themed as a travel commercial for the Star Tours Company, a new video promotes the destinations of Bespin, Endor and Alderaan ("recently voted Safest Planet in the Galaxy by 'Hyperspace Traveler'").

A closer look. The grounds resemble a stage set from 1983's "Episode 6: Return of the Jedi." Near a village of Ewoks (the teddy-bear-like creatures that helped save the day in that film) is a captured Imperial Walker, the empire's elephant-like All Terrain Armored Transport (AT-AT) that walked on giant mechanical legs. It was introduced in 1980's "Episode 5: The Empire Strikes Back." At night, guests hear the Ewoks talking and drumming in their tree huts.

Creating a space fantasy that takes place "a long time ago, far, far away," the "Star Wars" movies tell a tale of good versus evil. Combining a space-opera plot—similar to those of the Buck Rogers movie serials of the 1930s and 1940s—with special effects and modeling inspired by the 1968 film "2001—A Space Odyssey," the films' mix of wit, mythology and simulated reality has entranced audiences for more than three decades. One of the key elements of the "Star Wars" universe is the Force, an omnipresent, controllable energy field that, as described in the first film, "binds the galaxy together."

Enclosed machines about the size of garbage trucks, motion simulators create the sensation of flight by synchronizing tilts, dives and other movements to a video that simulates the view out of a windshield.

Where to sit. Choose a middle row for a fun ride that won't make you sick, or a back seat for lots of rock and roll. The front row is the most calm, but may be too close for voyagers to fully enjoy the 3-D effects.

Family matters. Perfect for snapshots, a climb-on reproduction of a Speeder bike—the woods-weaving motorcycle-like vehicle seen in the movie "Return of the Jedi"—sits across from the ride entrance.

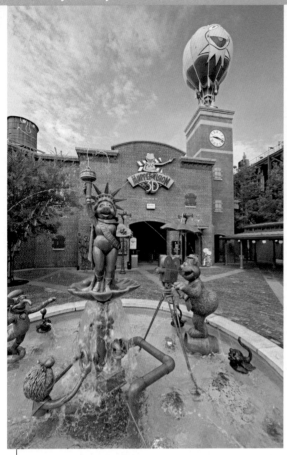

Re-creating her role in the finale of the MuppetVision 3-D movie, Miss Piggy poses as "Ms." Liberty in a fountain in front of the theater. Other Muppets film the pig as she stands on a half shell, an homage to the 1879 William Bouguereau painting "The Birth of Venus."

Jim Henson's MuppetVision 3-D

★ ★ ★ ★ ✔ **Streets of America** 25 min including preshow. Capacity: 584. Indoor, air-conditioned queue; also rarely used shaded outdoor area. Fear factor: None. Access: Guests may remain in wheelchairs, ECVs; assistive listening, reflective and activated video captioning, Audio Description. Debuted: 1991.

"We invited distinguished scientists from all over the world to come and work here," Kermit the Frog says as he introduces a secret research facility in this 3-D movie. "Unfortunately, none of them showed up."

Undeterred, Kermit emcees a demonstration of the inventions of bumbling Dr. Bunsen Honeydew, which cause so much havoc they nearly destroy the theater. Along the way, guests get squirted with water, showered with bubbles and caught in a crossfire of cannonballs. And despite Kermit's promises that "at no time will we be stooping to cheap 3-D tricks," Fozzie Bear and the rest of the cast do just that. In the theater (the red-velvet affair from the 1970s television series "The Muppet Show") formally-clad penguins make up a robotic orchestra, while cranky curmudgeons Statler and Waldorf toss barbs from a balcony box. Behind the audience, the Swedish Chef mans a haphazardly assembled projection booth where everything, at least at first, "is goin' der floomey floomey."

A very bad Mickey Mouse impersonator highlights an inventive preshow video. It's shown in a "prop warehouse" that holds real Muppet memorabilia.

Created in 1990, the movie hasn't aged perfectly. It stars two of Henson's least

Kermit the Frog, Miss Piggy and Fozzie Bear are among the stars of Jim Henson's MuppetVision 3-D. The theater includes robotic versions of Statler and Waldorf, who toss barbs from a balcony box.

appealing characters, Bean Bunny and Waldo C. Graphic, and its premise—that 3-D film technology is something new—is out of date. Timeless, however, are the show's charm, humor and sweetness. Digitally restored in 2010, both the preshow film and the main movie are once again bright and clear.

Where to sit. If you can, sit in the rear center of the theater. The film will be in great focus, and the 3-D effects more evident. Avoid the first few rows; the images separate when viewed too closely, and some require an audience in front of you to make sense.

A closer look. Created when digital animation was in its infancy, the Waldo character was the world's first digitized puppet, and, thanks to this film, the first digital 3-D character. To create its movements a puppeteer wore an electronic glove, which transmitted signals to a computer that generated a wireframe image. Digital artists then added color, detail and texture.

Other scenes were created with low-tech methods. When Miss Piggy sings "Dream a Little Dream of Me," the fluttering butterfly was planned as an expensive optical effect until Henson realized the comedic potential of making it merely a cloth insect on a string.

To create the illusion of Sweetums bouncing a paddleball into the audience, performer John Henson (Jim's son, then age 24) simply hit a real paddleball directly at the camera. Though his costume completely blocked his view, the young Henson hit the ball perfectly on the first take. The scene channels a famously pointless moment from the 1953 Vincent Price 3-D film, "House of Wax."

The outdoor queue and bus shelter are an homage to a closet. In 1963, when the Muppets were booked on NBC's "The Jack

Paar Program," Jim Henson and his associates mistakenly arrived six hours early. To kill time, they decorated a utility closet with Muppet touch-up paint, covering the walls and pipes with loopy designs and faces.

The show was Henson's last major project. He died suddenly just before it was finished. That's him you hear as the voice of Kermit as well as the Swedish Chef.

Fun finds. ❶ An outdoor staircase leads to the show's projection room, from which the Swedish Chef runs an editing-and-catering business. Its slogan: "Frøöm Qüick Cüts tø Cöld Cüts." ❷ An Acme anvil honors classic Warner Bros. cartoons. ❸ Atop a side wall, large planters hold ice cream sundaes. One is half-eaten. ❹ In the entryway, a Security Office "Key Under Mat" sign isn't lying. ❺ Inside the office is a wanted poster for Fozzie (for impersonating a comic) and a Piggy pinup calendar. ❻ A directory case lists Statler and Waldorf's Institute

Average wait times

Time	Standby line	Fastpass time
9:00a	0 min	(n/a)
10:00a	5 min	(n/a)
11:00a	5 min	(n/a)
Noon	15 min	(n/a)
1:00p	20 min	(n/a)
2:00p	20 min	(n/a)
3:00p	20 min	(n/a)
4:00p	15 min	(n/a)
5:00p	5 min	(n/a)
6:00p	5 min	(n/a)
7:00p	5 min	(n/a)
8:00p	(closed)	(n/a)
9:00p	(closed)	(n/a)

IN SPACE, NO ONE CAN HEAR YOU "MEEP"!

BEAK·E

Whimsical pipes and posters line the outdoor queue area of Jim Henson's MuppetVision 3-D. Out front, a Hidden Mickey image of Mickey Mouse appears on a ring float in a fountain.

of Heckling and Browbeating and Gonzo's Dept. of Poultry and Mold Cultivation. **7** A sign above the 8-foot entrance archway reads "You must be shorter than this to enter." A chipped top indicates someone didn't see it. **8** A door leading to the MuppetLabs' Dept. of Artificial Reality reads "This is not a door." **9** In the queue room, hanging from the ceiling is a net full of Jell-O, a reference to 1950s Mouseketeer Annette Funicello. **10** Next to it is a bird cage with a perch—a fish. **11** A box for the Swedish Chef from Oompah, Sweden's "Sven & Ingmar's Kooking Kollection" holds "Der Noodle Frooper." **12** Catwalks hold toy soldiers and frontiersmen from the film's finale and the "Pigs in Space" SwineTrek spaceship from "The Muppet Show." **13** Along the walls are large reprints of the Henson Company's "Kermitage Collection" calendar portraits from 1984. They include parodies of Henri Rousseau ("The Sleepy Zootsy") and Hans Holbein ("Jester at the Court of Henry VIII")—a painting of Fozzie holding a banana up to his ear which includes the Latin phrase Bananum In Avre Habeo ("I'm holding a banana in my ear"). **14** A photo of a banjo-playing Jim Henson Muppet from a "Muppet Show" band hangs from the ceiling. **15** Down front is a "2-D Fruities" box that contains flat cutouts of a banana, cherry and lemon; a hydraulic tube from the film's MuppetVision machine; a box of Gonzo's props labeled "mold, fungus, helmets, helmets covered with fungus and mold, helmets with mold—no fungus" and "fungus and mold—no helmets;" and a crate of emergency tuxedos for the penguins stamped "Open in

the event of an event." **16** The birds' food has arrived in a container from Long Island Sound and Seafood Supplies ("Everything from Hearing to Herring"). **17** A sarcophagus peers through 3-D glasses. **18** In the movie, a Beethoven bust wears 3-D glasses on its head, as does a brass bald eagle. **19** The orchestra penguins cackle at Statler and Waldorf's barbs and cough when squirted by Fozzie's boutonniere. One gets sucked up by Beaker's VacuuMuppet. **20** Two goldfish eventually swim in a beaker above Chinese takeout boxes. **21** Statler and Waldorf gape at the MuppetVision machine, nod as Waldo bounces off people's heads, duck from the VacuuMuppet and hide when the Chef brings out his cannon. **22** Miss Piggy loses her head as she is pulled into the lake. It falls backward. **23** Some members of the marching band aren't wearing pants. **24** When the penguin orchestra fires a cannon at the Swedish Chef, he yells "Schtupid crazy birds!" **25** At the exit, a poster for penguin outfitter Frankie reads: "Large formalwear for the hard-to-fit. Small formalwear for the hard-to-find." **26** In the adjacent Stage 1 Company Store, the Muppet lockers and Happiness Hotel front desk from 1981's "The Great Muppet Caper" form a back corner. **27** Nearly two dozen silly signs in the store include one over a doorway that reads "Absolutely no point beyond this point."

Hidden Mickeys. 1 On Gonzo's ring float in the fountain. **2** In a small sketch of a DNA model in the "5 Reasons" poster along the outdoor queue. **3** As a test pattern in the early moments of the preshow video.

Looks can be deceiving in the Streets of America, a backlot-style walk-through area. Detailed facades, authentic props and painted flats create illusions of New York and, above, San Francisco.

Streets of America cityscapes

★ ★ ★ **Streets of America** Unlimited; allow 15 minutes. No wait. Fear factor: None. Access: Guests may remain in wheelchairs, ECVs. Debuted: 1989.

The illusion may fool you, especially in photographs. Using forced perspective techniques, skillful artwork and lots of detailing, the Streets of America section of the park re-creates cityscapes of New York City and San Francisco. The buildings are facades, as the place is meant to represent a movie set.

The area is dominated by Beaux Arts-style New York Street, a 500-foot thoroughfare based on the Big Apple's West 40th Street. The north end, a three-dimensional background piece, includes flat representations of the Chrysler, Empire State and Flatiron buildings. Recalling San Francisco, the cross street appears to be a hilly boulevard complete with a cable car on its back flat.

Other details include graffiti, soot stains and, on New York Street, a sidewalk stairwell that looks like it leads to a subway terminal. A corner drugstore's windows show antique merchandise, as do most shop windows. The antique stoplights were used on New York City roadways during the 1930s. Background noise rounds out the realism; Big Apple sound effects include honking horns, playing children, screeching buses, murmuring crowds and whistling police.

The area's best detail is an umbrella that hangs off a lamppost near the entrance to the Lights, Motors, Action stunt show. Meant to recall the 1952 movie "Singin' in the Rain," it often mists guests who stand under it.

Between Thanksgiving and New Year's Day the area is lavishly decorated for the holidays with the Osborne Family Spectacle of Dancing Lights. Christmas music—and Disney-fied "snow"—fills the air.

When the park opened New York Street was part of a two-hour Studio Backlot Tour, a tramway that was closed to other guests. That soon changed, creating today's huge pedestrian walkway. The cross street was re-themed as San Francisco in 2004; its left side was originally designed to look like London. The area has been used sporadically in the past as an actual movie and commercial set. Most notably, some of the outdoor scenes of the 1990 Warren Beatty/Madonna vehicle "Dick Tracy" were filmed here.

Tip. Bring a camera. Used as a background for snapshots, the area creates a sense of place that's sure to fool friends back home.

A car jumps through fire in the finale of the Lights, Motors, Action! stunt show. Other high points include tightly choreographed chase scenes involving multiple cars and motorcycles.

Lights, Motors, Action!

★★ **Streets of America** 33 min. Capacity: 5,000. Outdoor, shaded queue. Fear factor: Some gunshots; action is far from the seating area. Closed during rain. Access: Guests may remain in wheelchair, ECVs. Assistive listening. Debuted: 2005.

Vehicles fly through the air in this loud outdoor stage show, as stunt drivers demonstrate how chase scenes are created for action-adventure films. The stunts are elaborately choreographed: buzzing cars synchronize their spins, motorcycles skid in unison. Two guys end up on Jet Skis.

The premise is the filming of a European spy thriller in which a hero receives an envelope and bad guys try to stop him. After a film crew captures the stunts on video, the clips appear to be combined into a completed scene which plays on a wall-sized screen.

There are four segments. First, six Opel Corsas—two-stroke models specifically built for this show—race around in an orchestrated chase. The cars return to jump over a blockade of produce stands and trucks. Then three motorcycles arrive, one jumping through what appears to be a plate-glass window as the cars drive on two wheels. One man, then another, races on Jet Skis in

a short canal in the front of the stage. This scene ends as a motorcyclist falls and, thanks to a special jumpsuit, appears to catch on fire. For the finale, a car jumps directly at the audience as 40-foot fireballs billow in the air.

There's also a car that breaks in half, and a confusing segment where the crew plays a trick on a child volunteer.

Unfortunately, most of the action takes place far from the viewing area, making the show one of Disney's least immersive experiences. Narration is often drowned out by the revving motors and gunshots.

The set resembles a seaside village marketplace in southern France (one shop is the Café Fracas, the "restaurant of the noisy rumpus"). The show debuted at Disneyland Paris, hence the French connection.

Family matters. Surprising for a Disney production, the show displays a cavalier attitude toward violence. There's lots of gunplay, none of which is played for laughs.

Hidden Mickeys. ❶ A full-figure Mickey appears in the window of the Antiquites Brocante shop. ❷ The three-circle shape is formed by a gear and two circular belts in a corner of the window of the motorcycle shop.

Children race around a huge can of Play-Doh at the "Honey, I Shrunk the Kids" playground. A cushy floor makes falls relatively painless. Other props include a climb-on ant and a sneezing dog.

'Honey, I Shrunk the Kids' Playground

★★★ **Streets of America** Unlimited. Capacity: 240, including parents. No wait. Fear factor: None. Access: Guests may remain in wheelchairs, ECVs. Debuted: 1990.

Children can pretend they are the size of bugs at this outdoor playground, an over-sized backyard filled with plants, insects and discarded toys, each piece enlarged about 1,000 times beyond normal. Towering blades of grass curve overhead as kids scamper through dimly lit "ant tunnels" and get dribbled on by a dripping garden hose. Hidden among it all are many nooks and crannies.

Huge props include an Oreo cookie, a Super Soaker water gun, a climb-on ant and a slide that appears to be a roll of camera film. Today's kids may wonder about that last one.

The area stays pretty cool even on the hottest days. The massive faux plants block most of the sun, electric fans create a breeze, water areas spray and mist guests and, unlike the asphalt and concrete walkways everywhere else in the park, the playground's cushy floor doesn't retain heat. Water fountains are scattered throughout. Parents will find lots of places to sit and relax; on oversized twigs, pebbles and especially by a dog's paw-print.

The playground is the most fun early in the day, when the sky is overcast, or very late in the afternoon. It offers a great chance for children to burn off energy, something that many kids need at this particular theme park, since the Studios is relatively small and has so many attractions which require kids to sit still for long periods.

The playground is based on Disney's 1989 live-action movie "Honey, I Shrunk the Kids." In that flick, Inventor Professor Szalinski (Rick Moranis) mistakenly uses a new invention—the Electromagnetic Shrinking Machine—to zap his children down to the size of insects. The shrunken kids soon get lost in their own backyard.

Family matters. Bring a camera. Children can pose for memorable snapshots throughout the area, including on a giant spiderweb and atop fiddlehead ferns. It's easy for parents to lose sight of their children in this 11,000-square-foot play area, though there's only one exit (the narrow entrance) which is always monitored by a Disney cast member.

Fun find. Walk up to the top of the back wall to find the nose of a huge dog. It sniffs you, then sneezes.

© Disney

An earthquake, fire and flood occur back-to-back-to-back at the appropriately named Catastrophe Canyon, a special-effects stop on the Studio Backlot Tour tram ride

Studio Backlot Tour

★ **Streets of America** 30–40 min. Capacity: 1,000. Open 10a–6p. Outdoor, shaded queue. Fear factor: Simulated disasters. Cancelled during thunderstorms. Access: Guests may remain in wheelchairs, ECVs. Handheld and activated video captioning. Debuted: 1989, revised 2004.

To paraphrase Richard Nixon, let us be perfectly clear—this theme park has no backlot and therefore offers no tour through it. There used to be a backlot here, as well as real soundstages and an animation studio, but Disney shut all that down years ago. What's left is a water-effects tank, a staged prop room, a stop at a fancy faux disaster set and a peek into theme-park costume and set shops.

First up is a demonstration of how water cannons and fire bursts can simulate torpedo and bombing attacks, as volunteers get splashed on a PT boat. (Want to volunteer? Tell a cast member at the tour entrance.)

After walking through a dusty prop room, guests take a tram to Catastrophe Canyon, a special-effects area that simulates an earthquake, fire and flood. As the tram returns it passes some movie props as well as Walt Disney's personal jet. The exit is an American Film Institute Showcase exhibit of movie-villain costumes and antique film equipment.

Fun finds. The prop room holds ❶ cans of eyeballs and glue from 1988's "Who Framed Roger Rabbit," ❷ a tiny Austin of England taxi from the 1984 movie "The Muppets Take Manhattan" and ❸ furniture from the set of the television show "Dinosaurs."

Hidden Mickeys. ❶ In the prop room, on the "Marvin's Room" refrigerator and as hanging cannon balls. ❷ At Catastrophe Canyon, as gauges on your right atop a barrel.

Average wait times

Time	Standby line	Fastpass time
9:00a	(closed)	(n/a)
10:00a	15 min	(n/a)
11:00a	15 min	(n/a)
Noon	20 min	(n/a)
1:00p	25 min	(n/a)
2:00p	30 min	(n/a)
3:00p	35 min	(n/a)
4:00p	25 min	(n/a)
5:00p	15 min	(n/a)
6:00p	(closed)	(n/a)
7:00p	(closed)	(n/a)
8:00p	(closed)	(n/a)
9:00p	(closed)	(n/a)

Mickey Mouse is a puppet in Disney Junior—Live on Stage, a show that features the stars of "Mickey Mouse Clubhouse," "Handy Manny" and other television programs for young children

Disney Junior—Live on Stage!

★★★★★ **Animation Courtyard** 22 min. Capacity: 600. Shows 10a–5p. Outdoor shaded queue. Fear factor: None. Access: Guests may remain in wheelchairs, ECVs; assistive listening, reflective and activated captioning. Debuted: 2001, revised 2008, 2011.

Little children get to clap, dance, sing, shake, twist, call out their names, wave their arms, bounce and chase bubbles, leaves and streamers during this lively puppet show, which teaches gentle lessons about working together. When the host talks directly to the kids—not their parents—they know this is a show all their own.

The puppet show features the stars of four Disney Junior television programs— "Mickey Mouse Clubhouse" (Mickey and his pals help young viewers learn how to solve problems; when they need help they shout "Oh Tootles!" which brings forth a magical flying machine equipped with mouse-ka-tools; a clubhouse appears when they call "Meeska, Mooska, Mickey Mouse!"), "Handy Manny" (bilingual handyman Manny Garcia solves problems with talking tools), "Little Einsteins" (four young world travelers enjoy art and classical music) and "Jake and the Never Land Pirates" (in a story inspired by

Disney's 1953 film "Peter Pan," youngsters learn to solve problems as they try to outsmart Captain Hook and his sidekick Mr. Smee).

Production values are the equal of any Disney performance. The stage features an innovative sliding walkway that allows the human host to magically walk on the same floor as the puppets. The puppets' eyes blink and their mouths move.

Sound is crisp, and nearly a hundred spotlights ensure that everything—including, at times, the audience—is well lit.

Best of all, the show treats its young audience with respect. The stories are lessons, not lectures, as characters use teamwork to achieve their goals. The host addresses the children as equals, and bounces into the crowd to meet a few face-to-face.

The audience sits on a flat, carpeted floor, which makes it easy for children to get up and boogie. The semicircular stage curves into the seating area, so even those who arrive at the last minute are still fairly close to the action.

Family matters. Don't sit in the first three rows. Since the stage is elevated, children who do often can't see the characters.

Conceptual art and other memorabilia from Disney and Pixar movies is displayed in glass cases inside The Magic of Disney Animation building. The exhibits change often.

The Magic of Disney Animation

★★★★ ✔ **Animation Courtyard** Allow 45 min (film 10 min, Animation Academy 10 min, rest self-guided). Often opens at 10 a.m. Capacity: Theater 150; Animation Academy 50. Outdoor shaded queue. Fear factor: None. Access: Guests may remain in wheelchairs, ECVs; lap boards available for drawing; reflective, video captioning; Audio Description. Debuted: 1989, revised 2004.

You'll learn how Disney develops an animated character and then draw one yourself in this building. It also contains exhibits of concept art, character-greeting spots and some kids' touch-screen activities. The highlight is an "Animation Academy" drawing lesson. Paper and pencil in front of you, you'll draw a particular Disney character as a live host provides step-by-step instructions. Best of all, you keep your sketch.

Meet-and-greet characters here include Mickey Mouse in his Sorcerer's Apprentice garb (lines are relatively short) and the stars of the latest Disney animated film.

Displays feature art from Disney films. Concept art from 1937's "Snow White and the Seven Dwarfs" lines the exit hall. Also displayed are Oscar statuettes, including those Disney won for creating Mickey Mouse (1932) and the World War II short "Der Fuehrer's Face" (1943). Another exhibit promotes Disney's latest animated movie.

A closer look. The building is the former East Coast home of Disney Feature Animation. Working in the area that now holds the touchscreens and character spots, artists created the movies "Mulan" (1998), "Lilo & Stitch" (2002), "Brother Bear" (2003) and "Home on the Range" (2004); portions of "The Little Mermaid" (1989), "Beauty and the Beast" (1991), "Aladdin" (1992) and "The Lion King" (1994); and the Roger Rabbit cartoons "Tummy Trouble" (1989) and "Roller Coaster Rabbit" (1990). At its peak the studio had a staff of 350. Disney closed it in 2004.

To wait, or not to wait. The main entrance (expect about a 15-minute wait) leads first to a short, hosted film. "Drawn to Animation" shows how animators created Mushu, the dragon sidekick in the 1998 movie, "Mulan." A second entrance, which rarely has a line, heads directly to the rest of the building.

Family matters. Is your child a budding artist as well as a Disney fan? Have her draw a character at the Animation Academy, and then get it signed by that character at a meet-and-greet spot later in the day. The result makes a great souvenir.

"I want more!" Gadgets and gizmos aren't enough for Ariel, a teenage mermaid who longs to be human. A live actress portrays the character in the "Voyage of The Little Mermaid" stage show.

Voyage of The Little Mermaid

★★★★ ✓ *FASTPASS* **Animation Courtyard** 17 min. Capacity: 600. Queue partially outdoors in shade, partially indoors and air-conditioned. Fear factor: Scary Ursula appearance and voice causes some toddlers to cry. Access: Guests may remain in wheelchairs, ECVs; assistive listening, reflective captioning. Debuted: 1992.

A live actress portrays Ariel, the star of the 1989 movie "The Little Mermaid," in this multimedia stage show. Entertaining for all ages, it features a talented singer, imaginative puppetry and some creative effects. The show takes place in a comfortable, misty theater that appears to be underwater. After a rousing blacklight puppet version of "Under the Sea," Ariel belts out "Part of Your World" like a Broadway star. A huge robotic octopus, Ursula the Sea Witch slithers in to sing "Poor Unfortunate Soul" and con Ariel out of her voice. Video clips (blurry and faded) advance the plot to the finale, where Ariel grows her gams and hugs her honey, Prince Eric.

A closer look. In the Disney movie, Ariel, 16, is the daughter of King Triton. Though her dad forbids human contact, Ariel swims to the surface and saves the life of Prince Eric. Chaos ensues after a sea witch makes Ariel human, but eventually true love prevails. The story is based on an 1836 fairy tale by Hans Christian Andersen.

Family matters. Small children should sit in the middle of the theater. Front rows are too close for small folks to see onto the stage.

Fun find. A replica of P.T. Barnum's infamous 1842 "FeeJee Mermaid" hides in the waiting room above the theater's right entrance door. Half dead monkey, half dried fish tail, it toured the U.S. as the real thing.

Average wait times

Time	Standby line	Fastpass time
9:00a	0 min	10:05a
10:00a	20 min	11:05a
11:00a	25 min	12:15p
Noon	25 min	1:15p
1:00p	30 min	2:05p
2:00p	25 min	3:40p
3:00p	20 min	4:50p
4:00p	25 min	6:05p
5:00p	25 min	7:05p
6:00p	15 min	8:05p
7:00p	20 min	8:50p
8:00p	15 min	(out)
9:00p	10 min	(out)

Just a few inches tall, a model boat awaits guests in the original 1954 concept diorama for Disney's Jungle Cruise ride. The hand-built piece is displayed at Walt Disney: One Man's Dream.

Walt Disney: One Man's Dream

★★★★ ✓ **Mickey Avenue** (the walkway between Animation Courtyard and Pixar Place) Allow 35 min. Capacity: 200. Fear factor: None. Access: Guests may remain in wheelchairs, ECVs. Assistive listening, handheld and reflective captioning; Audio Description. Debuted: 2001, revised 2010.

A salute to the life and dreams of Walt Disney, this multimedia gallery combines memorabilia exhibits with a short film. The attraction has 400 artifacts in its collection, though many are rotated on and off display.

The most interesting new display is the actual Abraham Lincoln figure that starred in the 1964-65 New York World's Fair. Here shown without clothing, this robotic Honest Abe is mostly skinless except for its head and hands. An adjacent control board has buttons that read "elbow" and "finger."

Other artifacts include the desk Walt used as a Missouri second-grader, his studio desk from the 1930s and his (re-created) office from the 1960s. Motion-picture memorabilia includes props and costumes from 1954's "20,000 Leagues Under the Sea," as well as an Academy Award that movie won.

Disney's hand in theme-park history is well represented. Built by Disney himself in 1949,

a hand-wired wooden diorama displays his early ideas for multiple-room attractions such as Snow White's Scary Adventures. Nearby, a "Dancing Man" electronic marionette tested figure-movement techniques that led to the development of Disney's Lincoln and other Audio-Animatronics robots. Display cases hold tabletop models used to build the Main Street U.S.A. area of California's Disneyland, as well as that park's Jungle Cruise and Peter Pan's Flight attractions. Another display portrays the creation of "it's a small world."

A simulated television studio shows Walt Disney filming a video that he used to interest investors in his ultimate, unful-filled dream of the Experimental Prototype Community of Tomorrow, or EPCOT.

A 200-seat theater shows a moving bio-graphical film. Narrated by Disney himself through an assemblage of audio clips, the inspirational 16-minute movie is surprisingly straightforward.

Family matters. The movie includes advice that's especially useful to high-school and college students. Recounting a business setback early in his career, Walt Disney says "I think it's important to have a good, hard failure when you're young."

"Hey young lady. Yes, you, in the red..." A robotic Mr. Potato Head chats with guests in the Toy Story Mania queue. The five-foot spud is Disney's most interactive Audio-Animatronics character.

Toy Story Mania!

★★★★★ ✓ *FASTPASS* **Pixar Place** 7 min. (game play 5 min.) Capacity: 108. Indoor, air-conditioned queue; over-flows into outdoor area. Fear factor: None. Vehicles move from game to game in a jerky, funhouse fashion. Access: Offline loading area for disabled guests, into special vehicles equipped with guns that have buttons as well as pull strings. ECV users must transfer. All ride vehicles offer closed captioning. Debuted: 2008, revised 2010.

You'll pitch baseballs at flying plates, shoot darts at moving mine cars, hurl eggs at scurrying animals and toss hoops over Little Green Men in this ride-through 3-D shooting arcade, in which "Toy Story" characters host virtual midway games on a series of large screens. Using what appear to be spring-action shooters, two guests sit side-by-side to compete against each other. Thanks to some impressive tech, players see the objects they launch leave their guns and travel into the screens. Water sprays enhance virtual explosions; blasts of air heighten the sensation that some targets pop off their screens.

Easy to play, the games offer secret bonus levels. Lay gamers may feel rushed, as each screen plays out in less than a minute.

Fastpass mania. The ride's biggest challenge is avoiding a long wait to get on it. On a typical day (when the park opens at 9 a.m.), the standby wait will be a half-hour by 9:05 a.m., an hour by 10 a.m. The entire supply of Fastpasses is usually distributed by 11:30 a.m.

How to skip the line. You can avoid the long wait, or get an early Fastpass return time, by rushing to the ride when the park opens. If you do be prepared to take part in a stampede. For best results get to the park 45 minutes early to be first in the line at the turnstiles, and know ahead of time whether

Average wait times

Time	Standby line	Fastpass time
9:00a	35 min	10:40a
10:00a	60 min	4:00p
11:00a	60 min	7:15p
Noon	75 min	(out)
1:00p	90 min	(out)
2:00p	130 min	(out)
3:00p	130 min	(out)
4:00p	140 min	(out)
5:00p	95 min	(out)
6:00p	115 min	(out)
7:00p	110 min	(out)
8:00p	85 min	(out)
9:00p	75 min	(out)

Andy's Wanted poster for nefarious "One Eyed-Bart" (who, as die-hard fans know, has two eyes when he is in disguise) stands alongside the Toy Story Mania standby queue. The poster appears in the opening moments of the first "Toy Story" movie.

you're headed directly to the ride (stay on the left side of the crowd as you pass the entrance to One Man's Dream) or to its Fastpass machines (stay to the right). When entering the line for a particular Fastpass machine try to avoid getting behind a tour-guide leader; they often get 100 or more passes at a time.

Skillful use of the attraction's Fastpass system also gives a guest the chance to take in the ride multiple times in a day, and therefore more fully enjoy the experience—something many children will insist on.

Only want to ride it once? Then there's no need to rush—as long as you plan to be in the park all day and don't plan to see the Fantasmic evening spectacle. Just stop by the attraction anytime before 11 a.m. or so to get a Fastpass for late in the day.

Talking potato. If you do end up in the standby line, you'll be treated to Disney's most interactive Audio-Animatronics character. Acting as the ride's carnival barker, a 5-foot 2-inch Mr. Potato Head chats with guests personally. His eyes can look at the person he's speaking to; his mouth can move to form vowel sounds and words. He occasionally sings a song, and sometimes takes off his ear or hat. The voice comes from a library of audio clips recorded for the attraction by comedian Don Rickles, the voice of Mr. Potato Head in the "Toy Story" movies.

Fun finds. ❶ Across from the ride entrance, some Green Army Men are in the process of hanging a Scrabble board. Spelling out the message "You've got a friend in me," it hints at the teamwork the ride requires to get a high score. **❷** A second hint: Andy has left a note on the door of the back of the Pixar Place entrance gate that describes the board

as a "top secret message decoder." **❸** In the standby queue, a huge pink crayon is the only unused crayon in the boy's collection. **❹** Andy's drawing of "Wanted" Mr. Potato Head that opened 1995's "Toy Story" sits along the queue line. **❺** Near the end of the line Andy has painted the clownfish Nemo from 2003's "Finding Nemo." **❻** In the games themselves, at the Green Army Men Shoot Camp hit either of the two yellow plates to have an adjacent cannon fire a shot at you. **❼** At Buzz Lightyear's Flying Tossers, hoop one of the aliens wearing a jetpack to have it fly over your head. **❽** Hoop one of the rockets to have it shoot toward you. **❾** As your vehicle moves to Woody's Rootin' Tootin' Shootin' Gallery, a wall mural of a carnival includes Toy Story Mania as an attraction. **❿** At the Shootin' Gallery, a bank-robbing squirrel pops out of the bank when you hit the target next to it. **⓫** Hitting the target by the bird nest causes the bird to pop up in the air. Sequential targets make baby birds fly away. **⓬** A beaver pops up when you hit the target on the dam. Sequential targets make the beaver squeak. **⓭** In the attraction's exit area, two blocks facing the exit walkway show the letters "C" and "U." **⓮** As you leave, a "Tin Toy" Little Golden Book has jammed Andy's bedroom door closed, so the toys can play with his new game indefinitely.

Hidden Mickeys. ❶ Near the end of the standby queue, upside down, as a paint splotch under the tail of a clownfish. **❷** In the boarding area mural, as frames on the Toy Story Midway Games Playset box. **❸** After the final game, on a mural to your right as the dot in the exclamation point of the phrase "Circus Fun!"

You've got a friend in... your partner!

BY MICAELA NEAL There are three keys to getting a high score on Toy Story Mania: Shoot constantly (your cannon can fire six objects per second), know where the high-value targets are, and... teamwork! To get a top score, you have to work together with the person sitting next to you. That way, the two of you can hit multiple targets simultaneously, which will reveal hidden levels of the game.

GAME BOOTH	HIGH-VALUE INITIAL TARGETS	HOW TO REVEAL BONUS TARGETS
HAMM AND EGGS	❶ In the doorway of the barn is a 500-point horse. ❷ The green ducks in the lake are also 500 points. ❸ A 500-point squirrel runs up both the left and right edges of the screen. ❹ Three gophers repeatedly pop up along the bottom. The brown gophers are worth 500 points; the gray ones 1000 points. ❺ The animals in the tree are 1000 points each. A 1000-point goat peers out of the barn window. A 1000-point mouse skitters along the barn's roof.	❶ Hit the mouse (see Tip No. 5 at left) and the barn will rotate to reveal its interior, which is filled with 2000-point rats. Hit every barn rat and more rats appear in the grass as 1000-point targets. ❷ Hit the fox on top of the henhouse (in the bottom left corner of the screen) and three hens will scurry out. The first is worth 1000 points; the second is worth 2000 points; the third 1000 points. ❸ Hit the 500-point donkey that walks along the hills and the animal will turn and run the other way as a 2000-point target.
REX AND TRIXIE'S DINO DARTS	❶ 500-point targets are in the lava streams of the volcano, on dinosaur eggs at the bottom left, held by two red dinosaurs at the bottom center and tied onto a blue stegosaurus and red raptors in the back. ❷ A blue dinosaur on the right chews 1000-point targets, others are tied to a pink brontosaurus in the background. ❸ Pterodactyls hang from the sky with 500- and 1000-point targets.	**Team up with your partner** to hit the lava flows until the volcano erupts. Then hit the two meteors on the left and right of the volcano three times each (the last two meteors, worth 500 points each, must be hit within one second of each other). This will cause three large comets (spheres formed by 1000-point balloons) to crash into the screen.
GREEN ARMY MEN SHOOT CAMP	❶ Helicopters hover with plates worth 1000 points. Other 1000-point plates appear within the mass of plates, while more are carried by trucks along the bottom. ❷ Airplanes tow plates worth 2000 points. Others are tossed up on either side of the mountain.	**Team up with your partner** to simultaneously hit the two 2000-point plates that are tossed up from the sides of the mountain (see note at left) at the same time. Doing so will open the mountain and reveal a tank that shoots plates toward you worth 5000 points each.
BUZZ LIGHTYEAR'S FLYING TOSSERS	❶ Meteors near the sides of the screen are 500 points. ❷ Rockets are 1000 points. ❸ Jetpack aliens are worth 2000 points. ❹ Aliens at the top corners of the screen are 5000 points.	**Team up with your partner** to simultaneously hoop all of the aliens in the large central rocket to launch the rocket and reveal a huge robot. When the robot's mouth opens, toss rings into it to score—if you reveal the robot early enough—up to 2000 points per toss.
WOODY'S ROOTIN' TOOTIN' SHOOTIN' GALLERY	All initial targets are worth 100 points each.	❶ Each 100-point target triggers a series of bonus targets worth up to 1000 points each. ❷ As your vehicle moves from screen 1 to 2 (or from screen 2 to the Woody's Bonus Roundup screen), hit two 100-point or 500-point targets close together to reveal a 2000-point target.
WOODY'S BONUS ROUNDUP	The second-to-last mine cart on each track is always worth 2000 points.	❶ Hit 1000-point targets above the carts by two bats to awake them and reveal 5000-point targets. ❷ Hit all of the carts on a track and the last one will be worth 5000 points. ❸ The final target is worth 2000 points if you hit it often enough.

Toy Story Mania logo © Disney

A colorful stage musical, Beauty and the Beast—Live on Stage retells Disney's version of the famous fairy tale. Above, chefs welcome Belle to dinner in "Be Our Guest."

Beauty and the Beast—Live on Stage

★ ★ ★ ★ ★ ✔ **Sunset Boulevard** 25 min. Capacity: 1,500. Outdoor queue. Fear factor: During "The Mob Song" Gaston stabs the Beast, but you don't see the wound. Access: Guests may remain in wheelchairs and ECVs. Assistive listening. Audio Description. Debuted: 1991, revised 2001.

The love story between a beautiful bookworm and blighted beast is retold in this lavish stage show, which re-creates the spirit of Disney's 1991 animated movie by focusing solely on its music. It tells its story through colorful, choreographed productions of "Belle," "Gaston," "Be Our Guest," "Something There," "The Mob Song" and the title song, "Beauty and the Beast." The inspiration for Disney's acclaimed Broadway version of the tale, this lively theme-park production is thoroughly entertaining, as good as ever after 20 years.

The show's colorful costumes and creative lighting lend a true theatrical feel. Supporting dancers wear a crayon box of hues; in the ballroom scene Belle's signature gold gown is offset by her maids' vivid pink dresses. Re-creating the look of the famed Hollywood Bowl, an arch above the stage flashes during "Be Our Guest," later dappled lights add dramatic color to "The Mob Song."

A revolving cast is always outstanding. Whoever plays her, Belle always sings with skill and expression; Gaston ad-libs lines and shamelessly flirts with females in the audience. Also notable are the supporting cast members. A delight to watch all by themselves, they faint, fight, jump, kick, swoon, twirl and waltz as they portray villagers and castle attendants.

While the Belle and Gaston performers sing live, the supporting characters rely on the prerecorded vocals from the film. These voices include Robby Benson as the Beast, the late great Jerry Orbach as Lumiere and Angela Lansbury as Mrs. Potts, who sings the Academy Award-winning song "Beauty and the Beast." (Three tunes in the movie were nominated for Best Song; the others were "Belle" and "Be Our Guest.")

The open-air theater is covered, but the waiting area is simply a sidewalk that's at the mercy of the weather. Arrive 30 minutes early for a good seat; for the full experience get in line 45 minutes before showtime and sit down front. As you wait, one member of your group can go get ice cream for the others; there's a hard-ice-cream stand directly across Sunset Boulevard from the theater.

Clockwise from right: Local girls dismiss the "most peculiar mademoiselle," Gaston believes "it's not right for a woman to read," Belle falls in love with her captor after he gives her a book during "Something There"

A closer look. Originally a story for adults, "Beauty and the Beast" became a children's fairy tale in 1756, when French tutor Jeanne-Marie Leprince de Beaumont wrote a version to prepare girls for arranged marriages. Wanting her charges to believe love can make any man princely, Beaumont contrasted Beauty's beastly fate with that of her two sisters: the first marries a handsome man who thinks only of himself, the second weds a smart man who belittles his bride. "Many women," her Beauty observes, "are made to marry men far more beastly than mine." The author's own arranged marriage had been annulled when her philandering husband contracted a venereal disease. To encourage girls to read, Beaumont makes Beauty a book lover.

Set in what its heroine describes as a "poor, provincial town," Disney's version of the tale replaces the sisters with street-tart village girls and creates a new character, the vain hearthrob Gaston. The story kicks off with Gaston, "setting his sights" on Belle, an intelligent book reader who dismisses him. Later, she finds herself imprisoned in a castle of a prince who has been cursed for his selfishness and transformed into a hideous beast—his cooks, maids and other attendants transformed into objects—until he learns how to love someone and earns their love in return. Quicker than you can say "Stockholm Syndrome," Belle falls for her captor, Gaston tries kill him, and Belle and the dying creature exchange words of love.

Visually, the song "Be Our Guest" is a tableware take on Busby Berkeley's "By a Waterfall" sequence in 1933's "Footlight Parade." Voiced by the late Broadway vet and "Law and Order" TV star Jerry Orbach, enchanted candelabrum Lumiere blends dashing Maurice Chevalier from 1958's "Gigi" with Pepé Le Pew, Warner Brothers' Looney Tunes scent-imental skunk created in 1945.

Fun finds. ❶ The show begins with a pun: a ringing bell. **❷** "The Mob Song" includes a quote from Shakespeare. As he rallies villagers to kill the Beast, Gaston commands "Screw your courage to the sticking place," the same phrase Lady MacBeth uses to urge her husband to kill Duncan. **❸** Thirty television stars have left handprints in an entrance plaza. "Star Trek's" Scotty, James Doohon, added "Beam Me Up." "Jeopardy" host Alex Trebek wrote "Who is Alex Trebek?"

A 40-foot guitar graces the entrance facade to Rock 'n' Roller Coaster Starring Aerosmith. The ride hits a top speed of 57 mph and is the only Disney World coaster that goes upside down.

Rock 'n' Roller Coaster Starring Aerosmith

★★★★★ ✓ **FASTPASS Sunset Boulevard** 1 min 22 sec. Capacity: 120 (5 24-seat vehicles). Single Rider line. Indoor, air-conditioned queue. Fear factor: Anticipating launch scares many. Guests should be free from motion sickness; pregnancy; high blood pressure; heart, back or neck problems. Access: ECV users must transfer. Height min: 48 min. Debuted: 1999.

You go upside down twice on this dark, indoor roller coaster. The beginning is the scariest part: a powered launch that hurls you forward to a speed of 57 mph in just 2.8 seconds. It's followed by a half-mile of twists and turns, two loops and a tight corkscrew. As Aerosmith music pounds from speakers in what looks like a Cadillac convertible limousine, you pass through two famous L.A. landmarks, the iconic "Hollywood" sign and the huge doughnut that, in real life, promotes Randy's Donuts. Plenty thrilling for most guests, the ride gets mixed reviews from hardcore coaster freaks, as it slows down considerably after the first loops.

"Make it a super stretch." The grins begin as you enter the building, the headquarters of mythical "G-Force Records." Step through the lobby and you're off on a time-warp to the 1970s. Along the walls are displays of real vintage recording and playback gear. Soon you come to Studio C, where you find the rock band Aerosmith (via video) mixing the rhythm tracks to their "new" number "Walk This Way." Suddenly the guys have to leave; they're late for a show. But no worries: since the band members "can't forget our fans," they offer you—and everyone else in line—backstage passes. As the manager phones for a car she counts the crowd, then tells the limo company "We're going to need a stretch. In fact, make it a super stretch."

You're then ushered into a grimy back alley, where up pulls your ride. Squealing off into the darkness, the limo takes you to the backstage entrance of an L.A. arena, where a red carpet leads to (a video of) the band performing on stage.

When Disney chose Aerosmith as the band for the attraction, initially the company couldn't reach frontmen Steven Tyler and Joe Perry. Unbeknownst to Disney, the two were vacationing with their families at the time... at Walt Disney World.

© Disney

Resembling vintage Cadillac convertibles, Rock 'n' Roller Coaster cars loop and corkscrew through a Hollywood night. Unlike a conventional coaster, the ride doesn't start off with a lift hill. Its launch is powered by a magnetic linear induction system imbedded in the track. Vehicles accelerate by being quickly pushed and pulled from one hidden magnet to another. An earlier version of linear induction powers Magic Kingdom's PeopleMover ride. *Disney photo illustration.*

Fun finds. ❶ Mimicking guitar necks, columns in the standby lobby have fret boards and strings. ❷ The first display case in the standby area holds a 1958 Gibson Les Paul Standard guitar as well as a disc cutter, a device that "cut records" by etching sounds from a mixing console onto a master disc. ❸ Record players in the second case range from a 1904 external-horn Edison Fireside to a 1970s Disc-O-Kid. ❹ Put your ear to doors marked "Studio A" or "Studio B" to hear Aerosmith rehearsing. ❺ In the alley, signs on the rear of the G-Force building indicate that repair work has been done by Sam Andreas and Sons Structural Restoration, the garage is run by Lock 'n' Roll Parking Systems and that its dumpster is owned by the Rock 'n' Rollaway Disposal Co. ❻ A glass case displays rates for Wash This Way Auto Detail. ❼ Limo license plates sport messages such as 2FAST4U and H8TRFFC. ❽ The disc jockey heard on the car radio is longtime Los Angeles rock jock Uncle Joe Benson. ❾ The concert video loop shows Tyler screaming "Rock 'n' Roller Coaster!!!"

Hidden Mickeys. Twice on the building sign: ❶ Tyler's shirt has Mickey silhouettes; ❷ the boy wears mouse ears. ❸ As tile pieces in the foyer floor. ❹ In the carpet of the first queue room. ❺ As cables on the recording-studio floor. ❻ On the registration stickers of the limos' rear license plates. ❼ As the "O" in "Box #15" on an exitway trunk.

Average wait times

Time	Standby line	Fastpass time
9:00a	0 min	10:30a
10:00a	45 min	12:20p
11:00a	50 min	2:15p
Noon	65 min	4:15p
1:00p	75 min	6:30p
2:00p	80 min	8:00p
3:00p	75 min	(out)
4:00p	80 min	(out)
5:00p	70 min	(out)
6:00p	80 min	(out)
7:00p	70 min	(out)
8:00p	80 min	(out)
9:00p	80 min	(out)

According to Disney legend, the Hollywood Tower Hotel lost its front wings during a lightning strike. The building and its backstory provide the setting for The Twilight Zone Tower of Terror. Below, a statue of Demeter—the goddess of the cycle of life and death—stands in the 'long-abandoned' grounds.

The Twilight Zone Tower of Terror

★★★★★ ✔ **FASTPASS Sunset Boulevard** 4 min. Capacity: 84. Indoor, air-conditioned queue; overflows into shaded outdoor queue. Fear factor: Darkness. Ascents and drops are smooth, but mind games are intense. Guests should be free from motion sickness; pregnancy; high blood pressure; heart, back or neck problems. Access: ECV users must transfer. Activated captioning. Height min: 40 in. Debuted: 1994, revised 1996, 1999, 2002.

You plummet—and soar—up to 130 feet aboard a pitch-black freight elevator in this fully realized thrill ride. Both the falls and lifts are unpredictable, as the sequence is randomly selected by a computer. Loaded with special effects and superb detailing, the ride appeals to nearly everyone except those with an intense fear of falling.

The attraction is designed to freak you out. It's set in what appears to be an abandoned hotel, covered in cobwebs and stuffed with strange artifacts from episodes of the 1960s television series, "The Twilight Zone." The queue snakes through a spooky library and an unwelcoming basement boiler room. The rusty elevator creaks as its doors shut. The ride itself is filled with creepy images and has doors that open by themselves.

And there's just the right amount of perfectly timed... silence.

A 'somewhat unique' story. Meant to recall the eerie style of "The Twilight Zone," the experience is even more fun if you know its story. According to Disney lore, the extravagant 12-story Hollywood Tower Hotel opened in 1917 as a gathering place for

Purposely covered in dust and grime, the lobby of Disney's "Hollywood Tower Hotel" recalls the splendor of luxurious Southern California retreats of the early 20th century

Tinseltown elite. Two decades later, on Oct. 31, 1939, the hotel hosted a Halloween party in its rooftop lounge. But at precisely 8:05 p.m. a huge lightning bolt hit the building, dematerializing two elevator shafts and the wings they supported. Among the victims were five people riding in an elevator—a child actress with her nanny, a young Hollywood couple and a bellhop.

The hotel stood deserted for decades, but now, Disney says, has mysteriously reopened, just in time for your visit. As you arrive to check in, a bellhop asks you to wait in the library, where, as the power goes out, a black-and-white television shows the beginning of what appears to be an episode of "The Twilight Zone." But as host Rod Serling describes a "somewhat unique" story about a maintenance service elevator, he adds, "We invite you, if you dare, to step aboard, because in tonight's episode, you are the star."

Boarding the elevator, you enter that episode yourself, traveling past strange images as you journey to a mysterious 13th story. After your elevator car unexpectedly moves forward, its doors slam shut and soon it is tossed—violently—up, down—down, up—up, up, down.

Every ride is different. Occasionally other doors open, revealing the open sky and the theme park down below. Those five victims from 1939 may appear again, or rain may fall, or an odd smell may waft around you. After about a minute the madness stops, and you calmly arrive... in the basement.

"The next time you check into a deserted hotel," you hear Serling say, "make sure you know just what kind of vacancy you're filling. Or you may find yourself a permanent resident of... 'The Twilight Zone.'"

A closer look. "There is a fifth dimension beyond that which is known to man." Along with a four-note theme song ("do-do-do-do, do-do-do-do..."), those words welcomed viewers to "The Twilight Zone," a television anthology that aired on the CBS network from 1959 to 1964. Placing ordinary people into extraordinary situations, the episodes often had mind-bending twists.

Host Rod Serling created the show. The footage of Serling used in the ride is from the introduction of the 1961 episode, "It's a Good Life." Though Serling originally said "This, as you may recognize, is a map of the United States," on the video the clip cuts away just as he begins to pronounce the word "map" and instead you hear him say "maintenance service elevator." Serling's lines are voiced by impersonator Mark Silverman.

Some Tower trivia: The cast members' break room is between the drop shafts; when you scream they hear it. The tower is 199 feet high, just short enough to not need aircraft

Average wait times

Time	Standby line	Fastpass time
9:00a	0 min	10:15a
10:00a	50 min	12:00p
11:00a	60 min	12:55p
Noon	60 min	2:30p
1:00p	55 min	3:15p
2:00p	55 min	5:40p
3:00p	45 min	7:30p
4:00p	50 min	(out)
5:00p	60 min	(out)
6:00p	35 min	(out)
7:00p	50 min	(out)
8:00p	70 min	(out)
9:00p	65 min	(out)

warning lights. It was struck by lightning in 1993, as it was being built.

The science of spooky. Hidden behind all the theming is a unique mix of innovative engineering, classic special effects and modern math. Combining three distinct ride systems, the attraction's mechanics represent a novel example of applied science. Its elevators go up, move forward, then plummet down and soar up a second shaft, all in a seamless experience.

The first system is obvious: an elevator. When guests leave the boiler room, they are in a standard, 50-foot elevator shaft, with sliding doors and two stops.

The second system kicks in at the top of the shaft. As the elevator car (an independent vehicle, which rode up the shaft in a cage) moves forward, it's using the technology of a self-guided palette driver. Controlled by a computer, it rolls on wheels and gets its power from an on-board battery.

The third system is Disney's own. Once the cabin enters the drop shaft, it's silently locked into a second cage that is tightly suspended on a looped steel cable. Pulled by high-speed winches and motors, the cage "falls" faster than the pull of gravity (it reaches 37 mph in 1.5 seconds, about a quarter of a second faster than a free fall) and shoots up with similar speed. The result: though guests never are free of the ride's grasp, they feel completely out of control.

Most of the elevator effects are created by simple, time-tested methods. At the first stop, a long corridor filled with translucent and disappearing objects is really a shallow area filled with see-through screens showing images from hidden projectors. Though it looks far away and 8 feet tall, the end of the hall is actually just a few feet away, and only 4 feet high. Once the elevator moves forward, mirrors on the floor and ceiling make it seem like those planes have disappeared. The characters to the side are simply moving plastic cutouts, split down the middle to make them look warped. In front, the changing star field comes from synchronized fiber-optic lights built into the doors to the final drop zone.

Each ride is different, as a computer system chooses the particulars of each fall using a random-number generator based on modulo functions—calculations that search for two numbers which, when divided by a third number, have the same remainder.

The attraction has a reprogrammable ride system, which Disney has used to keep the ride fresh. At first the experience was one plummet of about 100 feet. A 1996 revision added a half drop and a false fall. Three years later Disney debuted a seven-fall experience that brought faster acceleration, more weightlessness and more shaking. Finally, on New Year's Eve 2002, the company introduced "Tower of Terror 4," the current mix of random drops and special effects.

Family matters. If your child is a little uneasy about riding but still wants to go, have her sit at the end of one of the rows of seats in the elevator, by the side wall. Each of these seats has a handle to hold onto.

Fun finds. ❶ To the right of the lobby reception desk, a plaque from the American Automobile Association honors the hotel's "13-diamond" status. An actual award, it was presented to Disney when the ride opened. ❷ A mah-jongg game is in progress on a nearby table. The pieces are properly positioned. ❸ On the library television, the Rod Serling footage has been altered to remove a cigarette from his right hand. ❹ The little girl sings the nursery rhyme "It's Raining, It's Pouring" in the video (as well as during her appearance on the fourth floor). ❺ In the boiler room, though the dials of the service elevators go to "12," their arrows will point to an unmarked "13." ❻ As the doors to your elevator close, a hint at your destination (a "1" on the left door and a "3" on the right) disguises itself as a "B," the elevator's letter. ❼ The clock in the basement office (the "Picture If You Will" souvenir-photo area) is stuck on 8:05, the time of the lightning strike in the hotel storyline. ❽ The gift shop's outdoor display windows are still decorated for the Halloween of 1939, the night of the lightning strike.

Hidden Mickeys. ❶ In the hotel lobby, as a pair of folded wire-rim glasses on the concierge desk (the temples form Mickey's face, the eye rims make his ears). ❷ 1932's "What! No Mickey Mouse?" is the song featured on some sheet music in the left library, on a bookcase directly in front of the entrance door. ❸ The little girl in the TV video is holding a 1930s Mickey Mouse doll. ❹ As large, round ash doors beneath a fire box on a brick furnace in the boiler room (on your right just after you've entered the basement). ❺ As water stains just to the left of a fuse box on the boiler room's left wall, just past the spot where the queue divides. ❻ On the 13th floor, in the center of the star field as it comes together in a pinpoint.

Mickey Mouse wields a magical sword in the evening spectacle Fantasmic. Filled with a variety of scenes and many Disney characters, the multimedia show tells a story of good versus evil.

Fantasmic!

★★★★ **Sunset Blvd** 25 min. Capacity: 9,900 (6,900 seats). Arrive 90 min early for the best seats. Outdoor queue. Cancelled during rain. Fear factor: Loud noises, bright flashes, villains may frighten small children. Access: Guests may remain in wheelchairs, ECVs; assistive listening, reflective captioning. Debuted: 1998 (Disneyland 1992).

Held in a large open-air amphitheater, this lavish evening spectacle includes boats, cannons, characters, fireworks, fountains, laser beams, music, smoke, water screens and before you can say "great balls of fire!" one of those, too. It tells a story of good versus evil, as Mickey Mouse dreams of colorful animals and princesses but also of battles with scheming Disney villains. Most of the action takes place on a 60-foot-tall mountain that's ringed by a narrow lagoon.

Though confusing, the show is a visual delight. It begins as Mickey, dressed as the Sorcerer's Apprentice from the 1940 movie "Fantasia," conducts water fountains like instruments in an orchestra. As his powers increase, Mickey imagines live-action flowers and animals that perform a version of "I Just Can't Wait to be King," from the 1994 film "The Lion King."

The mouse's dream becomes a nightmare as a video version of Monstro the whale (1940's "Pinocchio") lunges at the audience and the amphitheater turns dark. Live-action villains include Gov. Ratcliffe (1995's "Pocahontas"), the Evil Queen (1937's "Snow White and the Seven Dwarfs"), Jafar (1992's "Aladdin") and Maleficent (1959's "Sleeping Beauty"), who transforms into a dragon and ignites the lagoon with her fiery breath.

All ends well, of course. A boat parade has Ariel (1989's "The Little Mermaid"), Belle (1991's "Beauty and the Beast") and Snow White. The finale is a now-you-see-him, now-you-don't, now-you-do Mickey farewell.

A snack bar sells hot dogs and other snacks. Souvenir hawkers roam the stands.

Fantasmic plays only a few times a week, but often twice a night. During busy periods the first show often fills to capacity; when there are two shows the second one is always less crowded. A dinner package (407-939-3463) includes reserved seating for the first show and a meal at your choice of three of the park's table-service restaurants.

Hidden Mickey. Pinocchio's water bubble forms Mickey's head; two others his ears.

"Often imitated, never nominated" film director Alberto Dante and script girl Paige Turner ("I'm not a wannabe, I'm a gonna-be!") interact with guests as members of the Citizens of Hollywood

Street performers and parade

Citizens of Hollywood ★★★★★ ✔ Hollywood Blvd., Sunset Blvd 30-min shows. This improv troupe portrays the residents of a 1940s Tinseltown. Performing skits and chatting up guests, they appear as film crews, has-beens, wannabes, boys off the bus and inept public-works employees. A nightly "99" contest ("99 footballs walk into a bar…") is a crowd favorite.

Disney Channel Rocks ★★★ Sorcerer's Hat. 20-min shows. Fourteen lively singers and dancers perform choreographed routines in this street concert, which features songs from Disney Channel shows such as "Camp Rock," the "High School Musical" series, "Sonny With a Chance" and "StarStruck." Children are invited onstage to learn some moves.

A six-minute procession, the Pixar Pals Countdown to Fun Parade features characters from the movies "A Bug's Life," "The Incredibles," "Monsters, Inc.," "Ratatouille," "Toy Story" and "Up."

Mulch, Sweat and Shears ★★★★ ✔ Streets of America 30-min shows. Driving into the Streets of America a few times each day as landscape workers, Mulch, Sweat and Shears is actually a humorous live rock band ready to "Rake 'n' Roll." As its vehicle transforms into a stage and power source, the group cranks out a set of classic tunes and medleys, grabbing audience members to play cow bells and air guitars. The group changes some lyrics to make them more family-friendly: lead singer and wannabe comedian Morris Mulch delivers a line from the Eagles' 1977 hit "Life in the Fast Lane" as "They had one thing in common, they were good… at sports!"

Pixar Pals Countdown to Fun Parade ★ Hollywood Blvd, Echo Lake 6 min. Carl, Russell, Remy and other Pixar characters appear in this short afternoon procession. Riding on floats and dancing on the street, characters from "A Bug's Life," "The Incredibles," "Monsters, Inc.," "Ratatouille," "Toy Story" and "Up" quickly travel down Hollywood Boulevard and alongside Echo Lake. Fans of those films may enjoy it—the character costumes look exactly like their animated inspirations—but others will be disappointed. A low-budget gutting of the park's former Block Party Bash, it re-uses the costumes and floats from that street party but cuts its acrobats, many of its dancers and all of its interaction. Lifted from a segment of the far more elaborate Pixar Play Parade in California, the soundtrack features a version of the 1983 Todd Rundgren anthem "Bang the Drum All Day" as well as, inexplicably here, shouts of "Play! Play! The Play Parade!"

Mulch, Sweat and Shears

Star Wars: Jedi Training Academy ★★★★ Outside Star Tours, Streets of America 30-min shows. Age 4–12. Children learn lightsaber techniques from a Jedi Master during this outdoor stage show. Donning signature brown robes, young Padawans learn basic movements and duel Darth Vader. Approximately 15 children are chosen for each show. Sign up your child very early in the day to get a spot; he or she will be assigned a showtime for later in the day.

A live street concert, Disney Channel Rocks relies on music from the "Camp Rock" movies. Other songs come from "Jump In," "The Cheetah Girls: One World," "Sonny With a Chance," "StarStruck" and "High School Musical."

Disney's Animal Kingdom

Animal lovers and conservationists will adore this theme park. All of its rides and shows focus on animals and their habitats, and live creatures fill the park's lush landscape. Attractions include Disney's typical mix of thrill rides, live shows and carnival-style fun, but in this case everything has a wildlife theme. Among the highlights are a roller coaster that changes direction, two Broadway-quality live shows and a truck ride through a convincing re-creation of wild Africa. Real-life issues of habitat destruction and poaching dominate the park's storylines.

With over 1,700 exotic creatures living on its grounds, the park offers guests encounters with live animals at most every turn. Many of

The King of Beasts eyes an approaching truck at the Kilimanjaro Safaris attraction

its 250 species are either endangered or the biggest, tallest, smallest or most colorful of their kind. Guests see these animals up close, in natural habitats. The park's combination of live creatures and conservation themes can be especially inspiring to children, though visitors of all ages come away with an appreciation of the animal world.

Accredited by the Association of Zoos and Aquariums, the park also conducts animal research, breeds endangered species and contributes to conservation efforts.

Best reasons to go

Kilimanjaro Safaris: A giraffe—or rhino, or ostrich—may come right up to your truck on this open-air ride. Traveling through 110 acres of an African jungle and savanna that are both brimming with free-roaming animals, Kilimanjaro Safaris delivers a different experience with each trek.

Stellar live stage shows: A dazzling musical revue, Festival of the Lion King rouses its audience with circus acts, a fire dancer, wildly creative costumes and great music. Finding Nemo: The Musical re-imagines the beloved Pixar film in song, using huge imaginative puppets and a wealth of live singers.

The gorillas: The park's walk-through African habitat—the Pangani Forest Exploration Trail—features two gorilla groups. One is a family, with a giant silverback, females and children; the other a lively bachelor troupe. The family's youngsters wrestle and play, moms nurse and tend their brood (a baby girl joined the family in 2010), the massive father calmly oversees. Just a few feet away from their human onlookers, the gorillas look at you with eyes and expressions that are oh-so-human.

The slower pace: The self-guided nature of the many animal exhibits slows down the pace and lends itself to a more relaxing day.

The tropical landscaping: You'll want bamboo in your yard after visiting this park (at least if, like the author, you live in Florida). Lush foliage dotted with streams and waterfalls creates an Eden-like atmosphere. Plants, flowers and trees disguise the hard divisions between animal enclosures, which adds to the feeling of being in a natural environment. It's almost impossible to picture the flat Florida pastureland that used to be here.

The walking trails: Shady paths in the park's Africa, Asia and Discovery Island areas make you feel like you're creeping up and spying on animals in the wild. The lavishly re-created habitats encourage natural behaviors from the bats, hippos, gorillas, kangaroos, tigers and myriad other live beasts.

The coaster: With an 80-foot drop and dizzying backward plunge, Disney's Expedition Everest roller coaster treks into and out of a mountain range. An angry yeti appears to tear up your track, and almost destroys your trip.

Disney's village of Harambe represents a former gold-and-ivory trading post that's creating a new economy based on ecotourism. Buildings display authentic African architecture.

Worst aspects of the park

The walking: This 500-acre park requires lots of foot travel. It's a half-mile from the entrance to the back attractions and a half-mile from one side of the park to the other. There is no transportation inside the park except for a train that shuttles guests even farther out, to an animal-care center and petting zoo.

The heat: Guests spend more time outdoors at this park than any other at Disney World, which can be a real problem between April and October, when the weather is almost always hot and humid. Summer afternoons can be especially challenging.

Getting oriented

Disney's Animal Kingdom is divided into seven themed areas:

Oasis: Bordered by tropical animal enclosures, two shady walkways lead to Discovery Island.

Discovery Island: This central hub contains the park's biggest shops, two restaurants and a 3-D movie. It's also home to the huge Tree of Life, the park icon. Trails wind around the tree, passing animal enclosures that are often nearly hidden.

Camp Minnie-Mickey: Meant to evoke an Adirondack summer camp where Mickey Mouse and his friends have gone on vacation, this is the park's least defined area.

It's home to The Festival of the Lion King theatrical show and some shady character meeting spots.

Africa: With its architecture, artisans, dancers, musicians and native African staffers, Disney's village of Harambe is the most fully-realized section of the park. Attractions consist of a realistic safari ride through acres of forest and savanna—past elephants, giraffes, lions and dozens of other creatures—and a walking trail alongside gorillas. Africa has a good buffet restaurant, with characters at breakfast. The mythical town struggles to convert its economy to ecotourism.

Rafiki's Planet Watch: Guests board an African train to get to this conservation-themed area, which features a veterinary and research facility, petting zoo and a character meet-and-greet area.

Asia: This land is home to the park's biggest thrill ride—a roller coaster that goes forward and backward—along with a raft ride, bird show and animal exhibits. A good restaurant has both indoor and outdoor areas. The setting is comprised of two fictional rural towns—the riverside kingdom of Anandapur and mountainside village of Serka Zong. Like Africa's Harambe village, these communities wrestle with economic and environmental issues.

The park icon, the Tree of Life rises from Discovery Island. More than 300 sculpted animals emerge from its gnarled branches, roots and trunk. The massive structure resembles an African baobab. Narrow surrounding walkways wind past wildlife habitats.

DinoLand U.S.A.: This tongue-in-cheek land celebrates the public's curiosity about all things dinosaur. The Dino Institute represents a scientific approach, with a lighthearted indoor thrill ride and an elaborate playground. The adjacent Dino-Rama re-creates a tacky roadside carnival with a spinning roller coaster, hub-and-spoke ride and midway games. The incongruent Theater in the Wild presents a stage musical based on 2003's "Finding Nemo." A fast-food restaurant sells burgers and chicken.

What if it rains?

With its large size and few indoor attractions, Disney's Animal Kingdom makes it tough to ignore the weather. No park attraction closes due to rain, but Mickey's Jammin' Jungle Parade can be cancelled. Roller coasters Expedition Everest and Primeval Whirl temporarily close when lightning is in the area, as does The Boneyard, Kali River Rapids and TriceraTop Spin. Ironically, Kilimanjaro Safaris rides are often better during a rain, as its savanna animals are usually more active.

Family matters

All of the park's thrill rides have height minimums—40 inches for Dinosaur, 44 inches for Expedition Everest, 38 inches for Kali River Rapids and 48 inches for Primeval Whirl. With frightening in-theater effects that include threatening robotic insects, the 3-D movie It's Tough to Be a Bug is too intense for some children.

Every park restaurant offers a children's menu. The park has one character meal: Donald's Safari Breakfast at Africa's Tusker House, with Donald Duck, Daisy Duck, Mickey Mouse and Goofy.

A Magical Day

8:15a: Arrive at the parking lot, then be first in line at the turnstiles. As you wait for the gates to open (typically at 8:50 a.m.), pick up a Times Guide from Guest Relations at your left. Rolls and coffee are sold at a snack kiosk.

9:00a: As one member of your party gets Fastpasses for Expedition Everest, the rest walks to Dinosaur.

9:10a: Ride Dinosaur.

9:30a: Ride Primeval Whirl.

10:15a: Arrive for the 10:30 a.m. show of Finding Nemo—The Musical.

11:00a: Use your Fastpasses to ride Expedition Everest. Get Fastpasses for a second ride later in the day.

11:30a: Walk through the Maharajah Jungle Trek.

12:30p: Lunch at either Yak & Yeti or Tusker House. As you wait for a table, have one member of your party get Fastpasses for Kilimanjaro Safaris.

1:45p: Walk through the Pangani Forest Exploration Trail.

2:15p: Use your Fastpasses to ride Kilimanjaro Safaris.

3:00p: Arrive for the 3:30 p.m. show of Festival of the Lion King.

3:45p: Walk through the Discovery Island Trails. Find the kangaroos.

4:15p: Arrive for the 4:45 p.m. show of Flights of Wonder.

5:30p: Use your Fastpasses to ride Expedition Everest a second time.

6:15p: Play Fossil Fun Games.

7:30p: Dinner at Boma, at the nearby Animal Kingdom Lodge.

Prayer flags decorate Serka Zong, a Himalayan village which serves as the starting point of Animal Kingdom's Expedition Everest attraction. Buildings nestle within exotic plants and trees.

A Baby Care Center (behind Discovery Island's Creature Comforts store) provides changing rooms, nursing areas, a microwave and a playroom. It sells diapers, formula, pacifiers and over-the-counter medications.

Six Kids' Discovery Club stations offer hands-on activities for children. Open from 10 a.m. to 5 p.m., the stations are geared to kids ages 3 to 8. Early each morning, friendly college interns hold small animals and artifacts for youngsters to examine on the Oasis walkways. Later they're stationed alongside other animal habitats, in DinoLand U.S.A. beside Dino Sue and in Africa at the Harambe School presentation area.

Restaurants and food

The park has two table-service restaurants, a buffet (with a character breakfast) and four fast-food spots—two indoor, two outdoor. Make reservations at 407-939-3463 or online at disneyworld.com/dining.

See the chapter **Restaurants and Food.**

A closer look

It's a novel concept—the Third World as theme park. Unlike the fantasized American and European focus in Disney's other parks, Animal Kingdom depicts realistic towns in African and Asian countries. Nothing looks new; signs are dented and rusty, paint is cracked, copper green. Light bulbs hang down from ceilings. Faded posters curl up on patched walls. Indentations of bare feet, fallen leaves and bike tracks crisscross dried-mud roads. Authentic artifacts mix with spot-on replicas, surrounding guests with a fascinating peek into unfamiliar cultures.

Worn and weathered by decades of rain and sand storms, the African village of Harambe represents an old gold-and-ivory trading post that's attempting to build a new economy based on ecotourism. Typical of Swahili construction techniques, the buildings appear to have coral-rock substructures that, for the most part, are covered with plaster and topped with corrugated-metal or reed-thatch roofs. Foundations of former buildings are visible in the main streets, while lampposts bear the phrase "Harambe 1961," a reference to the year the village gained independence from Great Britain. Vintage tin signs (mostly real) and Kenyan-English advertising posters (mostly fake) hang throughout the town.

Dominating Disney's Asia are the faux rural villages of Anandapur and Serka Zong, which also struggle economically. Hooting gibbons live on two monument areas, one Thai and one Nepalese. Supposedly built in 637 A.D., the temples are covered in bamboo scaffolding as cash-starved villagers try

Step right up! DinoLand U.S.A.'s Dino-Rama carnival area includes midway-style tests of luck and skill. Each Fossil Fun Game costs between $2 and $3 to play. Winners take home prizes such as stuffed dinosaurs.

to restore them. Nearby, bells celebrate answered prayers on a crumbling Indian tiger shrine decked with scarves and garlands.

Other lands focus on building styles found in the Caribbean (Discovery Island), rustic Northeastern areas of the United States (Camp Minnie-Mickey) and kitschy roadside carnivals (DinoLand U.S.A.).

The Tree of Life. This 14-story man-made structure towers over Discovery Island and serves as the park's centerpiece. Sculpted animals cover its massive roots, trunk and branches. The tree symbolizes the diversity and grandeur of animal life, and embodies the idea that all life is interconnected and therefore equally deserving of respect.

Workers built the tree over 18 months, using a support structure similar to an off-shore oil rig. It has a 50-foot-wide trunk, 8,000 branches and 103,000 polyurethane leaves.

Three hundred and twenty-five animals emerge from the bark. Among the best: Visible from the trail on the back side of the tree, ❶ the bottom of a large tree branch forms the underside of a rearing horse, just above a lion; ❷ a shark rises over the walkway next to a 20-foot waterfall; ❸ and a young chimp hangs from a branch inches from the same waterfall. On the kangaroo trail, ❹ a manatee mother and calf swim in a root above a waterfall visible from a foot-bridge just past a swan exhibit; ❺ a dolphin rides on a crest of wood that looks like a wave above a flying bald eagle on the trunk; and ❻ a branch turns into a snake—look for an ant, follow the branch it is on up the tree, and watch as the wood turns reptilian.

Fun finds. Discovery Island: ❶ Murals in the front dining room of the Pizzafari restaurant

Park Resources

ATMs: Park entrance, on the right; also outside Dinosaur Treasures gift shop.

First Aid: For minor emergencies. Registered nurses. Behind Creature Comforts, Discovery Island.

Guest Relations: Walk-up window outside the turnstiles, office inside. General questions, dining reservations, currency exchange. Maps, Times Guides for all WDW parks. Stores items found in park that day. Multilingual.

Locker rentals: Next to Guest Relations inside the park entrance ($7/day plus $5 deposit).

Package pickup: Merchandise bought in the park can be sent to the entrance to pick up later. No charge; allow 3 hours. Packages can be delivered the next day to Disney hotels or shipped nationally.

Parking: $14/day per car. Free for Disney hotel guests.

Stroller rentals: At Garden Gate Gifts inside the park entrance (Singles $15/day, $13/day length of stay. Doubles $31, $27). Replacements at Mombasa Marketplace.

Tip Board: Shows attraction wait times. Discovery Island.

Transportation: Buses serve all Disney resorts, Magic Kingdom (via TTC), Epcot, Hollywood Studios and Blizzard Beach; no direct service to Downtown Disney, Typhoon Lagoon or ESPN Wide World of Sports.

Wheelchair, scooter rentals: At Garden Gate Gifts inside the park entrance. Wheelchairs $12/day, $10/day length of stay. 4-wheel scooters $50/day, $20 deposit.

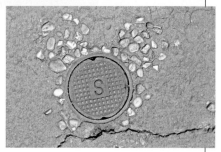

Clockwise from top left: A "Cementosaurus" at DinoLand U.S.A., posters in Harambe village, a Hidden Mickey in an African walkway, rearranged letters on a travel trailer in DinoLand U.S.A.

include only one animal that is right side up: toward the back, a small blue bug stands upright under a purple bird, on a header that frames the rear seating area. On the opposite side of that header, an opossum tail without a body appears between the second and third opossums from the right. ❷ Dozens of animals hide in the murals in the large rear dining room. They include two bitterns standing in the reeds under the orange fox; a frog, resting on the tree trunk under the brown leopard; and a stickbug posing on a leaf at the top of a plant to the left of the orange tiger. **Camp Minnie-Mickey:** ❸ As the walkway crosses the Discovery River, a stone dragon lies along the right bank. What starts in the woods as scattered slabs of stone forms into its head. **Africa:** ❹ The sounds of residents of a boarding house sometimes can be heard behind the back door of Tusker House. Sometimes there's knocking on a door: a landlady trying to collect back rent. ❺ A tribute to Animal Kingdom's chief design executive appears in the "open-air market" (the serving area) of the Tusker House restaurant. On the market's second

floor, the Jorodi Masks & Beads shop is an homage to famed Disney Imagineer Joe Rohde. Posters for the shop are plastered throughout the village of Harambe. **Asia:** ❻ Each Anandapur business displays a tax license featuring the fictional kingdom's king and queen. The bigger the license, the more taxes that business pays. **DinoLand U.S.A.:** ❼ Two baby dinosaurs hide underneath the Cementosaurus folk-art sculpture. One is hatching. Archeological and dinosaur references abound in the Restaurantosaurus fast-food eatery. Among the best: ❽ The shapes formed by greasy hand prints on the walls of the Quonset hut; ❾ the cans of Sinclair Litholine Multi-Purpose Grease and Dynoil ("keep your old dinosaur running") on the shelves of that room; ❿ the song titles in the Hip Joint rec room juke box (such as "Dust in the Wind"); ⓫ posters in that room for bands Dinosaur Jr. and T Rex; and the ambient music, which includes ⓬ the 1988 Was Not Was hit "Walk the Dinosaur." ⓭ The letters A-I-R-S-T-R-E-A-M on the front of the restaurant's travel trailer have been rearranged to spell the phrase I ARE SMART.

A face painter transforms a girl into a tiger in Animal Kingdom's Harambe Village. Designs include tigers, monkeys, even dinosaurs. Prices range from $10 to $15. The process takes about 10 minutes.

⑭ Four hanging signs above the entrance to the Dinosaur Treasures gift shop read, from one direction, "When in Florida... Be sure to... Visit... Epcot." ⑮ Plastic toy dinos ride trains, snow ski and flee lava flows above the shop's main room. ⑯ An oil funnel and gas-pump nozzle are among items that have been turned into dinosaurs on the shop's walls. ⑰ Ambient music includes bone-themed country songs (played on radio station "W-BONE") such as "I Like Bananas Because They Have No Bones," an actual 1935 ditty by the Hoosier Hot Shots novelty band.

Hidden Mickeys. Discovery Island: ❶ In the Pizzafari restaurant, as an orange firefly in the nocturnal room, to the left of a large tiger, behind a frog. **Camp Minnie-Mickey:** ❷ A profile appears as the hole of a bird-house that hangs in the courtyard. ❸ In the carved woodwork of the ice cream stand, as sideways accents. **Africa:** ❹ In Harambe, as a large shape of gray pavement in front of Harambe School, behind the Fruit Market. ❺ As a drain cover (marked with a "D") and two ear-shaped pebble groupings, to the left of the main entrance to Mombasa Marketplace, across from Tusker House. ❻ As another drain cover (this one with the letter "S", shown on the opposite page) and two pebble groupings in front of Tamu Tamu Refreshments, facing Discovery Island. **DinoLand U.S.A.:** ❼ As cracks in the asphalt parking area next to the Cementosaurus, to the right of Dinosaur Treasures. ❽ On a Steamboat Willie cast member pin on the right of the fourth back hump on the Cementosaurus. ❾ As small black scales on the back of the hadrosaurus at the start of the Cretaceous Trail.

Notable Shops

Art of Disney boutique: Lithographs, oils, porcelain, 2-ft. character figurines. Inside Disney Outfitters shop (see below), Discovery Island.

Beastly Bazaar: Candy, Disney Christmas items, housewares, pet goods. Discovery Island.

Bhaktapur Market: Asian books, silk wraps, teapots, impulse items. Yak & Yeti merchandise. Asia.

Chester and Hester's Dinosaur Treasures: Candy, caps, hats, toys. DinoLand U.S.A.

Creature Comforts: Children's wear, books. Discovery Island.

Dino Institute gift shop: Dinosaur-themed toys, T-shirts, children's books. DinoLand U.S.A.

Disney Outfitters: Children's wear, fashion apparel, fine jewelry, menswear, watches. Disney World's most attractive, comfortable store. Discovery Island.

Island Mercantile: Main souvenir store. Discovery Island.

Mandala Gifts: Jewelry, unusual Asian sundries. Asia.

Mombasa Marketplace / Ziwani Traders: Books, children's wear, fashion apparel, jewelry, toys. African art, musical instruments. Kilimanjaro Safaris merchandise. Africa.

Rainforest Cafe gift shop: Wildlife-themed books, children's wear, toys. No Disney items. At park entrance, inside restaurant; before turnstiles.

Serka Zong Bazaar: Expedition Everest, Mt. Everest, Yeti merchandise. Hindu prayer flags. Asia.

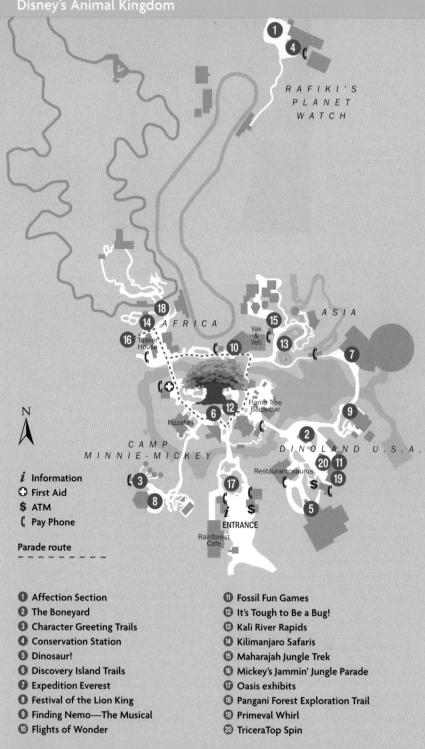

RAFIKI'S PLANET WATCH

ASIA

AFRICA

Yak & Yeti

Tusker House

Flame Tree Barbecue

Pizzafari

DINOLAND U.S.A.

CAMP MINNIE-MICKEY

Restaurantosaurus

N

i Information

✚ First Aid

$ ATM

☏ Pay Phone

Parade route

- - - - - - - - -

ENTRANCE

Rainforest Cafe

❶ Affection Section
❷ The Boneyard
❸ Character Greeting Trails
❹ Conservation Station
❺ Dinosaur!
❻ Discovery Island Trails
❼ Expedition Everest
❽ Festival of the Lion King
❾ Finding Nemo—The Musical
❿ Flights of Wonder

⓫ Fossil Fun Games
⓬ It's Tough to Be a Bug!
⓭ Kali River Rapids
⓮ Kilimanjaro Safaris
⓯ Maharajah Jungle Trek
⓰ Mickey's Jammin' Jungle Parade
⓱ Oasis exhibits
⓲ Pangani Forest Exploration Trail
⓳ Primeval Whirl
⓴ TriceraTop Spin

Attractions at a Glance

Animal exhibits

❶ Affection Section: ★★★ ✔ Petting zoo
Domestic animals, mostly free-roaming, for petting, brushing. Allow 15 min. No wait. Rafiki's Planet Watch.

❹ Conservation Station: ★★★★ ✔
Research, vet center Actual animal-care facility has viewable procedures, exhibits, presentations. Allow 90 min. No wait. Rafiki's Planet Watch.

❻ Discovery Island Trails: ★★★★ ✔ Animal habitats Walkways wind through tropical garden, massive Tree of Life roots, past kangaroos, exotic wildlife. Allow 20 min. No wait. Discovery Island.

❶❹ Kilimanjaro Safaris: ★★★★★ ✔ FASTPASS
Animal-spotting truck ride Bouncy open-air trip roams a forest and savanna; encounters elephants, giraffes, lions, rhinos, more. 22 min. Avg wait 25 min. Preshow video shows killed animals. Africa.

❶❺ Maharajah Jungle Trek: ★★★★★ ✔
Animal habitats Trail around crumbling palace. Passes tigers, other Asian animals, through aviary. Allow 30 min. No wait. Asia.

❶❼ Oasis exhibits: ★★★★ ✔ Animal habitats
Park entrance; lush garden hosts unusual animals such as giant anteater, spoonbills. Allow 15 min. No wait. Oasis.

❶❽ Pangani Forest Exploration Trail:
★★★★★ ✔ Animal habitats Shady walkway past African animals; through aviary. Large gorilla habitat. Allow 30–45 min. No wait. Africa.

Bird show

❶❶ Flights of Wonder: ★★★★ ✔ Comedic
natural-behavior demonstrations Funny, with conservation theme. Birds fly over audience members. 25 min. Avg wait 15 min. Asia.

Carnival games

❶❶ Fossil Fun Games: ★★★ ✔ Midway games
Winners get prizes. Extra charge; $2 to $3 per game. Allow 15 min. No wait. DinoLand U.S.A.

Character-greeting attraction

❸ Character Greeting Trails: ★★★ Meet-and-greet gazebos Characters can include Chip 'n Dale, Donald Duck, Daisy Duck, Goofy, Koda and Kenai, Mickey and Minnie Mouse, Pocahontas. Avg wait 15 min. Camp Minnie-Mickey.

Parade

❶❻ Mickey's Jammin' Jungle Parade:
★★★★★ ✔ Character procession, animal

floats Safari-themed procession has huge mechanical puppets, humorous character SUVs. 15 min. Arrive 15–30 min early. Circles Discovery Island; starts, and ends, in Africa.

Playgrounds

❷ The Boneyard: ★★★★ ✔ Themed play area
Dig-site playground has climbing zone, slides, tunnels. Allow 15–30 min. No wait. DinoLand U.S.A.

Rides

❺ Dinosaur!: ★★★★ ✔ FASTPASS Indoor jerky
ride Open vehicle searches for dinosaurs in the dark. 3 min, 30 sec. Avg wait 20 min. Height min 40 in. Intense, bouncy. DinoLand U.S.A.

❼ Expedition Everest—Legend of the Forbidden Mountain: ★★★★★ ✔
FASTPASS Indoor-outdoor roller coaster Smooth; speeds into, out of mountain; goes backward, zooms past robotic Yeti. 3 min. Avg wait 40 min. Height min 44 in. High lift, dark, backward motion, threatening giant monster, one steep drop. Asia.

❶❸ Kali River Rapids: ★★★★ ✔ FASTPASS
Flume ride Raft floats down threatened rainforest river. 6 min. Avg wait 40 min. Height min 38 in. Jerky, wet. Asia.

❶❾ Primeval Whirl: ★★★ FASTPASS Spinning coaster Kitschy "Wild Mouse"-style ride spins its cars. Time-travel theme. 2 min, 30 sec. Avg wait 20 min. Height min 48 in. Jerky, spins, one steep drop. DinoLand U.S.A.

❷❶ TriceraTop Spin: ★★★ Hub-and-spoke ride
Four-seat cartoon-dinosaur vehicles. 90 sec. Avg wait 9 min. DinoLand U.S.A.

Theatrical shows

❽ Festival of the Lion King: ★★★★★
✔ Stage musical Rousing in-the-round revue includes stilt walkers, acrobats, fire-baton twirler. Based on 1994 film "The Lion King." 28 min. Avg wait 25 min. Camp Minnie-Mickey.

❾ Finding Nemo—The Musical: ★★★★★
✔ Puppet and stage show Spectacle retells 2003's "Finding Nemo" with huge puppets, live singers. Broadway quality. 30 min. Avg wait 45 min. DinoLand U.S.A.

3-D movie

❶❷ It's Tough to Be a Bug!: ★★★ FASTPASS
Comedic animal revue Playfully sadistic film displays insect survival skills. Stars characters from 1998's "A Bug's Life." 8 min. Avg wait 8 min. Intense for preschoolers. Discovery Island.

The babirusa (above left) is a wild pig. The Patagonian cavy (top right) is related to the guinea pig. Pointed snout scales identify the rhinoceros iguana (bottom right).

The Oasis

★★★★ ✔ Allow 15 min. 3 trails (1200 ft), 13 viewing areas, 17 species. Fear factor: None. Access: Wheelchair, ECV accessible. Debuted: 1998.

The thematic entrance to the park, this zoological area connects Animal Kingdom's turnstiles and guest services area with its Discovery Island hub. Lush tropical and subtropical plants from throughout the world — flowering trees, vines and shrubs such as jacarandas, tabebuias and orchids as well as bamboo, eucalyptus, palms and broad-canopied evergreens—combine to create a natural entranceway. A man-made haven of pools, streams and waterfalls creates, in essence, a small zoo, with animals from Africa, Asia and South America. College interns greet early-morning guests with terrariums and hand-held wildlife exhibits.

Animal guide

❶ **Admin's stork:** Defecates on legs to maintain body temp (evaporative cooling).
❷ **Babirusa:** Wild pig—the name means "pig deer" in Malay language—found on Indonesian islands. Up to a foot long, males' upper tusks extend through snout and curve back toward face. Eats clay to cleanse system.

Ducks: ❸ **Chiloe wigeon.** Small dabbling duck. Metallic green head, white cheeks. Male whistles; female quacks. ❹ **Indian spotted duck.** Has orange, yellow spots on bill. ❺ **Rosybill pochard.** Dark plumage is offset by bright pink-red bill.
Macaws: ❻ **Hyacinth macaw.** World's largest parrot. Cobalt blue with no blue plumage pigment; feather structure produces blue cast. ❼ **Military macaw.** Olive-green feathers resemble fatigues. ❽ **Scarlet macaw.** Brilliant multicolored plumage. Longest tail feathers of any macaw.
❾ **Patagonian cavy:** One of the world's largest rodents; just under 3 ft long. Related to guinea pig, but resembles small deer with rabbit head. Long legs let it run up to 28 mph and leap up to 6 ft.
❿ **Reeve's muntjac:** Called "barking deer" due to call it makes when alarmed. Male has short antlers to throw rivals off-balance, large canine teeth that curl from lips like tusks used to injure enemies.
⓫ **Rhinoceros iguana:** Large lizard. Pointed snout scales resemble rhino horns.
⓬ **Southern giant anteater:** Up to 9 ft long. Devours 30,000 ants, termites a day by flicking 2-ft-long tongue 160 times a minute. Walks on

Disney's roseate spoonbills (right) hatch eggs and raise young in view of guests. Parents regurgitate food for newborns. The Southern giant anteater (below) walks on its front knuckles. In the wild, it consumes up to 30,000 ants and termites a day by flicking its 2-foot tongue.

front knuckles to protect claws, which are the largest of any mammal. Uses tail as blanket.

Spoonbills: These tall wading birds feed by swinging their open spoon-shaped bills in water. In mating ritual, males offer female sticks for nest; when she accepts she has chosen mate. Lines nest with leaves. ⓭ **African spoonbill.** White. ⓮ **Roseate spoonbill.** Pink, red and orange plumage; rosy color comes from algae eaten by crustaceans on which bird feeds. South American; also found along U.S. Gulf Coast.

⓯ **Swamp wallaby:** Small kangaroo cousin. Protects itself by jumping up and kicking and scratching the faces of predators in mid-air. Can drink sea water. Also known as the black wallaby and, due to musky odor, "the stinker."

Swans: ⓰ **Black swan.** Longest swan neck. ⓱ **Black-necked swan.** White body; large red knob on bill. Parents piggyback young to protect from cold, predators.

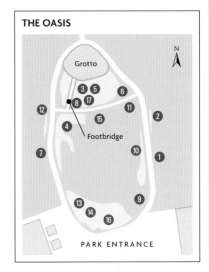

THE OASIS

Micaela Neal

Clockwise from top left: A sculpted gavial emerges from a Tree of Life root, two red-fronted macaws, the Galapagos tortoise is the world's largest tortoise, the African crested porcupine

Discovery Island Trails

★★★★ ✔ **Discovery Island** Allow 20 min. Garden plus 2 trails (1680 ft), 9 viewing areas, 15 species. Fear factor: None. Access: Guests may stay in wheelchairs, ECVs. Debuted: 1998.

Located in the center of the park, these three walking paths offer close-up views of flamingos, kangaroos and other odd creatures living in idyllic hideaway habitats. Landscaped with what appear to be tropical rolling hills dotted with streams, grottos and waterfalls, the area is fully realized, but its walkways are tough to find. On the plus side, once you "discover" an animal, often no one else will be there.

Kangaroo trail. So hidden few guests notice it, a trail off the park's walkway to Africa leads to a kangaroo habitat. The narrow path weaves through the huge roots of the Tree of Life and winds past a waterfall. Its entrance is just past the Pizzafari restaurant.

Back trail. Parrots, porcupines, storks and tortoises inhabit the grounds along a walkway that runs behind the Tree of Life, alongside the Discovery River. It leads from the park's Africa gate to its Asia gate.

Tree of Life garden. A small walkway directly in front of the park's huge Tree of Life offers a nice view of a variety of

creatures. Stately crested cranes strut around up front, while kangaroos hop on a small hill behind them. Flamingos and whistling ducks hang out in a pond to the left, near a cotton-top tamarin habitat. Next to that—and completely unmarked—is a shady otter habitat with an underwater viewing area.

Family matters. Small children can easily view most of the animals, but may have a hard time seeing the kangaroos. Their viewing spot sits high above their habitat, but behind a concrete wall that's about 4 feet tall.

Animal guide

❶ **African crested porcupine:** Largest, heaviest African rodent; up to 60 lbs. Covered with barbed quills 1–12 in long. Shoulder quills stand erect to form crest. Other quills lie flat but are raised when alarmed. Animal does not shoot quills. Quills easily fall out, can get imbedded in predator's skin; scales on tips lodge like fishhooks. New quills replace those lost. Newborns have soft spines that harden.
❷ **Asian catfish:** The largest scaleless freshwater fish. Up to 10 ft long, 650 lbs. Travels yearly up to 600 miles, from the South China Sea up the Mekong River.

Named for the puffy crest of white fur on top of its head, the squirrel-sized cotton-top tamarin (right) mates for life; older siblings care for infants. A very rare monkey, it is more common today in captivity than in the wild. The donkey-faced gray kangaroo (below) is rarely found in U.S. zoos.

❸ **Asian small-clawed otter:** World's smallest otter at 2 to 11 lbs. Playful; chases other otters on land and in water at speeds to 18 mph. Unique (for otters) non-webbed front paws look like hands.

❹ **Axis deer:** Females fight like boxing kangaroos, pawing at each other while standing on hind legs. Male has branched antlers, ruts almost constantly, makes loud, bugle-like bellow. Also known as the chital.

❺ **Cotton-top tamarin:** See Conservation Station.

Ducks: ❺ **Eyton tree duck.** Spends most time on land, not water. Long tan plumes on wings.

❻ **White-faced whistling duck.** High-pitched three-note whistle sounds like a squeak toy.

❼ **Galapagos tortoise:** World's largest tortoise at 5 ft long. Herbivore. Lives only in Galapagos ("tortoise") archipelago, 600 mi west of Ecuador. Can live to 150 yrs. Top speed 0.16 mph. At night sleeps partially submerged in mud, water or brush. Can retain so much water can go without eating, drinking for a year. Peaceful life; males "fight" by facing, opening mouths, and stretching heads; highest stretch wins.

❽ **Helmeted guinea fowl:** Common bird in southern, western Kenya. Call is a grating, rasping, staccato "kek-kek-kek." Nest is shared among females, can hold 50 eggs.

❾ **Kangaroos:** Only large mammal that hops; can jump 9 ft, leap 40 ft, run 30 mph. Back-leg tendons act as springs. Can outpace racehorse. At rest, weight is supported by tripod of hind legs, tail. Licks forearms to stay cool. Cannot walk backward. Inch-long hairless newborn still developing, resembles jellybean, has no back legs; crawls into mom's pouch, stays 9 mo. Mother produces unique milk for each joey; controls pregnancy progress so each has open teat; gestation (typ. 35 days) can be delayed 11 months. Males box.

Micaela Neal

The ring-tailed lemur (left) uses its long tail as a signal flag. The lesser flamingo (center) is the pinkest flamingo species. The West African crowned crane (right) has a golden, halo-like crown.

Red kangaroo. World's largest marsupial. Can stand 7 ft, weigh 200 lbs. Color matches Australian outback. Can go without water if green grass available. **Western gray kangaroo.** Least common kangaroo in U.S. zoos. ⑩ **Lappet-faced vulture:** Skin folds hang off bare, pink head. Unlike other vultures, will eat live prey. Wingspan 9 ft. **Lemurs:** ⑪ **Collared lemur.** In the wild, will salivate on poisonous millipedes, roll them between hands before eating, possibly to remove toxins. Reddish-blond beard, long furry tail. ⑫ **Ring-tailed lemur.** Uses long tail as flag to signal location or warn of danger. Females dominant. Male competes for female by rubbing tail with wrist-gland odor, arching tail over back and shaking it at other males while baring teeth. Golden eyes. Long tail; black and white tail rings.

⑬ **Lesser flamingo:** Smallest, pinkest, most numerous flamingo. Color from diet of algae, aquatic insects, crustaceans. Rests on one leg. Lives in groups up to tens of thousands. Ritualized displays of head-flagging (stretching neck, rhythmically turning side to side), wing salutes (tail cocked, neck outstretched), group marching with abrupt direction changes. In E Africa up to a million gather to form world's largest flock.
⑭ **Red-fronted macaw:** Smallest standard macaw. Mostly green; brilliant red forehead, crown, ear patches; turquoise flight and tail feathers; and neon orange under the wings. **Storks:** ⑮ **Painted stork.** Pink patch on back during breeding season. Young make loud call to attract parents; by 18 mos practically voiceless. ⑯ **Saddle-billed stork.** Black-and-orange bill topped with distinctive thick yellow "saddle." Builds one-egg stick nest in top of tall trees. ⑰ **White stork.** Lives in African grasslands. Legend of birds bringing human babies to homes comes from migration of this bird from Africa to N Germany to nest on chimneys and roofs in spring, a time of many human births. Lifelong mates share incubating, feeding. Chicks mew; do not cheep or squawk.
⑱ **Tambaqui:** Freshwater fish; looks like the smaller piranha. Mostly eats plants.
⑲ **West African crowned crane:** Halo-like golden crown; red face patch. Mostly gray, white; some golden tail feathers.

DISCOVERY ISLAND

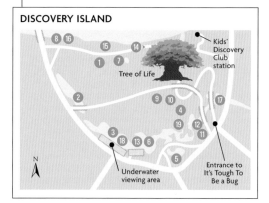

Kids' Discovery Club station

Tree of Life

Underwater viewing area

Entrance to It's Tough To Be a Bug

N

Insects seem to join the audience in the comical 3-D movie "It's Tough To Be a Bug." Though most adults enjoy the show, children are often frightened. (Disney photo illustration)

It's Tough to Be a Bug!

★ ★ ★ *FASTPASS* Discovery Island, inside Tree of Life 8 min. Capacity: 430. Mostly shaded outdoor queue. Fear factor: Intense for many children, with darkness, fog, cartoonish menacing bugs. Access: Guests may remain in wheelchairs, ECVs; assistive listening, reflective captioning, Audio Description. Debuted: 1998.

It was awesome!" said the 8-year-old girl, leaving the theater with her parents. "I hated it!" said the 7-year-old boy next to her, crying to his parents. Different children have different reactions to this 3-D movie, which demonstrates how insects defend themselves by pretending to torture its audience. Special effects make it seem like guests are sprayed with acid and attacked by poison quills. Two characters from the 1998 movie "A Bug's Life" appear in the theater as robotic figures—mild-mannered ant Flik (the host) and grasshopper villain Hopper. Once state-of-the-art, the show is blurry compared to modern 3-D efforts. For the best focus sit in the center of a back row.

Character voices include those of actors Dave Foley (Flik), Cheech Marin (Chili the tarantula) and Kevin Spacey (Hopper).

Family matters. Outside the exit, a Kids Discovery Club station (ages 3–5; 10a-5p) has real-life grasshoppers and tarantulas.

Fun finds. ❶ Outside the lobby a plaque honors Dr. Jane Goodall's work with chimpanzees. ❷ Lobby posters promote previous shows such as "Beauty and the Bees" and "Little Shop of Hoppers." Ambient music is from those shows. ❸ The theater is an anthill; its projection booth a wasp nest. ❹ As the show ends, fireflies swarm to exit signs.

Hidden Mickey. As spots on a root in the lobby, to the left of the handicapped entrance.

Average wait times

Time	Standby line	Fastpass time
9:00a	0 min	10:10a
10:00a	5 min	11:20a
11:00a	5 min	11:30a
Noon	10 min	12:30p
1:00p	15 min	1:45p
2:00p	10 min	2:40p
3:00p	10 min	3:40p
4:00p	5 min	4:45p
5:00p	5 min	5:35p
6:00p	5 min	(out)
7:00p	5 min	(out)
8:00p	(closed)	(closed)
9:00p	(closed)	(closed)

At Festival of the Lion King: Emcee Timon (above left), a fire-baton twirler performs to "Be Prepared" (above center), a Tumble Monkey acrobat prepares to fly through the air (above right)

Festival of the Lion King

★★★★★ ✓ **Camp Minnie-Mickey** 28 min. Capacity: 1,375. Partially shaded outdoor queue. Fear factor: None. Access: Guests may remain in wheelchairs, ECVs; assistive listening, handheld captioning. Debuted: 1998.

Fans of Disney's 1994 movie "The Lion King" will love this rousing musical spectacle. Filled with energized renditions of the best songs from the film, it manages to combine the pageantry of a parade, the wit of a Catskills comic and the emotions of a gospel revival. The revue is presented in-the-round in an air-conditioned theater.

The show begins with an evocative take on the film's opening scene, as animal-costumed dancers create an abstract sunrise to "The Circle of Life." A chorus of "I Just Can't Wait To Be King" brings in nearly 50 more performers, including the emcee, the wisecracking meerkat Timon. Parade floats carry Simba, Pumbaa, an elephant and a giraffe.

From then on, singers, dancers, acrobats, stilt-walkers and giant puppets fill your field of vision. After Timon sings "Hakuna Matata," flying "Tumble Monkey" acrobats perform trapeze acts to a wacky Spike Jones-style medley that includes a *gargled* version of the 1937 Duke Ellington classic, "Caravan."

Next, a fire-baton twirler performs to "Be Prepared," a ballerina soars in the air to "Can You Feel the Love Tonight?" and the audience sings along to "The Lion Sleeps Tonight."

Best is the finale, a twirling celebration that becomes a kaleidoscopic circle of life.

Where to sit. The theater has four seating areas. To see the show the way it's intended, sit in the quadrant at the back right. Timon faces this area during his "Hakuna Matata" number, and it's right next to the talking puppets of Pumbaa and Simba.

When to go. Though the most spirited shows are those with a full house, the first show of the day is the easiest to get into; it's often less than half full. Other shows often play to a full house; arrive at one of those 40 minutes early to get the best seats.

Family matters. Watch the movie first, as the show's more fun if you are well acquainted with the film. Another tip: learn the hand jive. It will come in handy during the Tumble Monkey segment.

Fun finds. ❶ Timon cracks up watching the Tumble Monkeys, trembles during "Be Prepared" and swoons throughout "Can You Feel the Love Tonight?" ❷ The float giraffe often mouths the words to the songs. ❸ The Tumble Monkeys "pick bugs" off guests and each other. ❹ After the show a backstage microphone picks up Timon's aside, "Could somebody hose down those tumble monkeys? They're starting to smell a little gamey." ❺ Puppeteers work in all four floats and can see out; their animals can respond to guests who wave at them, especially after the show.

Facing page: Festival of the Lion King dancers channel wild animals.

A white rhino crosses the path of a safari truck on Disney's Kilimanjaro Safaris attraction. Animals always have the right-of-way; trucks are sometimes forced to stop and wait for them to move.

Kilimanjaro Safaris

★★★★★ ✓ *FASTPASS* **Africa** 22 min. Capacity: Apx 36 per truck, max 4,320 guests per hr. Closes at dusk. Covered outdoor queue. Fear factor: Queue video briefly shows slaughtered animals; finale has audible gunshots. Access: ECV users must transfer; assistive listening; hand-held, activated captioning. Debuted: 1998.

One of the best zoological attractions in the United States, this open-air truck ride takes you through a seamless re-creation of African jungles and savannas that are filled with free-roaming wildlife. There are no visible fences, and many animals, including giraffes and rhinos, can come up to your vehicle. Other creatures include crocodiles, elephants, hippos, lions, warthogs and many species of antelope. Rutted roads, creaky bridges and blind corners lend a sense of adventure.

Animals are most lively first thing in the morning (they're often feeding), when skies are cloudy and during a rain that comes after a few hours of hot sunshine. Gorillas are visible after the ride, along the exit walkway.

Geography buffs will notice that, despite its name, the attraction has nothing to do with any African mountain.

The ride appears to be a trip through an African wildlife preserve, an effort by

Disney's village of Harambe to replace its timbering economy with eco-tourism. Though drivers say the journey will take two weeks and cover 800 square miles, it's actually a 22-minute trip through about 100 acres.

Poachers may be involved. The ride's story begins in the queue, as videos show, somewhat graphically, how poachers are killing the preserve's animals. Once underway, your driver makes contact with the head warden, who supposedly is flying above you

Average wait times

Time	Standby line	Fastpass time
9:00a	20 min	10:10a
10:00a	30 min	11:15a
11:00a	30 min	12:20p
Noon	25 min	1:30p
1:00p	35 min	2:20p
2:00p	45 min	3:30p
3:00p	25 min	4:10p
4:00p	20 min	5:20p
5:00p	15 min	6:10p
6:00p	20 min	(out)
7:00p	10 min	(out)
8:00p	(closed)	(closed)
9:00p	(closed)	(closed)

Open-sided safari trucks wind through a re-created Serengeti savanna, a grassland plain where free-roaming ankole cattle, antelopes, gazelles, giraffes, impala and wildebeest forage for food. Giraffes often feed directly in the path of the trucks.

in a spotter plane. Eventually he sees some poachers who have captured a baby elephant, and asks for your driver's help to rescue it. (The plot was originally more gruesome. Until 2007 the warden reported that the baby's mother had been shot.)

Family matters. As you board the truck, place your children on the outside of your row so their views will be unobstructed.

Animal guide

① African elephant: Largest land animal, to 20 ft long, 14,000 lbs. Communicates by trumpets, grunts, low-frequency rumbles inaudible to people but heard by other elephants 5 mi away. Sensitive skin; can feel a fly. Few natural enemies but hunted to near extinction for tusks, which are made of same material as human teeth, ivory dentine. Both sexes have tusks. Trunk holds 3 gal of water and has more muscles (40,000) than human body, combines long nose with upper lip; two finger-like projections at tip can pluck grasses, manipulate small objects. Females breed only 3–6 days every 4 yrs, gestation 21 mo. Bulls find mates by listening for female rumbles, can hear for miles. During mating entire herd often takes part in noisy "mating pandemonium"—females, calves mill, circle, wave trunks, trumpet for up to hour. Five babies have been born at Disney; 2 males (2003, 2008), 3 females (2004, 2005, 2010); habitat has backstage pool for calves to learn to swim.

② Ankole cattle: Huge whitish horns are hollow, full of blood vessels, which cool cow on hot days. World's largest horn circumference: up to 28 in. Also known as Watusi cattle.

③ Bontebok: Rarest antelope. Extinct in wild. Chocolate-brown coat, purplish sheen. Both sexes: backswept, ringed horns.

④ Cheetah: Fastest land animal; can accelerate from 0–70 mph in 3 sec. Slightly curved non-retractable claws help traction. Balances with long tail. Pale gold coat, black spots. Hunts in daylight; Disney's cheetahs often eye intended prey, though can't reach it.

Ducks: ⑤ Northern pintail duck. Brown and gray body; white breast. **⑥ Red-billed teal.**

The world's largest antelope, the eland can be 6 feet tall and weigh 2,200 pounds. The word "eland" comes from the Dutch word for moose.

An African elephant (above left) splashes in a pool, the mandrill (center) is the world's largest monkey, the reticulated giraffe sports knobby skin-covered ossicones on its forehead (right)

Mallard-like; brown-gray plumage, brown cap. ⑦ **White-faced whistling duck.** Odd three-note whistle sounds like a squeeze toy. ⑧ **Yellow-billed duck.** Only African duck with yellow bill. Dark gray plumage. ⑨ **Egyptian goose:** Sacred in ancient Egypt. Tan, chestnut eye mask; pink legs. ⑩ **Eland:** Largest antelope, up to 2,200 lbs, 6 ft tall. Can jump over each other from standstill; survive a month without water, gets liquid from plants. Both sexes have spiraled horns.

KILIMANJARO SAFARIS

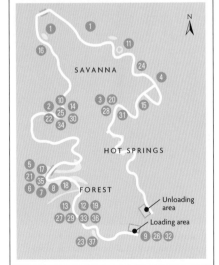

⑪ **Greater flamingo:** Largest, palest flamingo, mainly found in Africa. Can live 75 years. See lesser flamingo, Discovery Island. ⑫ **Greater kudu:** Antelope. Can leap 8-ft fence. Reddish-tan, 6–10 white stripes. Males have spiraling horns up to 5 ft long. ⑬ **Helmeted guineafowl:** Calls with a grating, rasping, staccato "kek-kek-kek." ⑭ **Impala:** The most agile antelope; can jump 8 ft straight up, run 40 mph, bound 40 ft, change direction midair. A male attracts female, scares off other males, by repeatedly sticking out tongue. Males have curving, ridged horns. ⑮ **African lion:** Largest African predator, up to 550 lbs. Most social big cat, forms prides of 5–10. Female hunts herd animals, will steal prey from others; male defends pride, bushy mane protects neck. Can run 37 mph, leap 40 ft. Sleeps up to 20 hrs a day. Roar can be heard 5 mi away. ⑯ **Mandrill:** World's largest, most colorful monkey, up to 85 lbs. Non-aggressive, social; bares massive canine teeth as greeting, with corners of mouth open like smile. Energetically beats on ground when upset. Ground-dwelling. Bright red, blue markings on muzzle, rump. Most colorful are males who have mated with many females. Main inspiration for Rafiki, wise mandrill with baboon tail, in Disney's 1994 film "The Lion King." ⑰ **Nile crocodile:** Larger, more aggressive than American alligator, up to 20 ft long. Hatchlings call to mother from inside eggs before hatching; both parents roll eggs in mouths to crack shells. Mother carries newborns in jaws to water; guards for up to 6 mo.

Clockwise from top left: An impala can leap 40 feet, Ankole cattle have the world's thickest horns, the bontebok is the world's rarest antelope, a crouching cheetah eyes intended prey.

Nile hippopotamus: Most aggressive African animal. Can outrun man over short distance. Largest mouth of any land mammal. Spends day in water, grazes on land at night on up to 150 lbs of vegetation. Ears, eyes, nose on top of head; can keep track of surroundings while hiding bulk under water. Webbed feet. Can hold breath 12 min. Up to 15 ft long, 8,000 lbs. Closest relatives: whales, dolphins. Said to sweat blood due to oozing of pinkish oil that moisturizes skin. Disney World hippo herd is largest in U.S.

Okapi: Only mammal that grooms ears, eyelids with tongue, which can be 14 in long. Solitary, lives in Congo's dense Ituri Forest. Sleeps 5 min daily. Giraffe relative; appearance combines giraffe body, face, ossicones, walk (moves front, hind leg on same side of body simultaneously) with zebra striped rear. Identified as species in 1900.

Ostrich: World's fastest two-legged animal; top speed 45 mph. World's largest bird, 8 ft tall. Widest eyes (2 in) of any land creature. Largest eggs (2.5 lbs) of any land animal. Too heavy to fly; fans body to stay cool. Contrary to myth, does not stick head in sand, rather "hides" by laying head on ground.

Pink-backed pelican: Gray and white. Feeds in groups by herding fish.

Reticulated giraffe: Tallest animal; up to 20 ft; on avg 6-ft legs, 6-ft torso, 6-ft neck, 1 ft head. Longest tail (8 ft) of any land mammal, feet 1-ft wide. Generally quiet; adults can grunt, hiss, moo, snort. Calves bleat. Stride 15 ft, can run 45 mph. Tongue to 20 in. Heart 2-ft wide. Neck has 7 vertebrae, same as human. Splays legs to lower head to ground. Females give birth standing; newborns avg 6 ft tall, drop head first, grow 1 inch a day. Knobby skin-covered ossicones (head knobs).

Rhinoceros: Has existed 60 million years. Today 10,000 left (less than 15% of 1970 pop.); poached for its two muzzle horns, alleged aphrodisiac in Asia. Actually horns are same material as human nails (keratin), like nails would grow back if poachers let animal live. Herbivore. Wallows in mud for protection from sun, insects; sensitive hide appears armored. Can charge at 40 mph.

Black rhinoceros. Up to 3,200 lbs. Solitary. Uses hooked upper lip like a finger to select leaves, twigs. Horns to 4 ft. **White rhinoceros.** Largest rhino; up to 5,000 lbs. Sociable. Hide is gray to yellow-brown. Name mistranslation of Afrikaans "wijt" ("wide"), a reference to its mouth.

Sable antelope: Aggressive. Males drop to knees to clash. Stout, ringed horns. At rest, adults lie in ring around young, horns out. Symbol of Disney's mythical preserve.

Sacred (royal) ibis: Worshipped as god Thoth in ancient Egypt, said to protect it

Clockwise from top left: African lions, white-bearded wildebeest, white rhinoceros, warthogs, Nile crocodiles and black rhinoceros can be seen on the Kilimanjaro Safaris attraction

from plagues, serpents. Often mummified, placed in pharaohs' tombs. Alongside queue.

㉗ **Saddle-billed stork:** Builds a large stick nest atop tall tree; lays one egg. Colorful black, red bill has yellow top portion that resembles a horse saddle.

㉘ **Scimitar-horned oryx:** Extinct in wild due to poaching of long scimitar-sword-like horns. Specialized for desert, sweats only when body temp exceeds 116° F.

㉙ **Stanley crane:** Blue-gray, black tail, white cap. When courting, a pair simultaneously picks up grass clumps and tosses in air. South Africa's national bird.

㉚ **Thompson's gazelle:** Small antelope, 2–4 ft tall. Can run 50 mph, bounds into air. Most common E African gazelle; favorite prey of cheetahs. Pointed horns.

㉛ **Warthog:** Only grassland pig. Has knee pads for grazing, tough snout roots underground stems. Male has wart-like facial growths, two 6-in lower tusks, two curved upper tusks that can grow to 2 ft. Male courts with rhythmic grunts.

㉜ **West African crowned crane:** Halo-like golden crown; red face patch. Mostly gray, white; some golden tail feathers.

㉝ **Western bongo:** Largest forest antelope. Up to 8 ft tall, 900 lbs. Shy; known as Ghost of (Kenyan) Forest. Chestnut coat usually has 13 white stripes; "Bongo" is Swahili for "thirteen." Long backswept horns.

㉞ **White-bearded wildebeest:** Called "gnu" for call. Social, sleeps in rows, births in groups. Migrates in world's largest wildlife movement, herd up to 1.5 million. Cow-like horns.

The scimitar-horned oryx (left) is extinct in the wild. The saddle-billed stork (center) lays one egg per nest. To protect their young, sable antelopes (right) lie in a ring around them, horns out.

Newborn runs day born. Partial inspiration for Beast in 1991 film "Beauty and the Beast."
㉟ **White-breasted cormorant:** Diver, fishes with hooked bill. Intertwines necks to court.
㊱ **Yellow-backed duiker:** World's largest duiker, up to 175 lbs. Brown coat has yellow patch on rounded back. Duikers ("divers" in Afrikaans) are named for habit of diving into underbrush when startled.
㊲ **Yellow-billed stork:** White; red face and legs, large yellow bill. Stirs up water and mud with foot to flush out prey.

Fun facts. ❶ Disney created the rutted road by coloring concrete to look like soil, then rolling truck tires through it and tossing in dirt, stones and twigs while it was still wet. ❷ Not everything is real. There's a reason your driver says the termite mounds are "as hard as concrete." A pile of ostrich eggs is equally tough to crack. The first baobab tree on the route is actually a storage shed. ❸ The acacia trees are actually Southern live oaks with their lower branches removed. ❹ The safari has the largest North American collection of Nile hippos and African elephants. ❺ The first hippo pool contains all males; the second females. ❻ The animals respond to sound cues to come in at night. Elephants hear drums, hippos a triangle, crocodiles a metal bar banging in water. ❼ Kilimanjaro Safaris is the largest Disney attraction in the world. The entire Magic Kingdom would fit inside it.

Fun find. "Prehistoric" drawings appear on a gate past the flamingos and on rocks to the right as trucks pass the lions.

Hidden Mickeys. ❶ Just beyond the clay pits past a baobab tree, as a puffy spot between a split branch, opposite the main elephant area. ❷ As the flamingo island. ❸ Just past that island but before the next gate, as an indentation in a right boulder.

Micaela Neal

Grant's zebras often roam a Kilimanjaro Safaris savanna far behind the main elephant habitat

Sharing a tropical habitat with his family, a male gorilla eyes human onlookers along the Pangani Forest Exploration Trail. The gorilla is the largest and most powerful primate, but also the least aggressive. Below, the gerenuk can stand to eat high leaves, thanks to swiveling hips that align its backbone with its hind legs.

Pangani Forest Exploration Trail

★★★★★ ✔ **Africa** Allow 30–45 min. 1 trail (2100 ft), 9 viewing areas, 10 species plus aviary, indoor exhibits. Fear factor: None. Access: Guests may stay in wheelchairs, ECVs. Audio Description. Debuted: 1998.

Streams and waterfalls weave through the grounds of this self-guided tour of African animals, including gorillas, hippos and meerkats. The entire trail is shady, and benches are scattered throughout. Presented as a series of research areas, the trail has a scientific theme. The word "pangani" is Swahili for "place of enchantment."

A replica research station features naked mole rats, interactive displays and child-level cages and tanks that hold creatures kids find fascinating: plate-sized giant African bullfrogs, hissing cockroaches and dung beetles.

Exhibits shed light on subjects as diverse as bushmeat overhunting and baobab trees. One display recalls the African fable "When The Hippo Was Hairy."

A 40-foot glass wall lets guests view hippos underwater. It's best early, when the 100,000-gallon tank is clear. A suspension bridge and viewing island divide two large gorilla habitats. One holds a family (a silverback, two moms and four youngsters); the other has a bachelor troupe.

Animal guide

❶ **African cichlid:** Small, striped lake fish.
❷ **African lungfish:** Eel-like "salamanderfish" has retained lungs, can breathe air. Lives in pools that often evaporate; uses long, fleshy fins to plod in mud.

Micaela Neal

Clockwise from top left: A Nile hippopotamus has the largest mouth of any land mammal; a sentry meerkat guards a community burrow; the African green pigeon can grind fig seeds

❸ Angolan black and white colobus monkey: Tree dweller. Uses branches as trampolines to leap 50 ft. Has no thumbs.

❹ Gerenuk: Antelope stands to reach leaves; hips swivel to align backbone with hind legs.

❺ Nile hippo: See Kilimanjaro Safaris.

❻ Okapi: See Kilimanjaro Safaris.

❼ Slender-tailed meerkat: Lives in multifamily burrows of up to 30, which divide duties.

❽ Stanley crane: See description at Kilimanjaro Safaris.

❾ Western lowland gorilla: The largest (up to 450 lbs), most powerful primate; also least aggressive despite chest-beating display. The western lowland is the most populous gorilla; its wild population is 94,000. Shared traits with humans include abilities to stand upright, use tools and learn a sign language; both also share 32 teeth, fingerprints, 28-day menstruation cycle, same 9-month gestation, puberty age. Mature males have a silver back. Adult male is typically twice the size, weight of female.

❿ Yellow-backed duiker: See description at Kilimanjaro Safaris.

⓫ Aviary birds: Include the taveta golden weaver, hammerkop stork.

Hidden Mickeys. ❶ In the research station as a small shape on a backpack to the left of the naked mole rat exhibit. **❷** In the same room, as an "O" in the word "Asepco" on a box of antiseptic soap on a small ledge behind the desk lamp; Mickey's ears are formed by two paper-reinforcement rings.

PANGANI FOREST EXPLORATION TRAIL

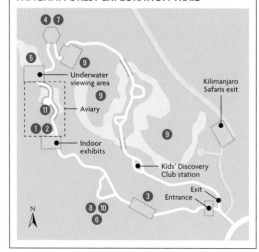

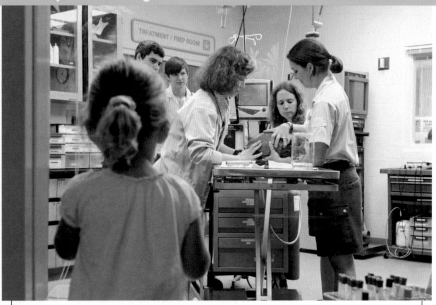

Animals are examined, and sometimes operated on, directly in front of guests at Conservation Station's veterinary care center. The procedures only take place in the morning.

Conservation Station

★★★★ ✓ **Rafiki's Planet Watch** Allow 90 min. 49 species. 9:30a-dusk. Fear factor: none. Access: Guests may stay in wheelchairs, ECVs. ECV users must transfer to a wheelchair to enter petting zoo. Debuted: 1998.

This modern air-conditioned pavilion houses straightforward exhibits, a veterinary care center and a few character-greeting spots. A petting zoo sits next to it. The area is inconveniently located and much of what it offers can also be seen at a typical zoo. Animal lovers, however, may find it fascinating, especially its veterinary procedures. To get to the area guests take a train from the park's Africa section, a "Wildlife Express" that, despite its name, offers no wildlife views except some backstage Kilimanjaro Safaris pens.

Indoor areas. Bizarre snakes, spiders, frogs and insects sit in child-height viewing tanks. Windows peer in on animal-behavior researchers and a food-preparation area. Exhibits include rainforest sound booths, remote-control video feeds from park habitats and telephones that play messages from environmental leaders such as Dr. Jane Goodall. A short film offers a look at endangered creatures. A Caring for the Wild display has a telescope used by Dr.

Goodall and notebooks used by Dian Fossey. Docents invite guests to touch some animals, including lizards, snakes and owls. Meet-and-greet characters include Jiminy Cricket, Pocahontas and Rafiki.

Guests can view gorillas, tigers and other animals undergoing medical procedures each morning, typically from 10 a.m. to noon. Vets explain what's going on, while overhead cameras offer up-close views. Expect to see anything from a bandage change to a root canal. About three animals are treated daily.

Petting zoo. Guests can touch, and brush, goats and sheep at the Affection Section.

Family matters. Conservation Station is the only place in the park where guests can touch an animal. The area includes drinking fountains and restrooms, but there's no restaurant or snack bar. Carts sell ice cream and hot dogs; an outdoor gift stand has a tiny selection of snacks. Young children can search for (faux) backyard animals at a Kids Discovery Club station on the walkway.

Animal guide

Cotton-top tamarin: Squirrel-size monkey. Very rare; more in captivity than wild. Puffy crest of fur on head. Mates for life; lives as

The Gulf Coast native sheep (above) is the oldest breed in North America; the African pygmy goat (top right) has a large beard; the axolotl (above right) remains in larval form throughout its life

family. Older siblings help care for infants. Black face; mottled gray-brown shoulders, back and rump; white stomach and limbs. Long dark tail. Habitat Habit walkway exhibit. Also at Discovery Island.

Dexter cow: Smallest N American cow; 3 ft tall. Most daily milk for its size of any cow; avg 1.5–2.5 gal. Originally from S Ireland. Most are black; some red. Both sexes have horns. Affection Section.

Goats: Associated with devil since domesticated 10,000 years ago, as Satan was thought able to transform into goat at will; and was often portrayed with creature's hooves and horns. Farmer myths claimed owning goat would protect from devil, and that when a goat could not be found it was meeting with him. A sailors' belief that having a goat on board ensured a calm sea led to the animal becoming common in N America. No goats are native to the continent. **African pygmy goat:** Barrel shape makes it appear perpetually pregnant. **Nigerian dwarf goat:** Slim, rare. Raises hackles when alarmed. Fleshy wattles. **San Clemente goat:** Rare; descended from wild goats on San Clemente Island, Calif.; Spanish seafarers in 1500s placed it there as food source. Affection Section.

Llama: S American member of camel family. Domesticated in 16th century. Pack animal, can carry 100 lbs. Brought to U.S. in 1920s by William Randolph Hearst for private zoo at his California estate. Affection Section.

Sheep: Gulf Coast native sheep: Brought to SE U.S. by Spanish in 1500s. Oldest known N American breed. Wool-free face, legs, belly. Both sexes horned. **Tunis sheep:** One of oldest U.S. breeds; in 1799 given as gift to Penn. man from ruler of Tunisia. Affection Section.

Sicilian miniature donkey: Known for dark cross-shaped stripe along back, shoulders. According to Christian lore, Mary rode this donkey the night Jesus was born; mark is said to be Christian cross. Affection Section.

Indoor exhibits vary, but often include the American alligator, Asian giant centipede, Burmese python, desert hairy scorpion, the 11-inch European fire salamander, poison dart frogs, tarantulas and the cute axolotl.

Hidden Mickeys. ❶ At the Rafiki's Planet Watch railroad station, as blue circles in the rafters' cross beams. ❷ As overlapping circles in the grates of trees in Affection Section as well as those in the Conservation Station lobby. ❸ Throughout the Conservation Station entrance mural (more than a dozen examples). ❹ Throughout the Song of the Rainforest display. ❺ As a pattern on a sheared sheep (often) in Affection Section. ❻ As orange spots on the wall of the outdoor stage, to the right of a lizard door.

Micaela Neal

Micaela Neal

Clockwise from top: A crow returns a stolen dollar to a Flights of Wonder audience volunteer; a parrot appears to answer math questions; a trainer holds Hope, an American bald eagle

Flights of Wonder

★★★★ ✔ **Asia** 25 min. Capacity: 1,150. Outdoor, shady queue. Fear factor: None. Access: ECV, wheelchair accessible. Assistive listening. Debuted: 1998.

Birds fly inches over your head in this entertaining live show. It demonstrates natural bird behaviors as it promotes the intrinsic value of these animals and the need to protect them from the abuses of man. Altogether you'll see about 20 birds, including a bald eagle. Though the subject is serious, the presentation is anything but. After the host tosses a grape for a hornbill to catch, she asks for a child to come down and try it. "I'll toss the grape," the host says, "you fly up and get it."

Shows take place in a shaded outdoor theater and are held rain or shine. If it rains, the regular show is often scrapped and trainers simply walk through the audience with birds on their wrists.

Arrive 15 minutes early to see a brief preshow in front of the theater with a great horned owl. When the main show is over, handlers also bring out a bird or two for a brief meet-and-greet session.

Family matters. Families should plan to arrive at least 20 minutes before showtime so they can sit close to the stage. Since the seating area is flat, small children can't see the show well except from the first few rows.

Tigers appear to roam freely through Disney's realistic Maharajah Jungle Trek habitats. No two cats have the same black stripe pattern, which appears on the animal's skin as well as its fur.

Maharajah Jungle Trek

★★★★★ ✓ **Asia** Allow 30 min. 1 trail (1500 ft), 7 viewing areas. 14 species plus aviary. Fear factor: None. Access: Guests may stay in wheelchairs, ECVs; Audio Description. Debuted: 1998.

Tigers, giant fruit bats and other exotic Asian animals line this shady winding walkway. Other animals include a Komodo dragon (the world's largest living lizard), a Malayan tapir and some unusual deer and cattle. A lush aviary is filled with beautiful birds, including golden pheasants. The mammals and dragon are often sedentary most of the day, but unpredictably lively early in the morning and, in the case of the tigers, late in the afternoon. Docents are stationed at key viewing spots. Large overhead fans help keep you cool in the bat pavilion, the attraction's only indoor area.

A closer look. The circular walkway winds through the ruins of a mythical hunting lodge, which, in one of Disney's more inspired architectural efforts, has been taken over by the forces of nature. After centuries of exposure to wind and water, its walls have eroded and crumbled. Trees have taken root within towers, bursting their seams from within. Birds have moved into the grand ballroom, which has lost its roof but not all of its columns and floor tiles. Eventually, the story goes, the lodge was donated to the local village, which uses it today as a wildlife refuge.

What looks like a prayer-flag-covered footbridge over the last tiger habitat is actually the top of a solid wall that separates the big cats from other animals.

Family matters. Elevated walkways and low walls and windows make it easy for children to see the animals. The trail has no bathrooms, but there is a water fountain halfway through. Benches are scattered throughout. Some children are afraid of the bats, but there is no need to be.

Animal guide

❶ **Asian giant centipede:** Aggressive; poisonous. Also at Conservation Station.
❷ **Banteng:** Shy ox. Grazes in swamp forests; bamboo jungles. Shoulder hump. Both sexes have horns. First endangered species to be successfully cloned.
❸ **Bar-headed goose:** One of world's highest-flying birds, migrates seasonally over Himalayas from Nepal to India. Body pale gray; head has black bars.
❹ **Bats:** The only flying mammals. Hands form into wings; skin stretched between

A vegetarian, the Rodriguez fruit bat (left) is harmless to man. Only a few hundred remain in the wild. Weighing up to 1,200 pounds, the Malayan tapir (below) is one of the largest nocturnal hoofed mammals. Though often mistaken for a pig or anteater, it is actually related to the horse and rhinoceros.

Micaela Neal

fingers, body, hind legs. Roosts, feeds hanging by hind feet; circulatory valves keep blood from rushing to head. Uses echolocation to navigate in darkness. Groom, lick each other to express affection, pairs often nuzzle snouts. More closely related to humans than rodents. **Malayan flying fox:** World's largest bat. 6-ft wingspan is so massive bat cannot take off from ground. Vegetarian; can eat to body weight daily. No threat to man. **Rodriguez fruit bat:** Can hover. Wingspan 3 ft. Only eats fruit; spits out hard pulp, seeds, skin, often in tidy mouth-shaped pellet. Only few hundred remain in wild; only found on Rodriguez Island in Indian Ocean. No threat to man.
❺ **Blackbuck:** In Hindu mythology, transports moon goddess Chandrama, bestows prosperity to areas it lives. Most hunted animal in India 18th, 19th, 1st half of 20th century. Females tan, males dark brown. Males have ringed, spiraling horns.

❻ **Blood python:** Up to 50 lbs; 8 ft long.
❼ **Elds deer:** Most endangered deer. Lives only in eastern India, in 15-sq-mi Loktak Lake marsh. Wide spreadable hooves. Antlers sport at least six points.
❽ **Java green peafowl:** Most vivid green peafowl. Ventriloquist. Found in Java, on Malay Peninsula. Only 1,000 exist in wild.
❾ **Komodo dragon:** World's largest living lizard; up to 250 lbs. Can reach 10 ft long. Aggressive. Saliva contains lethal bacteria. Juvenile rolls in feces to avoid being eaten by adult. When fleeing attacker, will vomit to increase speed. Dangerous to man.
❿ **Malayan tapir:** World's largest tapir, up to 1,200 lbs. Black with white saddle and elephant's trunk. Related to horse, rhino.
⓫ **Sarus crane:** Tallest flying bird at 6 ft; 8 ft wingspan. During courtship, pair will bow; hop, strut, flap wings as it circles; pair will also perform coordinated honks.

Clockwise from upper left: Entrance to the Maharajah Jungle Trek walking trail; the Komodo dragon is the world's largest lizard; the beautiful Mandarin duck; the banteng grazes in forests

⑫ Tiger: World's largest cat at up to 660 lbs. Can leap 30 ft, drag up to 3,000 lbs. No two have same black stripe pattern, which is on both fur and skin. Ears turn individually, can rotate 180 degrees.

⑬ White-lipped tree frog: World's largest tree frog, meows when disturbed.

Aviary birds include many of Asia's most beautiful creatures, including the amazingly colorful golden pheasant, the striking mandarin duck, the iridescent Nicobar pigeon and the five-colored black-browed barbet.

Fun finds. ❶ After the tiger footbridge, an environmental history of man is shown in a sequence of carvings on a wall to the right: man emerges out of the water; comes to a paradise rich with wildlife; chops down its tree; faces floods, death and chaos; and finally gains happiness when he learns to respect nature. ❷ Guests enter the aviary via the tomb of Anantah, the first ruler of Disney's Anandapur kingdom. His ashes are said to be in the room's (real) fertility urn.

Hidden Mickeys. ❶ At the second tiger viewing area, in the first mural on the right as swirls of water under a tiger. ❷ As a maharajah's golden earring in the first mural on your left. ❸ As three small bushes in that same mural. ❹ As rocks in a mountain range

above a flying dove in the second mural on your left. ❺ As swirls in a cloud formation in the second mural on your right. ❻ Past the tigers, as a leaf in a mural to your left, about 9 feet off the ground. ❼ In the top right of a mural behind the Elds deer habitat, as an orange flower and two leaves.

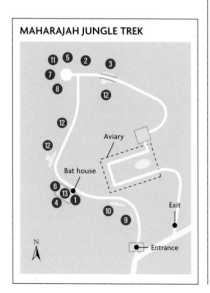

MAHARAJAH JUNGLE TREK

Aviary

Bat house

Exit

Entrance

N

Churning waters splash guests on Kali River Rapids. The turbulent raft ride carries a conservation message, as key scenes depict the clear-cutting and burning of a rainforest.

Kali River Rapids

★★★★ ✓ *FASTPASS* Asia 6 min. Capacity: 240 (20 12-person rafts). Outdoor queue mostly shaded. Fear factor: Bumpy, splashy; one steep drop. Guests should be free from motion sickness; pregnancy; high blood pressure; heart, back or neck problems. Closed during thunderstorms. Access: ECV users must transfer. Height min: 38 in. Debuted: 1999.

This raft ride takes guests down a turbulent jungle river that has many twists and turns as well as a 25-foot drop. Erupting springs, spraying water jugs and squirting statues ensure all riders get wet, many soaked. Each raft holds twelve people, and has a central storage area to help keep valuables dry.

The ride carries a strong conservation message, as it graphically depicts the process of deforestation. Though the ride begins with a 90-foot ascent through a lush jungle, when guests reach the river's headwaters they witness the illegal operations of a logging business. In its never-ending quest to harvest tropical hardwoods, the company has clear-cut a pristine section of a rainforest, setting ablaze any wood that doesn't have commercial value. The logging company's chainsaws can be heard throughout Disney's mythical Asian land.

Family matters. If your children get drenched on the ride, stick them under one of Disney's high-speed hand dryers. They're located in most park bathrooms, including the one directly across from the ride's exit.

Animal guide

Located in front of the ride, two monument towers are home to gibbons. These lower apes are the only true brachiators—animals who swing hand over hand through the trees:

Average wait times

Time	Standby line	Fastpass time
9:00a	15 min	10:10a
10:00a	15 min	11:25a
11:00a	30 min	11:55a
Noon	55 min	1:10p
1:00p	75 min	2:40p
2:00p	50 min	4:05p
3:00p	45 min	5:20p
4:00p	50 min	6:30p
5:00p	35 min	(out)
6:00p	30 min	(out)
7:00p	10 min	(out)
8:00p	(closed)	(closed)
9:00p	(closed)	(closed)

Clockwise from above: Buttons on an exit bridge spray water on unsuspecting riders, Michael Jackson is among the raft riders in a queue-room mural, raft names include "Papa-Do Ran-Rani"

Siamang: Largest and loudest gibbon. Inflates throat sac to size of a grapefruit; produces a hoot that can reach 113 decibels, nearly as loud as a jet aircraft at 100 yards. A family's adult female will start a group morning call that can last 30 minutes. Monogamous mates sing duets to express affection. Females dominant. Father shares in raising baby and takes over care after an infant's first year.

White-cheeked gibbon: Territorial call is crescendo of siren-like whoops. Males and juveniles are black with white cheeks. Females and newborns are blond. In the wild, travels up to a mile each day.

Fun finds. ❶ Thousands of real Asian artifacts and props, including some parade masks, sit in small buildings that form the standby queue. ❷ One of the queue buildings, Mr. Panika's Shop, sells "Antiks Made to Order." ❸ Pop star Michael Jackson is among the raft riders in a mural in the last queue room; the late King of Pop sits at the top right with his hands raised. The art was created in Nepal by a Jackson fan. ❹ Raft names include "Sherpa Surfer," "Papa-Do Ran-Rani" and "Khatman-Doozi." ❺ On the exitway, buttons on a bridge over the river shoot sprays of water on unsuspecting riders. Children (of all ages) love to push them.

Micaela Neal

A male white-cheeked gibbon looks to be wearing mutton chops. Its territorial call is a crescendo of siren-like whoops. The ape is monogamous, which is rare among primates.

© Disney

The Expedition Everest entrance area and gift shop appear to be part of a small Himalayan village. Coaster trains climb 200 feet to reach the top of Disney's "Forbidden Mountain."

Expedition Everest

★★★★★ ✔ *FASTPASS* Asia 3 min. Capacity: 170. Indoor, outdoor queue is mostly covered. Fear factor: High lift, dark backward travel 10 sec, one turning drop; ride creates intense pressures that some will find unpleasant. Guests should be free from motion sickness; pregnancy; high blood pressure; heart, back or neck problems. Closed during thunderstorms. Access: ECV and wheelchair users must transfer. Height min: 44 in. Debuted: 2006.

This high-speed roller coaster climbs forward, zooms backward in the dark and takes some steep sweeping turns. What appears to be an old tea train zips guests in, around and through a snow-capped mountain and narrowly escapes a snarling beast. Though it doesn't go upside down, the 4,000-foot journey climbs 200 feet, stops twice, takes an 80-foot drop and hits a top speed of 50 miles per hour.

Sit in the back for the wildest ride; you'll get whipped harder and fall faster. If you can, ride it at night; though the mountain is lit in eerie orange and purple, the track stays dark.

"Disco Yeti." One note about the Yeti: it doesn't always work. Designed to be a moving figure that lunges at passing trains, the 25-foot-tall, 20,000-pound Audio-Animatronics creature is usually motionless.

To give it a somewhat menacing look, Disney has posed the huge beast with one arm outstretched and lit it with strobe lights, earning it the unofficial nickname, "Disco Yeti."

A monster myth. The ride is more fun when you know its story, the "Legend of the Forbidden Mountain." It begins in the 1920s, as tea plantations flourished in Disney's imaginary Asian kingdom of Anandapur. Private steam trains carried the tea to villages, where it was shipped to distant markets. Soon, however, the railroads were plagued with strange track snaps and other accidents. Some locals blamed the British, claiming their attempts to reach the summit of nearby Mt. Everest had angered the Yeti, a creature that was said to guard the area.

The tea train has been shut down until today. "Bob," a bohemian American, has just teamed up with a local entrepreneur to restore the line and create Himalayan Escapes Tours and Expeditions, a business that makes it easy for mountain trekkers to get to Everest quickly. Local fears have fallen on deaf ears.

The Yeti legend. Yetis are not real; scientists agree there is no credible evidence they exist. The Yeti *legend*, however, is quite

Nine out of ten riders agree... Expedition Everest's 80-foot drop is a highlight of their Animal Kingdom day. Warnings from locals try to convince riders to "respect tradition" and cancel their trip (bottom) to avoid angering the "guardian of the realm of the snows."

real. For hundreds of years, Himalayans have told stories about a humanoid monster that fiercely guards the area around Mt. Everest. The reports increased in the 20th century, when Westerners began seeing an "Abominable Snowman." Interest peaked in 1960, when Sir Edmund Hillary led a fact-finding trip to the peak. Equipped with trip-wire and time-lapse cameras, he found nothing.

Still, the legend lives. The villain of 1964's stop-motion classic "Rudolph the Red-Nosed Reindeer" is a Yeti named Bumbles. The 2001 Disney/Pixar film "Monsters, Inc." includes a disgruntled Abominable Snowman voiced by John Ratzenberger. "'Abominable!'" he complains. "Why can't they call me the 'Adorable Snowman,' or the 'Agreeable Snowman,' for crying out loud? I'm a nice guy!"

Hidden Mickeys. ❶ In the queue, as a Mickey hat on a Yeti doll and ❷ as water bottle caps in a display of patches. ❸ As a dent and two holes in a tea kettle in the queue museum. ❹ On the left wall after the museum, with a sorcerer's hat, as wood stains in a photo.

Average wait times

Time	Standby line	Fastpass time
9:00a	20 min	10:10a
10:00a	35 min	11:40a
11:00a	50 min	12:60p
Noon	45 min	2:30p
1:00p	60 min	4:10p
2:00p	50 min	5:10p
3:00p	40 min	6:00p
4:00p	35 min	6:40p
5:00p	35 min	7:10p
6:00p	40 min	(out)
7:00p	30 min	(out)
8:00p	(closed)	(closed)
9:00p	(closed)	(closed)

An angry carnotaurus threatens guests on Dinosaur. The ride's "Time Rover" vehicle uses an onboard hydraulic system to simulate the pitch, roll and yaw of a slippery offroad adventure.

Dinosaur!

★★★★ ✔ **FASTPASS** DinoLand U.S.A. 3 min, 30 sec. Capacity: 144. Indoor, air-conditioned queue. Fear factor: Dark, loud, threatening. Can terrify children. Guests should be free from motion sickness; pregnancy; high blood pressure; heart, back or neck problems. Access: ECV, wheelchair users must transfer. Assisted listening, video captioning. Height min: 40 in. Debuted: 1998.

Ferocious dinosaurs chase you in this tense dark ride. As your vehicle careens through a primeval forest, asteroids rain from the sky, hissing raptors prepare to pounce and an angry carnotaurus tries to hunt you down. Air and smoke cannons, large strobes and loud sound effects ratchet up the thrills.

The adventure begins as you enter the Dino Institute Discovery Center, a tongue-in-cheek take on a serious museum. A multimedia show explains the theory that an asteroid shower wiped out dinosaurs long ago. Moving to an orientation room, guests meet director Dr. Helen Marsh (Phylicia Rashad) via a video feed. She announces that, thanks to a new time-traveling vehicle (the Time Rover), visitors can now travel back to the age of dinosaurs. Dr. Marsh plans to send you back to a tranquil era, but then her assistant (Wallace Langham of "CSI")

secretly reprograms your mission to a time just before the asteroids hit.

Soon a flashing, smoky time tunnel sends you 65 million years back in time. As you enter a dark forest you see many dinosaurs, but suddenly a huge one starts chasing you. Then it gets worse: your power starts to fail. As a massive meteor destroys your trail, it appears that you, too, are about to become extinct.

The attraction is themed to Disney's year-2000 animated movie "Dinosaur."

Average wait times

Time	Standby line	Fastpass time
9:00a	0 min	10:10a
10:00a	20 min	10:40a
11:00a	30 min	11:40a
Noon	25 min	12:50p
1:00p	35 min	1:40p
2:00p	40 min	2:40p
3:00p	25 min	3:45p
4:00p	15 min	4:45p
5:00p	20 min	(out)
6:00p	20 min	(out)
7:00p	10 min	(out)
8:00p	(closed)	(closed)
9:00p	(closed)	(closed)

A cast of a T-Rex skeleton dominates a queue room for the Dinosaur attraction. Below, guests enter an "underground research facility" to travel back in time. An orange flashing portal sends riders to the late Cretaceous era.

Dino-Sue. A cast of the largest and most complete Tyrannosaurus rex fossil ever found (Sue, South Dakota, 1990) stands in front of the ride. Named after paleontologist Sue Hendrickson, the 67-million-year-old creature was 45 feet long. Much of its bone-work was done in front of Disney guests where today's Dino-Rama carnival sits. The skeleton stands at Chicago's Field Museum.

Cretaceous Trail. This shady paved path meanders through ancient plant species that replicate a dinosaur-era jungle. The greenery includes conifers, ferns, mosses, more than 20 magnolia species and the third largest cycad collection in North America.

Family matters. Outside seats provide the most intense experience. Timid children should sit in the center of the vehicle.

Animal guide

A 1970s-style exhibit sits in the grounds of the Dino Institute, between Restaurantosaurus and the Dinosaur attraction.

American crocodile: Much larger than alligator. Can grow to 15 ft, 2,000 lbs. Can go 2 yrs without eating, using tail fat for nourishment. Bony, platelike body scales; long, powerful tail. No sweat glands; cools by opening mouth. Can't chew; kills large prey by drowning then letting carcass rot. Young chirp before hatching; mother rolls eggs in mouth to open; carries hatchlings to water in mouth; guards 6 mos. Only about 500 left in U.S., all in South Florida. **Asian brown tortoise:** World's most primitive tortoise. Largest in Asia, with heavy, overlapping scales.

Fun finds. ❶ Trees that appear to be behind the building are actually on its roof; they create the illusion that the structure is much smaller than it is. ❷ A dedication plaque is dated April 22, 1978, exactly 20 years before the attraction opened. ❸ In the boarding area, three red, yellow and white pipes are labeled with the chemical makeup of ketchup, mustard and mayonnaise, a nod to the ride's original sponsor, McDonald's. ❹ Gift shop monitors show the ride's iguanodon wandering the building. ❺ A cast of an ancient sea turtle hangs from the gift shop ceiling.

Hidden Mickey. The shape appears as marks on a tree trunk in a lobby mural.

A 1970s Jeep Wrangler sits "stuck in the mud" of The Boneyard playground, which is themed to be a dinosaur-bone dig site. Two distinct areas are connected by an overhead footbridge.

The Boneyard

★★★★ ✓ DinoLand U.S.A. Allow 15–30 min. Capacity: 500. Fear factor: None. Closed during thunderstorms. Access: Guests may remain in wheelchairs, ECVs. Debuted: 1998.

Geared for toddlers through elementary-age kids, this large outdoor playground is themed to be a dinosaur-bone dig site. Two distinct areas are connected by an overhead footbridge. Highlights include a three-story tower of nets and slides (parents can lead kids up to the slide entrances) and a sandy pit where kids can dig for mammoth bones.

Extras include a maze of walk-through tunnels, walls embedded with dinosaur skeletons, climb-on bones and rocks, steep net and rope-climbing ramps and waterfalls sized just right to drench a young head. Mesh canopies filter the sun, and the flooring is a spongy material that stays cool and won't harm tumbling youngsters. There's never a wait, and the playground is rarely overcrowded.

Family matters. The playground offers plenty of spots for parents to get off their feet. Overhead fans keep things breezy. An abundance of nooks and crannies makes it easy to lose sight of your child, but there's only one exit, and its shut gate is monitored.

Fun finds. ❶ Notes sound when kids bang a "xylobone" embedded in a wall near the Jeep. ❷ Nearby, dinosaur tracks trigger loud roars when kids step on them. ❸ Though it looks like the shoulder bone of a stegosaurus, the marquee is actually in the shape of the theme park as it appeared before the addition of Asia. An "N" points north. ❹ Three fictional grad students and their professors have posted work schedules and notes about their dig findings on a whiteboard along the top back wall. ❺ Their notes to each other and personal possessions are scattered about the playground, on the bulletin board at the DinoLand U.S.A. entrance and in the nearby Restaurantosaurus, where they supposedly live in the rafters. ❻ Ambient music (courtesy of radio station w-dino) includes "Brontosaurus," a 1970 U.K. hit for the Move, a band that would later become the Electric Light Orchestra.

Hidden Mickeys. ❶ Near the entrance, as a stain under a drinking fountain. ❷ As a quarter and two pennies on a table in a fenced-off area on the second level in the back, by the slides. ❸ As a fan and two hardhats in a fenced-off area at the back of the sand pit.

Disney whirled: Primeval Whirl "Time Machines" spin as they zig-zag down the ride's narrow track. The roller coaster is the signature attraction of Animal Kingdom's Dino-Rama carnival.

Primeval Whirl

★★★★ *FASTPASS* DinoLand U.S.A. 2 min, 30 sec. Capacity: 52 on each of two tracks. Covered outdoor queue. Fear factor: One steep drop. Jerky. Spinning can affect those with inner-ear issues. Guests should be free from motion sickness; pregnancy; high blood pressure; heart, back or neck problems. Closed during thunderstorms. Access: ECV and wheelchair users must transfer. Height min: 48 in. Debuted: 2002.

This quirky roller coaster—a kitschy timetrip back to the days when dinosaurs became extinct—combines the thrills of a Wild Mouse carnival ride with the spins of a Disney tea cup. Riders continually feel like they are about to fall off the narrow track, as the wide cars whip around turns as they slowly build speed.

Lining the course are cartoon clocks, spinning vortices and cheesy dinosaur cut-outs warning "The End is Near." Eventually a meteor shower hits.

A closer look. The makeshift time machine of a wacky professor, each candy-colored coaster car features the fins and chrome of a 1950s automobile and the huge reflectors of an old bicycle. On the dash sits an alarm clock, a clock radio and an egg timer. Egg beaters and hubcaps adorn the professor's time portal, which sits alongside the queue.

A takeoff on the story told at the nearby Dinosaur attraction, Primeval Whirl is the work of local low-brows Chester and Hester, who wanted a time-travel ride for their Dino-Rama carnival. Lacking the ability to actually send guests back in time, the gas-station owners built a cheap rip-off.

Family matters. The ride makes for a good introduction to roller coasters, as it's not that high or fast. Unsure children can watch others ride it beforehand.

Average wait times

Time	Standby line	Fastpass time
9:00a	10 min	10:10a
10:00a	30 min	10:40a
11:00a	20 min	11:40a
Noon	25 min	12:45p
1:00p	35 min	1:40p
2:00p	25 min	2:45p
3:00p	15 min	3:40p
4:00p	20 min	4:40p
5:00p	15 min	(out)
6:00p	10 min	(out)
7:00p	15 min	(out)
8:00p	(closed)	(closed)
9:00p	(closed)	(closed)

TriceraTop Spin may not have the classic charm of Dumbo the Flying Elephant, but it does seat four, there's rarely a long line, and a covered queue area has huge fans to keep guests cool

TriceraTop Spin

★★★ **DinoLand U.S.A.** 1 min, 30 sec. Capacity: 64. Covered outdoor queue. Fear factor: None. Closed during thunderstorms. Access: ECV users must transfer. Debuted: 2001.

Circling around a colorful spinning-top tin toy, you and up to three other passengers ride in a chubby triceratops that climbs, dips and dives at your command. Extra eye candy includes playful dinosaurs that pop out of the top, flying cartoon comets that circle around it and, at night, white light bulbs lining the hub and spokes. Manic banjo and fiddle music adds a wacky cornpone touch.

Though the ride doesn't have the classic charm of Magic Kingdom's similar Dumbo the Flying Elephant, it is easier to enjoy. There's never a long wait; in fact there's often no wait at all, especially first thing in the morning or during evening Extra Magic Hours. And since each vehicle seats four, small families can ride together. Many Disney purists dismiss the ride as too cheesy, but younger children will love it, and after all, cheesy is the point of the whole Dino-Rama area, which is Disney's riff on a cheap roadside carnival. The vehicles circle the top once every 13 seconds. That's the same speed as Dumbo and Magic Kingdom's

Magic Carpets of Aladdin, half the pace as that theme park's Astro Orbiter.

A closer look. Hub-and-spoke rides have been around since traveling carnivals first appeared in the 1890s. The first rider-controlled version was The Jet Planes, a 1952 U.K. contraption that was around for 30 years.

Family matters. TriceraTop Spin is the only ride at Disney's Animal Kingdom that is completely toddler friendly. The attraction has no height minimum and isn't at all scary.

Average wait times

Time	Standby line	Fastpass time
9:00a	0 min	(n/a)
10:00a	5 min	(n/a)
11:00a	5 min	(n/a)
Noon	10 min	(n/a)
1:00p	20 min	(n/a)
2:00p	15 min	(n/a)
3:00p	15 min	(n/a)
4:00p	10 min	(n/a)
5:00p	10 min	(n/a)
6:00p	5 min	(n/a)
7:00p	5 min	(n/a)
8:00p	5 min	(n/a)
9:00p	(closed)	(n/a)

Colorful stuffed dinosaurs are among the prizes at Disney's Fossil Fun midway games. Contests such as the mallet-strike game Whac-A-Pachycephalosaur are easy for children to play.

Fossil Fun Games

★★★ ✔ **DinoLand U.S.A.** Allow 15 min. Capacity: 1–10 per game. Fear factor: None. Access: Guests may remain in wheelchairs and ECVs. Debuted: 2002.

These whimsical midway games offer children and adults the chance to win stuffed animals and other prizes. Unlike those at many real carnivals, the games aren't rigged and are relatively easy to beat.

Three games are designed specifically for children: the watergun Fossil Fueler, the ball-rolling racing derby Mammoth Marathon and the mallet-strike game Whac-A-Pachycephalosaur ("Whacky Packy" for short). Two others—a ball toss and basketball throw—require serious skill to win. Contestants use a mallet to send a weight up a pole at Dino-Whamma, a strongman game that's unfortunately almost always closed.

Games cost $2–$3 to play. Operators don't accept cash; instead, guests buy vouchers at a cart or at the Dinosaur Treasures gift shop; both take credit cards. Smaller prizes can be combined and traded for larger ones, and can be sent to Package Pickup free of charge, so you don't have to carry them with you.

Part of the Dino-Rama carnival set up by gas-station owners Chester and Hester,

the games sit on what appears to be an old asphalt parking lot. The area also includes funhouse mirrors and a photo booth.

Family matters. Each of the three children's game requires only two players and always awards a prize. In other words, if one of the games has no one else waiting to play it—a common situation, especially early in the morning—you and a child can spend $5 and one of you will absolutely win a small stuffed dinosaur worth at least that much.

The authors' daughter (above) has played the three games for nearly a decade, and offers these tips on how to score high:

Fossil Fueler: For the most accurate shooting, use your free hand to cradle the barrel of your gun.

Mammoth Marathon: Roll the balls gently to keep your mammoth moving fast. If you use too much force your ball will go into a hole with a lesser value, which will move your creature too slowly to win the game. To help hone your child's skill, have her ask for a practice ball before her race begins.

Whac-A-Pachycephalosaur: Wait until you actually see a dinosaur head pop up before you swing at it; don't anticipate.

When curious clownfish Nemo (left) defies his overprotective father in "Finding Nemo—The Musical," each takes off on a journey that ultimately teaches them to understand each other

Finding Nemo—The Musical

★ ★ ★ ★ ★ ✔ **DinoLand U.S.A.** 30 min. Capacity: 1,500. Outdoor queue is not shaded; doors open 25–30 min before showtime. Indoor, air-conditioned theater. Fear factor: None. Access: ECV, wheelchair accessible. Reflective captioning. Debuted: 2007.

Shimmying sharks, body-surfing turtles and a bicycle-riding stingray star in this colorful, whimsical stage show, which re-creates the 2003 Pixar movie "Finding Nemo" as a musical. Nine songs tell the story with help from acrobats, dancers and huge mechanical puppets. Broadway quality but for its length, the show is funny, touching and a visual treat.

Principal characters are represented by live performers, who act out their roles while simultaneously operating large puppet versions of themselves. Other characters are portrayed with a variety of puppetry styles, including rod, shadow and bunraku, a Japanese form in which one huge puppet is operated by multiple puppeteers.

Crowds. The production takes place in the Theater in the Wild, an enclosed, air-conditioned theater. Long lines form for most performances; the last one of the day is usually the least crowded. Arrive at least 45 minutes early for a good seat, even earlier during holiday and other peak periods. Food is allowed in line but not inside the theater.

Where to sit. If you can, sit in the middle of the auditorium to see the full spectacle, or along the center catwalk to be immersed in it.

A closer look. Songs were composed by Robert Lopez and Kristen Anderson-Lopez. The husband-and-wife team took the project "as seriously as we would a Broadway show," says Anderson-Lopez. Robert Lopez won a 2004 Tony Award for "Avenue Q." The puppets were designed by Michael Curry, who created the floats and puppets for Mickey's Jammin' Jungle Parade as well as those used in the Broadway version of "The Lion King."

Family matters. As children wait for the show to begin, many love to find Nemo swimming. The clownfish passes through oversized bubbles on the sides of the stage.

Fun find. As you leave, the movie's gulls ("Mine! Mine!") bid you "Bye! Bye!" They're voiced by Andrew Stanton, the director of the "Finding Nemo" movie.

Hidden Mickey. As three blue bubbles, two lit and one drawn, at the bottom left of the stage wall.

Performance artist DiVine blends into the foliage along the Africa-Asia walkway. Internationally acclaimed percussionist Mor Thiam performs in Harambe. He invites children to drum with him.

Street performers

Asian cultural representatives ★★★★ Asia, next to Yak & Yeti restaurant 20-min shows. Natives from Bali, Thailand and other countries chat about their homelands. At noon and 1 p.m. they tell children's folk tales.

DiVine ★★★★ ✓ On walkway between Africa and Asia 20-min shows. Covered in realistic leaves, grapes and flowers, this sinuous stilt-walker blends into the dense foliage.

Gi-Tar Dan ★★★★ ✓ Camp Minnie-Mickey courtyard 20-min shows. Mon–Fri. Funnyman guitarist sings animal songs, invites children to join in. Often improvises lyrics to include a child's name, clothing or hometown.

Harambe School ★★★★ ✓ Africa, Harambe Village 20-min shows. Approachable young Botswanans, Namibians and South Africans talk about their countries at this three-bench "classroom." Presentations vary; 1 p.m. class is a history of Disney's Harambe village.

Mor Thiam ★★★★★ ✓ Africa, Harambe Village 20-min shows. So unassuming you'd never guess he's been called Africa's greatest percussionist, this living legend often invites children in the audience to join in. A master of the Djembe drum, Mor Thiam (pronounced "Chahm") has played with B.B. King and toured Europe with the Alvin Ailey Dance Company. His son is the R&B artist Akon.

Pipa the Talking Recycling Bin ★★★★ Conservation Station 20-min shows. Roving trash chats and jokes with guests as it wanders the area. Encourages guests to recycle. Pipa means "barrel" in Swahili.

Smear, Splat & Dip ★★★★ DinoLand U.S.A. at Dinosaur Treasures gift shop 20-min shows. Disguised as three wacky painters, this balance and juggling trio uses painters' tools to perform a funny musical mime routine.

Tam Tams of Congo ★★★★★ ✓ Africa, Harambe Village in front of Tusker House restaurant 20-min shows. Rousing native percussion quintet brings guests of all ages on stage for quick lessons in West African dances. Show includes calls, shouts, whistles.

Tropicals ★★★★ DinoLand U.S.A. 20-min shows. Strolling acoustic steel-drum band performs calypso, reggae and world-music tunes.

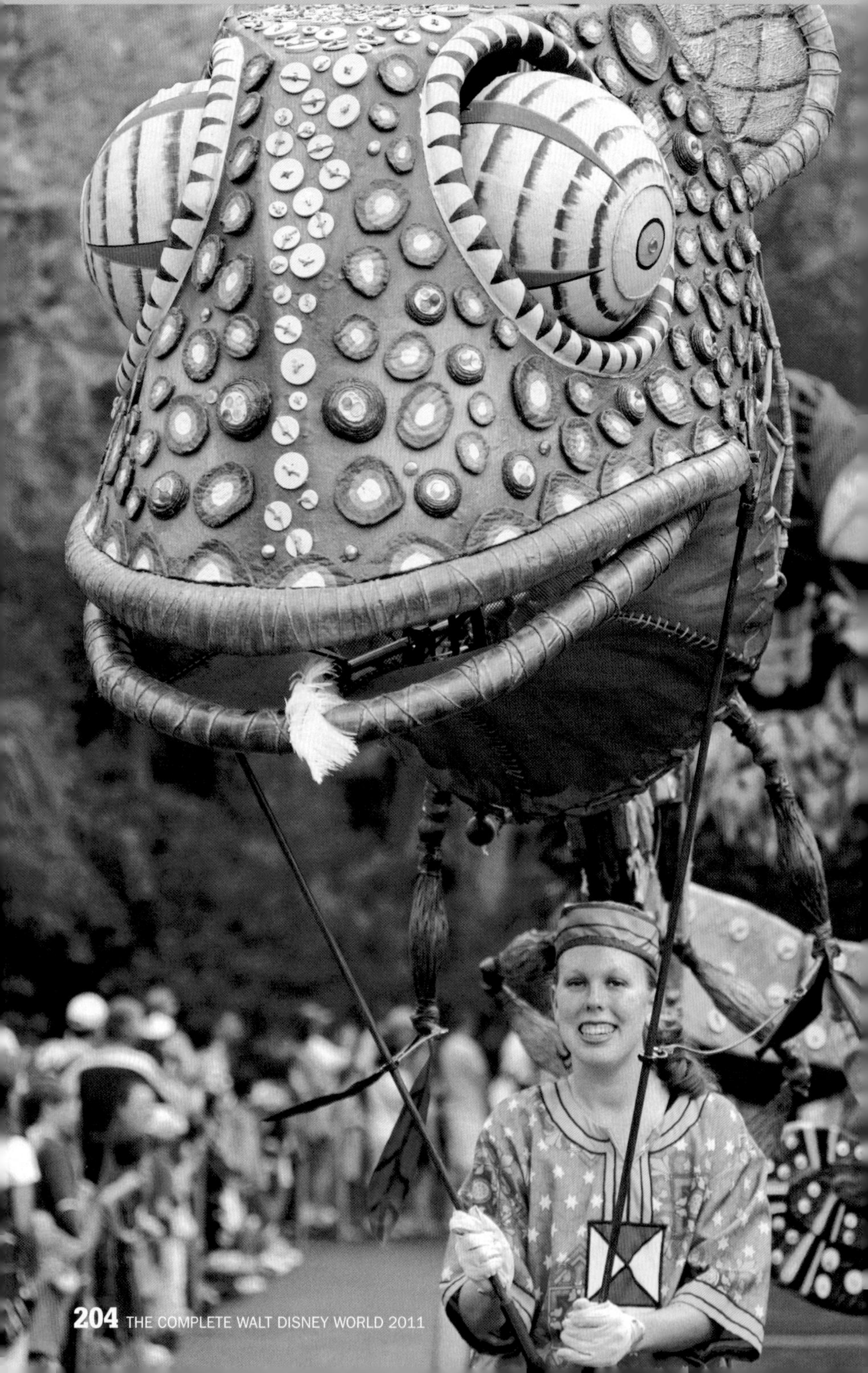

With help from its puppeteer, a chameleon is ready to snag insects off guests with his feathered tongue (facing page); a stiltwalker channels a bird; characters include King Louie, Baloo and Chip

Mickey's Jammin' Jungle Parade

★★★★★ ✓ **Africa, Asia, Discovery Island** 15 min. Circles Discovery Island. Starts, exits, in Africa. Arrive 15 min early for good spot, 30 min for best spots. Cancelled during rain. Fear factor: None. Access: Special viewing locations for those in wheelchairs, ECVs. Assistive listening. Debuted: 2001.

A chameleon may snatch a fly off your head in this lively parade, which combines Disney animal characters, whimsical mechanical puppets, stilt-walkers, dancers and infectious music to celebrate the harmony between man and animals. Quite up close and personal, the procession winds along shady pathways that are often just 12 feet wide. It begins and ends in Africa's Harambe Village; crowds are light for the return trip.

Disney characters ride in safari-themed SUVs. As the story goes, Mickey Mouse and Rafiki—the wise mandrill from 1994's "The Lion King"—are taking Minnie Mouse, Donald Duck and Goofy camping, though none of the three know how to pack. Donald totes a leaky boat, Minnie brings a bathtub. Goofy's packing list apparently included everything—even, literally, his kitchen sink.

Dancing alongside are stilt-walking animals, safari guides and characters such as Pluto, Chip 'n Dale, Timon ("The Lion King"), Terk (1999's "Tarzan"), Baloo and King Louie (1967's "The Jungle Book") and Brer Bear and Brer Rabbit (1946's "Song of the South").

A toe-tapping soundtrack features Disney versions of the 1954 New Orleans standard "Iko Iko," South African legend Miriam Makeba's 1960s tune "Pata Pata" and "Mas Que Nada," the 1966 signature song of Brazil's Sergio Mendes.

Created by Broadway designer Michael Curry, the huge handcrafted puppets use leaves for feathers, vines for tails and sharpened twigs for teeth. Curry also created the puppets for Finding Nemo—The Musical as well as those used in the Broadway version of "The Lion King."

Selected at random by Disney cast members, up to 25 park guests ride along in the parade in rickshaws and trailers.

Family matters. Stand right up front and your children will almost be guaranteed to slap hands with characters.

Fun finds. ❶ Minnie Mouse's bathtub blows bubbles and has a Donald Duck rubber ducky. **❷** Goofy's hood ornament, a Most Dangerous Bowler trophy, topples over as his engine overheats. **❸** Strapped onto the truck are Aladdin's lamp and carpet and a Donald life preserver. **❹** The driver of the hippo rickshaw is the animal's pic-pic bird. **❺** The kangaroo float has a spring for a tail and a drummer in its pouch. **❻** Timon's backpack is full of bugs. **❼** Brooms create the mane and tail of the zebra stilt-walker.

Hidden Mickeys. ❶ As the grill and headlights of the lead vehicle. **❷** As flashing foglights of Mickey's truck.

Water Parks

Giggles, laughs and squeals fill the air at Blizzard Beach and Typhoon Lagoon, the two most popular water parks in the world. Close your eyes and you'll hear happy people enjoying life, perhaps more so than anywhere else you've ever been. Why? Because it's just so much fun to ride a water slide, float down a lazy river or splash in a pool, especially when you're with family or friends in such a fantasy environment. The United States has more than a thousand water parks, but few offer the immersive decor and detailing of these two Disney efforts. Thanks to some first-class landscaping, plastic culverts appear to be streams and rivers, their steel supports completely hidden under rolling, forested hills. The air is filled with calypso and reggae tunes, everywhere you look is

A young boy enjoys the Mayday Falls tube ride at Disney's Typhoon Lagoon water park

opens, which is typically 9 or 10 a.m. Be among the first hundred or so guests in and you will have your choice of primo spots to establish a base, and the waiting lines for rides will be, for the first hour or two, nonexistent.

Be prepared for a day that wears you out. Though Blizzard Beach and Typhoon Lagoon are smaller than any of Disney's theme parks and require much less walking, their rides are much more physical and consume significantly more energy. What's more, queue lines often wind up stairs, sometimes in direct sun, and you'll be outside all day.

Cooler days can be more enjoyable than you might think. With one exception (the pools of Typhoon Lagoon's Shark Reef), all of the water in Disney's flumes, pools and rivers is heated to 80 degrees.

What to bring with you. We say travel light—just a cap or hat, wallet or purse with a charge card, a swimsuit and sunscreen. A towel is a must, but you can rent one for $2. Disney does not allow swimsuits with rivets, buckles, or exposed metal; consider rash guards to protect skin from burns, scrapes and scratches (especially for children).

Want to bring more? Disney allows guests to bring in picnic coolers, food, small conventional toys, strollers, towels and wheelchairs, but not boogie boards, tubes or water toys, glass containers or alcohol. Be careful carrying items with you on rides; Disney sells a small plastic storage container you can hang around your neck for $5, but it can pop open.

Lockers. Small lockers rent for $10 a day, which includes a $5 deposit. Large lockers go for $12. Rental stands typically open 15 minutes before the official park opening time.

Avoiding crowds. Water-park crowds are a different animal than those at theme parks. On one hand, they are sometimes easy to ignore—there's almost always room in a wave pool or lazy river for a few extra people. On the other hand, they're more often in your face—clogging up all the good beach chairs and picnic tables and making the waiting lines for the most popular rides ridiculously long (at a theme park, few people would wait in line 40 minutes for a ten-second ride, but at water parks people do it every afternoon). Worse, there's no such thing as a Fastpass.

The best way to avoid a crowd is to arrive early (see above); do the slides before noon, the lazy rivers and playgrounds after lunch. Second best: stop by after an afternoon thunderstorm, which clears out many guests. In general the parks are least crowded on Tuesdays, Wednesdays and Thursdays.

spic-and-span and everywhere you go is decidedly family oriented.

How do the parks compare? Blizzard Beach has more sun; longer, faster slides; and a great preteen spot. Typhoon Lagoon offers more shade, bigger waves, a better toddler spot and a unique snorkeling experience.

Planning your day. To get the most out of your visit, arrive 30 minutes before a park

On busy days Disney's water parks often fill to capacity—and close to additional guests—by 11 a.m. Visitors already inside are not asked to leave. Typically, the parks reopen later in the day.

Weather closures. Blizzard Beach and Typhoon Lagoon typically stay open when it rains. However, if there is lightning within five miles a park will close its rides and clear its pools. The attractions reopen once the lightning is more than five miles away.

Rain checks: If the attractions are closed for 30 minutes or more, a guest who has been inside the park less than three hours can get a complimentary rain check, with no expiration date, good for a future entry; all members of that party then have to leave. Rain checks are issued from Guest Relations or any ticket booth. Disney will not issue a rain check if the park entry was free, such as with another rain check.

Seasonal closures. Both parks close for annual refurbishments, but they don't shut down at the same time. Typhoon Lagoon usually closes during November and December, Blizzard Beach in January and February.

Family matters. Almost nowhere offers a better place for families to bond than a Disney water park. There are, however, a few issues parents should be aware of:

Life jackets: Disney offers use of standard life jackets at no charge. The parks do permit water wings, though these swimming aids are easy to puncture.

Lost children: Disney staffers—very approachable for children, and easy to identify by their uniforms and name tags—take lost children to marked areas (often covered picnic tables) at the front of each park; sandwich-board signs read "Lost Children." Some families arrange ahead of time to meet in a specific spot in case one of their members gets lost.

Rafts and toys: Neither park allows guests to bring in rafts or other air-filled toys. The parks provide the use of rafts, tubes and mats at rides that are designed for them.

Swim diapers: Infants and toddlers who are not potty-trained are required to wear plastic swim diapers. The water parks sell the diapers at their main gift shops.

Disney lifeguards assist guests with tubes, keep swimmers safe and answer questions

Facing page: A dad and daughter await a wave at the Typhoon Lagoon surf pool

Summit Plummet rises high above Melt-Away Bay, a swimming pool that appears to be created by streams of melting snow. Bobbing waves wash through the pool for 45 minutes of each hour.

Blizzard Beach

The second-most-popular water park in the world—No. 1 is Typhoon Lagoon—66-acre Blizzard Beach attracts nearly 2 million guests a year. Embracing one of Disney's zaniest park themes, it has the look of a melting snow-ski resort. Disguised as ski slopes and watery gullies, body and tube slides line the sides of Mt. Gushmore, a 90-foot snow-capped peak; guests reach its summit on a ski-resort chair lift. In front is a bobbing-wave pool; wrapping around it is a lazy river and children's areas. About a mile from Disney's Animal Kingdom, Blizzard Beach is just down the road from the Coronado Springs Resort.

Attractions. Blizzard Beach includes two intense body slides, two tube slides, two mat slides, a raft ride, bobbing wave pool, lazy river, great preteen spot and a toddler area.

Cross Country Creek ★★★★ ✓ Floating stream 25 min roundtrip. 3,000 ft, 15-ft wide, 2.5-ft deep, max speed 2 mph. Fear factor: None. Circling the park, this shady stream has seven entry points, each with a stack of tubes. Lined with palms and evergreens, it flows under bridges, over springs, past a squirting snowmaking machine and through a cave with icy dripping water. Photopass photographers are on hand.

Downhill Double Dipper ★★★ Steep, enclosed, side-by-side tube slides 6 sec. 230 ft, 50-ft drop, max speed 25 mph. Fear factor: For thrill lovers only. Height min 48 in. This side-by-side racing run takes riders through a tunnel with two steep drops before shooting them through a curtain of water. Just like at an alpine competition, cowbells cheer on the racers as they leave the gate. Times are shown at the finish line. Pull up on your tube handles just before the catch pool to fly across the water. **Family matters**: Thrill-seeking youngsters love this ride; for others the experience is too short.

Melt-Away Bay ★★★★ ✓ Bobbing-wave pool Unlimited time. 1 acre. Fear factor: None. Nestled against the base of Mt. Gushmore, this swimming pool appears to be created by streams of melting snow that wash down into it. Bobbing waves wash through the water for 45 minutes of every hour. Lined by a sandy sunbathing beach, most of the pool is just a few feet deep. Photopass photographers are available. **Family matters:** A shallow slope makes it easy for young children to have fun.

Runoff Rapids ★★★★ ✓ Three banked tube slides 600 ft. Fear factor: May frighten young children. You climb 127 steps to ride these three flumes, but they're worth every huff and puff. Two

Though her boyfriend chickened out moments earlier and had to take the "walk of shame" down the ride's entrance steps, a teenager still prepares to brave Summit Plummet (right), one of the tallest, fastest water slides in the United States. Below, another guest takes the plunge.

outdoor slides allow two-person tubes, a third enclosed one is like Space Mountain, dark except for some pinlights. Steeply banked curves make riders feel like bobsledders.

Ski Patrol Training Camp ★★★★★ ✓ **Preteen area** Unlimited. 8 ft deep in drop area. Fear factor: None. This inventive collection of experiences for preteens is a gem. Children can see each ride before choosing which ones to try:

Fahrenheit Drop: Kids hang on to a cabled T-bar that drops them into an 8-foot pool. Two bars hang at different heights.

Thin Ice Training Course: A slippery walk on floating "icebergs" has overhead rope grids for support, a pool to fall into.

Snow Falls: These wide slides are designed for parents and children to ride together (in separate tubes). Parents can wait for young children in the catch pool.

Cool Runners: These two short tube slides offer brief, but bumpy, rides.

Frozen Pipe Springs: This short covered body slide ends a few inches above its pool.

Slush Gusher ★★★★ ✓ Steep body slide 2 drops. 11–13 sec. 250 ft, 90-ft drop, max speed 50 mph. Fear factor: For thrill lovers only. Height min 48 in. Looking like a melting snow-banked gully, this slide starts off slow, but riders get some airtime off its second drop. A viewing area at the end has covered bleachers. A Photopass photographer is often on hand. **Family matters:** The ride is viewable without getting in line, so it's easy for children to evaluate. The smaller the child, the milder the ride.

Snow Stormers ★★★★ ✓ High-banked mat slide 15–20 sec. 350 ft. Fear factor: Fast, disorienting. You lie face-first as you race down snow-gully S-curves. The three tracks are fast. As you careen up corners splashing water makes it tough to see; a horizontal line on the wall provides a point of reference. To win your race, keep your elbows on your mat and your

Clockwise from top left: A chair lift takes guests up Mt. Gushmore, a rider gets airborne on Slush Gusher, riders are timed on Downhill Double Dipper, two teens race on Toboggan Racers

feet up. **Family matters:** A family of three can ride at the same time.

Summit Plummet ★★★★★ ✔ **Steep body slide** 9–10 sec. 360 ft, 66° 120-ft drop, max speed 60 mph. Fear factor: For thrill lovers only. Height min 48 in. One of the tallest, fastest water slides in the United States, this 12-story tower of terror is the scariest ride in Walt Disney World. Lying down at the top of the ramp, you cross your arms and feet then push yourself over the edge. There's a blur of sky and scenery as you fall; a roar of water as you splash down. The impact can send much of your swimsuit where the sun never shines; wear a T-shirt or rash guard to avoid stinging your skin.

The fall is so intense even some of its designers don't care for it. "I made the mistake when we were building it of going up the stairs and looking down," says Disney Imagineer Kathy Rogers. "I thought, 'There's no way I'd put my body in there!' I did it once and said, 'Done!'"

The ride has no exit stairs; those who chicken out at the last second squeeze back down the entrance stairway in what cast members privately call "the walk of shame."

A mock ski jump, the launch tower rises only 30 feet above Mt. Gushmore but seems much, much higher. There's an observation deck and viewing area at the end of the slide; a display shows rider speeds. **Family matters:** It's easy for children (and adults) to determine whether Summit Plummet is a ride they can handle, as it's viewable from below without getting in line.

Tikes Peak ★★ **Toddler area** Unlimited time. Fear factor: None. Height max: 48 in for slides. Gentle slides, rideable baby alligators and an

Above left, the author's daughter hangs in there on the Thin Ice Training Course at the Ski Patrol Training Camp. Above right, Blizzard Beach tubers take it easy on Cross Country Creek.

ankle-deep squirting "ice" pond highlight this unshaded preschool playground. There's a fountain play area, a little waterfall, sand boxes, lawn chairs, chaise lounges and picnic tables. Kids should wear water shoes; the pavement can get hot. **Family matters:** Unlike Typhoon Lagoon's inspired Ketchakiddee Creek area, Tikes Peak offers few ways for parents and children to spend time together.

Teamboat Springs ★ ★ ★ ★ ★ ✔ Family raft ride 1,200 ft. Min 4 people in rafts, so some groups ride together. Fear factor: Rough ride; unavoidable water sprays. All ages smile on this, the world's longest family raft ride. Sitting in a raft the size of a kiddie pool, you slide down a high-banked course, spinning on tight curves which toss you up on their steep walls. Thirty holes in each raft's bottom edge make sure your rear end gets soaked. A 200-foot ride-out area takes you under a collapsing roof that's dripping with cool water. There's often a minimum of four riders per tube, when smaller groups ride together. **Family matters:** It's tough to find another spot at Disney where families have such a good time together. The ride is so long that parents and children have time to chat.

Toboggan Racers ★ ★ ★ ★ ★ ✔ 8-lane mat slide 10–20 sec. 250 ft. Fear factor: None. Based on an amusement park gunnysack slide, this straight, 8-lane mat slide has guests race down its two dips face first. To go fast, push off quickly then lift up the front of your mat slightly so it doesn't dig in the water. Regardless of technique, the heaviest riders usually win. **Family matters:** Loads of fun for families, Toboggan Racers is more joyful than scary, a sweet spot of fun for all ages. Since multiple riders go at once, whole families can compete against each other.

Characters. Goofy often greets guests next to the Lottawatta Lodge fast food restaurant (in the park's Alpine Village entrance area) and wanders down nearby walkways. He's usually out for half an hour at a time.

Food. Three year-round and two seasonal fast-food spots offer hamburgers, hot dogs, sandwiches, salads and personal pizzas ($4–$9). Snack stands sell hot mini donuts, cotton candy, funnel cakes, ice cream treats, nachos and snow cones. Other spots offer coffee, tea, pastries and beer and rum drinks.

Shopping. Located near the park entrance, Beach Haus has beach and swimwear from Quiksilver, Roxy and Element. Across from the changing rooms, the Shade Shack offers beach towels and sundries; North Pearl sells Japanese akoya pearls in their oysters (6–9 mm, $15), settings and pearl jewelry.

A preschooler plays at Tikes Peak, above left. The Beach Haus gift shop rents lockers and towels, top right. An Alpine Village snow family makes a great photo prop, above right.

A closer look. According to the Disney legend, a freak winter snowstorm hit central Florida in the mid-1990s. Gazing outside their windows, Disney "Imagineers" had a brainstorm: "Let's build a ski resort!"

Within days they built a small mountain and topped it with a ski jump, slalom and bobsled courses, but just as they finished the warmth returned. As workers boarded things up, however, they spotted a lone alligator, still blue from the cold, who had somehow strapped on a pair of skis. He careened down the jump, flew through the air, landed on the restrooms, crashed into the gift shop...

Blizzard Beach average wait times

This table shows the average wait time (in minutes) for each Blizzard Beach ride that has a wait. Guests rarely, if ever, have to wait in line for Cross Country Creek, Melt-Away Bay, the Tikes Peak toddler playground or many of the attractions at the Ski Patrol Training Camp.

ATTRACTION	9A	10A	11A	Noon	1P	2P	3P	4P	5P	6P	7P	8P
Chair lift	0	5	10	20	25	25	20	15	15	10	10	5
Downhill Double Dppr	0	5	5	10	10	15	20	15	10	15	5	5
Fahrenheit Drop	0	5	5	5	5	5	10	10	10	5	5	5
Runoff Rapids	0	0	10	15	15	15	15	15	15	15	15	5
Slush Gusher	0	5	15	20	25	20	25	10	15	20	10	5
Snow Stormers	0	0	10	10	15	15	15	15	15	15	15	5
Summit Plummet	0	5	20	30	40	35	35	20	30	25	20	10
Teamboat Springs	0	5	10	20	30	25	25	10	20	15	10	5
Thin Ice Training Camp	0	5	5	5	5	5	10	10	10	5	5	5
Toboggan Racers	0	5	5	10	10	10	15	10	10	15	5	5

Data based on surveys taken on random days during the summer of 2010.

Teamboat Springs is a 1,200-foot-long family raft ride. A raft the size of a kiddie pool spins down curves and slides up banks. A ride-out area travels under a collapsing roof that's dripping ice water. The trip is so long riders have time to chat.

and emerged with a smile. Watching this "Ice Gator," the Imagineers realized their failed ski resort would make a great water park—the jump could be a body slide; the slalom, bobsled and sledding runs could be mat and tube rides; the slushy creek a lazy river. Naming their creation Blizzard Beach, the Imagineers opened it to the public—on April Fools Day, 1995.

Fun finds. ❶ At the Alpine Village, Ice Gator's ski tracks appear on the roof of the women's dressing room, behind a sign that reads "Caution: Low Flying Gator." ❷ Across the walkway, his silhouette forms a hole in the side of the Beach Haus shop. It's also on the weathervane. ❸ An eclectic soundtrack mixes summertime tunes with Christmas ditties, including the Beach Boy's version of "Frosty the Snowman." ❹ Barrels of equipment and "Instant Snow" from the fictional Joe Blow Snow Co. line the walkways to Slush Gusher, Summit Plummet and Teamboat Springs. ❺ Equipment from the Sunshine State Snow Making Co. sits along the bank of Cross Country Creek and along the queue for the Toboggan Racers mat slide. ❻ Across from the entrance to the Downhill Double Dipper slide, melting snow drips off a roof of a small building marked "Safe to Approach Unless Melting." ❼ "Ancient" drawings on the walls of the Cross Country Creek cave include a beach chair with an umbrella and a skier with a leg cast. ❽ The Northern Lights shine through the cave ceiling. ❾ "B-r-r-r-occoli" and "Sleet Corn" are planted in Ice Gator's garden along Cross Country Creek, just past Manatee Landing. ❿ As guests float by the nearby home of the alligator, they often hear him sneeze and ask "Anybody got a hanky?"

Blizzard Beach Resources

ATM: At the Guest Relations kiosk, located just outside the entrance turnstiles.

Cooler policy: Coolers with up to two wheels are allowed. The park has no place to store medication coolers.

First-aid supplies: To the right of the Beach Haus shop, Alpine Village.

Guest Relations: A kiosk just outside the entrance turnstiles.

Life jackets: Complimentary, offered at Snowless Joe's, Alpine Village.

Locker rentals: At the Beach Haus and Snowless Joe's in Alpine Village. Lockers are located next to Snowless Joe's and near the Ski Patrol Training Camp and Downhill Double Dipper attractions.

Lost children: Taken to a marked picnic table in Alpine Village, between the changing rooms and Lottawatta Lodge.

Lost and Found: At Guest Relations.

Parking: Free.

Phone number: 407-560-3400.

Strollers: Strollers are welcome, though many sandy areas are tough to navigate. No rental strollers are available.

Towel rentals: Rentals at the Beach Haus and Snowless Joe's, Alpine Village.

Transportation: Disney buses shuttle guests to Blizzard Beach from all Disney resorts and Disney's Animal Kingdom theme park. There is no official service to other parks or Downtown Disney, but all Disney buses that travel to Animal Kingdom stop at Blizzard Beach.

Wheelchairs: No wheelchairs are available for rent. Wheelchairs are welcome, though many sandy areas are tough to navigate.

Braced for impact, a crowd at the Typhoon Lagoon surf pool awaits a breaking wave. Few guests body surf but many love to be knocked around. Wave height varies throughout the day.

Typhoon Lagoon

The most popular water park in the world, Typhoon Lagoon draws more than 2 million visitors a year. With an atmosphere that's one part Hawaii and two parts "Gilligan's Island," it's a shady, silly escape. Thorough landscaping immerses guests in a tropical environment, though all the greenery makes it tough to see some of the slides before you go on them. Located along the eastern side of Disney World property, the 61-acre park is located across the street from Downtown Disney, within easy access of Interstate 4.

Attractions. Typhoon Lagoon features a signature surf pool that's the largest in the United States, a saltwater-snorkeling experience and an absolutely terrific water playground for toddlers. It also includes three body slides (one of which is intense), three tube slides (one of which is a water coaster), a raft ride and a lazy river:

Bay Slides ★★★ **Children's body slides** 10 sec. 35 ft, max speed 7 mph. Fear factor: None. Height max: 60 in. At secluded corner of Surf Pool. These two short slides are for children who are too old for Ketchakiddee Creek but a little too young for the Storm Slides, Humunga Kowabunga or the big waves of the main area of the surf pool. One slide is uncovered with a few gentle bumps; the other has a 4-foot tunnel. The slides are in the calm left corner of the Surf Pool, an area called Blustery Bay. **Family matters:** Though parents lose sight of their kids on the walkway up to slides for a few seconds there's little need for concern; the path is just 10 steps and leads only to the slides. Many parents wait in the water.

Castaway Creek ★★★ ✔ **Floating stream** 25 min (roundtrip). 2,100 ft, 15-ft wide, 3-ft deep, max speed 2 mph. Fear factor: None. This shady palm-lined journey circles the surf pool. Expect to get misted, drizzled on and, as you enter a cave, maybe completely drenched. Shoreline sights include three crashed boats and the Ketchakiddee Creek playground; once high above you is a suspension bridge. The creek splits in two for a short distance. There's never a wait, though the creek gets crowded on summer afternoons. There are seven entry points; some tubes hold two people.

Crush 'n' Gusher ★★★★★ ✔ **Water-coaster tube ride** 30 sec. 420 ft, max speed 18 mph. 2-, 3-person tubes. Covered queue. Fear factor: Chaotic, disorienting; few visual reference points. Height min 48 in. Debuted 2005. With both lifts and dips, these three flumes offer roller coaster thrills. A conveyer

Clockwise from top left: Two girls enjoy the surf pool, Miss Tilly spouts every half hour, the park ticket booth, a surf pool warning is sometimes not heeded, side coves have calm entrances.

belt lowers you onto a slide, then water jets thrust you upward. Each ride is more thrilling than it looks from the entrance area; it's hard to tell how fast the tubes go because the flumes aren't steep. To stay in control, push your feet down into the front of your tube. A Photopass photographer is often available. The three flumes offer slightly different rides:

Banana Blaster: Includes 1 long, 2 med tunnels; slightly longer track than other flumes; 2-person rafts only.

Coconut Crusher: Includes 3 tunnels of various lengths.

Pineapple Plunger: Includes 2 peaks, 3 short tunnels. Lean back to catch air.

The attraction is meant to be the hurricane-ravaged remains of the (say it slowly) Tropical Amity fruit-packing plant. The flumes are spillways that once cleaned fruit before it was shipped. Aptly named Out of the Way Cay, the 5-acre setting for Crush 'n' Gusher is hidden from the rest of the park, tucked behind the main locker area. **Family matters:** Note that if there are three people in your group you can all ride together; in general the more people on a tube the more fun the ride. Besides the ride, the area includes a shallow gradual-entry swimming pool lined with beach chairs and chaise lounges, a perfect place for parents and toddlers to play while big kids check out the ride.

Gangplank Falls ★★ Family raft ride 30 sec. 300 ft, avg speed 7 mph. 4-person rafts. Fear factor: Rough ride; unavoidable water sprays. This wide waterway goes under waterfalls, a small cave and past squirting pipes, but its ride is too short for its

Clockwise from top left: The Gangplank Falls tube slide has rafts that hold up to five people, Mayday Falls can turn riders backwards, Keelhaul Falls is the park's tamest full-size tube slide.

typically long wait. Ride it first thing in the morning, or late in the day, to make it worthwhile. A Photopass photographer is often on hand. **Family matters:** The rafts are too small to hold families with more than four people.

Humunga Kowabunga ★★ Steep enclosed body slides 7 sec. 214 ft, 60° 50-ft drop, max speed 30 mph. Fear factor: For thrill lovers only. Height min 48 in. These three identical tubes offer a one-dimensional experience: a short, straight drop. **Family matters:** A shady viewing area has two spots to watch from: one standing, one seated.

Keelhaul Falls ★★ Gentle C-curve tube slide 50 sec. 400 ft, avg speed 6 mph. Fear factor: None. Tubes slowly build speed on this short course, the park's tamest full-size tube slide. Guests get one small thrill, as they slightly slide up its final banked turn.

Ketchakiddee Creek ★★★★★ ✓ **Toddler area** Unlimited time. 18 activity spots. Fear factor: None. Height max: 48 in for slides. What was once, according to Disney lore, a no-man's land of volcanoes and geysers is now an elaborate kiddie water park all its own. Lined with palms, a 100-foot tube slide has three little dips, and a surrounding area of low bubbly fountains and ankle-deep streams and pools. More adventurous toddlers will hurl themselves down two slip 'n' slides—cushy 20-foot mats with 20-degree drops. Older kids have a blast at the S.S. Squirt, an oversized

"sand sculpture" where guests battle each other with swiveling water cannons. Nearby, water hoses shake, shimmy and squirt atop a 12-foot-tall Blow Me Down boiler. **Family matters:** The area has shady chairs and picnic tables; many families build sandcastles. Ketchakiddee Creek is so popular it often gets too crowded in the afternoons; Disney doesn't enforce the requirement that children are shorter than 48 inches, so older kids sometimes play here, too.

Mayday Falls ★★★ Swervy, rippled "white water" tube slide 30 sec. 460 ft, avg speed 10 mph. Fear factor: Rough ride. This triple vortex can turn guests around and has one small waterfall; unfortunately the inches-deep water makes the trip uncomfortable.

Mt. Mayday Trail ★★★★ Scenic walkway Fear factor: None. Located between Gangplank Falls and Humunga Kowabunga, this hidden fern-and-hibiscus-lined path—not an attraction per se—travels close to the park's iconic impaled Miss Tilly shrimp boat, with a view of the entire park. Tiny streams splash through it. Crossing a suspension bridge high over Castaway Creek, the walkway is often vacant even on the most crowded days.

Shark Reef ★★★★ ✓ Saltwater snorkeling pool Fear factor: Cold saltwater. Guests swim above tropical fish (including "smiling" rainbow parrotfish), rays, and small—and quite

Clockwise from above left: Shark Reef snorkelers swim with tropical fish, rays and sharks; they drift past a (real) overturned tanker; water jets propel Crush 'n' Gusher riders uphill

passive—leopard and bonnethead sharks, any of which may come close to guests who stay still. The artificial reef has a small central resting area; use of masks, snorkels, life vests, changing areas and outdoor showers is complimentary. An optional Supplied Air Snorkeling adventure includes use of an air tank, regulator, flippers and instruction ($20, 30 min, summer only, ages 5 and up, run by the National Association of Underwater Instructors, money goes to a conservation program). **Family matters:** You can watch your child in the water from a bridge above the reef, or from underwater viewing windows in a (real) capsized tanker.

Storm Slides ★ ★ ★ ★ Shady, high-banked body slides 15 sec. 300 ft, max speed 20 mph. Fear factor: May frighten young children. At the boarding area of these, the most interesting body slides in the park, guests choose from three courses: Rudder Buster (on the left) has a small tunnel; Stern Burner (middle) has a longer, dark tunnel; Jib Jammer (right) has no tunnel at all. **Family matters:** Parents who don't wish to ride can wait for their children—and watch them splash into the catch pool—from unshaded bleachers.

Surf Pool ★ ★ ★ ★ ✔ **Wave pool** Unlimited time. Waves 2–6 ft. Fear factor: Waves intimidate some guests, can topple those even in shallow areas. Young children should stay with parents. Body-surfable

waves sweep down this large pool, making it a popular hangout among teens and young adults, as well as a fun spot for families to play together. Few guests body surf but many love to be knocked around by the waves. The surf is created in a closed-off deep end, as 12 backstage collection chambers repeatedly push out 80,000 gallons of water through two underwater doors. Wave size varies throughout the day; a chalkboard in front of the area shows the daily schedule.

The largest wave pool in the United States in terms of guest capacity, water volume and wave height, the scallop-shaped concrete pool is 115 feet wide by 395 feet long. Side areas offer protected wading zones and kid-sized slides. The 2.5-acre area resembles a tropical cove, with a real sandy beach, infant-friendly bubbling "tide pools" (with tiny climb-on boats) and an artificial sand bar about 50 feet "offshore." Surfing lessons (see the chapter "Activities") are often held in the pool early in the day, before the park opens.

Characters. Lilo and Stitch often greet park guests at a spot next to High 'N Dry Towels. They appear for 20 minutes at a time.

Food. Three year-round fast-food counters and two seasonal spots serve hamburgers, hot dogs, sandwiches, salads and personal

New Jersey's Amanda Mathus, 14, braces for splashdown on the Stern Burner Storm Slide, above left. Dads join in the water-cannon fun at the Ketchakiddee Creek children's area, above right.

pizzas ($4–$9). The largest variety of items is at the Leaning Palms counter, located in the far left side of the main Harbor Village area. Snack stands serve hot mini donuts (pretty good when fresh), cotton candy, funnel cakes, hot dogs, pretzels and ice cream treats. Other stands sell coffee, tea and pastries, and, from a converted "Surf Doggies" surf scooter, beer and decent rum drinks. Typhoon Lagoon has two designated picnic areas, though guests can set up a meal virtually anywhere.

Shopping. Located near the park entrance in the Harbor Village area, Singapore Sal's is stocked with beach- and swimwear from Quiksilver, Roxy and Element, Disney beach towels and sundries. At the entrance to the Shark Reef attraction, a Pearl Factory stand sells Japanese akoya pearls in their oysters (6–9 mm, $15), settings and pearl jewelry.

A closer look. According to Disney lore, the Placid Palms resort was once nestled in

Typhoon Lagoon average wait times

This table shows the average wait time (in minutes) for each Typhoon Lagoon attraction that has a wait. Guests rarely, if ever, have to wait in line for the Bay Slides, Castaway Creek, Ketchakiddee Creek, the Mt. Mayday Trail or the Typhoon Lagoon Surf Pool.

ATTRACTION	9A	10A	11A	Noon	1P	2P	3P	4P	5P	6P	7P	8P
Crush 'N Gusher	0	5	10	10	10	10	15	15	15	10	10	5
Gangplank Falls	0	5	20	30	40	35	35	20	30	25	20	10
Humunga Kowabunga	0	0	5	5	5	10	15	15	15	10	5	5
Keelhaul Falls	0	0	10	10	15	15	15	15	15	15	15	5
Mayday Falls	0	0	10	15	15	15	15	15	15	15	15	5
Shark Reef	0	0	10	10	10	10	15	10	15	10	5	5
Storm Slides	0	5	5	10	10	10	15	10	10	15	5	5

Data based on surveys taken on random days during the summer of 2010.

Orlando's Rathbun family relaxes under the lush landscape of Castaway Creek. Shoreline sights include three crashed boats, a suspension bridge high overhead and the Ketchakiddee Creek playground. Some tubes hold two people.

a tranquil valley next to a volcanic mountain. Over the years the resort had been subject to a few earthquakes and geothermal rumblings, but overall life remained, well, placid. Then, in 1955, Hurricane Connie struck. The massive storm blew boats through buildings, sliced surfboards through trees, impaled a shrimp boat, cut an adjacent harbor off from the Atlantic (trapping many fish) and nearly destroyed a fruit processing plant. Crates of fireworks blew in from some nearby island warehouses owned by a Mr. Merriweather Pleasure; at the time he put on a nightly fireworks show. After the storm swept out to the sea, villagers remained upbeat. Sign paint in hand, they renamed their resort "Leaning Palms" and, barely bothering to clean up, transformed it into a topsy-turvy tropical playground—a sunny, but shady, water park. Typhoon Lagoon opened on June 1, 1989.

Fun finds. ❶ To the right of the entrance turnstiles, hanging nautical flags secretly spell out "PIRANHA IN POOL." ❷ The surf pool wall resembles a wooden levee ready to burst; water spits out between its planks. ❸ An alligator totem stands under the clock tower, near the shack of park mascot Lagoona Gator. ❹ Inside the shack are posters and flyers for The Beach Gators ("So cold blooded, they're hot!") and the film "Bikini Beach Blanket Muscle Party Bingo"; a Surfin' Reptile magazine includes the article "How to Get a Golden Tan Without Being Turned into a Suitcase." ❺ In front of the Happy Landings snack bar, guests can squirt water at Castaway Creek floaters through props of real outboard motors. ❻ Ripped open, a "shark-proof" cage sits along the Shark Reef walkway, past the showers.

Typhoon Lagoon Resources

ATM: At Singapore Sal's, entrance area

Cooler policy: Coolers with up to two wheels are allowed. The park has no place to store medication coolers.

First-aid supplies: Behind the Leaning Palms fast-food restaurant.

Guest Relations: A kiosk just outside the entrance turnstiles.

Life jackets: Complimentary; offered at Singapore Sal's and High 'N Dry Towels, both at the entrance area.

Locker rentals: At Singapore Sal's at the entrance area. Most lockers are nearby; some are near the Shark Reef attraction.

Lost children: Taken to a marked area in front of Singapore Sal's.

Lost and Found: At Guest Relations.

Parking: Free.

Phone number: 407-560-7223.

Strollers: Strollers are welcome, though many sandy areas are tough to navigate. No rental strollers are available.

Towel rentals: Rentals at Singapore Sal's, at the entrance area.

Transportation: Disney buses shuttle guests to Typhoon Lagoon from all Disney-owned resort hotels. Before 10 a.m. the buses drop off guests at Typhoon Lagoon and then continue to Downtown Disney; after 10 a.m., they stop first at Downtown Disney. There is no direct service between Disney theme parks and Typhoon Lagoon.

Wheelchairs: No wheelchairs are available for rent. Wheelchairs are welcome, though many sandy areas are tough to navigate.

Downtown Disney

This lakeside commercial center offers unusual dining, entertainment and shopping for all ages. Located near the northeast corner of Disney property along the 43-acre Village Lake, the 120-acre strip is divided into three sections, each with its own parking lot.

Marketplace. Originally called the Walt Disney World Shopping Village, this 48-acre open-air shopping mall has been a Disney fixture since the 1970s. Rough-hewn buildings are covered in cedar-shake shingles.

Pleasure Island. Built in 1989 as a night-club district but today largely vacant, this 6-acre area sits in the center of Downtown Disney. By 2013, the site will have morphed into Hyperion Wharf, a "nostalgic yet modern" take on an early-20th-century port city and amusement pier. At night, thousands

Cirque du Soleil's La Nouba begins with an invasion by the lock-step Urbanites

Photo © Cirque du Soleil / Disney

of lights will transform the spot into what Disney calls "an electric wonderland."

West Side. Downtown Disney's largest section, this 66-acre area has many creative restaurants and some unusual entertainment options, including a Cirque du Soleil show.

Complimentary pontoon-boat water taxis shuttle guests between the Marketplace and West Side areas.

Restaurants and food. With a dozen table-service restaurants and a handful of fast-food eateries, there are lots of dining choices at Downtown Disney. Several have music and dancing, a couple are on the water and some have elaborately themed interiors that re-create a rain forest or a dinosaur habitat. Most are not owned by Disney, and therefore are not on the Disney Dining Plan.

See the chapter **Restaurants and Food.**

Entertainment

Downtown Disney offers many entertainment options, both expensive and affordable:

AMC 24 Theater ★★★★ ✓ Movie theaters $6 before noon; A $8.50, C 2–12 $7.50 noon–4p; A $10.50, C 2–12 $7.50 after 4p; Sr. 60+ $6 on Tuesdays. Digital 3-D movies $3 addl.; in ETX auditorium $5 addl. Annual/Seasonal Passholders get $2 off adult evening admission price after 6p. Hours vary. 24 theaters, 18 with stadium seating, 2 3-story auditoriums with balconies. Audio: THX Surround Sound, Sony Dynamic Digital Sound. Listening devices available. Guests may remain in wheelchairs, ECVs. 110,000-sq-ft complex. Seats 5,390. AMC movie listings: 888-262-4386. Local box office: 407-827-1308. West Side. This cineplex is the only public movie theater on Disney property. Redone in 2010, auditorium No. 1 has the first Enhanced Theater Experience in the United States, with a 20 percent larger floor-to-ceiling screen, 12-channel audio and ultra-high resolution digital projection. New concession stands offer gourmet popcorn, ice cream, specialty coffees and 106 flavors of Coca-Cola. New for 2011, six Fork & Screen auditoriums deliver food to guests seated at tables.

Bongos Cuban Cafe ★★★ Restaurant with live band, dancing No cover. Latin traditional and pop music, dance floor, dancing starting at 10p Fri, Sat. All ages. Created by pop star Gloria Estefan and her husband, Emilio. Seats 560. Info: 407-828-0999. West Side.

Characters in Flight ★★★ Tethered helium balloon rides A $18, C 3–9 $12. Sun–Thur 10:30a–11p; Fri–Sat 10:30a–mid. 9-min rides (2 min ascent, 5 min at 400 ft, 2 min descent). Flights, times subject to change due to weather. Capacity: winds 0–3 mph: up to 30; 3–12 mph up to 20; 12–22 mph up to 10; over 22 mph does not fly. Access: Guests may stay in wheelchairs, ECV users must transfer to a wheelchair. Children under 12 must fly with adult. Weather refunds day of purchase only. West Side. The world's largest tethered gas balloon silently lifts a 30-person gondola 400 feet in the air. Waist-high walls are topped with loose-weave netting. A certified pilot rides along. Guests see up to 10 miles. The balloon glows at night.

DisneyQuest ★★ Electronic games A $42, C $36. Sun–Thurs 11:30a–10p, Fri–Sat to 11p. Height min: 51 in.

The five-story DisneyQuest building anchors the Downtown Disney West Side. Inside is a variety of video games and virtual-reality experiences.

for CyberSpace Mountain, Buzz Lightyear's AstroBlaster; 48 in. Mighty Ducks Pinball Slam; 35 in. Pirates of the Caribbean. Children under 10 must be accompanied by an adult. No strollers. Complimentary coat check. 2 counter cafes. 407-828-4600. West Side. Virtual reality experiences highlight this five-story arcade, which was state-of-the-art about a decade ago. Admission includes unlimited experiences. Evening crowds can create long waits for popular games; the complex is least crowded on fair-weather afternoons. Games include:

Aladdin's Magic Carpet Ride: A virtual reality hunt through the alleys of Agrabah for a magic lamp. 2nd floor.

Animation Academy: 30-minute class teaches how to draw Disney characters. Printouts $5, $12 with pen. 2nd floor.

Buzz Lightyear's AstroBlaster: Cannon-firing bumper cars. 3rd floor.

CyberSpace Mountain: Design a roller coaster, then "ride" it in a motion simulator. DVD of your ride: $12. 2nd floor.

Invasion! An ExtraTERRORestrial Alien Encounter: Battle virtual aliens on a spaceship. 5th floor.

Kid's Zone: Games for ages 2 to 7. 4th floor.

Living Easels: Guests place images into backgrounds using touch screens, with printouts available for $5. 2nd floor.

Mighty Ducks Pinball Slam: Guests stand on a giant joystick and steer themselves among other guests on a huge screen in this life-sized pinball game. 3rd floor.

Pirates of the Caribbean: Battle for Buccaneer Gold: The best DisneyQuest game, this virtual boat ride puts a crew of four into a 3-D pirate battle. 1st floor.

Radio Disney SongMaker: Create your own song, buy it for $12. 2nd floor.

Replay Zone: Classic games such as Asteroids, Centipede, Donkey Kong, Frogger, Pac-Man, Space Invaders and Tron. 3rd, 4th, 5th floors.

Ride the Comix: Guests don virtual reality helmets to battle supervillains. Up to six can play as a team. 4th and 5th floors.

Sid's Create-a-Toy: Make a toy from mismatched parts. Buy it for $10. 2nd floor.

Virtual Jungle Cruise: Guests row a raft down a prehistoric river past dinosaurs, getting splashed along the way. 1st floor.

House of Blues ★★★★ ✔ **Music Hall** $8–$95. Showtimes typ 7–9:30p. Gen adm; restaurant diners get priority. Doors open 1 hr before showtime weekdays, 90 min early weekends. All ages. Capacity 2,000 (tables and stools seat 150, standing room 1,850). 407-934-2583 or hob.com. West Side. One of a handful of music halls created by Hard Rock Cafe founder Isaac Tigrett and entertainer Dan Aykroyd, this two-story venue books a range of acts; blues and rock dominate. A folk-art decor, hardwood floors and quality sound and light systems add to the experience. An adjacent restaurant has acoustic entertainment on a Front Porch bar from 6–11 p.m., a plugged-in show Thurs–Sat 10:30 p.m. to 2 a.m.

La Nouba ★★★★★ ✔ **Musical European Circus** A $76–$132, C $61–$105. Tues–Sat 6p, 9p. Arrive 30 min early. 90-min show, no intermission. Best ages 4+. Snack stand. Seats 1,671. Tickets avail 6 mos in adv at 407-939-7600, cirquedusoleil.com or at the box office. Blending the traditions of a European circus with modern acrobatics, dance and street entertainment, this invigorating Cirque du Soleil spectacle fills nearly everyone with delight. Costumes, choreography, music and stagecraft are all world-class. Designed for a Disney audience, the show's purpose is to "wake up the innocence in your heart." You'll be surprised how well it succeeds.

The opening portrays a meeting of two worlds, a modern urban society that toes society's line and a hundred-year-old circus troupe in which each member marches to his or her own beat. The finale features a surreal ballet in which acrobats dive into, and out of, large window frames. Other highlights include tightrope walkers, trapeze artists and, in the show's most beautiful moment, hanging aerialists wrapped in huge red-silk ribbons. Stealing the show is a group of four ever-smiling young Asian girls, who dance, flip and climb on each other as they play Diabolo.

Each scene is presented as a figment of the imagination of a cleaning lady, who eventually finds herself in the fairy tale "The Princess and The Frog."

Sideshow characters include a quartet of all-white simpletons and a flightless, envious Green Bird. Clowns Balthazar and Sergei entertain between acts.

Movie buffs will find references to 1997's "The Fifth Element" in La Nouba's odd music and warbling diva, and influences of 1998's "Dark City" in its looming cityscapes and unexpected moving floors. Art lovers will note homages to Calder and Matisse.

Lacking a master of ceremonies, the show is abstractly narrated by musicians who perform in towers alongside the stage. Their mix of classical, jazz, hip hop, klezmer, techno and bluegrass adds a zesty accent to each performer. Some songs have vocalists—an androgynous high-alto male and a spirited Gospel female. Nonsensical lyrics sound vaguely French. Acoustics are crystal clear.

Every seat is good, but spending the money to sit down front does pay off—you'll see every costume and makeup detail, every smile and grimace, every tensed muscle.

You'll hear the acrobats shout verbal cues. Front-row center is Row 1, Section 103. Tickets go on sale six months in advance.

Raglan Road ★★★★★ ✔ **Irish pub with live band, dancers** No cover. Band plays 7p–1:30a Mon–Sat, Irish table dancers every half hour. All ages. Seats 600. Direct res: 407-938-0300. Pleasure Island. A cheerful crowd sings along to an Irish band at this gem of a spot, a favorite hangout of off-duty Disney cast members. Brought over from the Emerald Isle, 3-piece house band Creel starts off with acoustic Irish tunes; later its Irish rock sets get rowdy. A dancer performs on a small table (an old parson's pulpit) in the middle of the room; additional dancers go through their paces in front of the band.

Downtown Disney Resources

ATMs: The Marketplace section of Downtown Disney has three ATMs—near the Tren-D store, next to the Ghirardelli chocolate shop and inside the World of Disney. The West Side area has two ATMs: at the House of Blues Company Store and the Wetzel's Pretzels snack shop.

First-aid supplies: At the Marketplace, aspirin, Band-Aids and similar items are sold at World of Disney, Tren-D and the marina. In the West Side you'll find them at Mickey's Groove, DisneyQuest and the Cirque du Soleil box office.

Guest Relations: At the Marketplace between Team Mickey's and Arribas Brothers, 8:30a–11p Sun–Thurs, to 11:30p Fri–Sat. At the West Side across from Wetzel's Pretzels, 9a–11:45p.

Locker rentals: At the Marketplace marina near Cap'n Jack's Restaurant.

Mailbox: At the Marketplace next to the fountain in front of World of Disney.

Parking: Free.

Stroller rentals: At the Marketplace at Disney's Design-A-Tee Shop; at the West Side at the DisneyQuest Emporium ($15 day plus $100 deposit).

Transportation: Boats lead to Old Key West, Port Orleans and Saratoga Springs resorts. Disney buses serve all Disney resorts, Magic Kingdom (via TTC), Epcot, Animal Kingdom, Blizzard Beach and Typhoon Lagoon; no direct service to ESPN Wide World of Sports.

Wheelchair rentals: At the Marketplace at Disney's Design-A-Tee Shop; at the West Side at the DisneyQuest Emporium ($12 day plus $100 deposit).

Downtown Disney shops

Marketplace

Arribas Brothers: Hand-cut crystal, hand-blown glass. Engraving. Artisans work in front of guests.

The Art of Disney: Disney-themed oil paintings, animation cels, lithographs, theme-park attraction posters, Lenox china figurines, plates, vases and other quality art pieces fill the walls.

Basin: All-natural massage and shampoo bars, bath bombs, body butters, lotions, salt and sea scrubs. Make-your-own candle station. Intoxicating aroma.

Design-A-Tee Shop: Personalized T-shirts.

Disney's Days of Christmas: Holiday shop has ornaments, collectibles, figurines, Mickey-eared Santa hats. Embroidery, engraving. Disney's largest holiday shop.

Disney's Pin Traders: Open-air pin shop.

Ghirardelli: Candy, fudge sauce, cocoa, hot-chocolate mix. Free samples.

Goofy's Candy Co.: Custom apples, cookies, marshmallow treats. Jellybeans, lollipops, coffees.

LEGO Imagination Center: World's largest Pick-A-Brick wall has 320 bins. Giant display creations. Outdoor play area.

Little Miss Matched: Socks and accessories for adults and children.

Mickey's Mart: Discount Disney items.

Mickey's Pantry: Mickey Mouse-styled housewares. Non-Disney cookware, food, tableware, wine. New spice and tea section features "create-your-own" blends.

Once Upon a Toy: 16,000-sq-ft toy store has theme-park items, Hasbro items. Build-Your-Own Mr. Potato Head station.

Rainforest Cafe: Shop within restaurant has Rainforest Cafe and animal-themed apparel, plushies, toys. Animated decor.

T-REX Dino-Store: Shop within restaurant has dinosaur children's apparel, toys. Build-A-Bear Workshop "Build-A-Dino" area. Kids search for faux fossils in outdoor "sand" pit and sluice.

Team Mickey's Athletic Club: Disney, ESPN sportswear, sporting goods. Custom Louisville Slugger bats.

Tren-D: Stylish Junior apparel. Disney, Billabong, Hurley, Roxy brands.

World of Disney: Disney department store has rooms dedicated to "Princesses" (girls), Ladies and Juniors, Boys, Men, Infants, Hats and T-shirts, Housewares, Home Accessories, Jewelry and Pins, Candy and Snacks, Souvenirs. Bibbidi Bobbidi Boutique (10 chairs, 407-939-7895, reservations book quickly) is makeover salon mainly for young girls.

Pleasure Island

Curl by Sammy Duvall: Beachwear. Youth fashion apparel, purses, hats, jewelry, sunglasses, surf boards, skate boards.

Fuego By Sosa: Hand-rolled cigars, 100 varieties. Cocktail lounge.

Orlando Harley-Davidson: Motorcyle-themed apparel for men, women, kids. Collectibles, pet items. No bikes for sale.

Shop for Ireland: Irish apparel, infantwear, mugs, cookbooks. At Raglan Road.

West Side

Bongos shop: Cuban apparel, mugs, margarita glasses, maracas, coffee.

Candy Cauldron: Jellybeans, candied apples, chocolate-covered strawberries made in front of guests. Recalls Evil Queen's dungeon in 1937's "Snow White and the Seven Dwarfs."

Cirque du Soleil Boutique: Apparel, accessories. Stunning Cirque-branded scarves, purses, fashion apparel, masks, figurines, circus caps. La Nouba souvenirs.

D Street: Vinylmation collectibles, apparel.

DisneyQuest Emporium: Disney items.

House of Blues Co. Store: Blues CDs, cornbread mix, folk art, hot sauce, incense.

Hoypoloi: Home-accent gallery offers unusual clocks, figurines, fountains, lamps, paintings, pottery, windchimes.

Magic Masters: Magic tricks demonstrated live. Replicates Harry Houdini's private library, has "secret" door. Books, DVDs.

Magnetron Magnetz: Tiny shop has 50,000 quirky refrigerator magnets, knickknacks.

Mickey's Groove: General Disney items.

Pop Gallery: Signed paintings, three-dimensional wall hangings, wild glass sculptures. Small champagne bar.

Ridemakerz: Customized R/C toy cars.

Sosa Family Cigars: Cigars; hand-rolling demonstrations. Adults can smoke.

Sunglass Icon: Sunglasses; Ray-Ban, Maui Jim, Oakley brands.

Facing page: Fashion apparel store Tren-D, Downtown Disney Marketplace

ESPN Wide World of Sports

Showcasing athletes who range from 8-year-old Jr. Pee Wees to adult professional superstars, this sports complex attracts two million guests a year and hosts more than 300 annual events. For youth sports, the 220-acre venue is the most popular place to play in the United States.

The complex has a distinct ESPN feel. Competition highlights, player and coach interviews air in a "SportsCenter"-style broadcast that airs continuously on video monitors throughout the grounds. Robotic cameras and roving reporters and videographers capture the action.

Nicely landscaped with many palm trees, most of the complex uses a Mediterranean style of architecture. Highlights include Spanish-style towers, archways and roofing.

The multi-sport Jostens Center has 45,000 square feet of indoor competition space

A yellow color scheme is offset by blue and green accents. Disney calls the style Florida Picturesque. Architect David Schwarz also designed Rangers Ballpark in Arlington and the American Airlines Center in Dallas.

Admission. Though the public is welcome as spectators ($13.50 ages 10 and above, $10 for ages 3–9), courts and fields are open only to groups participating in official events.

Restaurants and food. The complex has one restaurant (the ESPN Wide World of Sports Grill; no reservations taken); carts and stands offer snacks and beverages on event days.

See the chapter **Restaurants and Food.**

Shops. The ESPN Clubhouse Shop offers complex, network and sports-team merchandise. The shop has two locations: next to the box office and inside Champion Stadium. Next to the restaurant, a Custom Tee Center by Champion lets guests customize event T-shirts by adding "1st Place," "Champions," a team caption or one of 50 pre-made designs.

Family matters. Moms might find it tough to nurse in Champion Stadium; the baseball park has few private spots beyond restrooms, especially out of the heat. The best options are inside the stadium's ESPN Clubhouse Shop or next door at the ESPN Wide World of Sports Grill.

Venues

Consisting of eight distinct venues with another on the way, ESPN Wide World of Sports includes an array of courts and fields.

Baseball Quadraplex. These four baseball fields are accompanied by an adjacent half field that is designed for infield drills. The quad hosts camps, clinics and tournaments for amateur players, and is used by pros during Gulf Coast League and Fall Instructional League seasons. The Atlanta Braves use it for its annual Spring Training.

Bowling center. Announced to open as early as 2012, a state-of-the-art bowling alley is planned to include 100 lanes.

Champion Stadium. This retro-style ballpark hosts Atlanta Braves Spring Training and numerous amateur tournaments. Eighty percent of its 9,500 seats are located behind or alongside the infield. A grass berm in left field offers seating for an additional 2,000 fans.

Hess Sports Fields. These four defined fields and seven large grass surfaces host baseball, cricket, field hockey, football, lacrosse, rugby, soccer and softball games. Bleachers can hold 10,000 spectators.

HP Field House. With high arches and trusses reminiscent of a 1950s arena, this versatile 165,000-square-foot facility (formerly the Milk House) accommodates most indoor sports. Its main arena can seat 5,500 for a single basketball game or hold multi-court events. Another two courts are upstairs.

Jostens Center. This 80,000-square-foot fieldhouse can be configured for two

© Disney

The Spring Training home of the Atlanta Braves, Champion Stadium is the only minor league baseball park with an upper deck. The ESPN complex can hold up to 9 baseball fields altogether.

roller-hockey rinks, six basketball courts or a dozen volleyball courts. Unlike the HP Field House, it doesn't convert to a single arena and does not have multiple seating levels.

Softball Complex. Six fields can accommodate fastpitch and slowpitch softball; baseball for players ages 12 and younger.

Tennis Complex. Set within palm-lined grounds, these ten green-clay courts (including one stadium court) have hosted events ranging from youth clinics to major professional tournaments.

Track & Field Complex. Designed consistent with Olympic track and field venues, this 400-meter polyurethane area meets IAAF standards and measurements. It has an adaptable cross-country course.

Events

Amateur competitions. The complex draws amateur athletes from more than 70 countries. Signature events include:

Cheerleading World Championships. The Super Bowl of cheerleading competitions, this April event include more than 8,500 cheerleaders; 100 teams from 40 countries.

AAU Boys National Basketball Championships. Elite high school players compete in front of top NCAA coaches in this July collegiate recruiting showcase, one of many Amateur Athletic Union (AAU) events at the complex. Many future NBA stars—including the likes of Lebron James, Dwight Howard, Chris Paul, Dwyane Wade—have been in the spotlight during this national competition.

ESPN RISE Games. Anchored by the AAU U-17 Boys Basketball Super Showcase, the Under Armour High School Softball All-American Game and the Gridiron Kings 7-on-7 football event, this July multi-sport festival has open divisions in baseball, basketball, field hockey, lacrosse and track and field.

Old Spice Classic. Featuring Division I collegiate basketball teams, this pre-season November event is an eight-team, 12-game men's tournament that takes place over Thanksgiving weekend.

Pop Warner Super Bowl. After advancing through regional competitions, 64 top youth football teams compete in these December week-long championships. Four divisions play for national crowns, divided by size and age: Jr. Pee Wee (ages 8–11 years), Pee Wee (9–12 years), Jr. Midget (10–13 years) and Midget (11–15 years).

Pop Warner National Cheer & Dance Championships. Held during the Pop Warner Super Bowl, this December event brings together about 500 young cheer and dance squads. Teams compete in the same four age ranges as the football players—Jr. Pee Wee,

The leading youth sports facility in the United States, the ESPN Wide World of Sports complex hosts more than 300 events a year, more than 11,000 individual games and contests. At right, U-14 Girls compete in a national soccer championship.

Pee Wee, Jr. Midget and Midget—as well as squad size (Small and Large) and three competition categories (Novice, Intermediate and Advanced).

Disney's Soccer Showcase. The top elite youth soccer tournament in the nation, this December event features more than 500 high-school-age teams, roughly 9,500 athletes. About 800 college coaches also attend, recruiting top college prospects.

Atlanta Braves Spring Training. After two weeks of Spring Training workouts, the Atlanta Braves baseball team plays a 15- or 16-game schedule in February and March against other Grapefruit League competitors, including the New York Yankees, Boston Red Sox and St. Louis Cardinals. The afternoon and evening contests include in-game entertainment and Disney characters;

after each game children are invited onto the field to run the bases. Tickets ($28–$39 reserved; $15–$19 general adm. lawn seats) are sold through Ticketmaster (800-745-3000, ticketmaster.com) and at the complex box office (prerecorded 407-828-3267; live voice 407-939-1500 or 407-939-4263) starting the first week in January. Group tickets and three- and six-game packages are available. Games against the most popular teams (those mentioned above) sell out. Travel packages are sold through Spring Training USA (springtrainingtours.com).

Tom Shaw Performance Camps. Since 2006, speed and conditioning coach Tom Shaw has trained some of the top NFL players at the complex, including 9 Super Bowl MVPs and over a hundred first-round draft picks. Notable students have included Deion

The main arena of the HP Field House can accommodate 5,500 spectators. With the highest row of seats only 35 feet off the ground, everyone gets a close view of the action. An adjacent smaller gymnasium offers additional court space.

The ESPN Wide World of Sports production center mixes feeds from 42 robotic cameras and various field reporters to generate coverage of events at the complex. It appears on display boards throughout the grounds.

Sanders and Santonio Holmes. Open to amateurs and professionals alike, Shaw's camps run from April through September. For more information call 407-739-3958.

'Look, I'm on TV!'

Designed to make its amateur athletes feel like they've made it to the "big time," the complex incorporates many signature elements of the ESPN television network. Video coverage includes a daily "SportsCenter"-style program with highlights and interviews and many live national broadcasts.

Video screens. Positioned along walkways throughout the complex, 40 video display boards let athletes, coaches and fans see themselves and their teams on TV. A continuous "SportsCenter"-style program includes highlights from recent action, interviews with coaches and players, an ESPN-style "bottom line" ticker of game results and other complex news, and local weather. The content is updated constantly—from the time a game ends to the time its highlights appear is usually less than 45 minutes. Twelve to 15 clips are produced each day.

Guests staying at Disney resort hotel can watch the highlight coverage on Channel 42 on their in-room televisions.

Other digital signage includes large video displays at the Welcome Center and the HP Field House.

Nationwide broadcasts. Family and friends who can't attend events in person can follow the action, too. Many Wide World of Sports contests—more than 200 hours a year—are carried live on ESPN3.com, the network's broadband channel that reaches 50 million homes nationwide. Games and highlights can also be viewed on X-Box Live and various YouTube channels. Occasionally highlights appear on the main ESPN network, often as part of a review of the top sports plays of the day. The annual ESPN RISE Games (see Events) are often broadcast on the ESPNU network as well as ESPN3.com.

Behind the scenes. Rebranded with the ESPN name in 2010, the complex gets a lot of national attention for its Innovation Lab and 3-D efforts (see next page), but the facility's backstage production center may be its most impressive new addition. Operating out of a nondescript series of small buildings tucked

The ESPN Innovation Lab pioneers broadcast technologies by using the sports complex as a testing center. Currently the lab is developing 3-D technology. Located near the tennis center, it is closed to the public.

within Champion Stadium, a small team of ESPN staffers controls 42 robotic cameras (each of which can pan, tilt and zoom) that are scattered throughout the various playing venues, as well as a 20-zone audio system. Mixing in additional coverage from up to 40 field videographers and four studio cameras, they generate a nearly continuous stream of news, highlights and live broadcasts. Each live event is covered with an average of seven cameras, two more than the typical ESPN college-football telecast. With all of its work produced in high definition, the 2,500-square-foot center has more fiber-optic cable than the new Cowboys Stadium in Dallas.

The center also serves as a broadcast distribution hub for the ESPN network, one of five in the United States. Using one of four fiber-optic feeds, programming originating throughout the Florida region is routed to ESPN's main facilities in Bristol, Conn., New York and Los Angeles.

ESPN Innovation Lab. Located near the tennis center, the ESPN Innovation Lab develops broadcast technologies by using the complex as a testing center. So far the results have included Ball Track, a Doppler-radar system that can continuously update the distance and height of a baseball in flight; the ESPN Snap Zoom, a freeze-frame technology for football plays that zooms in on an area to provide more insight on the action; and the EA Virtual Playbook application, which allows studio analysts to bring to life key match-ups, formations and game action with multi-dimensional animation. Currently the lab is developing telecast systems for ESPN 3-D, the industry's first 3-D television network. Other companies also use the facility for 3-D research. It is closed to the public.

Wide World of Sports Resources

ATM: Inside Champion Stadium.

Cooler policy: Each guest may bring in a 1-gallon for personal use; each coach can bring in a 5-gallon cooler. No coolers are allowed in the Jostens Center.

First-aid supplies: Guests needing basic supplies such as over-the-counter pain medication or bandages should contact a Disney cast member. The entrance gift shop sells these items.

Guest Relations: A Welcome Center serves as a guest relations office. Cast members help with theme-park tickets, transportation and reservations for dining, golf and other recreation options.

Locker rentals: The complex has no public locker or storage facilities.

Parking: General parking is free; paid valet parking is available for select event dates.

Strollers: Strollers are welcome in most areas though prohibited inside the Jostens Center and HP Field House; designated stroller parking is available outside these venues. No strollers are available for rent.

Transportation: Complimentary Disney bus service to the complex is available from Disney's Hollywood Studios (daily, 8a–8p); and from Disney's All-Star, Caribbean Beach and Pop Century resorts (Thurs–Mon 5–11p, and when sports events are taking place from one hour prior to the complex opening to 11 p.m. or closing time, whichever is later).

Wheelchair rentals: A limited number of complimentary wheelchairs are at the entrance turnstiles. No wheelchairs are available for rent.

Activities

Sports and Recreation

Archery. Fort Wilderness offers archery lessons followed by target practice. Children's bows are smaller; special left-handed bows available; all are in bright colors. Arrows have rounded tips. Check in at the Bike Barn. If you are driving to the resort give yourself 45 minutes from the time you park until class starts ($25, 90 min, Thurs–Sat 2:45p. Ages 6 and up. 10 students max per class. Reservations taken 90 days in advance at 407-939-7529).

Bicycle and surrey rentals. Ten Disney hotels rent bikes and/or multi-seat surreys: BoardWalk, Caribbean Beach, Coronado Springs, Fort Wilderness, Old Key West, Polynesian (surreys only), Port Orleans, Saratoga Springs, Wilderness Lodge and Yacht and Beach Club (bikes only) (Bicycles: $9 hr, $18 day; surreys $20–$22, 30 min).

Boat charters. Most Disney boat charters are evening trips to view fireworks:

Pontoon boats. The Pirates and Pals Fireworks Voyage views Magic Kingdom's Wishes fireworks. It includes an onboard pirate storyteller and onshore character greetings (Nightly. $54 A, $31 C 3–9. Fri.–Mon., nightly over holidays. Contemporary Resort marina. 407-939-7529). View Wishes or IllumiNations with up to 9 friends from a guided pontoon boat ($275–$325. 1 hr. Snacks. Wishes: Contemporary, Grand Fla., Polynesian, Wilderness Lodge marinas. Illuminations: Yacht Club dock. 407-939-7529).

Inboard. The Breathless II is a 26-foot mahogany replica of a 1930s Chris-Craft inboard (Ages 3 and older; up to 7 people. 30 min. ride: $95 per group. 90 min. IllumiNations cruise: $275. Yacht Club marina. 407-939-7529).

Yacht. Grand 1, a 52-foot Sea Ray yacht, cruises Seven Seas Lagoon and Bay Lake ($480 per hr, up to 18 people. Includes captain, deckhand. Food, butler optional. Grand Floridian marina. 407-824-2682).

Facing page: A snowy Cinderella Castle highlights a hole at Winter Summerland

Boat rentals. Disney World has the world's largest rental-boat fleet. Boats vary by marina; call 407-939-7529 for details.

Canoes and kayaks. $7 per 30 min.

Two-seat outboards. Small Sea Raycers. $32 per 30 min., $45 per hr. Ages 12–15 may drive with a licensed driver. Min height 60 in. Max weight 320 pounds per boat.

Center-console outboards. 17-foot Boston Whaler Montauks, $45 per 30 min.

Pedal boats. $6.50 per 30 min. The Walt Disney World Swan and Dolphin has swan boats at twice the price; $12–$14 per 30 min.

Personal watercraft. 3-seat Sea-Doos. Non-guided rides $80 per 30 min, $135 per hr. 1-hr a.m. group rides into Seven Seas Lagoon $135. Max. 3 riders per vehicle, max .combined weight 400 lbs. Sammy Duvall's Watersports Centre, Disney's Contemporary Resort.

Pontoon boats. 21-foot SunTrackers, $45 per 30 min.

Sailboats. 12-foot Sunfish $20 per hr., 13-foot Hobie Cats $25 per hr. Operator must be 16 with valid driver's license; renters must be 18. 407-939-0754.

Campfires. Held at a small amphitheater at Fort Wilderness, Chip 'n Dale's Campfire Sing-a-Long includes a marshmallow roast, 30-min. sing-a-long with the chipmunks (sit on the benches to meet one) and a movie. A snack bar sells s'mores kits, marshmallows and sticks (Free. Schedule: 407-824-2727). Port Orleans Riverside offers a campfire sing-a-long (no movie) seasonally. Outdoor movies are shown seasonally at seven resorts—the Beach Club, Contemporary, Grand Floridian, Old Key West, Saratoga Springs, Wilderness Lodge and Swan and Dolphin.

Carriage and wagon rides. Available at the Fort Wilderness, Port Orleans Riverside and Saratoga Springs resorts, horse-drawn carriages hold up to four adults or a small family ($45 per carriage. 25 min. 5:30–10p, those under 18 must ride with adult; reservations accepted 90 days in advance at 407-939-7529; same-day availability at 407-824-2832). Fort Wilderness has 32-passenger wagons ($8 A, $5 C 3–9. Under 3 ride free. 45 min. 7p, 9:30p. Fireworks rides are often available. Pioneer

Clockwise from above: Catching bass is easy on a Disney fishing trip; Danielle Finke, 20, stands up on her second attempt at Typhoon Lagoon surfing; DiveQuest scuba pals at Epcot

Hall. Children under 11 must ride with adult. No reservations. Group rides with 24 hours notice: 407-824-2734).

Diving and snorkeling. Guests spend 40 minutes inside a 5.7-million-gallon saltwater aquarium during Disney's DiveQuest experience held at Epcot's The Seas with Nemo & Friends pavilion. The tank contains more than 65 species, including sharks, rays and sea turtles. ($175, 40 min. in water, 3 hr. total experience. Inc. gear, lockers, showers, pavilion overview. Park admission not required. Opt. video. Up to 12 divers per group. Ages 10 and up. Ages 10, 11 must dive with adult. Open-water certification required. 407-939-8687).

The Epcot Seas Aqua Tour puts you in the tank with scuba-assisted snorkel (SAS) equipment ($140, 30 min. in water, 2.5 hr. total. Inc instruction. Park admission not required. Ages 10 and up; under 18 must dive with adult. 407-939-8687). Proceeds from the experiences go to the Disney Worldwide Conservation Fund.

Dolphins in Depth. You'll spend 30 minutes in knee-deep water with Epcot's bottlenose dolphins, learn about their anatomy and behavior and watch biologists do research. No interaction is guaranteed, but then again you may get to feel a dolphin's heartbeat. Trainers work with guests individually. Proceeds go to the Disney Wildlife Conservation Fund ($194, 3 hrs. Inc. T-shirt, photo of guest with dolphin, refreshments, use of wetsuit. No swimming. Park admission not required. Ages 13 and up. Those under 18 must be with adult. 407-939-8687).

Fishing. Disney offers both guided fishing trips and pole rentals to fish from the shore. Either way, catching a fish is almost a certainty, as all Disney fishing areas are stocked (with bass, bluegill and catfish), all fish must be released and only a handful of anglers are fishing at any one time

Guided excursions. Guests routinely catch largemouth bass weighing 2 to 8 lbs on these guided pontoon-boat trips. Most trips catch five to 10 fish; guests average 2.5 fish per hour. Bay Lake and Seven Seas Lagoon are teeming with bass; the largest fish (up to 14 lbs.) are in the Crescent and Village lakes. The Bass Anglers Sportsman Society runs the programs ($235–$270 2 hrs, $455 4 hrs, addl hrs. $110. Up to 5 guests. Inc. bait (shiners addl.), guide, equipment, refreshments, digital camera. No license req. Trips on Bay Lake, Seven Seas Lagoon, Crescent Lake, Village Lake and the Coronado Resort's Lago Dorado. Leaves early and mid a.m., early p.m. 407-939-2277. Reservations taken 2 wks in advance).

Photos © Disney

Disney's five golf courses are designated wildlife sanctuaries, home to alligators, deer and egrets. A bunker at the Magnolia course's No. 6 green—the "mouse trap"—resembles Mickey Mouse.

Shoreline fishing. Available at the Fort Wilderness and Port Orleans Riverside resorts (Cane poles $4 30 min., $9 day, 4–6 pole pkg. $14 30 min., $28 day. Rods $6 30 min., $10 day. Bait inc. No lic. required. Fort W: 407-824-2900, Riverside: 407-934-6000).

Golf. Grouped into three facilities, Walt Disney World's five golf courses each offer a different experience. There's the long course, the short course, the flat course, the water course... and the child-friendly 9-hole. Home to deer, egrets, herons, otters, alligators and an occasional bald eagle, each course is designated as a wildlife sanctuary by the Audubon Cooperative Sanctuary System. All but the Lake Buena Vista course roam away from civilization. All Disney greens have ultra-dwarf TifEagle Bermuda grass, which offers a true, fast roll.

The best months to play golf at Disney are September, April and May, when the weather is nice and good tee times are easy to book. Build extra time into your round, as the pace may be slower than you expect (Greens fees: 18-hole courses $39–$180 req. cart rental inc; 9-hole Oak Trail course $38, $20 for under 18. Club, shoe rental avail. Proper golf attire req. 18-holes have putting greens, driving ranges. Free transportation from Disney-owned resorts. Reservations 90 days in adv. for Disney resort guests, 60 days other players. Cancellations require 48 hrs. notice. $50 Fla. resident Annual Golf Membership saves up to 60% on greens fees after 10a for member, up to three guests. Addl. summer savings. 407-939-4653, disneygolf.com).

Lake Buena Vista course. Disney's least forgiving course has narrow, tree-lined fairways and small greens. Play demands accuracy on tee shots and approaches. Errant shots can hit windows. Signature hole No. 7 has an island green; No. 18 is a 438-yard dogleg to the right. Ten holes have water hazards. You tee off at Disney's Saratoga Springs Resort then weave through Old Key West Resort lodging areas (Yardage: 5,204–6,802. Par: 72. Course rating: 68.6–73.0. Slope rating: 122–133. Designer: Joe Lee. Year open: 1972. At the Saratoga Springs Resort).

Magnolia course. How's that shoulder turn? It needs to be efficient on this long-game course, a rolling terrain amid more than 1,500 magnolia trees. The Magnolia has elevated tees and greens and 97 bunkers, the most of any Disney course. Greens are quick. Host to the final round of Disney's PGA Tour tournament stop since 1971, the course has tested most top-name pros (Yardage: 5,232–7,516. Par: 72. Course rating: 69.4–76.5. Slope rating: 125–140. Designer: Joe Lee. Year open: 1971. Across from Disney's Polynesian Resort).

© Disney

Fort Wilderness outdoor experiences include Chip 'n' Dale's Campfire Sing-a-Long—in which guests roast marshmallows and watch a movie— and horseback rides on shady pine trails

Oak Trail 9-hole course. A walking course, Oak Trail is nice for a quick nine or practice. With small greens and two good par 5s, the course requires accuracy with short irons. The longest hole, the 517-yard No. 5, has a double dogleg. Water hazards cross three fairways. Most greens and tees are elevated. The scorecard lists separate pars for children 11 and under and 12 and over. Golf shoes must be spikeless; tennis shoes are permitted. (Yardage: 2,532–2,913. Par: 36. Course rating: 64.6–68.2. Slope rating: 107–123. Designer: Ron Garl. Year open: 1980. Next to Shades of Green, across from Disney's Polynesian Resort.)

Osprey Ridge course. Set within beautiful rolling terrain, this challenging course winds through dense vegetation, oak forests and moss hammocks. More than 70 bunkers, mounds and a meandering ridge provide obstacles, banking and elevation changes. Some tees and greens are 20 feet above their fairways. The course often has swirling winds. One bit of relief: fairway waste bunkers have hard sand, so you can play out of one with a more-normal swing. (Yardage: 5,402–7,101. Par: 72. Course rating: 69.5–74.4. Slope rating: 123–131. Designer: Tom Fazio. Year open: 1992. Just east of Fort Wilderness.)

Palm course. Pretty palms. Ugly hazards. This course has both. Water hazards line seven holes and cross six. Shorter and tighter than the nearby Magnolia, the Palm course has a few long par 4s and a couple of par 5s that can be reached in two using a fairway wood. The large, elevated greens can be maneuvered with good lag putting. Save a sprinkle of pixie dust for hole No. 18. A long par 4, it has been rated as high as fourth toughest on the PGA Tour. The Palm is rated one of Golf Digest's Top 25 Resort Courses. (Yardage: 5,311–6,957. Par: 72. Course rating: 69.5–73.9. Slope rating: 126–138. Designer: Joe Lee. Year open: 1971. Next to Shades of Green, across from Disney's Polynesian Resort.)

Golf lessons: PGA pros offer year-round instruction. Choose from one-on-one training focused on a specific skill, video swing analysis or on-course lessons that include course management and strategy, club selection and short-game skills. ($50–$150, 45 min lesson for single golfer $75, $50 ages 17 and under. Shades of Green center. All ages, skills. Individual lessons, clinics: 407-939-4653. Group lessons: 407-938-3870. $50 Fla resident Annual Golf Membership saves 20 percent.)

Horseback riding. Guides lead small groups down shady pine and palmetto trails at the Fort Wilderness Resort & Campground. Excursions start at the Tri-Circle D Livery at

Located at Disney's Contemporary Resort, Sammy Duvall's Watersports Centre offers activities such as water skiing and parasailing as well as personal watercraft rentals

the resort entrance. Go early and you'll likely see wildlife such as snakes and deer ($46, 45 min. Daily starting at 8:30a. Ages 9 and up. Height min. 48 in. Max weight 250 lbs. Closed-toe shoes required; no sandals or flip-flops. No trotting. Required reservations can be made 30 days in advance at 407-939-7529). Smaller children can take a short pony ride at the resort's petting farm; a parent walks the pony ($4, cash only. Ages 2–8. Max. height 48 in. Max weight 80 lbs. 10a–5p daily. 407-824-2788.

Miniature golf. Two themed mini-golf complexes on Disney property make it easy to take a break from theme-park activities ($13 A, $11 C. 10a–11p. Last tee time 30 min. before close. 2nd rounds 1/2 price if same day or next day. In-person same-day reservations accepted. 407-939-7529).

Fantasia Gardens. Across the street from the Walt Disney World Swan and Dolphin, this two-course complex (407-560-4753) is busy at night, when tee-time waits can be an hour. Splashing brooms and dancing-ostrich topiaries line a Gardens course, which is themed to Disney's 1940 movie "Fantasia." A Fairways course replicates real links with bunkers, roughs, undulating hills and holes up to 103 feet long. The Gardens course closes at 10:30p.

Winter Summerland. Next to Blizzard Beach, these two courses (407-560-7161) are

often deserted at night. Themed to the activities of elves who, as the story goes, vacation here (Santa bought them the course as a respite from their duties at the North Pole), the courses are dotted with tiny elf trailers and Christmas decor. Getting a hole-in-one is easy, as greens often funnel into cups.

Stock car driving. The engine rumbles… you tremble with excitement… then zoom! You put pedal to the metal and tear down a race track at over 100 mph, all by yourself in a 630-hp. stock car. Held at the Walt Disney World Speedway, the Richard Petty Driving Experience kicks off with a training session. Then, wearing a driving suit, fire cap and helmet, you climb through the window of a stock car, pop on a steering wheel, strap in and take off. With your car almost always in a turn, you drive behind your instructor, who paces you in his own car (when the author took a car out she averaged 122 mph—fastest in her class!—and passed a guy). NASCAR-style vehicles have tube frames, huge V-8s, 4-speed manual transmissions and product logos plastered everywhere. The doors don't open; that's why you climb in. Also available: no-training-required 3-lap ride-alongs with a professional driver, with speeds up to 150 mph. (Rides $110. Drives $450–$1380 for 8–30 laps. Hrs: 9a–4p. Duration: 30 min–1 hr for rides includes 3 min in car; 3–4 hrs for drives inc 10–15 min driving car. Gift cards available. Drives require reservations, include training. Ride-along trips don't require reservations. Adjacent to Magic Kingdom parking lot. Must be 16 or older to ride, 18 or older to drive. One-day Safe Driving Program in May for those 15 to 25: $329–$399. Spectators welcome. 1-800-237-3889, 1800bepetty.com.)

Surfing lessons. Know how to swim? Fit? If so, then you are almost guaranteed to learn how to ride the crest of a wave at the Craig Carroll Surfing School. It holds instruction at dawn in the surf pool of Typhoon Lagoon, before the water park opens to the public. Conducted on dry land, a step-by-step introduction is followed by many in-pool attempts. After each one, Carroll critiques you from the lifeguard stand then an instructor in the water adds advice. Waves average about 5 feet for adults; half that for children. About 70 percent of all students succeed; females tend to do better. "Girls don't think as hard about it, and try to do exactly what you say," Carroll explains. "Boys tend to think it's a macho thing." ($150. Must be 8 yrs or older, strong swimmer. Most students have never surfed. Days, hrs. vary with season. 2.5-hr. lesson has 30 min. on land, 2 hrs. in water. Surfboards provided. Spectators permitted. Maximum 12 students per class; sessions sell out quickly. Reservations accepted 90 days early at 407-939-7873).

Tennis. Disney has 34 lighted tennis courts for recreational guest use, all at resort hotels. Use is complimentary except at the Grand Floridian ($13/hr., same-day reservations at 407-621-1991). Some resorts restrict court use to their own guests, though the BoardWalk, Contemporary, Fort Wilderness and Yacht Club welcome other Disney-resort guests on a first-come, first-served basis. Organized programs for all ages and abilities are offered at the Grand Floridian; a pro shop there rents rackets and ball machines and re-strings and re-grips guest rackets (private lessons $90/hr., "Play the Pro" hitting lessons $90/ hr., group clinics $15 per person, convention-style group tourneys $25 hr. 407-939-7529; parking available at Disney's Wedding Pavilion).

Water sports. Many activities are available at Sammy Duvall's Watersports Centre (407-939-0754) located at Disney's Contemporary Resort. A legendary skier himself, Duvall has won more than 80 pro championships.

Parasailing. Soaring high beneath an open parachute will give you a birds-eye view of Walt Disney World. Hundreds of feet above the 450-acre Bay Lake, you can see the entire property as you're pulled by a powerboat. You never get wet, as you take off and land from the boat (Single riders $95 for 8–10 min at 450 ft; $130 for 10–12 min at 600 ft. Tandem riders $170 for 8–10 min at 450 ft; $195 for 10–12 min at 600 ft. Weight per flight 130–330 lbs).

Other water sports. Kneeboard, wakeboard or go tubing or water-skiing behind a MasterCraft inboard. Friendly instructors are patient, especially with kids (Per boat: $85 30 min., $165 1 hr., $135 per addl. hr.; water-skiing apx $20 addl. Up to 5 skiers. Inc equipment, driver, instruction. Extra charge if picked up from Fort Wilderness, Grand Floridian, Polynesian or Wilderness Lodge).

Tours

Organized tours offer a closer look at Walt Disney World and often include backstage trips. Unless indicated below, tours are for guests age 16 and older. To book any tour listed below except a VIP tour call 407-939-8687. Note: Tours that go backstage do not allow photography. Photo IDs are required.

Around the World at Epcot. A group Segway trip through World Showcase. Training, safety equipment provided ($99, Park admission required. 2 hrs. Daily. Must weigh 100–250 lbs).

Backstage Magic. Goes backstage at all four theme parks to view creative and technical operations. The longest Disney World tour ($224, Whispering Canyon lunch includded, park admission not required. 7 hrs. Mon–Fri).

Backstage Safari. Tours the vet hospital, elephant barn and other facilities of Disney's Animal Kingdom ($72, park admission required. 3 hrs Mon, Wed, Thr, Fri).

Behind the Seeds. An inside look at the four greenhouses and fish farm at The Land pavilion ($16 adults, $12 children 3–9, park admission required. 1 hr. Daily. All ages).

Disney's Family Magic Tour. A Magic Kingdom scavenger hunt to capture a dastardly villain; a skip (literally) through the park for families with small children ($34, park admission required. 2 hrs. Daily. All ages, best for ages 4 to 10).

ESPN Wide World of Sports Guided Tour. An inside look at the athletic complex, held on selected days when events are scheduled (Complimentary. 1 hr. All ages).

A swaying rope bridge crosses over a crocodile habitat on the Wild Africa Trek, a guided journey through remote forest and savanna areas of the Kilimanjaro Safaris attraction at Disney's Animal Kingdom (photo by Rebekah Moseley)

© laughingplace.com

Gardens of the World. A Disney horticulture expert shows how the Epcot gardens and landscaping is created and maintained. Tour includes backstage looks, lunch ($69, park admission required. 3 to 3.5 hrs. Seasonal).

Holiday D-Lights. Tours backstage decorations shop, Main Street U.S.A., Osborne Dancing Lights; includes seats for the Candlelight Processional. A light buffet is provided ($199, no park admission required. 4.5 to 5 hrs. Mon, Wed. 4p. Late Nov–Dec).

Inspiration Through Walt's Eyes. Explores how Walt Disney was motivated to achieve his dreams. The tour visits Disney's Hollywood Studios, goes backstage at Disney's Event & Decorating Support and travels into Magic Kingdom's underground Utilidor areas ($99, no park admission required. 3 hrs, Mon, Wed, Thr, Fri).

Keys to the Kingdom. Guides discuss Magic Kingdom's history, philosophies; travels into Magic Kingdom's underground Utilidor areas ($74, includes a lunch at Columbia Harbour House, park admission required. 4 hrs. Daily).

The Magic Behind Our Steam Trains. Shows how Magic Kingdom's antique steam trains are prepped for operation; also discusses Walt Disney's love of trains ($49, park admission required. 3 hrs. Mon, Tue, Wed, Thr, Sat. Ages 10 and up).

Mickey's Magical Milestones. Visits Magic Kingdom areas that trace the career of Mickey Mouse ($25, park admission required. 2 hrs. Mon, Wed, Fri. Ages 16 and under must be with adult. Best for ages 10 and up).

Nature–Inspired Design. Guests ride a Segway as they learn how Epcot design uses the concepts of air, land and sea ($124, park admission required. 3 hrs. Includes stops at Soarin', The Land greenhouses, goes backstage. Tue, Sat. 8:15a).

UnDISCOVERed Future World. Learn of the planned Experimental Prototype Community of Tomorrow, visit all Future World pavilions, go backstage ($55, park admission required. 4 hrs. Mon, Wed, Fri).

VIP Tours. Guided custom tours based on your custom itinerary ($175–$315 per hr, min 6 hrs, park admission required. Daily. All ages. 407-560-4033).

Wild Africa Trek. Small groups take personalized, guided treks through the wildlife-filled forest and savanna of the Kilimanjaro Safaris at Disney's Animal Kingdom. The tour begins on foot, as trekkers navigate winding pathways. Guests clip onto a lifeline to lean over a cliff to see hippos and crocodiles. A special open-air truck ride explores the savanna. Finally, guests unwind at a covered viewing area that's stocked with appetizers. (Price varies by season; apx. $150 per person, park admission required. 3 hrs. Multiple times daily. Ages 8 and up. Maximum of 12 guests per trek. Includes photographer.)

Wild by Design. Covers the art, architecture, storytelling and animal care at Disney's Animal Kingdom ($60, includes light breakfast, park admission required. 3 hrs. Mon, Wed, Thr, Fri. Ages 14 and up. Guests under 16 must be with adult).

Wilderness Back Trail Adventure. Ride a Segway X2 through shady off-road Fort Wilderness trails ($90. 2 hrs. Tue–Sat; 8:30, 11:30a. Max weight 250 lbs. Same-day walk-up reservations at Fort Wilderness marina).

Yuletide Fantasy. Tours holiday decorations of Magic Kingdom, Epcot and a few Disney resorts ($84, late Nov–Dec, no park admission required. 3 hrs. Mon–Sat).

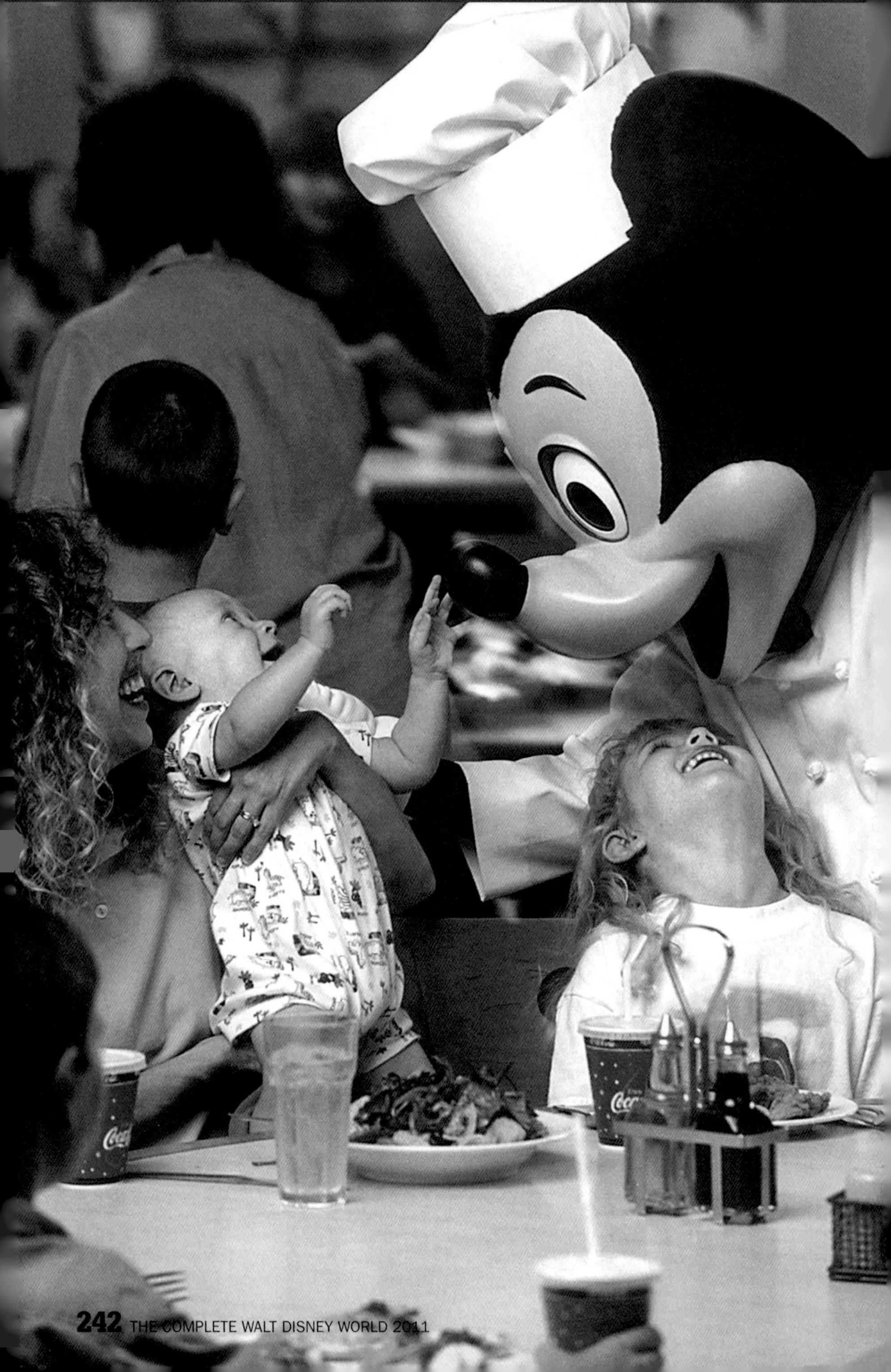

Restaurants and Food

Theme parks

Magic Kingdom. Walt Disney World's signature character meal highlights the dining choices at The Most Magical Place On Earth.

Cinderella's Royal Table. ★★★ Character meals $$$$$ Cinderella in lobby, other princesses in dining room. B: $45 (children $30), 8–11:15a. L: $49 (children $31), Noon–3p. D: $55 (children $34), 4p–park close. Seats 184. At Cinderella Castle, Fantasyland. Disney Signature, 2 credits on Disney Dining Plan. Perfect for princess fans, this restaurant inside Cinderella Castle offers a magical character meal. Sweet princesses circulate through a lovely dining room; Cinderella stays downstairs posing for (complimentary) photos. The atmosphere is rowdy, not romantic; the food is good but beside the point. Very girly, quite expensive, but those who love it. Tall windows overlook Fantasyland. The best time to dine is 8 a.m., before the park opens. Meals are fully booked months in advance (often six months early); reservations must be guaranteed.

Crystal Palace. ★★ Character buffet $$$$ Winnie the Pooh, Tigger, Eeyore, Piglet. B: $23 (children $13), 8–10:30a. L: $25 (children $14), 11:30a–2:45p. D: $37 (children $18), 3:45p–park close. Seats 400. Main Street U.S.A. Disney Dining Plan. Even the adorable Winnie the Pooh can't redeem this loud, overpriced cafeteria. The crowds and tightly-packed tables mean the characters are spread too thin. The buffet has many basic food choices, some good meats and salads, some salty soups and vegetables. High ceilings and marble tabletops look nice but add to the din. For the nicest time reserve for 8:05 a.m. (the first breakfast seating), 10:30 a.m. (the last) or 3:45 p.m. (the first dinner seating).

Liberty Tree Tavern. ★★★ ✔ American $$$$ L: $11–$19; 11:30a–2:45p. D: $30 (children $15), 4p–park close. Seats 250. Liberty Square. Disney Dining Plan. Hearty comfort food and a cozy atmosphere make Liberty Tree Tavern a relaxing break in a hectic theme-park day. This unpretentious New England eatery resembles a home; six separate rooms keep the noise level low. Despite its name, no liquor flows. Best bet at lunch: the tender pot roast. Dinner is a

Facing page: Guests meet Mickey Mouse at the Chef Mickey's character meal

fixed-price, family-style Thanksgiving feast. Window-side tables overlook the parade route. Friendly servers wear Colonial garb.

The Plaza. ★★★ American $$ L,D: $10–14. 11a–park close. Seats 94. Main Street U.S.A. Disney Dining Plan. The food screams diner—good basic hamburgers, sandwiches and sundaes—but the calm atmosphere fits in a more upscale eatery. The Victorian cafe's pleasant decor includes carpeted floors, padded wrought-iron chairs and faux-marble tabletops. Hand-dipped milkshakes, splits and sundaes come from the adjacent ice cream parlor. A trip to the restroom takes you outside and around the corner.

Tony's Town Square. ★★★ ✔ Italian $$$$ L: $11–$17; 11:30a–2:45p. D: $17–$28; 4:30p–park close. Seats 286. Main Street U.S.A. Disney Dining Plan. Fans of 1955's "Lady and the Tramp" may not recognize this comfortable café as the restaurant from that film though a window in back looks into the movie's alley. Its location near the park entrance makes Tony's popular for dinner as guests exit. Lunch often has tables available, especially at 11:30 a.m. The traditional Italian fare is good but not exceptional. Portions are generous. The lovely open-glassed solarium can be sunny and too warm during the day.

Fast food. Main Street U.S.A.'s **Casey's Corner** ✔ offers decent hot dogs in a worn atmosphere. A large screen plays a Goofy sports reel (11a–park close. Seats 123 inc. 43 inside. Main Street U.S.A. Disney Dining Plan Quick Service). Straddling the border between Liberty Square and Fantasyland, **Columbia Harbour House** ✔ has chicken, fish and good vegetarian chili. It's peaceful upstairs (L,D: 10:30a–park close. Seats 593. Liberty Square. Disney Dining Plan Quick Service). Across from the Tomorrowland Speedway, noisy **Cosmic Ray's Starlight Cafe** sells chicken, burgers, ribs and kosher meals. A robotic lounge singer performs in the front dining area (10:30a–park close. Seats 1,162. Tomorrowland. Disney Dining Plan Quick Service). Open seasonally, the **Diamond Horseshoe** ✔ serves sandwiches and salads (Seats 300. Frontierland. Disney Dining Plan Quick Service). Main Street U.S.A.'s **Main Street Bakery** ✔ offers pastry, breakfast quiche and yogurt parfaits (Park open–close. Seats 29. Main Street U.S.A. Disney

Diners eat fish while they watch fish at Epcot's Coral Reef Restaurant. Windows look into the main aquarium of The Seas with Nemo & Friends pavilion.

Dining Plan Quick Service). Next door to the Country Bear Jamboree, **Pecos Bill Cafe** has burgers, wraps and salads. Rooms on the right are the quietest (10a–park close. Seats 1,107. Frontierland. Disney Dining Plan Quick Service). Adjacent to It's a Small World, **Pinocchio Village Haus** offers individual pizzas, chicken and salads. Murals depict scenes from 1933's "Pinocchio" (10:30a–park close. Seats 400. Fantasyland. Disney Dining Plan Quick Service). Offering hand-dipped treats, the **Plaza Ice Cream Parlor** ✔ is next to the Plaza Restaurant (Seats 40. Main Street U.S.A. Disney Dining Plan Quick Service).

As for outdoor fast-food spots, **Tortuga Tavern** ✔ offers decent tacos and taco salads (Open seasonally. Shares seats with Pecos Bill Cafe. Adventureland. Disney Dining Plan Quick Service). Next to Astro Orbiter, **The Lunching Pad** sells hot dogs and frozen drinks (Seats 83. Tomorrowland. Disney Dining Plan Quick Service). Near Main Street U.S.A., **Tomorrowland Terrace** serves a variable menu (Open seasonally. Seats 500. Shaded seating. Tomorrowland. Disney Dining Plan Quick Service).

Snack stands. Notable options include **Aloha Isle** ✔ and its legendary Dole Whip pineapple vanilla soft-serve ice cream; the counter also offers juice, pineapple spears and floats across from the Swiss Family Treehouse (Adventureland). At the entrance to Liberty Square, **Sleepy Hollow** ✔ offers fresh hot funnel cakes (Seats 51, Liberty Square).

Epcot. The seafood restaurant Coral Reef tops the options at this theme park.

Akershus Royal Banquet Hall. ★★ Character dining; American breakfast, American/ Norwegian lunch and dinner. $$$$ Five characters rotate among Alice ("Alice in Wonderland"), Ariel ("The Little Mermaid"), Aurora ("Sleeping Beauty"), Belle ("Beauty and the Beast"), Cinderella, Esmerelda ("The Hunchback of Notre Dame"), Jasmine ("Aladdin"), Mary Poppins, Mulan. B: $29 (children $18), 8:30–10:45a. L: $35 (children $21), 11:10a–4p. D $40 (children $22), 4:15–8:40p. Seats 255. Norway pavilion. Disney Dining Plan. Five Disney princesses visit your table at this Princess Storybook Dining Experience. Breakfast is American, all-you-can-eat but brought to the table. For lunch and dinner guests order an entree and help themselves to a buffet of cold Norwegian appetizers and salads. The noisy rooms have closely-packed tables. The last lunch and dinner seatings often have walk-up tables available. The price includes a photo.

Biergarten. ★★★ ✔ German buffet, with live band $$$$ L: $26 (children $14), noon–3:45p. D: $35 (children $17), 4–9p (last show 8:05p). Seats 400. Germany pavilion. Disney Dining Plan. A live oompah band rolls out a barrel full of polkas and waltzes at this boisterous Oktoberfest buffet. Musicians lead toasts and demonstrate bizarro instruments. Parties smaller than eight dine at a long table with others. The buffet features lots of sausages and other meats, unusual salads and desserts. Order beer; skip the seafood. The dining room simulates a medieval Rothenburg outdoor courtyard at night; the moon and stars glow overhead. Cheery servers wear traditional German garb.

Bistro de Paris. ★★★★ Gourmet French $$$$$ D: $33–$54, 5–9p. No children's menu. Seats 120. France pavilion. Gourmet foodies will best appreciate the inventive creations at this quiet formal eatery. An ever-changing menu typically includes top-notch shellfish and seafood dishes, as well as venison and other meats. The escargot and chocolate soufflé are always good. A three-course, prix-fixe meal is offered with and without wine pairings. The intimate second-floor dining room overlooks the World Showcase promenade. A refined decor features white linens and tuxedoed servers. Like the lower-level Chefs de France, Bistro de Paris is owned by legendary French chefs Paul Bocuse (who visits now and then), and Roger Vergé. The late Gaston LeNotre was a founding partner.

Chefs de France. ★★★ ✔ French $$$$ L: $12–$20; Noon–3p. D: $19–$37; 5–9p. Seats 266. France pavilion. Disney Dining Plan. Traditional French food fans will enjoy this sophisticated eatery, which offers everything from sandwiches to quiche to seafood. Good appetizers include lobster bisque; for dessert the signature créme brulee is rich and silky. Big kids will love the adult menu's mac and cheese, made with cream and gruyere. Tile floors and high tin ceilings are nice but noisy.

Coral Reef. ★★★★★ ✔ Seafood $$$$ L: $12–$29; 11:30a–3:30p. D: $19–$32; 4–8:50p. Seats 275. The Seas with Nemo & Friends pavilion. Disney Dining Plan. Seafood fans will love this dimly lit hidden treasure, which looks into The Seas with Nemo & Friends aquarium with its 85 different tropical fish species. Non-seafood choices include chicken, pork, steak and a vegetarian dish. The signature appetizer is a creamy lobster soup. Brushed-metal tables are trimmed in light woods. Arrive at 11:30 a.m. and you may walk right in; otherwise book lunch two weeks early, dinner 60 to 90 days out. Ask for an aquarium-front table or a booth near the tank.

Garden Grill. ★★★ ✔ Character buffet $$$$ Farmer Mickey Mouse, Pluto, Chip 'n Dale. D: $31 (children $15), 4–8p. Seats 150. The Land pavilion. Disney Dining Plan. Children and adults alike will love this family-style country-themed dinner. The menu includes grilled steak, turkey and fish; some food comes from the pavilion's own greenhouses. As you dine, characters mosey up to say hi. Thanks to the restaurant's

small size you see the characters often, at least three times each if you stay an hour. The circular dining area rotates around the kitchen, circling completely every two hours. The outside rim overlooks the Living with the Land dioramas. Ask to sit on the outside of the ring and your booth's high-backed seats will block your family's view of the rest of the restaurant, making every character visit a delightful surprise. If you pose for the optional photo package, you'll get a tableside sales pitch.

La Hacienda de San Angel. ★★★ ✔ Mexican $$$$ D: $23–$26; 4p–9p. Seats 250. Mexico pavilion. Disney Dining Plan. Opened in 2010, this inviting spot offers good food and tasty drinks. The varied menu offers authentic Mexican fare. Best bets include the fresh salsas, creative appetizers and flavorful on-the-rocks margaritas—six varieties of which were developed with an expert mixologist. A tequila ambassador helps guests choose a flight from among 17 choices. The waterfront eatery was designed to emulate a cozy hacienda, with original artwork and unusual blown-glass light fixtures. Oversized windows provide a nice view.

Le Cellier. ★★★ ✔ Steaks $$$$ L: $14–$31; 11:30a–3p. D: $20–$37; 4–9p. Seats 156. Canada pavilion. Disney Signature; requires 2 credits on the Disney Dining Plan at dinner, 1 credit at lunch. Ideal for diners who want comforting, non-adventurous food, this steakhouse is the toughest World Showcase reservation to nab. Alberta-beef steaks are aged 28 days. Other entrees include fish, seafood, chicken and sandwiches. Made with Moosehead beer, a cheddar-cheese soup makes a nice makeshift dip for complimentary soft breadsticks. The low-ceilinged, stone-walled eatery resembles a chateau wine cellar; it's cozy and a little claustrophobic.

Nine Dragons. ★★★ ✔ Chinese $$$$ L: $13–$22; Noon–3:45p. D: $13–$27; 4–9p. Seats 300. China pavilion. A 2008 refurbishment at this China Company eatery has brightened its decor and livened up its menu with modern dishes. New entrees are light and savory; holdovers include honey-sesame and stir-fried Kung Pao chicken. Direct from China's National Guest House, a small cucumber stack appetizer is an indulgence. Highlights include good teas and light desserts. Servers are helpful and polite. Window tables make for good people-watching.

Restaurant Marrakesh. ★★★ ✔ Moroccan $$$$ L: $15–$28; Noon–3:30p. D: $21–$42; 3:30–8:45p. Seats 255. Morocco pavilion. The comfort food served here uses the same ingredients as

Epcot's La Hacienda de San Angel sits lakeside on the World Showcase promenade. Oversized windows provide a good view of the park's nightly IllumiNations spectacle.

those in American cooking, and flavors are mild. The lamb shank couscous is like your mom's pot roast, complete with roasted carrots and meat that falls off the bone, but tossed in light fluffy wheat instead of potatoes. Lunch includes beef and fish dishes; dinner adds sampler platters. A belly dancer shimmies in front of a small band (on the hour 1–8p except at 4p), her moves more graceful than sexy. Children can join in. Ceilings are intricately decorated; walls are covered in tiles. As Moroccan cuisine is unfamiliar to many Americans, this is the least crowded Epcot eatery. Ask to sit by the dance floor.

Rose & Crown Dining Room. ★★★ ✔ British $$$$ L: $13–$19; Noon–3:30p. D: $15–$27; 4–9p. Seats 242, inc 40 on covered porch. United Kingdom. Disney Dining Plan. Fans of hearty food will enjoy this comfortable eatery. Good choices include deliciously creamy potato soup, bangers and mash and shepherd's pie. Young servers exude British charm. The little covered patio is one of Disney's best outdoor dining spots.

San Angel Inn. ★★★ ✔ Mexican $$$$ L: $17–$24; 11:30a–4p. D: $24–$30; 4:30–9p. Seats 156. Mexico pavilion. Disney Dining Plan. Good choices at this relaxing spot include tortilla soup and a steak that tastes like it's straight off a backyard grill. Traditional recipes use ingredients such as spicy chocolate mole sauce. Sitting on padded chairs and benches

around a lantern-lit table, guests dine in a faux moonlit courtyard so dark it can be tough to see the menu. The backdrop is a rumbling volcano, part of the Gran Fiesta Tour ride. Down a couple of margaritas and its lava flow looks real.

Teppan Edo. ★★★ ✔ Teppanyaki (Hibachi) $$$$ L,D: $16–$30 (children $$9–12); noon–9p. Seats 192. Japan pavilion. Disney Dining Plan. Kids love the entertaining tableside chef who may juggle knives or make a "smoking Mickey train" out of onion stacks. Using a grill set into your table, the chef's hands fly fast as they slice, dice and stir-fry your choice of chicken, beef, pork, seafood or vegetables. The light desserts include a silky green tea pudding. The cocktail menu features sake and Kirin beer. You share your table with other guests in a stunning red-and-black dining room.

Tokyo Dining. ★★★★ ✔ Japanese, sushi $$$$ L,D: $15–$28; noon–9p. Seats 116. Japan pavilion, Disney Dining Plan. With good food, a calm atmosphere and great service, this is what a World Showcase restaurant is supposed to be: a non-threatening way to experience a foreign cuisine. Entrees include a tender beef teriyaki and light shrimp tempura. Unsure what to get? You can't miss with the Bento Box. Diffused lighting, dark tables and a tile floor create a peaceful mood. A friendly staff bows to diners at every opportunity.

Tutto Italia Ristorante. ★★★★ Italian $$$$$
L: $16–$31; 11:30a–3:30p. D: $22–$36; 3:30–8:45p. Seats 300.
Italy pavilion. Disney Dining Plan. Pricey yes, but this
is the best Italian spot on Disney property,
thanks to its imported pastas, delicate sauces
and handmade mozzarella. Meat and fish
entrees are good too. Desserts are luscious.
Entree salads use ingredients like asparagus,
curly endive and fava beans. A young Italian
wait staff is friendly. An elegant decor has
dark woods, chandeliers and Roman murals.
Via Napoli. ★★★ Pizza, pasta $$$$ L,D: $16–$26;
11:30–9p. Seats 400. Italy pavilion. Disney Dining Plan. New
as of 2010, this sophisticated pizzaria serves
good Neopolitan pies. The flavorful, charred
crust is made from caputo flour imported from
Naples. Pizzas come in three sizes: Individual,
large (eight slices) and 1/2 meter (12 slices).
Three wood-burning ovens are named after
the active volcanoes in Italy: Etna, Vesuvio
and Stromboli; the flames inside are framed
by oversized faces with gaping mouths.

Fast food. In Future World, **Electric
Umbrella** offers run-of-the-mill burgers, salads and sandwiches (11a–9p. Seats 426. Innovations
Plaza. Disney Dining Plan Quick Service). Way better,
the **Sunshine Seasons** ✔ food court serves
grilled meats, noodle dishes, salads, sandwiches, soups and breakfast inside The Land
pavilion (B: 9–11a. L,D: 11a–9p. Seats 707. The Land
pavilion. Disney Dining Plan Quick Service). Serving
hand-dipped treats, the **Fountainview Ice
Cream Shop** ✔ specializes in made-to-order
ice-cream sandwiches (10:30a–9p. Seats 108, inc.
68 outside. Innovations Plaza. Disney Dining Plan Quick
Service). In World Showcase, **Liberty Inn** serves
uninspired burgers, chicken and salads as
well as a kosher meal (11:30a–9p. Seats 710. American
Adventure pavilion. Disney Dining Plan Quick Service).
Just inside the Morocco pavilion, **Tangierine
Café** ✔ offers chicken and lamb platters,
pastries, tea, liqueur coffees and beer (11:30a–9p.
Seats 101. Morocco pavilion. Disney Dining Plan Quick
Service). Perched in a garden setting, **Yakitori
House** ✔ has beef, chicken, noodles, packaged
sushi, beer and wine. The miso soup is tasty
(11:30a–9p. Seats 94 inc. 36 outside. Japan pavilion).

Outdoor fast-food choices at Epcot include
Boulangerie Patisserie ✔ at the France
pavilion, which offers cheese plates, pastries
and quiche. Ordering is indoors, seats are
outside as well as in the adjacent gift shop
(11a–9p. Seats 24). On the promenade, Mexico's
re-done **Cantina de San Angel** sells empana-
das, nachos, tacos, churros, margaritas and
beer (11a–9p. Seats 150). In front of the American
Adventure pavilion, **Fife & Drum** sells hot
dogs, turkey legs, smoothies and beer (11a–9p.

Disney Dining Plan Quick Service). Serving good
fresh pastries and sandwiches, Norway's
Kringla Bakeri Og Kafe ✔ has a rich school
bread treat. As in France, ordering is indoors,
seating outdoors (11a–9p. Seats 50. Shaded seating.
Disney Dining Plan Quick Service). China's **Lotus
Blossom Café** has egg rolls, chicken, stir-fry
and specialty drinks (11a–9p. Seats 106). Serving
hot dogs, turkey legs, smoothies and beer,
Promenade Refreshments sits just inside
World Showcase near the Canada pavilion
(11a–9p. World Showcase Plaza. Disney Dining Plan
Quick Service). Tucked under a covered patio,
Germany's **Sommerfest** ✔ sells bratwurst,
frankfurters, pretzels, desserts and, of
course, beer (11a–9p. Seats 24. Disney Dining Plan
Quick Service). The U.K.'s **Yorkshire County
Fish Shop** ✔ offers fish and chips and Bass
ale (11a–9p. Seats 30. Disney Dining Plan Quick Service).

Snack stands. Notable choices include
Japan's **Kaki Gori** with its tasty shaved ice
and, right nearby, the American Adventure's
ice-cream-optional **Funnel Cake Kiosk.**

Disney's Hollywood Studios. A lovingly
replicated Hollywood icon, a sadistic little
café and a straightforward Italian eatery are
among the best options at this park.

50's Prime Time Cafe. ★★★★★ ✔ American
$$$ L: $11–17, 11a–4p. D: $12–21, 4p–park close. Seats 225,
also 14 at bar. Echo Lake. Disney Dining Plan. Fried
chicken, meatloaf, pot roast—it's all good, but
expect trouble if you put your elbows on the
table or don't eat your vegetables. Servers
portray fussy relatives you never knew you
had (request one with "a lot of theming" to
get the full treatment); formica tables, sparkly
vinyl chairs and period knickknacks re-create
1950s dinettes. Ask for a TV table to sit by
a black-and-white set playing food-related
vintage sitcom clips.

Hollywood & Vine. ★★★ Character buffet
$$$$ "Little Einsteins" June, Leo; Handy Manny; Oso from
"Special Agent Oso." B: $27 (children $15), 8–11:20a. L: A
$29 (children $15), 11:40a–2:25p. ★★ American buffet
$$$$ D (no characters): $33 (children $16). 3:30p–30 min
before park close. Seats 468. Echo Lake. Disney Dining Plan.
Preschoolers dance and sing with characters
at breakfast and lunch; sparse crowds allow
plenty of interaction. Food is standard buffet
fare. A character-free dinner is overpriced.

The Hollywood Brown Derby. ★★★★ ✔
American $$$$ L,D: $15–40, 11:30a–park close. Seats 224.
Hollywood Blvd. Disney Signature, 2 credits on Disney
Dining Plan. A homage to the 1929 second loca-
tion of the famous eatery, this fine-dining
spot offers an excellent Cobb salad, a fine
grouper dish and a tart grapefruit cake. A

"Iron Chef" Cat Cora presides over Kouzzina. The BoardWalk Resort eatery mixes flavors from Greece and the American South.

white-tablecloth ambience belies the bustle outside. Walls hold 1,000 caricatures. Talk to the hostess and your child (of any age) will get a tableside call from Goofy.

Mama Melrose's Ristorante Italiano. ★★★★ ✔ California Italian $$$ L,D: $12–$20, noon–1 hr before park close. Seats 250. Streets of America. Disney Dining Plan. Hidden in a rear corner of the Streets of America area, this gem serves some of the best food in the park. Flatbreads, made-from-scratch sauces and desserts are especially good. Resembling a converted warehouse, the dining room has wood tables, chairs and floors. Christmas lights hang from open ceilings. Walls are covered with Californian and Italian pop-culture relics.

Sci-Fi Dine-In Theater Restaurant. ★★ ✔ American $$$ L: $12–22, 11a–4p. D: $12–23, 4p–park close. Seats 252. Commissary Lane. Disney Dining Plan. A starlit dining room channels a 1950s drive-in theater, with a huge movie screen showing trailers from kitschy sci-fi films, newsreels, intermission bumpers and odd space-age cartoons. Sound comes from real drive-in speakers; some servers roller skate. Diners sit two abreast in miniature convertibles. As for food, stick to the hamburger and milkshake. Ask for a car seat when you check in, otherwise you may get a plain-Jane patio table.

Fast food. Next to The Great Movie Ride, the **ABC Commissary** offers burgers, chicken and fish. Cushioned booths and chairs and a carpeted floor make for a comfortable place to eat, though ceiling-mounted televisions play annoying ABC-TV hype. Service is slow at peak periods (L,D: 11a–park close. Seats 562 inside, 16 outside. Commissary Lane. Disney Dining Plan Quick Service). Tucked in between the Indiana Jones stunt show and Star Tours, **Backlot Express** has burgers, hot dogs, grilled sandwiches and salads. Themed as a crafts shop, it's decorated with real clutter such as the Toon Patrol truck and a small stunt car from 1988's "Who Framed Roger Rabbit" (11a–8p. Seats 600. Echo Lake. Disney Dining Plan Quick Service). Across from the MuppetVision 3-D attraction, the **Toy Story Pizza Planet Arcade** is a noisy gameroom (that looks nothing like the one in the 1995 movie "Toy Story") that sells individual pizzas and salads. Tables sit upstairs, but an open floor plan amplifies the racket (11a–7:30p. Seats 584. Streets of America. Disney Dining Plan Quick Service).

As for outdoor fast food, **Min and Bill's Dockside Diner** sells shakes, pretzels, beer, frozen lemonade across from the American Idol Experience (10a–8p. Seats 140. Looks like a boat. Echo Lake). Next to the Brown Derby, **Starring Rolls Cafe** ✔ has good pastries, sandwiches and coffee (B: 9–11:30a. L: 11:30a–4p. Seats 60. Uses Brown Derby kitchens. Sunset Blvd. Disney Dining Plan Quick Service). Across from the Backlot Tour attraction, **Studio Catering Co.** serves sandwiches, chili dogs, salads and desserts (11:30a–7p. Seats 498. Shaded seating. Adj outdoor bar. Streets of America. Disney Dining Plan Quick Service). Across from the Beauty and the Beast stage show, the **Sunset Ranch Market** is an outdoor food court. Various stands offer breakfast bagels, burgers, fresh fruit, hot dogs, pizza, salads, sandwiches, turkey legs and hand-dipped ice cream (B: park open–10:30a. L,D: 10:30a–park close. Seats 400. Sunset Blvd. Disney Dining Plan Quick Service).

Snack stands. The **Writer's Stop** recreates the atmosphere of a small bookstore café (once the one in the sitcom "Ellen") with baked goods, coffee and frozen drinks in between the Streets of America and the Sci-Fi Dine-In (Seats 15. Commissary Lane). **Peevy's Polar Pipeline** serves up frozen soft drinks from behind Hollywood Boulevard's Keystone Clothiers (Echo Lake).

Disney's Animal Kingdom.
A good buffet and an interesting Asian option are the two best choices at this theme park.

Rainforest Café. ★★ American $$$$ (B: $9–$14, 8:30–10a. L,D: $13–$43, 10a–park close. Seats 985, 72 at bar.

Run by outside company; direct reservations: 407-938-9100. Entrance plaza. Disney Dining Premium, Platinum plans only). The atmosphere is the draw at this kid-friendly spot, where robotic animals come to life in a dense faux jungle inside the dining room. Every 22 minutes the animals shriek as a thunderstorm strikes. Huge aquariums hold exotic fish. The food is fine if uninspired, generous portions delivered by friendly servers. It's overpriced, but you're paying for the hooting chimp as well as the sandwich or pasta.

Tusker House. ★ ★ ★ ★ ✔ Character buffet $$$ Donald Duck, Daisy Duck, Mickey Mouse, Goofy. B ("Donald's Safari Breakfast"): $21 (children $12), opt. photo package. 8–10:30a. ★ ★ ★ ✔ African-flavored buffet $$$$ L: $21 (children $12), 11:30a–3:30p. D: $29 (children $14), 4p–park close. Seats 1,206. Bar seats 256. Africa. Diners who enjoy fresh vegetarian dishes will enjoy this varied, well-prepared buffet. Standouts at lunch and dinner include the couscous, hummus, tabbouleh and salads; the carving station meats and desserts are also good. At breakfast Donald Duck hosts a character meal with standard American fare. Mickey Mouse leads a conga line in the dining room with kids playing instruments. The "Safari Orientation Centre" of mythical Harambe village, the dining area is lined with real African artifacts, faux maps and notices.

Yak & Yeti. ★ ★ ★ ★ ✔ Pan-Asian $$$$ L,D: $16–25. 11a–park close. Seats 250, 8 at bar. Same management as Rainforest Cafe. Direct reservations: 407-824-9384. Asia. Disney Dining Premium, Platinum plans only. With life-sized golden statues, other authentic Asian artifacts and lots of mismatched lighting and chairs adding interest to the rooms, Yak & Yeti is themed to be a guest home that's been turned into a restaurant (and hotel). The comfortable eatery satisfies both adventurous and timid diners. The large, interesting menu has both traditional Asian dishes and American standards such as baby back ribs, shrimp and steak. Best bets are the flavorful egg rolls with chili-plum dipping sauce and the cheesecake-like mango pie. Upstairs tables are quietest; window seats overlook Asia's walkway.

Fast food. Animal Kingdom has two indoor fast-food restaurants. On Discovery Island next to the walkway to Camp Minnie-Mickey, **Pizzafari** ✔ offers breakfast standards, individual pizzas, salads and sandwiches. Beautiful murals, floor mosaics and ceiling art add to a clean, cool, relaxing feel (B: 9–10:30a. L,D: 10:30a–park close. Seats 680. Discovery Island. Disney Dining Plan Quick Service). Tucked into a corner of DinoLand U.S.A., **Restaurantosaurus** has

Yak & Yeti, a Pan-Asian restaurant in Disney's Animal Kingdom, is filled with authentic Asian artifacts, including life-sized golden statues

burgers, chicken and salads as well as a lavishly wacko theme—an excavation-student dorm was a former dinosaur institute. The right-corner Hip Joint "rec room" stays peaceful and cool (L,D: 11a–park close. Seats 750. DinoLand U.S.A. Disney Dining Plan Quick Service).

Want to eat outside? On Discovery Island next to the walkway to DinoLand U.S.A., **Flame Tree BBQ** ✔ sells barbecue meats, baked beans, corn on the cob. Except when the weather is very hot and humid, its shady garden dining pavilions are pleasant; some sit on a lake (L,D: 11a–4p. Seats 500. Shaded seating. Discovery Island. Disney Dining Plan Quick Service). Next to Yak & Yeti, the **Local Food Cafes** offer Asian pork, lo mein, egg rolls and desserts. The mango pie is not the same served inside (L,D: 11a–4p. Seats 350. Shaded seating. Adj outdoor bar. Discovery Island. Disney Dining Plan Quick Service).

Snack stands. Notable spots include Africa's **Kusafiri Coffee Shop and Bakery,** which serves warm baked pastries, desserts, coffee and hot chocolate from a window adjacent to Tusker House and, across from the Yak & Yeti restaurant in Asia, the **Royal Anandapur Tea Co.** ✔, which offers a nice variety of hot individually-brewed teas (great on a cool day), specialty and iced coffees, pastries and smoothies.

Decked out with period knickknacks, formica tables and vinyl chairs, seating areas at the 50's Prime Time Café recall vintage dinettes. Black-and-white televisions play old sitcom clips.

Disney resort hotels

All-Star Resorts

In the All-Star Sports Resort, the **End Zone Food Court** offers standard American fare (B: 6:30–11a. L,D: 11a–mid. Seats 550. Disney Dining Plan Quick Service); similar is the All-Star Music Resort's **Intermission Food Court** (B: 6:30–11a. L,D: 11a–mid. Seats 550. Disney Dining Plan Quick Service). Best of the bunch—in food and atmosphere—is the **World Premiere Food Court** at the All-Star Movies Resort (B: 6:30–11a. L,D: 11a–mid. Seats 550. Disney Dining Plan Quick Service).

Animal Kingdom Lodge. All the choices at this resort are outstanding.

Boma—Flavors of Africa. ★★★★★ ✓ Africa/American buffet $$$ Breakfast buffet: $19 (children $11), 7:30–11a. D: $33 (children $17), 4:30–9:30p. Seats 400. Jambo House. Disney Dining Plan. This lavish buffet combines American comfort food with outstanding, non-exotic African options (our favorites are the roasted meats, the breakfast pap and grilled tomatoes and the dinner soups). The buffet area resembles an outdoor market, with each serving station in its own hut or "makeshift" stand. Several seating areas sit under abstract thatched ceilings with hand-cut glass and tin fixtures. Servers, many of which have been here for ages, are extraordinarily friendly and prompt.

Jiko—The Cooking Place. ★★★★ ✓ African fusion $$$$$ D: $26–$41, 5:30–10p. Seats 300. Jambo House. Disney Signature Restaurant, 2 credits on Disney Dining Plan. Sophisticated, relaxing and romantic, this Disney jewel specializes in unusual flavor combinations: cherries with goat cheese, roasted sweet potatoes with spiced yogurt, filet mignon with macaroni and cheese. The South African wine selection is the largest in the United States. Hanging from the ceiling are sculpted kanu birds, flying over diners to bring them good luck. Representing a sunset, the back wall slowly changes color.

Sanaa. ★★★★★ ✓ Indian-inspired East African $$–$$$$ L: $11–$19; 11:30a–3p. Bar only: 3–5p, desserts, beverages. D: $14–$28; 5–9p. Seats 124, 24 in lounge. Kidani Village. Disney Dining Plan. Serving a delicious cuisine that features dishes both spicy and mild, this colorful dining room comes with an added bonus: those with window seats can watch exotic animals roaming a savanna. The optional bread service is a must, as is a chai cream dessert. A stylized decor recalls an African marketplace, lights that resemble ripe fruit hang from acacia trees.

Fast food. Spacious and relaxed, **The Mara** ✓ at Jambo House offers American/African options with good fresh soups. Cartoons play on televisions. (7a–11:30p. Bakery 6a–11:30p. Small store has fruit, snacks, S African wines. Seats 250. Disney Dining Plan Quick Service).

BoardWalk Resort. All of these restaurants are located on the resort's boardwalk: **Big River Grille & Brewing Works.** ★★★ American $$$ L: $9–$26, 11:30a–4p. D: $11–$26, 4–11p. Seats 190, including 50 outside. Disney Dining Plan. Sporting Disney World's only micro brewery, this classy little franchise also offers down-to-earth food and free Wi-Fi. Food—grilled meats, seafood, pasta, sandwiches—is fine if not unique, though prices are lower than comparable Disney eateries. Small gunmetal tables make it noisy when crowded. Serves dinner later (11 p.m.) than most Disney restaurants. Equipped with two televisions, the small bar can be a less-crowded sports-bar alternative to the nearby ESPN Club.

ESPN Club. ★★ Sports Bar $$ L,D: $10–21, 11:30a–11p. Seats 450. Disney Dining Plan. This casual, noisy eatery combines a sports bar with a second room that hosts radio talk shows. It has 123 television monitors. Weekends can be packed. Basic bar chow includes burgers, hot dogs, ribs, salmon and steaks.

Flying Fish Cafe. ★★ Seafood $$$$$ D: $28–42, 5:30–10p. Seats 193. Disney Signature, 2 credits on Disney Dining Plan. Cramped, crowded, bright and loud, the atmosphere at this pricey nightspot interferes with enjoyment of its food. The onstage kitchen boosts the noise, but adds a nice aroma. Sit in back for the best and calmest experience. Good bets include the calamari, crabcakes, scallops and, interestingly for a seafood spot, the steak. Fish is better at Kouzzina. A six-course prix fixe Chef's Tasting Wine Dinner is available.

Kouzzina. ★★★★★ ✔ Mediterranean/American $$$$ B: $10–$12, 7:30–11a. D: $16–$28, 5–10p. Seats 232. Disney Dining Plan. Opa! People who like bold flavors—especially Greek ones—will raise their glasses to Kouzzina ("koo-ZEE-nah"). The first restaurant of Cat Cora, the only female winner of the television series "Iron Chef," it mixes Greek cuisine with southern staples such as greens and sweet potatoes. Entrees, all of which are full of flavor, include a whole fish (my husband's favorite), meats, pasta and a vegetarian option. A plaster ceiling and wood floors, tables and chairs create a bustling noise that adds a sense of camaraderie. A private room is available.

Fast food. A Pizza Window offers slices or full pies (Disney Dining Plan Quick Service). For snacks try the **Belle Vue Room** ✔, an intimate lounge with pastries and coffee in the morning, mixed drinks at night (B: 8–11a, drinks 4p–mid. Disney Dining Plan Quick Service) and the **BoardWalk Bakery** ✔, which has fresh-baked pastries and treats all day, hot breakfast sandwiches and cold lunch sandwiches (6:30a–varies. Disney Dining Plan Quick Service).

Caribbean Beach Resort. Both food options are just so-so at this resort.

Shutters. ★★ American/Caribbean $$$$ D: $18–$28, 5–10p. Seats 132. Disney Dining Plan. With premade food that can be served within a minute of ordering, this pricey eatery is in the lower tier of Disney's resort restaurants. The steak, chicken, ribs, pasta and seafood are just a step up from frozen food. Very few choices; there are only six entrees on the menu. A bright spot is the tres leches cake. The small room is well-staffed. Bland but pleasant, the decor includes big tables and wide padded chairs.

Fast food. The **Centertown Food Court** offers standard, but uninspired, American fare (B: 6:30–11:30a. L,D: 11:30a–11p. Seats 500. Disney Dining Plan Quick Service). A small food store sells fruit and snacks. Designed to look like an outdoor market, the two-story interior walls are building facades with balconies, shuttered windows and thatched roofs. The blue ceiling looks like the sky.

Contemporary Resort. Here are two good modern restaurants and a crowded signature character buffet.

California Grill. ★★★★ ✔ New American/California fusion $$$$$ D: $28–$44, 5:30–10p. Seats 156. Disney Signature, 2 credits on Disney Dining Plan. Superb fare is matched by an entertaining view at this Disney landmark, perched atop the resort's A-frame. Sushi is prepared by Okinawa's Yoshie Cabral, famous for her sauces and use of fruit. The menu has many vegetarian options and an extensive wine list. Guests watch Magic Kingdom's fireworks show from inside or rooftop walkways, with the show's music audible. A stylishly modern decor uses honey woodwork. Diners check in on the hotel's 2nd floor.

Chef Mickey's. ★★ Character buffets $$$$ Mickey, Minnie Mouse; Donald Duck; Goofy; Pluto. B: $27 (children $14), 7–11:30a. D: $34 (children $17), 5–9:30p Seats 405. Disney Dining Plan. This popular spot features Mickey Mouse as a chef and his pals as cooks. Unfortunately, each dining room often has only one character at a time, who during busy periods has to divide time among 100 diners. Huge buffets include PB&J pizzas for breakfast, good meats and salmon for dinner. Expect to be asked to pose for an optional non-character photo package, then asked to buy it while you eat.

The Wave. ★★★★ ✔ American $$$$ B: $7–$18, 7:30–11a. L: $12–$21, noon–2p. D: $18–$29, 5:30–10p.

Located at Animal Kingdom Lodge, Sanaa serves Indian-inspired East African food. Its colorful decor was inspired by African markets. Diners with window seats view exotic animals.

Lounge: noon–mid. Buffet, private rooms avail. Seats 222 plus 100 in lounge. Disney Dining Plan. This upscale eatery serves fresh, healthy food. Its menu emphasizes sustainability, local produce and organic ingredients. Highlights include intense dessert flights and Southern hemisphere wines. The open dining room has a sophisticated decor but no windows. Typically uncrowded, the Wave is a relaxing way to escape theme-park frenzy.

Fast food. The **Contempo Cafe** offers little to recommend it. Its food is uneven, its electronic ordering confusing (6a–10p. Light fare 10p-mid. Seats 112. Disney Dining Plan Quick Service). In the lobby near the Convention Center, the **Contemporary Grounds** coffee bar is open early; cartoons play on a television (6:30a–5p).

Coronado Springs Resort. Most eateries at this resort include Mexican dishes.

Maya Grill. ★★★ **American/Latin $$$$** B: $8–$16; 7–11a. D: $15–$29, 5–10p. Seats 220. Disney Dining Plan. Breakfast dishes include a Kobe brunch burger and Huevos Rancheros. Dinners come with delicious breads and a chimichurri dipping sauce. Meat dishes dominate entrees; juicy prime rib is a good bet. The open kitchen has a wood-burning oven. Expect attentive, friendly service.

Fast food. The **Pepper Market Food Court** offers American/Mexican dishes that are mall-quality at best. There's an automatic 10 percent service charge (B: $3–$11, 6–10:30a. L,D: $10–$22, 11a–11p. Seats 420. Disney Dining Plan Quick Service). **Café Rix** serves pastries, sandwiches and gelato (B: $5–$7, 6:30–11a. L,D: $7–$11, 11a–mid. Seats 50. Disney Dining Plan Quick Service). Ritzy **Rix Lounge** serves appetizers, has a nightly DJ and, sometimes, a live band; corporate bigwigs can indulge in VIP tables and private rooms (5p–2a Wed–Sun. Seats 220. $15 cover; VIP tables, which seat up to 12, have $500 min).

Fort Wilderness Resort. Down-home cooking characterizes these choices:

Hoop-Dee-Doo Musical Revue. ★★★ Dinner show $$$$$ D: $53–$62 (children $27–$32), 2-hr shows at 5, 7:15, 9:30p. Tues–Sat. Seats 360. Pioneer Hall. Disney Dining Plan. This rootin' tootin' institution has been performed 35,000 times since 1974. Children often think it's the funniest show ever; they love the six exuberant performers and the rat-a-tat jokes. The songs and skits aren't really that good, but it's all so silly you can't help but have fun. Vittles include all-you-can-eat tin pails of fried chicken and ribs with lots of fixin's and, if you want, unlimited draft beer and wine.

Mickey's Backyard Barbecue. ★★★ Character country show, buffet $$$$$ Mickey Mouse, Minnie Mouse, Goofy, Chip 'n Dale. D: $51 (children $21). 2-hr show at 6:30p. Thurs, Sat except Jan, Feb. Seats 300.

The Settlement. Disney Dining Plan. Hosted by live performers Tumbleweed Will and Cyclone Sally, this old-fashioned country show is especially fun for children. Held in a large outdoor pavilion, it includes a live band, a trick roper and a big ol' dollop of patriotism. Highlights include the exuberant hosts and the characters, who dance with guests. Ever wanted to get down and boogie with Mickey Mouse? This is your chance. A so-so buffet offers pork ribs, chicken, corn on the cob, watermelon and beer. Diners share long tables. Arrive early; it's first come, first seated, and the initial group sits right next to the stage and dance floor.

Trail's End Restaurant. ★★ American, **buffet $$$$** B: $18 (children $11), 7:30–11:30a. L: $13–$18, 11:30a–2p. D: $25 (children $14), 4:30–9:30p Sun–Thurs, 4:30–10p Fri–Sat. Take-out service: $8–$9, noon–2p daily, 4:30–9:30p Sun–Thurs, 4:30–10p Fri–Sat. Seats 192, 6 at bar. The Settlement. Disney Dining Plan. The food is a step up from what you might expect at this overpriced, Cracker Barrel-esque eatery. The potatoes are creamy, the vegetables have flavor; but you expect more for the price. Breakfast and dinner are buffets with fried chicken and other comfort food; lunch is a la carte. Friendly servers add to a down-home ambience. A separate take-out counter offers sandwiches, salads and pizzas. Restrooms are outside and around the corner.

Fast food. Crockett's Tavern serves up nachos, pizza and chicken wings (Pioneer Hall, Disney Dining Plan Quick Service).

Grand Floridian Resort. Disney's signature resort has multiple fine-dining choices.

1900 Park Fare. ★★★★★ ✓ Character buffets $$$$$ Breakfast characters: Mary Poppins, Winnie the Pooh and Tigger, Alice and Mad Hatter. Dinner characters: Cinderella, Prince Charming, others such as stepsisters Anastasia and Drizella, Lady Tremaine, Gus, Jacques. B ("Supercalifragilistic Breakfast"): $25 (children $14), 8–11:30a. D ("Cinderella's Happily Ever After Dinner"): $36 (children $18), 4:30–8:30p. Seats 270. Disney Dining Plan. These joyous character meals are the best at Disney World. Breakfast serves standard American fare and a standout lobster Benedict. At dinner, everyone's favorite princess is on hand, of course, but also her fascinating family; bickering stepsisters Anastasia and Drizella usually steal the show. Varied buffet choices are delicious; the strawberry soup and prime rib are especially good. The elegant dining room has a turn-of-the-century amusement park theme.

Cítricos. ★★★★ ✓ Mediterranean $$$$$ D: $22–$46, 5:30–10p. Seats 190. Disney Signature, 2

credits on Disney Dining Plan. Lit with a soft yellow glow, this overlooked gem doesn't have Narcoossee's view or the over-the-top glam of Victoria & Albert's, but does offer imaginative, market-fresh dishes in what might be the most comfortable setting of any Disney Signature restaurant. The Mediterranean menu excels in seafood with citrus notes and seasonal soups. Try the outstanding lemon cheesecake with raspberry sauce. Tall windows overlook the main pool and marina. The pace is so slow and relaxing, you'll spend more time here than you might think.

Grand Floridian Café. ★★★ ✓ American $$$ B: $11–$17, 7–11:30a. L: $14–$25, 11:30a–2p. D: $17–$26, 5–9p. Seats 326. Disney's Dining Plan. This pleasant spot is the best general-purpose restaurant on the Magic Kingdom monorail loop. It's what Magic Kingdom's Plaza Restaurant aspires to be. Best bets include the fluffy citrus pancakes for breakfast, the tuna niçoise salad at lunch, and the steak and pasta dishes for dinner. Efficient servers are sometimes too absent. Floral wallpaper and thick carpeting heighten the calm, comfortable atmosphere.

Narcoossee's. ★★★★★ ✓ Seafood $$$$$ D: $22–$59, 5:30–10p. Seats 270. Disney Signature, 2 credits on Disney Dining Plan. Although pricey, this pretension-free seafood spot is one of the best seafood restaurants at Walt Disney World, with good meats as well. Wood floors and peaked ceilings look nice but make the dining room noisy and echoey. The circular building sits over the Seven Seas Lagoon; its view of Magic Kingdom's Wishes fireworks show includes beautiful reflections in the water. Ask for a windowside table. ✓

Victoria & Albert's. ★★★★★ ✓ Gourmet $$$$$ D: $125, $185 w/wine pairings (Chef's Table $200, $295 w/pairings). Two seatings. Formal dress. Jackets required for men; loaners available. Harpist. Women receive roses. Private restroom. No children under 10. Seats 90, inc. 10 at Chef's Table. Not on Disney Dining Plan. For an evening to remember, this formal restaurant is the most expensive on Disney property, and worth it. You'll have perhaps the best meal you've ever had; it's like having "Top Chef" winners cook just for you. A six-course dinner is created to match your personal tastes. A four-hour Chef's Table option includes more courses, a kitchen tour and a chat with the cooks. Service is exemplary.

The elegant, cozy **Garden View Tea Room** overlooks lovely gardens. English-style delicate tea sandwiches, scones, tarts, hot teas and specialty coffees are served on flowery china. Many choices have three courses (L: $14–$25. 2–6p. Disney Dining Plan Quick Service).

Princess Jasmine (from the 1992 film "Aladdin") appears at Cinderella's Royal Table and Akershus Royal Banquet Hall character meals

Fast food. Although its diners sit in an arcade, the noisy **Gasparilla Grill and Games** has good food (24 hrs. Seats 150. Disney Dining Plan Quick Service).

Old Key West Resort. This resort's table-service restaurant is one of the author's favorites for breakfast.

Olivia's Cafe. ★★★ ✓ American $$$$ B: $11–$16, 7:30–10:30a. L: $11–$20, 11:30a–5p. D: $17–$29, 5–10p. Seats 156, inc. 22 outside. Disney Dining Plan. Jimmy Buffett would feel right at home in this Keys-inspired eatery. The menu is a nice mix of standard American fare and regional recipes that use lots of shrimp and conch, with tropical accents such as mango glaze. Breakfast in particular has unusual choices such as a shrimp and conch Benedict. Dinner offers more traditional fare. The homey decor includes a tin ceiling and mismatched padded chairs.

Fast food. Offering burgers, hot dogs, salads and sandwiches, **Good's Food To Go** is an outdoor counter (B: 7–10:30a. L,D: 11:30a–10p. Disney Dining Plan Quick Service).

Polynesian Resort. For families, the best bet here is the character breakfast.

Kona Cafe. ★★ Pan-Pacific American $$$$ B: $9–$14, 7:30–11:30a. L: $11–$19, noon–3p. D: $17–$30,

5–10p. Seats 163. Disney Dining Plan. This pricey coffee shop is packed during peak periods, though its food is generally mediocre. Those in the know get the macadamia-pineapple pancakes for breakfast, a sandwich at lunch, the good sushi at dinner. New seafood additions are worthwhile, too. Friendly servers aim to please. A few comfy booths sit within a subdued (and carpeted) coffee-themed decor. Kona coffee is available.

'Ohana. ★★★ Character breakfast $$$ Lilo, Stitch, Mickey Mouse, Pluto. B ("Mickey and Friends Character Breakfast"): $25 (children $14), 7:30–11a. ★★ **Family-style dinner $$$$** D: $35 (children $16), 5–10p. Seats 300. Disney Dining Plan. Highlighted by fresh coconut-pineapple bread, breakfast is one of Disney's most popular character meals. Every hour characters lead kids in a maraca-shaking parade. Carnivores, come hungry for dinner, when skewers of Polynesian-flavored meats and seafood are grilled over a fire and continually delivered to your table. Kids participate in coconut races and hula contests.

Spirit of Aloha. ★★ Dinner show $$$$$ D: $53–62 (children $27–$32), 2-hr shows at 5:15p, 8p. Tues–Sat. Seats 420. Luau Cove, Disney Dining Plan. A dancing, drumming and musical tour of Hawaii, New Zealand, Samoa, Tahiti and Togo, this venerable dinner show features skimpy traditional costumes and lots of booty shaking. The story of a native girl returning to her roots has a corny first half of sitcom-style skits. Later, children are invited onstage to learn the hula. The meal is an all-you-can-eat feast of uninspired pork ribs and chicken. Service is perfunctory. If you go, splurge for the front-of-the-house seats; folks who sit in back have a hard time hearing.

Fast food. The only place outside Magic Kingdom to get the Dole Whip pineapple treat, **Captain Cook's Snack Co.** also has standard American fast food plus flatbread, stir-fry dishes and packaged sushi (6:30a–11p. Seats 150. Disney Dining Plan Quick Service). In the morning, the **Kona Island Cafe Coffee Bar** serves pastries; it transforms into the **Kona Island Cafe Sushi Bar** ✓ in the evening, also serving alcoholic beverages (B: 6:30a–4p. Sushi: 5–10p. Seats 16. Disney Dining Plan Quick Service).

Pop Century Resort

The **Everything Pop! Food Court** ✓ offers standard American fare plus some usually good salads and flatbreads; the bakery is especially good (B: 6:30–11a. L,D: 11a–mid. Seats 650. Disney Dining Plan Quick Service). The carpeted dining area has many comfortable booths, and vintage Top 40 ambient music.

Port Orleans Resorts. Riverside has a nice restaurant; French Quarter only a food court. **Boatwright's Dining Hall.** ★★★ ✔ Southern American $$$$ D: $17–$28, 5–10pm. Seats 206. Disney Dining Plan. This underrated eatery serves fish, a grilled meat, pasta, a vegetarian dish—all with down-home side dishes. A bit pricey, but recipes are delicate. A 46-foot boat hangs above the dining room; ship-building tools adorn walls. The back room has a fireplace. Faux-wood tables sit on tile floors.

Fast food. The **Sassagoula Floatworks & Food Factory** food court is themed as a Mardi Gras float warehouse (B: 6–11a. L,D: 11a–mid. Seats 550. French Quarter. Disney Dining Plan Quick Service). Made-to-order beignets are mouth-watering; the rest of the offerings are poor, even by the standards of a shopping mall. Resembling a cotton mill, the spacious **Riverside Mill** food court has a large water wheel with working gears. It serves fine standard American fare (B: 6–11a. L,D: 11a–mid. Seats 550. Riverside. Disney Dining Plan Quick Service).

Saratoga Springs Resort. Choices are a masculine restaurant and nice fast-food spot. **Turf Club Bar & Grill.** ★★★ ✔ American $$$ L: $10–$19, Noon–5p. D: $17–$32, 5–9p. Seats 146, inc. 52 outside. Disney Dining Plan. Great food at decent prices makes this cozy country-club-style retreat worth seeking out. Lunch attracts golfers; this overlooked gem sits above the pro shop of the Lake Buena Vista golf course. Dinner has steaks that are worth the money. While waiting for a table, guests can shoot billiards or watch sports at the adjacent bar. An outdoor balcony overlooks the golf course, a small lake and Downtown Disney.

Fast food. The nice **Artist's Palette** food court ✔ offers above-average flatbreads and a nice dining area with padded booths. Drawing easels are set up for children. A store sells fruit, snacks and limited groceries (11a–11p. Seats 112. Disney Dining Plan Quick Service).

Wilderness Lodge. A rowdy barbecue restaurant highlights the choices here. **Artist Point.** ★★★★ ✔ American/Pacific Northwest $$$$$ D: $25–$43, 5:30–9:30p. Seats 225. Disney Signature, 2 credits on Disney Dining Plan. Foodies will love this rustic restaurant offering fine meals in a relaxed atmosphere. Inspired dishes include cedar plank-roasted salmon, grilled buffalo and Artist Point cobbler, featuring house-made black raspberry ice cream. The waitstaff is knowledgeable and pleasant. The L-shaped dining room mixes landscape murals with blond and cherry woods and a soaring ceiling. Large windows offer views of the courtyard and pool.

Whispering Canyon Cafe. ★★★ ✔ American barbecue $$$$ B: $10–$12, 7:30–11:30a. L: $12–$19, 11:30–2:30p. D: $19–$32, 5–10p. Seats 281. Disney Dining Plan. "Let's hand over the menus; no free souvenirs at Disney World." The brusque, loud servers keep the one-liners coming at this entertaining and tasty barbecue spot. Signature all-you-can-eat skillets are overpriced, but many good choices are not. Try the grilled quinoa cakes for lunch, the meatloaf for dinner, or the trout anytime. The comedic wait staff doesn't let the schtick interfere with the good service. The cowboy decor is bold yet, believe it or not, tasteful.

Fast food. Noisy **Roaring Fork Snacks** serves grilled foods, pizza, salads and sandwiches (B: 6–11a. L,D: 11–mid. Seats 250. Disney Dining Plan Quick Service).

Yacht and Beach Club Resort. These sister resorts offer some of Disney's best meals. **Beaches & Cream.** ★★★★ ✔ Soda shop $$ L,D: $6–$24, 11a–11p. Take-out counter. Seats 48. Next to Stormalong Bay, Beach Club. Disney Dining Plan. Gigantic sundaes are the draw at this old fashioned soda shop, which also serves good burgers and sandwiches. The claim to fame is the ridiculous $24 Kitchen Sink sundae that's served, literally, in a kitchen sink. It's a tiny spot, with just three booths and six small tables. A tin ceiling has a tray center with elaborate moldings. Guests can choose songs from a classic jukebox.

Cape May Café. ★★★ ✔ Character breakfast buffet $$$ Goofy, Minnie Mouse, Donald Duck. B ("Goofy's Beach Club Breakfast"): $20 (children $12), 7:30–11a. ★★★ Dinner buffet $$$$ D: $27 (children $13), 5:30–9:30p. Seats 235. Beach Club. Disney Dining Plan. This relaxed restaurant is the only Disney-operated character meal not in a theme park or on the monorail loop. Small parties can often get in without a reservation. Breakfast offers American standards and Mickey Mouse waffles. Though billed as a clambake, the dinner devotes less than 10 percent of its buffet line to clams, mussels, crab legs and shrimp; the standout item is a carved-to-order top sirloin. Subdued lighting and sounds of sea gulls make the café a pleasant place to recover at the end of a day.

Captain's Grille. ★★★ ✔ American $$$$ B: buffet: $20 (children $11); a la carte $9–$14, 7:30–11:30a. Only buffet from 11–11:30a. L: $11–$19, 11:30a–2p. D: Prix fixe meal w/app, entree, dessert $28 (children $9); a la carte $16–$30, 5–9p. Seats 280. Yacht Club. Disney Dining Plan. This grade-A restaurant makes a sincere effort to be a destination eatery, although it gets ignored by sitting next to the outstanding Yachtsman Steakhouse. Despite its nautical name, its cuisine is not focused on seafood. Choices also include beef, chicken, pork and a vegetarian option. Portions are generous, dishes distinctive. Decor is inspired by 1930s New England, with nice lighting, padded chairs and gleaming brass.

Yachtsman Steakhouse. ★★★★★ ✔ Steaks $$$$$ D: $24–$44, 5:30–10p. Seats 286. Yacht Club. Disney Signature, 2 credits on Disney Dining Plan. Disney World's best steakhouse hits the trifecta—exceptional food, attentive service and a warm, inviting atmosphere. Generous portions of grain-fed beef steaks are of the highest quality. Those in the know rave about the desserts. The simple, elegant dining room has honey-colored wood, leather and brass. A glass-walled butcher room lets you see your steak being prepared. Half of the restaurant is on a wood floor; the other half is carpeted.

Fast food. The **Beach Club Marketplace** offers pastries, salads, sandwiches and soups; a small food store sells fruit and snacks (B: 7–11a. L,D: 11a–10p. Seats 16 outside. Disney Dining Plan Quick Service).

Other locations

Downtown Disney. Only one restaurant—Capt'n Jack's—is owned by Disney at this shopping and entertainment complex:

Bongos Cuban Cafe. ★★ Cuban $$$$ L: $8–$17, 11a–4p. D: $14–$33, 4–11p Sun–Thurs, 4p–mid Fri–Sat. Seats 560, including 60 outside and 87 at the bar. No reservations. Info: 407-828-0999. West Side. The Cuban food isn't as impressive as the architecture and decor in this eatery, created by singer Gloria Estefan. Housed in a whimsical building dominated by a three-story adobe pineapple, bamboo bars and mosaic murals recall the B.C. (Before Castro) Cuba of the 1940s and 1950s. Good side dishes include yuca and plantains; entrees are inconsistent. Ask to sit in the pineapple or on the second-story patio. Friday and Saturday nights can be loud, especially next to the dance floor. An outside bar serves sandwiches, desserts and drinks.

Cap'n Jack's. ★★ Seafood $$$$ L,D: $13–$24, 11:30a–10:30p. Seats 113, also 15 at bar. Direct res: 407-828-3971. Marketplace. Disney Dining Plan. Though its worn wood decor is due for a makeover, this unpretentious 1970s throwback has good basic food. The limited menu has only six entree choices, half seafood but with no lobster or oysters offered. The pot roast falls apart in your mouth. Nearly every table has

a nice view of the water. Disney is missing an opportunity here—Cap'n Jack's has nothing to do with everyone's favorite Pirate of the Caribbean, Capt. Jack Sparrow.

Fulton's Crab House. ★★ Seafood $$$$$ L: $10–$18, 11:30a–3:30p. D: $20–$74, 4–11p. Seats 660, including 24 outside. Direct res: 407-934-2628. Pleasure Island. Accepts Disney Dining Premium, Platinum plans only. OK for lunch, expensive for dinner, this white-tablecloth spot offers lots of crab dishes as well as lobster, shrimp and steaks. Best bets include the filling crab-and-lobster bisque and Lobster Narragansett. Although it looks just like an old paddlewheeler from the outside, it was built by Disney as a restaurant and, despite appearances, is not floating. Ask to sit on the lake side of the semicircular Constellation Room on the second deck; its ceiling glows blue at night.

House of Blues. ★★★★★ ✔ Southern Creole/American $$$ L,D: $11–$27, 11:30a–11p Sun–Mon, 11:30a–mid Tue–Wed, 11:30a–1:30a Thurs–Sat. Seats 578, including 158 at outside tables and 36 at outdoor bar. No reservations. Gospel brunch with live music Sun. 10:30a, 1p, in Music Hall, 250 seats. A: $34, C: $17. Info: 407-934-2583. West Side. With spicy jambalaya, flavorful cornbread and walls and ceilings covered with folk art, this down-home eatery is a perfect antidote to too much Disney. The funky atmosphere makes for one of the more relaxed meals at Disney World. Wood floors and tables make the restaurant noisy when crowded. Live free music plays late some evenings in the dining area; a concert hall sits next door. Kids love to pick through the lobby's bucket of crayons to make their own folk art.

Paradiso 37. ★★★ ✔ American/Latin American $$$ L,D: $10–27, Sun–Wed 11:30a–mid, Thr–Sat 11:30a–1a. Seats 250, 100 outside, 20 stools at bar. Live entertainment nightly: 6–11:30p Sunday–Thursday, 6–12:30a Friday and Saturday. Direct res: 407-934-3700. Pleasure Island. This classy lakefront eatery is a good alternative to the more touristy restaurants nearby. The menu represents the 37 countries of the Americas. An eclectic mix of dishes focuses on "street" food, from hamburgers and hot dogs to Peruvian beef skewers and Chilean-style salmon. Thirty-seven tequilas ($8–$50 a glass) are displayed in a two-story lighted wall bar with thousands of color-changing LEDs. Loud world music thumps day and night. Servers are friendly.

Planet Hollywood. ★ American $$$ L,D: $12–$27, 11a–1a; bar only until 2a. Seats 800. Info: 407-827-7827. West Side. Disney Dining Plan. Shaped like a planet, this three-story cafe is chock full of celebrity and movie memorabilia, including a blue gingham dress Judy Garland wore in 1939's "The Wizard of Oz." Other than good hamburgers, the menu is lame, the atmosphere loud, the service irritating. On the plus side, it's open late, and the props and costumes are interesting.

Portobello. ★★★ Italian $$$$$ L: $10–$24, 11:30a–3:45p. D: $10–$37, 4–11p. Seats 414, including 86 outside. Direct res: 407-934-8888. Pleasure Island. Accepts Disney Dining Premium, Platinum plans only. Italian-food lovers will best appreciate this comfortable eatery. Themed to be a Tuscan country trattoria, it offers a variety of antipasti and entrees inspired by dishes of Milan, Rome and Tuscany. Pasta dishes dominate the menu; other offerings include pizzas from the wood-burning oven and, for dinner, chicken, fish or steak. Portions are on the small side. Meals come with good bread and a roasted garlic spread; salads are not included. Formerly Portobello Yacht Club.

Raglan Road. ★★★★★ ✔ Irish pub, restaurant $$$$ L: $12–$16, 11a–3p. D: $14–$28, 3–11p. "Pub Grub" 11p–1:30a. Live band, table step-dancers evenings Mon–Sat. Children welcome. Seats 600, including 300 outside. Direct res: 407-938-0300. Pleasure Island. Disney Dining Plan. Run by Irish proprietors, this pretension-free spot offers sophisticated comfort food. Tops are tender meats, creamy soups and sinful bread pudding. The bar serves many beers and whiskeys. Meals come with a delicious Guinness-reduction-and-olive-oil dip and hearty Irish soda bread. The antique decor includes two 130-year-old bars from Ireland complete with traditional leaded-glass dividers. A live band and Irish table dancer entertain every night but Sunday. One of our favorite places to eat.

Rainforest Café. ★★ American $$$$ L,D: $13–$43, 11:30a–11p Sun–Thurs, till mid Fri, Sat. Seats 575. Direct res: 407-827-8500. No same-day reservations. Marketplace. Accepts Disney Dining Premium, Platinum plans only. The atmosphere is the draw at kid-friendly Rainforest Café, where robotic animals come to life in a dense faux jungle inside the dining room. Every 22 minutes the animals move and shriek when a thunderstorm strikes. Huge aquariums hold exotic fish. The food is fine if routine, generous portions are delivered by friendly servers. The food is overpriced, but you're paying for the monkeys as well as the meatballs.

T-REX. ★★★ ✔ American $$$$ L,D: $12–$30, 11a–11p Sun–Thurs, till mid Fri, Sat. Small playground adjacent. Seats 626, including 26 at bar. Direct res: 407-828-8739. Marketplace. Accepts Disney Dining Premium, Platinum plans only. Young dino fans will love this big, brash take on its sister restaurant, Rainforest Café. In both eateries, you're paying for the

experience as well as the food. Dining areas include a geothermal room, a glowing blue ice cave, and sea-life spot with aquariums. A "meteor shower" hits every 21 minutes, with accompanying loud dino roars. The best bet on the huge, varied menu—blackened fish tacos. A free fossil dig site for kids provides a slot for shoes and a place to wash up.

Wolfgang Puck Café. ★★ California Fusion $$$$ L: $11–$25, 11:30a–4p. D: $13–$29, Sun–Mon 4–10:30p, Tue–Thurs till 11p, Fri, Sat till 11:30p. Weekend lunch serves dinner menu. Takeout window. Private room for groups. Seats 586, including 30 at sushi bar. Direct res: 407-938-9653. West Side. Disney Dining Plan. This loud, pricey eatery often has slow service. Signature dishes (i.e. crusted chicken, pumpkin ravioli, veal weinerschnitzel) are mild yet flavorful. The fried chicken is outstanding, but nearly $30. Topped with breadcrumbs, a creamy macaroni and cheese tastes homemade. Sadly, sushi bar selections are routine.

Wolfgang Puck Dining Room. ★★★ California Fusion $$$$$ D: $25–$60, 6–9p Sun–Thurs, 6–10p Fri–Sat. Seats 120. Direct res: 407-938-9653. West Side. Disney Dining Plan. This white-tablecloth eatery blends flavors into sophisticated entrees that feature chicken, fish, steak and veal. Prices and quality are higher than at the more boisterous Café downstairs. Located on the second floor of the Puck building—above the Café—the room's orange walls are dominated by a gigantic ornamental hookah (though sadly, no giant ornamental caterpiller). The restaurant was inspired by Puck's signature Spago and Chinois eateries.

Fast food. Between Tren-D and Once Upon a Toy, **Earl of Sandwich** ✔ offers tasty hot sandwiches, crusty bread and steaming creamy-orange tomato soup. Morning fare includes a breakfast BLT (B: $2–$5, 8:30a–10:30a. L,D: $5–$6, 10:30a–11p. Seats 190 including 65 outside. Marketplace). Next to Basin, the **Ghirardelli Soda Fountain** ✔ serves luscious ice cream treats. The hot fudge sauce is made daily (10:30a–11p Sun–Thurs, till 11:30a–mid Fri–Sat. Seats 88, including 22 outside. Marketplace. Disney Dining Plan Quick Service). **Wolfgang Puck Express** ✔ offers an imaginative mix of pasta, pizza, salads, sandwiches and soups, including signature Crispy Cornflake French Toast and silky butternut squash soup. Hardwood tables and a concrete floor keep the dining area noisy, as does loud ambient music (B: $9–$11, 9a–11a. L,D: $10–$16, 11a–11p. Seats 184, including 96 outside. Marketplace). A part of the Raglan Road enterprise, **Cookes of Dublin** ✔ has a surprisingly large menu, offering fish and chips, a hand-battered beef burger and

Irish sausages, with deep-fried candy bars for dessert (L,D: 11a–11p. Seats 20, with stand-up bar tables. Pleasure Island).

Downtown Disney's best snacks are the hot, soft treats at **Wetzel's Pretzels,** which also offers fresh-squeezed lemonade and Haagen-Dazs ice cream (10:30a–11p Sun–Thr, to mid Fri, Sat. 36 outdoor seats. West Side).

ESPN Wide World of Sports

A fast-food spot where diners order at a counter but get food delivered to their tables, the **ESPN Wide World of Sports Grill** (★ ★ ✔ **American $** L,D: $7–$10, 11a–7p; on slow days will close early or have limited menu. Seats 350, 48 in the bar. Disney Dining Plan). shows sports channels as well as events from within the complex on six huge television screens that surround diners. Though most items are made to order, waits are typically 10 minutes or less. The menu offers chicken wings, individual pizzas, salads and hot and cold sandwiches; best bets are the roast beef and blackened fish sandwiches. The grill can host live ESPN radio broadcasts and has a photo prop that looks like a "SportsCenter" desk. More TVs are at the separate bar, which serves liquor as well as brewed coffee. Relatively unknown outside the complex, the Grill is a secret spot to watch NFL, NBA, MLB and college games. An adjacent small PlayStation Pavilion offers free access to various sports titles—some not yet released— on 17 PS3 consoles.

Policies

Disney-operated restaurants share a variety of policies and procedures.

Dress codes. Most Disney World restaurants have a casual dress code, equal to that of the theme parks. With the exceptions of Cinderella's Royal Table and the Hollywood Brown Derby, all Disney Signature Restaurants have a business casual dress code. For men, that means jeans, dress shorts, dress slacks or trousers; and a shirt with a collar or T-shirt underneath. Women are required to wear jeans, dress shorts or a skirt with a blouse or sweater, or a dress. Not permitted: Cut-offs, men's caps or hats, swimsuits, swimsuit cover-ups, tank tops or torn clothing. Victoria & Albert's (Grand Floridian) requires jackets for men and dresses or dressy pants suits for women.

Gratuities. Disney adds an automatic 18 percent gratuity to dining bills for parties of 8 or more. In general, tip 15–20 percent for good service; 10 percent for mediocre.

Reservations. Having a dining reservation is often a must at Disney, even for restaurants in your hotel. The best eateries often book to capacity far in advance, especially for popular dining times. During peak periods many don't accept walk-up diners regardless of how long a guest is willing to wait.

Making a reservation: Reservations can be made up to 180 days in advance (190 days for Disney resort guests) at 407-939-3463 or at disneyworld.com as well as at most restaurant check-in counters and resort concierge desks. Some restaurants require a credit-card guarantee; some charge a cancellation fee. Reservations for parties of 13 or more always require a credit card, as do dinner shows and Grand Gathering Experiences.

Cancellation policy: Each Disney restaurant has its own reservation cancellation policy. In general, if a credit card isn't required to guarantee a reservation, there is no cancellation fee.

Holding time: Most Disney restaurants will hold your reservation for 15 minutes beyond its stated time.

When to arrive: Plan to arrive at least 5 minutes before your seating time. Your party will be seated at the next available table that can accommodate your group.

Toughest reservations: Cinderella's Royal Table inside Magic Kingdom's Cinderella Castle is the toughest reservation to nab. It often books in full on the first day of availability. Its meals are charged at the time you book them. Other hot spots include California Grill and Chef Mickey's (at the Contemporary Resort), Le Cellier (Canada pavilion, Epcot) and Victoria & Albert's (Grand Floridian Resort). The toughest reservation time is 7 to 8 p.m. To eat at that hour make a reservation at least a few days early, especially for a party of six or more.

Gastric-bypass surgery guests. Those who have had gastric-bypass surgery should bring a weight-loss-surgery card issued by their doctor or hospital with them to Disney restaurants. Present it to a server to pay the child price for an adult meal at buffets, or to possibly order from a kids menu at non-buffet meals.

Children's meals. Disney Kids' Picks meals include many nutritious entrees. Each comes with unsweetened applesauce, baby carrots or fresh fruit (your choice of two) and a beverage of low-fat milk, juice or water. Less than 35 percent of a Kids' Picks meal's calories come from fat, and of those, no more

One McDonald's sits on Disney property. Located in front of Disney's All-Star Resorts at Osceola Parkway and Buena Vista Drive, the fast-food spot is open 24 hours. Between 3 and 4 a.m. it often only takes cash. A clean, expansive dining area has many video screens.

Micaela Neal

than 10 percent come from saturated fat and sugar. French fries and soft drinks can be substituted. Kids' Picks meals are available throughout Disney World theme parks as well as at Disney resort hotels.

Special diets. No-sugar, low-fat, low-sodium, vegetarian or vegan diets can be met at table-service restaurants by telling a reservation clerk, host or server. Dinner shows need 24 hours notice.

With three days notice, Disney restaurants accommodate dietary needs such as allergies to gluten or wheat, shellfish, soy, lactose or milk, peanuts, tree nuts, fish or eggs. Many counter-service restaurants offer low-fat or vegetarian options. No Disney restaurant serves food with added trans fats or partially hydrogenated oils.

Kosher meals: Glatt kosher meals are available at most full-service Disney restaurants with 24 hours notice at 407-939-3463. Requests require a credit-card guarantee and have a 24-hour cancellation policy. Kosher fast-food meals are always available—without notice—at Cosmic Ray's Starlight Café (Magic Kingdom), Liberty Inn (Epcot), ABC Commissary (Hollywood Studios), Pizzafari (Animal Kingdom) and the food courts at the All-Star, Caribbean Beach, Pop Century and Port Orleans Riverside resorts. Disney's kosher food is prepared in Miami.

Discounts. Disney's Tables in Wonderland discount card ($75–$100 annually, available to annual passholders and Florida residents only, 407-566-5858, weekdays 9 a.m. to 5 p.m.) saves its holder and up to nine guests 20 percent off food and beverage during non-holiday periods at most DisneyWorld table-service

restaurants and a handful of other spots, including the food courts at Disney Value Resorts. An 18 percent gratuity is added.

Discounts for annual passholders are typically 10–20 percent off lunch or dinner at the following locations:

Magic Kingdom: Tomorrowland Terrace.

Epcot (World Showcase): Biergarten, Nine Dragons, Restaurant Marrakesh, San Angel Inn, Teppan Edo, Tokyo Dining, Tutto Italia.

Disney's Hollywood Studios: Disney's Hollywood & Vine.

Disney's Animal Kingdom: Rainforest Café, Yak & Yeti.

Downtown Disney: Cap'n Jack's restaurant, Ghirardelli Soda Fountain, House of Blues, Paradiso 37, Planet Hollywood, Portobello Trattoria, Rainforest Café, T-REX Café, Wolfgang Puck Café.

Disney resorts: Animal Kingdom Lodge (Sanaa), BoardWalk (Kouzzina, ESPN Club), Contemporary (The Wave), Fort Wilderness (Trail's End Restaurant), Grand Floridian (Grand Floridian Café), Old Key West (Olivia's Café), Saratoga Springs (Turf Club), Wilderness Lodge (Whispering Canyon Café) and Yacht & Beach Club (Captain's Grille).

Other locations: Osprey Ridge Golf Club (Sand Trap Bar and Grill).

Specialty promotions. The official Walt Disney World website (disneyworld.com) often offers dining deals under a "Special Offers" link on its home page.

About these listings. Restaurants are rated from one to five stars (★) for quality and value; checkmarks (✔) indicate the authors' personal favorite places to eat.

Accommodations

As the most popular vacation destination on the planet, Walt Disney World has no shortage of places to stay. Disney itself owns and operates 19 resort hotels on its property—combined, they have enough rooms to hold 120,000 people—and dozens of brand-name hotels are just a few miles away.

Disney resort hotels

It's not just the theme parks that are magical. The themed architecture, decor, swimming pools, lush landscaping and, in many cases, quality restaurants at a Disney resort hotel immerse you in a unique vacation experience. Their reputation as clean, family environments is well-deserved; during most mornings grounds crews and maintenance workers seem to be everywhere. Fancier spots offer a variety of recreation options and sometimes character meals, where guests can meet Mickey Mouse and other beloved stars in person.

Categories. The Walt Disney company runs 19 resorts on its Florida property, which it divides into four categories. These group the resorts by price, amenities, and, in most cases, the number of people that guest rooms will accommodate.

Value Resorts (Disney's All-Star Resorts, Pop Century Resort). With rack rates starting as low as $89 a night, these huge motel-like complexes are the least expensive Disney-owned places to stay on Disney World property. Most rooms sleep four, feature double (not queen) beds, and are relatively small at 260 square feet. The All-Star Movies Resort also offers 520-square-feet suites that sleep up to six. Amenities are limited, but do include swimming pools, playgrounds and food courts. Luggage service is hourly. Parking lots are near lodging buildings.

Oddly, the Value Resorts are the only Disney hotels that have an obvious Disney theme; at both, many buildings are trimmed with gigantic statues and other props that recall Disney movies. Both properties are

Facing page: A whirlpool bath in a one-bedroom villa at Disney's BoardWalk Resort

popular with large youth groups, especially the All-Star complex.

Expected to open by the end of 2012, Disney's Art of Animation Resort will be Walt Disney World's third Value Resort complex. To be located next to the Pop Century Resort, the new property will have nearly 900 standard rooms and over 1,100 family suites. Like Disney's other Value properties, the motel-style complex will have budget rates and limited amenities, and feature larger-than-life icons masking its outdoor elevator platforms and stairwells. Areas will be themed to the movies "Cars," "Finding Nemo," "The Lion King" and "The Little Mermaid." Though it will have its own entrance, the resort will use land and buildings originally meant to be the second phase—the "Legendary Years" area—of the Pop Century Resort.

Moderate Resorts (Disney's Caribbean Beach Resort, Coronado Springs Resort, Fort Wilderness Resort & Campground and Port Orleans Resorts). With rack rates starting at $154 a night, these large complexes offer distinctive geographical themes, more elaborate swimming pools and, in most cases, a table-service restaurant. Most rooms are 314 square feet and come with two queen beds; some at Disney's Port Orleans Riverside Resort sleep five thanks to trundle beds; Fort Wilderness cabins sleep six. Amenities include on-site recreation options. Parking lots are near lodging buildings.

Deluxe Resorts (Disney's Animal Kingdom Lodge, BoardWalk Inn, Contemporary Resort, Grand Floridian Resort & Spa, Polynesian Resort, Wilderness Lodge Resort and Yacht and Beach Club Resort). Serious architecture, lush landscaping and a wealth of amenities distinguish Disney's top-of-the-line resort hotels; rack rates start at $250. Rooms sleep five, and vary in size from 340 to 415 square feet. Amenities include fine restaurants, elaborate swimming pools, on-site recreation, full room service, club levels, fitness centers and valet parking. Restrooms in public areas offer cloth towels and hand lotion. Located in front of large resort entrance areas, parking lots are away from lodging buildings; non-valet spots can require a short hike to get to.

Towers of time front the registration building at Disney's Pop Century Resort. The budget property is themed to American pop culture of the late 20th century.

Deluxe Villas (Disney's Old Key West Resort and Disney's Saratoga Springs Resort; sections of Disney's Animal Kingdom Lodge, Beach Club Resort, BoardWalk Inn, Contemporary Resort and Wilderness Lodge). These Disney Vacation Club (DVC) timeshare units are often available nightly; rack rates start at $280. Units vary from studios to multi-story suites that can sleep twelve. All have kitchens. DVC buildings are usually adjacent to Deluxe Resorts and share those amenities. Old Key West and Saratoga Springs have amenities similar to Deluxe Resorts, though their parking lots are usually next to their lodging buildings.

Disney occasionally groups its resort hotels geographically. Some Disney highway signs refer to the properties in this fashion:

Magic Kingdom Area Resorts: Disney's Contemporary Resort, Grand Floridian Resort & Spa, the Polynesian Resort, Wilderness Lodge and Fort Wilderness Resort & Campground.

Epcot Area Resorts: Disney's BoardWalk Resort, Caribbean Beach Resort and Yacht and Beach Club Resort. (In reality, Caribbean Beach is closer to Hollywood Studios than it is to the entrance of Epcot.)

Downtown Disney Area Resorts: Disney's Old Key West Resort, the Port Orleans Resorts and Saratoga Springs Resort.

Animal Kingdom Area Resorts: Disney's All-Star Resorts, Animal Kingdom Lodge, Coronado Springs Resort and Pop Century Resort. (In truth, Pop Century is closer to Hollywood Studios—and Downtown Disney—than it is to Animal Kingdom.)

Benefits of Disney hotels. Staying on Disney property is certainly convenient. The location makes it easy to get to a theme park early in the morning, and to return to your hotel during the day. Other benefits include:

Extra Magic Hours. Each day, one of the four Walt Disney World theme parks has extended hours, opening one hour early, or staying open up to three hours late for Disney resort guests with theme-park tickets. Water parks also participate. These Extra Magic Hours offer you uncrowded time in the parks and make it easier to plan out your vacation.

Complimentary transportation. Disney boats, buses and monorails take you to all theme and water parks as well as Downtown Disney at no additional charge. In some cases, it takes just a few minutes to get from your hotel room to a theme park.

Magical Express. With this complimentary service, when guests bound for Disney hotels are traveling via commercial airline to Orlando International Airport (OIA), they can check their bags at their hometown airport,

A hammock hangs over a beach at the moderately priced Disney's Caribbean Beach Resort. Other Disney resort hotels with beach hammocks include the moderate Coronado Springs convention complex and the deluxe Polynesian near Magic Kingdom.

bypass baggage claim and board buses for complimentary transportation to their Walt Disney World resort hotel, where their bags "magically" appear. When it's time to leave, many guests can check their baggage for the return flight at their Disney resort.

See chapter **Walt Disney World A-Z.**

Key to the World. This small plastic card acts as a room key, theme-park ticket and charge card. Each Disney resort guest gets one at check-in, even children.

Package delivery. Anything a Disney resort guest buys at a Disney theme park can be delivered to their resort free of charge.

Guaranteed admission. If they have tickets, Disney resort guests are guaranteed entry into Disney theme parks, even, in most cases, when those parks are officially filled to capacity. Visiting at Christmas, the Fourth of July or another peak period? This matters.

Special deals. Disney resort guests can prepay for their meals through the Disney Dining Plan and get preferred tee times and discounts at Disney's four golf courses.

See chapters **Activities** and **Walt Disney World A-Z.**

About these listings. On the following pages, resorts are rated from one to five stars (★) for quality and value; checkmarks (✓) indicate the authors' favorite places to stay. "Rack" room rates are the standard prices quoted by Disney before taking into account any deals or promotions, "discount" rates are the actual range of prices charged through TripAdvisor and other online travel agencies over the past year. All Disney hotel addresses listed are in the city of Lake Buena Vista, Fla., ZIP code 32830. All Disney resort phone numbers connect to the same switchboard.

Guests at Disney's Contemporary, Grand Floridian and Polynesian resorts are whisked to Magic Kingdom and Epcot on elevated monorail trains. Other resorts are served by Disney buses and boats. All Disney transportation is complimentary.

A giant jukebox rises at the All-Star Music Resort. A huge megaphone covers a stairwell at All-Star Sports. Sheriff Woody graces All-Star Movies. Each All-Star guest room has two double beds.

All-Star Resorts

★★ **Rates:** Rack: $82–$179. Suites $194–$365. Discount (i.e., online travel agency): $57–$179. **Hotel type:** Value resort hotel with clustered, multistory lodging buildings. **Location:** Located southwest on WDW property, near Animal Kingdom. **Distance to theme parks:** Magic Kingdom 5 mi; Epcot 5 mi; Hollywood Studios 3 mi; Animal Kingdom 1 mi. Other destinations: Blizzard Beach 1 mi; Typhoon Lagoon 4 mi; Downtown Disney 4 mi; ESPN Wide World of Sports 3 mi. **Address:** All-Star Movies: 1901 W Buena Vista Drive, All-Star Music: 1801 W Buena Vista Drive, All-Star Sports: 1701 W Buena Vista Drive, 32830. **Size:** 5,740 rooms, 298 suites, 246 acres. **Amenities:** Each resort has a food court, two swimming pools and one kiddie pool. Arcade, jogging trail, playground. Laundromat, laundry service. Shop with groceries. **Children's programs:** Pool activities. **Transportation:** Disney buses shuttle guests to theme parks, water parks and Downtown Disney. All-Star Sports is the first stop for buses, All-Star Music second, All-Star Movies last. **Built:** 1994 (All-Star Movies 1999). **Renovated:** 2007–2009. **Check In:** 3p. **Check Out:** 11a. **Phone:** Movies: 407-939-7000. Music: 407-939-6000. Sports: 407-939-5000. **Fax:** All-Star Movies: 407-939-7111. All-Star Music: 407-939-7222. All-Star Sports: 407-939-7333.

Cramped rooms, bad food and cheap decor make these three Disney Value Resorts poor places to stay. These are really just basic motel buildings disguised by superficial theming. However, the pools are nice for the price, with fountains and children's activities. Youth groups such as marching bands and soccer teams often stay here.

Highs: Good rates; child-friendly Disney theme; McDonald's adjacent; large swimming pools; All-Star Music has family suites, the only Disney Value suites.

Lows: No table-service dining; childish theming; unshaded bus stops; lodging elevators not air-conditioned; small guest rooms; long lines at food courts and bus stops, especially in the morning.

What's new: Rooms were refurbished in 2007 and 2009.

In the rooms: Rooms are fairly plain and modestly decorated; the decor is not subtle. All three resorts use stars in their decorating, as well as honey-colored wood and cheery colored walls (260 sq ft. Sleep 4. Two double beds. Accessed by outdoor walkways. All-Star Music has family suites: 520 sq ft. Sleep 6. 1 king bed, 1 sleeper-sofa double bed, 2 single beds convert from chair and ottoman, kitchenette, 2 full baths).

Grounds. Built to compete with the rash of discount motels on nearby U.S. 192 (most of which have since fallen into disrepair), each All-Star Resort is laid out like a typical budget complex, but on a giant scale. A central building holds the registration area, food court and bus station, and fronts the main swimming pool. Boldly decorated three-story lodging buildings spread out from there, with parking lots nearby. Structurally little different from those at a Holiday Inn Express, each lodging building is coated with bright paint, and its stairwells and elevator entrances are hidden by way-larger-than-life icons—either Disney film characters (All-Star Movies), musical instruments (Music) or sports gear (Sports). Landscaping is often sparse, though native pine trees cover much of the grounds.

Swimming pools. Each All-Star Resort has two themed pools, one with a kiddie pool behind its central hall and a second deeper within. No pool has a slide, but the central ones have fountains that shoot water over swimmers' heads. All-Star Movie's "Fantasia" pool is themed to that film; the smaller "Mighty Ducks" Duck Pond pool is shaped like a hockey rink. All-Star Music's Calypso Pool is guitar shaped; a smaller Piano Pool has a cushy keyboard. All-Star Sport's Surfboard pool looks like a beach; the smaller Grand Slam pool is shaped like a baseball diamond.

Food. Each resort has a food court which serves all three meals, as well as a bakery, convenience store and small bar open to its main pool. Room service (pizza, salads, desserts) is available from 4 p.m. to midnight.

See chapter **Restaurants and Food.**

Family matters. Each resort has a sandy playground with climbing areas, monkey bars and slide. Organized children's activities at each resort's main pool are posted on a poolside board each morning. Occasionally each resort shows outdoor movies.

Animal Kingdom Lodge

★★★★★ ✔ **Rates:** Rooms: Rack: $250–$615. Discount (i.e., online travel agency): $144–$615. Suites: Rack: $740–$2990. Discount: $422–$2990. Villas: Rack: $280–$2330. Discount: $160–$2330. **Hotel type:** Deluxe resort hotel with main lodge, secondary lodge curving around wild animal savannas. **Location:** Southwest corner of WDW, near Disney's Animal Kingdom. **Distance to theme parks:** Magic Kingdom 6 mi; Epcot 5 mi; Hollywood Studios 3 mi; Animal Kingdom less than 1 mi. Other destinations: Blizzard Beach less than 1 mi; Typhoon Lagoon 5 mi; Downtown Disney 5 mi; ESPN Wide World of Sports 9 mi. **Address:** 2901 Osceola Parkway, 32830. **Size:** 762 rooms, 19 suites, 708 villas, 74 acres. **Amenities:** Jambo House has two restaurants, fast-food cafe, two lounges; Kidani Village has one restaurant. Each section has a pool with slide, hot tubs, kiddie pool, play area. Animal viewing (24 hours), arcade, children's programs, night-vision animal spotting, playground, poolside crafts. Sunrise truck ride through disney's Animal Kingdom habitat; sunset ride into resort savannas (both extra charge). Business center. Laundromat,

Disney's All-Star Movies Resort is dominated by gigantic Disney movie characters, such as Pongo from 1961's "101 Dalmatians"

laundry service, massages, shops. Kidani Village: BBQ pavilion; basketball, shuffleboard, tennis courts. Kidani Village Community Hall has games, activities. **Children's programs:** Many organized activities (daily, some have a small fee) include African cultural activities, arts and crafts and pool games. **Transportation:** Disney buses shuttle guests to theme parks, water parks and Downtown Disney, as well as between Jambo House and Kidani Village. **Built:** Jambo House 2001, Kidani Village 2009. **Renovated:** Jambo House 2007. **Check In:** 3p. **Check Out:** 11a. **Phone:** 407-938-3000. **Fax:** 407-938-4799.

A giraffe may wander behind your balcony at this African-themed complex. Consisting of the original Jambo House and newer Kidani Village, it features savannas filled with free-roaming exotic animals behind most guest rooms. Viewing walkways extend into the habitats.

If you can afford it, Jambo House is a no-brainer: a fully realized resort with comfortable rooms, first-class dining and a good pool. Children will love the all-suite Kidani Village, but parents paying the bill may find it disappointing. Not at all like a village, Kidani Village is one long building—over a half mile in length—with a parking garage underneath. Guests there must take a bus to Jambo House to eat breakfast, and the lunch and dinner restaurant, though excellent,

© Disney

Clockwise from top left: Disney's Animal Kingdom Lodge has its own wildlife preserve and a huge swimming pool. A Jambo House room hints at African adventure, as does a Kidani Village villa.

serves an African/Indian cuisine that may not be everyone's cup of tea. Kidani Village does have a pool with a fun winding slide and a water-park-like kiddie play zone.

Highs: Wild animals roam savannas behind the lodging buildings, superb restaurants, rooms at each area are easily accessible since they are all in the same building, good pools, child-care center onsite, Kidani's larger suites are stunning. **Lows:** Distant location; Kidani Village has limited dining and no breakfast, its small suites are cramped.

What's new: Kidani Village, a Disney Vacation Club complex, opened in 2009. It has its own parking lot, pool and savanna.

In the rooms: Rooms have multicolored fabrics and dark wood furniture hand-crafted in Africa. Above the first floor, rooms have balconies which extend about 4 feet; the few on the ground level have patios. Most overlook wildlife savannas, though some face the pool or parking lot. Club level available. Jambo House suites are at prime locations at the end of animal trails. Some have pool tables. Kidani Village has 492 villas; Jambo House has 109 (340 sq ft. Sleep 4. Two queen beds, or one

Facing page: Exotic chandeliers top the lobby of Jambo House at Animal Kingdom Lodge

queen plus bunk beds, small refrigerator. Suites: 1-, 2- and 3-bedroom units sleep up to 9. Villas: Studio, 1-, 2- and 3-bedroom units sleep up to 12).

Grounds. At Jambo House, 19 interconnected lodging buildings arc into a 33-acre savanna, home to non-aggressive African animals. Kidani Village is a Disney Vacation Club (timeshare) complex that often offers nightly rentals. It's surrounded on three sides by its own 13-acre savanna populated with exotic animals. Common areas are less elaborate than the original Jambo House.

Swimming pools. Refurbished for 2010, the Jambo House pool is the largest at any Disney World resort. Open 24 hours a day, it has a 67-foot water slide as well as a "zero-entry" gradual ramp. A kiddie pool, two isolated hot tubs and a shady playground are nearby. A Kidani Village swimming complex adds a 4,200-square-foot interactive water-play area.

Food. The resort has a buffet and two table-service restaurants. All are terrific. Room service is available 6 a.m. to midnight. See chapter **Restaurants and Food.**

Family matters. Children's activities range from African cultural lessons to after-dark animal spotting with night-vision goggles. Kids play games and experience African culture at Camp Kidani ($30; $27 for DVC members, ages 5–12, 6–8p nightly, at Kidani Village, 407-939-3463).

Disney's BoardWalk Resort features a lakefront promenade with restaurants, shops and midway games. Accommodations include garden suites. Guest rooms are trimmed in yellows and greens.

BoardWalk Inn and Villas

★★★★★ ✓ **Rates:** Rooms: Rack: $345–$995. Discount (i.e., online travel agency): $204–$995. Suites: Rack: $675–$2865. Discount (i.e., online travel agency): $405–$2865. Villas: Rack: $345–$2330. Discount (i.e., online travel agency): $204–$2330. **Hotel type:** Deluxe resort hotel with interconnected, multistory lodging. **Location:** Centrally located on WDW property, between Hollywood Studios and Epcot. **Distance to theme parks:** Magic Kingdom 4 mi; Epcot less than 1 mi; Hollywood Studios less than 1 mi; Animal Kingdom 4 mi. Other destinations: Blizzard Beach 2 mi; Typhoon Lagoon 2 mi; Downtown Disney 2 mi; ESPN Wide World of Sports 4 mi. **Address:** 2101 N Epcot Resorts Blvd, 32830. **Size:** 378 rooms, 20 suites, 533 villas, 45 acres. **Amenities:** Four restaurants, pizza window, snack shops, lounge. Three pools. Main pool has a clown-faced slide, kiddie pool, playground. Arcade, BBQ grill, bike and surrey rentals, fitness center, lighted tennis courts. Two nightclubs. Laundromat, laundry service. Shop with groceries. Conference center (9,600 sq ft, ballroom, 14 breakout rms). Business center. **Children's programs:** Organized activities (daily, some have a small fee) include arts and crafts, pool games. **Transportation:** Boats go to Epcot, Hollywood Studios. Disney buses shuttle guests to theme parks, water parks and Downtown Disney. When the boats can't operate (during lightning), buses take guests to Epcot, Hollywood Studios. **Built:** 1996. **Renovated:** 2009. **Check In:** 3p (Villas 4p). **Check Out:** 11a. **Phone:** 407-939-5100. **Fax:** 407-939-5150.

Disney cut no corners when it built this turn-of-the-century Deluxe Resort, a recreation of the golden days of Atlantic City. Rooms that are pretty as well as comfortable and authentic period architecture create a cozy, immersive experience. A wide lakeside promenade is lined with quaint shops, interesting restaurants, even a dance hall and dueling-piano bar. The pools are small, but have a fun amusement-park theme. The location is terrific: within walking distance of Disney's Hollywood Studios as well as the back entrance to Epcot.

Highs: Great dining variety, quality; within walking distance to Epcot, Hollywood Studios; evening entertainment on boardwalk; lovely setting on a lake.

Lows: Lodging buildings are far from the parking lot, no restaurants are within the hotel interior, there's no Disney transportation to the main entrance of Epcot.

What's new: Rooms and suites were refurbished in 2009.

In the rooms: Rooms feature plush mattresses on wood-framed beds and marble sinks. A Club level is available. Two-story garden suites have individual front lawns with white picket fences. Timeshare villas, some two-story, are often available for nightly rentals. (Standard room: 385 sq ft. Sleep 5. Two queen beds, sleeper sofa, small refrigerator.

Suites: Sleep 4–9. Villas: Studio, 1-, 2- and 3-bedroom units sleep 4–12).

Grounds. Surrounded by water on three sides, the property includes a hotel, time-share villas and a conference center. The boardwalk level holds restaurants, shops and entertainment venues; rooms, suites and villas—some up to six stories tall—rise behind. Most rooms and suites spread out among two semicircular arcs of interconnected buildings. Some overlook the lake, though most face landscaped areas or pools. Meant to resemble a 1940s Atlantic City, N.J. oceanside resort, the BoardWalk has the look of a community that has grown over time. "Newer" structures appear unrelated to their neighbors; mom-and-pop shops have tucked themselves into residential buildings.

Swimming pools. The Luna Park swimming pool area features a 200-foot slide that looks like a 1920s wooden roller coaster, with small dips and sweeping turns. Nearby is a kiddie pool, playground and sunny hot tub. Two quiet pools are somewhat different—the Villas one is nicely landscaped with a large grill, the Inn has a lesser version of the same thing: smaller pool, fewer trees, no grill.

Food. A variety of good dining choices includes a Disney Signature seafood eatery, a celebrity chef-designed Mediterranean restaurant and good sandwich spots. Room service is available 24 hours a day at the Inn; 6 a.m. to midnight at the Villas.

See chapter **Restaurants and Food.**

Family matters. Organized children's activities (daily, some have a small fee) include arts and crafts and pool games. The Villas Community Hall has board and video games.

Caribbean Beach

★★★ ✓ **Rates:** Rack: $154–$309. Discount (i.e., online travel agency): $104–$309. **Hotel type:** Moderate resort hotel with clustered, multistory lodging buildings. **Location:** Centrally located on WDW property, near Hollywood Studios. **Distance to theme parks:** Magic Kingdom 5 mi; Epcot 4 mi; Hollywood Studios 3 mi; Animal Kingdom 5 mi. Other destinations: Blizzard Beach 3 mi; Typhoon Lagoon 1 mi; Downtown Disney 2 mi; ESPN Wide World of Sports 3 mi. **Address:** 900 Cayman Way, 32830. Size: 2,112 rooms, 200 acres. **Amenities:** Restaurant, food court. Central pool w/slide, kiddie pool, hot tub. Each lodging area has basic pool; playgrounds at Barbados, Jamaica, Trinidad, Old Port Royale areas. Arcade, beach, bike rentals, boat rentals, guided fishing trips, hammocks, picnic area, sand volleyball court, surrey rentals, walking trail. Laundromat, laundry service. Shop

The slide is the tongue of a clown on the Keister Coaster, a feature of the main swimming pool of Disney's BoardWalk Resort

with groceries. **Children's programs:** Pontoon-boat adventure; complimentary arts and crafts, beach and pool activities. **Transportation:** Disney buses shuttle guests to theme parks, water parks and Downtown Disney. A separate shuttle circles within the resort. **Built:** 1988. **Renovated:** 2008. **Check In:** 3p. **Check Out:** 11a. **Phone:** 407-934-1000. **Fax:** 407-934-3288.

A nice mix of value and convenience, this Disney Moderate Resort is a good choice for families who want the resort experience but don't want to bust their bank account, especially if they want to see some palms on their vacation. Colorful metal-roofed buildings add to the exotic look. Rooms are comfortable, though their decor is unsophisticated.

Highs: Decent rates, convenient by car to all theme parks, many rooms are near parking lots, tropical landscaping lends a distinct vacation feel.

Lows: Dining facilities are too small, especially at breakfast; weak food court; many lodging buildings are far from bus stops; superficial theming; room decor may be too childish for guests without children.

What's new: As of 2009 all guest rooms are specifically themed (see below).

In the rooms: Most rooms have a bright decor with subtle "Finding Nemo" trim, 384 rooms in the Trinidad South lodging

Disney's Caribbean Beach Resort has tropically colored buildings. Its main swimming pool appears to surround a stone fort. Standard rooms have a "Finding Nemo" decor; others have a pirate theme.

village have a strong "pirate" decor, with molded-plastic beds that resemble ships, dressers that look like old crates and skull-and-sword drapes that close off vanities. Except for their furnishings and decor, all Caribbean Beach rooms are identical (314 sq ft. Sleep 4. Two queen beds, small refrigerator. Accessed by outdoor walkways).

Grounds. Disney's second largest hotel complex, the 200-acre Caribbean Beach Resort is landscaped with palms and native pines. Lodging buildings cluster into six self-contained "villages" which wrap around a 42-acre man-made lake; each has its own parking area. Footbridges over the lake lead to a one-acre island, Caribbean Cay, a flowery spot dotted with benches and hammocks. A dining, shopping and recreation center ("Old Port Royale") is centrally located. Its indoor area ("Centertown") is designed to look like an outdoor market—walls have faux second-story balconies, windows and thatched roofs, hallways are strung with tin street lamps.

The resort's check-in counters and main concierge center are in the Custom House, a building along the entranceway that is removed from other areas.

Swimming pools. The central swimming pool appears to sit within an old stone fort. Cannons spray swimmers; a small slide has a 90-degree turn. Nearby is a kiddie pool and hot tub. A few feet away, a small water playground for young children looks like a wrecked pirate boat, with mini-slides, fountains and a barrel that dumps water from above; wading water is ankle deep, nearby are shady spots for adults to sit. Less crowded, smaller basic pools sit within each lodging area.

Food. Shutters, a small restaurant, is open only for dinner; a food court serves all three meals. Room service (pizza, salads, desserts) is available from 4 p.m. to 11:30 p.m.

See chapter **Restaurants and Food**.

Family matters. Children's activities include the Islands of the Caribbean Pirate Adventure Cruise, a pontoon-boat treasure hunt ($34, ages 4–12, 2 hours, reservations at 407-939-7529).

Contemporary

★★★★ **Rates:** Rooms: Rack: $300–$885. Discount (i.e., online travel agency): $171–$885. Suites: Rack: $645–$3040. Discount: $368–$3040. Villas: Rack: $395–$2550. Discount: $226–$2550. **Hotel type:** Deluxe resort hotel with two towers and a separate 3-story wing. **Location:** Northwest corner of WDW property, near Magic Kingdom. **Distance to theme parks:** Magic Kingdom less than 1 mi; Epcot 4 mi; Hollywood Studios 4 mi; Animal Kingdom 7 mi. Other destinations: Blizzard Beach 5 mi; Typhoon Lagoon 6 mi; Downtown Disney 7 mi; ESPN Wide World of Sports 7 mi. **Address:** 4600 N. World Drive, 32830. **Size:** 632 rooms, 23

Disney's Contemporary Resort features a 15-story central A-frame; guest rooms have a modern Asian decor. Villas at the adjacent, rounded Bay Lake Tower have a bright, lively style.

suites, 295 villas, 55 acres. **Amenities:** Three restaurants, fast-food cafe, snack shops, lounges. Two pools, kiddie pool. Also private Bay Lake Tower complex; Bay Lake Tower Community Center has video, board games. Arcades; beach; boat rentals; evening beach campfire with movie; guided fishing trips; tennis, beach volleyball courts; water sports. Fitness center, hair salon, laundromat, laundry service. Convention center (120,000 sq ft, 4 ballrooms, 1,600 sq ft stage, 33 breakout rms). Business center. **Children's programs:** Arts and crafts, beach and pool activities. **Transportation:** Monorail goes to Magic Kingdom, Epcot; Grand Floridian, Polynesian resorts. Boats travel to Wilderness Lodge, Fort Wilderness resorts. Disney buses shuttle guests to Hollywood Studios, Animal Kingdom, water parks and Downtown Disney. **Built:** 1971. **Renovated:** 2008–2009. **Check in:** 3p (Bay Lake Towers 4p). **Check out:** 11a. **Phone:** 407-824-1000. **Fax:** 407-824-3539.

It's on the monorail route, it has comfortable rooms and a character meal, but overall this Deluxe Resort still fails to deliver a magical Disney experience. An abundance of glass, carpet and sprayed plain concrete lends an impersonal feel to most public areas, while the resort's restaurants are pricey and the pools plain. As for being contemporary, each guest room has its own computer as well as a modern Asian theme, but the rest of the resort seems more like a coldhearted office complex straight from the 1970s. Ceilings are often acoustical tile, escalators connect lower floors in the A-frame.

Highs: On monorail route, within walking distance to Magic Kingdom, big comfortable rooms, great recreation, lakeside.
Lows: Corporate feel, pricey dining, poor counter-service eatery, plain pools.
What's new: A new kiddie pool area has a splash pad and water cannons.
In the rooms: Asian-inspired modern decor features tan fabrics and dark woods. Club level available. Sitting above the atrium, 14th-floor suites serve as convention hospitality rooms. The size of three standard rooms, one-bedroom suites have Scandinavian decors. Opened in 2009, Bay Lake Tower has 295 modern villas. (Standard rooms 394 sq ft. Sleep 5. Two queen beds, daybed, small refrigerator. Suites: Sleep 4–8. Villas: Studio, 1-, 2- and 3-bedrm units sleep up to 12.)

Grounds. The resort includes a distinctive 15-story A-frame, a garden-wing annex, and Bay Lake Tower, a new crescent-shaped timeshare tower. The Contemporary is the only hotel from which guests can walk to Magic Kingdom, and the only one with direct monorail service from an indoor train station. The lakefront resort has the most extensive water recreation of any Disney hotel complex and a large convention center. A restricted Disney Vacation Club complex, Bay Lake Tower has its own recreation area and a rooftop lounge with a fireworks-viewing deck.

Disney's Coronado Springs Resort has a Spanish Colonial style. Rooms have a modern Mexican decor with turquoise and orange accents. The registration area has an open-beamed ceiling.

Swimming pools. The main swimming pool has a 17-foot-high spiraling slide, a large central fountain and a row of smaller sprays. A second pool sits next to the lake. It's round, and gets deeper in its center. Cabana tents are available for rent (407-939-7529; 407-824-2464 same-day). Nearby are a beach volleyball court and a new kiddie pool area with a splash pad and fun water cannons. A Bay Lake Tower pool includes a "zero-entry" side and a 20-foot-high spiraling slide wrapped in a glass block. A hot tub, Mickey Mouse-shaped kids fountain, shuffleboard and bocce ball courts and a barbecue pavilion with shaded picnic tables are nearby.

Food. The resort is home to two iconic Disney restaurants: California Grill and Chef Mickey's, and a pricey but tasty choice in The Wave. Room service is available 24 hours.

See chapter **Restaurants and Food.**

Family matters. Children's activities include arts and crafts, pool games and a beach campfire with a movie. The Electrical Water Pageant passes by nightly at 10:05 p.m.

Coronado Springs

★★★ ✔ **Rates:** Rack: $154–$310. Discount (i.e., online travel agency): $108–$310. Suites $350–$1320. **Hotel type:** Moderate resort hotel with clustered, multistory lodging buildings in three separate themed areas. **Location:** Next to WDW's Western Way entrance, near Hollywood Studios. **Distance to theme parks:** Magic Kingdom 4 mi; Epcot 3 mi; Hollywood Studios less than 1 mi; Animal Kingdom 2 mi. Other destinations: Blizzard Beach less than 1 mi; Typhoon Lagoon 3 mi; Downtown Disney 4 mi; ESPN Wide World of Sports 5 mi. **Address:** 1000 W. Buena Vista Drive, 32830. **Size:** 1,877 rooms, 44 suites, 125 acres. **Amenities:** Restaurant, food court, fast-food cafe, lounge. Large outdoor recreation complex with swimming pool, children's programs, playground, sand volleyball court, large hot tub. Three smaller pools in lodging areas. Arcades; beach; bike, boat, surrey rentals; fitness center, guided fishing trips, hammocks. Hair salon, laundromat, laundry service. Shop with groceries. Convention center (220,000 sq ft, ballroom, exhibit hall, 45 breakout rms). Business center. **Children's programs:** Organized activities (daily, some have small fee) include arts and crafts, pool games. **Transportation:** Disney buses shuttle guests to theme parks, water parks and Downtown Disney. **Built:** 1997. **Renovated:** 2009. **Check In:** 3p. **Check Out:** 11a. **Phone:** 407-939-1000. **Fax:** 407-939-1001.

This sprawling Spanish Colonial convention complex offers a quality place to stay at a decent price. Rooms have comfortable beds and calm decors; most are close to parking lots but a long walk from many amenities. Swimming pools are excellent, and include a large central one with many features. Dining options are poor, but there's a McDonald's down the street. The Disney Moderate Resort has little Disney atmosphere, but its tropical landscaping is well-maintained. The resort is Disney's only mid-priced convention property.

Highs: Family-friendly despite convention location, many rooms are near parking lots, fun themed pool, close to McDonald's, 22-person hot tub one of WDW's largest.

Lows: Dining facilities limited, weak food court, lodging buildings distant. Guests using Disney's Magical Express service have a long walk from the bus depot.

What's new: The Coronado's rooms were refurbished in 2009.

In the rooms: A modern Mexican decor combines dark woods with blue, green and yellow fabrics. Club-level rooms have DVD players. (314 sq ft. Sleep 4. Two queen beds, small refrigerator. Accessed by outdoor walkways.)

Grounds. The complex consists of an amenities and convention center and three distinct lodging areas, all of which circle outward around a 15-acre lake. Rooms and suites are grouped into an urban-styled Casitas area near the convention center; a Ranchos section that has an American Southwest landscape of sagebrush, cactus and gravel; and a Cabanas area that suggests Mexico's Gulf Coast.

Swimming pools. With old-fashioned swing sets, treasures buried in the sand and a sneaky spitting jaguar next to a winding swimming-pool slide, children may never realize they're at a convention hotel if they hang out at the resort's first-rate recreation area. Adjacent to the Ranchos lodging buildings, it also includes a large swimming pool (a waterfall flows into it off a four-story pyramid), a kiddie fountain pool, a 22-person hot tub, a sand volleyball court and an indoor arcade. Smaller quiet pools are located in each lodging area.

Food. The Disney touch is absent at the Coronado's dining choices, which are run by an outside company. Room service is available 7 a.m. to 11 p.m.

See chapter **Restaurants and Food.**

Family matters. A soft-surfaced playground at the rec center has swings and a sandbox with hidden faux artifacts.

Fort Wilderness

★★★★ ✔ **Rates:** Campsites: Rack: $46–$125. Cabins: Rack: $275– $450. Discount (i.e., online travel agency): $193–$450. **Hotel type:** Moderate resort hotel with campsites and cabins. **Location:** Northwest corner of WDW property, southeast of Magic Kingdom. **Distance to theme parks:** Magic Kingdom 2 mi; Epcot 4 mi; Hollywood Studios 4 mi; Animal Kingdom 6 mi. Other

A towering Mayan pyramid sets the stage for the swimming pool at the Coronado Springs recreation complex

destinations: Blizzard Beach 4 mi; Typhoon Lagoon 6 mi; Downtown Disney 6 mi; ESPN Wide World of Sports 6 mi. **Address:** 3520 N Ft. Wilderness Trail, 32830. **Size:** 784 campsites, 409 cabins, 740 acres. **Amenities:** One buffet restaurant, two dinner shows (1 seasonal), lounge. Central pool with a slide, nearby kiddie pool with splash zone, hot tub. Smaller pool near cabins. Organized children's activities include arts and crafts and pool games. Arcade, archery instruction, beach, bike rentals, dog park, golf cart rentals, picnic areas, playgrounds, Segway tour, stable, surrey rentals, walking trail, watercraft rentals. Basketball, horseshoes, tennis, tetherball, volleyball courts. Cane-pole fishing, guided fishing trips. Carriage, wagon, trail, pony rides. Nightly campfire with Chip 'n Dale, movie. Laundromat. Two stores with groceries, camping supplies. **Children's programs:** Complimentary arts and crafts, pool activities, campfire / movie with characters. **Transportation:** Boats take guests to Magic Kingdom. Disney buses shuttle guests to all Disney World theme parks, water parks and Downtown Disney. A separate shuttle bus circles within the resort. **Built:** 1971. **Renovated:** 2009. **Check In:** 3p. **Check Out:** 11a. **Phone:** 407-824-2900. **Fax:** 407-824-3508.

Everything you expect a campground to be, Fort Wilderness is a huge swath of wooded land with a wide range of recreation options, fair-to-middlin' dining choices and plain-Jane swimming pools. Campsites are decent, but cabins are small and cheap for the high

Disney's Fort Wilderness Resort & Campground has full hook-up campsites as well as "log" cabins with living rooms, kitchens and bedrooms furnished with one double bed and two bunk beds

price. Still, the resort offers a unique family-friendly experience many guests treasure. You certainly feel removed from civilization, especially when you try to get back to it. Headed to a theme park? Leave early.

Fort Wilderness is the only Disney resort that takes pets ($5/day). They are allowed at some campsites but not in cabins. Leashed dogs are allowed on golf carts; dogs can run free at a dog park.

Highs: Relaxed wooded setting, huge variety of outdoor recreation, only campsite on Disney property, dogs welcome at select spots, dog park.

Lows: Inconvenient to travel inside or outside resort; many lodging areas are far from bus stops, dining, shops; cabins cheap for the price; complicated bus transportation; limited dining options.

What's new: The main swimming pool was refurbished in 2009. Cabins (see below) were updated in 2008–2009. The resort's kennel closed in 2010.

In the cabins: Though still worn, cabins got new furniture, carpeting, fixtures and paint in 2008–2009. Cabins are located in the front of the resort; some sit in a drained swamp (504 sq ft. Sleep 6. Living room w/ Murphy bed, kitchen, bath, bedroom w/ one double and two bunk beds, deck, picnic table, outdoor grill. A/C, vaulted ceilings, daily housekeeping).

The center of the resort is filled with campsites for recreational vehicles (picnic table, outdoor grill; concrete pad) with full hook-up (water, electric and sewer). Usually the choice of large RV owners, "preferred" sites sit closest to the Settlement and include cable-television and Internet service. All sites are near air-conditioned comfort stations with private showers, ice dispensers, laundromats and vending machines.

Partial hook-up tent sites (water, electric, level pads) line the sides of the property. Groups of 20 or more can reserve the tents-only Creekside Meadow. If you don't have a tent, Disney will rent you one for $32 a night.

Grounds. Fort Wilderness is tucked into a thick pine forest and, in some cases, the remains of a drained cypress wetland. Lined with creek-like canals, it sits on a 450-acre natural lake. The registration building and riding stables are at the entrance. From there, three roads branch off into 28 loops, each of which is lined with either cabins or campsites. In back, a commercial "Settlement" area includes a restaurant, general store, music hall and marina, from which boats ferry guests to Magic Kingdom. Like all the resort's other public areas, the Settlement has no parking lot. Though buses shuttle guests around the area, many guests rent golf carts to get around.

Disney's Grand Floridian Resort recalls fabled Florida seaside retreats of the late 19th century. Spacious grounds include large greens, two nice swimming pools and a white-sand beach.

Swimming pools. The main swimming pool at Fort Wilderness has a water slide, hot tub and children's splash zone. A smaller quiet pool sits in the cabin area.

Food. Dining choices are relatively limited, with a buffet restaurant and two dinner shows. The resort has no room service.

See chapter **Restaurants and Food.**

Family matters. The resort offers a huge number of family-friendly activities, including a free outdoor movie/campfire with characters, fishing, horseback riding and much more. Disney's Electrical Water Pageant passes the resort nightly at 9:45 p.m.

Grand Floridian

★★★★★ **Rates:** Rooms: Rack: $440–$1145. Discount (i.e., online travel agency): $246–$1145. Suites: Rack: $1140–$3145. Discount: $638–$3145. **Hotel type:** Deluxe resort hotel with clustered, multistory lodging buildings. **Location:** Northwest corner of WDW property, near Magic Kingdom. **Distance to theme parks:** Magic Kingdom less than 1 mi; Epcot 4 mi; Hollywood Studios 4 mi; Animal Kingdom 7 mi. Other destinations: Blizzard Beach 5 mi; Typhoon Lagoon 7 mi; Downtown Disney 7 mi; ESPN Wide World of Sports 7 mi. **Address:** 4401 Grand Floridian Way, 32830. **Size:** 842 rooms, 25 suites, 40 acres. **Amenities:** Six restaurants (including Disney Signature eateries), snack bar, tea room, lounges. Two swimming pools, hot tub; main pool has long slide with

waterfall. Kiddie pool, splash zone; children's programs. Arcade, beach, boat rentals, guided fishing trips, tea parties, tennis courts and clinics, walking trail. Child-care center, hair salon, laundromat, laundry service, spa. Shop with groceries. Convention center (40,000 sq ft, 2 ballrooms, 16 breakout rms). Business center. **Children's programs:** Pontoon-boat adventure; complimentary pool activities. Child-care facility onsite. **Transportation:** Monorail goes to Magic Kingdom, Epcot; Contemporary, Polynesian resorts. Boats travel to Wilderness Lodge, Fort Wilderness resorts. Disney buses shuttle guests to Hollywood Studios, Animal Kingdom, water parks and Downtown Disney. **Built:** 1988. **Renovated:** 2009. **Check In:** 3p. **Check Out:** 11a. **Phone:** 407-824-3000. **Fax:** 407-824-3186.

Offering many of the same benefits as the nearby Polynesian Resort, this high-class resort adds beauty but loses some charm, has better and more varied food choices but smaller rooms. The signature Disney World resort, it lives up to its promise as the rooms are comfortable and the refined atmosphere truly Grand. The genteel lodging buildings are surrounded by canary palms, Southern magnolias and formal gardens. There are two nice pools, one calm, one lively.

Highs: On monorail, big beautiful rooms, great dining options, lakeside, wedding pavilion, unique children's programs.

Lows: Expensive, self-parking distant from resort, more formal than fun.

Grand Floridian guest rooms are highlighted by light woods and fabrics. Rooms on top floors have gabled ceilings.

What's new: New marble flooring in lobby has inlaid Disney characters.

In the rooms: Situated in four detached buildings, rooms have a Victorian decor with light woods and fabrics, ceiling fans and marble-topped sinks. Each room has live plants and special touches such as iPod docks in clock radios. A Club level is available. (Standard rooms: 440 sq ft. Sleep 5. Two queen beds, some daybeds, small refrigerator. Suites: Sleep 2–8.)

Grounds. With its gabled roofs, clapboard siding and miles of moldings, scrolls and turnposts, the Grand Floridian brings a Victorian era back to life. The luxe amenities include direct monorail access, a lovely little conference center and full-service spa. Next door is Disney's Wedding Chapel. A five-story atrium, the lobby is topped with three illuminated stained-glass domes. An afternoon grand pianist and retro orchestra entertain.

Swimming pools. A calm swimming pool sits in a central courtyard, surrounded by a kiddie pool and hot tub. A second beachside pool, however, is the family favorite. It has a swerving 181-foot slide that takes 12 seconds to travel, as well as a 20-foot waterfall. A fountain play area keeps little ones entertained; a "zero-entry" side welcomes wheelchair

guests. (Cabanas available for rent; deluxe accoutrements and attendant among options: Call 407-939-7529 in advance or 407-824-2464 for same-day reservations.)

Food. The many dining options, featuring three high-roller restaurants and two relative bargains, include Disney World's best character-meal breakfast and dinner. Room service is available 24 hours a day.

See chapter **Restaurants and Food.**

Family matters. Children's activities include specialty teas and a Pirate Adventure pontoon-boat treasure hunt ($34, ages 4–12, 2 hours, reservations at 407-939-7529). There's a child-care facility onsite. Disney's Electrical Water Pageant passes the resort nightly at 9:15 p.m.

Old Key West

★★★★ ✓ **Rates:** Rack: $305–$1780. Discount (i.e., online travel agency): $177–$1780. **Hotel type:** Deluxe Villas resort with clustered, multistory lodging buildings. **Location:** In the eastern part of WDW property, between Downtown Disney and Port Orleans French Quarter. **Distance to theme parks:** Magic Kingdom 4 mi; Epcot 2 mi; Hollywood Studios 3 mi; Animal Kingdom 5 mi. Other destinations: Blizzard Beach 4 mi; Typhoon Lagoon 2 mi; Downtown Disney 2 mi; ESPN Wide World of Sports 3 mi. **Address:** 1510 N Cove Road, 32830. **Size:** 761 villas, 74 acres. **Amenities:** Restaurant, fast-food cafe, lounge. Four pools, each with a hot tub. The main pool has a giant sandcastle slide with nearby kiddie pool. Arcades, bike rentals, boat rentals, Community Center, DVD rentals, fitness center, guided fishing trips, marina, playground, surrey rentals. Basketball, shuffleboard, volleyball courts; 3 tennis courts, 2 lighted. Laundromat, laundry service. Shop with groceries. **Children's programs:** Arts and crafts, pool activities, sandcastle building. **Transportation:** Boats go to Downtown Disney; Old Key West, Port Orleans French Quarter and Riverside, and Saratoga Springs resorts. Disney buses shuttle guests to all theme parks, water parks and Downtown Disney. A separate shuttle circles within the resort. **Built:** 1991. **Renovated:** 2010. **Check In:** 4p. **Check Out:** 11a. **Phone:** 407-827-7700. **Fax:** 407-827-7710.

Floridians will feel right at home amid this resort's tropical landscaping, Olde Florida facades and Victorian trim with gingerbread accents. The newly renovated, spacious villas, all which have a view of the woods, a canal or the Lake Buena Vista golf course, are lovely and relaxing. Everywhere you look are swaying fronds and falling pine needles. Like other Disney Vacation Club resorts, it offers nightly rentals as owner bookings permit. Old Key West Resort was Disney's first timeshare property.

Disney's Old Key West Resort features a small marina, a decorative lighthouse at its main swimming pool and Olde Florida lodging buildings. Villas are especially roomy.

Highs: Spacious Old Key West villas with expansive closet space, good restaurant, parking is within steps of each villa cluster, palm-filled tropical landscaping lends a distinct vacation feel to non-Floridians.

Lows: Pools are small, simple and few for a property this size; limited dining options do not include an indoor fast-food spot; location is distant to all theme parks except Epcot; a lack of indoor common areas, especially during the summer; villa clusters distant, a car may be necessary for convenience.

What's new: Refurbished in 2010, villas now have new hardwood floors and granite countertops.

In the rooms: Most villas have a tropical color scheme, in peach and turquoise with upholstered furniture. Light woods look weathered. The resort is notable for its roomy accommodations—bedrooms so big that, even with two queen beds, they still look empty. Each villa has a balcony overlooking a private courtyard. Grand Villas have the largest living areas of any Disney World timeshare units. (Studios 376 sq ft; sleep 4. 1-bedroom 942 sq ft; sleep 4. 2-bedroom 1,333 sq ft; sleep 8. 2-story 3 bedroom 2,202 sq ft; sleep 12. Accessed by outdoor walkways.)

Grounds. Inspired by Florida's Tropical Victorian architecture, building exteriors combine tin roofs with clapboard siding, shuttered windows and gingerbread accents. Two- and three-story lodging buildings—many of which back up to Disney's Lake Buena Vista golf course—cluster into small groups along three roadways. A central Hospitality House contains a registration area, restaurant, gift shop, community hall, fitness center and marina.

Swimming pools. The main swimming pool, at Conch Flat Community Hall, has a water slide designed to look like a giant sandcastle. A faux lighthouse sits nearby, along with a kiddie pool, playground and hot tub. Three quiet pools are scattered among the villages.

Food. Small Olivia's Café is the lone restaurant; the only other option is an outdoor snack bar. Room service (pizza, salads, sandwiches, desserts) is available from 4 p.m. to midnight.

See chapter **Restaurants and Food.**

Family matters. Conch Flat Community Hall features organized children's activities each day, including arts and crafts, bingo, foosball, ice-cream making, ping pong and a variety of board games. Tennis, basketball, shuffleboard and bike and surrey rentals are available. The resort schedules a Disney "Movie Under the Stars" campfire and movie some nights.

The lakefront Polynesian Resort features a main swimming pool nestled against a simulated volcano. Spacious guest rooms have dark woods, tall headboards and exotic-print fabrics.

Polynesian

★★★★★ ✔ **Rates:** Rooms: Rack: $365–$1020. Discount (i.e., online travel agency): $219–$1020. Suites: Rack: $845–$3100. Discount: $507–$3100. **Hotel type:** Deluxe resort hotel with main lodge, multistory lodging buildings. **Location:** Northwest corner of WDW property, near Magic Kingdom. **Distance to theme parks:** Magic Kingdom 1 mi; Epcot 4 mi; Hollywood Studios 4 mi; Animal Kingdom 6 mi. Other destinations: Blizzard Beach 5 mi; Typhoon Lagoon 6 mi; Downtown Disney 6 mi; ESPN Wide World of Sports 7 mi. **Address:** 600 Seven Seas Drive, 32830. **Size:** 853 rooms, 5 suites, 39 acres. **Amenities:** Two restaurants, character meal, dinner show, snack shop, sushi bar, lounge. Two swimming pools; main pool has a two-story slide and waterfall. Kiddie splash zone, children's programs, playground, hot tubs. Arcade, beach, boat rentals, campfire, guided fishing trips, hula dancing and lessons, surrey rentals, 1.5-mile-long walking trail. Child-care center, laundromat, laundry service. **Children's programs:** Complimentary arts and crafts, beach and pool activities. Child-care facility onsite. **Transportation:** Monorail goes to Magic Kingdom, Epcot; Contemporary, Grand Floridian resorts. Disney buses shuttle guests to Hollywood Studios, Animal Kingdom, water parks and Downtown Disney. **Built:** 1971. **Renovated:** 2006–2007. **Check In:** 3p. **Check Out:** 11a. **Phone:** 407-824-2000. **Fax:** 407-824-3174.

It's the definitive Disney vacation: a room at a get-away-from-it-all resort hotel with easy monorail trips over to Magic Kingdom.

And that's exactly what you get at this, Walt Disney World's original family resort. The vintage 12-building complex is themed to the South Seas, with many palms, waterfalls and torch-lit walkways. Huge rooms and a fun pool add value; child-friendly-but-mediocre eateries and a confusing, sprawling layout detract from it. High in quality but not overtly luxurious, the resort has a distinctive laid-back attitude.

Unique complimentary activities include hula dancing, where guests can join in (lobby, Tues–Sat, 3:45p) or hula lessons with friendly resort icon Auntie Kaui (lobby, Sat, 11a). An evening torch-lighting ceremony features a fire-baton twirler. Later, a musician often entertains in the lobby.

Highs: On monorail, huge beautiful rooms, lakeside, good sushi bar, Kona coffee, relaxed child-friendly ambience, tropical landscaping, good swimming complex.
Lows: Uneven dining options, large confusing layout.
What's new: A sushi bar opened in 2009. Guest rooms were redone in 2006 and 2007.
In the rooms: Rooms have hand-carved furniture and batik-print fabrics. A Club level is available. (415 sq ft. Sleep 5. Two queen beds, some daybeds, small refrigerator. Suites: Sleep up to 9).
Grounds. Walt Disney World's original family hotel, the Polynesian consists of

standard 1970s-style lodging buildings, but they're disguised by lots of wood trim and sit within a spacious and lush landscape. Torch-lit walkways wander through the grounds, which are anchored by a central building with restaurants, shops and monorail station. A 40-foot-tall atrium lobby includes a rocky waterfall.

Swimming pools. Nestled against a simulated volcano, the Nanea swimming pool is centrally located behind the lobby. Kids love standing underneath its waterfall and taking repeat trips down its slide—a slippery two-story tunnel with squirting water and eerie colored lights. Listen closely to hear the pool's underwater music. One end is a "zero-entry" gradual ramp for disabled users. Nearby is a kiddie sprinkler area and hot tub. Tucked in to a lodging area, the smaller East pool is less crowded. Hidden behind its lounge chairs are six shady open huts, each with its own table and ceiling fan.

Food. A fun character meal and a nice little sushi bar are the dining highlights. Room service is available 6:30 a.m. to midnight.

See chapter **Restaurants and Food.**

Family matters. Children's activities include hula dancing lessons, arts and crafts, beach and pool games. Child-care facility onsite. Disney's Electrical Water Pageant passes the resort nightly at 9 p.m.

Pop Century

★★★★ ✔ **Rates:** Rack: $82–$179. Discount (i.e., online travel agency): $57–$179. **Hotel type:** Value resort hotel with clustered, multistory lodging buildings. **Location:** Close to Interstate 4, near Hollywood Studios and ESPN Wide World of Sports. **Distance to theme parks:** Magic Kingdom 6 mi; Epcot 5 mi; Hollywood Studios 3 mi; Animal Kingdom 4 mi. Other destinations: Blizzard Beach 4 mi; Typhoon Lagoon 2 mi; Downtown Disney 3 mi; ESPN Wide World of Sports 2 mi. **Address:** 1050 Century Drive, 32830. **Size:** 2,880 rooms, 177 acres. **Amenities:** One food court. Three themed swimming pools with adjacent kiddie pools. Arcade, beach, playground, Memory Lane walking trail IDs yearly events 1950 to 1999. Laundromat, laundry service. Shop with groceries. **Children's programs:** Pool activities. **Transportation:** Disney buses shuttle guests to theme parks, water parks and Downtown Disney. **Built:** 2003. **Renovated:** 2007. **Check In:** 3p. **Check Out:** 11a. **Phone:** 407-938-4000. **Fax:** 407-938-4040.

Your children will know they are someplace special if you stay at this Disney Value Resort. Though meant to appeal to nostalgic adults, it looks—at least to young eyes—like a child designed it. Poster-paint buildings

© Disney

Monorail trains connect the Polynesian Resort with Magic Kingdom, Epcot, the Contemporary Resort and the Grand Floridian Resort

feature towering props of toys and cartoon characters. Everywhere you turn is a spirit of playful tackiness. Close to the ESPN Wide World of Sports complex, Pop Century is popular with youth athletic groups.

Highs: Decent dining, colorful large swimming pools and a fun theme make this the best Disney budget resort. Good rates, good food court, covered bus stops, non-stop bus routes to nearly all destinations.

Lows: No table-service dining; childish theming; lodging elevators not air-conditioned; small guest rooms; no suites; long lines at food courts and bus stops, especially in the morning.

What's new: Refurbished in 2010, guest rooms have new carpet, comforters, dressers, flat-screen televisions, mattresses and paint. A curtain now hangs between the bedroom and bathroom.

In the rooms: Basic rooms are cheaply decorated. Those in the 1960s section ($10 surcharge) are closest to the bus stand, food court and lobby. 1950s rooms (no extra charge) are almost as close. (260 sq ft. Sleep 4. Two double beds. Accessed by outdoor walkways.)

Grounds. Grouped into five areas, the lodging area is a collection of four-story motel buildings, each decorated to illustrate

Surreal sights such as a huge Mickey Mouse telephone, a giant bowling pin and a massive yo-yo decorate the grounds at Disney's Pop Century Resort. Guest rooms are plain.

a particular decade of American popular culture, from the 1950s to the 1990s. The buildings are adorned with gigantic props such as 41-foot Rubik's Cubes, 65-foot bowling pins and iconic Disney characters, and topped with huge words and phrases such as "Flower Power" and "Do the Funky Chicken." A central complex holds a food court, arcade and gift shop. Out front is the bus station, in back the main swimming pool.

Swimming pools. The resort has three themed pools, with adjacent kiddie pools. The 1960s Hippy Dippy pool has four giant metal flowers that spray swimmers—the kiddie pool with a neon-blue flower shower. The 1950s pool is shaped like a bowling pin. The 1990s pool (a rectangle) has a spongy keyboard deck. A Goofy-themed water-jet playground fountain sits between the 1960s and 1970s areas.

Food. Disney's nicest food court serves all three meals, as well as a bakery, convenience store and small bar open to its main swimming pool. Room service (pizza, salads, desserts) is available 4 p.m. to midnight.

See chapter **Restaurants and Food.**

Family matters. Organized children's activities at the resort's main pool are posted on a poolside board each morning. Kids can join food court cast members doing the Twist at 8 a.m. and the Hustle at 6 p.m. daily.

Port Orleans Resorts

French Quarter: ★ **Riverside:** ★★★ ✔ **Rates:** Rack: $154–$274. Discount (i.e., online travel agency): $104–$274. **Hotel type:** Moderate resort hotels with clustered, multistory lodging buildings. **Location:** Northeast on WDW property, near Downtown Disney. **Distance to theme parks:** Magic Kingdom 4 mi; Epcot 2 mi; Hollywood Studios 4 mi; Animal Kingdom 6 mi. Other destinations: Blizzard Beach 4 mi; Typhoon Lagoon 2 mi; Downtown Disney 2 mi; ESPN Wide World of Sports 4 mi. **Address:** French Quarter 2201 Orleans Dr, 32830; Riverside 1251 Riverside Drive, 32830. **Size:** French Quarter: 1,008 rooms, 90 acres; Riverside: 2,048 rooms, 235 acres. **Amenities:** French Quarter: Food court, lounge. Central swimming pool with slide, hot tub, kiddie pool. Riverside: Restaurant (dinner only), food court, lounge. Large outdoor "swimming hole" recreation complex with swimming pool, slide, kiddie pool, hot tub; five basic pools in lodging areas. Bike, boat, surrey rentals; guided fishing trips, cane-pole fishing. Carriage rides (same-day reservations available at 407-824-2832). Both complexes: Arcade, playground. Laundromat, laundry service. Shop with groceries. **Children's programs:** Pontoon-boat adventure; complimentary pool activities. **Transportation:** Boats take guests to Downtown Disney; Old Key West, Saratoga Springs resorts and between Port Orleans French Quarter and Riverside. Disney buses shuttle guests to theme parks, water parks and Downtown Disney. **Built:** French Quarter 1991, Riverside 1992. **Renovated:** French Quarter 2004, Riverside 2001.

Rooms at the Port Orleans French Quarter Resort (left side, above) sleep four. Those in the Alligator Bayou area of the Port Orleans Riverside Resort (right) sleep five thanks to trundle beds.

Check In: 3p. **Check Out:** 11a. **Phone:** French Quarter 407-934-5000; Riverside 407-934-6000. **Fax:** French Quarter 407-934-5353; Riverside 407-934-5777.

These two sister resorts are quite different. Corners are cut everywhere at Port Orleans French Quarter, with few amenities and a sub-standard food court but no restaurant. Port Orleans Riverside is a significant step up. This spacious Southern resort is dotted with magnolia and live oak trees. It's the only Disney Moderate Resort with rooms that sleep 5. Amenities include both a food court and a restaurant, a fun main pool and shady quiet pools set within the lodging areas, and a wealth of recreation options.

Highs: French Quarter: Rooms are close to fast-food dining and the limited recreation, hot fresh beignets. Riverside: Great pools, some rooms sleep 5, lovely grounds.

Lows: French Quarter: Uninspired rooms, sub-standard food court, no restaurant, grounds are a little shabby, superficial theming. Riverside: Rooms are in need of refurbishment, getting to your room can be quite a hike if you don't have a car.

What's new: Riverside's Boatwright's Dining Hall discontinued breakfast in 2009; it now just serves dinner.

In the rooms: French Quarter rooms have cherry woods, pastel bedspreads and dark blue carpet. Riverside rooms vary; those in its Magnolia Bend area have cherry woods and tapestries while those in Alligator Bayou have a backwoods feel with hickory furnishings and quilted bedspreads. These rooms sleep five, thanks to the addition of trundle beds. (Standard rooms: 314 sq ft. Sleep 4. Two double beds, small refrigerator. Riverside Alligator Bend rooms: 314 sq ft. Sleeps 5. Two queen beds, small refrigerator. All rooms accessed by outdoor walkways.)

Grounds. Port Orleans French Quarter has narrow, tree-lined walkways, lots of wrought-iron railings and some intimate gardens. The pool area is themed to a Mardi Gras parade; the food court looks like it's a warehouse for Mardi Gras parade props. Port Orleans Riverside has two lodging areas. Set within shady live oaks and other hardwoods, Magnolia Bend has four distinct sections, each with a trim lawn and adjacent parking lot. Buildings recall Southern plantations, with white columns and sweeping entrance facades. Riverside's smaller Alligator Bayou area has a completely different feel. Leading to faux-rustic lodging buildings, walkways meander through an unkempt landscape of palmettos, pines and pine needles.

Swimming pools. A huge dragon winds through, and forms the slide of, the French Quarter's Doubloon Lagoon area, as an alligator jazz band strolls the grounds. At

Parking lots are convenient to the lodging buildings at Disney's Saratoga Springs Resort. Elevated 10 feet off the ground, "cabin casual" Treehouse Villas blend into their forest environment.

Port Orleans Riverside, an Ol' Man Island recreation area includes a pool with the most waterfalls of any Disney hotel swimming spot; a swerving slide dribbles water on those who go down it. Peaceful quiet pools sit between the lodging sections.

Food. Riverside has a dinner restaurant. Both resorts have food courts; Riverside's is bigger and better. Room service (pizza, salads, desserts) is available 4 p.m. to midnight.

See chapter **Restaurants and Food.**

Family matters. Children's activities include the Bayou Pirate Adventure, a pontoon-boat treasure hunt that tells the story of John Lafitte ($34, ages 4–12, 2 hours, reservations at 407-939-7529). A Riverside dock rents cane fishing poles and sells bait.

Saratoga Springs

★★★ **Rates:** Rack: $305–$1708. Discount (i.e., online travel agency): $177–$1708. **Hotel type:** Deluxe Villas resort with clustered, multistory lodging buildings. **Location:** In the eastern part of WDW property, north of Downtown Disney. **Distance to theme parks:** Magic Kingdom 5 mi; Epcot 3 mi; Hollywood Studios 4 mi; Animal Kingdom 6 mi. Other destinations: Blizzard Beach 4 mi; Typhoon Lagoon 2 mi; Downtown Disney 2 mi; ESPN Wide World of Sports 4 mi. **Address:** 1960 Broadway, 32830. **Size:** 828 villas, 65 acres. **Amenities:** Restaurant, food court, lounge. Four pools, each with a hot tub.

The main pool has a short slide, kiddie pool, children's programs, sand volleyball court, two playgrounds. Three smaller pools in lodging area, hot tub, BBQ area. Arcades, bike rentals, Community Center, fitness center, guided fishing trips, surrey rentals. Basketball, shuffleboard courts, full-service spa, two lighted tennis courts, two walking trails. Lake Buena Vista 18-hole golf course. Laundromat, laundry service. Shop with groceries. **Children's programs:** Arts and crafts, pool activities. **Transportation:** Boats go to Downtown Disney; Old Key West, Port Orleans French Quarter and Riverside resorts. Disney buses shuttle guests to all theme parks, water parks and Downtown Disney. A separate shuttle circles within the resort. Treehouse Villas guests go to bus stops in either The Springs or The Grandstand parking lots. **Built:** 2004. **Renovated:** 2009. **Check In:** 4p. **Check Out:** 11a. **Phone:** 407-827-1100. **Fax:** 407-827-1151.

This equestrian-themed condo complex is the most tranquil Walt Disney World resort, with pleasant grounds, good food and upscale, comfortable suites. It's also the only Disney resort with a golf course. A Disney Vacation Club complex, Saratoga Springs often offers nightly rentals. Despite its name, there are no springs, no horses except in the decor and nothing New York.

Located behind Downtown Disney on the shores of Village Lake, Saratoga Springs is as far away as you can be from a theme park and still stay at a Disney-owned resort. The resort also includes the Treehouse Villas, a small nearby complex of elevated dwellings set in a pine forest.

Highs: Tranquil, upscale comfortable villas, many adjacent to parking lots; lush landscaping; great fitness center and spa; direct golf access.

Lows: Theme, room decor will be of little interest to some children, far from theme parks, no room service, main swimming pool is small and crowded.

What's new: A separate Treehouse Villas section opened in 2009.

In the rooms: Timeshare villas feature large, masculine furniture; all are furnished with table and chairs, kitchen facilities. Larger units have whirlpool tubs. Three-bedroom Grand Villas feature two-story living rooms. Rustic Treehouse Villas have cathedral ceilings and granite countertops. (Studios 365 sq ft; sleep 4. 1-bedroom 714 sq ft; sleep 4. 2-bedroom 1,075 sq ft; sleep 8. 3-bedroom 2,113 sq ft; sleep 9–12. Accessed by outdoor walkways.)

Grounds. Saratoga Springs includes the clubhouse of an 18-hole golf course, clubhouse restaurant with a pool table and bar and a full-service spa. Though quite spread out, the resort has many small gathering spots that give it a cozy feel. Lodging buildings cluster into five sections that horseshoe around a recreation center. Thematically unrelated, a separate Treehouse Villas area is nestled into a wooded area; its 60 stand-alone octagons are elevated 10 feet off the ground. The property sits on the grounds of the former Disney Institute.

Swimming pools. The main swimming pool has a 126-foot slide between cascading waterfalls, an interactive fountain area and a "zero-entry" gradual ramp. It often shows Disney movies at night; guests float while they watch. Nearby is a kiddie pool, playground and two hot tubs. A water play area has hand-held squirters that look like stick ponies. Three quiet pools are scattered in the lodging areas, each with a hot tub and barbecue area.

Food. Saratoga Springs has a good steak restaurant and nice food court. There is no room service; grocery delivery is available. See chapter **Restaurants and Food.**

Family matters. A Community Hall features children's activities each day, including arts and crafts, bingo, foosball, ice-cream making, ping pong and a variety of board games. Tennis, basketball, shuffleboard and bike rentals are available. The food court has easels set up for young artists.

An open ceiling highlights a three-bedroom villa at Disney's Saratoga Springs Resort. Its masculine decor is unusual for Disney.

Wilderness Lodge

★★★★★ ✔ **Rates:** Rooms: Rack: $250–$840. Discount (i.e., online travel agency): $144–$840. Suites: Rack: $555–$1500. Discount: $333–$1500. Villas: Rack: $340–$1245. Discount: $198–$1245. **Hotel type:** Deluxe resort hotel with main lodge with two wings; condominium-style villas. **Location:** Northwest corner of WDW property, southeast of Magic Kingdom. **Distance to theme parks:** Magic Kingdom 1 mi; Epcot 3 mi; Hollywood Studios 4 mi; Animal Kingdom 6 mi. Other destinations: Blizzard Beach 5 mi; Typhoon Lagoon 5 mi; Downtown Disney 5 mi; ESPN Wide World of Sports 7 mi. **Address:** 901 Timberland Drive, 32830. **Size:** 701 rooms, 27 suites, 136 villas, 65 acres. **Amenities:** Three restaurants, snack bar, lounge. Two pools, three hot tubs, kiddie pool. Main pool has slide. Arcade, beach, bike and surrey rentals, fitness center, guided fishing trips, lobby tour, trail to Ft. Wilderness. Community Center. Child-care center, laundromat, laundry service. **Children's programs:** Organized free children's activities, 2:30–4 p.m. Campfire, movie at night. **Transportation:** Boats take guests to Magic Kingdom; Contemporary, Fort Wilderness resorts. Disney buses shuttle guests to all Disney World theme parks, water parks and Downtown Disney. **Built:** 1994. **Renovated:** 2006. **Check In:** 3p (Villas 4p). **Check out:** 11a. **Phone:** 407-824-3200, Villas: 407-938-4300. **Fax:** 407-824-3232.

Lincoln Log fans will love this secluded resort. A dead ringer for one of the rustic

Disney's Wilderness Lodge channels the historic lodges of our Western national parks. Beds have padded headboards topped with carved panels. A portion of the resort is a DVC property.

park service lodges of the American West, it sits on a lakefront spot tucked into a pine forest. A lobby atrium is dominated by four 60-foot bundled log columns which appear to support a wood truss. Though rooms are comfortable and, since they are all in the same building, easy to access, their decor suffers from a mismatched cowboy theme. Restaurants and amenities are top-notch. Magic Kingdom is a pleasant boat ride away.

Highs: Stunning lobby, good, child-friendly restaurants; easily accessible rooms; fun boat ride to Magic Kingdom; nice pool; quiet atmosphere; great views; child-care facility; convenient self-parking.

Lows: Room decor can look cheap.

What's new: Rooms were redone in 2006.

In the rooms: Decorated with Native American and wildlife motifs, rooms have vibrant quilts, plaid drapes, Mission-style furniture and handcrafted embellishments; colors and patterns clash. Beds have padded headboards topped with carved upper panels. (344 sq ft. Sleep 4. Two queen beds, small refrigerator. Villas: Studio, 1- and 2-bedroom units sleep 4 to 8.)

Grounds. Nestled in a forest along 450-acre Bay Lake, the four-building complex consists of a central eight-story lodge and three guest wings, one of which is a five-story Disney Vacation Club timeshare property. The lobby is highlighted by a three-sided stone fireplace, the layers of which illustrate the geological history of the Grand Canyon. The fourth-floor indoor balcony has cozy sitting areas and front and back porches. The fifth floor has a small back balcony. A simulated hot spring in the lobby creates a stream that appears to flow outside, over a waterfall and eventually into the swimming pool.

Swimming pools. Portrayed as part of a mountain stream, a large swimming pool features a curving slide that sprays riders with mist. Nearby are two hot tubs (one hot, one cold), a kiddie pool, and a geyser that erupts hourly. The Villas area has a smaller quiet pool with four bubbling "springs" and a 15-person whirlpool.

Food. Guests can choose from two terrific restaurants—one rowdy, one fine dining—plus a snack bar. Room service is available 7 a.m. to 11 a.m. and 4 p.m. to midnight.

See chapter **Restaurants and Food.**

Family matters. The Cub's Den child-care center offers free activities from 2:30–4 p.m., paid care in the evenings. The resort also has a 24-hour playground, bike and watercraft rentals and fishing. Disney's Electrical Water Pageant passes by nightly at 9:35 p.m.

Facing page: The Wilderness Lodge lobby is highlighted by a massive stone fireplace

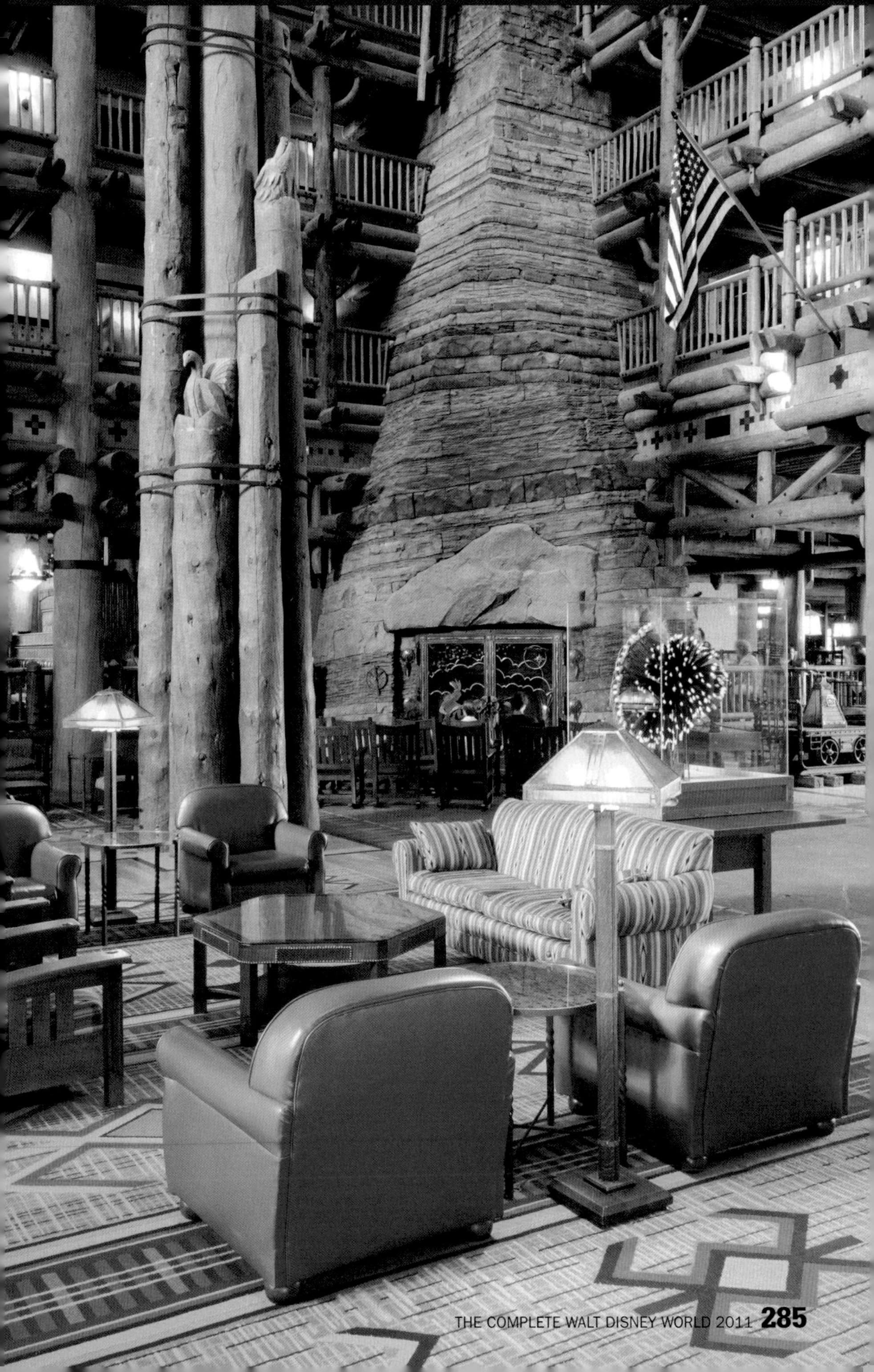

Clockwise from top left: The lawn behind the Yacht Club. Chaise lounges sit in the sand behind the Beach Club. Beach Club rooms have a cottage style, those at the Yacht Club are more formal.

Yacht and Beach Club

★★★★★ ✔ **Rates:** Rooms: Rack: $335–$815. Discount (i.e., online travel agency): $204–$815. Beach Club suites: Rack: $620–$2690. Discount: $379–$2690. Yacht Club suites: Rack: $650–$2875. Discount: $390–$2875. Beach Club Villas: Rack: $345–$1250. Discount: $211–$1250. **Hotel type:** Deluxe resort hotel with adjoining multistory lodging buildings. **Location:** Centrally located on WDW property, next to the back entrance of Epcot. **Distance to theme parks:** Magic Kingdom 5 mi; Epcot (by car) 4 mi; Hollywood Studios 2 mi; Animal Kingdom 5 mi. Other destinations: Blizzard Beach 3 mi; Typhoon Lagoon 3 mi; Downtown Disney 3 mi; ESPN Wide World of Sports 5 mi. **Address:** Beach Club: 1800 Epcot Resorts Blvd. Yacht Club: 1700 Epcot Resorts Blvd, 32830. **Size:** 1,197 rooms, 112 suites, 208 villas, 30 acres. **Amenities:** Five restaurants, lounges. Sprawling outdoor recreation swimming complex, children's programs, playground, hot tubs. Sand volleyball, croquet, tennis courts. Arcades, beach, boat rentals, boat rides, child-care center, Community Center, guided fishing trips, walking trail. Hair salon, laundromat, laundry service. Shop with groceries. Conference center (73,000 sq ft, 2 ballrooms, banquet space for 3,000, 21 breakout rms), business center. **Children's programs:** Pontoon-boat adventure; complimentary arts and crafts, beach and pool activities. Child-care facility onsite. **Transportation:** Boats take guests to Epcot, Hollywood Studios. Disney buses shuttle guests to Magic Kingdom, Animal Kingdom, water parks and Downtown Disney. When the boats can't operate (during lightning), buses take guests to Epcot and Hollywood Studios. **Built:** 1990. **Renovated:** 2009. **Check In:** 3p. **Check Out:** 11a. **Phone:** Beach Club: 407-934-8000. Villas: 407-934-2175. Yacht Club: 407-934-7000. **Fax:** Beach Club: 407-934-3850. Yacht Club: 407-934-3450.

Families will have a ball at these side-by-side resorts. Kid-friendly benefits include comfortable rooms that are easy to get to, an uncrowded character meal, a soda shop that offers what might be the world's largest ice cream sundae and Disney World's best swimming complex. The Disney Deluxe complex is adjacent to Epcot via that theme park's back-entrance walkway; the Beach Club is literally next door.

Highs: Within walking distance to Epcot, Hollywood Studios; evening entertainment at the BoardWalk; lovely lakeside setting; best Disney swimming complex; good food at all price levels.

Lows: No transportation to main entrance of Epcot; limited breakfast choices.

What's new: Guest rooms were refurbished in 2009.

In the rooms: Rooms have nautical motifs, with ceiling fans and white furniture. A Club level is available. Suites share the salty theme, as do Beach Club timeshare villas, which are often available for nightly rentals. (381 sq ft. Sleep 5. Two queen beds, some daybeds, small refrigerator. Suites: Sleep 4–8. Villas: Studio, 1- and 2-bedroom units sleep 4–8.)

With features much like those of a water park, 3-acre Stormalong Bay includes a meandering central pool, a lazy river, a shallow sandbar inlet, a huge water slide through a shipwrecked pirate galleon and many fountains and waterfalls.

Grounds. Five-story, nautical-themed compounds with clapboard trim, the resorts evoke the look of 1870s summer homes on Martha's Vineyard and Nantucket. Behind the Yacht Club is a lighthouse marina; the Beach Club has a white-sand beach. Inside, the Yacht Club is trimmed with gold-fringed drapes and a red-white-and-blue carpet that seems straight from the The Hall of Presidents, while the Beach Club has a casual interior fit for Coastal Living magazine.

Swimming pools. Themed to look like a Nantucket lagoon, 3-acre Stormalong Bay is a miniature water park. It includes a meandering central pool, lazy river, shallow inlet with a real sandbar, a shady hot tub and an assortment of fountains, waterfalls and bridges. A spiral staircase on a life-sized simulated shipwreck leads to a 300-foot slide. Starting off in a dark tunnel (the inside of the ship's fallen mast) it plummets into daylight at a rocky outcropping. Riders get showered by two waterfalls before splashing into the central pool. A large kiddie pool has overhead sprinklers and a sandy play spot; a second kiddie pool on the pirate ship has a tiny slide.

Food. The Yacht and Beach Club Resort offers an excellent steakhouse, a fun soda shop and a good character meal. The only flaw: Breakfast. The Yacht Club buffet is uninspired; the only Beach Club breakfast—the character meal—grows old after a visit or two. Fast-food breakfast items are sold in gift shops. Room service is available 24 hours.

See chapter **Restaurants and Food.**

Family matters. Children's activities include the Albatross Treasure Cruise, a pontoon-boat treasure hunt ($34, ages 4–12, 2 hours, reservations at 407-939-7529). A child-care facility is onsite.

Beach Club Villa kitchens have colorful cabinets, granite countertops, glass-panel cabinet doors and open shelves. The studio, 1- and 2-bedroom units sleep between four and eight people.

Photos (except Dolphin ext.) © Starwood Hotels

The Walt Disney World Swan (left) and Dolphin (right) are the signature properties of Starwood Hotels, the company that includes the Sheraton and Westin chains. Rooms have "heavenly" beds.

Other hotels

For those visitors who prefer not to stay at a Disney-owned resort, choices include many offerings on Disney property and, within 10 miles, nearly every major hotel franchise.

Walt Disney World Swan and Dolphin

★★★★ **Rates:** Rooms: Rack: $279–$555. Discount (i.e., online travel agency): $99–$555. Suites: Rack: $350–$1320. Discount: $125–$1320. **Hotel type:** Large, luxurious convention hotel. A Starwood Resort. **Location:** Centrally located on Disney property, just east of Disney's Hollywood Studios. **Distance to theme parks:** Magic Kingdom 4 mi; Epcot (by car) 3 mi; Hollywood Studios 1 mi; Animal Kingdom 4 mi. Other destinations: Blizzard Beach 2 mi; Typhoon Lagoon 2 mi; Downtown Disney 3 mi; ESPN Wide World of Sports 4 mi. **Address:** 1500 Epcot Resorts Blvd, Swan: 1300 Epcot Resorts Blvd, 32830. **Size:** 2,265 rooms, 191 suites, 87 acres. **Amenities:** Nine restaurants, lounges. Elaborate swimming area with 5 swimming pools (2 are lap pools), 5 hot tubs, kiddie pool and play area, playground, basketball court, sand volleyball court. Arcades, beach, pedal-boat rentals, fitness centers, 4 tennis courts. Hair salon, laundromat, laundry service, massage services, full-service spa. Disney's Fantasia Gardens miniature golf across street. Disney World's largest convention center (254,000 sq ft, 9,600-sq-ft ballroom, 3 other ballrooms, exhibit hall, 84 breakout rms). Business centers. **Children's programs:** Child-care facility onsite. **Transportation:** Disney boats

take guests to Epcot and Disney's Hollywood Studios. Disney buses shuttle to Magic Kingdom, Animal Kingdom, water parks and Downtown Disney. When the boats can't operate (during lightning), buses take their place. **Built:** 1990. **Renovated:** 2006. **Check In:** 3p. **Check Out:** 11a. **Phone:** Dolphin: 407-934-4000, Swan: 407-934-4499. **Fax:** Dolphin: 407-934-4884, Swan: 407-934-4710.

Giant swan statues, huge fish figurines, a towering triangular roof—the architecture of these adjacent convention resorts is one-of-a-kind. The Swan and Dolphin are the signature properties of Starwood Hotels, the company that includes the Sheraton and Westin chains. In fact, more Starwood Preferred Guests use their points to stay at these two hotels than at any of the other 925 Starwood properties in 95 countries worldwide. The Swan is quiet and intimate. The Dolphin, with twice as many rooms and a large convention center, is boisterous and impersonal.

Designed by Michael Graves—an accomplished architect ironically best known for his line of housewares sold at Target stores—the Swan and Dolphin feature playful "entertainment" architecture with details that include enormous statues and fountains. The tallest structure at Walt Disney World, the Dolphin's 27-story-tall triangular tower sits between two wings topped with 20-foot tulip fountains and 56-foot statues of dolphinfish, or mahi mahi. In back, a nine-story

Chaise lounges tuck under a waterfall at the Grotto pool shared by the Swan and Dolphin. The huge water complex has five standard pools, two lap pools, five hot tubs and a kiddie pool. During the summer, the Grotto pool shows a movie on Saturday nights.

waterfall cascades down giant clamshells. The 12-story Swan has two seven-story wings crowned with 47-foot swan statues. Its wings have 20-foot clamshell spouts. The buildings are connected by a palm-lined promenade that splits a lagoon. Seen together, abstract designs on the buildings define the Dolphin as a tropical mountain surrounded by huge banana palms. Its waterfall splashes into the lagoon and onto the Swan, a huge sand dune.

Highs: Within walking distance to Epcot, Hollywood Studios; nearby evening entertainment at the BoardWalk; great swimming complex; comfortable rooms.

Lows: Convention vibe is awkward for families; restaurant prices, parking fees.

What's new: The complex began hosting its own version of Epcot's Food and Wine Festival in 2010.

In the rooms: Featuring "heavenly" beds with pillow-top mattresses and goose-down comforters, rooms have pale woods, muted floral carpeting, pastel drapes and maple bureaus with frosted glass accents (360 sq ft. Sleep 5. Club level available. Dolphin rooms have two double beds, Swan rooms two queens. Suites sleep five to ten.)

Swimming pools. An elaborate swimming area (5 pools, 5 hot tubs, kiddie pool) arcs between the resorts. A meandering Grotto pool has a waterfall and slide. Tiny waterfalls splash near a volleyball net that extends over a narrow area. A Disney movie plays at the pool every Saturday night in the summer. The area also includes a spring pool and two lap pools. A circus-themed beach area has two volleyball nets, a basketball court and a boat-like playground piece with covered slides. Children will enjoy finding the statue of a seal that sprays water out of its nose.

Shades of Green ★ ★ ★ ★ $ Exclusively for use by active and retired members of U.S. military, accompanying families, friends. Rates based on rank. This relaxed resort is the only Armed Forces Recreation Center in the continental United States. Comparable in scope to a Disney Deluxe Resort, it has large rooms, full-service restaurants and a great location, though it lacks themed architecture or memorable decor. Close to Magic Kingdom, Shades of Green sits directly across from the Polynesian Resort and next to Disney's Palm, Magnolia and Oak Trail golf courses. About 750,000 military guests stay here annually.

Room rates are based on rank and pay grade; top brass pay the most. Eligible guests and dependent spouses can each "sponsor" up to three rooms at a time to accommodate nonmilitary friends and family members. Huge and comfortable, rooms feature light oak woods (455 sq ft. Sleep 5. Two queen beds, small refrigerator, daybed, balcony or patio. Suites sleep 6 to 8.)

Built in 1973 as the Disney Golf Resort (a country club with no guest rooms), Disney added a lodging area and renamed it the Disney Inn in 1993. In 1996 Disney sold the complex to the feds, who enlarged it in 2004. The resort's name refers to the fact that, regardless of branch, all U.S. military standard uniforms include some shade of green.

Downtown Disney hotels. Situated near Downtown Disney at the northeast corner of Disney World, these independent hotels lack the ambience of Disney resorts but offer better rates and often have rooms available when Disney properties are full. A complimentary shuttle bus stops at each one then heads to theme parks. The area was developed in the 1970s as Disney's Hotel Plaza.

Best Western Lake Buena Vista ★★★ $55–$121 (rack $89–$121). Suites $209–$220. 321 rooms, 4 suites, 12 acres. Rooms, suites: Sleep 4–5, 2 queen beds, balconies or patios. Cherry-walnut furniture, granite counter tops, Italian tile bathrooms. 2 restaurants, snack bar, Pizza Hut Express. Swimming pool, kiddie pool. Arcade, child-care service, fitness center, playground, tennis courts. Business center, car-rental counter, cyber cafe, laundromat. Garden gazebo. Lakefront. Check in: 3p. Check out: 11a. Phone: 407-828-2424. Fax: 407-827-6390. 2000 Hotel Plaza Blvd, 32830.

Buena Vista Palace and Spa ★★★★ $89–$355 (rack $189–$355). Suites $259–$1535. 890 rooms, 124 suites, 27 acres. 27 stories. Rooms: Sleep 4, 2 queen beds, balconies or patios, refrigerator. Suites: Sleep 4–8. Ergonomic Herman Miller chairs. Two restaurants including Disney character breakfast on Sundays, mini-mart. Three swimming pools (one partially covered), hot tub. Arcade, fitness center, playground, sauna, full-service spa (407-827-3200). Basketball, tennis, volleyball courts. Business center, car-rental counter, convention center, cyber cafe, laundromat, laundry services, salon. Check in: 4p. Check out: 11a. Phone: 407-827-2727. Fax: 407-827-3136. 1900 Buena Vista Dr, 32830.

Doubletree Guest Suites ★★★ $79–$434 (rack $135–$434). 229 suites, 7 acres. 7 stories. Suites: Sleep 6, 1 or 2 bedrooms, Sweet Dreams bedding, microwave, refrigerator, 2 TVs, B&W bathroom TV-radio. 1 restaurant, mini-mart. Swimming pool, kiddie pool, hot tub. Fitness center, playground, pool table, tennis courts. Business center, car-rental counter, child-care service, laundromat, laundry services, meeting rooms. The only all-suite hotel on Disney property. Renovated in 2006, 2007. Check in: 4p. Check out: 11a. Phone: 407-934-1000. Fax: 407-934-1015. 2305 Hotel Plaza Blvd, 32830. Florida Green Lodging hotel.

Hilton ★★★★ $99–$249 (rack $139–$249). Suites $229–$339. 704 rooms, 110 suites, 23 acres. 10 stories. Rooms: Sleep 4, 2 double beds, mini-bar, MP3 clock-radio. Suites: Sleep 4–6. Club level. 7 restaurants inc Benihana, Disney character breakfast buffet Sun (no res); mini-mart. 2 swimming pools, kiddie pool with spray area. Arcade, fitness center, golf pro shop, pool table. Business center, car-rental counter, child-care services, concierge, cyber cafe, laundromat, salon. Most upscale Downtown Disney hotel; only one that offers Disney's Extra Magic Hours benefit. Renovated in 2008. Check in: 3p. Check out: 11a. Phone: 407-827-4000. Fax: 407-827-3890. 1751 Hotel Plaza Blvd, 32830. Florida Green Lodging hotel.

Holiday Inn ★★★ $60–$119 (rack $79–$119). 323 rooms, 1 suite, 10 acres. 14 stories. Rooms: Sleep 4 to 5, 2 queen beds, sleeper sofa, pillow-top mattresses, small refrigerator, work desk. Restaurant, Kids Eat Free program (2–12 yrs). "Zero-entry" swimming pool with whirlpool. Business center, health club, laundromat, meeting rooms. Business center, fitness center, laundromat, laundry services. Newly renovated. Check in: 4p. Check out: 11a. Phone: 407-828-8888. Fax: 407-827-4623. 1805 Hotel Plaza Blvd, 32830.

Royal Plaza ★★★ $50–$209 (rack $159–$209). Suites $219–$229. 394 rooms, 23 acres. 17 stories. Rooms: Sleep 5, 2 double beds, pillow-top mattresses, sleeper sofa. Some kitchenettes, wet bars, whirlpool tubs. Standard rooms are largest of any Downtown Disney hotel. Suites: Sleep 4–5. Restaurant (children 10 and under eat dinner free with paying adult), mini-mart. Swimming pool. Arcade, fitness center, tennis courts. Business center, laundromat, meeting rooms. Check in: 4p. Check out: 11a. Phone: 407-828-2828. Fax: 407-827-6338. 1905 Hotel Plaza Blvd, 32830. Florida Green Lodging hotel.

Wyndham Lake Buena Vista ★★★ $55–$137 (rack $81–$137). Suites $409–$497. 619 rooms, 7 suites, 13 acres. 19 stories. Rooms: Sleep 4, 2 queen beds, flat-screen TV, MP3 clock-radio. Suites: Sleep 4–6. Restaurant; English pub; Disney character breakfast Tue, Thur, Sat. 2 swimming pools, kiddie pool, water playground for children. Fitness center, playground. Basketball, shuffleboard, tennis, volleyball courts. Business center, car-rental counter, currency exchange, laundromat, laundry services, meeting rooms. Formerly Regal Sun, before that The Grosvenor. A favorite of British guests. Renovated 2007. Check in: 3p. Check out: 11a. Phone: 407-828-4444. Fax: 407-828-8192. 1850 Hotel Plaza Blvd, 32830. Florida Green Lodging hotel.

Hotels within 10 miles

Bohemian Celebration Hotel ★★★★ ✔ $$$ **Celebration:** Some suites. Restaurant. Swimming pool. Fitness, laundry service. Meeting rooms, business center. 407-566-6000. 700 Bloom St, 34747. Shuttle $15 roundtrip. WDW 4 mi. In heart of small walkable downtown with restaurants, shops and a movie theater; pleasant commute to Disney through pretty Disney-developed residential community. Rooms sleep up to 6. Nostalgic Old Florida decor; good, though pricey, breakfast.

Buena Vista Suites ★★★ ✔ $$ **World Center Dr:** All suites. Restaurant, free b'fast buffet. Swimming pool, hot tub. Basketball, tennis courts. Fitness center. Meeting rooms. 800-537-7737. 8203 World Center Dr, 32821. Fla. Green Lodging hotel. Free WDW shuttle. WDW 2 mi. Clean, nicely updated; easy access to Disney World. Affordable rates and free, if limited, breakfast make the hotel an attractive alternative to Disney options.

Caribe Royale All-Suite Resort ★★★★ $$$ **World Center Dr:** 3 restaurants, 2 lounges. Swimming pool w/waterfalls, 75-ft slide, kiddie pool; 2nd villas pool. Fitness center, laundromat, laundry services. Basketball, tennis courts. 150,000-sq-ft meeting space, business center. 800-823-8300. 8101 World Center Dr, 32821. Fla. Green Lodging hotel. Free shuttle. WDW 2 mi.

The Best Western Lake Buena Vista sits on Disney's Hotel Plaza Boulevard. Nearby are the Buena Vista Palace and Spa, Doubletree Guest Suites, Hilton, Holiday Inn, Royal Plaza and Wyndham. Complimentary bus service takes guests to Disney World destinations.

Comfort Inn ★★★ $ Some suites. Restaurant, Kids Eat Free, free breakfast. Swimming pool. **Int'l. Dr.:** 407-313-4000. 8134 Int'l. Dr, 32819. Shuttle $8. WDW 8 mi. **Lake Buena Vista:** 800-999-7300. 8442 Palm Parkway, 32836. Free shuttle. WDW 1 mi. **Universal Studios area:** 407-363-7886. 6101 Sand Lake Rd, 32819. Free shuttle. WDW 9 mi.

Country Inn & Suites ★★★ $ Some suites. Kitchenettes. Free cont. b'fast. Swimming pool. Fitness center. Meeting room. **Lake Buena Vista:** 407-239-1115. 12191 S. Apopka-Vineland Rd, 32830. Free shuttle. WDW 1 mi. **Int'l. Dr. area:** 407-313-4200. 7701 Universal Blvd, 32819. Free shuttle. WDW 8 mi. **U.S. 192 area:** 407-997-1400. 5001 Calypso Cay Way, 34746. Pet fee. Free shuttle. WDW 5 mi.

Courtyard By Marriott ★★★ $ 24/7 market. Swimming pool. Fitness center. Business center. **Lake Buena Vista:** 407-239-6900. 8501 Palm Pkwy, 32836. Free shuttle to outlet mall, WDW. WDW 1 mi. **Little Lake Bryan area:** 877-682-8552. 8623 Vineland Ave (Marriott Village), 32821. Shuttle $5 roundtrip. WDW 1 mi.

Embassy Suites ★★★ $$ All 2-room suites. Restaurant. Free cooked-to-order breakfast. Evening Mgrs Reception w/free beverages. Swimming pool. Fitness center. Business center. Fla. Green Lodging hotels. **Int'l. Dr area (2 locations):** 407-352-1400. 8978 Int'l. Dr, 32819. Free shuttle. WDW 5 mi. Also: 407-345-8250. 8250 Jamaican Ct, 32819. WDW 6 mi. **Lake Buena Vista:** 407-239-1144. 8100 Lake Ave, 32836. Free shuttle. WDW 3 mi.

Floridays Orlando ★★★★ $$$ **SeaWorld area:** All suites. Condo rentals. Restaurant. Swimming pool, lap pool, kiddie area w/water cannons. 2-person jetted tubs. 866-994-6307. 12550 Floridays Resort Dr, 32821. Fla. Green Lodging hotel. Free Epcot shuttle. WDW 3 mi.

Gaylord Palms ★★★★ $$$$ **Adjacent to WDW:** Opulent convention resort. Glass-enclosed 5-acre atrium has alligators, koi, snakes, lagoons, streams. Nightly entertainment. Some suites. 7 restaurants inc sushi bar. Swimming pool, kiddie pool, play area. Golf putting course, sand volleyball court, spa. Fitness center, laundromat, laundry services. 400,000-sq-ft convention space, business center. 407-586-0000. 6000 W. Osceola Pkwy, 34746. Fla. Green Lodging hotel. Free shuttle. WDW 1 mi.

Grand Beach ★★★ $$$ **Little Lake Bryan area:** All suites, condos. Restaurant. Swimming pool. Lakefront, water sports, spa. Fitness center, laundromat. 407-238-2500. 8317 Lake Bryan Beach Blvd, 32821. WDW 2 mi.

Hawthorn Suites by Wyndham ★★★ $ **Lake Buena Vista:** All suites. Kitchens, free hot breakfast. Swimming pool. Basketball court. Barbecue, fitness center, laundromat, laundry services. 1,800 sq ft of meeting space. 407-597-5000. 8303 Palm Pkwy, 32836. Fla. Green Lodging hotel. Free Epcot shuttle. WDW 1 mi.

Hilton Garden Inn ★★★ $$ Restaurant, 24/7 market. Swimming pool, hot tub. Meeting space, business center. Fla. Green Lodging hotels. **SeaWorld area:** 407-354-1500. 6850 Westwood Blvd, 32821. WDW 4 mi. **Universal Studios area:** 407-363-9332. 5877 American Way, 32819. WDW 9 mi.

Hilton Orlando Bonnet Creek ★★★★ $$$$ Adjacent to WDW between Disney's Caribbean Beach Resort and Typhoon Lagoon water park, largest Hilton in the mainland U.S. Opened Nov. 2009. Sister hotel is adjacent Waldorf Astoria; they share amenities. Some suites. Six restaurants, mini-mart. 2 swimming pools, water slide (lagoon-style 2-acre pool has a zero-entry side). Golf course; tennis, volleyball courts; spa. Fitness center, laundromat, laundry services. 122,000 sq ft of convention space, business center. 407-597-3600. 14100 Bonnet Creek Resort Ln, 32831. Free shuttle. WDW 1 mi.

Homewood Suites ★★★ $$ All suites. Free hot b'fast. Swimming pool. Fitness center, laundry services.

Meeting space, business services. Fla. Green Lodging hotels. **Int'l. Dr.:** 407-248-2232. 8745 Int'l. Dr, 32819. WDW 5 mi. Free shuttle. **Universal Studios area:** 407-226-0669. 5893 American Way, 32819. WDW 9 mi.

Hyatt Regency Grand Cypress ★★★★ ✓
$$$$ Lake Buena Vista: 1,500 acres, private 21-acre lake. Extensive recreation: 4 Jack Nicklaus golf courses inc 18-hole. Shares amenities with Villas at Grand Cypress. Some suites. 6 restaurants inc sushi bar. Nightly entertainment. Swimming pool has 2 slides, 12 waterfalls, suspension bridge. Racquet club has 12 tennis courts, 2 racquetball courts, basketball court. Spa, water sports. Trails for biking, hiking. Fitness center, laundromat, laundry services. 65,000 sq ft convention space, business center. 407-239-1234. One Grand Cypress Blvd, 32836. Fla. Green Lodging hotel. Free shuttle. WDW 1 mi.

JW Marriott Grande Lakes ★★★★★ ✓ $$$
SeaWorld area: Luxurious, shares amenities, inc Greg Norman-designed golf course, with adjacent sister hotel Ritz-Carlton Grande Lakes. Some suites. Six restaurants. 3 tennis courts, sand volleyball courts, fly-fishing school, fly-fishing onsite, golf course, spa. Life-size chess board. Ropes course w/zip line, giant swing. Fitness center, laundromat; laundry services. 100,000 sq ft meeting space, business center. 407-206-2300. 4040 Central Florida Pkwy, 32837. Fla. Green Lodging hotel. WDW 7 mi.

Marriott Cypress Harbor ★★★★ $$$ Lake Buena
Vista: All suites. 3 restaurants. 3 swimming pools, hot tub. Lake, water sports. Fitness center, laundry services. 540 sq ft meeting space. 800-845-5279. 11251 Harbour Villa Rd, 32821. Fla. Green Lodging hotel. WDW 4 mi.

Marriott Grande Vista ★★★★ $$$ SeaWorld
area: Two restaurants, food court, market. Four swimming pools, hot tub. Lake, some kitchens and kitchenettes, sauna. Golf course, golf academy. Tennis, volleyball courts. Lake, water sports. Fitness center, laundry services. 407-238-7676. 5925 Avenida Vista, 32821. Fla. Green Lodging hotel. WDW 5 mi.

Marriott World Center Orlando ★★★★ ✓
$$$ World Center Dr.: Lavishly appointed, lushly landscaped. Some suites. 5 restaurants, food court. 6 pools (waterfalls, slides, one indoor), 6 hot tubs. Golf course, miniature golf course. Fitness center, spa, laundry services. 450,000 sq ft of convention space, business center. 800-228-9290. 8701 World Center Dr, 32821. WDW 2 mi.

Monumental Hotel ★★★ $ Int'l. Dr.: 1 restaurant.
Swimming pool, hot tub. Laundry services. 3,000 sq ft meeting space, business center. 407-239-1222. 12000 Int'l. Dr, 32821. Formerly Crowne Plaza. WDW 4 mi.

Nickelodeon Family Suites ★★★ $$ World
Center Dr. area: All suites, some bunk beds. 6 restaurants,

Nickelodeon character breakfast buffet (reservations req), mini-mart. 2 mini water parks w/13 slides, 2 hot tubs, kids spa. Basketball court, miniature golf, pool table. Fitness center, laundromat. Business center. 877-387-5437. 14500 Continental Gateway, 32821. Fla. Green Lodging hotel. Free shuttle. WDW 1 mi. Run by Holiday Inn, this family-focused resort offers wacky fun including a daily mass sliming and Nickelodeon shows starring guests. Children's bedrooms are decorated with SpongeBob SquarePants and other Nick cartoon characters.

Omni Orlando Resort ChampionsGate
★★★★ $$$ SW of WDW: Some suites. 5 restaurants, sushi bar. 3 swimming pools w/lazy river, slides. 2 golf courses, golf academy, spa. Fitness center, laundry services. 70,000 sq ft meeting space, business center. 407-390-6664. 1500 Masters Blvd, 33896. Fla. Green Lodging hotel. Free shuttle. WDW 7 mi.

Peabody Orlando ★★★★ $$$ Orlando Convention
Cntr area: Some suites. 3 restaurants, market. Swimming pool, kiddie pool with waterfall, hot tub. Spa, fitness center, laundry services. 300,000 sq ft convention space, business center. Club level. Mallard march at fountain twice daily. 800-732-2639. 9801 Int'l. Dr, 32819. Fla. Green Lodging hotel. Shuttle $10 roundtrip. WDW 6 mi.

Renaissance Orlando ★★★★ $$ SeaWorld area:
Some suites. 2 restaurants, sushi bar. Tennis, volleyball courts. Spa. Fitness center, laundry services. Across street from SeaWorld. 185,000 sq ft meeting space, business center. 800-327-6677. 6677 Sea Harbor Dr, 32821. Fla. Green Lodging hotel. WDW 4 mi.

Residence Inn By Marriott ★★★ $$$ All suites.
Free breakfast, grocery delivery service. Swimming pool, hot tub. Fitness center, laundry services. Meeting space, business center. Fee for pets. **Int'l. Dr. area:** 407-226-0288. 8800 Universal Blvd, 32819. Free shuttle. WDW 7 mi. **Lake Buena Vista:** 407-465-0075. 11450 Marbella Palm Ct, 32836. Free Epcot shuttle. WDW 1 mi. **SeaWorld area:** 800-889-9728. 11000 Westwood Blvd, 32821. Free shuttle. WDW 4 mi.

Ritz-Carlton Grande Lakes ★★★★★ $$$$
SeaWorld area: Luxurious, shares amenities inc Greg Norman-designed golf course w/adj JW Marriott Grande Lakes. Some suites. 5 restaurants. Swimming pool w/zero entry, kiddie pool. 3 tennis courts, sand volleyball courts, fly-fishing w/school, golf course, spa. Life-size chess board. Ropes course w/zip line, giant swing. Fitness center, laundromat; laundry services. 47,000 sq ft meeting space, business center. 800-576-5760. 4012 Central Florida Pkwy, 32837. Fla. Green Lodging hotel. WDW 7 mi.

Rosen Centre ★★★ $$$$ Orlando Convention Cntr
area: Some suites. 4 restaurants, sushi bar. Swimming pool, kiddie pool, hot tub. Spa. Fitness center, laundry services.

The Marriott World Center Orlando (right) is 2 miles from Disney. Other nearby Marriott properties include the stunning JW Marriott Grande Lakes, the Marriott Grande Vista with its golf academy, the all-suite Marriott Cypress Harbor, and the multi-hotel Marriott Village.

100,000 sq ft convention space. 800-204-7234. 9840 Int'l. Dr, 32819. Fla. Green Lodging hotel. WDW 6 mi.

Rosen Plaza ★★★ $$ **Orlando Convention Cntr area:** Some suites. 4 restaurants, nightclub. Swimming pool w/ waterfall, hot tub. Fitness center, laundry services. 60,000 sq ft meeting space. 800-627-8258. 9700 Int'l. Dr, 32819. Fla. Green Lodging hotel. WDW 6 mi.

Rosen Shingle Creek ★★★ $$$ **Orlando Convention Cntr area:** Some suites. 4 restaurants, piano bar. 3 pools, 2 hot tubs. Basketball, tennis, volleyball courts. Golf course, academy. Fitness center. 445,000 sq ft convention space, business center. 407-996-9939. 9939 Universal Blvd, 32819. Fla. Green Lodging hotel. WDW 7 mi.

Sheraton Safari ★★★ $$ **Lake Buena Vista:** Some suites. 3 restaurants. Swimming pool w/python slide, kiddie pool, hot tub. Fitness center. 13,000 sq ft meeting space, business center. Pets to 80 lbs w/fee. 407-239-0444. 12205 S. Apopka-Vineland Rd, 32836. Fla. Green Lodging hotel. Free shuttle. WDW 1 mi.

Sheraton Vistana Resort Villas ★★★ $$ **SeaWorld area:** All suites, condos. Restaurants, market. Swimming pool, 9 hot tubs. Basketball, tennis courts. Miniature golf. Fitness center, laundromat. Business center. 407-239-3100. 8800 Vistana Centre Dr, 32821. Fla. Green Lodging hotel. Free shuttle. WDW 4 mi.

SpringHill Suites ★★★ $$ **Orlando Convention Cntr area:** Free continental breakfast. Swimming pool. Volleyball court. Fitness center. 407-938-9001. 8623 Universal Blvd, 32819. Fla. Green Lodging hotel. WDW 7 mi.

Staybridge Suites ★★★ $$$ Free continental breakfast. Swimming pool, kiddie pool, hot tub. laundromat. **Int'l. Dr. area:** 800-238-8000. 8480 Int'l. Dr, 32819. WDW 7 mi. **Lake Buena Vista:** 800-238-8000. 8751 Suiteside Dr, 32836. Free shuttle. WDW 1 mi.

Villas of Grand Cypress ★★★★ $$$$ **Lake Buena Vista:** All suites. Many whirlpool baths, fireplaces. 2 restaurants. Swimming pool. Shares amenities with Hyatt Regency Grand Cypress. Laundry services. 14,000 sq ft meeting space, business center. 2 golf courses. 800-835-7377. 1 N. Jacaranda St, 32836. Fla. Green Lodging hotel. Free shuttle. WDW 4 mi.

Waldorf Astoria Orlando ★★★★★ $$$$ **Adjacent to WDW:** Between Disney's Caribbean Beach Resort and Typhoon Lagoon water park, elegant, first Waldorf Astoria built outside NYC. Opened Nov. 2009. Rees Jones 18-hole golf course. Formal swimming pool circled by private cabanas, personalized service. Like NY Waldorf, lobby has hand-crafted clock. Adj Hilton Orlando Bonnet Creek shares amenities. Some suites. 4 restaurants. 2 swimming pools, water slide, private cabanas. Tennis, volleyball courts; spa. Fitness center, laundromat, laundry services. 28,000 sq ft meeting space, business center. 407-597-5500. 14200 Bonnet Creek Resort Ln, 32831. Free shuttle. WDW 1 mi.

WorldQuest Resort ★★★★ $$$ **World Center Dr. area:** All suites. Condo rentals. 24/7 market. Swimming pool. Fitness center, laundromat. 877-987-8378. 8849 Worldquest Blvd, 32821. Free shuttle. WDW 2 mi.

Wyndham Bonnet Creek Resort ★★★ $$ **Adjacent to WDW:** Located between Disney's Caribbean Beach Resort and Typhoon Lagoon water park. All suites. Spa tubs. 2 swimming pools with lazy river, wading pool, 3 hot tubs. 18-hole miniature golf. Fitness center, laundry services. 407-398-4090. 9560 Via Encinas, 32830. Fla. Green Lodging hotel. WDW 1 mi.

Wyndham Orlando Resort ★★★ $$ **Int'l. Dr.:** Some suites, bunk beds. 3 restaurants. 3 swimming pools, hot tub. Fitness center. Meeting rooms, business center. Pet to 60 lbs w/fee. 407-351-2420. 8001 Int'l. Dr, 32819. WDW 8 mi.

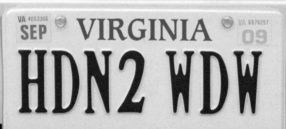

Planning Your Trip

With just a little bit of preparation, it's easy to put together a terrific Walt Disney World vacation. Planning your trip isn't brain surgery—all you need is this book, the Internet and a cell phone (Disney World phone and internet directories appear at the back of this book). Ideally you should put your plan together a year early. As your vacation nears, doing Disney World-focused activities with your family will help everyone look forward to it. For basic planning, here's a step-by-step strategy:

1. Decide when to go. You can have a good time at Disney World any day of the year, but if you've got the flexibility, the first two weeks of December is the best time to go. It's not too crowded, and there's more to see and do than any other time of the year, thanks to special holiday decor and entertainment. Crowds are also light, and hotel rooms less expensive, from mid-January to Valentine's Day, late April to late May and between Labor Day and mid-November (it's not all good: some attractions close during these periods for maintenance; Magic Kingdom often closes at 6 p.m.). The least crowded week of the year is the one that starts the day after Labor Day.

The worst times to visit? July and early August, when crowds are thick and the air thicker, and the week between Christmas and New Year's, when crowds are horrid and temperatures can be near freezing.
See the chapter **Walt Disney World A-Z.**

2. Decide how long to stay. Want to see the best of everything Disney has to offer? You'll need at least a week. Each theme park takes a day or more to fully enjoy. You can easily spend a day at each water park. Diversions such as fishing, horseback riding, golf and water sports add variety to your trip. It's also worthwhile to linger at character meals or take a backstage tour. If you can't stay a week, three days is enough to get a decent dose of Disney.

As for daily schedules, you'll find "Magical Day" theme-park plans in this book at the start of each theme-park chapter.

Headin' to Walt Disney World? This chapter makes it easy, and fun, to plan your trip.

3. Decide where to stay. You have hundreds of choices. Disney itself operates 19 resorts, and nearly every hotel chain known to man has at least one property within 10 miles. Disney resorts are most convenient, of course, and offer other benefits such as Extra Magic Hours (additional time in the parks before or after closing time), free transportation and packaged dining and recreation options. Off-property accommodations run the gamut from very cheap (and often very poorly maintained) motels to huge luxurious convention complexes. This book's Accommodations chapter reviews every Disney World resort and lists every hotel of at least 3-star quality within 10 miles.
See the chapter **Accommodations.**

4. Buy your airline tickets. The Orlando International Airport is 19 miles east of Walt Disney World, about a 30-minute drive. It's served by 35 airlines, including American, Delta, Frontier, Southwest, United, U.S. Airways and Air Canada. Driving to Disney? Walt Disney World sits alongside Interstate 4, 15 miles southwest of downtown Orlando and 70 miles northwest of Tampa.
See the chapter **Walt Disney World A-Z.**

5. Decide what you want to do. Thumb through this book and check out the official Disney website disneyworld.com. If you have children, let them pick out their favorites.

6. Choose your park tickets. Disney offers a variety of options, including packages with pre-paid dining and recreation for guests staying at Disney resort hotels. Tickets are priced by the number of days they are good for; the longer you stay, the better the value.
See the chapter **Walt Disney World A-Z.**

7. Make a plan. Check the calendar at disneyworld.com for park hours, fireworks schedules and special events. Talk with your family about having a day or two when you don't visit a park (after all, this is a *vacation*). Keep your plan flexible in case of bad weather. If you will be staying at a Disney hotel, check for Extra Magic Hours schedule at disneyworld.com.

8. Book it! Purchase your park tickets and reserve your Disney room at 407-934-7639 or disneyworld.com. Call between 7 a.m. and 10 p.m. Eastern time.

Wacky Star Wars Weekends storm Disney's Hollywood Studios each spring. Other seasonal events include Epcot's spring Flower & Garden Festival and fall Food & Wine Festival.

9. Make other reservations. Make reservations for restaurants as soon as possible. Character meals, dinner shows and key dining times for regular restaurants fill up months in advance for peak periods. Meals that book quickest include those at Cinderella Castle and Epcot's Le Cellier steakhouse. You can book a table as early as 190 days in advance if you're staying at a Disney resort (407-939-3463 or at disneyworld.com). Many entertainment, sports and recreation choices require reservations, too. The best seats for the Cirque du Soleil production La Nouba get nabbed months in advance, as do prime golf tee times.

See the chapters **Activities, Restaurants.**

10. Rent a car, maybe. Disney has such an extensive transportation system that you may not need to rent a car. The company's unique Magical Express bus service shuttles guests from the Orlando International Airport, and complimentary boats, buses and monorails move guests around Disney World property. However, those with cars get around quicker, and have the option to visit areas outside Disney. You can rent a car from the airport or from many locations on Disney property.

See the chapter **Walt Disney World A-Z.**

What to pack. Walt Disney World visitors often underestimate the heat and humidity inherent in Central Florida, and can be unprepared for the amount of outdoor exposure a Disney vacation requires. Therefore, they pack poorly. Here are some packing tips that recognize that Florida is indeed the Sunshine State:

For all ages. Suitcase fundamentals include T-shirts, loose-fitting cotton tops, capris and shorts with large pockets, baseball caps and swimsuits, and broken-in walking shoes (pack two pair per person, so if it rains everyone still has a dry pair). Flip-flop sandals are a bad idea; they create blisters when used this intensely. In the winter guests need clothes to layer, such as jackets, sweaters and sweatshirts, as days start off cool but warm quickly. January mornings can be below freezing at 9 a.m. but 60 degrees by noon. Temperatures at 7 p.m. will be no higher than the 50s through March. (For detailed Disney weather data log on to weather.com, type in the ZIP code 32830 and then scroll down to the tab "Averages.")

Other essentials include an umbrella, sunglasses and sunscreen. Guests can keep their hands free by using a backpack or waist pack instead of a purse. Don't forget tickets, reservation confirmations and all the various battery chargers a modern life requires. And don't splurge on those specs—sunglasses are the No. 1 item guests lose at Disney World. Cast members find hundreds of pairs a day.

Though popular, thong-style sandals can leave feet sore and blistered—the average Disney World guest walks seven miles a day. A better choice is broken-in walking shoes worn with socks.

For children. Guests should dress their children like they dress themselves, casually and comfortably, but with more protection from the sun. Wide-brimmed hats help. Bring snacks (granola bars, raisin boxes) and, for autographs, a fat Sharpie pen (pick a thick pen so furry characters can hold it easily).

Most forgotten item. The most common item Disney World visitors mistakenly leave at home—and at the end of the trip, the item they most often leave behind in their hotel rooms—is a cell phone charger.

Family Activities

Like looking forward to Christmas day, anticipating a Walt Disney World vacation can be nearly as much fun as the event itself. Build your family's excitement with these ideas and activities:

Announcing the trip. "We're going to Disney World!" Letting your children know about an upcoming Disney trip can be a thrilling moment all on its own. Here are some creative ways to spring the good news:

Quiz cards. Create a quiz with questions for children to answer on Disney characters, movies or on Disney World itself. Each question is on the front of a card laid face up on a table; its answer is on the back. When a child answers a question correctly, he or she turns over that card. When all the cards are revealed, they spell out a message such as: "We Are Going to Disney World on Tuesday!" (For help coming up with questions, see this guidebook's theme-park chapters and Character Guide.)

Scavenger hunt. Create a scavenger hunt that uses clues about Disney characters or quotes from Disney movies. Make each "find" a Disney trinket that has a card attached with the next clue. The final card—announcing the trip—can be attached to a helium-filled Mickey balloon tucked inside a new suitcase. When the suitcase is opened, the balloon

Smart snacks
Nut packs, fruit and nut bars and raisin boxes are easy to stuff into a backpack or fanny pack, offer tasty and nutritious energy, and can help avoid expensive and time-consuming stops at snack stands.

Some families save for their Disney vacation by creating a special Disney Fund. A homemade container makes it easy to collect extra money or spare change. The cash can be used as spending money for children or as a way to afford bonus activities.

floats up. The child can then use the suitcase to pack for the trip.

Letter from Mickey Mouse. Mail your child a letter or postcard that appears to be from Mickey Mouse, Cinderella or another Disney character and reads "can't wait to meet you at Disney World!" (Mickey could add ""See ya real soon!").

Backpack with Disney World stuff. As a present, fill a new backpack with Walt Disney World items such as an autograph book, several Disney Dollars and a T-shirt. Your child will quickly figure out where they are headed.

Jigsaw puzzle. Create a personalized jigsaw puzzle that, when assembled, announces the trip. Paint—or use felt-tip markers to write— "We're going to Disney World tomorrow!" (or "next week!," "at Easter!" etc.) on the pieces. Perhaps give the puzzle as a Christmas or birthday present.

Change the destination. Announce in advance that the family is going on a trip to a bland, fictitious destination—"This weekend we're going to visit your Great Aunt Harriet!" On the way to the airport, give them goodie bags for the plane ride filled with Disney activities, games, snacks and trinkets. Goodie bags can be made from brown paper lunch bags and craft supplies.

Sources for these materials. Disney items for most of the above ideas are available online at disneystore.com or over the phone at 407-363-6200; choose option 3 to reach a live operator. At press time, Walt Disney World postcards were sold only over the phone. Disney Dollars can be purchased through

Facing page: A tiny princess views Magic Kingdom's Cinderella Castle early one morning

Walt Disney World Ticketing at 407-566-4985. Uninflated Disney Mylar balloons can be ordered online through many sources, including Amazon.com, for less than $10; the balloon can be inflated at most any florist or card shop for a token fee. Dick Blick Art Supplies (800-828-4548, dickblick.com) sells pre-cut Create-A-Puzzle kits.

Saving for the trip. Want to teach your kids the value of a dollar? A Disney trip gives parents a great opportunity to do just that. The more involved children are in budgeting for the vacation, the more they'll learn the benefits of saving and wise spending.

Disney Fund. Once a vacation is in the works, the family can create a special "Disney Fund" to help pay for the entire trip or for special parts of it such as a character meal, a backstage tour, a fireworks cruise or a horseback ride. Start with a large can (a coffee can will do), then cover it, decorate it and label it "Disney Fund." Put it in a visible spot in your kitchen, so it's easy for everyone to toss in extra money and spare change. Over time, the fund grows.

The fund can also be used for spending money for children. Cash can be turned into Disney Dollars (see above) or Gift Cards.

Countdown meals. Look forward to your Disney World trip by creating meals and activities inspired by Disney movies and characters. These occasions can be once a week, once a month or on particular dates (i.e., 120 days before your vacation, 90 days before, etc.). Our thanks to DisBoards contributor Princess Tiger Lily for her great ideas.

"Aladdin": *Food*—Kabobs with couscous; baklava for dessert. *Activity*—Cut pieces

To make Mickey Mouse pancakes, pour batter to create a large circle for the face and—quickly—two smaller circles for the ears. Disneystore.com often sells Mickey-shaped molds.

of felt into "magic carpets" to sit on. Cut slits on each end to add fringe. Decorate with fabric paint or other pieces of felt.

"Alice in Wonderland": *Food*—Make tea sandwiches (ham and cheese, PB&J) with Cheshire Cat smiles (slices of melon). Decorate sugar cookies with gel frosting so they read "Eat Me;" tape "Drink Me" signs on juice boxes. Make an Unbirthday cake. *Activity*—Build a house of cards.

"A Bug's Life": *Food*—Dirt Torte (layers of chocolate pudding, crushed Oreos and gummy worms). *Activity*—Play Cootie. The game is available at many retailers.

"Cars": *Food*—Checkered flag sandwiches (tuna or chicken salad on pumpernickel and white breads—cut into cubes and arrange to look like a checkered flag). *Activity*—Using a round cookie or biscuit cutter (or the top of a glass), make stop lights out of green, red and yellow Jello.

"Cinderella": *Food*—A Royal Banquet. Serve a fancy meal on good china with cloth napkins. *Activity*—Slipper Hunt. Separate pairs of mom's high heels and hide the shoes around the house. Compete to see who can find the most pairs.

"Dumbo": *Food*—Circus food, such as hot dogs, popcorn and peanuts. *Activity*—Have someone draw Dumbo on a large poster board, get a feather and play Pin the Feather on the Dumbo (the correct spot: the trunk). Use the same rules as the game Pin the Tail on the Donkey.

"Finding Nemo": *Food*—Sprinkle goldfish crackers over macaroni and cheese to create Nemo and friends on a sea anemone. Put gummy fish in blue Jello and serve it in clear cups to create an undersea world. *Activity*—Tape strips of pink crepe paper onto pink helium-filled balloons to turn your family room into an ocean of jellyfish. Kids can pretend they are Dory and Marlin swimming through the ocean.

"Lilo & Stitch": *Food*—Peanut butter and banana sandwiches (the favorite food of Lilo's idol, Elvis Presley). *Activity*—Make crepe paper hula skirts.

"The Lion King": *Food*—Ants on Logs: celery strips filled with peanut butter topped with raisins. *Activity*—Create lion masks with paper plates, construction paper, pipe cleaners, markers and glitter.

"Mary Poppins": *Food*—Serve scones, fruit, tea sandwiches and tea to create an English tea party. Use china plates. *Activity*—Make and fly paper kites. Or go out to a park and feed the birds.

Mickey Mouse: *Food*—Mickey Mouse-shaped pancakes. *Activity*—As a family, make Mickey Mouse-shaped Rice Krispy treats. Use microwave dipping chocolate to dip the ears, then sprinkle with mini chocolate chips and mini M&Ms.

"Peter Pan": *Food*—Fruit on a Sword. Put slices of fruit on wooden skewers. Make a dip using 8 ounces of fat-free Cool Whip mixed with 6 ounces of fruit yogurt; refrigerate one hour. *Activity*—A treasure hunt. Create what looks like an old worn map by first cutting a map shape out of a brown paper grocery bag, then wetting it slightly and crumpling it. After a few minutes, flatten it out to dry. Then draw a treasure map on it with an "X" that marks the spot in your house where you've hidden treasure, such as a bag of gold-wrapped "pirate coin" chocolates from a candy or party shop.

"Pirates of the Caribbean" films: *Food*—Serve apple juice "ale" in mugs or goblets, along with turkey legs or fish sticks. Create Pirate Treasure by crumbling graham crackers to make a "beach" and giving each person chocolate coins; serve alongside blue Jello to depict the water's edge. *Activity*—Make a treasure map and have a treasure hunt (see the description above under "Peter Pan").

"Sleeping Beauty": *Food*—Create a birthday cake that is half blue, half pink. *Activity*—Have everyone come to the dinner table wearing their pajamas.

"Snow White and the Seven Dwarfs": *Food*—Apple pie. *Activity*—Bob for apples. Or tie a string to a stem of an apple, hang it up, and have everyone take turns to eat it without using their hands.

"The Three Caballeros": *Food*—Make-your-own tacos, served with Spanish rice. *Activity*—Make Mexican paper flowers from tissue paper and pipe cleaners. Put them in a terra cotta pot decorated with acrylic paint; hold the flowers in place by putting Styrofoam in the pot's bottom. Makes a colorful centerpiece.

"Toy Story" movies: *Food*—Pizza, a la Pizza Planet. *Activity*—Get down on the floor and play with your children using "Toy Story" dolls and action figures—Woody, Buzz Lightyear, Mr. and Mrs. Potato Head, even Barbie and Ken.

Countdown chain. "How long until Disney World?" One consequence of planning a trip to Walt Disney World with your family is hearing this question. Endlessly.

A countdown chain is a fun way to answer it. Especially when your family makes this craft project together. Here's how you do it:

Using construction paper, create a chain that has the same number of links as the number of days until your trip. Number the links consecutively on one side. Decorate the other side with glitter, markers, paint and stickers. Perhaps give each link its own theme, such as a particular character or ride. Make special links for birthdays and holidays, as well as milestones such as "One Month To Go" or "One Week To Go." Hang the chain in a conspicuous spot, such as the kitchen ceiling.

Each day tear off one of the links, perhaps at bedtime or first thing in the morning. Remove the last link right before leaving for your trip.

Disney World movie nights. Sitting down with the family for a few Walt Disney World movie nights—watching films that form the basis of the rides and shows you're about to experience—is a great way to get in the right state of mind for a trip to the Vacation Kingdom, and will make the trip itself more fun. In fact, many Disney attractions make

A homemade Walt Disney World countdown chain helps younger children look forward to their upcoming vacation

© Warner Home Video

"My goodness. I can talk again!" Dorothy (Judy Garland) and the Scarecrow (Ray Bolger) bring the Tin Man (Jack Haley) back to life in 1939's "The Wizard of Oz." The classic family film is featured at the Great Movie Ride attraction at Disney's Hollywood Studios theme park.

little or no sense to those guests who don't already know their characters, backstories or music. By the way, not every choice needs to be a Disney movie. Some Disney World attractions are based on films from other studios, such as "Raiders of the Lost Ark" and the "Star Wars" series.

To make your movie nights truly special, schedule them when everyone can relax together. Before a movie begins, parents and children alike should get all of their distractions out of the way—no e-mails, no chores, no homework, no texting! Set a start time, turn down the lights and make sure everyone has a comfortable seat. Schedule an intermission for bathroom runs and snack grabs.

The list at right shows every movie that is referenced at Disney World theme parks. All but one—"The Song of the South"—are available on Amazon.com or Netflix.

Helping children face their fears. Many kids are nervous about going on particular rides or even meeting characters. One way to allay these fears is to take away the mystery and become familiar with the attraction ahead of time.

YouTube. This video-sharing website includes many amateur ride-through videos of Disney World attractions as well as some of guests meeting characters. When searching it, include the phrase "Disney World" to filter out experiences at California's Disneyland.

This book. Flip through the theme-park, water-park and character-guide pages of this guidebook with your children. Even toddlers will enjoy looking at the pictures. Tips on meeting characters as well as a table that lists Disney's scariest attractions for children appear in the upcoming chapter Walt Disney World A–Z.

DVD images © Walt Disney Home Entertainment

The fab four
The four most-referenced movies at Walt Disney World are also four of Disney's best animated films—"Aladdin," "Beauty and the Beast," "Cinderella" and "The Lion King."

Family Activities

Theme park movie references

"2001: A Space Odyssey": Magic Kingdom: Space Mountain.

"Aladdin": Magic Kingdom: Afternoon parade, Magic Carpets of Aladdin, Mickey's PhilharMagic, Move It! Shake It! Celebrate It!, Wishes. Disney's Hollywood Studios: Fantasmic.

"Alice in Wonderland": Magic Kingdom: Afternoon parade, Mad Tea Party, Main St. Electrical Parade, Move It! Shake It! Celebrate It!

"Alien": Studios: The Great Movie Ride.

"Beauty and the Beast": Magic Kingdom: Afternoon parade, Mickey's PhilharMagic, Move It! Shake It! Celebrate It!, Wishes. Studios: Beauty and the Beast Live on Stage.

"A Bug's Life": Disney's Animal Kingdom: It's Tough to Be a Bug. Studios: Pixar Pals parade.

"Casablanca": Studios: Great Movie Ride.

"Cinderella": Magic Kingdom: Afternoon parade, Dream Along with Mickey, Main St. Electrical Parade, Prince Charming Regal Carrousel, Wishes.

"Dinosaur": Animal Kingdom: Dinosaur.

"Dumbo": Magic Kingdom: Dumbo the Flying Elephant.

"Fantasia": Magic Kingdom: Mickey's PhilharMagic, Wishes. Studios: Fantasmic, The Great Movie Ride.

"Finding Nemo": Animal Kingdom: Finding Nemo–The Musical. Epcot: The Seas with Nemo & Friends pavilion.

"Footlight Parade": Studios: The Great Movie Ride.

"Honey, I Shrunk the Kids": Studios: "Honey, I Shrunk..." playground.

"The Incredibles": Magic Kingdom: Move It! Shake It! Celebrate It! Studios: Pixar Pals parade.

"The Jungle Book": Magic Kingdom: Afternoon parade, Move It! Shake It! Celebrate It!

"Lilo & Stitch": Magic Kingdom: Afternoon parade, Stitch's Great Escape.

"The Lion King": Magic Kingdom: Mickey's PhilharMagic. Epcot: Circle of Life movie. Studios: Fantasmic. Animal Kingdom: Festival of the Lion King, Mickey's Jammin' Jungle Parade.

"The Little Mermaid": Magic Kingdom: Afternoon parade, Mickey's PhilharMagic, Move It! Shake It! Celebrate It!, Wishes. Studios: Voyage of the Little Mermaid.

"Mary Poppins": Magic Kingdom: Afternoon parade. Studios: The Great Movie Ride.

"Monsters, Inc.": Magic Kingdom: Laugh Floor. Studios: Pixar Pals parade.

"Mulan": Studios: The Magic of Disney Animation.

"Peter Pan": Magic Kingdom: Afternoon parade, Dream Along with Mickey, Main St. Electrical Parade, Mickey's PhilharMagic, Peter Pan's Flight.

"Pete's Dragon": Magic Kingdom: Main St. Electrical Parade.

"Pinocchio": Magic Kingdom: Afternoon parade, Main St. Electrical Parade, Wishes. Studios: Fantasmic.

"Pirates of the Caribbean" series: Magic Kingdom: Pirates of the Caribbean.

"Pocahontas": Studios: Fantasmic.

"The Princess and the Frog": Magic Kingdom: Afternoon parade.

"Public Enemy": Studios: The Great Movie Ride.

"Raiders of the Lost Ark": Studios: The Great Movie Ride, Indiana Jones Epic Stunt Spectacular.

"Ratatouille": Studios: Pixar Pals parade.

"Singin' in the Rain": Studios: The Great Movie Ride.

"Sleeping Beauty": Magic Kingdom: Dream Along with Mickey. Studios: Fantasmic.

"Snow White and the Seven Dwarfs": Magic Kingdom: Afternoon parade, Main St. Electrical Parade, Snow White's Scary Adventures, Wishes.

"Song of the South": Magic Kingdom: Splash Mountain.

"Star Wars" series: Studios: Star Tours.

"Swiss Family Robinson": Magic Kingdom: Swiss Family Treehouse.

"Tarzan and His Mate": Studios: The Great Movie Ride.

"The Three Caballeros": Epcot: Gran Fiesta Tour.

"Toy Story" series: Magic Kingdom: Buzz Lightyear's Space Ranger Spin, afternoon parade, Move It! Shake It! Celebrate It! Studios: Toy Story Mania, Pixar Pals parade.

"Up": Studios: Pixar Pals parade.

"Winnie the Pooh and the Blustery Day": Magic Kingdom: The Many Adventures of Winnie the Pooh.

"The Wizard of Oz": Studios: The Great Movie Ride.

Walt Disney World special events

January–March

Walt Disney World Marathon Weekend:
January 6–9. A pair of running events—a
26.2-mile full marathon and a 13.1-mile
half marathon—highlight this athletic
festival. The full route goes through all
four Disney theme parks; the half marathon covers Magic Kingdom and Epcot.
Typically more than 30,000 athletes
compete. There's also a 5K Epcot run
for families (Disney's Family Fun Run), a
series of small races for children (Mickey's
Marathon Kids' Fest) and a three-day
health and fitness expo. Details are at
rundisney.com or 407-938-3398.

Disney Princess Half Marathon Weekend:
February 25–27. This female-focused
weekend features a half marathon that
winds through Magic Kingdom and
Epcot. On-course princess-themed
entertainment includes Prince Charming.
Other events include a 5K race, kids'
races and a health and fitness expo. Men
are not excluded, but are not eligible for
individual awards. Details are at rundis-
ney.com or 407-938-3398.

Atlanta Braves Spring Training: February–
March. The Atlanta Braves Major League
Baseball club holds its 14th consecutive
Spring Training season at ESPN Wide
World of Sports. Workouts start in
February. Fifteen or 16 Grapefruit League
exhibition games follow in March. Details
and tickets ($28–$39 reserved; $15–$19
gen adm lawn seats, packages available,
on sale first week in January) at dis-
neysports.com, the ESPN Wide World of
Sports Box Office (prerecorded 407-828-
3267; live voice 407-939-1500 or 407-939-
4263) and Ticketmaster (800-745-3000).

**Epcot International Flower & Garden
Festival:** March 2–May 15. Disney's most
elaborate one-park event, this 75-day
garden party includes seminars, demonstrations and celebrity guest speakers, as
well as character topiaries, floating water
gardens and 30 million flowers. Themed
weekends celebrate art, bugs and
Mother's Day. Friday–Sunday concerts
feature vintage "Flower Power" acts such
as former Monkees singer Davy Jones. A
butterfly garden often includes a live cat-
erpillar/chrysalis exhibit. Vendor booths
line walkways. Standard park admission
required. Details at 407-934-7639.

ESPN the Weekend: Early March.
Legendary athletes join popular ESPN
broadcasters during this no-extra-charge
fan-fest at Disney's Hollywood Studios.
Events include Q&A sessions, celebrity
motorcades, hands-on sports activities
and live ESPN telecasts. Coincides with
Atlanta Braves Spring Training. Standard
park admission required. Details at es-
pntheweekend.com.

St. Patrick's Day: March 17. Special events
mark this Irish holiday at two Disney
World locations: the Raglan Road restaurant at Downtown Disney and the U.K.
pavilion at Epcot's World Showcase.

April–June

Easter Weekend: April 23–24. Outfitted in
colorful homemade dresses, the Azalea
Trail Maids from Mobile, Ala., greet
guests at Magic Kingdom and lead its
Easter Day parade. Joining them are Mr.
and Mrs. Easter Bunny, who meet and
greet guests all day. At Epcot, children
hunt for Easter eggs at the American
Adventure Pavilion (ages 3–9) and participate in Easter egg relays at Future World
West Garden (age 6-12). Standard theme
park admission required.

Grad Nights: April 29, 30; May 6, 7. High
school seniors celebrate graduation
at these after-hours parties at Magic
Kingdom, which include multiple dance
floors, live musical performances, Disney
character greetings and special Grad
Night merchandise for sale. Select attractions are open. Separate ticket required.
Information and tickets at 800-544-7646.

Star Wars Weekends: May–June. This
Disney's Hollywood Studios fan-fest
celebrates the "Star Wars" movie saga.
Highlights include celebrity motorcades,
roving characters, Q&A and autograph
sessions, trivia games and children's
activities. Many guests wear costumes.
Get there when the park opens to nab
the best autographs, take advantage of
all the activities and be greeted at the
entrance by wisecracking stormtroopers.
Standard theme park admission required.
Details at 407-827-2799.

Gay Days: May 31–June 6. Tens of thousands
of gay adults come to Walt Disney World
during the first week in June, most wearing red shirts in a sign of celebration and

solidarity. Groups gather Thursday, June 2 at Disney's Animal Kingdom; Friday, June 3 at Disney's Hollywood Studios; Saturday, June 4 at Magic Kingdom; and Sunday, June 5 at Epcot. Disney does not sponsor the event but doesn't interfere with it. Details at gaydays.com or 407-896-8431.

Sounds Like Summer Concert Series: June–August. Cover bands perform timeless tunes from acts such as U2, Elton John and The Supremes. Three shows nightly at Epcot's American Gardens amphitheater. Standard park admission required.

July–September

Independence Day Weekend: July 2–4. Usually the most crowded days of the year, Independence Day weekend features a spectacular Magic Kingdom fireworks show on Sunday and Monday nights that surrounds guests watching from Main Street U.S.A. Disney's Hollywood Studios has a fireworks show too. Historic characters share their stories at Epcot's American Adventure.

Night of Joy: September 9–10. Live concerts by many Contemporary Christian artists highlight this Magic Kingdom event. Most major attractions are open. Info and tickets ($45 one night; $76 two nights) at nightofjoy.com or 407-827-7200.

Mickey's Not-So-Scary Halloween Party: September–October. There's nothing but fun during these all-ages Magic Kingdom evenings, held on select dates from 7 p.m. to midnight. Included is a terrific parade that starts with a galloping headless horseman, costumed Disney characters, a spectacular fireworks show and many free-candy stations. Most attractions are not crowded. Thousands of children and some adults wear costumes, many of which are homemade. Tickets are $64 for adults; $58 for children 3–9. Many dates offer $6 advance savings. Parties held on Fridays near Halloween, and the one on Halloween itself, often sell out. Information and tickets at 407-934-7639.

October–December

Wine & Dine Half Marathon Weekend: September 30–October 1. Races include a family 5K through Magic Kingdom and culminate in an evening half marathon through multiple parks which finishes inside Epcot for an exclusive Food & Wine Festival experience. Details at disneywinedinerun.com or 407-938-3398.

Epcot International Food & Wine Festival: September 30–November 13. Dozens of World Showcase booths offer food and drink samples from around the world. Events include cooking demonstrations and (pricey!) dinners and wine seminars. Free concerts feature vintage pop acts such as Kool & The Gang and David Cassidy. Standard park admission required. Details at disneyworld.com/foodandwine or 407-939-3378.

Festival of the Masters: Mid-November. This Downtown Disney open-air festival features over 100 artists, each of whom has won a primary award at a juried art show within the past three years. Self-taught creators are at the adjacent House of Blues folk-art festival. Cirque du Soleil artists perform in front of their theater each afternoon. Chalk artists cover 6,000 square feet at the Marketplace. Held annually since 1975. No charge. For more information call 407-824-4321.

Children's Miracle Network Golf Classic: Mid-November. Fans are just a few feet away from the top names in men's golf with a pass to this PGA Tour tournament, held on Disney's Magnolia and Palm golf courses. Proceeds benefit local Children's Miracle Network hospitals. Info and tickets ($20 daily, $30 full week; food packages available) at 407-824-2250.

Mickey's Very Merry Christmas Party: November–December. Held every few nights from early November through just before Christmas, these 7p–mid Magic Kingdom parties have light crowds (10,000–25,000). They offer a great parade and fireworks, special stage shows and complimentary cookies and hot chocolate. It "snows" on Main Street U.S.A. All major attractions are open; lines are short. For the best time arrive before 6 p.m. and see the less-crowded second parade. The least-crowded parties are those before Thanksgiving; those on December Fridays and Saturdays sell out early. Info and tickets ($62 adults; $56 children 3–9, bought in advance; $6 more day of party) at 407-934-7639. Other Christmas events are in the section Walt Disney World A–Z.

Walt Disney World A–Z

Airports. Orlando has two main commercial airports. Most U.S. airlines fly into the huge Orlando International Airport, while some international carriers use the smaller Orlando Sanford International airport.

Orlando International. Located 19 miles east of Disney World, Orlando International is among Florida's busiest airports, handling an average of 80,000 passengers a day. Its hub-and-spoke layout features a large central "landside" terminal that's connected by elevated trains to four remote "airside" concourses. The terminal is divided into two sides ("A" and "B") and has two lobbies, one with a Hyatt Regency hotel on its upper floors, the other with a Chili's Too restaurant.

The airport's confusing IATA code— "MCO"—refers to its former life as McCoy Air Force Base, a Strategic Air Command installation that closed in 1976. During the Cuban Missile Crisis of October, 1962, McCoy was the primary forward operating base for U-2 reconnaissance aircraft. Today's terminal was built in 1981; the last gate opened in 2000 (One Airport Blvd., Orlando, 32827; 407-825-2001; orlandoairports.net).

Chapel: Open to all faiths, the airport chapel is in the terminal just past the west security checkpoint (Gates 1–59). Any passenger with a boarding pass is welcome. Catholic mass is Sundays at 8:15 a.m. and noon.

Checking in: The airport's governing body, the Greater Orlando Aviation Authority, advises passengers to arrive two hours before a domestic departure; three hours for an international flight.

Child ID cards: In general children under age 18 are not required to have photo identification for domestic flights. Airlines have more specific requirements.

Flight arrivals: Information is available at 407-825-8463 and on the airport's home page (orlandoairports.net).

Highway tolls: Two toll booths sit between Walt Disney World and the airport; each requires a toll of $1.25, in each direction.

No credit cards are accepted. Vehicles enrolled in Florida's E-PASS/SunPass program are charged automatically and therefore don't have to stop.

Internet access: Free Wi-Fi is available in all public airport areas. Several kiosks offer wired connections. Dial-up service is offered in pay phones via RJ-11 jacks.

Lost and found: The lost and found office (8a–9p, 407-825-2111) is located in Terminal B, across from the food court.

Operating hours: The airport is open 24 hours a day. Each airline within it sets its own hours of operation.

Parking: Daily rates range from $10 to $25. Parking lots accept cash, major credit cards and Florida's E-PASS/SunPass transponders. Valet parking services can include auto detailing. Details at orlando-airports.net/ops/parking.

Rental cars: Most car rental companies are located in a parking garage adjacent to the terminal. Rental counters are on both sides of the terminal on the Ground Transportation level.

See also **Rental Cars** under **Transportation.**

Directions to Disney World: The simplest route (25 min): Take the airport's South Exit road 4 miles to Florida 417 (a toll road), go west 13 miles to Osceola Parkway (Exit 3), then west again 2 miles.

Transportation to Disney: Travelers can get to Disney World by taxi ($55–$65, Mears Yellow Cab: 407-422-2222), 4-person town car ($80–$90, Mears: 407-423-5566), 8-person van ($80–$90, Mears: 407-423-5566) or shuttle bus ($20 per adult, Mears: 407-423-5566). Guests staying at Disney resorts can use Disney's free Magical Express bus system.

See also **Magical Express, Transportation.**

Orlando Sanford International. Located 48 miles northeast of Walt Disney World, this smaller airport (IATA code "SFB") serves 5,000 passengers a day. It was created as a Naval Air Station during World War II (1200 Red Cleveland Blvd., Sanford 32773; 407-585-4000; orlandosanfordairport.com).

Major airlines: Primarily British carriers, airlines include Allegiant (702-505-8888), Direct Air (877-432-3473), Icelandair

Facing page: A "Cursed Pirate" admires his look at The Pirates League makeover salon

The Orlando International Airport is located 19 miles from Walt Disney World. The third-largest airport in the United States, the facility covers 23 square miles.

(800-223-5500), Monarch (44-0-1582-398-036), Thomas Cook (44-0-870-750-0512) and Thomson (44-0-871-231-4691).

Directions to Disney World: The simplest route (50 min): Take the airport's exit road to Florida 417 (a toll road), go south 16 miles to Florida 408, continue west 8 miles to Interstate 4, then south 16 miles.

Alcohol. Visitors are not allowed to bring alcoholic beverages into any Disney World theme or water park, though guests of legal age can carry open containers of purchased alcoholic drinks at any park that sells them. There are no liquor stores on Disney property although Disney hotels sell beer, wine and liquor, as do all theme and water parks except Magic Kingdom. It is illegal to carry open containers of alcohol in a car or public area in Central Florida. The legal age to purchase and consume alcohol in Florida is 21.

AA meetings. Local meetings of Alcoholics Anonymous are held daily at the Royal Plaza Hotel near Downtown Disney (3p Mon–Sat, 10a Sun; 1905 Hotel Plaza Blvd., 32830; 407-828-2828). Friends of Bill W. Orlando (friendsofbillworlando.org) meets in a small room between the hotel's restaurant and Giraffe Lounge and provides rides for those without transportation from anywhere in the Disney World area. Catering to travelers, the group has had over 10,000 visitors since it formed in 1992. Disney does not sponsor the meetings.

Birthdays. Walt Disney World offers many ways to help celebrate a birthday.

Balloons. At Disney resort hotels, concierge staff can often have balloons delivered to a room or a hotel birthday meal.

Buttons. Available at no charge from theme-park Guest Relations offices, Happy Birthday buttons cue Disney cast members to recognize the celebrants.

Cakes. All Disney table-service restaurants except Victoria & Albert's offer 6-inch birthday cakes ($21, chocolate or vanilla, no notice required, larger cakes avail.). Guests who use Disney's Cake Hotline (407-827-2253, requires 48 hrs. notice) choose the filling, icing and personalized decorations. Those staying at Disney hotels can order cakes through room service or guest services.

Cruises. Fireworks cruises are available to view Magic Kingdom's Wishes display or Epcot's IllumiNations. One-hour pontoon-boat trips include snacks and drinks ($275 for up to 8 people on 21-foot boat; $325 for up to 10 people on 25-foot boat. $25 additional for decorative banner and balloons. Cakes available through Disney's Cake Hotline (see details above). Reservations available 180 days in advance at 407-939-2329; 2-day cancellation policy.

Flowers and gift baskets. Adult and child styles are available at Disney Floral & Gifts (407-827-3505, disneyflorist.com).

Gifts. Personalized presents can be delivered throughout the Walt Disney World property. Contact Disney Dream Makers at 407-939-4438 or disneyworld.com.

Goodie bags. Standard bags contain a party hat, game, coloring book and crayons; deluxe bags add a magnet activity set and Mickey-shaped straw. Order at 407-939-3463.

Goofy telephone call. Goofy will call your Disney hotel room with a free birthday greeting. To arrange it call 407-824-2222.

Parties. Four Walt Disney World locations offer organized celebrations:

Located in both terminal lobbies of the Orlando International Airport, two Disney stores stock popular Walt Disney World merchandise. The shops also sell theme-park tickets and will ship any item bought on Disney property.

Blizzard Beach: A 90-minute party on the water park's Lottawatta Lodge deck includes pizza, drinks and cake. Park admission required ($16 per person, min 5 guests, max 30 guests. 407-560-3400).

Goofy's Candy Co.: A private room at this Downtown Disney shop is the setting for a 90-minute birthday party with balloons, favors, hot dogs or pizza, ice cream, drinks and a cake as well as invitations and thank-you notes. The birthday child gets extra goodies. Goofy and Cinderella themes available. ($25 per person, 12–15 guests, ages 3 and up. Reservations available 90 days in advance at 407-939-2329).

Neverland Club: This Peter Pan-themed childcare center at the Polynesian Resort offers a two-hour party with pizza, drinks, cake and an activity such as a craft project or face painting. Various themes available ($34 per child, min 10 guests, weekends only. Reservations available 90 days in advance at 407-939-2329). A premium party adds two half-hour appearances by a Disney character ($69 per child, reservations must be made a week early, $400 additional for a second character).

Winter Summerland: A two-hour party at this miniature golf course includes a round of golf, pizza, drinks, cake and favors ($20 per person, 10–40 guests. Reservations need to be made at least a week early at 407-939-7529).

Room decorations. Disney resort guests can have their rooms decorated in personalized birthday themes. Contact Disney Dream Makers at 407-939-4438.

Characters. Although fantasy-free adults may not think so, the Disney walk-around

Orlando International airlines

Nearly three dozen airlines serve the Orlando International Airport. Most have toll-free telephone numbers:

Aer Lingus	800	474-7424
AeroMexico	800	237-6639
Air Canada	800	247-2262
Air Jamaica	800	523-5585
Air Transat	877	872-6728
AirTran	800	247-8726
Alaska Airlines	800	252-7522
Allegiant	702	505-8888
American Airlines	800	433-7300
Bahamas Air	800	222-4262
British Airways	800	247-9297
Continental Airlines	800	525-0280
Copa Airlines	800	359-2672
Delta	800	221-1212
Frontier	800	432-1359
GOL	55 11	5504-4410
Interjet	866	285-9525
JetBlue Airways	800	538-2583
Lufthansa	800	645-3880
Martinair	800	627-8462
Mexicana	800	531-7921
MiamiAir International	305	871-3300
Midwest Airlines	800	452-2022
Southwest Airlines	800	435-9792
Spirit Airlines	800	772-7117
Sun Country Airlines	800	359-6786
SunWing	800	761-1711
TACA Airlines	800	400-8222
TAM Airlines	888	235-9826
United Airlines	800	241-6522
U.S. Airways	800	428-4322
Virgin America	877	359-8474
Virgin Atlantic	800	862-8621
Volaris	866	988-3527
West Jet	800	538-5696

© Disney

Cinderella signs an autograph for a young fan at Epcot. Disney characters greet guests daily throughout all four theme parks. Autograph books are sold at shops throughout Walt Disney World, including at Disney-owned resort hotels.

characters are *real* to many visitors, especially children—that's not a sweaty young woman in a fur suit, *that's Pluto!!!* Dozens of Disney stars appear in shows and parades and personally greet guests at theme parks, water parks and resort hotels.

Disney has two types of walk-around characters, "face" and "fur." The costume of a face character, such as Cinderella, shows the actual face of the performer, who can talk and interact fully with guests. Fur characters, such as Mickey Mouse, have a fully costumed head and don't speak. They interact with guests purely through mime.

Meet-and-greet lines. Most Disney characters pose for photos and, in most cases, sign autographs at designated locations, many of which draw long lines. Guests with autograph books should bring a pen or, better, a Sharpie marker. Some characters don't sign because of costume limitations. It's fine to hug, kiss or pat characters, but not to give them gifts. A Disney PhotoPass photographer is often on hand, although guests are welcome to take photos themselves.

Character meals. A handful of Disney buffet and table-service restaurants offer "character meals," in which an assortment of characters come up to each table to greet guests as they eat. Each theme park has at least one character-meal restaurant, as do many Disney resort hotels.

How to find a character. Characters most often appear at attractions that relate to them. For example, French princess Belle of "Beauty and the Beast" can be found at Epcot's France pavilion. If you can't find a particular character, most cast members can easily track down that star's schedule.

See also **Character Guide.**

How to help your child interact. Though face characters rarely intimidate children, the fur folks, with their cartoonishly large heads, sometimes do. To help your child feel comfortable, talk with her beforehand so she knows what to expect. For meet-and-greet lines, buy her an autograph book to give her something to focus on besides the face-to-fur encounter. When it's her turn don't push her; the characters are patient and are trained to be sweet. Approach a character from the front. Fur characters in particular often cannot see guests standing behind or beside them.

Children. As you might guess, many special services are available for Walt Disney World guests with children.

Babysitters. Disney works with two in-room childcare providers. Kids Nite Out (800-696-8105, 407-828-0920, kidsniteout.com) supplies babysitting and childcare for kids ages 6 weeks to 12 years, including those with special needs. Caregivers bring age-appropriate toys, activities, books, games and arts and crafts. Rates start at $16 per hour with a 4-hour minimum, plus a $10 transportation fee. All About Kids (800-728-6506, 407-812-9300, all-about-kids.com) offers child-sitting services; rates start at $13 per hour with a 4-hour minimum, plus a $12 transportation fee.

Caricatures. Caricaturists offer their services in all theme and water parks, at most Disney-owned hotels and at Downtown Disney. Finished portraits come with storage tubes ($15–$90, based on number of people and whether black-and-white or color).

Childcare centers. Five Disney-owned hotels include an evening childcare center:

© Starwood Hotels/Disney

Pluto greets guests during a character meal at the Garden Grove restaurant at the Walt Disney World Swan. Each Disney theme park has at least one character-meal restaurant, as do many resort hotels.

Disney's Animal Kingdom Lodge, Beach Club, Grand Floridian, Polynesian and Wilderness Lodge. Each has a secure room staffed by adults and stocked with arts and crafts, books, games, toys and videos ($11.50 per hr per child, 2-hr min, includes dinner 6–8p. Children must be toilet trained, no pull-ups, 4–12 years old. 4p [sometimes 4:30p] to mid. 407-939-3463. Reservations required). The Walt Disney World Dolphin also has a childcare center, Camp Dolphin ($10 per hr per child, 2-hr min, includes dinner 6:30–7:30p. Ages 4–12, must be toilet trained, no pull-ups. 5:30p–mid. 407-934-4241. Reservations req).

Child swap. This complimentary, unpublicized service allows two parents to enjoy a ride even if they have a child who can't (or doesn't want to) ride who they don't want to leave unattended. To use it, parents tell a cast member at the ride's entrance of their situation, then one parent gets in line while the other waits with the child and gets a FastPass to ride later. The guest's park ticket is not used to get the FastPass, so the ability to get other FastPasses is not affected. If the attraction does not offer FastPasses the whole family waits in line once, with the child. One parent rides while the other stays with the child. When the first parent returns, the waiting spouse rides immediately.

Equipment rentals. Outside companies below deliver to hotels throughout Walt Disney World and the surrounding area.

Cribs and rollaway beds: Disney resorts offer free use of Pack 'n Play Playard cribs; guests may request one when making a reservation. Rollaway beds typically incur an extra fee ($20–$30). Standard crib rentals are available at Baby's Away (407-334-0232, 888-376-0084, babysaway.

Height minimums

Magic Kingdom

Big Thunder Mountain Railroad	40 in.
Space Mountain	44 in.
Splash Mountain	40 in.
Stitch's Great Escape	40 in.
Tomorrowland Speedway	
To ride alone	54 in.
To ride as a passenger	32 in.

Epcot

Mission Space	44 in.
Soarin'	40 in.
Sum of All Thrills (Innoventions)	48 in.
Test Track	40 in.

Disney's Hollywood Studios

Rock 'n' Roller Coaster	48 in.
Star Tours	40 in.
The Twilight Zone Tower of Terror	40 in.

Disney's Animal Kingdom

Dinosaur	40 in.
Expedition Everest	44 in.
Kali River Rapids	38 in.
Primeval Whirl	48 in.

Blizzard Beach

Chairlift	32 in.
Downhill Double Dipper	48 in.
Slush Gusher	48 in.
Summit Plummet	48 in.

Typhoon Lagoon

Crush 'n' Gusher	48 in.
Humunga Kowabunga	48 in.

DisneyQuest

Buzz Lightyear's AstroBlaster	51 in.
CyberSpace Mountain	51 in.
Mighty Ducks Pinball Slam	48 in.
Pirates of the Caribbean: Battle for Buccaneer Gold	35 in.

© Disney

Young girls are transformed into princesses at the Bibbidi Bobbidi Boutique, a fantasy makeover salon. One boutique is in Magic Kingdom's Cinderella Castle; another is inside Downtown Disney's World of Disney store.

com) and All About Kids (800-728-6506, 407-812-9300, all-about-kids.com).

Strollers: Single and double strollers can be rented just inside the entrance at all Disney theme parks (singles $15/day, $13/day length of stay; doubles $31/day, $27 length of stay). Single strollers are available at Downtown Disney ($15/day, $100 refundable deposit). For multiple-day rentals, a length-of-stay ticket allows guests to make a one-time payment for as many days as needed (single strollers $13/day, doubles $27/day); guests show their ticket each day at the rental location and are expedited through the queue. Note: Disney's molded-plastic strollers are not designed for infants. To rent infant strollers try Orlando Stroller Rentals (800-281-0884; orlandostrollerrentals.com), Baby's Away or All About Kids (see above).

Other equipment: Baby's Away and All About Kids (see above) rent car seats, high chairs, playpens and the like. Most local car-rental companies lease infant or child safety seats for a minimal charge (per day $2–$10) with an advance reservation. See also **Rental Cars** under **Transportation**.

Face painting. Children can get their faces painted ($10–$15) at all Disney World theme parks, Downtown Disney and on the boardwalk at Disney's BoardWalk Resort. Theme-park stands offer designs themed to their particular areas—animal styles are available at Disney's Animal Kingdom, Star Wars faces at Disney's Hollywood Studios.

Infant care. Diaper-changing stations are in men's and women's restrooms throughout Disney World. Moms can nurse babies anywhere on Disney property without hassle. Each theme park also has a Baby Care Center, which provides changing rooms, nursing areas, a microwave and a playroom, as well as diapers, formula, pacifiers and over-the-counter medications for sale.

Lost children. If a child becomes lost, parents should report it to Guest Relations or any Disney cast member; children should tell a cast member if they become separated from their family. Upon arrival at a park, some parents introduce their children to a cast member and point out the worker's distinctive name tag, and use a permanent marker to write their cell-phone number on the child's arm. Lost children in a theme park are usually taken to its Baby Care Center.

Makeover salons. Disney offers two types of fantasy makeover salons, one focused on princesses, the other pirates.

Bibbidi Bobbidi Boutique: Little girls turn into princesses and pop stars at this female-focused salon. Three packages are available: Coach ($50, hairstyle and shimmering makeup), Crown ($55, adds nails) and Castle ($190, adds costume and photo package). Photo packages can be bought separately. A Cool Dude boys package ($8) has hair gel and confetti. (Ages 3 and up. Reservations up to 180 days in advance, 407-939-7895. At Magic Kingdom inside Cinderella Castle; Downtown Disney Marketplace at World of Disney store.)

Pirates League: Makeover salon transforms adults and children into swashbucklers. Packages ($30) include a choice of five facial effects, reversible bandana, earring and eye patch, sword, temporary tattoo, pirate coin necklace, personalized pirate oath and official pirate name. Costumes, headwear and photo packages also available. Participants can join a daily

Scary moments in Disney attractions

Some Disney attractions have frightening elements or unusual movement which might be too intense for children.

Magic Kingdom

Astro Orbiter: Height and steep angle bother some children, even some adults.
Big Thunder Mountain Railroad: Jerky, violent turns toss you around in your seat; many sharp hills and sudden dips.
The Enchanted Tiki Room—Under New Management: A threatening goddess lingers, thunderstorm effects.
The Haunted Mansion: Dark, ominous atmosphere; some screams, scary ghosts.
Jungle Cruise: A trip through a dark temple gets close to some unrealistic snakes.
Mad Tea Party: Spinning, jerky motion can cause motion sickness.
The Many Adventures of Winnie the Pooh: Some sudden mild effects; nightmare scene can disorient toddlers.
Mickey's PhilharMagic: Sudden images, briefly totally dark.
Pirates of the Caribbean: Short, dark drop; realistic cannon battle; simulated fire.
Snow White's Scary Adventures: Scares many young children; dark, threatening scenes, some with loud screams. To many toddlers the scariest ride at Disney.
Space Mountain: Dark drops and turns, coaster doesn't go upside down.
Splash Mountain: A small drop is completely dark; big drop can scare adults.
Stitch's Great Escape: Restrictive shoulder harnesses, dark periods.
Tom Sawyer Island: Young children can get temporarily lost in cave's side niches.
Wishes: Loud explosions.

Epcot

Ellen's Energy Adventure: The Big Bang portrayal is loud, dark.
Captain EO: Some children will be scared by the movements of the seating area or by the freakish villain.
IllumiNations: Loud bright explosions, fire can scare toddlers, some preschoolers.
Journey Into Imagination... with Figment: A dark room has the loud clamor of an oncoming train; blast of air emits odor of a skunk; the last scene has a sudden flash.
Maelstrom: Often dark, some scary faces. Film has two loud, jolting flashes.

Mission Space: "Orange" version is intense, can cause disorientation, headaches, nausea, worse. Take posted warnings seriously: those with health issues or head colds should pass.
Soarin': Can be troubling for some who fear heights.
Test Track: Can be intense for those scared by speed or for children who believe they really will crash into a wall.

Disney's Hollywood Studios

Beauty and the Beast—Live on Stage: Ominous "Mob Song" scene. Gaston stabs the Beast, wound isn't visible.
Fantasmic: Loud noises, bright flashes, fire, scary villains may frighten small children.
The Great Movie Ride: Intense for preschoolers. "Alien" creature moves toward you from the ceiling, then appears suddenly out of the right wall. The Wicked Witch looks real.
Rock 'n' Roller Coaster Starring Aerosmith: Anticipating the launch scares even adults. Total darkness. Coaster goes upside down.
Star Tours: Vehicle's unpredictable sways and dives can cause motion sickness.
Studio Backlot Tour: Flames, simulated disasters may frighten young children.
The Twilight Zone Tower of Terror: Sudden, smooth drops and ascents, ominous atmosphere, intense mind games.
Voyage of the Little Mermaid: Ursula's scary appearance and threatening voice cause some toddlers to cry.

Disney's Animal Kingdom

Dinosaur: Dark, loud, threatening, intense with pursuing dinosaurs; can be terrifying for young children.
Expedition Everest: The lift rises high over the ground; coaster travels backwards in darkness 10 sec.; one big turning drop.
It's Tough To Be a Bug: Dark, intense for preschoolers. Fog, cartoonish menacing bugs. Sadistic tone.
Kali River Rapids: Bumpy; one steep drop.
Kilimanjaro Safaris: Queue video shows slaughtered animals, finale of ride has audible gunshots.
Primeval Whirl: One steep drop; jerky spinning can seriously affect those with inner-ear issues.

© Disney

Magic Kingdom's Cinderella Castle appears to be draped in icicles during the Christmas season. Each evening at twilight, the Fairy Godmother waves her wand to turn on 200,000 tiny "dreamlights."

Adventureland Pirate Parade. Ages 3 and up. At exit of Pirates of the Caribbean, Magic Kingdom. Reservations up to 180 days in advance at 407-939-2739.

Reduced rates. Disney offers reduced prices for children ages 3 to 9 for park tickets, food and dining plans and paid-recreation options. Older children are charged adult rates. Those younger than age 3 are admitted free into Disney theme and water parks.

See also **Disney Dining Plan, Tickets** and the chapter **Activities.**

Restaurants. Most Disney restaurants offer kids' menus and high chairs. Only one excludes children: Victoria & Albert's at the Grand Floridian. Restaurants outside Disney are generally accepting of children, though many fancy spots do not offer kids' menus.

Silhouettes. Paper artists cut out profiles of children ($8 plus optional frame) at Magic Kingdom (on Main Street U.S.A. and in Liberty Square), Epcot (France pavilion) and at Downtown Disney (Marketplace).

Christmas. Even the most stubborn Scrooge will warm up to Disney in November and December. Each theme park offers special entertainment, and holiday decor is often so elaborate it seems to be everywhere.

Magic Kingdom. The mood is most contagious at Disney World's signature park, which focuses its decor on Main Street U.S.A. Rows of thick garlands hang over it, poinsettias hang from its lampposts, some second-story windows display Menorahs. Inside stores, garland embellishments match merchandise themes. A 65-foot Christmas tree stands in Town Square, a spruce so thoroughly decorated most guests don't notice that it's artificial. A toy train circles its base.

At night, Cinderella Castle looks draped in icicles thanks to a transparent net of 200,000 tiny white lights.

Celebrate the Season: ★★★★ ✓ Outdoor stage show Mickey and Minnie Mouse, Donald Duck, Chip 'n Dale, Pluto, Goofy. 20 min. Cinderella Castle forecourt. Remember when your neighbors got together for holiday sing-a-longs? When carolers came to your door? When your town held its Santa Claus parade? No? Well Disney does, and brings that spirit back with a campy musical revue of hoofing horses, dancing reindeer and some very merry elves. Nighttime shows are best, as spotlights add a theatrical flair.

Cinderella's Holiday Wish: ★★★ Outdoor stage show Cinderella, Fairy Godmother, Mickey Mouse. 20 min. Cinderella Castle forecourt. 5:45p. When Cinderella wants her home to sparkle for the holidays, the Fairy Godmother waves her wand to light it up.

Holiday Wishes: ★★★★★ ✓ Fireworks 15 min. Synced to Christmas music, fireworks form holiday shapes while projected images decorate Cinderella Castle in this memorable extravaganza. During "O Christmas Tree" the castle becomes an abstract Christmas tree: a star explodes above it while flood lights turn it green. The best viewing spot is on Main Street U.S.A. on the bridge to the castle hub. Arrive 15 minutes early for a good spot.

Mickey's Once Upon a Christmastime Parade: ★★★★★ ✓ Santa Claus parade 15 min. Starts in Frontierland, to Liberty Square, down Main Street U.S.A. This lively procession includes horse-drawn sleighs; marching toy soldiers; dancing reindeer, snowflakes and gingerbread men; elves; plenty of Disney characters; and, of course, Mr. Santa.

Toy soldiers from Disney's 1961 movie "Babes in Toyland" come to life in Magic Kingdom's Once Upon a Christmastime Parade. The procession also includes dancing gingerbread men, prancing reindeer, horse-drawn sleighs and Santa Claus.

Good seats get taken about 45 minutes ahead of time.

A Totally Tomorrowland Christmas: ★★★ **Outdoor stage show** Stitch, Buzz Lightyear, Mike Wazowski. Tomorrowland Stage. A *fer-sure* live singer hosts this comedic musical revue, in which the characters discover the true meaning of the season. Giant-eyeball Mike Wazowski plays the role of Rudolph.

Epcot. Decorations include a huge holiday tree in World Showcase Plaza trimmed in a world motif and trees, wreaths and garlands in the courtyard of the Germany pavilion (lovely at night), with the nearby miniature train village with its own decorations and tree lot. Inside American Adventure's Liberty Inn fast-food restaurant, a gingerbread house sells cider and hot chocolate.

Holidays Around the World Storytellers: ★★★★★ ✔ **Cultural storytellers** 20 min. World Showcase pavilions. Hourly noon–dusk. Sharing the seasonal legends and traditions of cultures from throughout the world, these actors perform to small crowds outside each World Showcase pavilion. *Canada*—Comic lumberjack Nowell describes Boxing Day, the Inuit's impish Nalyuks and the legend of "people who come to homes dressed in strange outfits. We call them... relatives!" *United Kingdom*—Father Christmas tells how holiday cards and decorating with holly and mistletoe began in his countries. *France*—Pére Noël comically explains how children leave shoes on their doorsteps for him to put presents in. *Morocco*—A drummer describes the Festival of Ashura, which gives presents to children who behave well. *Japan*—A vendor explains Daruma dolls, pupil-free charms that children

paint eyes on as they make wishes. *The American Adventure*—One storyteller explains Hanukkah, another Kwanzaa. *Italy*—Good witch La Befana, who slides down chimneys to leave treats, explains why she travels on the anniversary of the day the Three Kings came to Bethlehem. *Germany*—St. Nicholas fills you in about the first Christmas tree and Nutcracker as well as the Christmas pickle, a hidden tree ornament that rewards its finder with an extra present. *China*—The Monkey King spins a tale of how he defeated a monster and found a magic stick. *Norway*—Farm girl Sigrid is sure Gnome Julenissen doesn't exist, though you can see him easily. The strangest, and most fun, Holiday Storyteller skit. *Mexico*—The Three Kings explain the customs of Posada.

Candlelight Processional: ★★★★ **Religious pageant** 60 min. Three times nightly. America Gardens amphitheater, American Adventure pavilion. This inspirational show recounts the birth of Jesus with a 50-piece orchestra, 400 singers and a celebrity narrator. Though free with park admission, the show is so popular that on peak evenings the only guaranteed way to see it is to buy a Candlelight Processional Dinner Package (407-939-3463), uses two Disney Dining Plan credits), which includes dinner at an Epcot restaurant. Otherwise you wait in line for up to two hours, with no guarantee of admission (hence, only four stars).

Disney's Hollywood Studios. Straight out of a 1940s holiday musical, silver strands form garlands above Hollywood Boulevard while red and silver stars hang from Sunset Boulevard lampposts; out front is a period-perfect 65-foot-tall tree.

La Befana

Father Noel

The Monkey King

Each storefront window, balcony and brownstone along the Streets of America is decorated to reflect the life of its tenant. One celebrates Hanukkah. Oversized bulbs and a giant Santa decorate other buildings. At night thousands of lights cover the facades in the **Osborne Family Spectacle of Dancing Lights.** Hanging from the rooftops in huge nets, they flash rhythmically to holiday tunes. Displays above include a spinning carousel and rotating globe. Rope-light angels fly over a town square; others pray to a creche. Snow-like soap bubbles spray from overhead spouts. The spectacle once graced the home of Little Rock, Ark., businessman Jennings Osborne.

Citizens of Hollywood: ★★★★★ ✓ **Street performers** 20 min. Hollywood Blvd, Sunset Blvd. Show times at Guest Relations. Portraying directors, starlets, script girls and wanna-bes, these improvisational actors perform holiday street skits with audience participation. As the Hollywood Glee Club, they sing the lyrics to "Jingle Bells" to the music of "Joy to the World."

Disney's Animal Kingdom. Entrance areas and hub walkways display natural decorations. A 65-foot-tall tree is adorned with primitive metal and wood animals; gift-shop garlands are filled with berries, flowers, grain stalks and straw. At Dinoland U.S.A., the tongue-in-cheek Dino-Rama carnival is trimmed with shredded-plastic trees, candy canes and a huge cheesy snowman. The Dinosaur Treasures gift shop has plastic Santas, Santa heads and a tree with pink flamingos and Styrofoam snowmen. Each tree at Camp Minnie-Mickey belongs, on close inspection, to a Disney character. The ornaments on Lilo's tree include her handmade doll and Elvis records.

Ambient music features flute-and-drum traditionals such as "Silent Night" in the entrance area, and obscure ditties such as Spike Jones' 1956 "My Birthday Comes on Christmas" and Augie Rios' 1958 "¿Donde Esta Santa Claus?" at Dinoland U.S.A.

Mickey's Jingle Jungle Parade: ★★★★ ✓ **Character parade** 15 min. Circles Discovery Island. Starts, exits in Africa. Choose a viewing spot 30 min early to get a shady seat. A reworking of the theme park's regular safari-themed Mickey's Jammin' Jungle Parade, this 12-minute procession finds Mickey Mouse and Rafiki (from 1994's "The Lion King") leading Minnie Mouse, Donald Duck and Goofy in an SUV parade that's headed out for a rustic holiday adventure. You can smell the chocolate when candy-making Minnie passes by in her truck; Donald's vehicle will spray you with artificial snow. Giant mechanical puppets include a partridge in a pear tree. Selected at random each day, up to 25 guests ride in the parade in giant rickshaws and open-top trailers.

Campfire Carolers: ★★★★ ✓ **A cappella singing group** 20 min. Camp Minnie-Mickey These youthful singers aren't above cracking a few jokes as they belt out holiday pop tunes. When one sings that she wants an "opotamus" for Christmas, the others correct her. "You must mean a hippopotamus!" "No, he doesn't have to be very cool." Crowds are small; you'll sit, or stand, just a few feet from the performers.

Disney resort hotels. All Disney-owned lodging complexes are decorated for the

The Osborne Family Spectacle of Dancing Lights sparkle on New York Street in Disney's Hollywood Studios. Towering above are a spinning carousel, giant rotating globe and other animated displays.

holidays. The largest Christmas trees are at the Contemporary (75 feet tall, with 77,000 lights), Wilderness Lodge (50 feet, 52,000 lights) and Grand Floridian (45 feet, 45,000 lights). Many resorts have confectionery displays; a 16-foot-tall gingerbread house sits in the Grand Floridian lobby. Miniature villages stand at Animal Kingdom Lodge and the Contemporary Resort, there's a Santa's workshop at the BoardWalk Resort, a sugary mountain at the Yacht Club and a life-size candy carousel at Disney's Beach Club.

Avoiding the holiday crush. The week between Christmas and New Year's is Disney World's most crowded time of the year. Not only does Magic Kingdom often close around lunchtime (after reaching its 80,000-person capacity), the throng includes many people who appear to have IQs somewhere south of Goofy's. Aimlessly wandering the park, they fill walkways, clog rides and crowd shops and restaurants. We've even seen guests drunk.

If you must visit Magic Kingdom during this week, arrive at the park by 7:30 a.m. Use the morning to see most attractions and to collect Fastpasses for the major attractions. See the noon parade, then use your Fastpasses—you should have about 3 per person by then. After dark see the castle show and Holiday Wishes.

The week *before* Christmas is, overall, a much better time to visit; as all the holiday events are happening but the monster crowd hasn't arrived yet.

See also **Calendar.**

On tape with Regis and Kelly. Though ABC-TV implies that it airs the Walt Disney World Christmas parade live on Christmas Day, the event is taped the first weekend in December. Usually hosted by Regis Philbin

and Kelly Ripa, the production fills Magic Kingdom's Main Street U.S.A. and the Cinderella Castle stage with cameras, crews and celebrities for hours. Want to be on camera? Come early, wear festive clothes without advertising slogans and look happy. Special access may be available at www.lightshiptv.com.

Fun facts. Walt Disney World displays more than 1,500 Christmas trees during the holiday season, as well as 15 miles of garland and 170 miles of ribbon. Each of Disney World's signature theme-park trees weighs at least 28,000 pounds.

Convention attendees. Convention and conference centers at the Walt Disney World Swan and Dolphin and four Disney hotels—the BoardWalk, Contemporary, Coronado Springs, Grand Floridian and the Yacht and Beach Club—draw many business guests. At the Disney hotels, discounted room rates can be applied to additional days. Other attendee discounts include savings on golf (20 percent off greens fees; free club rental, range balls, transportation) and park tickets.

Discounted park tickets. Attendees of nearly any meeting or convention in Central Florida can buy Meeting/Convention theme-park passes for themselves, friends and families. The Disney Dining Plan is not available as an option. These special passes are sold at disneyconventionears.com or at 407-939-4686 option 3, but not at theme parks.

After 2 p.m. ticket: Admits one adult or child to one theme park from 2 p.m. until park closing. Approximately $18 cheaper than a regular 1-day, 1-park ticket.

After 4 p.m. tickets: Admits one adult or child to one Disney theme park from 4

Four Disney resort hotels have business facilities, such as the Disney's Yacht Club Conference Center (left). Business guests often get discounted room rates, special theme-park-ticket deals and savings on golf.

p.m. until park closing. Approximately $30 cheaper than a normal 1-day, 1-park ticket. **Multi-day tickets:** For theme-park visits before or after a meeting or convention; first use must be within seven days of the meeting or convention. Savings depend on number of days purchased. Ticket must be purchased at least 24 hours in advance.

More information is on the web sites disneymeetings.com, disneyconventionears.com and swandolphinmeetings.com, or call 321-939-7129 for Disney facilities, 407-934-4000 for the Swan and Dolphin.

Crowd patterns. In general Walt Disney World's theme parks are the most crowded whenever schools in the United States are not in session. During peak periods the wait times at major attractions can exceed three hours, popular Fastpasses run out early in the day and restaurants are booked months in advance. The hotter the weather, the more crowded the water parks.

Least crowded times of year: The day after Labor Day (the slowest day of the year) until Epcot's Food & Wine Festival and mid-January through the first week in February.

Most crowded times of year: The week between Christmas Day through New Year's Day and Independence Day weekend; also the Spring Break period (typically from the third week of March through the third week of April), holiday weekends, Presidents' week, Marathon Weekend.

Least crowded time of day: First two hours of the day; last hour of the evening.

Most crowded time of day: Afternoons.

Least crowded day of week: Monday.

Most crowded days: Weekends, followed by Thursday and Friday.

Disability services. Disney offers a variety services for guests with hearing, mobility, visual or other disabilities. Many employ Disney's Handheld Device, a wireless gadget available on a daily, park-specific basis from Guest Relations offices for a $25 deposit.

Hearing services. Disney offers many services for the hearing impaired:

Assistive listening: Disney's Handheld Device amplifies the audio at select stationary attractions.

Handheld captioning: The Device displays captions at narrated moving attractions.

Closed captioning: The Device turns on captions on video monitors in some pre-show areas. Single-button activators are also available.

Reflective captioning: At many theatrical attractions, cast members can supply handheld acrylic panels that reflect captions from an LED display on a back wall

Sign language: Live interpreters typically appear at live shows at Magic Kingdom (Mondays, Thursdays), Epcot (Tuesdays, Fridays) Disney's Hollywood Studios (Sundays, Wednesdays) and Disney's Animal Kingdom (Saturdays). With 14 days notice guests can request interpretation at other events including the Hoop-Dee-Doo Revue and Spirit of Aloha dinner shows. For a schedule or to request a show be interpreted call 407-824-4321 (voice), 407-827-5141 (TTY). Cast members with sign language abilities wear identifying pins.

TTY telephones: Pay phones with amplified handsets and Text Typewriters are located throughout Walt Disney World.

Guest Assistance Packet: Available at many attractions, this notebook contains a script, flashlight, pen and paper. Cast

A quarter-million square feet of meeting and exhibit space is available at the Walt Disney World Swan and Dolphin Resort, Walt Disney World's largest convention facility. The Dolphin's Atlantic Hall (right) consumes 60,000 square feet.

members supply them on request and write on the pads to communicate with guests who can't hear well.

Mobility services. Disney rents wheelchairs and four-wheel electric scooters (called "Electric Convenience Vehicles," or ECVs). Both are available on a first-come, first-serve, same-day basis (no reservations are accepted) and neither requires any proof of need. Disney's wheelchairs and ECVs may not be transferred from park to park, but the deposit ticket from a first rental will let a guest rent one on the same day at another park at no extra charge if one is available.

Wheelchairs: All Disney theme parks rent wheelchairs ($12/day). Complimentary chairs are available for guests to travel between parking lots and rental locations. Wheelchairs are also available at Disney hotels ($315 deposit). At ESPN Wide World of Sports complimentary wheelchairs are available at the entrance turnstiles.

Electric Convenience Vehicles: Arrive early to rent an ECV ($50/day, $20 deposit), especially at Magic Kingdom. The scooters are very popular with both disabled as well as obese guests.

Off-property companies: The best way to guarantee the use of a chair or ECV throughout a visit is to reserve one through a local rental company. These include Apria Health Care (407-291-2229, 800-338-1640; apria.com), Care Medical Equipment (407-856-2273, 800-741-2282; caremedicalequipment.com), Turner Drugs (407-828-8125; turnerdrug.com) or Walker Mobility (407-518-6000, 800-726-6837; walkermobility.com).

Transferring: Certain attractions require guests to transfer from wheelchairs or

ECVs to a ride vehicle. Disney cast members are not allowed to lift guests.

Special treatment: Guests in wheelchairs and ECVs and their parties may avoid long waiting lines, as they often enter attractions through alternate entrances (usually exits), especially at Magic Kingdom. Parade routes and some attractions have designated viewing areas for wheelchair/ECV parties of up to six people.

Visual disability services. Guests who are visually impaired can take advantage of Braille devices, audio guides and tours, and Disney's Audio Description service:

Braille maps: Stationary maps are located in theme parks near Guest Relations offices and tip boards as well as at Downtown Disney. Large print is covered with a clear Braille overlay and some raised graphics.

Handheld braille guides: Available at Guest Relations offices ($25 deposit).

Audiotape guides and tours: Guides orient users to a park and summarize its services. Tours offer routes, distances between attractions and key stopping spots. At Guest Relations offices ($25 deposit).

Audio Description: Disney's Handheld Device provides audio descriptions of 33 attractions for visually impaired guests.

Guest Assistance Cards. Each Guest Relations office has complimentary Guest Assistance Cards for visitors with non-apparent assistance needs, such as autism or heart conditions. About the size of a Pop Tart, the cards offer custom privileges such as waiting in shaded areas or entering through auxiliary entrances. They are good for parties of up to six people.

Disability parking. Designated parking areas for guests with disabilities are located

Disney's Handheld Device (that's the actual name) combines multiple functions—assistive listening, handheld captioning, closed captioning activation, Audio Description—into one unit. The device is slightly larger than a smart phone.

throughout Disney property. A valid disability parking permit is required. Theme-park disability parking is available adjacent to entrance complexes, though courtesy trams do not serve these areas.

Disney resort hotels. Resort-wide features include complimentary valet parking where valet service is offered, wheelchair-accessible bathrooms and Braille on signage and elevators. Room amenities can include bathroom features (wider doors, portable commodes, rails, roll-in showers, shower benches, hand-held shower heads), bed features (adjustable bed, lower bed, rails, rubber bed pads, shaker alarm), double-door peep holes, door-knock and phone alerts, strobe-light fire alarms and smoke detectors and in-room TTYs. For details on particular resorts call the Special Reservations hotline at 407-939-7807 (voice) or 407-939-7670 (TTY).

Restrooms. All of Disney's public restrooms have wheelchair-accessible stalls.

Service animals. Trained and leashed (or harnessed) service animals are welcome throughout Disney. Guests with service animals often enter attractions through an alternate entrance, usually the exit. Service animals aren't permitted on the following attractions; in these cases a member of the guest's party must remain with the animal:

Magic Kingdom: Big Thunder Mountain Railroad, Peter Pan's Flight, Space Mountain, Splash Mountain.

Epcot: Mission Space, Soarin', Test Track.

Disney's Hollywood Studios: Rock 'n' Roller Coaster Starring Aerosmith, Star Tours, The Twilight Zone Tower of Terror.

Disney's Animal Kingdom: Affection Section, Dinosaur, Expedition Everest, Kali River Rapids, Primeval Whirl.

Each park has designated locations for service animals to relieve themselves.

Transportation. Monorails are accessible by entrance ramps or elevators. Bus routes include buses that can accommodate wheelchairs and ECVs; the standard lift is 32 x 48 inches. Watercraft access depends on the type of boat and existing water levels and conditions.

Disney Dining Plan. Disney hotel guests and Disney Vacation Club members can add this prepaid meal plan (which can include recreation options) to their park-ticket purchase. Over a hundred restaurants participate. Five packages are available:

Basic Plan: Provides a table-service meal, a fast food ("quick-service") meal and a snack per each nightly stay.

Deluxe Plan: Provides three daily table-service meals, two snacks and a refillable drink mug for use at your resort.

2011 Dining Plan prices (per day)

Plan	Adults	Children 3–9
Basic		
Regular	$48	$13
Discount	$46	$12
Deluxe	$79	$22
Quick Service	$35	$12
Premium	$169	$119
Platinum	$229	$160
Wine & Dine opt	$45	(n/a)

Basic plan discount periods are Jan. 1–Feb 11, April 11–June 3 and Aug. 18–Dec 16. Platinum Plan available only to guests at Disney Deluxe and Vacation Club resorts.

Quick-Service Plan: Provides two fast food meals and two snacks per day, plus a refillable mug.

Premium Plan: Provides three daily table-service meals, unlimited use of many recreation options, vouchers to La Nouba, unlimited use of child-care facilities and unlimited theme-park tours. Requires purchase of at least a one-day park ticket. Buy it six months early to cherry-pick recreation times.

Platinum Plan: The Premium Plan with extras like an itinerary planning service, a spa treatment and a fireworks cruise.

Available with any plan, a Wine & Dine option adds a bottle of wine each evening of your stay, redeemable at a range of restaurants and merchandise locations.

How the Dining Plan works. You can use Disney Dining Plan meals and snack credits in any combination during your stay. For example, you can eat all table-service meals one day, all fast-food meals the next, and nothing but snacks the day after that. If one person in your party uses up his or her plan, others can continue to use theirs. Disney defines a breakfast meal as one entree and one beverage; or a combo meal and a beverage or juice. Lunch and dinner are defined as one entree, one dessert and one beverage; or a combo meal, dessert and beverage. The Dining Plans have four key conditions:

They are sold per party, not per person: If one person in your group buys a Dining Plan, everyone else must, too. The only exception: children under age 3 can eat from an adult's plate at no extra charge.

Kids are kids: When their parents are using a Dining Plan, children 3–9 must order from a kid's menu when one is available. Likewise, those over 9 can't.

Some restaurants charge two credits: These include all Disney Signature restaurants, dinner shows and Cinderella's Royal Table at Magic Kingdom. Room-service meals at Disney Deluxe Resorts charge two credits, too.

You can't take it with you: Just like the magical accoutrements of Cinderella, unused meals and snacks expire at midnight on your checkout date.

To use the plan, guests present a Key to the World card (room key) to a cashier or server. Food usage is tracked electronically; balances are available from hotel concierge.

Getting your money's worth with the Disney Dining Plan

If you take advantage of it, the Disney Dining Plan will give you great food and memorable meals. Handle it poorly, however, and your magical vacation can include a frustrating waste of time and resources. Here are four keys to getting the most for your money:

1. Don't overestimate your hunger

When determining which plan to purchase, keep in mind that it's tough to eat enough food to justify three table-service meals a day. It's also difficult to dine at more than one Signature restaurant a day, as each takes awhile to fully experience.

2. Use your credits efficiently

Except for those at Signature restaurants, the plan considers nearly all table-service meals equal. In most cases, dining with a princess, Mickey Mouse or Lilo and Stitch at an all-you-can-eat feast uses no more credits than getting a hamburger and fries at Magic Kingdom's Plaza Restaurant.

3. Know where the deals are

Though the Dining Plan charges you the same amount— one credit—for most meals, some restaurants offer better values. Great breakfast buffets include Boma at Animal Kingdom Lodge and the 1900 Park Fare character meal at the Grand Floridian Resort. For lunch, try Coral Reef at Epcot and Sanaa at Disney's Animal Kingdom Lodge. For dinner, consider Boma, 1900 Park Fare or Kouzzina at the BoardWalk Resort. Good quick-service choices include Sunshine Seasons at The Land pavilion at Epcot, Pizzafari at Animal Kingdom and Earl of Sandwich at Downtown Disney.

4. Make reservations far in advance

Disney World restaurants get booked to capacity sometimes months early, especially for the most popular dining times. Make your reservations as early as possible to ensure you can dine at places, and times, that best suit your needs.

Nearly every Disney-owned restaurant participates in the Dining Plan, as do snack locations such as food carts and sweet shops. Tips are not included; neither are alcoholic beverages, some bottled drinks, souvenir or refillable drink mugs (except in the Deluxe and Quick-Service plans) or snacks and beverages from recreation rental counters.

Extra Magic Hours. Each day at least one Disney theme or water park opens many of its attractions an hour early, or keeps them open three hours later, for those guests staying at Disney-owned resorts, the Walt Disney World Swan and Dolphin, Shades of Green or the Downtown Disney Hilton. To take advantage of an extra morning hour, guests simply arrive at its turnstiles with a valid park ticket and resort I.D. During evening hours, guests present resort I.D.'s at each attraction. Note: On a day when a park offers an Extra Magic Hour in the morning, that park will be more crowded than usual during regular hours.

Fastpass. This free reservation system lets guests skip the regular waiting line at top theme-park attractions, and instead use an express line during a one-hour window later in the day. To get a Fastpass, a guest inserts a park ticket into a Fastpass machine, which are located at the entrance of many attractions. The machine returns the ticket with a Fastpass good for a time to experience that ride or show later in the day. Guests can't choose a particular return time, but displays show what it will be (this book includes average Fastpass return times on each attraction page). Guests can get Fastpasses throughout a day, but usually have to wait an hour or two between acquisitions. The Fastpass service is not well understood, so only about half of all visitors use it.

How to take advantage of it. Follow these three tips to save hours waiting in line:

Assign a Fastpass manager: Designate someone in your group as your Fastpass manager. This person will hold everyone's park tickets, head off now and then to get more Fastpasses, and keep track of when each pass is valid and when to get more.

Always have at least one Fastpass: This way, your group is always on the clock for at least one attraction. Get your first set when you arrive at a park, then others as soon as possible throughout your day. Try to use the service for every popular Fastpass attraction except those you will be riding before 10 a.m.

Know this one secret: Miss your Fastpass time window? No worries, Disney doesn't actually enforce the end time. In other words, if the return time on your Fastpass reads "10:10 a.m.–11:10 a.m.," your Fastpass will be good anytime from 10:10 a.m. to closing time of that day.

Floral services. Disney Floral & Gifts (407-827-3505, 8a–6p daily, disneyflorist.com) sells floral arrangements, gift baskets, balloons, fruit, liquor, plants and business products, each with as much, or little, Disney theming as desired. Delivery is available to guests at Disney theme parks, resorts and Downtown Disney. Its Disney Dream Makers division decorates guest resort rooms before arrival or for special occasions. The Disney Event Group has arrangements for business gatherings (407-939-7129, disneymeetings.com); Disney's wedding planners help with bridal displays (407-939-4610, disneyweddings.com).

Gasoline stations. Three Hess stations sit on Disney property, all open 24 hours with self-serve gasoline and a convenience store. Gas prices are often a nickel or dime per gallon cheaper than stations outside of Disney.
Magic Kingdom: On the parking-lot exit road, next to the AAA Car Care Center (1000 W. Car Care Dr, 32801; 407-938-0143).
Disney's Hollywood Studios: Corner of Buena Vista Drive and Epcot Resorts Boulevard. Car wash available (300 East Buena Vista Dr. 32801; 407-938-0151).
Downtown Disney: Across from Pleasure Island, Downtown Disney (1475 Buena Vista Dr., 32801; 407-938-0160).

Gay and lesbian travelers. Gay adults of all ages come to Walt Disney World (especially Magic Kingdom) during the first week in June for Gay Days (407-896-8431, gaydays.com); most wear red shirts in a sign of celebration and solidarity. Disney does not sponsor the event but doesn't interfere with it. GayCities Orlando (orlando.gaycities.com) has a list of LGBT-friendly Orlando accommodations, bars and restaurants.

Grand Gatherings. Designated parties of eight or more (3 years of age and up) staying at a Disney-owned resort can book adjoining

Facing page: A Fastpass reserves a window of time for a park guest to experience an attraction. Toward the bottom, it states the time that guest can get another Fastpass.

BIG THUNDER
Mountain Railroad

FASTPASS®
Return Anytime Between
11:55 AM
AND
12:55 PM

Riders must be at
least 40"(102cm)
to experience
Big Thunder Mountain

Another FASTPASS® ticket
will be available
after 11:55am
SUN JUN 22
WMK:CAS009 06/05/2008 T 12
TD2-H4
06/22/2008   11:17

The ready-to-eat department at Whole Foods (7 miles from Walt Disney World off Interstate 4) includes hot and cold sandwiches, hand-tossed pizzas and a massive self-service area. The bakery offers artisanal breads.

rooms and get special dining and entertainment options. These can be booked 180 days in advance, up until three days before arrival at 407-939-7526.

Good Morning Gathering: Held at Tony's Town Square in Magic Kingdom, this breakfast includes songs by Tony, a character styled from Disney's 1955 movie "Lady and the Tramp." Mickey Mouse, Goofy, Pluto, and Chip 'N Dale show up for autographs and photos. Afterward guests watch Mickey's PhilharMagic from a special area (Adults $39, children 3–9 $23; one Disney Dining Plan credit).

International Dinner: A dinner buffet at Epcot's Odyssey Center features an international cuisine, Disney characters and chatty Auntie Roz ("everyone's favorite aunt") who tells stories and interacts with guests. Afterward the group gets a private dessert viewing of IllumiNations (Adults $74, children 3–9 $36; two Disney Dining Plan credits).

Safari Celebration Dinner: A Kilimanjaro Safaris truck takes longer than the regular Animal Kingdom ride and stops a few times for guests to take photos. Dinner at Tusker House follows; characters such as Timon and Terk pose for photos and sign autographs in the foyer, cast members hold small creatures on the patio for guests to get an up-close view (Adults $74, children 3–9 $36; two Disney Dining Plan credits).

Grand Gatherings guests can order unique personalized merchandise by calling 407-827-7600 at least 10 days prior to arrival. Hours are 8:30 a.m. to 5 p.m. Monday through Friday.

Groceries. There are a number of ways for Disney World visitors to get groceries:

At Disney resorts. Many Disney resorts have shops that offer limited groceries. Stores in resorts that offer suites and kitchen facilities have more variety.

Outside Disney. Many supermarkets are within a few miles of Disney World:

Gooding's Supermarket: Close to Disney in the Crossroads Shopping Center; prices are 20–25 percent higher than Publix or Winn-Dixie (12521 SR 535, Lake Buena Vista 32830; 407-827-1200; 24 hr).

Publix: Conveniently located near the community of Celebration at the corner of International Drive and U.S. Highway 192, Publix has decent prices and a wide variety of items (2925 International Dr., Kissimmee 34746; 407-397-1171; 7a–11p).

Whole Foods: Near Disney property at the intersection of Interstate 4 and Sand Lake Road; quality natural and organic groceries. The produce department has over 75 locally grown types of fruits and vegetables. A 136-seat indoor-outdoor dining area offers a convenient spot to chow down on the large selection of to-go items (8003 Turkey Lake Rd., Orlando 32819; 407-355-7100; 8a–10p).

Winn-Dixie: A mile north of the Crossroads center (11957 S Apopka Vineland Rd., Orlando 32836; 407-465-8600; 7a–mid).

Delivery services. Gardengrocer.com offers 4,700 different products on its website. Categories include "park essentials," baby care, natural and organic, fresh produce and household products. The service delivers to hotels (866-855-4350, min. order $40, delivery fee $12, orders over $200 delivered free). Guests can also order online at the Gooding's Supermarket website (goodings.com, min. order $50, $25 delivery fee).

Some fast-food restaurants near Walt Disney World offer free Wi-Fi Internet service to their customers. Located across Interstate 4 from Disney on U.S. 192, the Celebration Chick-fil-A provides service that blocks pornographic websites.

Highways. Two major limited-access highways border Walt Disney World.

Interstate 4. The main drag across Central Florida, Interstate 4 runs along the southeastern edge of Disney World, connecting it to Orlando (18 miles northeast) and Tampa (53 miles southwest). Technically the highway runs east to west, but through the Disney and Orlando areas it often aligns more north and south.

Florida 429. A toll road opened in 2007, this highway runs along the southwestern edge of Disney property, creating a shortcut for those coming from the north on Florida's Turnpike. Taking it saves about a half-hour compared to continuing on the turnpike into Orlando, and instead of congested urbania offers a drive past farms and orange groves. To use this route, take the turnpike south to Exit 267A, then head southeast on Florida 429 11 miles to Exit 8, which leads to Disney's Western Way entrance. The toll for 429 is $1. As you drive it, after about 4 miles you can see, off to your left, Cinderella Castle, Space Mountain, the Contemporary Resort, Spaceship Earth and the Walt Disney World Dolphin Resort.

Holidays. Disney visitors are affected in a variety of ways during major holiday periods—the day that surround Martin Luther King Jr. Day, Presidents Day, Good Friday, Easter, Memorial Day, Independence Day, Thanksgiving as well as the week between Christmas Day and New Year's Day:

Crowds. Reservations for air travel and accommodations fill up fast for these dates. Theme parks will be packed.

Costs. Room rates will be at their most expensive, as will many places to eat. Disney often temporarily increases prices for dining at its buffet restaurants during these times (typically $4 for adults, $2 for children), and charges a premium for its dining plan.

Hours. Disney World theme parks have extended hours during holiday periods, and are often open late into the night.

Festivities. Depending on the holiday, Disney schedules additional activities and entertainment, and decorates the entrances to its theme parks and hotel lobbies.

Restrictions. Seasonal annual passes often cannot be used during holiday periods. On peak days, neither can the Tables in Wonderland restaurant discount card.

International travelers. Wireless "Ears to the World" headsets ($100 deposit) provide translation of Disney attraction audio into French, German, Japanese, Portuguese or Spanish. Other Disney services include multilingual theme-park guidemaps, restaurant menus, tours and cast members (those fluent in languages other than English have nametags with gold badges).

Internet access. Still charging for wired and wireless connections in its hotels, Walt Disney World lags behind the times when it comes to Internet access:

Hotels. Disney hotels offer in-room wired high-speed access, with a cable provided to attach to a laptop ($10 24 hr). At some Disney resorts—the BoardWalk, Contemporary, Coronado Springs, Fort Wilderness, Grand Floridian and Yacht & Beach Club—Wi-Fi service is available in lobbies, lounges, at swimming pools and other common areas ($10 24 hr, $5 1 hr). All rooms have data ports on their telephones; to access the Internet using one a guest needs a dial-up account

Arriving Magical Express guests check in at a Welcome Center at the Orlando International Airport, located on Level 1 of the B side of the main terminal.

and a local access number; Disney does not charge for the local call. Preferred campsites at Fort Wilderness offer high-speed access through use of a modem kit ($125 deposit). Internet access is free for DVC members when staying at a DVC resort on points.

Many non-Disney resorts offer in-room wired access; some do so free of charge.

Business centers. Internet-connected computers ($10 15 min or $40 hr; $1 per page to print. 9a–4p daily) are available at Disney's Animal Kingdom Lodge, Beach Club, Contemporary, Coronado Springs, Grand Floridian and Yacht Club resorts.

ESPN Wide World of Sports. This complex offers free Wi-Fi throughout its grounds.

At the airport. Wireless Internet access is available free of charge in all public areas of the Orlando International Airport. Several kiosks offer wired Internet connections in addition to standard dial service provided via RJ-11 jacks in pay phones.

Other areas. Branches of the Osceola County Public Library (osceolalibrary.org) have free access; the closest to Disney is at Water Tower Place in Celebration (6070 W. Irlo Bronson Hwy, 34747, 407-742-8888, Mon–Sat 10a–7p). For a complete list of free-Wi-Fi businesses check out wififreespot.com or jiwire.com.

Lost and found. At Disney theme parks, water parks and Downtown Disney, guests can inquire about items lost the same day at Guest Relations. Disney resort hotels have their own internal lost and found facilities. At the ESPN Wide World of Sports complex lost items are held at the Welcome Center.

After one day items move to the Theme Park Lost and Found office (407-824-4245,

9a–7p daily, shipping at no charge), located at the former Magic Kingdom kennel next to the Transportation and Ticket Center. It keeps most items 30 days. Cameras, credit cards, prescription eyeglasses, purses and wallets are kept 90 days; hats, strollers and sunglasses just one week. Tip: If you've lost your purse and it had, say, a wallet and iPhone inside, ask Lost and Found for all three items. Sometimes only one is found, or one is still stored inside another.

Magical Express. With this free service, guests bound for Disney-owned hotels traveling via commercial airline to the Orlando International Airport can skip the airport's baggage claim area and take a shuttle bus to their hotel, where their bags then "magically" appear. When it's time to return home, guests board buses back to the airport; those traveling on participating airlines can check their bags for their flight at their hotel. For guests planning to spend their entire vacation at Disney, the service makes traveling to Disney World much easier, and eliminates the need to rent a car. The service carries over 2.2 million passengers a year.

Eligibility. Magical Express is available for guests staying at any Disney-owned resort. Guests of the Walt Disney World Swan and Dolphin, Shades of Green and the Downtown Disney hotels are not eligible.

Booking. Guests can reserve the service when booking their Disney hotel accommodations, or do so anytime at least 10 days in advance at 866-599-0951.

Arrivals. Upon landing at the airport, domestic guests go directly to the Magical Express Welcome Center (on Level 1 at the B side of the terminal) to check in and board

Magical Express buses carry guests of Disney-owned resort hotels to and from the Orlando International Airport. The complimentary service also delivers luggage directly from arriving flights to the hotels, so guests can bypass Baggage Claim.

their shuttle bus. Luggage is delivered to their hotel within three hours after resort check-in for flights arriving between 5 a.m. and 10 p.m. daily. For later arrivals guests collect their bags at baggage claim, bring the luggage themselves to the Welcome Center, and carry it into the resort with them. International guests always claim their own baggage.

Departures. As their vacation draws to a close, guests receive a Magical Express Transportation Notice advising them of the time they are scheduled for a bus back to the airport. With some airlines—Airtran, Alaska Airlines, American Airlines, Continental, Delta Air Lines, JetBlue, Southwest, United and US Air—guests can check their bags and get boarding passes at their hotel, eliminating those chores at the airport. Departing guests need to stop by their hotel's Resort Airline Check-In Desk three hours prior to their flight time; a valid government-issued photo I.D. and a Disney resort room key must be shown.

Maps. Though the maps in this book should suffice for many planning needs, larger, more detailed maps are available from Disney.

Customized maps. Potential visitors can create free customized maps of all Disney World theme parks at disneyworld.disney. go.com by selecting "My Disney Vacation" then "Customized Maps." Choices also include a map of the entire property. The full-color maps can be printed, or Disney will mail 14-by-20-inch copies free of charge. Allow 2 to 4 weeks for delivery.

For Disney hotel guests. Guests staying at a Disney-owned hotel can request a map of the grounds when making reservations. It shows lodging areas with room numbers, restaurants, shops, pools, smoking areas,

recreation locations and transportation. Also available: a set of Disney's theme-park guide maps that are distributed in the parks.

Medical services. Walt Disney World has many first-aid stations and AEDs. Hotel prescription delivery and in-room care are easy to arrange, and doctors, dentists and a major hospital are all just a few miles away.

Automated External Defibrillators. Disney World has 700 Automated External Defibrillators (AEDs). Designed to aid a person suffering from cardiac arrest, an AED is easy to use even without training. When one is pulled off the wall, it automatically calls 911 and gives responders its location. All include instructions for use; in general don't push the "Shock" button if the collapsed person is awake, and make sure no one is touching the victim before administering a shock.

Clinics. Florida Hospital's Centra Care Walk-In Medical Clinics offer free transportation; call 407-938-0650 for pick-up. Two locations are close to Disney World:

Formosa Gardens shopping center: On U.S. 192 south of Disney. 7848 W Irlo Bronson Hwy, Kissimmee 34747. 8a–5p daily. 407-397-7032.

Lake Buena Vista: Near Downtown Disney. 12500 S. Apopka Vineland Rd, Orlando 32836. 8a–mid. Mon–Fri.; 8a–8p Sat–Sun. 407-934-2273.

Dental services. Regular and emergency care is available at the Celebration Dental Group, Florida Hospital at Celebration Health, 400 Celebration Place, Celebration 34747; 407-566-2222.

Equipment rentals. Portable commodes, crutches, nebulizers, oxygen, scooters, walkers and wheelchairs are available from:

The Reedy Creek Fire Department provides Disney guests with EMT (Emergency Medical Technician) and paramedic treatment and transport. The department has four fire stations, including one near Downtown Disney (left).

Apria Health Care: 407-291-2229 or 800-338-1640, after hours 407-297-0100; apria.com.
Care Medical Equipment: 407-856-2273 or 800-741-2282; caremedicalequipment.com.
Turner Drugs: 407-828-8125; turnerdrug.com (see Pharmacies, below).
Walker Mobility: 407-518-6000 or 800-726-6837; walkermobility.com.

Hospitals and EMS. The closest hospital to Disney is Florida Hospital at Celebration Health (emergencies: 407-303-4034). Reedy Creek Emergency Services dispatches paramedics (407-560-1990 via Disney Security).

In-room care. For non-emergencies, in-room medical care is available from:
Centra Care: 407-238-2000.
Doctors on Call Service: 407-399-3627.
EastCoast Medical: 407-648-5252.

Pharmacies. Turner Drugs delivers prescription and OTC medications (Mon–Fri 8a–9p, Sat–Sun 8a–7p. 407-828-8125, fax 407-828-8027; turnerdrug.com). There's a $5 charge to deliver to Disney resorts; orders are left at concierge and charged to guests' room accounts. Turner Drugs has walk-in locations at 12500 Apopka-Vineland Road, Orlando 32836 (Mon–Fri 8a–mid, Sat–Sun 8a–8p) and 1530 Celebration Blvd, Celebration 34747 (Mon–Fri 9a–7p, Sat–Sun 9a–5p).

Vision services. The closest optometrist to Disney is Celebration Eye Care, 741 Front St, Celebration 34747; 407-566-2020.

Money. Cash and credit and debit cards are accepted at nearly every store, restaurant and snack stand at Disney World as well as throughout Central Florida. Instances that require cash can include paying tips, highway tolls, some taxi and limousine services and parking fees at Disney theme parks.

ATMs. Chase Bank automated teller machines (ATMs) are sprinkled throughout Disney property. The machines accept cards from the Plus and Cirrus systems. Withdrawals using out-of-state cards, or cards from a bank other than Chase, can incur surcharges of $1.50 to $2.50.

Banks. Locations of full-service banks closest to Disney property:
SunTrust Bank: Across from Downtown Disney (1675 E. Buena Vista Dr., Lake Buena Vista 32830. 407-828-6103. 8a–5p Mon–Thurs; 8a–6p Fri). Also in the Disney-developed community of Celebration off U.S. 192 in Water Tower Place, 4 mi. from Disney (74 Blake Blvd., Celebration 34747. 321-939-3970. 9a–4p Mon–Thurs; 9a–6p Fri).
Bank of America: In Celebration, 5 mi. from Disney World (700 Celebration Ave., Celebration 34747. 321-939-7677. 9a–5p Mon–Thurs; 9a–6p Fri, 9a–1p Sat).
Wachovia Bank / Wells Fargo: Near International Dr., 6 mi. from Disney (7740 W. Sand Lake Rd., Orlando 32819. 407-649-5800. 8a–6p Mon–Fri; 9a–2p Sat).

Credit / debit cards. American Express, Diners Club, Discover, Japan Credit Bureau (JCB), MasterCard and Visa cards are accepted at Disney World, even at snack stands. Renting a car requires a major credit card or debit card with major-credit-card backing; using a debit card will require a deposit (usually $200–$300) that will be credited back to the user's account a week or so after the car is returned.

Currency exchange. Foreign currency can be exchanged for U.S. dollars at the Orlando International Airport, main bank branches, theme park Guest Relations offices and Disney resort concierge desks.

Convenient to the resort hotels on the south side of Disney property, the Water Tower Place SunTrust bank sits off Highway 192, near the Disney-designed town of Celebration. The friendly bank is ideal for guests who need to conduct indoor business.

Disney Dollars. This whimsical script is accepted at all Disney World theme parks and Disney-owned resorts and gift shops. Popular as currency as well as souvenirs, the dollars are sold at Guest Relations offices, Disney concierge desks and the World of Disney store at Downtown Disney. Denominations are $1, $5 and $10; the exchange rate is always $1 for $1. Disney issues new designs nearly every year.

Gift cards. Disney gift cards can be used throughout Walt Disney World. Disney Dollars purchases are not eligible. The gift cards have no fees and don't expire; they are available online in set amounts from $25 to $500 (disneygiftcard.com).

Gratuities. Tips are included in the bill on room-service orders at Disney hotels and with use of a Tables in Wonderland discount card. Tips often will be refused by Disney concierge staff and other cast members; guests can express appreciation for cast-member service by emailing wdw.guest.communications@disney.com; comments can boost a career. Tips are accepted by valets, the non-Disney concierge staff at the Walt Disney World Swan and Dolphin Resort and employees of Downtown Disney hotels.

Traveler's checks. Nearly any Disney purchase can be paid for with a traveler's check. SunTrust Bank is the closest full-service bank that sells, replaces and redeems traveler's checks. For refunds on lost or stolen checks call American Express (800-992-3404) or Thomas Cook (800-287-7362).

Wire transfers. For most Disney guests, the Downtown Disney SunTrust Bank is the closest full-service bank that handles wire transfers. Gooding's Supermarket (in the CrossRoads Shopping Center near Downtown Disney, 8a-10p daily, 407-827-1200) offers Western Union (800-325-6000) transfers.

Obese guests. Guests of nearly all shapes and sizes can experience just about all Walt Disney World has to offer with no problem, as long as they heed Disney's medical advisories and use common sense. Here's what Disney offers for guests "at large."

Bench seats. On some Disney attractions an obese person should take a seat alone to fit comfortably. To make this easy, when a cast member at the loading area asks how many are in your party, say "1" and then the number of the rest of your party, such as "and 3."

Getting around. Probably the biggest challenge for overweight guests is handling all the walking involved. The typical theme-park guest walks miles a day, which can be difficult for anyone who isn't fit. The best

---

How much to tip?

Airport baggage handlers: $1 per bag
Airport parking shuttle: $1 per person
Hairstylists: 10 percent
Hotel bellmen: $1 per bag
Hotel concierge: $5–$10 per visit
Hotel housekeepers: $1–$3 per person, per night (left in a marked envelope)
Restaurants: 15–20 percent for good service; 10 percent for mediocre
Spa treatment: 15–20 percent for a full-service treatment
Taxi drivers: 10–15 percent
Valet parking: $1–$2 when car delivered
Typical amounts for Central Florida

Shuttle trams transport guests from parking lots at all Disney World theme parks. The vehicles have their own roadways. Due to their distinctive driver shades and large rear-view mirrors, the trams are nicknamed "Flying Nuns" by Disney cast members.

advice is to have a good plan, pace yourself and take breaks. Electric Convenience Vehicles (ECVs) and extra-wide wheelchairs are available to rent at the theme parks. On crowded days EVCs often sell out early.

Lap-bar rides. Many rides have bars guests control by pulling down as far as they feel comfortable. When two people share a restraint, an obese person should not share a seat with a small or skinny guest; the bar will stop and lock based on the large tummy, leaving the small person relatively unrestrained.

Recreation. *Epcot DiveQuest*—Disney supplies wetsuits for guests scuba diving at the Seas with Nemo & Friends; wetsuits are available up to size 5X. *Horseback riding*—The weight limit at Fort Wilderness Resort is 250 pounds. *Parasailing*—Guests taking flight at Disney's Contemporary Resort should weigh no more than 330 pounds.

Restaurants. Many Disney eateries use chairs with armrests, however hostesses can usually supply chairs without them.

Seatbelt rides. Pull the seat belt out all the way before sitting down. Hold it out while you sit, then fasten the buckle. Ask a family member to help attach the buckle if needed.

Disney cast members aren't allowed to help guests who struggle to buckle belts.

Shopping. Many shops sell large-sized Disney T-shirts, up to 3X. The three stores with the most variety are the Emporium at Magic Kingdom, MouseGear at Epcot and World of Disney at Downtown Disney. These stores commonly stock T-shirts, sweatshirts and jackets in sizes up to 4X and sometimes 5X. For details contact Disney Merchandise at 407-363-6200; choose Option 3 to immediately speak to a live operator.

Spas. The Grand Floridian and Saratoga Springs spas supply guests receiving treatments with robes in sizes up to 5X.

Theater seats. For attractions with armrests, obese guests may find it easier to sit on the front edge of a seat and then slide back, or sit sideways and then turn to squeeze in. Some theaters have narrow seats; the narrowest are those at Epcot's France pavilion.

Turnstiles. Magic Kingdom has the narrowest turnstiles at Disney; obese guests can turn sideways and squeeze through. Wheelchair and stroller entrances are often wider; obese guests can use them by asking cast members to open the gates.

A "VIP suite" for dogs at the Best Friends Pet Care Resort, the only kennel on Disney property. The 226-square-foot space includes an elevated bed, a flat-screen television that shows movies such as "Lady and the Tramp," and a small outdoor area.

Water parks. The weight limit to ride the Blizzard Beach chair lift is 375 lbs.

The independent website allearsnet.com has a terrific section for obese guests. Search "WDW at Large" and "At Large" trip reports.

Parking. And here's the most unplanned expense at Disney World: the price to park at the theme parks. Daily rates are $14 for cars, motorcycles or taxis; $15 for campers; $18 for buses and tractor-trailers. The fee provides access to all four theme-park lots for that day. Parking is free for those staying at Disney hotels or holding annual passes. Tables in Wonderland cardholders can park free too; they can receive a refund at Guest Relations offices with a table-service dining receipt.

Except for Magic Kingdom, all theme-park parking is just outside the main entrance to the park. At Magic Kingdom, the lot is located at the Transportation and Ticket Center; guests then take either a monorail or a ferry to the Magic Kingdom, which is a mile away.

Parking is free at Disney water parks and Downtown Disney. Most parking is complimentary at the ESPN Wide World of Sports, though premium spots may cost $5.

Hotel parking. Parking is complimentary at Disney-owned resort hotels for those staying there or coming to shop or dine. Shades of Green charges $5 for parking, the Walt Disney World Swan and Dolphin Resort charges $9 for overnight self-parking, $16 for overnight valet parking, $9 per exit for day self-parking, $12 per exit for day valet parking. Valet parking is offered at all Disney Deluxe Resorts; the fee is $12 daily, not including gratuity. Guests can use their hangtag to valet park at any other Disney resort (except for gratuity) for no additional

charge. Valet parking is complimentary for Tables in Wonderland cardholders with dining reservations and guests with a current handicap license plate or tag.

Pets. With the opening of the Best Friends Pet Care kennel in 2010, all other kennels at Disney have closed. The 50,000-square-foot facility is well maintained, and lets dog owners spend time with their pet unleashed in a grassy backyard that has its own water-play area. Billing itself as a "luxury pet resort," Best Friends refers to many of its 200-plus cages as "suites" and "condos" since they are divided into multiple spaces. Some spots include controlled access to small outdoor areas. Dog facilities also include 14 "vacation villas" (6-by-7-foot rooms with raised bedding and flat-screen TVs) and four larger rooms marketed as "VIP suites."

Birds stay in an area with hamsters, guinea pigs, rabbits, ferrets and other pocket pets (owners must supply cages, supplies and food). No primates or venomous pets are allowed; dogs and cats must be at least 4 months old. Optional services include daytime boarding; activities such as nature walks, grooming and playgroups; and pampering such as ice-cream treats and bedtime stories. (Dogs: overnight $34–$76, daycare $16–$69; optional services $5–$15. Cats: overnight $21–$30, daycare $15–$26; optional services $3–$8. Small animals: overnight $12–$23. Across from Disney's Port Orleans Resort at 2510 Bonnet Creek Parkway, Lake Buena Vista 32830; reservations 877-493-9738 or wdw.bestfriendspetcare.com)

At Disney resorts. Campers at Disney's Fort Wilderness Resort & Campground may keep their pet with them for $5 per day at

Disney PhotoPass photographers take snapshots of guests throughout Walt Disney World property without obligation. Guests pay for only those images they like.

select locations. Only service animals are allowed elsewhere.

Laws. It's illegal to leave a pet in a car in Florida with the windows up; the heat makes it dangerous for the animal, as temperatures can rise to unbearable degrees quickly.

Photography. Besides giving you the ability to record landmarks and character greetings, a still camera can capture spontaneous moments that create treasured memories. Consider giving children their own cameras and perhaps bringing waterproof models for swimming pools and water parks. Whatever shots you snap, take turns being the photographer; if dad takes all the pictures none will include dad. If you bring your charger with you, Guest Relations will often charge your camera batteries for free.

Digital prints and CDs. The Camera Centers at Magic Kingdom and Hollywood Studios and the Epcot ImageWorks area (at the Imagination pavilion) have Kodak PictureMaker kiosks. Simplified versions of machines found in drug and grocery stores, they create prints and burn CDs, and accept nearly every type of storage device.

Photographic services. Disney offers its own photo services in its parks, hotels, restaurants and at Downtown Disney:

Makeover salons: Some packages at the Bibbidi Bobbidi Boutique salons include photos. Details at 407-939-7895.

PhotoPass: With this service Disney photographers take shots of your group throughout Disney World property, but you pay for only those images you like. Photographers are stationed throughout Disney property, including at all theme-park icons and most character spots. Each photographer gives away free credit-card-like PhotoPasses, which guests then carry with them as digital IDs. Guests view the shots at theme-park Camera Centers or online at disneyphotopass.com. Note: PhotoPass is not a replacement for taking your own photos, as photographers shoot only posed shots at specific locations. If you use the service, write down your 16-digit PhotoPass ID number and save it. That way if you lose your card you won't lose track of your images.

Resort hotel sittings: Guests can have a portrait session with a PhotoPass photographer at five hotels: Animal Kingdom Lodge, Grand Floridian, Polynesian, Wilderness Lodge and Yacht & Beach Club. Guests consult about locations, themes and wardrobe, then pose at picturesque settings. Sessions ($100) last 20–30 minutes, and include a CD with 60 to 100 images and a select print package. Book up to 30 days in advance at 407-824-1700.

Restaurant souvenir photos: Diners at the following locations can purchase photos taken either tableside or before entering the dining room: Chef Mickey's (Contemporary Resort), Cinderella's Royal Table (Cinderella Castle, Magic Kingdom, photo charges included in meal price), Hoop-Dee-Doo Revue Dinner Show and Mickey's Backyard Barbecue (Fort Wilderness Resort & Campground), Planet Hollywood (Downtown Disney), Princess Storybook Dining (Akershus, Norway pavilion, Epcot, photo charges included in meal price), Spirit of Aloha Dinner Show (Polynesian Resort).

Thrill-ride souvenirs: At some rides an automated camera takes your picture

Old-fashioned mail boxes along Magic Kingdom's Main Street U.S.A. (right) and at the American Adventure pavilion at Epcot actually do accept mail. Disney delivers items placed into them to the U.S. Postal Service.

during a peak moment then an exit-way gift shop offers to sell you the shot: *Magic Kingdom*—Buzz Lightyear's Space Ranger Spin, Space Mountain, Splash Mountain. *Epcot*—Test Track. *Disney's Hollywood Studios*—Rock 'n' Roller Coaster Starring Aerosmith, The Twilight Zone Tower of Terror. *Disney's Animal Kingdom*—Dinosaur, Expedition Everest.

Pin trading. Disney World has sold collectible pins for years; in 1999 Disney began the tradition of pin trading. Many guests trade pins; many Disney cast members wear a lanyard of pins to trade with guests, and will agree to nearly any one-for-one offer.

Postal services. Access to the U.S. Postal Service is available throughout Walt Disney World and the surrounding area.

Sending mail. *Magic Kingdom*—Station Break, Main Street U.S.A. train station. Guests can drop stamped mail in old-fashioned Main Street letter boxes (postmarks read "Lake Buena Vista" not "Walt Disney World"). *Epcot*—Camera Center, under Spaceship Earth. *Disney's Hollywood Studios*—Oscar's Super Service, entrance plaza. *Disney's Animal Kingdom*—Garden Gate Gifts, entrance plaza. *Nearby U.S. Post Offices*—Lake Buena Vista: 13769 Apopka-Vineland Rd. in the Buena Vista Shopping Center, 407-238-0223, 9 a.m.–4 p.m., Sat 9 a.m.–noon. Full-service facility. Celebration: 610 Market St., downtown, 407-566-1145, 9 a.m.–4 p.m., Sat 8:30 a.m.–2 p.m. Full-service facility. Other locations at 800-275-8777, usps.com.

Stamps. *Magic Kingdom*—Newsstand, entrance plaza. *Epcot*—Camera Center, under Spaceship Earth. *Disney's Hollywood*

Studios—Oscar's Super Service, entrance plaza. *Disney's Animal Kingdom*—Garden Gate Gifts, entrance plaza. *Disney hotels*—Main gift shops. *Downtown Disney*—Guest Services, Marketplace. *Outside Disney*—U.S. Post Offices (see above).

Receiving mail. *Disney resort hotels*—Letters, packages and postcards can be sent to guests staying at any Disney resort. Mail should include the guest's arrival date if the item will be received before check-in. *Non-Disney hotels*—Nearly all area convention hotels accept mail for guests, as do some other properties. Contact the particular hotel. *General Delivery*—Guests can receive mail care of General Delivery at most major post offices. Guests must first complete an application in person and show two forms of ID and a temporary local address. The application is valid for 30 days. Mail is held for up to 15 days.

See also **Shipping**.

Pregnant guests. Walt Disney World's theme parks can be fun and safe places for expectant moms. Although roller coasters are off limits, there are numerous character greetings, fireworks, parades, shows, swimming pools and gentle rides that are easy for moms-to-be to enjoy. Pregnant visitors should check with their doctors first, heed Disney's advisories and use common sense.

Attractions to avoid. Pregnant guests should consider avoiding rides that have sudden stops or drops, rough motion, spinning or require significant exertion:

Magic Kingdom: Big Thunder Mountain Railroad, Mad Tea Party, Space Mountain, Splash Mountain, Swiss Family Treehouse (lots of steps), Tomorrowland Speedway.

Current wait times are posted in front of nearly all Walt Disney World theme-park attractions. Water parks post wait times on central chalkboards.

Epcot: Mission Space, Sum of all Thrills (an Innoventions exhibit), Test Track.

Disney's Hollywood Studios: Rock 'n' Roller Coaster, Star Tours, Twilight Zone Tower of Terror.

Disney's Animal Kingdom: Dinosaur, Expedition Everest, Kali River Rapids, Primeval Whirl and Kilimanjaro Safaris (the bumpy ride is smoothest for those who sit in the front row).

Blizzard Beach: All slides.

Typhoon Lagoon: All slides, surf pool when waves are in effect.

Water. It's important for anyone to stay hydrated while outdoors in Florida, but even more vital for expectant moms. Guests can bring water into Disney World theme parks (though not in glass containers or rolling coolers) and get free ice water (on request) from counter-service restaurants. Water fountains dot each park.

Snacks. To head off morning sickness, expectant moms may want to carry some light snacks, such as granola bars, crackers or fresh fruit. It's fine to bring in food to a theme park as long as there are no glass containers. Each park has a variety of snack stands, some of which sell fresh fruit.

Baby Care Centers. All theme parks have Baby Care Centers which serve pregnant guests. Quiet air-conditioned spots provide expectant women with a relaxing way to get off their feet.

Magic Kingdom: Next to the Crystal Palace restaurant, off Main Street U.S.A.

Epcot: Inside the Odyssey Center, a building that sits between Test Track and the Mexico pavilion.

Disney's Hollywood Studios: At the park's entrance, next to Guest Relations.

Disney's Animal Kingdom: Behind the Discovery Island store Creature Comforts.

Disney resort hotels. Staying at a hotel on Disney property—especially one on the monorail loop—will make it more convenient to return to your room in the middle of the day for a rest. Expectant guests can request extra pillows from housekeeping for additional support. Many Disney resorts have great swimming pools, a fact which can be especially important for pregnant guests; the buoyancy of the water can help take strain off aching backs.

Shopping. Disney offers some unusual opportunities to shop for the baby:

Autographs: Some parents-to-be buy an autograph book and have characters sign it. The completed book—plus character photos with dad and mom—can make a unique gift later for the new addition.

Infant merchandise: A few theme-park stores carry unique (and usually, good quality) Disney infant apparel and other merchandise. *Magic Kingdom*—The Emporium, Pooh's Thotful Shop; *Epcot*—MouseGear, Showcase Station East Port, World Showcase has some hard-to-find infant items such as Steiff teddy bears (Germany pavilion) and puffin plushies (Norway pavilion); *Disney's Hollywood Studios*—L.A. Cinema Storage, Stage 1 Co. Store; *Disney's Animal Kingdom*—Creature Comforts.

Queues. Guests at Walt Disney World commonly have to wait in line for attractions, since the number of people who can experience its rides and shows at any one time is far less than the number of people Disney allows in its theme parks. For example, the

Disney's attraction waiting lines are often designed to be part of the experience. The queue for Rock 'n' Roller Coaster Starring Aerosmith winds through a recording studio before entering a grimy back-alley boarding area (right).

total capacity of the rides and shows at Magic Kingdom is about 9,500, though on average that park contains about 30,000 guests and can hold at least twice that many.

Wait times. A sign at each attraction displays its current wait time. At some rides, an easy way to avoid that wait is to use Disney's Fastpass system, a sort of virtual queue that is completely free of charge. Guests still wait their turn, but don't have to physically be in line while they do. In this book's theme-park chapters, the average wait time and Fastpass return time for each attraction appears on that attraction's page.

See also **Children (Child Swap), Fastpass.**

Single Rider lines. A few attractions have a third entrance, a "Single-Rider" line for guests who don't mind experiencing a ride by themselves. During peak periods, using it can cut your wait time by at least 30 minutes. Three rides have one: Test Track in Epcot; Rock 'n' Roller Coaster Starring Aerosmith at Disney's Hollywood Studios; and Expedition Everest at Disney's Animal Kingdom. There is also a single-rider line at the Blizzard Beach chair lift, which offers a speedy way up to that water park's main body and mat slides.

How Single-Rider lines work: When ride operators can't fill a vehicle from guests in a regular line without breaking up a group, they take a guest from the single-rider line. Groups can wait in the line together, but will be split up.

Quinceañera celebrations. Traditional Quinceañera parties celebrate Latina girls turning 15. Walt Disney World offers three packages, each available year-round:

Belle of the Ball (La Bella del Baile): A ball complete with dinner and dancing.

Dancing With a Star (Bailando con una Estrella): Dance party with a bilingual DJ. **Reflection of You (Un Reflejo de Ti):** A dessert party in Epcot and private viewing of IllumiNations.

Families can also create their own package. For details call 321-939-4555.

Refurbishments and rehabs. For operational updates call 407-939-6244 or check online at disneyworld.com.

Shipping. The closest Fedex Office location to Disney is near Downtown Disney at 12181 S Apopka Vineland, Orlando, 32836

Radio stations in Orlando

AM Stations

580	WDBO	News Talk
660	WORL	Sports
740	WQTM	Sports
990	WDYZ	Radio Disney

FM Stations

88.3	WPOZ	Christian Contemp.
89.1	WLAZ	Spanish
90.7	WMFE	National Public Radio
92.3	WWKA	Country
95.3	WPYO	Hip Hop, R&B
96.5	WHTQ	Classic Rock
98.9	WMMO	Soft Rock
100.3	WEBG	Latin Hits
101.1	WJRR	Rock
103.1	WLOQ	Smooth Jazz
104.1	WTKS	Talk
105.1	WOMX	Adult Contemporary
106.7	WXXL	Top 40
107.7	WMFG	Soft Rock

Magic Kingdom's largest gift shop, The Emporium extends the length of Main Street U.S.A. Although it appears to be a series of small stores, in reality the shop is one big interconnected space. It sells nearly every type of Disney merchandise.

(407-465-0085, open 24 hrs). The closest UPS spot is at 8131 Vineland Ave, Orlando, 32821 (407-465-1700, 8a–7p Mon–Fri, 9a–5p Sat, noon–5p Sun). About four miles from Disney, it's behind the Orlando Premium Outlet Mall.

At Disney hotels. Ask the front desk or concierge for instructions. Some resorts have a business center or desk with shipping supplies. Expect to pay a handling fee.

Shipping luggage to a hotel can often be cheaper than checking it as airline baggage. Send packages in enough time so they arrive a couple of days early; use FedEx or UPS for the most reliable service. To be sure the hotel will hold your package until your arrival, address the shipping label as follows:

    Guest's name (same as on reservation)
    c/o Name of hotel
    Hold for guest arrival on 0/00/0000
    Reservation #000000000
    Hotel street address
    Lake Buena Vista, FL 32830

At Disney theme parks. Package Pickup at each theme park can ship purchases made in that park to a guest's Disney-owned resort hotel or, via UPS or Fedex, to any domestic or international address.

At Downtown Disney. Stores can deliver purchases to a Disney resort or ship them elsewhere via UPS or Fedex.

See also **Postal Services.**

Shopping. Walt Disney World has hundreds of stores, selling everything from hand-rolled cigars to the largest selection of Mickey Mouse merchandise in the world. Non-Disney apparel is sold at Downtown Disney, Disney Deluxe resorts, at Epcot's World Showcase and at water parks. Some theme-park shops sell World Wildlife Fund T-shirts. Ralph Lauren men's dress shirts are sold at the Commander's Porter shop at Disney's Grand Floridian Resort (9a–10p).

Disney return policy. Disney-owned stores will accept returns on merchandise within 90 days of purchase with a valid receipt. Items that cannot be returned include those marked "as is" or "all sales final," original artwork, fine jewelry and special orders. A guest returning an item without a receipt receives credit based on its selling price at the time of the return. Some stores on Disney World property—including many in Epcot's World Showcase and at Downtown Disney—are not run by Disney; return policies at these shops vary.

Disney Store returns: In most cases, Disney Stores across the U.S. accept returns of items bought at Disney-owned Disney World stores with a valid receipt.

Nearby retailers. Popular stores close to Walt Disney World include:

Barnes & Noble: 7900 W. Sand Lake Rd, Orlando 32819, 7 mi. from WDW (407-345-0900; Sun–Thur 9a–10p, Fri–Sat 9a–11p).

Best Buy: 4155 Millenia Blvd, Orlando 32839; 16 mi. from WDW (407-248-2439; Mon–Sat 10a–10p, Sun 10a–7p).

Mall at Millenia: 4200 Conroy Rd, Orlando 32839; 16 mi. from WDW (407-363-3555; Mon–Sat 10a–9p, Sun noon–7p).

Target: 4750 Millenia Plaza Way, Orlando 32839; 16 mi. from WDW (407-541-0019; Mon–Fri 8a–11p, Sat 8a–11p, Sun 8a–11p).

Walgreens: 7767 W. Irlo Bronson Blvd. (U.S. 192), Kissimmee 34747; 3 mi. from WDW (407-390-1701; 24 hr).

Whole Foods: 8003 Turkey Lake Road, Orlando 32819; 7 mi. from WDW (407-355-7100; daily 8a–10p daily).

The Mall at Millenia (right) includes Ann Taylor, Apple, Bloomingdale's, Coach, Gap, Juicy Couture, Macy's and Quiksilver stores. Nearby are Barnes & Noble, Best Buy and Target. In Kissimmee, Eli's Orange World sells and ships fresh citrus.

Outlet Mall: The Orlando Premium Outlet Mall has 150 stores, including Ann Taylor, Burberry, Coach, Gap Outlet, Giorgio Armani, Nike and Polo Ralph Lauren. 8200 Vineland Ave. at I-4 exit 68; 5 mi. from WDW (407-238-7787; Mon–Sat 10a–10p (11p in summer), Sun 10a–9p).

Smoking. Florida law requires that all restaurants be smoke-free. Smoking is allowed in freestanding bars that earn less than 10 percent of their income from food.

On Disney property. Smoking areas are available throughout. All shops are non-smoking except Fuego at Downtown Disney.

All Disney hotel rooms, balconies and patios are smoke-free. Smoking is permitted at Fort Wilderness campsites and on cabin porches. A $250–$500 "room recovery fee" is charged to guests who smoke in hotel rooms.

Tobacco sales. No tobacco products are sold in Disney theme parks. They are often sold, but not displayed, at Disney hotel gift shops and Downtown Disney. The Disney Hess stations sell smoking products openly.

Spas. Disney World has three full-service spas. All offer aromatherapy, boutique products, exercise facilities, facials, manicures and pedicures, massages and both adult and child services; robes and slippers are provided for body treatments.

Grand Floridian Spa. Treatments include signature citrus-zest facials. Couples can get massages together in a candle-lit room (407-824-2332, at the Grand Floridian Resort; parking at Disney's Wedding Pavilion).

Mandara Spa. This Asian-inspired spa has two indoor gardens. Services include seaweed wraps and stone therapies (407-934-4772, at the Walt Disney World Dolphin Resort).

Saratoga Springs Spa. Popular treatments include a maple sugar body polish, Adirondack stone therapy massage, mineral springs hydrotherapy and signature Mystical Forest. A French whirlpool has 72 jets (407-827-4455, at the Saratoga Springs Resort).

Taxes. Two types of taxes are of concern to most Disney visitors: sales and hotel.

Sales taxes. Nearly all of Walt Disney World sits in Orange County, Fla., where the sales tax rate is 6.5 percent. A portion of Disney property is in Osceola County, which has a sales tax of 7 percent. This area includes Disney's All-Star Resorts and the ESPN Wide World of Sports complex.

Hotel taxes. The hotel tax rate is a combination of the sales tax rate (above) and the resort tax rate, which in Central Florida is 6 percent.

Sun protection
Florida visitors should use a sunscreen with a high SPF rating and quality ingredients (such as No-Ad 50, above left). Aloe-based after-sun products (above right) ease pain and help repair skin.

Telephone services. No cell-phone towers stand on Disney property, but since the land is flat the signals from adjoining towers are usually available. Guests in cars will typically have decent reception, but service can be poor or even nonexistent in many Disney buildings, especially hotel rooms. Verizon has the most extensive network for the area; AT&T and Sprint have secondary coverage. All Disney parks can have weak cell-phone service on their most crowded days; reception can be awful just before or after parades or fireworks, when usage is at its peak.

Cell-phone stores. Good locations relatively close to Walt Disney World include:

AT&T: Directly across from Celebration Ave. on U.S. 192. (6081 W. Irlo Bronson Memorial Hwy., Kissimmee 34747; 407-566-0650. 10a–9p Mon–Thr, 10a–7p Fri, 10a–9p Sat, noon–6p Sun), 4 miles from Disney World.

Sprint: Next to WalMart on a service road alongside Interstate 4 (8910 Turkey Lake Rd., Orlando 32819; 407-351-5155; 10a–8p Mon–Fri, 10a–7p Sat, noon–5p Sun), 7 miles from Disney World.

Verizon Wireless: Near North John Young Parkway at 1340 West Osceola Parkway #101, Kissimmee 34741; (407) 343-0516; 9a–9p Mon–Sat, 11a–6p Sun, 12 miles from Disney World.

Disabled guests. Telecommunications Devices for the Deaf (TDD) are available for hearing-impaired guests at Guest Relations offices in the theme parks and Downtown Disney. Many pay phones in the parks are also equipped with amplifying headsets.

Local calls. Callers must include the area code—"407" for all Disney numbers—in all local calls. It is not necessary to dial "1" first.

Hotels. Area hotels often add a hefty service charge on telephone calls made from a room phone. Check the telephone information card near the room phone for a list of all the costs involved.

Pay phones. Pay telephones are found in all Disney theme parks, Downtown Disney, local shopping centers, gas stations and many other places. Local calls, including all calls within Disney property, cost 50 cents.

Prepaid phone cards. Private prepaid phone cards are sold at Disney World gift shops and Guest Relations offices. Outside Disney they're available at convenience stores, supermarkets and pharmacies.

Theme park policies. Though they aren't heavily publicized and enforcement can vary,

Can you hear me now? Wireless service inside the Disney theme parks can be spotty. Since there are no cell-phone towers on Disney property, service depends on signals from adjacent, often distant, locations.

Walt Disney World does have specific policies regarding park closures, dress codes, and items allowed in the parks.

Park closures. During peak periods the Disney parks can fill to capacity and close to additional guests, even those who have purchased tickets. Closures for capacity typically occur only on the busiest days such as Independence Day, Christmas Eve, Christmas and New Year's Eve. Disney closes its theme parks for capacity in five distinct phases:

Phase 1: The park stays open to any additional guest who has already purchased a park pass, though Disney stops ticket sales at that location.

Phase 2: Open to only those additional guests who have multi-day park passes or are staying at a Disney-owned resort.

Phase 3: Open to only those additional guests who are using the last day of a multi-day park pass or are staying at a Disney-owned resort.

Phase 4: Open to only those additional guests who are staying at a Disney resort.

Phase 5: No additional entry available; the park is at capacity.

Before employing the steps above, occasionally the Magic Kingdom will first close its parking lot to new cars, then stop using Disney transportation (monorail, buses, boats) to shuttle in new guests.

Guests who are already in a Disney theme park when it closes for capacity are not asked to leave. To learn if a Disney theme park is currently closed, call 407-939-4636.

Dress codes. As family-oriented environments, the Disney World parks have long had a policy of refusing, or revoking, admission to anyone managers deem not appropriately dressed or whose appearance could create a distraction to others, especially if another guest complains and the guest refuses suggestions to comply. In the case of offensive T-shirt graphics, an offender may be asked to turn the shirt inside-out. Other unacceptable attire includes clothing displaying offensive messages or language or that is made with offensive material (i.e. transparent), excessively torn or exposes inappropriate portions of the body (i.e., string bikini tops, excessively cropped tops, G-strings); and adult costumes or clothing that can be viewed as a costume (does not include special events such as Mickey's Not-So-Scary Halloween Party or makeovers from the Pirates League in Magic Kingdom; children under age 10 can wear costumes at Disney any day of the year).

All park guests are required to wear shirts and shoes. Women may wear swimsuit tops if they are covered by other clothing. Guests wearing formal wedding attire are "discouraged" from entering the parks.

Items allowed in theme parks. You can bring a lot into a Disney World theme park:

Coolers: Those that don't have wheels and are smaller than 24 in. long by 15 in. wide by 18 in. high are OK. (This isn't true at Disney's Animal Kingdom, however, which prohibits all coolers except for those needed for medications.)

Food: Guests are welcome to bring in any snacks, foods or beverages (except alcoholic) that do not require heating.

Medications: Necessary medications are allowed. Medication coolers may be stored in a locker or at Guest Relations.

Umbrellas: Most any umbrella is allowed.

Items not allowed in theme parks. Just have to bring that folding chair? Sorry. Other prohibited items include:

Fingerprint file: At Disney World theme and water parks, biometric scanners identify guests by matching their fingerprints to data on their park tickets. Each guest inserts his or her ticket into a slot, then places an index finger onto the device.

Alcoholic beverages: You can buy them at every park except Magic Kingdom.
Glass containers: Excluding baby food jars and perfume bottles.
Oversized items: For example, strollers larger than 36 in. by 51 in.; backpacks, coolers or suitcases larger than 24 in. long by 15 in. wide by 18 in. high.
Pets: Except for service animals.
Pulled items: Guests are not permitted to pull any item behind them in a Disney theme park, including a stroller, wagon or any trailer-like object that is pushed or towed by an ECV, wheelchair or stroller.
Weapons: Of any kind.
Most wheeled items: Such as inline skates, scooters, skateboards, shoes with built-in wheels, suitcases, wagons, wheeled backpacks or coolers. No two-wheeled or three-wheeled conveyances except ECVs, strollers and wheelchairs.
At Disney's Animal Kingdom: Balloons, coolers and plastic drink lids and plastic straws (even the little straws attached to juice boxes) are not permitted for the safety of the wildlife.
Operating hours. Theme-park operating hours vary throughout the year. Guests staying at Disney resorts can take advantage of Extra Magic Hours. The operating hours listed below are approximations.
Magic Kingdom: The world's most popular theme park is typically open 9a–10p. It can, however, open as early as 7a and close as late as 4a. Magic Kingdom's operating hours have the greatest variance of any Disney World theme park.
Epcot: 9a–9p. Future World is open 9a–9p; though some minor attractions may close at 7p. World Showcase is open 11a–9p.

Disney's Hollywood Studios: 9a–7p.
Disney's Animal Kingdom: 9a–5p.
Water parks: 10a–5p.
For more operating-hours information call 407-824-4321 or log on to disneyworld.disney.go.com/calendars and click "Park Hours and Updates."

Tickets. Though Disney World's unconventional "Magic Your Way" ticketing concept is promoted as a way to let guests create tickets that match their particular needs, it's also so complicated that, at first glance, it can seem impossible to understand.
In a nutshell, Disney's plan lets you tailor tickets to include from one to 10 days of theme-park visits, and then add options such as the ability to visit more than one park a day or spend time at Disney's water parks. You can also add a prepaid dining plan (the Disney Dining Plan), itself with various options including recreation activities.
To buy tickets from the Disney company go to disneyworld.com or call 407-934-7639 from 7 a.m. to 10 p.m. Eastern time. Orlando Fun Tickets sells Disney tickets at a small discount at orlandofuntickets.com or 866-225-4712.
Theme-park tickets. The basic theme-park ticket—the "base ticket"—provides admission to one Disney theme park per day, and is good for up to 10 days. The more days the ticket includes the cheaper it is on a per-day basis; the difference between a three-day ticket and a seven-day ticket is only $23. The days the ticket is used do not need to be consecutive, but it expires 14 days after its first use.
Base Tickets have three options:
Park Hopper: This option lets you visit more than one theme park in the same day. Its price ($54) is the same regardless

Theme park ticket prices for 2011

This table shows Walt Disney World ticket prices as of January 1, 2011. Other annual and seasonal options are available for Florida residents and military personnel. For more information go to disneyworld.disney.go.com/tickets-passes or call Disney at 407-934-7639.

GENERAL PUBLIC	1-Day	2-Day	3-Day	4-Day	5-Day	6-Day	7-Day	8-Day	9-Day	10-Day
Base ticket ages 10+	$82	$162	$224	$232	$237	$242	$247	$252	$257	$262
Base ticket ages 3–9	$74	$146	$202	$209	$214	$219	$224	$229	$234	$239
Park Hopper option	$54	$54	$54	$54	$54	$54	$54	$54	$54	$54
Water Park Fun & More	$54	$54	$54	$54	$54	$54	$54	$54	$54	$54
No expiration	(n/a)	$22	$28	$67	$95	$106	$142	$182	$208	$213

Tickets expire 14 days from date of first use unless the No Expiration option is purchased. Tax not included.

FLORIDA RESIDENTS	1-Day	2-Day	3-Day	4-Day	5-Day	6-Day	7-Day	8-Day	9-Day	10-Day
Base ticket ages 10+	$74	(n/a)	$135	$168	$201	$216	$219	(n/a)	(n/a)	(n/a)
Base ticket ages 3–9	$67	(n/a)	$122	$151	$172	$184	$187	(n/a)	(n/a)	(n/a)
Park Hopper option	$27	(n/a)	$27	$27	$27	$27	$27	(n/a)	(n/a)	(n/a)
Water Park Fun & More	$27	(n/a)	$27	$27	$27	$27	$27	(n/a)	(n/a)	(n/a)
No expiration	(n/a)	(n/a)	$24	$36	$46	$76	$112	(n/a)	(n/a)	(n/a)

Tickets expire 6 months from their activation date unless the No Expiration option is purchased. Available pre-arrival at disneyworld.com, 407-934-7639, AAA in Florida, The Disney Stores in Florida and military bases in Florida; **no discounted one-day tickets sold on-site.** Tax not included.

U.S. MILITARY	1-Day	2-Day	3-Day	4-Day	5-Day	6-Day	7-Day	8-Day	9-Day	10-Day
Base ticket ages 10+	$82	$162	$215	$221	$224	$227	$230	$233	$235	$238
Base ticket ages 3–9	$70	$138	$183	$189	$191	$194	$197	$200	$203	$206
Park Hopper option	$54	$54	$54	$54	$54	$54	$54	$54	$54	$54
Water Park Fun & More	$54	$54	$54	$54	$54	$54	$54	$54	$54	$54
No expiration	(n/a)	$22	$28	$67	$95	$106	$142	$182	$208	$213
Stars & Stripes ages 10+	(n/a)	$252	$307	$314	$319	$323	$328	$332	$337	$342
Stars & Stripes ages 3–9	(n/a)	$236	$286	$292	$297	$301	$306	$310	$315	$319

Standard tickets expire 14 days from date of first use unless the No Expiration option is purchased. Tax not included. Stars & Stripes ticket entitles military guest staying at Shades of Green or Disney-owned resort to unlimited admission to all Walt Disney World theme and water parks, DisneyQuest and Disney's ESPN Wide World of Sports complex as well as complimentary parking, except activities and events separately priced. Expires one day longer than the number of days on the ticket. Tax not included.

ANNUAL PASSES	10+	3–9	10+ R	3–9 R	10+ D	3–9 D	10+ DR	3–9 DR	10+ C	3–9 C
Regular	$499	$450	$459	$415	$399	$360	$354	$320	$399	$360
Premium	$629	$567	$579	$523	$504	$454	$464	$419	$504	$454
Fla. Resident Regular	$379	$342	$344	$312	(n/a)	(n/a)	(n/a)	(n/a)	$305	$276
Fla. Resident Premium	$499	$450	$454	$411	(n/a)	(n/a)	(n/a)	(n/a)	$399	$360
Fla. Resident Seasonal	$259	$234	$231	$209	(n/a)	(n/a)	(n/a)	(n/a)	(n/a)	(n/a)
Fla. Res. Weekday Seasonal	$174	$157	(n/a)	(n/a)	(n/a)	(n/a)	(n/a)	(n/a)	(n/a)	(n/a)
Fla. Resident Epcot After 4	$144	$130	(n/a)	(n/a)	(n/a)	(n/a)	(n/a)	(n/a)	(n/a)	(n/a)
U.S. Military Regular	$480	$424	(n/a)	(n/a)	(n/a)	(n/a)	(n/a)	(n/a)	(n/a)	(n/a)
U.S. Military Premium	$607	$536	(n/a)	(n/a)	(n/a)	(n/a)	(n/a)	(n/a)	(n/a)	(n/a)
Military/FL Res. Reg.	$362	$319	(n/a)	(n/a)	(n/a)	(n/a)	(n/a)	(n/a)	(n/a)	(n/a)
Military/FL Res. Seasonal	$229	$203	(n/a)	(n/a)	(n/a)	(n/a)	(n/a)	(n/a)	(n/a)	(n/a)

R: Renewal. D: DVC member. DR: DVC member renewal. C: Charter. Annual Pass entitles guest to unlimited admission for 365 days from the activation date (except activities/events separately priced) to all Walt Disney World theme parks and free parking. Premium passes add admission to water parks, Disney's Oak Trail golf course, DisneyQuest and Disney's ESPN Wide World of Sports complex. No blockout dates. Seasonal Pass blockout dates are March 27–April 9, June 12–Aug. 19, Dec. 18–Jan. 1. Epcot After 4 pass includes unlimited admission to Epcot after 4 p.m. for 1 year. Tax not included.

Monorail trains run through Disney's Contemporary Resort (left). Other stations are at the Grand Floridian and Polynesian resorts, Magic Kingdom, Epcot and the Transportation and Ticket Center. Many areas are served by Disney buses and boats.

of the number of days the ticket is good for. Practical benefits include the ability to go to one park during the day then another at night to see its fireworks show, sample a variety of theme parks during a short visit and easily revisit favorite attractions.

Water Park Fun & More: This adds admission to Disney World's water parks, DisneyQuest, the ESPN Wide World of Sports complex and/or rounds of golf at Disney's 9-hole Oak Trail golf course. Like the Park Hopper option, the Water Parks Fun & More price ($54) is fixed, but the number of admissions it provides varies by how long the base ticket is good for. Regardless, if you use this option at least twice during your visit it pays for itself.

No Expiration: This add-on ($22–$213) means unused days never expire. You can add the option anytime within 14 days of first use. The cost is based on the number of days the ticket was originally valid. See also **Disney Dining Plan.**

Annual passes. An annual pass includes admission to the four theme parks, plus perks such as theme-park parking and discounts on dining, entertainment and merchandise.

A Premium option adds admission to water parks, DisneyQuest and ESPN Wide World of Sports; seasonal passes are available. Florida residents, members of the U.S. military, Disney Vacation Club members and charter annual passholders can get discounts.

Monthly payments: Floridians can buy annual passes and pay for them monthly. Disney requires a down payment of $82 for adult passes, $74 for those for children. The down payment and first monthly payment are made at the time of purchase. There is no interest fee. Calculate it out, and it means a Florida resident can buy a Regular Annual Pass for $106.75 upfront and then $24.75 per month for 11 months.

Discounts and upgrades. Disney offers discounts for Florida residents and members of the U.S. military. Once you buy a ticket you can always upgrade it but can't downgrade it.

Transportation. Though many guests get around Disney's 47-square-mile property in cars, there are many other options.

Disney buses. A huge fleet of diesel buses connect Disney's resorts with all theme and water parks and Downtown Disney, and also between some parks. Some buses run to character breakfasts. Buses typically arrive every 20 to 30 minutes, from one hour before park opening until one hour after closing.

Though Disney buses run from theme park to theme park, and from any theme park to Blizzard Beach, they do not go from all theme parks to Downtown Disney or Typhoon Lagoon and serve ESPN Wide World of Sports only from Disney's Hollywood Studios (8a–8p) and Disney's All-Star, Caribbean Beach and Pop Century resorts (5p–11p Thurs–Mon).

There is also no direct Disney bus service between resort hotels.

Except during thunderstorms, buses do not run from the Epcot resorts (BoardWalk, Yacht and Beach Club, Walt Disney World Swan and Dolphin) to Epcot or Disney's Hollywood Studios. Guests at those resorts travel to those parks via ferry boat or on foot. They enter Epcot through its rear International Gateway entrance into World Showcase.

Disney monorails. These electric trains connect Disney's Transportation and Ticket Center (TTC) with Magic Kingdom and the Contemporary, Grand Floridian and Polynesian resorts; a separate line runs to Epcot. Monorails run from approximately 7 a.m. until two hours after park closing.

Disney boats. Ferry boats connect Magic Kingdom with the TTC and the resorts on Seven Seas Lagoon and Bay Lake; Epcot and Hollywood Studios with resorts between those parks; and Downtown Disney with the Port Orleans, Old Key West and Saratoga Springs resorts.

For more detailed Disney transportation information call 407-824-4321.

Rental cars. Orlando is the largest rental-car market in the world. At the Orlando International Airport—which rents more

Rental car companies at OIA

Eleven rental-car agencies serve the Orlando International Airport:

Advantage	407	857-1999
Alamo	800	327-9633
Avis	800	331-1212
Budget	800	527-0700
Dollar	800	800-4000
Enterprise	800	325-8007
E-Z	800	277-5171
Hertz	800	654-3131
L and M	407	888-0515
National	800	227-7368
Thrifty	800	367-2277

A 'huge loaf of bread'

It's the future of transportation—as imagined in the 1870s. It's the elevated monorail.

The concept of a small train straddling an elevated beam debuted in 1876, at Pennsylvania's American Centennial Exposition. Inventor LeRoy Stone argued that a single beam was cheaper than a two-rail system, and that elevating it made it fit into America's growing cities. Two years later a 4-mile system was built, running between Bradford and Gilmore, Penn. The train was a hit—until it blew off its tracks.

The idea reemerged after World War II. As traffic jams began to clog rebuilt German cities, industrialist Dr. Axel Wenner-Gren thought a monorail train—with additional horizontal stabilizing wheels that hugged its beam—would be just the ticket. Working near Cologne, he built an elevated track and boxy test train in 1957. A few months later, who should come driving through the area but the vacationing Walt and Lillian Disney. Glancing out his side window, Walt noticed a "huge loaf of bread" gliding above the treetops. He followed it to a service yard, to the office of Dr. Wenner-Gren and his company, Alweg Research.

Wenner-Gren had his first sale. Making just one change—the bodies would be redesigned to look like sleek Buck Rogers spaceships—Walt purchased an Alweg system for his Disneyland theme park in California. Debuting as a Tomorrowland ride in 1959, the 4,200-foot monorail was a serious demonstration of a future transportation system. It had overpasses, steep grades and tight turns.

Alweg built two other demo trains (for the 1961 Expo Italia fair in Turin, Italy and the 1962 Century 21 Exposition in Seattle), but never sold a system to a city. Wenner-Gren died in 1961; his test track was demolished in 1967 to make room for a subdivision.

The Disney World monorail comes close to fulfilling the doctor's dreams—it's a real transportation system, used by an average of 200,000 passengers a day. The two-track, 14-mile "highway in the sky" has six public stations. Today's trains are built by Bombardier, with a look that's similar to that company's Learjets. Each is 203 feet long, has six cars, eight 113-hp electric motors and can carry 360 passengers. Top speed is 45 mph; without equipment each fiberglass body weighs only 800 pounds.

The Orlando International Airport is the largest rental-car facility in the world, renting over 2 million cars a year, nearly 5,500 a day. Most major rental companies (including Hertz, left) are located in an adjacent parking garage.

than 2 million cars a year—most major rental companies have their cars in the adjacent parking garage, which eliminates the need for a shuttle bus. Rental-car counters are located on the Ground Transportation Level (Level 1) of each side of the terminal.

For guests already at Disney, the most convenient place to rent a car may be Disney's Car Care Center, which sits at the exit of the Magic Kingdom parking lot. A counter (407-824-3470) offers Alamo and National vehicles and shuttles guests from all Disney hotels. Satellite desks are at the Walt Disney World Dolphin (407-934-4930) and the Buena Vista Palace (407-827-6363). Four other hotels on Disney property have car-rental counters: the Downtown Disney Hilton (Avis, 407-827-2847), Doubletree Guest Suites (Budget, 407-827-6089), Wyndham (Dollar, 407-583-8000) and Shades of Green (Hertz, 407-938-0600).

Local rental-car customers pay a 6 percent sales tax, a $2.05 daily "road impact fee" and a 10 percent surcharge to the Greater Orlando Aviation Authority.

Taxicabs and town cars. Taxicabs, town cars and other vehicles are available for travel around Disney and the surrounding area, including airports. Mears Transportation—the largest transportation operator in the area, and the only contracted provider for Disney—has the most choices (24-hour reservations 407-423-5566, taxicabs 407-422-2222 or 407-699-9999, mearstransportation.com). To get a cab with a child's car seat, ask for one when you make your reservation.

Airport shuttle service. Mears offers group transportation from the Orlando International Airport to Disney-area resorts. Passengers wait on a bus or van at the airport until the vehicle is full. On the return trip,

shuttle passengers are picked up three to four hours before their flight times. Fares: One-way: $20 adult, $16 child. Round trip: $33 adult, $26 child. Children under 3 ride free.

Taxicabs. Mears taxis operate under the Yellow Cab, Checker Cab and City Cab brands. Transportation within Disney property should cost $10–$20; the fare for traveling between the Orlando International Airport and Disney is typically $55–$65. For groups of 5 or more, vans hold up to 8 people for $80–$90. Note: Though Mears is the only contracted taxi provider for Disney property, other cabs lurk in the area. These "gypsies" often have higher rates and may take only cash.

Town cars. Many area upscale resorts have Mears town cars available 24 hours a day. Mears airport town car service includes a driver who will meet a guest at baggage claim with a personalized sign, and transportation in a luxury sedan to the guest's resort; the fare to Walt Disney World resorts is typically $80–$90 for up to four passengers.

Vehicle charters. Mears has 55-passenger buses, 25-passenger mini-buses, 11-passenger vans and 8-passenger limos. Fares and policies are at mearstransportation.com.

Weddings. Up to a dozen couples tie the knot at Walt Disney World every day. And no wonder—Disney has unrivaled facilities for a family gathering, good year-round weather and a one-stop Fairy Tale Weddings division. Most weddings are performed at Disney's Wedding Pavilion next to the Grand Floridian Resort and Spa. Several hotels—including the BoardWalk, Polynesian, Wilderness Lodge and Yacht Club—also host them.

Planning. Named after Martin Short's memorable wedding planner in Disney's

Brief thunderstorms are common at Walt Disney World during summer months. They typically last less than an hour. Disney sells plastic ponchos for about $8, umbrellas from $14 to $40.

1991 movie "Father of the Bride," Franck's Bridal Studio offers services to help couples design their wedding. These include arranging accommodations, cakes, flowers, music, photography and rehearsal dinners. The facility is next to the wedding pavilion.

Costs. Disney offers three wedding packages, which vary based on the number of guests and the level of services requested. The average wedding costs $27,000 and includes 100 people. Prices start at $4,500.

For more information call 321-939-4610 or go online to disneyweddings.com.

Honeymoons. Disney planning services includes an on-line registry (407-939-7776, disneyhoneymoonregistry.com), which lets couples create a wish list for their trip and have family and friends contribute. More honeymoon help is available at 800-370-6009 or online at disneyhoneymoons.com.

Youth groups. Disney World offers various activities and competitions for youth groups of 10 or more. Participants get discounted group rates for both accommodations and theme-park tickets. Opportunities include:

Disney Magic Music Days: This audition-based performance program invites community groups and middle- and high-school students to perform at Disney year round. Instrumental and vocal groups participate, as do dance ensembles (instrumental groups 866-242-3617, vocal 866-578-4823, dance 866-578-4827). Students can benefit from optional performance workshops conducted by Disney professionals (866-578-4830).

Festival Disney: Held each spring, this educational experience is open to middle-school, junior- and senior-high school concert bands, jazz ensembles, marching (parade) bands, orchestras, vocal ensembles, show choirs and auxiliary units. No audition is required; directors choose either competitive or non-competitive adjudication options. Performances take place at Disney's Saratoga Springs Resort, Disney's Hollywood Studios and Downtown Disney (877-939-6884).

Disney Jazz Celebration: Held in conjunction with Festival Disney, this event provides middle- and high-school instrumental and vocal jazz ensembles a chance to perform for recognized jazz educators and appear in evening performances (866-842-3340).

Disney Youth Education Series: These "YES" programs give elementary through senior high students real-world learning experiences at Disney World theme parks. Hands-on courses taught by specially trained Disney facilitators focus on Leadership & Careers, Arts & Humanities, Physical Sciences and Natural Sciences.

Walt Disney World weather

Month	Avg high	Avg low	Rain
Jan	72	48	2.4 in.
Feb	73	49	2.7 in.
Mar	77	53	3.3 in.
April	82	58	2.0 in.
May	87	64	3.8 in.
June	90	70	6.0 in.
July	92	72	6.6 in.
Aug	92	72	7.3 in.
Sept	90	71	6.0 in.
Oct	84	65	3.2 in.
Nov	79	57	2.4 in.
Dec	73	50	2.2 in.

Character Guide

More than 80 Disney characters greet guests at Walt Disney World theme parks, water parks and resort hotels. Here's a list of the ones who appear most often, and where you're most likely to find them:

Aladdin: Arab "street rat," star of 1992's "Aladdin." Wins love of princess Jasmine after learns to be true to himself. **Magic Kingdom:** Magic Carpets of Aladdin, Adventureland. **Epcot:** Morocco pavilion.

Alice: Appears at Walt Disney World as star of 1951's animated "Alice in Wonderland." Curious, proper English girl dreams of non-sensical Wonderland. **Magic Kingdom:** Mad Tea

Magic Kingdom: Fairytale Garden, Fantasyland. **Grand Floridian Resort:** 1900 Park Fare dinner.

Annie: Disney Junior TV series "Little Einsteins" co-star, 4-year-old blonde likes to sing, loves most animals (esp. horses), fears spiders. Leo's little sister. **Disney's Hollywood Studios:** Animation Courtyard.

Ariel: Rebellious redheaded teen, star of 1989's "The Little Mermaid." "Sick of swimmin,'" loves all things human. Falls in love with Prince Eric. Best friend is a fish, Flounder. Wears seashell bikini top as mermaid, turquoise gown as human. **Magic Kingdom:** Fantasyland (after expansion). **Epcot:** Akershus Royal Banquet Hall meals (often), Norway pavilion.

Aurora: Blameless blond princess of 1959's "Sleeping Beauty" awakened from cursed coma by Prince Phillip's kiss. Also known as Briar Rose. Pink gown. **Magic Kingdom:** Exposition Hall; Cinderella's Royal Table breakfast, lunch (often), Cinderella Castle. **Epcot:** France pavilion; Akershus Royal Banquet Hall meals (often), Norway pavilion.

Baloo: Happy-go-lucky, lazy bear in 1967's "Jungle Book" teaches "man-cub" Mowgli how to relax, live in wild. Loves to scratch back on trees. **Disney's Animal Kingdom:** On trail off Asia-Africa walkway.

Beast: Selfish prince is transformed by witchy woman into hideous creature in 1991's "Beauty and the Beast." Has face of wildebeest; tusks of boar; mane of lion; body of bear, legs, tail of wolf. Transforms back into prince after learns to be kind and earns love of Belle. **Epcot:** France pavilion.

Belle: Co-star of 1991's "Beauty and the Beast," bookish brunette falls in love with beastly captor. Stands up for herself. Wears golden gown or turquoise dress with white apron. **Magic Kingdom:** Exposition Hall; Cinderella's Royal Table breakfast, lunch (often), Cinderella Castle. **Epcot:** France pavilion; Akershus Royal Banquet Hall meals (often), Norway pavilion. **Disney's Hollywood Studios:** Sorcerer's Hat, Hollywood Blvd.

Jasmine and Aladdin appear together at Magic Kingdom's Adventureland and Epcot's Morocco pavilion

Party, Fantasyland. **Epcot:** The Toy Soldier, U.K. pavilion; Akershus Royal Banquet Hall meals (often), Norway pavilion. **Grand Floridian Resort:** 1900 Park Fare breakfast.

Anastasia and Drizella: Conniving stepsisters to Cinderella in 1950's "Cinderella," daughters of Lady Tremaine. Redhead Anastasia is spiteful; brunette Drizella disorganized.

Buzz Lightyear: Deluded "Toy Story" space ranger is Woody's best friend. **Magic Kingdom:** Carousel of Progress, Tomorrowland. **Disney's Hollywood Studios:** Woody's Picture Shootin' Corral, Pixar Place.

Captain Hook: Snide pirate dandy in 1953's "Peter Pan"; intent on defeating Peter Pan, fending off ticking crocodile that has

Baloo

Buzz Lightyear

Donald Duck

Photos: Micaela Neal

swallowed alarm clock. Has hook for hand from previous encounter with Peter; looks, voice of Wendy's father. **Magic Kingdom:** Pirates of the Caribbean, Adventureland.

Chip 'n Dale: Playful chipmunks in 1940s–1950s cartoons. Smarter, sneakier Chip has small black nose that resembles chocolate

Micaela Neal

Chip 'n Dale. Can't tell them apart? Chip, left, has a black nose, while Dale's is red, and larger.

"chip." Goofier Dale has large red nose, two separated buck teeth. **Magic Kingdom:** Town Square, Main Street U.S.A.; Tomorrowland Plaza, Tomorrowland. **Epcot:** Garden Grill dinner, The Land pavilion. **Disney's Hollywood Studios:** Sorcerer's Hat, Hollywood Blvd. **Disney's Animal Kingdom:** Character greeting trails, Camp Minnie-Mickey. **Fort Wilderness Resort:** Mickey's Backyard Barbecue dinner show.

Cinderella: Definitive rags-to-riches heroine, upbeat blonde saved by Prince Charming from life of stepmother servitude in 1950's "Cinderella." Friend to animals, especially Gus, Jaq and other castle mice. Lives in Cinderella Castle; wears light blue gown at Disney World. **Magic Kingdom:** Exposition Hall; Cinderella's Royal Table, Cinderella Castle. **Epcot:** Akershus Royal Banquet Hall meals (often), Norway pavilion. **Grand Floridian Resort:** 1900 Park Fare dinner.

Daisy Duck: Donald Duck's impatient girlfriend in 1940s–1950s cartoons. Likes shopping, flowers. Best friend of Minnie Mouse. **Magic Kingdom:** Town Square outside Expo Hall, Main Street U.S.A. **Disney's Hollywood Studios:** Sorcerer's Hat, Hollywood Blvd. **Disney's Animal Kingdom:** Character greeting trails, Camp Minnie-Mickey; Donald's Safari Breakfast, Tusker House, Africa.

Donald Duck: He's rude, he's crude, he doesn't wear pants. He shouts, pouts and loses his temper at the drop of a pin. He likes to be mean. Yet who doesn't love Donald Duck, a character who responds to life the way we want to, but rarely dare? Created in 1934 as a foil for Mickey Mouse, Donald soon emerged as Disney's most popular star. The "duck with all the bad luck" is known for his "hopping mad" boxing stance, a leaning, jumping

Photos: Micaela Neal

Fairy Godmother   Frozone   Handy Manny

posture with one arm straight, the other twirling like a windmill. **Magic Kingdom:** Across from Frontierland Shootin' Gallery (frontier clothing). **Epcot:** Mexico pavilion (garb from 1944's "The Three Caballeros"). **Disney's Hollywood Studios:** Sorcerer's Hat, Hollywood Blvd. **Disney's Animal Kingdom:** Character greeting trails, Camp Minnie-Mickey. **Beach Club Resort:** Cape May Cafe breakfast. **Contemporary Resort:** Chef Mickey's meals.

Dopey: Sweet dimwit of 1937's "Snow White and the Seven Dwarfs" is film's only clean-shaven dwarf. Large ears. Has crush on Snow White. **Magic Kingdom:** Town Square, Main Street U.S.A. Epcot: Germany pavilion.

Eeyore: Gloomy stuffed toy donkey in 1977's "The Many Adventures of Winnie the Pooh." Speaks in depressed monotone. Devoted to friends. Tied with pink bow, tail often falls off. Magic Kingdom: Crystal Palace meals, Main Street U.S.A. Disney's Animal Kingdom: Boat landing across from Flame Tree BBQ, Discovery Island.

Esmerelda: Beautiful gypsy of 1996 movie "The Hunchback of Notre Dame" helps Quasimodo gain confidence to escape evil master Frollo. Musical free spirit, loves soldier Phoebus. **Epcot:** Akershus Royal Banquet Hall meals (often), Norway pavilion.

Fairy Godmother: Absent-minded fairy helps Cinderella go to ball in 1950's "Cinderella." Rotund, grandmotherly, uses wand to make magic with a "Bibbidi, bobbidi boo!" **Magic Kingdom:** Cinderella Castle (back left corner), Fantasyland; Cinderella's Royal Table dinner, Cinderella Castle.

Flik: Inventive, optimistic ant of 1998's "A Bug's Life." Crush on Princess Atta; friends

with circus bugs; nemesis is grasshopper Hopper. **Disney's Animal Kingdom:** River overlook off Asia-Africa walkway.

Flynn Rider: Charming bandit captured by Rapunzel in 2010's "Tangled." Inspired by dashing real-life screen legend Errol Flynn. **Magic Kingdom:** Fairytale Garden, Fantasyland.

Friar Tuck and Little John: Merry men from 1973's "Robin Hood." Jolly badger Tuck is a former monk; big bear John tries to keep his friend Robin out of trouble. **Disney's Hollywood Studios:** Sorcerer's Hat, Hollywood Blvd.

Frozone: Superhero name of Lucius Best, a confident speed-skater and best friend to Mr. Incredible in 2004's "The Incredibles." Can freeze moisture in air, make snow. **Disney's Hollywood Studios:** The Magic of Disney Animation, Animation Courtyard.

Genie: Steals the show in 1992's "Aladdin." Witty, fast-talking blue genie channels his voice talent, Robin Williams. Can reshape body. Grants Aladdin three wishes. **Magic Kingdom:** Magic Carpets of Aladdin, Adventureland. **Epcot:** Morocco pavilion.

Geppetto: Kindly woodcarver makes a puppet boy in 1940's "Pinocchio," wishes on star for the puppet to be his human son. **Disney's Hollywood Studios:** Sorcerer's Hat, Hollywood Blvd.

Goliath: Adorable loyal lion is the pet, and the conscience, of JoJo the Clown in Disney Junior TV show "JoJo's Circus." Playfully hides from JoJo. **Disney's Hollywood Studios:** Animation Courtyard.

Jiminy Cricket   Lady Tremaine   Leo

Goofy: Good-hearted country simpleton appeals to your inner idiot. Clumsy and gullible, has hard time concentrating. Has bad posture, ill-fitting clothes, big stomach yet always mugs for camera. Many physical characteristics of dog; first known as Dippy Dog in 1930. Later hosted series of "How To" sports parodies, in 1950s was transformed into suburban everyman George Geef. **Magic Kingdom:** Left of Splash Mountain, Frontierland. **Epcot:** Character Spot, Innoventions Plaza. **Disney's Hollywood Studios:** Sorcerer's Hat, Hollywood Blvd. **Disney's Animal Kingdom:** Character greeting trails, Camp Minnie-Mickey; Donald's Safari Breakfast, Tusker House, Africa. **Beach Club Resort:** Cape May Cafe breakfast. **Contemporary Resort:** Chef Mickey's meals. **Fort Wilderness Resort:** Mickey's Backyard Barbecue dinner show.

Gov. Ratcliffe: Corrupt, pompous Jamestown leader in 1995's "Pocahontas." Nearly starts war between settlers and Indians until Pocahontas steps in. **Disney's Hollywood Studios:** Sorcerer's Hat, Hollywood Blvd.

Green Army Men: Molded-plastic "Toy Story" soldiers often comically shout orders, directions to Disney World guests. **Disney's Hollywood Studios:** Pixar Place.

Handy Manny: Star of Disney Junior TV show "Handy Manny," bilingual Hispanic handyman Manny Garcia uses talking tools. **Disney's Hollywood Studios:** Animation Courtyard; Play 'N Dine character meals, Echo Lake.

Jasmine: Spirited 16-year-old princess in 1992's "Aladdin." Long black ponytail. Wears aqua bedlah with pouffy pants. Has pet tiger. **Magic Kingdom:** Magic Carpets of Aladdin, Adventureland; Cinderella's Royal Table breakfast, lunch (often), Cinderella Castle. **Epcot:** Morocco pavilion; Akershus Royal Banquet Hall meals (often), Norway pavilion.

Jessie: Plucky yodeling "Toy Story" cowgirl. Woody's exuberant friend; has secret crush on Buzz Lightyear. **Magic Kingdom:** Splash Mountain, Frontierland.

Alice and the Mad Hatter. Walt Disney World characters are from the 1951 animated movie.

Meeko: Micaela Neal

Lilo   Meeko   Mickey Mouse

Jiminy Cricket: Dapper whistling cricket is Pinocchio's conscience in 1940's "Pinocchio." Always carries an umbrella, wears a top hat. **Disney's Animal Kingdom:** Conservation Station, Rafiki's Planet Watch.

JoJo: Curious, energetic 6-year-old clown JoJo Tickle in Disney Junior television show "JoJo's Circus." **Disney's Hollywood Studios:** Animation Courtyard.

June: Black-haired 6-year-old from Disney Junior's "Little Einsteins" loves art, dancing, astronomy. **Disney's Hollywood Studios:** Animation Courtyard; Play 'N Dine breakfast, lunch, Echo Lake.

King Louie: Orangutan in 1967's "Jungle Book" plays practical jokes, kidnaps boy Mowgli in effort to gain knowledge of fire, and therefore learn to be like a human. **Disney's Animal Kingdom:** On trail off Asia-Africa walkway.

Lady Tremaine: Imperious, sarcastic stepmom in 1950's "Cinderella" treats Cinderella as servant. Mother of Anastasia, Drizella. **Magic Kingdom:** Fairytale Garden, Fantasyland. **Grand Floridian Resort:** 1900 Park Fare dinner.

Leo: Six-year-old redhead from Disney Junior's "Little Einsteins" loves to conduct music. Annie's big brother. **Disney's Hollywood Studios:** Animation Courtyard; Play 'N Dine character meals, Echo Lake.

Lightning McQueen: Hotshot stock-car star of 2006 Pixar movie "Cars." At first is arrogant; eventually becomes big-hearted, loyal. **Disney's Hollywood Studios:** Luigi's Garage, Streets of America.

Lilo: Lonely orphan of 2002's "Lilo & Stitch," 7-year-old Hawaiian loves Elvis Presley, surfing. Adopts alien as pet, names it Stitch. Lives with her older sister. **Disney's Hollywood Studios:** Sorcerer's Hat, Hollywood Blvd. **Disney's Animal Kingdom**: outside Island Mercantile, Discovery Island. **Polynesian Resort:** 'Ohana breakfast.

Mad Hatter: Manic milliner confuses Alice during "unbirthday" party in 1951's "Alice in Wonderland." Lisps; tall green hat bears "10/6" (ten shillings, six pence) price tag. **Magic Kingdom:** Mad Tea Party, Fantasyland. **Grand Floridian Resort:** 1900 Park Fare breakfast; Wonderland Tea Party.

Marie: White French kitten in 1970's "The Aristocats" thinks girls better than boys; bosses two brothers. Wears pink bows. **Epcot:** France pavilion (sporadically).

Mary Poppins: Magical nanny teaches uptight family to enjoy life in 1964's "Mary Poppins." Proper, kind, thinks for herself, flies with umbrella. **Magic Kingdom:** Town Square outside Expo Hall, Main Street U.S.A. **Epcot:** The Toy Soldier, U.K. pavilion. **Disney's Hollywood Studios:** Sorcerer's Hat, Hollywood Blvd. **Grand Floridian Resort:** 1900 Park Fare breakfast.

'Mater: Good ol' boy tow truck in 2006's "Cars." Sidekick to, best buds with, Lightning McQueen. Prankster. **Disney's Hollywood Studios:** Luigi's Garage, Streets of America.

Meeko: Friendly, silly raccoon in 1995's "Pocahontas" loves to eat. Pocahontas' pet and one of her best friends along with Flit the hummingbird. **Disney's Animal Kingdom:** Character greeting trails, Camp Minnie-Mickey.

Minnie Mouse

Mr. Incredible

Mulan

Photos: Micaela Neal

Mickey Mouse: Based in part on silent-film star Charlie Chaplin, debuted in 1928 as underdog who dreamed big. Looks are based on his predecessor, Oswald the Lucky Rabbit. His optimistic attitude was perfect antidote to 1930s Great Depression; at many theaters, the name "Mickey Mouse" would be in larger letters on marquee than stars of feature. In 1933 received 800,000 fan letters (more than any live-action Hollywood star); President Roosevelt later began showing Mickey cartoons at the White House. Happy-go-lucky, said to be Walt Disney's alter ego. World's most recognized and celebrated cartoon character, Americana pop-culture icon, corporate symbol. During World War II symbolized can-do spirit of U.S. Banned in Nazi Germany in 1933, the Soviet Union in 1936, Yugoslavia in 1937, Italy in 1938; in 1960s was embraced by counterculture as symbol of mischievous rebellion. **Magic Kingdom:** Exposition Hall. **Epcot:** Character Spot, Innoventions Plaza; Garden Grill dinner, The Land pavilion. **Disney's Hollywood Studios:** Sorcerer's Hat, Hollywood Blvd; The Magic of Disney Animation, Animation Courtyard (as Sorcerer's Apprentice). **Disney's Animal Kingdom:** Character greeting trails, Camp Minnie-Mickey; Donald's Safari Breakfast, Tusker House, Africa. **Contemporary Resort:** Chef Mickey's meals. **Fort Wilderness Resort:** Mickey's Backyard Barbecue dinner show. **Polynesian Resort:** 'Ohana breakfast.

Mike Wazowski: One-eyed green monster likes to get laughs in 2001's "Monsters, Inc." Quick-witted; Sulley's best friend, roommate. **Disney's Hollywood Studios:** Streets of America, at exit to Backlot Tour.

Minnie Mouse: Mickey's girlfriend. Flatters, swoons over her main squeeze. Quick-witted;

energetic; loves animals, cooking and gardening. Can play harmonica, guitar, piano. In early cartoons she gets mad: slaps Mickey after he forces her to kiss him in 1928's "Plane Crazy" then jumps out of their open-cockpit airplane; smashes a lamp on Mickey's head when he pulls her nose in 1930's "The Cactus Kid"; when she mistakenly thinks Mickey has given her a bone for a present in 1933's "Puppy Love" kicks him out of her house and sobs "I hate him! I hate all men!" Has an old flame (suave, tap-dancing Mortimer) in the 1936 cartoon "Mickey's Rival"; has children in 1933's "Mickey's Steam Roller." As portrayed in the 1928 cartoon "The Gallopin' Gaucho," Mickey and Minnie first meet in a bar in Argentina. When Minnie, a flirty tavern dancer, bats her eyes at Mickey, a cigarette-smoking outlaw(!), he watches her dance, chugs a beer, then grabs her for a dramatic tango. Later, he rescues her from a kitty kidnapper. Walt Disney originally voiced both characters. **Magic Kingdom:** Exposition Hall. **Epcot:** Character Spot, Innoventions Plaza. **Disney's Hollywood Studios:** Sorcerer's Hat, Hollywood Blvd. **Disney's Animal Kingdom:** Character greeting trails, Camp Minnie-Mickey; Donald's Safari Breakfast, Tusker House, Africa. **Beach Club Resort:** Cape May Cafe breakfast. **Contemporary Resort:** Chef Mickey's meals. **Fort Wilderness Resort:** Mickey's Backyard Barbecue dinner show.

Mr. Incredible: Frustrated claims adjuster, super-strong Bob Parr is devoted dad, husband, superhero in 2004 Pixar movie "The Incredibles." **Disney's Hollywood Studios:** The Magic of Disney Animation, Animation Courtyard.

Mrs. Incredible: Quick-witted mom, wife, superhero in "The Incredibles," Helen Parr's

Rafiki, Stitch: Micaela Neal

Rafiki

Snow White

Stitch

stretching ability gives her superhero name Elastigirl. **Disney's Hollywood Studios:** The Magic of Disney Animation, Animation Courtyard.

Mr. Smee: Captain Hook's bumbling, fumbling, cowardly first mate in 1953's "Peter Pan." Balding, fat. **Magic Kingdom:** Pirates of the Caribbean, Adventureland.

Mulan: Star of 1998's "Mulan"; brave Chinese girl pretends to be boy, joins army to take frail father's place. Quick-witted, strong. **Epcot:** China pavilion; Akershus Royal Banquet Hall (often), Norway pavilion.

Mushu: Fast-talking small dragon "protects" Mulan in 1998's "Mulan." **Epcot:** China pavilion.

Oso: Stuffed panda from Disney Junior TV show "Special Agent Oso" is bumbling agent trainee, enlists viewers to complete assignments such as cleaning their rooms, brushing teeth, using library. **Disney's Hollywood Studios:** Play 'N Dine character meals, Echo Lake.

Penguins: Dancing "Jolly Holiday" waiters in 1964's "Mary Poppins." **Magic Kingdom:** Town Square, Main Street U.S.A.

Peter Pan: Confident preteen of 1953's "Peter Pan" vows to never grow up. Loves adventure, bravely fights pirates, flies with Tinker Bell. **Magic Kingdom:** Pirates of the Caribbean, Adventureland.

Piglet: Stuffed pig faithful to Pooh in 1977's "The Many Adventures of Winnie the Pooh." Small, shy, fearful. **Magic Kingdom:** Crystal Palace meals, Main Street U.S.A. **Disney's Animal Kingdom:** Boat landing across from Flame Tree BBQ, Discovery Island.

Pinocchio: Wooden marionette given gift of life by Blue Fairy in 1940's "Pinocchio." Naively led astray; nose grows when tells lie. Best friend Jiminy Cricket is conscience. **Magic Kingdom:** Town Square, Main Street U.S.A. **Disney's Hollywood Studios:** Sorcerer's Hat, Hollywood Blvd.

Pluto: Mickey Mouse's pet dog; gangly yellow hound is only Disney Fab Five character who doesn't speak or walk upright (except at theme parks). Licks, sniffs, romps and runs in a fashion recognizable to dog lovers everywhere. Always thinking, as cartoon dog is known for his vivid expressions. First appeared in 1930 cartoon "The Chain Gang" as an unnamed bloodhound, then briefly was Minnie's pet, named Rover. Once spoke: in 1931 short "The Moose Hunt" got down on knees and, doing an impersonation of Al Jolson, proclaimed "Mammy!"; later in same cartoon looked into Mickey's eyes and whispered "Kiss me!" Named for the now-demoted planet. **Magic Kingdom:** Town Square outside Expo Hall, Main Street U.S.A. **Epcot:** Character Spot, Innoventions Plaza; Garden Grill dinner, The Land pavilion. **Disney's Hollywood Studios:** Sorcerer's Hat, Hollywood Blvd. **Disney's Animal Kingdom:** DinoLand U.S.A. **Contemporary Resort:** Chef Mickey's meals. **Polynesian Resort:** 'Ohana breakfast.

Pocahontas: Brave, noble Indian maiden loves nature, animals (especially raccoon best friend Meeko), English captain John Smith in 1995's "Pocahontas." Spreads message of preserving, honoring nature. Long straight black hair. **Disney's Hollywood Studios:** Sorcerer's Hat, Hollywood Blvd. **Disney's Animal Kingdom:** Conservation Station, Rafiki's Planet Watch; Character greeting trails, Camp Minnie-Mickey.

Thumper   Tiana   Tinker Bell

Queen of Hearts: Fowl-tempered monarch of Wonderland in 1951's "Alice in Wonderland." Mean, vain, quick to command "Off with their heads!" Triggers Alice's return home. **Disney's Hollywood Studios:** Sorcerer's Hat, Hollywood Blvd.

Quincy: Appearing in Disney Junior's "Little Einsteins," African-American 5-year-old loves to play music. Afraid of dark. Named for musician Quincy Jones. **Disney's Hollywood Studios:** Animation Courtyard.

Rafiki: Wise shaman baboon who advises Simba's father Mufasa in 1994's "The Lion King." Carries gourd-topped walking stick. Magic Kingdom: Front entrance verandah, Adventureland. **Disney's Animal Kingdom:** Conservation Station, Rafiki's Planet Watch.

Rapunzel: Spunky teen with 70 feet of golden hair, star of 2010's "Tangled." Locked in tower for years, seeks escape by capturing charming, handsome bandit Flynn Rider. Magical hair has healing powers. **Magic Kingdom:** Fairytale Garden, Fantasyland.

Snow White: Gentle young princess whose stepmother tries repeatedly to kill her in 1937's "Snow White and the Seven Dwarfs." Befriends, mothers seven dwarfs; saved from death by "love's first kiss" by prince. White skin, raven-black hair. Most colorful princess gown; yellow skirt, white collar, blue bodice with red trim. **Magic Kingdom:** Town Square, Main Street U.S.A.; Cinderella's Royal Table meals (often), Cinderella Castle. **Epcot:** Germany pavilion; Akershus Royal Banquet Hall meals (often), Norway pavilion. **Disney's Hollywood Studios:** Sorcerer's Hat, Hollywood Blvd.

Stitch: Mischievous alien star of 2002's "Lilo & Stitch," known initially as Experiment 626. Escapes from outer space prison to Earth, where he is adopted and named by little girl Lilo. Bad-boy behavior includes picking nose, burping. **Magic Kingdom:** Carousel of Progress, Tomorrowland. **Disney's Hollywood Studios:** Sorcerer's Hat, Hollywood Blvd. **Disney's Animal Kingdom:** Outside Island Mercantile shop, Discovery Island. **Polynesian Resort:** 'Ohana breakfast.

Sulley: Good-natured giant monster James P. Sullivan in 2001's "Monsters, Inc." Has blue fur, purple spots. One-eyed Mike Wazowski is best friend, roommate. **Disney's Hollywood Studios:** Streets of America, at exit to Backlot Tour.

Terk: Smart-aleck tomboy gorilla in 1999's "Tarzan" likes to play pranks. Tarzan's best friend, cousin. **Disney's Animal Kingdom:** Across from Pizzafari, Discovery Island.

Thumper: Curious, talkative young rabbit befriends and shows forest to fawn Bambi in 1942's "Bambi." Thumps foot to send messages. **Disney's Animal Kingdom:** Plaza, Camp Minnie-Mickey.

Tiana and Prince Naveen: Stars of 2009's "The Princess and the Frog," Disney's first African-American (or, for that matter, American) princess, Tiana is an aspiring New Orleans restaurant owner who falls in love with funny, carefree, jazz-loving Prince Naveen. In a twist on the classic fairytale, when she kissed the frog prince she was turned into a frog herself. Tiana wears a pale green gown inspired by bayou elements. **Magic Kingdom:** Behind Ye Olde Christmas Shoppe, Liberty Square.

Photos: Micaela Neal

Wendy   White Rabbit   Woody

Tigger: Ebulliently optimistic toy tiger in 1977's "The Many Adventures of Winnie the Pooh loves to bounce. Tells Pooh false rumors about honey-thief "hefflalumps and woozles." Proud to be "onliest" tigger in the Hundred-Acre Wood. **Magic Kingdom:** Crystal Palace meals, Main Street U.S.A. **Epcot:** The Toy Soldier, U.K. pavilion. **Disney's Animal Kingdom:** Boat landing across from Flame Tree BBQ, Discovery Island. **Grand Floridian Resort:** 1900 Park Fare character breakfast.

Timon: Smart-aleck meerkat saves lion cub Simba with help from best-friend warthog Pumbaa in 1994 Disney movie "The Lion King." Has Catskills-comic personality; motto is "hakuna matata" (no worries). **Magic Kingdom:** Entrance verandah, Adventureland.

Tinker Bell and friends: Feisty, jealous pixie loyal to Peter in 1953's "Peter Pan." Jingles when moves; flies using magic pixie dust. Has talent for fixing things, hence "tinker" name. Dresses in bright green. Often appears at Disney World with acquaintances from current Disney Fairies movies and books, including tomboy Fawn (animal fairy loves playing games, speaks every animal language; wears long brown braid, orange and tan outfit), worrywart Iridessa (African-American light fairy; uses sunflower seed as button on golden yellow gown), sassy Rosetta (redheaded garden fairy, loves to give makeovers, tells bedtime stories to potted plants; dresses in pink), silly Silvermist (raven-haired water fairy, loves gossip, adds dewdrops to spider webs; dresses in blue) and kind Terence (helpful sparrow man, has crush on best friend Tinker Bell; wears acorn cap). **Disney's Hollywood Studios:** Location TBA.

Tweedledee, Tweedledum: Plump twin brothers in 1951's "Alice in Wonderland" dress identically. Always odd, sometimes menacing. Finish each other's sentences. **Disney's Hollywood Studios:** Sorcerer's Hat, Hollywood Blvd.

Wendy: Appearing in 1953's "Peter Pan," eldest Darling child is caring, sensible. Wears nightgown. Loves to tell stories. Close to Peter Pan; object of Tinker Bell's jealousy. **Magic Kingdom:** Pirates of the Caribbean, Adventureland.

White Rabbit: Nervous, worried rabbit continually declares that he's late in 1951's "Alice in Wonderland." Carries giant watch. Alice follows him down rabbit hole to Wonderland. **Magic Kingdom:** Mad Tea Party, Fantasyland.

Winnie the Pooh: Gentle, lovable stuffed bear in 1977's "The Many Adventures of Winnie the Pooh." Loves honey; fears heffalumps, woozles will steal it. Best friends Christopher Robin, Piglet. **Magic Kingdom:** Crystal Palace meals, Main Street U.S.A. **Epcot:** The Toy Soldier, U.K. pavilion. **Disney's Animal Kingdom:** Boat landing across from Flame Tree BBQ, Discovery Island. **Grand Floridian Resort:** 1900 Park Fare breakfast.

Woody: Practical, good-natured cowboy sheriff doll in Pixar's "Toy Story" trilogy. Favorite toy of boy Andy. Best friends with Buzz Lightyear, his former rival. Girlfriend is Bo Peep, a porcelain lamp base. Named for Woody Strode, an actor who appeared in 1939's "Stagecoach" and other classic Western movies. **Magic Kingdom:** Splash Mountain, Frontierland. **Disney's Hollywood Studios:** Woody's Picture Shootin' Corral, Pixar Place.

Telephone directory

AIRPORTS

Orlando International 825-2001
  Arrivals 825-8463
  Disney's EarPort store (East hall) 825-2339
  The Magic of Disney store (West hall) 825-2370
  Lost and Found 825-2111
  Paging 825-2000
Orlando Sanford International 322-7771

AUTOMOBILE RENTALS

Advantage Orlando Int'l Airport 857-1999
Alamo National toll-free 800 327-9633
  AAA Car Care Center 824-3470
  Buena Vista Palace 827-6363
  Walt Disney World Dolphin 934-4930
Avis National toll-free 800 331-1212
  Downtown Disney Hilton 827-2847
Budget National toll-free 800 527-0700
  Doubletree Guest Suites 827-6089
Dollar National toll-free 800 800-4000
  Regal Sun Resort 583-8000
Enterprise National toll-free 800 325-8007
E-Z National toll-free 800 277-5171
Hertz National toll-free 800 654-3131
  Shades of Green 938-0600
L and M Orlando Int'l Airport 888-0515
National National toll-free 800 227-7368
  AAA Car Care Center 824-3470
  Buena Vista Palace 827-6363
  Walt Disney World Dolphin 934-4930
Thrifty National toll-free 800 367-2277

AUTOMOBILE SERVICES

AAA Car Care Center 824-0976
  After hours 824-4777
AAA Emergency Road Service 800 222-4357
Pep Boys 70 Blake Blvd, Celebration 939-2581

BANKING SERVICES

Bank of America Celebration 321 939-7677
Disney Visa Card 800 222-1262
Suntrust Downtown Disney 828-6103
  Celebration Downtown 566-2265
  Celebration Water Tower Place 321 939-3970
  Toll-free 800 786-8787
Traveler's Checks
  American Express 800 992-3404
  Thomas Cook 800 287-7362
Wachovia/Wells Fargo Orlando 649-5800
Western Union wire transfers
  Gooding's Supermarket 827-1200

BUSINESS SERVICES

Disney Institute 566-2620
Disney Professional Seminars 824-7997

CHILDCARE SERVICES

All About Kids 812-9300
Baby's Away Equipment rental 334-0232
Kid's Nite Out 828-0920
Orlando Stroller Rentals 800 281-0884

CONVENTION PLANNING

Disney convention centers 321 939-7129
Gaylord Palms Resort 586-0000
Marriott World Center 238-8888
Orlando Convention Center 685-9800
Walt Disney World Swan
  and Dolphin 934-4290

DISABILITY SERVICES

Sign-language show schedule 824-4321
Special requests 939-7807
TDD numbers Disney information 827-5141
  Disney resort hotel reservations 939-7670
  Disney Vacation Club 566-3320

EDUCATIONAL SERVICES

Epcot Discovery Center For teachers 824-4321
Youth Education Series 877 343-5387

EMPLOYMENT

Disney College Program U.S. students 828-3091
  International students 828-2850
Walt Disney World JobLine 828-1000

ENTERTAINMENT

AMC movie theater Celebration 566-1405
  Downtown Disney 827-1308
  Movie listings 888 262-4386
Atlanta Braves Spring
  Training tickets 939-4263
  Ticketmaster 800 745-3000
Disney's BoardWalk Resort
  Entertainment hotline 939-3492
Chip 'n Dale's Campfire Sing-a-long
  Movie schedule 824-2727
Cirque du Soleil La Nouba Box office ... 939-7600
House of Blues Box office 934-2583

FLORIST

Disney Floral & Gifts 827-3505
  Disney Dream Makers 939-4438
  Convention services 827-1266
  Meetings and luncheons 939-7129
  Wedding services 939-4610

GASOLINE STATIONS

Hess Express Downtown Disney 938-0160
  Epcot Resort Area 938-0151
  Magic Kingdom 938-0143

GENERAL INFORMATION

AA meetings	828-2828
Poison Control Center	800 222-1222
Time and temperature	646-3131
Victim services Florida AG	800 226-6667
Walt Disney World Community relations	828-3453
Customer service (live operator)	824-2222
Hotel reservations	939-7429
Merchandise (Option 3 for live operator)	363-6200
Recreation reservations	939-7529
Restaurant reservations	939-3463
Technical support	939-7765
Theme-park ticket sales	934-7639
Vacation package booking	939-7675
Walt Disney World Travel Co.	939-6244
For Florida visitors	939-7718
For United Kingdom visitors	08702 424 900
Spanish-language	800 459-5432
Weather Weekly forecast	824-4104

GROCERIES

GardenGrocer Online service	866 855-4350
Gooding's Crossroads Shopping Center	827-1200
Publix 2925 International Dr	397-1171
2915 Vineland Rd	396-7525
7640 W Sand Lake Rd	226-3315
Whole Foods 8003 Turkey Lake Rd	355-7100
Winn-Dixie 11957 S Apoka-Vineland Rd	465-8600
7840 W Irlo Bronson Hwy (U.S. 192)	397-2210

HAIR SALONS AND BARBER SHOPS

American Beauty Salon & Barber	
Disney's Contemporary Resort	824-3411
Bibbidi Bobbidi Boutique	939-7895
Casa de Belleza Salon	
Disney's Coronado Springs Resort	939-3965
Harmony Barber Shop Magic Kingdom	824-6550
Ivy Trellis Beauty Salon	
Disney's Grand Floridian Resort	824-3000
Periwig's Beauty Salon	
Disney's Yacht Club Resort	934-3260
The Salon Walt Disney World Dolphin	934-4250

HOTELS AND RESORTS

Best Western Lake Buena Vista	
Downtown Disney	828-2424
Buena Vista Palace Downtown Disney	827-2727
Car rental (Alamo/National)	827-6363
The Spa	827-3200
Buena Vista Suites	
8203 World Center Dr	800 537-7737
Caribe Royale	
8203 World Center Dr	800 823-8300
Celebration Hotel 700 Bloom St	566-6000
Disney's All-Star Resorts	
All-Star Movies	939-7000
All-Star Music	939-6000
All-Star Sports	939-5000
Lost and found	939-6882
Disney's Animal Kingdom Lodge	938-3000

Lost and found	938-4778
Simba's Cubhouse childcare center	938-4785
Sunrise Safari Breakfast Adventure	938-4755
Wanyama Sunset Safari	938-4755
Zahanati Fitness Center	938-4715
Disney's BoardWalk Inn and Villas	939-5100
Entertainment hotline	939-3492
Lost and found	939-5116
Muscles and Bustles Health Club	939-2370
Disney's Caribbean Beach Resort	934-3400
Lost and found	934-3090
Disney's Contemporary Resort	824-1000
American Beauty Salon & Barber	824-3411
Lost and found	283-3659
Olympiad Fitness Center	824-3410
Disney's Coronado Springs Resort	939-1000
Casa de Belleza Salon	939-3965
La Vida Health Club	939-3030
Lost and found	939-3070
Disney's Fort Wilderness Resort	824-2900
Campfire movie schedule	824-2727
Electric cart rental	824-2742
Group camping	939-7807
Horseback riding	824-2900
Lost and found	824-2726
Pony rides	824-2788
Disney's Grand Floridian Resort	824-3000
Grand Floridian Spa	824-2332
Ivy Trellis Beauty Salon	824-3000
Lost and found	824-2988
Mouseketeer Clubhouse childcare center	824-2985
Disney's Old Key West Resort	827-7700
Lost and found	827-4942
Disney's Polynesian Resort	824-2000
Lost and found	824-2192
Neverland Club childcare center	824-2184
Disney's Pop Century Resort	938-4000
Lost and found	934-3090
Disney's Port Orleans Resorts	
French Quarter	934-5000
Riverside	934-6000
Lost and found	934-6000
Disney resort reservations Rooms only	939-7429
Package plans	934-7639
Photography sittings	824-1700
Disney's Saratoga Springs Resort	827-1100
Lost and found	827-4942
Saratoga Springs Spa	827-4455
Disney's Wilderness Lodge Resort	824-3200
Cub's Den childcare center	824-1083
Lost and found	824-4751
Sturdy Branches Health Club	938-4222
Wilderness Lodge Villas	938-4300
Disney's Yacht and Beach Club Resort	
Beach Club	934-8000
Beach Club Villas	934-2175
Sandcastle Club childcare center	934-6290
Yacht Club	934-7000
Periwig's Beauty Salon	934-3260
Ship Shape Health Club	934-3256

Lost and found................................. 934-1493

Doubletree Guest Suites
  Downtown Disney 934-1000
  Car rental (Budget) 827-6089
Gaylord Palms 6000 W Osceola Parkway 586-0000
Hilton Bonnet Creek 597-3600
  Downtown Disney 827-4000
  Car rental (Avis) 827-2847
Holiday Inn Downtown Disney....................... 828-8888
Hyatt Regency Grand Cypress
  1 Grand Cypress Blvd....................................... 239-1234
Marriott World Center
  8701 World Center Dr........................ 239-4200
Nickelodeon Suites Resort
  14500 Continental Gateway.......................... 387-5437
Royal Plaza Downtown Disney 828-2828
Shades of Green.. 824-3600
  Car rental (Hertz)......................... 938-0600
Waldorf Astoria Bonnet Creek 597-5500
Walt Disney World Swan and Dolphin
  Walt Disney World Dolphin....................... 934-4000
  Car rental (Alamo/National)....................... 934-4930
  Camp Dolphin childcare center................... 934-4000
  Mandara Spa.............................. 934-4772
  The Salon................................ 934-4250
  Walt Disney World Swan 934-4499
Wyndham Downtown Disney 828-4444
  Car rental (Dollar)............................ 583-8000

KENNEL
Best Friends Pet Care Center........ 877 493-9738

LOST AND FOUND
Disney's Animal Kingdom...................... 938-2785
Disney's Blizzard Beach........................... 560-5408
Disney's Hollywood Studios.................... 560-3720
Disney hotels See Hotels and Resorts
Disney's Typhoon Lagoon....................... 560-6296
Downtown Disney...................................... 828-3150
Epcot 560-6646
ESPN Wide World of Sports................... 541-5600
Magic Kingdom 824-4521
Main Disney office.................................... 824-4245

MEDICAL CARE
Centra Care in-room care 238-2000
Centra Care walk-in clinics 239-6463
  Formosa Gardens...................................... 397-7032
  Kissimmee.. 390-1888
  Lake Buena Vista....................................... 934-2273
  Vineland 351-6682
Dental emergencies Celebration Dental 566-2222
Doctors on Call Service (DOCS)................ 399-3627
EastCoast Medical In-room care.............. 648-5252
Florida Hospital Emergency Dept. 303-4034
Reedy Creek Emergency Paramedics... 560-1990

MEDICAL EQUIPMENT RENTALS
Apria Health Care 291-2229
Care Medical Equipment........................... 856-2273

Turner Drugs 828-8125
Walker Mobility 518-6000

PHARMACIES
Turner Drugs
  12500 S Apopka-Vineland Rd......................... 828-8125
  1530 Celebration Blvd.................................... 566-9060
Walgreens
  7767 W Irlo Bronson Hwy (U.S. 192) 390-1701

PHOTOGRAPHY SERVICES
Disney Photographic Services 827-5099
Disney's PhotoPass 560-4300

POLICE
Emergencies.. 911
Orange County Sheriff's Office.............. 254-7000
Osceola County Sheriff's Office............. 348-2222
Walt Disney World Security 560-7959
  Urgent matters... 560-1990

RECREATION
Boat rentals... 939-7529
Camping Groups.. 939-7807
Carriage rides 939-7529
Disney Cruise Line 566-7000
DisneyQuest Downtown Disney 828-4600
ESPN Wide World of Sports.................... 828-3267
  Live operator... 939-1500
  Youth group information 939-4263
Fishing Disney excursions 939-2277
Golf Disney tee-time reservations.................... 939-4653
Horseback riding Fort Wilderness............. 824-2900
Marathons and foot races....................... 938-3398
Miniature golf Fantasia Gardens................. 560-4753
  Winter Summerland..................................... 560-7161
Pony rides Fort Wilderness 824-2788
Reservations General Disney recreation 939-7529
Richard Petty Driving Experience
  Walt Disney World Speedway 800 237-3889
Surfing lessons Typhoon Lagoon 939-7873
Tennis Reservations, lessons 621-1991
Wagon rides... 824-2734
Walt Disney World Speedway 939-0130
Water Sports Sammy Duvall's...................... 939-0754

RESTAURANTS
Big River Grille BoardWalk Resort.............. 560-0253
Bongos Cuban Cafe Downtown Disney 828-0999
Cap'n Jack's Downtown Disney.................... 828-3971
Disney restaurants Reservations............... 939-3463
  Dietary requests 824-5967
  Tables in Wonderland discount card.............. 566-5858
Earl of Sandwich Downtown Disney 938-1762
ESPN Club BoardWalk Resort 939-1177
Fulton's Crab House Downtown Disney 934-2628
Fresh Walt Disney World Dolphin.................. 934-1609
Garden Grove Walt Disney World Swan....... 934-1609
Ghirardelli Soda Fountain
  Downtown Disney 934-8855

House of Blues Downtown Disney 934-2583
Il Mulino Walt Disney World Swan 934-1199
Paradiso 37 Downtown Disney 934-3700
Planet Hollywood Downtown Disney 827-7827
Portobello Downtown Disney 934-8888
Raglan Road Downtown Disney 938-0300
Rainforest Cafe Disney's Animal Kingdom... 938-9100
Downtown Disney 827-8500
Shula's Steak House
Walt Disney World Dolphin............................ 934-1362
T-REX Downtown Disney 828-8739
Todd English's bluezoo
Walt Disney World Dolphin............................ 934-1111
Wolfgang Puck Cafe Dining Room
Downtown Disney 938-9653
Wolfgang Puck Express
Downtown Disney 828-0107

RETAILERS NEAR WALT DISNEY WORLD
Apple Store Mall at Millenia........................ 241-5400
Barnes & Noble 7900 W Sand Lake Rd 345-0900
Best Buy 4155 Millenia Blvd.......................... 248-2439
Disney Store Florida Mall 240-4411
Seminole Towne Center.................................. 322-8220
West Oaks Mall.. 523-1234
Mall at Millenia 4200 Conroy Rd................. 363-3555
Office supply stores
FedEx Office, 12181 S Apopka-Vineland Rd.... 465-0085
Office Depot, 7600 Dr Phillips Blvd............... 248-1163
OfficeMax, 3107 W Vine St 870-2041
Staples, 8421 S John Young Prkwy 345-1006
Orlando Premium Outlet Mall
8200 Vineland Ave 238-7787
Target 4750 Millenia Plaza Way..................... 541-0019
Telephone stores
AT&T, 6081 W Irlo Bronson Hwy (U.S. 192)... 566-0650
Sprint, 8910 Turkey Lake Rd.......................... 351-5155
Verizon, 1340 W Osceola Prkwy #101 343-0516
Walgreens
7767 W Irlo Bronson Hwy (U.S. 192) 390-1701

SHIPPING SERVICES
FedEx 12181 S Apopka-Vineland Rd............... 465-0085
UPS 8131 Vineland Ave.................................... 465-1700
U.S. Postal Service........................... 800 275-8777
U.S. Post Office Celebration........................ 566-1145
Lake Buena Vista.. 238-0223

SPAS
Grand Floridian Spa.................................. 824-2332
Mandara Spa
Walt Disney World Dolphin............................ 934-4772
Saratoga Springs Spa.............................. 827-4455
The Spa Buena Vista Palace.......................... 827-3200

SPECIAL OCCASIONS
Birthday parties.. 939-2329
Floral arrangements 939-4610
Grand Gatherings...................................... 934-7639
Merchandise 827-7600

Reservations 939-7526
Honeymoons.................................... 800 370-6009
Disney Honeymoon Registry........................... 939-7776
Quinceañera events 321 939-4555
Special occasion cakes Ordering............. 827-2253
Weddings 321 939-4610
Marriage licenses, Orange County 847-1300
Osceola County 836-2067

THEME PARKS
Extra Magic Hours Schedule 824-4321
Capacity closures..................................... 939-4636
Refurbishments Schedule 824-4321
Ticket inquiries... 566-4985
Annual Passholder Hotline 827-7200
Ticket sales General................................. 934-7639
Convention attendees.................................... 939-4686
Orlando Fun Tickets............................. 866 225-4712
Tours 939-8687
VIP Tours 560-4033

TIMESHARES
Disney Vacation Club....................... 800 800-9100
Member services 939-3800
Sales information... 566-3100

TOURISM INFORMATION
Busch Gardens Tampa...................... 813 987-5082
Gay Days.. 896-8431
Kennedy Space Center.................. 877 313-2610
Kissimmee Convention and
Visitors Bureau 944-2400
Orange County Convention
& Visitors Bureau................................. 363-5871
Orlando Travel & Visitors Bureau 363-5872
SeaWorld Orlando 800 327-2424
Universal Studios Florida........................ 363-8000
Visit Florida.................................... 888 735-2872
Walt Disney World
Complimentary DVD planning kit........... 800 218-2004
For UK visitors 08705 000 000

TRANSPORTATION SERVICES
Disney's Magical Express 866 599-0951
Mears Transportation
Luxury sedans 423-5566
Airport and attraction shuttles...................... 423-5566
Group transportation sales............................. 839-1570
Taxicabs (Checker, City, Yellow Cabs)............ 422-2222
Walt Disney World Transportation 939-7433

YOUTH GROUPS
Disney Jazz Celebration 866 842-3340
Disney Magic Music Days 866 578-4830
Festival Disney Dance........................ 866 578-4827
Instrumental 866 242-3617
Vocal... 866 578-4823
General information 800 359-0509

Area Code 407 unless indicated

Internet directory

AIRLINES

Aer Lingus .... aerlingus.com
AeroMexico .... aeromexico.com
Air Canada .... aircanada.com
Air Jamaica .... airjamaica.com
Air Transat .... airtransat.com
AirTran .... airtran.com
Alaska Airlines .... alaskaair.com
Allegiant Air .... allegiantair.com
American Airlines .... aa.com
Bahamas Air .... bahamasair.com
British Airways .... britishairways.com
Continental Airlines .... continental.com
Copa Airlines .... copaair.com
Delta Airlines .... delta.com
Frontier Airlines .... frontierairlines.com
GOL Intelligent Airlines .... voegol.com
InterJet .... interjet.com
JetBlue Airways .... jetblue.com
Lufthansa .... lufthansa.com
Martinair .... martinair.com
Mexicana Airlines .... mexicana.com
Miami Air International .... miamiair.com
Midwest Airlines .... midwestairlines.com
Southwest Airlines .... southwest.com
Spirit Airlines .... spiritair.com
Sun Country Airlines .... suncountry.com
Sunwing Airlines .... flysunwing.com
TACA Airlines .... taca.com
TAM Airlines .... tam.com
United Airlines .... united.com
U.S. Airways .... usairways.com
Virgin America .... virginamerica.com
Virgin Atlantic .... virgin-atlantic.com
Volaris .... volaris.com
West Jet .... westjet.com

AIRPORTS

Orlando International
  Airport .... orlandoairports.net
Orlando Sanford International
  Airport .... orlandosanfordairport.com

AUTOMOBILE RENTALS

Advantage Rent a Car .... advantage.com
Alamo Car Rental .... alamo.com
Avis Car Rental .... avis.com
Budget Car Rental .... budget.com
Dollar Rent a Car .... dollar.com
Enterprise Rent-A-Car .... enterprise.com
E-Z Car Rental .... e-zrentacar.com
Hertz Rent-a-Car .... hertz.com
L & M Car Rental .... lmcarrental.net
National Car Rental .... nationalcar.com
Thrifty Car Rental .... thrifty.com

AUTOMOBILE SERVICES

AAA Emergency
  Road Service .... automotive.aaa.com

BANKING SERVICES

Disney Gift Cards .... disneygiftcard.com
Disney Visa Card .... mymickeycard.com

BUSINESS SERVICES

Disney Institute .... disneyinstitute.com

CHILDCARE SERVICES

All About Kids .... all-about-kids.com
Baby's Away Equipment rental .... babysaway.com
Kid's Nite Out .... kidsniteout.com
Orlando Stroller
  Rentals .... orlandostrollersrentals.com

CONVENTION PLANNING

Gaylord Palms .... gaylordpalms.com
Marriott World
  Center Resort .... marriottworldcenter.com
Orange County Convention Center .... occc.net
Walt Disney World .... disneymeetings.com
  Park tickets .... disneyconventionears.com
Walt Disney World Swan
  and Dolphin .... swandolphinmeetings.com

GENERAL DISNEY INFORMATION

All Ears Deb Wills' website has information on Walt
Disney World activities, hotels, planning and restaurants,
the latter complete with menus. The accommodations
section has dozens of photos of each property. The site
includes 10 blogs. Updated several times each week,
AllEars.net is one of the most reliable and thorough
unofficial Walt Disney World websites .... **allears.net**

The Daily Disney Timely news and blogs about Walt
Disney World from Disney experts at the Orlando
Sentinel newspaper. Reporters include Dewayne
Bevil, Kristin Ford, Steven Ford, Jason Garcia, Heather
McPherson and Matt Palm........... **thedailydisney.com**

Disney Information Station With 40 forums and over
200,000 fans, the DIS discussion boards are among the
liveliest and most popular in the Disney fan community.
The site includes a weekly DIS Unplugged podcast with
discussions on vacation planning .... **DISboards.com**

The Disney Blog John Frost's thoughtful, well-written
blog is "Disney News and Information by fans for fans."
Topics vary greatly. Included are comprehensive links to
other helpful Disney websites .... **thedisneyblog.com**

Disney Brit Podcast and forum about all things Disney
from the viewpoint of British visitors. The crew also
organizes meets at Disney parks .... **disneybrit.com**

Disney Food Blog In-depth food, restaurant news. Good
photos, incisive reviews.............. **disneyfoodblog.com**

Intercot The INTERnet Community of Tomorrow is one of the most helpful and popular Disney World fan sites. Its discussion boards are lively .... **intercot.com**

Jim Hill Media Jim Hill's website focuses on behind-the-scenes news and commentary about Disney and the general entertainment industry. Well-written articles dig deep to find inside information......... **jimhillmedia.com**

Laughing Place Doobie and Rebekah Moseley's website has the best news coverage of Disney parks and the Walt Disney Co. It includes breaking news and timely links to Disney stories in other media, as well as attraction ratings, discussion boards, photo galleries, an online store and a weekly podcast. Dozens of columns provide unique insight................................ **laughingplace.com**

Magical Mountain Founded by Nathan Rose, this thorough Don Rogers site has blogs, columns, discussion boards, movie reviews, shopping, vacation planning, the Magical Definition podcast and the cutest mascot, Shandy the Sugar Glider .... **magicalmountain.net**

Mice Age "A different look at Disney," focusing on literate columns from Kevin Yee and other Disneyphiles. Topics include Disney news, trip planning, behind-the-scenes analysis, taking photographs and history. Partner MiceChat has discussion boards .... **miceage.com**

Mouse Savers Full of money-saving ideas and tips, Mary Waring's site features a list of discounts and reservation codes for guests to use while planning their Disney World trip. The site also has discounts for AAA members and annual passholders......................... **mousesavers.com**

Northern Mouse Disney info with a Canadian twist, this site features a podcast, famous Disney Canadians and upcoming Canadian events......... **northernmouse.com**

Walt Disney Travel Co. .... **disneytravel.com**

Walt Disney World The official Walt Disney World website, with ticket purchasing, dining reservations, attraction descriptions (often with video), vacation planning assistance, much more .... **disneyworld.com**

Walt Disney World Community Relations .... **wdwpublicaffairs.com**

Walt Disney World DVD planning kit .... **disneyvacations.com**

Walt Disney World Moms Panel Sponsored by the Disney company, this helpful, timely vacation forum features advice from independent parents. Readers submit questions................... **disneyworldmoms.com**

WDW Magic Steve Fearson's comprehensive site includes information about accommodations, attractions, dining, news, recreation, reviews, shopping, trip planning and weather, as well as popular discussion boards, blogs, photo albums and a list of recent refurbishments at the Disney World theme parks........ **wdwmagic.com**

WDW News Today Run by Tom Corless, WDW News Today has daily news and information about Walt Disney World, including a popular podcast, many photos, videos and a discussion board.............. **wdwnewstoday.com**

WDW Radio Lou Mongello's comprehensive site includes message boards, Disney theme-park news, photos, trivia, video and the weekly WDW Radio Show podcast. Lou hosts live online video broadcasts from his studio and the parks. He also writes a blog................. **wdwradio.com**

EMPLOYMENT

Disney College Program
U.S. students.................... **wdwcollegeprogram.com**
International .... **disneyinternationalprograms.com**
Paid positions .... **disneyparks.jobs**

ENTERTAINMENT

AMC theaters.................................. **amctheaters.com**
Atlanta Braves Spring Training..... **espnwwos.com**
Cirque du Soleil La Nouba...... **cirquedusoleil.com**
House of Blues........................... **houseofblues.com**
Walt Disney World Live Entertainment Steve Soares publishes timely, accurate listings for Disney World theme parks, Downtown Disney, BoardWalk. Includes character greetings, fireworks, parades, street parties, events .... **pages.prodigy.net/stevesoares**

FLORIST

Disney Floral & Gifts.................... **disneyflorist.com**

GROCERIES

Garden Grocer Online delivery ..... **gardengrocer.com**
Gooding's Supermarket.................... **goodings.com**
Whole Foods...................... **wholefoodsmarket.com**

HOTELS AND RESORTS

Buena Vista Suites .. **buenavistasuitesorlando.com**
Caribe Royale .... **thecaribeorlando.com**
Comfort Inn & Suites...................... **comfortinn.com**
Country Inns & Suites................... **countryinns.com**
Courtyard by Marriott......................... **marriott.com**
Disney-owned resorts................. **disneyworld.com**
Doubletree Guest Suites .... **doubletree.com**
Downtown Disney
    hotels .... **downtowndisneyhotels.com**
Embassy Suites........................ **embassysuites.com**
Gaylord Palms............................ **gaylordpalms.com**
Hampton Inns................................. **hamptoninn.com**
Hawthorn Suites................................ **hawthorn.com**
Hilton Hotels.. **hilton.com**
Hilton Bonnet Creek .... **hiltonbonnetcreek.com**
Hilton Garden Inns .... **hiltongardeninn.com**
Homewood Suites................ **homewoodsuites.com**
Hyatt Regency .... **hyatt.com**
Marriott .... **marriott.com**
Nickelodeon Suites Resort.............. **nickhotel.com**
Radisson Hotels & Resorts .... **radisson.com**
Residence Inns................................... **marriott.com**
Shades of Green........................ **shadesofgreen.org**
Sheraton Hotels & Resorts .... **sheraton.com**
Sheraton Safari....................... **sheratonsafari.com**
Staybridge Suites............................. **staybridge.com**
Waldorf Astoria
    Bonnet Creek............ **waldorfastoriaorlando.com**
Walt Disney World Swan
    and Dolphin Resort .... **swandolphin.com**

INTERNET RADIO

Mouse World Radio Five stations play music heard at Walt Disney World................. **mouseworldradio.com**

KENNEL
Best Friends Pet Care Center
At Walt Disney World .... bestfriendspetcare.com

LEGAL SERVICES
Florida Attorney General
Div. of Victim Services.........myfloridalegal.com
Florida State Bar Association..........floridabar.org

MEDICAL CARE
Centra Care...centracare.org
Doctors on Call.............. doctorsoncallservice.com
EastCoast Medical ....themedicalconcierge.com
Florida Hospital........................floridahospital.com
Reedy Creek Fire Fighters.............. reedycreek.org

MEDICAL EQUIPMENT RENTALS
Apria Health Care .... apria.com
Care Medical
Equipment ....caremedicalequipment.com
Turner Drugs.......................................turnerdrug.com
Walker Mobility .... walkermobility.com

PHARMACIES
Turner Drugs ....turnerdrug.com
Walgreens ....walgreens.com

PHOTOGRAPHY SERVICES
Disney's Fine Art Photography
and Video.............. disneyeventphotography.com
Disney's PhotoPass.............. disneyphotopass.com

POSTAL AND SHIPPING SERVICES
FedEx...fedex.com
UPS ....ups.com
U.S. Postal Service ....usps.gov

RECREATION
ESPN Wide World of Sports Complex Events;
spectator, participant info ....disneysports.com
Richard Petty Driving Experience
Walt Disney World Speedway ....drivepetty.com
RunDisney Information, registration for marathons,
other Disney World running events....... rundisney.com
Sammy Duvall's Watersports Centre
Disney's Contemporary Resort........ sammyduvall.com

RESTAURANTS
Bongos Cuban Cafe............bongoscubancafe.com
Disney restaurants........................disneyworld.com
Earl of Sandwich.............. earlofsandwichusa.com
Fulton's Crab House .... fultonscrabhouse.com
House of Blues.................................houseofblues.com
Planet Hollywood.................planethollywood.com
Raglan Road.....................raglanroadirishpub.com
Rainforest Cafe.........................rainforestcafe.com
T-REX... trexcafe.com
Walt Disney World Swan and Dolphin
restaurants .... swandolphinrestaurants.com
Wolfgang Puck Cafe .... wolfgangpuckorlando.com

SHOPPING
Mall at Millenia.......................... mallatmillenia.com
Orlando Premium Outlets.... premiumoutlets.com
Walt Disney World
Merchandise................................disneystore.com

SPAS
Grand Floridian Resort & Spa .... relaxedyet.com
Mandara Spa
Walt Disney World Dolphin............... mandaraspa.com
Saratoga Springs Resort & Spa .... relaxedyet.com
The Spa Buena Vista Palace... buenavistapalace.com

SPECIAL OCCASIONS
Disney's Fairy Tale Honeymoons Planning ideas,
packages, tools, registry .....disneyhoneymoons.com
Disney's Fairy Tale Weddings Planning ideas,
packages, tools, blog .... disneyweddings.com

TIMESHARES
Disney Vacation Club......disneyvacationclub.com

TOURISM INFORMATION
Busch Gardens............................buschgardens.com
Gay Days...gaydays.com
Kennedy Space
Center ....kennedyspacecenter.com
Kissimmee Convention and
Visitors Bureau .... visitkissimmee.com
Orange County Convention
& Visitors Bureau.......................orlandoinfo.com
Orlando Travel &
Visitors Bureau ....orlandoinfo.com
SeaWorld Orlando ....seaworld.com
Universal Studios Florida............................usf.com
Visit Florida.. visitflorida.com

TRANSPORTATION SERVICES
American Automobile Assoc. .... travel.aaa.com
AAA Escape package savings .... aaasouth.com
Canada Automobile Association....................caa.ca
Florida's Turnpike Traveler info; construction updates;
toll rates, calculator; maps........floridasturnpike.com
Mears Transportation... mearstransportation.com
Orlando-Orange County Expressway Authority
Traffic, roadwork updates; maps, directions, toll
calculator .... expresswayauthority.com

WEATHER
The Weather Channel......................... weather.com

WI-FI LOCATIONS
Wi-Fi Free Spot.............................wififreespot.com

YOUTH GROUPS
Disney Jazz
Celebration ....disneyjazzcelebration.com
Disney Magic Music Days .... disneymmd.com
Disney Youth Groups....... disneyyouthgroups.com
Festival Disney.............................festivaldisney.com

Bibliography

Anderson, Philip Longfellow. "The Gospel in Disney: Christian Values in the Early Animated Classics." Augsburg Books, 2004.

"The Annotated Classic Fairy Tales," edited by Marie Tatar. W.W. Norton & Company Ltd., 2002.

Appelbaum, Stanley. "The New York World's Fair 1939/1940." Dover Publications, 1977.

Barrier, Michael. "The Animated Man: A Life of Walt Disney." University of California Press, 2008.

Borgenicht, David. "Classic Tales of Brer Rabbit." Running Press, 1995.

Brode, Douglas. "From Walt to Woodstock: How Disney Created the Counterculture." University of Texas Press, 2004.

Canemaker, John. "The Art and Flair of Mary Blair: An Appreciation." Disney Editions, 2003.

Canemaker, John. "Walt Disney's Nine Old Men and the Art of Animation." Disney Editions, 2001.

Capodagli, Bill. "The Disney Way." McGraw-Hill, 2006.

Dunlop, Beth. "Building a Dream: The Art of Disney Architecture." Harry N. Abrams, 1996.

"E.Encyclopedia Animal." DK, 2005.

Eisner, Michael. "Work in Progress." Random House, 1998.

Emerson, Chad Denver. "Project Future: The Inside Story Behind the Creation of Disney World." Ayefour Publishing, 2010.

Finch, Christopher. "The Art of Walt Disney." Harry N. Abrams, 2004.

Finch, Christopher. "Jim Henson: The Works: The Art, the Magic, the Imagination." Random House, 1993.

Fjellman, Stephen M. "Vinyl Leaves: Walt Disney World and America." Westview Press, 1992.

Flower, Joe. "Prince of the Magic Kingdom: Michael Eisner and the Re-making of Disney." Wiley, 1991.

Gabler, Neal. "Walt Disney: The Triumph of the American Imagination." Vintage, 2007.

Griswold, Jerry. "The Meanings of 'Beauty and the Beast,' A Handbook." Broadview Press, 2004.

Grover, Ron. "The Disney Touch: Disney, ABC and The Quest for the World's Greatest Media Empire." McGraw-Hill Trade, 1996.

Hahn, Don. "Disney's Animation Magic." Disney Press, 1996.

Harris, Joel Chandler. "The Complete Tales of Uncle Remus." Houghton Mifflin Company, 1955.

Hench, John. "Designing Disney: Imagineering and the Art of the Show." Disney Editions, 2003.

Kaufman, J. B. "South of the Border With Disney: Walt Disney and the Good Neighbor Program, 1941-1948." Disney Editions, 2009.

Koenig, David. "Realityland: True-Life Adventures at Walt Disney World." Bonaventure Press, 2007.

Kurtti, Jeff. "Since the World Began: Walt Disney World's First 25 Years." Hyperion, 1996.

Kurtti, Jeff. "Walt Disney's Legends of Imagineering and the Genesis of the Disney Theme Park." Disney Editions, 2008.

Lamb, Bob. "Field Guide to Disney's Animal Kingdom Theme Park." Roundtable Press, 2000.

Lambert, Pierre. "Mickey Mouse." Hyperion, 1998.

Lester, Julius. "Tales of Uncle Remus: The Adventures of Brer Rabbit." Puffin, 2006.

Malmberg, Melody. "The Making of Disney's Animal Kingdom Theme Park." Hyperion 1998.

Maltin, Leonard. "The Disney Films." Disney Editions, 1995, 2000.

Maltin, Leonard. "Of Mice and Magic: A History of American Animated Cartoons." Penguin Books, 1987.

Mannheim, Steve. "Walt Disney and the Quest for Community." Ashgate Publishing, 2002.

Marling, Karal Ann. "Designing Disney's Theme Parks: The Architecture of Reassurance." Hyperion, 1997.

Neary, Kevin and Smith, Dave. "The Ultimate Disney Trivia Book Vols. 1-3." Hyperion, 1992, 1994, 1997.

"Official Guide: New York World's Fair 1964/1965." Time Inc., 1964.

Paik, Karen. "To Infinity and Beyond!: The Story of Pixar Animation Studios." Chronicle Books, 2007.

Philip, Neil. "The Complete Fairy Tales of Charles Perrault." Albion, 1993.

Philip, Neil. "The Illustrated Book of Myths." DK, 1995.

Pinsky, Mark I. "The Gospel According to Disney: Faith, Trust, and Pixie Dust." Westminster John Knox Press, 2004.

Price, David A. "The Pixar Touch." Knopf, 2008.

Price, Harrison "Buzz." "Walt's Revolution! By the Numbers." Ripley Entertainment, 2004.

Rafferty, Kevin. "Walt Disney Imagineering." Disney Editions, 1996.

Ridgway, Charles. "Spinning Disney's World: Memories of a Magic Kingdom Press Agent." Intrepid Traveler, 2007.

Samuelson, Dale. "The American Amusement Park." MBI, 2001.

Schickel, Richard. "The Disney Version: The Life, Times, Art and Commerce of Walt Disney." Simon & Schuster, 1968, 1985, 1997.

Schroeder, Russell K. "Disney: The Ultimate Visual Guide." Dorling Kindersley Ltd., 2002.

Smith, Dave. "Disney A to Z: The Official Encyclopedia." Hyperion, 1998, 2006.

Smith, Dave. "The Quotable Walt Disney." Disney Editions, 2001.

Smith, Dave and Clark, Steven. "Disney: The First 100 Years." Hyperion, 1999.

Stewart, James B. "Disney War." Simon & Schuster, 2005.

Surrell, Jason. "The Disney Mountains: Imagineering At Its Peak." Disney Editions, 2007.

Surrell, Jason. "The Haunted Mansion: From the Magic Kingdom to the Movies." Disney Editions, 2003.

Surrell, Jason. "Pirates of the Caribbean: From the Magic Kingdom to the Movies." Disney Editions, 2005.

Telotte, J.P. "The Mouse Machine: Disney and Technology." University of Illinois Press, 2008.

Thomas, Bob. "Building a Company: Roy O. Disney and the Creation of an Entertainment Empire." Hyperion, 1998.

Thomas, Bob. "Walt Disney: An American Original." Hyperion, 1994.

Thomas, Frank and Johnston, Ollie. "The Illusion of Life: Disney Animation." Disney Editions, 1995.

Tieman, Robert. "The Disney Treasures." Disney Editions, 2003.

Twain, Mark. "The Adventures of Tom Sawyer." Fine Creative Media, 2003.

"25 Years of Walt Disney World." Disney's Kingdom Editions, 1996.

"Walt Disney Imagineering: A Behind the Dreams Look at Making the Magic Real." Hyperion, 1996.

"Walt Disney Resort: A Magical Year-By-Year Journey." Hyperion, 1998.

Zicree, Mark Scott. "The Twilight Zone Companion." Silman-James Press, 1982, 1989.

Zipes, Jack. "The Fairy Tales of the Brothers Grimm." Bantam, 1992.

Index

Micaela Neal

About the authors. Julie and Mike Neal (shown at left) have visited Walt Disney World more than 1,500 times. With an apartment in the adjacent town of Celebration, Fla., the husband-and-wife team stop by at least once a week. Both a roller coaster freak and a wildlife enthusiast, Julie lists Expedition Everest and Kilimanjaro Safaris as her favorite Disney attractions. Mike's top ride is Space Mountain, just like it has been since he first rode it in 1975. The Neals live on Sanibel Island, Fla., with their daughter Micaela—who contributes to this book when she's not scuba diving—and the world's sweetest chocolate lab, Bear.